The Celts

The Celts

History, Life, and Culture

VOLUME 2: I–Y

JOHN T. KOCH, GENERAL EDITOR
ANTONE MINARD, EDITOR

*Editorial Team: Thomas Owen Clancy, Petra S. Hellmuth,
Anne Holley, Glenys Howells, Marian Beech Hughes, Marion Löffler*

ABC-CLIO

Santa Barbara, California • Denver, Colorado • Oxford, England

Library of Congress Cataloging-in-Publication Data

The Celts : history, life, and culture / John T. Koch, general editor ; Antone Minard, editor.
  p. cm.
Includes bibliographical references and index.
ISBN 978–1–59884–964–6 (cloth : acid-free paper) — ISBN 978–1–59884–965–3 (e-book)
1. Civilization, Celtic—Encyclopedias. 2. Celts—History—Encyclopedias. I. Koch,
John T. II. Minard, Antone.
CB206.C48   2012
936.4—dc23   2012005137

ISBN: 978–1–59884–964–6
EISBN: 978–1–59884–965–3

16 15 14 13 12   1 2 3 4 5

This book is also available on the World Wide Web as an eBook.
Visit www.abc-clio.com for details.

ABC-CLIO, LLC
130 Cremona Drive, P.O. Box 1911
Santa Barbara, California 93116-1911

This book is printed on acid-free paper ∞

Manufactured in the United States of America

Contents

ICENI

The Iceni were an Iron Age tribe native to what is now eastern England. Numismatic evidence suggests the existence of a distinct tribal grouping in the area from *c.* 65 BC. By AD 50, the Iceni were under the control of Rome, though they retained the nominal title of independent allies until the death of king Prāstotagos. At that time, harsh enforcement of 'provincialization' by the Roman forces sparked off the famous revolt of AD 60/61 under Prāstotagos's widow, Boudīca.

The territory of the Iceni clearly included what is now Norfolk, northern Suffolk, and part of east Cambridgeshire. While the Iron Age archaeology of East Anglia shares, to some extent, the 'core' features of Continental influence in areas such as socio-political structure, COINAGE issue, and ceramic technology, the region also clearly possessed a strong individual identity expressed through the material remains.

The capital of the *civitas* of the Iceni under Roman rule, *Venta Icenorum*, was situated at Caistor St Edmund, a little to the south of Norwich. No Iron Age buildings have yet been uncovered at this site, but numerous Iron Age artefacts—including La Tène fibulae and COINAGE—have been recovered. A notable aspect of the culture of the Iceni appears to have been the extent of hoarding and expenditure of conspicuous wealth by the social élite. The site at Snettisham, which yielded more than 175 complete and fragmentary torcs of gold and electrum, illustrates this point well. Hoards of elaborate horse trappings, such as that from Westhall, also occur with unusual frequency in this region.

Icknield Way (Old English *Iccenhilde weg*), the English name for the ancient road running from Norfolk to Dorset, probably preserves the tribal name.

Simon Ó Faoláin

IMBAS FOROSNAI

Imbas forosnai (from *Old Irish imb-fhiuss/imb-fhess* 'encompassing knowledge' + *for-osna* 'lights [up], kindles'; hence 'encompassing enlightening knowledge' or, more simply, 'enlightening') was one of the three supernatural skills from which poets derived their special high status in early Ireland (Ériu); for other such powers, see SATIRE. In practice, this power allegedly enabled the poet to foresee future events and describe them in poetic form. The most complete description of how the power of *imbas forosnai* could be evoked is found in Sanas Chormaic ('Cormac's Glossary'). According to the glossary, the poet would chew a piece of the raw flesh of a pig, dog, or cat; offer the produce to the gods; and then put two palms around his cheeks and fall asleep. In his dream, future events would be revealed to him. Several examples of *imbas forosnai* occur in IRISH LITERATURE, particularly in the Finn Cycle.

Petra S. Hellmuth

IMBOLC

Imbolc (1 February) is the least understood of the Old Irish quarter days. It is associated with the feast-day of St BRIGIT (*Féil Lá Bríde*) and with Candlemas (2 February). SANAS CHORMAIC ('Cormac's Glossary') gives the name as *oí-melg* 'ewe-milk', but this seems to be a folk etymology. In contemporary Ireland (ÉIRE), the day is understood to be the first day of spring. A hedgehog emerging from its hole was interpreted as a weather omen, a possible origin of the American Groundhog Day. In some areas, work that required wheels was forbidden on St Brigit's Day. A common ritual associated with the day was the making of a diamond-shaped cross (*cros Bríde* or *bogha Bríde*) of straw, rushes, or wood. An 18th-century poem attributes these crosses with protecting the house from fire, and this belief is still current. Many other beliefs and traditions associated with St Brigit are also practised on this day.

Antone Minard

IMMRAM BRAIN MAIC FEBAIL

Immram Brain maic Febail (The voyage of Bran son of Febal) is the earliest extant voyage tale (*immram*, pl. IMMRAMA) in IRISH, possibly dating to the 7th or 8th century. It consists of two poems of twenty-eight stanzas each, together with introductory, linking, and final prose passages. The first poem is uttered by an OTHERWORLD woman to Bran mac Febail. She invites him to her paradisal island, a land without sickness or death.

On his voyage, Bran meets the sea-god MANANNÁN mac Lir driving a chariot across the sea. To Manannán, the sea is a flowery plain. He recites another poem to Bran describing his country as a 'plain of delights' (*Mag Mell*). Original sin has not come to this land, and the people enjoy a life of innocent sexual pleasure and general contentment. Manannán predicts the Fall, and prophesies both the birth of his son, Mongán mac Fiachnai, and the coming of Christ.

Bran and his companions reach their destination and remain there for many years, though it seemed to be only one year. On their return, one of the crew turns to ashes on touching Irish soil. Bran relates the story of his voyage, writes it down in OGAM, and sails away again.

Séamus Mac Mathúna

IMMRAMA

Immrama (sing. *immram*), meaning 'voyages', occurs in the medieval Irish TALE LISTS as one of the native categories of narratives; see ECHTRAI and VOYAGE LITERATURE. Extant *immrama* include *Immram Curaig Maíle Dúin* (The voyage of Mael Dúin's coracle) and IMMRAM BRAIN *maic Febail* (The voyage of Bran son of Febal); the

Hiberno-Latin 'Voyage of St Brendan' (Navigatio Sancti Brendani) is also indebted to the native genre. *Immram* is a noun derived from the verb *imb·rá*, 'rows around'.

John T. Koch

INDO-EUROPEAN

Indo-European is a related group (or 'family') of languages spread over large parts of Asia and most of Europe. By modern colonization, it has also been carried over to the Americas, Australia, and parts of Africa. It comprises a dozen major branches and several ill-defined minor groups (see map). The term 'Indo-European' or 'Proto-Indo-European' also refers to the common ancestral language, spoken in later prehistory, from which the attested members of the family descend. This common language was necessarily the cultural property of a community, and information about that language can reveal a picture of that community.

The principle with Proto-Indo-European and the Indo-European languages is essentially the same as that with Latin and the Romance languages of today (French, Italian, Spanish, and so on). In the case of Latin, we know that it was the language of ancient Rome, that it spread with the military expansion of the Roman Empire, and that it then broke up into local vernaculars in Europe after the Empire disintegrated. In the case of Indo-European, the common ancestor belonged to a much earlier horizon, before documentary records, and a process more or less analogous to that of the ebb and flow of Latin with the Roman Empire can only be inferred.

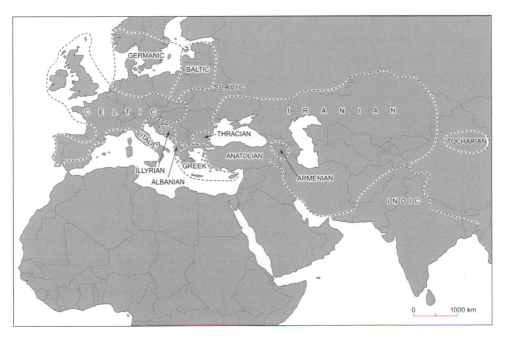

Approximate distribution of the major Indo-European branches or subfamilies at their earliest attestations. (Map by Ian Gulley and Antony Smith)

Celtic is one of the branches of Indo-European, and all Celtic languages are also Indo-European languages. Using the model of a human family, we may think of the CELTIC LANGUAGES as being more closely related to one another; for example, IRISH and WELSH would be siblings. A Celtic language would be more distantly related to a non-Celtic Indo-European language; for example, Irish and Hindi would be cousins, but neither is related to Hungarian or Tamil.

Reconstructing Proto-Indo-European

The existence of the Indo-European language family was already presumed by the first Europeans who learned Sanskrit, and anticipated by linguists of the 18th century. Sir William Jones (1746–94), a judge in India during British rule and an expert on Indian languages, clearly articulated the theory of the common ancestry of Sanskrit, Greek, and Latin. (A non-Welsh-speaking Welshman, *Cymro di-Gymraeg,* Jones was introduced to the King of France by the British ambassador as 'a man who can speak all languages but his own'.) Since then, further research has elucidated the principal details of the history of the whole group, and reconstructed the common ancestor, Proto-Indo-European. The workings of the Indo-European sound system are now understood in great detail. The morphology (i.e., such features as the personal and case forms of the verb and changes in the endings of the noun to express different grammatical functions) is known to a high degree, and much of the Proto-Indo-European vocabulary can be reconstructed with confidence. Basic patterns of Indo-European word order are implied by similarities in the early attested languages. Similarities in poetic formulae or stock phrases among such early texts as the Greek *Iliad*, the Vedic hymns, and Hittite religious formulae bring us to the threshold of recovering fragments of Proto-Indo-European traditional oral poetry.

Morphology

Indo-European is highly inflectional, and the grammatical elements (morphemes) usually express several functions at once. On the basis of the vocabulary of reconstructed Proto-Indo-European, we can gain an insight into the culture of the people who spoke it. Some scholars favour a date for Proto-Indo-European in the 3rd millennium BC, while others believe that the branches must already have separated by *c.* 3000 BC. The speed of linguistic change is unpredictable, and can vary tremendously between two neighbouring languages, or even within one single language. Social change often precipitates linguistic change; migration and substantial influence from other languages will also have effects. For example, English and Afrikaans have developed inflectional systems that are simpler than those of their relatives in the Germanic group.

Fame, hospitality, and truth are pivotal for Indo-European ethics, as shown by the concord of early poetry in the early Indo-European branches. Celtic shares this heritage fully. Nevertheless, as we see from anthropology, comparative religion, and comparative literature, these values are not confined to peoples who speak Indo-European languages.

Phonology

Proto-Indo-European had three distinct sets of consonants similar in sound to the English *k* and (hard) *g*. In the 'palatal' set, the top of the tongue was placed farther forward to the top of the mouth, on the hard palate. In the 'velar' set, the tongue was farther back on the velum or soft palate. This difference can be felt by noting the different position of the tongue in the initial consonant of English palatal *keel* versus velar *call*, or palatal *gill* versus velar *gull*.

A subgroup of Indo-European languages in the west, including Celtic, turned the IE palatals into velars. These are called *centum* languages, from the Latin word for 'hundred', pronounced /kentum/ in classical times, with an initial velar for an IE palatal; compare Welsh *cant* (also with *k*-) and Irish *céad* 'hundred'. The *centum* group contrasts with a *satem* group (mostly in the east of the Indo-European geographical range), named from the Old Iranian word for 'hundred'. In the *satem* group, the IE palatals have remained distinct from the velars.

Proto-Indo-European also had a series of voiced aspirated consonants: b^h, d^h, $g^{\cdot h}$, g^h, and g^{wh} (similar to English *su*b*human*, *a*d*here*, *pi*g*-headed*, *lo*g *house*, and *eg*g *white*).

Stefan Zimmer

INSCRIPTIONS, ANCIENT

Introduction

One of the widespread misconceptions concerning early Celtic culture is that it was almost entirely nonliterate. The Celtic epigraphic record, however, begins *c.* 575 BC, nearly as early as that of Rome.

The Iberian Peninsula

The majority of Hispano-Celtic (also known as CELTIBERIAN) inscriptions are engraved in a Celtic adaptation of Iberian script, with later-attested inscriptions appearing in Roman characters. They appear to date from *c.* 180 BC to *c.* 100 AD.

The best known of the Hispano-Celtic inscriptions are the three texts engraved on bronze tablets from BOTORRITA (ancient Contrebia Belaisca), which is located approximately 20 km to the southwest of Zaragoza. The most interesting of the three inscriptions is Botorrita I, which has 125 words of connected text on its front surface (face A) and 61 words on its reverse (face B). While it is now generally agreed that the text on face B is a list of 14 names, the content of the text on face A remains in dispute.

The most common type of inscription in the Hispano-Celtic corpus is the *tessera hospitalis*, a type of document that functioned as evidence of a pact between two parties—typically, an individual or family group and a community. Such texts vary from being composed of a single word to the 26 words of the inscription from Luzaga. They indicate the individual or family group and/or community participating in the pact and, occasionally, words explicitly signifying that the object upon which the inscription is engraved functioned as a *tessera hospitalis*.

Only one example of a funerary inscription appears in the Hispano-Celtic corpus. Discovered on the island of Ibiza, it is composed of the name of the deceased in the Celtiberian onomastic formula: *TiŕTanoś a PuloKum leTonTunoś Ke PeliKioś*, 'Tridanos of the Abulocoi, son of Letondu, a Beligian'. (The Celtiberian script characteristically does not distinguish between the sound *p* versus *b*, *k* versus *g*, and *t* versus *d*; therefore, modern Celtic scholars conventionally use uppercase *P* for the ambiguous *p/b* character, *K* for *k/g*, and *T* for *t/d*.)

At the site of Peñalba de Villastar, several inscriptions in Roman characters (as well as a few in Iberian characters) have been discovered. The best known, and longest, of these contains 19 words in two compound sentences and appears to involve, at least in part, a dedication to the pan-Celtic deity Lugus.

Finally, a significant number of legends are found on COINAGE and a small number of inscriptions appear on various types of ceramic wares and loom weights. The coin legends typically bear the name of the community where they were struck.

Transalpine Gaul

Transalpine Celtic inscriptions are attested as engraved in Greek capitals of the type used in Massalia (Marseille) and various forms of Roman script. The epigraphic tradition began *c.* 225 BC. It is difficult to know when it ended; the Plumergat (Pluvergad) inscription in Brittany (BREIZH) might be as late as the 4th century AD.

The most significant inscriptions are three lengthy texts engraved in Roman cursive from CHAMALIÈRES, Larzac, and Châteaubleau, France. The Larzac inscription is engraved on both sides of two lead plaques that were deposited in a tomb. It contains more than 160 words in two hands in *scriptio continua*, text without spaces. This inscription has not received as much attention as the Chamalières inscription, and its interpretation, unsurprisingly, has not been far advanced. It may have to do with female magicians.

Apart from these lengthy texts, one of the most common types of inscriptions from Transalpine Gaul is the dedicatory inscription. Among these is a series of 12 inscriptions, engraved in Greek characters, that are built around the core verbal expression ΔεΔε βατου Δεκαντε/ν *dede bratu dekantem/n* 'dedicated the tithe in gratitude'. These inscriptions usually provide the name(s) of the person(s) making the dedication in the nominative, often the name of the divine recipient with an inflected dative ending, and sometimes the name of the object dedicated in the accusative.

One of the most interesting Transalpine Celtic texts is the calendar of COLIGNY, which dates from the late second century AD. It contains roughly 60 words, often abbreviated, on 150 fragments (less than half of the original). These remains allow us to reconstruct a period of five years of 12 months each, plus two intercalary (inter-year) months. The months are divided into halves of 14 or 15 days.

A discrete body of inscriptions from the 1st- and 2nd-century AD ceramic factory at La Graufesenque (Aveyron) provide an interesting record of Transalpine Celtic and Latin in close contact. These graffiti are particularly important because they furnish us with a complete set of the names of the ordinal numerals from 'first' to 'tenth'.

Cisalpine Gaul

Approximately 150 Cisalpine Celtic inscriptions are known, which are almost exclusively engraved in the Lugano script—one of many derived from the northern variety of the Etruscan script. As is true of the Celtiberian script, SCRIPTS of the Etruscan type characteristically do not distinguish between the sound *p* versus *b*, *k* versus *g*, and *t* versus *d*; therefore, modern Celtic scholars conventionally use uppercase *P* for the ambiguous *p/b* character, *K* for *k/g*, and *T* for *t/d*. Of the total of 150 Cisalpine inscriptions, there are about 140 'LEPONTIC' inscriptions, which are attested from *c.* 575 BC to the end of the 1st millennium BC; the remaining 'Cisalpine Gaulish' inscriptions probably date from *c.* 150–*c.* 50 BC.

Most Cisalpine Celtic inscriptions are of the proprietary or funerary type. The proprietary inscriptions are typically composed of the name of the owner of the object that bears the engraving, in either the nominative case (the usual subject form) or the genitive case (the usual possessive form).

Funerary inscriptions are engraved on stone slabs or pillars or, more commonly, on funeral vases. They typically provide the name of the deceased in the nominative case. Some funerary inscriptions are of greater length. An inscription from Carcegna (S–122) provides not only the name of the deceased in the dative case, but also the names of the two dedicants, evidently his daughter and wife, in the nominative: *meTelui maeśilalui uenia meTeliKna aśmina KrasaniKna* 'U. daughter of M. (and) A. daughter of K. for M. son of M.'

The last of the longer funerary inscriptions is from Voltino and is interesting because the names of the deceased, evidently a married couple, are Latinized and engraved in Roman characters, with one Etruscoid character to represent the *tau Gallicum* sound (see CONTINENTAL CELTIC): TETVMVS SEXTI DVGIAVA SAŚADIS *tomedeclai obalda natina* 'T. son of S. (and) D. daughter of S.; O., their dear daughter, set me [= the stone] up'.

Finally, we may note that several coin legends are known, which bear 17 forms in total.

Other Locales

A few inscriptions attested elsewhere in Europe testify to the widespread geographic dispersal of the ancient Celts as well as the extent of literacy among them. The most interesting of these are what appear to be two curse tablets discovered at Aquae Sulis (modern BATH) in ancient BRITAIN, though so far the texts have resisted interpretation. There are also 260 coin legends with 61 forms attested in ancient Britain.

Ancient Celtic inscriptions have been discovered in the Balkans.

Joseph Eska

INSCRIPTIONS, EARLY MEDIEVAL

There are perhaps as many as 1,500 early medieval inscriptions surviving from Celtic-speaking regions. The majority are carved on public stone monuments, but the more than a handful of non-lapidary inscriptions known range from formal texts on deluxe metalwork to informal texts on domestic implements and graffiti. In general, the texts are short. As early witnesses unchanged by later scribes, inscriptions are of vital importance to the linguist and the historian. The majority of them employ forms of the Roman alphabet, though more than one fourth of the extant total are written in the OGAM alphabet, and a few Celtic names appear in runes.

The earliest post-Roman inscriptions date from the 5th and 6th centuries and are carved on undressed pillars, sometimes consisting of reused menhirs (prehistoric standing-stone monuments), prominently situated in the landscape. The texts are often written vertically rather than horizontally, and record individual personal names—most often male—in the genitive case. Several of these inscribed stones are explicitly funerary in purpose, but some performed additional functions. Their physical location implies that they laid claim to land. In formal terms, the parallels with PICTISH symbol stones are strong, and those might be included as individual inscribed memorials.

After the 7th century individual memorials are rare, and inscriptions are commonly to be found on dressed stone in a church setting. The simplest of these forms is the remarkable series of several hundred Irish monastic graveslabs, incised with a single name and a cross.

Katherine Forsyth

INSULAR CELTIC

Insular Celtic is used to refer to the CELTIC LANGUAGES and other types of cultural phenomena that are termed Celtic as they developed and emerged in Ireland (ÉRIU) and BRITAIN. The Insular Celtic languages consist of two major families: (1) GOIDELIC—that is, IRISH, SCOTTISH GAELIC, and MANX; and (2) BRYTHONIC—that is, WELSH, BRETON, CORNISH, and lesser-known CUMBRIC and PICTISH.

As languages that took shape in Britain and Ireland, the Scottish Gaelic of Canada and the Welsh of PATAGONIA are to be counted as Insular Celtic, even though these groups have now been outside the British Isles for generations (see CELTIC LANGUAGES IN NORTH AMERICA). At a greater time depth, Breton is classed as Insular Celtic rather than CONTINENTAL CELTIC, even though the home of the language and culture has been the European mainland for some 1,500 years.

Some scholars have argued that Insular Celtic was, in fact, a unified prehistoric proto-language, like INDO-EUROPEAN or PROTO-CELTIC; others argue that the similarities are areal features or the product of substrate languages. A third possibility is that there was neither an isolated Insular Celtic nor a Gallo-Brittonic proto-language, but rather a continuum of separating dialects in contact and incompletely sharing various linguistic innovations arising from various local centres, which then spread by trade and social interaction.

Of the several ancient Celtic languages, only Brythonic and Goidelic survived into the medieval and modern periods, at which time this Insular group became the only Celtic languages to develop extensive written literatures. They also shared in these periods such characteristic parallel developments as systematic losses of syllables and weakening of consonants.

John T. Koch

INTERPRETATIO ROMANA

Interpretatio Romana (Roman interpretation) is a Latin term used in CELTIC STUDIES to refer to widespread related phenomena in which a pre-Christian Celtic god was identified in ancient times, in one way or another, with one or more Roman or Greek god(s). The most usual types of identification include dedications in which the Roman and Celtic divine names are paired up. In some cases the equation can be inferred from incomplete evidence; for example, we may lack the Celtic name for the god, but the representation or its context is partly nonclassical and implies cultural hybrydization, which Roman religion itself underwent extensively through contact with Greek religion. For a believer in Graeco-Roman polytheism writing to an audience of believers and describing Celtic religion, such an effort would not have been a matter of impartially recording details like a modern anthropologist, but rather of determining to which of the various very real gods the alien Celtic names and unfamiliar cult practices referred. This mentality lay at the core of the genius of cultural assimilation that made the Roman Empire possible. For modern Celtic scholars, such classical tendencies have created the potential pitfall of making pre-Roman Celtic and Graeco-Roman religions appear more similar than they actually were.

John T. Koch

IONA

See Eilean Ì.

IRISH DRAMA

Irish drama encompasses non-theatre-based dramatic rites and performances, formal theatre, professional and amateur drama groups, and radio and television productions in the IRISH language (see also MASS MEDIA).

Introduction

Although the Irish did not develop conventional theatre until the 20th century, other forms of drama had flourished as part of Irish culture. Dramatic dialogues were common in the literary and oral traditions, as evidenced in *Aighneas an Pheacaig leis an m-Bás* (The contention between the sinner and death, 1899) by Pádraig Denn (1756–1828) and *Racaireacht Ghrinn na Tuaithe* (The humorous storytelling of the countryside, 1924) by Tadhg Ó Conchubhair (c. 1838–1925). Indigenous ritualistic forms of folk drama, such as *Brídeoga*, 'Biddy Boys' or 'Biddies', active on the eve of the festival of Brigit (31 January), and the Wren Boys on St Stephen's Day (26 December), were common. Popular assemblies associated with rites of passage, of which the merry wake is the most notable, featured dramatic amusements and games. The disguised participants in the CALENDAR activities were locally based, but the *crosáin* (sing. CROSÁN), professional entertainers, and other travelling performers are well documented in the tradition. Socio-political reasons ensured that these non-theatrical forms of drama gradually weakened, and from the 16th century onward there was no significant Irish-speaking urban middle class around which institutional theatre could develop.

Irish and the Theatre

It was with the first LANGUAGE REVIVAL at the close of the 19th century that activists sought to marry Irish and theatre. Douglas Hyde (Dubhghlas DE HÍDE) and other pioneering figures in Irish-language drama faced major challenges such as learning the basics of stagecraft. CONRADH NA GAEILGE (The Gaelic League) actively promoted drama at its annual Oireachtas competitions and gatherings (see FEISEANNA). In 1913, Na hAisteoirí (The actors) and Na Cluicheoirí (The players), dedicated drama troupes, were established in BAILE ÁTHA CLIATH (Dublin), but efforts to further the drama movement suffered in the turbulent period between 1916 and 1923 (see IRISH INDEPENDENCE MOVEMENT).

With the birth of the Free State (Saorstát na hÉireann), a drama co-operative called An Comhar Drámuíochta (The drama partnership) emerged in 1923 to stage plays at Dublin's Abbey Theatre (Amharclann na Mainistreach). Through the vision of Ernest Blythe (Earnán de Blaghd, 1889–1975), managing director 1941–67, the Abbey reconstituted itself as a bilingual national theatre with regular professional performances in Irish, though the Abbey gradually retreated from its mandate. It declined to stage multi-act Irish plays, limiting itself to its annual pantomime and to short plays staged after the curtain descended on productions in English.

Outside Dublin, An Taibhdhearc na Gaillimhe remained open in Galway, while the perseverance of the Donegal GAELTACHT's troupe, Aisteoirí Ghaoth Dobhair (The Gweedore actors), founded in 1932, was rewarded with its own theatre, Amharclann Ghaoth Dobhair (Gweedore theatre), in 1961. Yet, the decision by the cultural organization Gael Linn to lease a church basement on Dublin's St Stephen's Green as Amharclann an Damer (The Damer theatre) in 1955 was a fillip for Irish drama in the capital, and ushered in what is now recognized as the golden age of Irish theatre, 1955–70. The continuity provided by the Damer encouraged exciting and innovative work by a new generation of playwrights, including Seán Ó Tuama and Eoghan Ó Tuairisc.

Professional or high-quality productions in Irish in Dublin were scant in the 1980s. Professional theatre returned to Dublin in 1993 with the founding and funding of Amharclann de hÍde (Hyde's theatre). In the late 1990s, the professional group AISLING Ghéar (Keen vision) emerged in Belfast (Béal Feirste). However, the most dramatic change has come about with the arrival of TG4 (formerly Telefís na Gaeilge) in 1996. Apart from encouraging writing, TG4 has, through its major soap-opera *Ros na Rún* (Headland of secrets), provided opportunities for actors, directors, and technical staff and, in making a large television audience familiar with the series, has boosted stage productions involving cast members.

Irish Playwrights

As a form of artistic expression new to Irish at the end of the 19th century, aspiring writers had few models apart from earlier and contemporary English drama from which to learn their craft. The most successful early playwright, Douglas Hyde (Dubhghlas DE HÍDE), whose work benefited from collaboration with Lady Augusta Gregory and W. B. YEATS, penned ten short plays between 1901 and 1904. Drawing their inspiration from Irish folk culture and history, Hyde's pieces also mirrored the values of the Irish-Ireland movement. Hyde's first and most memorable work, *Casadh an tSúgáin* (The twisting of the rope, 1901), is now generally viewed as the prototype of the English-language peasant play for which the Abbey Theatre subsequently became (in)famous. Though Piaras Béaslaí (1883–1965) attempted to break away from peasant themes in his historical dramas, *Cormac na Coille* (Cormac of the wood, 1909), *An Danar* (The Dane, 1929) and *An Bhean Chródha* (The brave woman, 1931), these plays never matched the success of his comedies written for Na hAisteoirí (The actors) and An Comhar Drámuíochta (The drama partnership).

An Comhar and Galway's Taibhdhearc na Gaillimhe provided a stage for innovative work. *Dorchadas* (Darkness) by Liam Ó Flaithearta (Liam O'Flaherty) dealt with fratricide in the Gaeltacht and caused minor controversy when An Comhar staged it in 1926. Micheál Mac Liammóir's *Diarmuid agus Gráinne* (Diarmuid and Gráinne, 1935), a linguistically exuberant retelling of the Finn Cycle love story (see FIANNAÍOCHT; TÓRUIGHEACHT DHIARMADA AGUS GHRÁINNE) was staged in 1928.

Liam Ó Briain (1888–1974) produced a series of translations from French. Séamus de Bhilmot (1902–77); Máiréad Ní Ghráda (1896–1971), whose plays *An Triail* (The trial, 1978) and *Breithiúnas* (Judgement, 1978) discussed important contemporary social issues in the 1960s; and more recently, Antoine Ó Flatharta (1953–), who writes for stage and for television, have been exceptions. Other established writers have produced dramas: Críostóir Ó Floinn (1927–), Eoghan Ó Tuairisc, Seán Ó Tuama, and Brendan Behan, whose *An Giall* (1981) premiered at Amharclann an Damer (The Damer theatre) in 1958 and was subsequently reworked and repackaged in English as *The Hostage*. At present, prominent writers such as Biddy Jenkinson, Éilís Ní Dhuibhne (1954–), Liam Ó Muirthile (1950–), and Alan Titley (1947–) have turned to drama, resulting in several outstanding plays.

Pádraig Ó Siadhail

IRISH INDEPENDENCE MOVEMENT

The Irish independence movement (1900–23) was inspired by Theobald Wolfe TONE and the Young Ireland Movement of the 1840s, and built on the achievements of Charles PARNELL in the late 19th century (see also LAND AGITATION). At the end of the

19th century, the growing sense of Irish national identity found expression in organizations such as the Gaelic Athletic Association and CONRADH NA GAEILGE, as well as in the Irish literary renaissance. The early 20th century was a period of even greater activity, culminating in the turbulent period from 1914 to 1923, with the Home Rule Bill, the Easter Rising, the War of Independence, and the Irish Civil War.

A decisive step in the direction toward independence was taken in 1905, when Sinn Féin was founded by Art Ó Gríofa (Arthur Griffith) as an umbrella for the various nationalist organizations. The Irish Parliamentary Party introduced a Home Rule Bill to the British Houses of Parliament on 11 April 1912, polarizing pro- and anti-union positions, whose advocates began to demonstrate and to arm themselves.

The Home Rule Bill was passed by the British Parliament in 1914, but its implementation was postponed due to World War I. When the rebellion occurred on Easter Monday, 24 April 1916, the expected mobilization of forces took place only in BAILE ÁTHA CLIATH (Dublin). Irish Republican forces, numbering no more than 1,500, seized various public buildings in Dublin city centre. From the General Post Office, Patrick Pearse (Pádraig Mac Piarais) proclaimed the Irish Republic. The Easter Rising, as it became known, never spread beyond Dublin. The aftermath was bloody: Sixteen leaders were executed and more than 3,500 people imprisoned.

The heavy-handed way in which the British government crushed the Rising mobilized a much greater part of the Irish population for the cause of Irish independence. A radicalized Sinn Féin, now led by Eamon DE VALERA, swept to victory in the 1918 elections; out of 105 seats at Westminster, Sinn Féin won 73. Only parts of Ulster voted Unionist, returning six Members of Parliament. The Sinn Féin MPs refused to take their seats, instead constituting their own parliament, Dáil Éireann. It first assembled on 21 January 1919, marking the beginning of the Irish War of Independence. The Republican forces, now known as the IRISH REPUBLICAN ARMY (IRA), under Michael Collins, began a guerrilla war. The British government responded by sending troops and auxiliary police forces, the most notorious of whom, the 'Black and Tans', conducted a campaign of terror and arson against the population of the Irish Republic, including the original 'Bloody Sunday' of 21 November 1920.

Public opinion in Great Britain and the rest of the world soon turned against British military aggression in Ireland. The British government offered a truce that ended the War of Independence on 11 July 1921; the Anglo-Irish Treaty of 6 December 1921 granted dominion status to the twenty-six counties of the south of Ireland, thus creating the Irish Free State (see ÉIRE), but also upheld the partition of the island. Tension over this situation led to an attack by Michael Collins, Commander-in-Chief of the National Army, on the Four Courts garrison seized by the rebel IRA, which marked the beginning of the Irish Civil War in June 1922. Government forces soon prevailed; by 24 May 1923, the Civil War was over. It had claimed the lives of 927 people, among them Art Ó Gríofa, Michael Collins, and those executed by the Provisional Government. The young Irish state, however, had survived the war. Conversion from the 'Free State' to Republic began in 1932 with the victory of de Valera's Fianna Fáil party.

The Irish Republic (Éire) became, and remains, the only independent nation state with a Celtic language as its fully fledged national language. In practical terms, this development and the cultural NATIONALISM underpinning it have led to state support for Irish-medium EDUCATION at all levels, publishing and other MASS MEDIA in Irish, GAELTACHT communities, and Celtic scholarship. However, the nationalist hope that Irish could be easily revived as the everyday speech of the majority in an independent Ireland now appears naïve.

Marion Löffler

IRISH LANGUAGE

Introduction

Irish is spoken in Ireland (ÉRIU; ÉIRE). In the early Middle Ages, Irish was brought both to Scotland (ALBA) (5th century) and to coastal Wales (CYMRU) (6th century). Although Irish did not survive in Wales beyond the 9th century, in Scotland it developed into SCOTTISH GAELIC. Latin was an important language in both ecclesiastical and international contexts from the introduction of CHRISTIANITY, and Old Norse was spoken at least in the Viking centres of BAILE ÁTHA CLIATH (Dublin), Limerick (Luimneach), and Waterford (Port Láirge); the lexical input from these contacts was considerable. Even within the medieval period, English was beginning to have an effect, and in the Norman period it became increasingly influential. Within the modern period, English has become so dominant that it is feared Irish is dying out.

By convention, the history of Irish is divided into the following periods: Primitive Irish, from the separation of Goidelic and Brythonic up to the apocope or loss of final syllables; Early Old Irish (from the first appearance of syncope to the end of the 7th century); Classical Old Irish (8th and 9th centuries); Middle Irish (10th to 12th centuries); Classical (or Early) Modern Irish (13th to 16th centuries); and Modern Irish (17th century to the present).

Primitive Irish and Old Irish

Apart from the earliest names for Ireland and the Irish (see ÉRIU) and the names in the Greek script on Ptolemy's map, the earliest evidence for continuous Irish is written in OGAM.

The 5th and 6th centuries witnessed most of the major phonological changes in the language—for example, the phonemicization of lenition and palatalization following the loss of most final syllables. For the nonspecialist, these developments may be explained briefly as follows. In Primitive Irish, the consonant /t/ was a single grammatically significant sound or 'phoneme' and one letter; however, it had four actual sounds depending on where it occurred in a phrase. Thus, between vowels, and in some other positions, the phoneme /t/ had the weakened or lenited sound, tending to [θ], the *th* sound in English *ba<u>th</u>*. Before short and long *e* and *i*, both sounds of /t/ tended to be articulated more to the front of the mouth—that is, to be palatalized; thus unlenited palatal [t′] had roughly the sound in English *Christian* and lenited palatal [θ′] had the sound in *Scythia*. Nevertheless, these four sounds [t t′ θ θ′] were not grammatically significant and could still all be written with ogam T unambiguously. For a parallel situation, compare the American English pronunciation of *tater tot*. English speakers understand each /t/ to be the same letter and the same sound, but the sounds are objectively different depending on whether the /t/ is at the beginning, middle, or end of the word; a careful, slow pronunciation restores the basic /t/ sound.

In early Irish, vowels weakened and then disappeared (termed 'apocope' for final syllables and 'syncope' for medial syllables'), which had a dramatic effect on the language. The four articulations could now contrast in the same phonetic environment. At this point they became grammatically significant, and lenition and palatalization were thus 'phonemicized' or 'grammaticalized'. Some, but not all, of these contrasts are revealed in the ogam spelling system. Thus, we may compare ogam LUGUDECCAS with the Old Irish *Luigdech* /ˈluɣ′δ′əχ/, where the later form shows the effects of lenition, loss of final syllables, and syncope. In broad terms, then, ogam was originally used to write a language that had final case endings, no phonemic lenition of intervocalic consonants, and no syncope.

Phonological Features

All of the Insular Celtic languages were subject to a lenition of intervocalic consonants, whether within the same word or in the following word. Thus an initial consonant could weaken if preceded by a word with a final vowel; this situation, termed lenition, was originally simply a phonetic phenomenon. In Irish, lenition had the effect of reducing original voiced stops [b d g] to voiced fricatives [v δ f] and the voiceless stops [t k] to voiceless fricatives [θ χ]. The loss of final syllables had a profound effect on the language, including lenition, but it was not a single catastrophic event, nor did it affect all final syllables; final liquids /r r′ ll′/ and unlenited stops (e.g., /d d′/) seem to have protected the preceding vowel from loss, as in OIr. *bráthir* / *brāθir′*/ 'brother' < Proto-Celtic */brātēr/ (cf. Latin *frāter*, etc.). In essence, the vowels that were lost were final short vowels unprotected by a liquid or unlenited stops; other final syllables survived, as in OIr. *firu* < */wirūh/ < Celtic */wirūs/ 'men' (acc. pl.).

Another important development was the rise of a set of palatalized (slender, Irish *caol*) consonants side by side with the basic (broad, Irish *leathan*) set; for example, beside /p t k/ developed /p′ t′ k′/, which arose before a front vowel. The distinction between palatal and non-palatal consonants thereby became, in certain instances, grammatically crucial—for example, with OIr. *berait* /b′erəd′/ 'they carry': /b′erəd/ *berat* 'let them carry', /eχ/ *ech* 'horse' (nom. sing.): /eχ′/ *eich* 'of a horse' (gen. sing.) or 'horses' (nom. pl.). Phonemic palatalization is not very common, though it is found in other well-known languages such as Russian.

Following the loss of final syllables, the pressure of the initial stress accent had the effect of reducing polysyllabic words by the syncope of the second syllable, and of the fourth syllable in a five- or six-syllable word. The quality (palatal versus non-palatal) of the resulting consonant cluster was determined by the vanished (syncopated) vowel. It would appear that vowels in such syllables had been reduced either to a front vowel /I/ or a back vowel /a/, with the former leaving palatalization behind when it was syncopated, and the latter not; consider OIr. *toirthech* /tor′θ′əχ/ 'fruitful' (< */tor′ιθəχ/< *toret-āko-) beside *debthach* /d′eνθəχ/ 'contentious' (< */d′evaθaχ/ < *debutāko). The palatal form of a consonant has continued to be the marked variant even up to the modern language; for example, from Middle Irish onward, there has been a tendency to use palatalization to mark the feminine gender.

Morphology: The Nominal System

Irish inherited a series of nominal declensions corresponding to those attested in other Indo-European languages. For example, the declension of *fer* 'man' contains forms that display the effects of vowel affection and palatalization and also cause different mutations of the following closely associated words (as shown here by superscript letters—N for nasalization, L for lenition): *fer* (nom. sing.), *fer*[N] (acc. sing. / gen. pl.), *fir*[L] (gen. sing./ nom. pl), *fiur*[L] (dat. sing.), *firu* (acc. pl.), *feraib* (dat. pl.).

Morphology: The Verbal System

The verbal system of early Irish provides a full system of tenses, moods, and voices. A feature unique to the insular Celtic languages and most fully realized in Old Irish is the double system of 'absolute' and 'conjunct' verbal inflection. This system operated essentially as follows: When a simple verb was used in a declarative sentence with no negative or interrogative particle or conjunction, it occupied the first position in the sentence and took the 'absolute' form (e.g., *léicid* /′L′ēg′əδ′/ 'he leaves'), but if it was preceded by a particle of any sort, it took the 'conjunct'form (e.g., *ní·léici* /n′ī ′L′ēg′i/ 'he does not leave', *in·léici?* /in ′L′ēg′i/'does he leave?', and so on). In both cases, the stress was on the first syllable of the verbal element (*léic-*). Compound verbs worked in a similar way, except that the preverb (compounding preposition) took the place of the particle; thus *do·léici* 'he throws' had the same stress pattern as *ní·léici*. When the compound required another verbal particle, a negative, or an interrogative, however, the preverb was amalgamated with the verb (e.g., *ní·teilci* /n′ī ′t′el′g′i/ 'he does not throw'). Thus simple verbs had a double system of inflection, but the stem remained unchanged. Compound verbs had a double stem formation, conventionally known as deuterotonic and prototonic, respectively (referring to the moving position of the stress accent). The pretonic particles (those preceding the stress accent), whether preverbs or grammatical particles (such as the negative *ní*), also carried enclitic, infixed pronouns—elements that were always unstressed and often non-syllabic. In early Old Irish, a pronoun could be suffixed to a simple verb, as with *sástum* 'it feeds me' (*-um* 1st sing. pronoun), *léicthi* '(he) leaves it', *bertius* 'he carried them', but infixed into a compound verb, as with *dom·beir* /dom ′v′er′/ 'he gives me': *do·beir* 'he gives', and so on. By late Old Irish, an empty preverb *no* was used, as with *nos·bert* 'he carried them', *nom·sása* 'it feeds me', and so on.

Signpost in Irish and English. Place-names appear in both languages, but information intended for tourists ('Rent an Irish Cottage'; 'Scenic View') is not rendered in Irish. (Corel)

Sources

Given the attention usually devoted to Old Irish, the sources for the language are surprisingly thin, if our attention is to be restricted to texts written in the period from 700 to 900 and surviving in contemporary manuscripts. They amount to short passages in Old Irish in the Book of Armagh, the Cambrai Homily (both dating to the early 8th century), and the three main collections of glosses.

Middle Irish

The mixed nature of Middle Irish has long been recognized. The nature of the language varies considerably, depending on the text.

Phonology and Morphology

In comparison with early Irish, the developments within late Old and Middle Irish were far less catastrophic. With the apparent exception of /u/, internal vowels seem to have been reduced to /ə/ by the Classical Old Irish period, and their spelling then determined by the quality of the flanking consonants. Apart from the merger of /a/ and /o/, final vowels—where it was important to maintain the distinctions for as long as possible—seem to have survived as distinct entities into the early Middle Irish period, when they fell together as //. The consequences for nominal declensions where the grammatical distinctions were carried by final vowels were potentially catastrophic; for example, among the declensional forms of *céile* 'companion', *céile* (nom., acc., gen. pl.), *céili* (gen. sing., nom. pl.), and *céliu* (dat. sing., acc. pl.) were now all pronounced /k'ēl'ə/. It is possible that these changes took place as early as the 8th century in speech, though the distinctions may have been maintained in higher registers. What emerges from a consideration of Middle Irish nominal system is that the main preoccupation was avoidance of homophony, especially between singular and plural; accusatives and genitives could probably be distinguished by word-order patterns, and datives were by now almost entirely governed by prepositions, but distinctions of number were crucial. In Middle Irish, vowel-final nouns tended to acquire plural endings from consonant stem nouns, especially from the lenited dental stem nouns, as in OIr. *céile* (nom. sing.): *céili* (nom. pl.)—MIr. *céile* /k'ēl'ə/: *céileda* /k'ēl'ədə/.

Middle Irish witnessed some wholesale redevelopments of the verbal system. The loss of the neuter gender, together with the reduction of unstressed vowels to /ə/, reduced the series of infixed pronouns to chaos, out of which arose the modern system of independent, accented object pronouns. The breakdown of the infixed pronoun system was one factor in the erosion of the absolute/conjunct system (though it was preserved to a greater degree in Scottish Gaelic and MANX), as there was less need for pretonic perverbs in which to infix pronouns. The most frequent development was the creation of new simple verbs based on the prototonic forms of compound verbs, such as verbal nouns and imperatives—for example, OIr. *do·léici: · teilci*—MIr. *teilcid* 'throws'. The paradigm was further clarified by the development of clear single sets of endings, notably 3rd sing. *-enn/-ann*. The complex pattern of tense formations dependent on the class of verb was also ripe for simplification. For example, depending on the stem class of the verb, the Old Irish future was marked by an *f*-suffix, by reduplication of the initial of the verbal stem (with or without an *s*-suffix), or by a lengthened stem vowel—for example, *léicfid* 'he will leave': *léicid* 'he leaves'; *bebaid* 'he will die': *báid* 'he dies'; *memais* 'he will break': *maidid* 'he breaks'; and *béra* 'he will carry': *beirid* 'he carries'. Middle Irish displays a confused situation where each type seems to be becoming generalized at the expense of the others.

Sources

The sources for Middle Irish are far more substantial than for Old Irish, even if we apply the rule of contemporaneous manuscripts. The most important collections of material are those preserved in the main manuscripts of the 12th century: LEBOR NA HUIDRE ('The Book of Dun Cow'), Oxford, Bodleian Library, Rawlinson B 502, and the Book of Leinster (LEBOR LAIGNECH). Few texts can be firmly dated. In general terms, analysis of linguistic features is better at giving us a relative chronology of the texts than anything absolute; for example, studies of verbal systems or declensional forms may allow us to decide that the language of one text is more evolved in a particular direction than another, but not necessarily when it was composed.

Modern Irish

From the 12th century onward, a standardized (possibly artificial) form of language was developed for use in the poetical schools. In contrast to Old Irish, Classical

Modern Irish contained dialectal material from different areas, including Scotland. In addition, it contained a mixture of chronologically different forms and usages, some of which were recognizable from Old Irish and others which had developed in Middle Irish and were forerunners of modern forms. There was an archaic element of forms not in use in the spoken language (e.g., infixed pronouns and an inflected copula), though it is still possible to find instances of the modern uninflected copula and independent pronouns. At the same time, modern speech forms might be used beside older forms. There are also modern forms that show variation (perhaps dialectal), such as gen. pl. *teach/ teagh/ toigheadh*: OIr. *t(a)ige*.

In addition to the poetry preserved from this period, a valuable source for the spoken language of the period is the tracts of the bardic schools (see BARDIC ORDER), which were devised as the guides to proper usage—namely, the *Irish Grammatical Tracts* and the *Bardic Syntactical Tracts*. To teach proper usage, it was necessary on occasion to refer to inappropriate usage (labelling it *lochtach* 'faulty'). Thus, for example, we learn that in the spoken language (*Gaoidhealg*) the cluster of *-chth-* was pronounced as if it were *-ch-,* since that is stigmatized as *lochtach*.

Dialects in Modern Irish

It is customary to discuss Modern Irish in terms of three dialects: Munster (An Mhumhain), CONNACHT, and Donegal (Dún na nGall). Linguistically, the differences between the dialects conform to a broad (but not universal) principle that the Munster dialects are more conservative in morphology than Connacht and Ulster, but can be more innovative in phonology. A selection of features is considered here.

Phonology
   The position of the stress accent offers a useful range of comparative evidence. In Munster the stress is usually on the first syllable, as in *capall* /ˈkapəL/, but in a disyllabic or trisyllabic word it is on the second syllable if that syllable is long, as in *bradán* /ˈbrədān/. When the stress is on the second syllable and it begins with /r l n/, the preceding vowel is often syncopated, as in *cráiste* < *carráiste*. Elsewhere, the stress is invariably on the first syllable. The effect of the initial stress pattern seems to have been most strongly felt in the northern dialects where unstressed long vowels are shortened (e.g., *bradán* /ˈbradan/), though there is also a general tendency to shorten long vowels anyway (e.g., *lán* /lan/).

Nominal Morphology
   There is a general tendency for nominal morphology to become simpler as one moves farther north. For example, Munster still preserves relatively complex rules for the formation of the genitive singular: (a) broadening or palatalization of the final consonant—e.g., *capaill, brád, dóthan, athar*; (b) final consonant palatalized and *-e* added—e.g., *bróige*; (c) end consonant broadened and *-a* added—e.g., *feóla*; (d) consonant added to vowel—e.g., *ceártan, fiched*; (e) *-(e)ach* added—e.g., *catharach*; (f) stressed vowel altered—e.g., *laé*; and (g) no change—e.g., *rí, file, tine*. In northern dialects, the distinction between cases both in the singular and in the plural is greatly in decline, even in the genitive. As in Middle Irish, the crucial distinction to be maintained is

between singular and plural, and this has given rise to some very complex plural markers, especially in Connacht—for example, *lucht* 'load': pl. *luicht, luchtannaí, luchtaíl* (*-aíl* as a plural marker is unique to Connacht). Nevertheless, even in Munster, which tends to be more conservative, we find plural markers such as *-acha, -anna, -í, -íocha*. The short plurals do, however, survive in some dialects as the number form after numerals—for example, *ubh* 'egg': *sé uibhe* 'six eggs': *uibheachaí* 'eggs'.

Verbal Morphology
In all dialects, it is usual for the original 3 sing. *-idh* to be replaced by *-ann*.

Sources
There are two main sources of Classical Modern Irish: the vast quantities of bardic poetry preserved in manuscripts from the 16th century onward and the tracts of the bardic schools that were devised as the guides to proper usage.

Evidence for the spoken dialects has been preserved on tape in recordings from the early part of the 20th century onward. This rich collection of material has been exploited in various ways, from the detailed discussion of a single dialect to a survey of features throughout all the dialects.

Paul Russell

IRISH LITERATURE, CLASSICAL POETRY

Classical Irish poetry was the most highly prized and respected genre of IRISH writing during the period from approximately 1200 to 1650. It was the product of professional, trained poets working in a strictly regulated language, Classical Modern Irish (Gaoidhealg), and adhering to the strictest metrical code ever prescribed for the medium of poetry in the history of Irish literature (*dán díreach* 'straight verse'). This code was fixed around the beginning of the 13th century. At the beginning of the period, it would have been a regular lingua franca for the whole area it served (Ireland/ÉIRE and GAELIC Scotland/ALBA).

The poets (*filidh*), whose profession was hereditary, spent many years training in schools of poetry to master the language and the METRICS and, in particular, to familiarize themselves with the works of the master-poets of the genre (see BARDIC ORDER). Classical poetry tends to be 'conventional' rather than 'creative', though each official poem is a unique creation in itself. Most poets tended to use not only the same prescribed language and metrical form, but also a common stock of themes, motifs, and metaphors. Thus the genius of the gifted poet is seen in the ease with which he mastered the medium and the fresh expression he gave to well-known themes.

A well-wrought piece of craftsmanship by a master-poet could claim a considerable prize (twenty cows), so the poets guarded their profession jealously. The greatest prize of all, of course, was an appointment as official court poet (*ollamh flatha* 'professor to a prince'), which guaranteed not only full-time permanent employment but also a tax-free estate.

The poet's main duty was to validate his patron's position, usually as head of the family (*ceann fine*) in the form of a praise poem (*dán molta*). The qualities most commonly celebrated are valour, nobility, and, in particular, generosity. Anglo-Norman patrons could easily be accommodated in the scheme of things by an appeal to a well-known fact of Irish history and pseudo-history—namely, that successive invaders, including the Gaels, had established their rights by the sword and displaced the former occupants of their lands.

Damian McManus

IRISH LITERATURE, EARLY POETRY (*C.* 600–*C.* 1200)

Introduction

Verse in pre-literate Ériu (Ireland) was the particular preserve of a learned class whose members are usually referred to as 'poets': Irish *fili* (pl. *filid*) is the most common designation (see BARDIC ORDER). Unlike the BARD, who originally composed praise poetry, the *fili* merely used poetry as the form in which to transmit his message or teaching.

From the 6th century onward, there is evidence of literary activity in the Irish language in the monasteries. The monasteries were very much part of the rural communities in which they were situated, and they participated in local politics and even in wars. The large monasteries functioned much like wealthy landowners, acquiring clients who farmed monastic land and owed the same dues to the monastery as they would to a secular lord (see LAW TEXTS).

The Earliest Surviving Verse

The earliest surviving Irish verse, which has been dated to the second half of the 6th century, was partly social—probably composed by secular poets—and partly religious or ecclesiastical; it is, therefore, attributed to ecclesiastics who had a knowledge of Irish versification. The earliest poet known to us by name was Colmán mac Lénéni (†604) of Cloyne, Co. Cork (Cluain, Contae Chorcaigh).

Luccreth moccu Ciara, who is thought to have been a contemporary of Colmán mac Lénéni, left behind two important poems that claim an Ulster (ULAID) ancestry for certain population groups in the south of Ériu. One of these poems, *Conailla Medb Mí-Churu* ([Queen] MEDB had contrived injurious contracts), seems to represent, in very obscure language, a primitive version of the saga TÁIN BÓ CUAILNGE ('The Cattle Raid of Cooley'; see also ULSTER CYCLE).

Senchán Torpéist was a 7th-century poet who is better known for the rôle allotted to him in later tales such as *Scéla Cano meic Gartnáin* (The tales of Cano meic Gartnáin) and *Tromdám Guaire* (Guaire's band of poets) than for the verse attributed to him, most of which is clearly of a later date. The tales portray him as a cantankerous old man who flouts the hospitality of his royal hosts.

Royal Poets

It was not unusual for kings to have verse ascribed to them. The earliest of these royal poets is perhaps also the most interesting. Called Flann Fína in Irish, he is identified with Aldfrith, king of Northumbria from 685. His mother was said to have been Fín, daughter of Colmán Rímid, king of the Northern Uí Néill and uncle of Cenn Faelad mac Ailello. This would mean that Cenn Faelad and Aldfrith were first cousins.

An interesting series of more than a dozen poems is ascribed to Gormfhlaith (†948), daughter of Flann Sinna (†916), king of Teamhair. She was married in turn to three kings: Cormac ua Cuilennáin (†908), king of Cashel (Caisel Muman); Cerball mac Muirecain (†909), king of Leinster; and Niall Glúndub (†919), king of Tara. The poems seem to have formed part of a lost saga about Gormfhlaith that told of her fall from her royal estate to poverty in her later years. There are striking similarities between her life story and that of Suibne Geilt, the king who became a madman, in *Buile Shuibne* (Suibne's madness), which also consists of both prose and verse (see further Myrddin).

Religious Verse

A reflection of tensions between church and state can be seen in the verse attributed to Fothud na Canóne (†819). Two poems, *Cert cech ríg co réil* (The tribute of every king is clearly due) and *Eclas Dé bíí* (The church of living God), assert the rights of the church against the claims of kings. The latter poem claims the freedom of monks from military service—a dispensation credited also to Adomnán a century earlier.

In the early 9th century, Oengus mac Oengabann (Oengus Céile Dé) of the monastery of Clonenagh (Cluain-Eidhnech), a follower of the monastic reform movement identified with Mael Ruain (†792) of Tallaght, composed *Félire Oengusso* ('The Martyrology of Oengus'). This verse calendar included a quatrain for every day of the year commemorating the feasts of saints—Irish and foreign—and was based on the Martyrology of Tallaght.

In the later 10th century, Airbertach mac Coise Dobráin (†1016), teacher and later superior of the monastery of Ros Ailithir (modern Rosscarbery, Co. Cork [Ros Cairbre, Contae Chorcaigh]), was the author of a poem on the geography of the world and of several poems on biblical themes, including, most likely, the great epic *Saltair na Rann* (The verse psalter), on the creation, fall, and redemption of humankind, which was in the process of composition in 988. Mael Ísa Ua Brolcháin (†1086) of Armagh composed a poem of 40 lines in which the author addresses an old psalter as though it were a woman with whom he had slept when he was a child; as an older man, he is reunited with the book after it has belonged to four others, and he finds that age has taken its toll.

Historical Verse

In the period between the 10th and the 12th centuries, verse on historical topics predominated. The definition of 'history' to which these poets subscribed included mythological narrative and the Lebar Gabála Érenn ('The Book of Invasions') type of legendary history, which had emerged in monastic environments since the 8th century.

Dubliter ua Uathgaile (*fl. c.* 1100) of Killeshin is credited with a prose-and-verse tract on the Six Ages of the World. Gilla Mo Dubda ua Caisite, from Co. Meath

(Contae an Mhí), wrote in Daim-Inis, an island monastery in Loch Éirne, in 1147. His principal work is the *banshenchas*, a long poem commemorating the famous women of history and legendary history from Eve to the poet's own time, providing valuable information on the marriage patterns of the time.

The explanation of the origin of place-names was a favourite topic of verse (and prose) composition in the 11th and 12th centuries. Traditional stories explaining the origin of well-known place-names were not enough to satisfy the public taste for onomastic lore. Place-name literature was called DINDSHENCHAS (lore of high places) and exists in both verse and prose recensions. The Fenian tale *Acallam na Senórach* ('Dialogue of [or with] the Old Men'), though not primarily a *dindshenchas* document, contains many place-name stories and poems.

Saga Poetry

The earliest narrative prose texts, from the 8th and 9th centuries, contain occasional passages in verse. At first, the use of verse was restricted and many tales contain no verse. By the 11th and 12th-centuries, however, the tales consisted largely of verse connected by prose passages. The next step in this progression was the development of a free-standing narrative verse. This form appeared in the 12th and following centuries, exemplified principally by the FIANNAÍOCHT (Fenian) ballads, which provide an alternative narrative medium to the contemporary Fenian prose tales. It is not clear whether this narrative verse was a totally indigenous development or to what extent it was influenced by the growth of the international ballad at the same period.

Anonymous and Misattributed Verse

By far the greatest part of early Irish verse is anonymous; only in the 11th and 12th centuries did it become at all common for poets to identify themselves by giving their names in a stanza at the end of a poem. Earlier poets are identified in the headings prefixed to poems in the manuscripts. In many cases these attributions are patently false, as when poems are attributed to mythical or early historical characters or when the late language of a poem attributed to an early poet reveals the impossibility of such authorship.

The most pleasing poems of the whole early Irish corpus are the anonymous lyrics written in the Old Irish period and identified as NATURE POETRY or 'hermit poetry', whether or not they were written by real hermits. These short poems manifest familiarity with, and appreciation of, nature; the resulting well-crafted verse has a brightness lacking in most early verse. Other short poems deal with the great themes of love, mourning, and the passing of youth, and show a great depth of feeling.

Metrics and the Training of the Poets

The most common metre of the earliest poetry has seven syllables to the line and three syllables in the last word in the line. Other metres show a disyllabic or trisyllabic ending in a less structured line. In all of these verse forms, alliteration is prevalent, linking words within the line or linking lines together. Rhyme begins to appear in stanzaic poems. After the 7th century, stanzaic syllabic metres with rhyme and alliteration began to predominate. These models, in a wide variety of patterns, were the normal metrical forms in use between the 7th and the 17th centuries.

The poet received his training by belonging to the entourage of a senior poet for seven or more years. The subjects that he was expected to study are set forth in curricular form in the Second Metrical Tract (dating from the 11th century in its surviving form), while the First and Third Tracts list and exemplify the metres in use (see BARDIC ORDER; METRICS).

Gearóid Mac Eoin

IRISH LITERATURE, EARLY PROSE (*C.* 700–*C.* 1600/1650)

Introduction

The scope of this article is material written in the IRISH language (Old, Middle, and Early Modern Irish periods) in the broad category that we might term—from our own cultural perspective—literary prose fiction.

Texts and the Manuscript Tradition

Irish prose texts have been written in manuscripts since at least the 8th century. However, owing to both factors of historical discontinuity and climate, all Old Irish prose fiction survives only in later copies. Although we have no collection of tales surviving in a manuscript of the Old Irish period, we do know the name of one such important collection, now lost, but mentioned in later copies of the tales which it contained. This is CÍN DROMMA SNECHTAI ('The Book of Druim Snechta').

Categories

The early Irish writers had their own system of classification for the tales—for example, such categories as ECHTRAI 'adventures' and IMMRAMA 'voyage tales'. This system is well attested in the medieval Irish tale lists and is often confirmed in the traditional titles given to the individual tales. However, modern scholarship uses the following categories:

1. The MYTHOLOGICAL CYCLE: tales dealing with TUATH DÉ (tribe of the gods), whom many modern scholars have taken to be survivals of the ancient pre-Christian deities of Ireland
2. The ULSTER CYCLE: tales of the heroes of the legendary royal hall of EMAIN MACHAE, Red Branch (*Craebruad*), heroic tales about the ULAID (people of Ulster), whose central hero is CÚ CHULAINN
3. The KINGS' CYCLES: sagas about the ancient kings of Ireland
4. FIANNAÍOCHT, Fenian Cycle: tales and ballads about a war-band (FÍAN) led by the hero FINN MAC CUMAILL, also sometimes called the Ossianic cycle from Finn's son, the hero Oisín

5. Romances: beginning generally later (after the Anglo-Norman incursions from 1169) and showing inspiration from popular Continental and English tales of the High Middle Ages

The Mythological Cycle

The Irish Mythological Cycle may be defined as tales whose central characters are the *aes síde* (people of the SÍD mounds) or Tuath Dé. One of the leading figures of the Irish Tuath Dé is the omnicompetent LUG, whose name links him to the Gaulish and Celtiberian god LUGUS, and whose name and story are comparable to those of the figures of the Welsh MABINOGI, LLEU, and LLEFELYS.

Three tales from the Mythological Cycle that have received a fair amount of attention from modern scholars are CATH MAIGE TUIRED ('The [Second] Battle of Mag Tuired'), TOCHMARC ÉTAÍNE ('The Wooing of Étaín'), and *Aislinge Oengusa* ('The Dream of Oengus'; see AISLING; OENGUS MAC IND ÓC) from the 8th century.

The Ulster Cycle

The geographical setting for the Ulster Cycle is the southeastern part of the traditional province of Ulster (ULAID), the present-day counties of Armagh (ARD MHACHA) and Down (An Dún), as well as Louth (Lú) and Meath (An Mhí) (now considered Leinster [LAIGIN]). The central focus of the action is the royal court of Ulster's high-king CONCHOBAR at EMAIN MACHAE. Archaeology has recently shown that the high-status assembly centre at Emain Machae reached a climax of activity with a ritual destruction at 95/94 BC. Few would claim that the Ulster heroes clearly reflect actual historical figures, though the action is certainly set in the remote past.

Several elements distinguish the Ulster Cycle from other epic tales: (1) the warriors are consistently depicted as chariot fighters; (2) Cú Chulainn and the HEROIC ETHOS are key elements; and (3) heads of rivals are taken as trophies (see HEAD CULT).

The major tales from the Ulster Cycle that have received most attention from scholars are TÁIN BÓ CUAILNGE ('The Cattle Raid of Cooley'), FLED BRICRENN ('Bricriu's Feast'), SCÉLA MUCCE MÉIC DÁ THÓ ('The Story of Mac DáThó's Pig'), and several of the *remscéla* (fore-tales) that explain the background to the *Táin*.

The Kings' Cycles

In contrast to the Ulster Cycle, which deals mainly with the heroic ethos, the Kings' Cycles are legendary, more concerned with such issues as (1) the origins of peoples and dynasties; (2) anecdotes about famous representatives of various dynasties; (3) accounts about battles that altered the course of history in such a way as to explain doctrines relating to the *status quo* at the time the tale was written; and (4) anecdotes that explain customs and rites.

Examples of this genre include the following: (1) *Orgain Denna Ríg* ('The Destruction of Dind Ríg'), a version of the origin legend of the LAIGIN (LEINSTERMEN) composed in the 9th century; (2) *Longes Chonaill Corc* (The exile of Conall Corc), a tale from the 8th/9th century about the origin of the ÉOGANACHT dynasties of

Mumu (Munster); (3) *Fingal Rónáin* (The kin-slaying of Rónán), a tragic story set in the historical period of the killing of the prince Mael Fhothartaigh by his father Rónán, king of the Laigin (†624), which was written in the 10th century; and (4) *Buile Shuibne* (Suibne's madness), a 12th-century tale concerning Suibne, a fictional 7th-century king of east Ulster. Suibne was cursed by a saint and became mad after having witnessed the terrors of the battle of Mag Roth; thereafter, he lived in the wilderness among birds and animals. The Irish Suibne legend has close parallels with that of the mad Welsh poet and prophet, Myrddin.

In the 12th century, a significant change took place in the reception of Early Irish prose literature. One of the main reasons was the neglect of heroic literature such as the *Táin* and the Kings' tales. The political and ecclesiastical reality in Ireland in the central Middle Ages changed dramatically, which proved harmful to the native literary tradition.

The Fenian or Ossianic Cycle

The tradition about Finn and the Fían is given the Irish name Fiannaíocht, often but somewhat misleadingly translated as 'Fenian literature'. The name 'Ossianic' is used for this cycle as well, derived from Finn's son Oisín, but also referring to the controversial adaptation and publication of Scottish *Fiannaíocht* by James Macpherson.

The Fenian Cycle consists of prose tales and long passages of verse called *Laoithe Fianaigheachta* (Fenian lays/ballads). Recognized important tales within the cycle include *Finn agus Cúldub*, Tóruigheacht Dhiarmada agus Ghráinne ('The Pursuit of Diarmaid and Gráinne', which is not attested until the Classical Modern Irish period), and *Acallam na Senórach* ('Dialogue of [or with] the Old Men'). Oral *Fiannaíocht* did not depend on royal patronage or monastic scholarship for survival. These tales and songs continued to circulate vigorously in Ireland (Éire), Gaelic Scotland (Alba), and Nova Scotia well into the 20th century (see Celtic languages in North America).

The Romances

The development of Romances shows many parallels with contemporary Romances from France. Although these tales also concern heroes and adventures, the Romances contrast with the Ulster and Kings' Cycles in several respects. There is a preoccupation with love stories and miracles, and magic is a frequent element. The grandly heroic and archaic epic tone of the older tales is replaced by a more everyday register. The setting is often vague and unrealistic, in the manner of folktales. The structure of the narratives is more apparently a series of events, rather than the complex structures affected by deep-seated associations and traditions found in the older native tale types. The stories often conform to well-attested folklore types, both as collected in modern Ireland and found more broadly throughout Europe. The characters are usually more clearly depicted than in folk-tales, but they are less prominent than the episodes, themes, and motifs.

Irish-language versions and adaptations of British and Continental tales appear in the 12th century as well.

Peter Smith, Peter E. Busse, and John T. Koch

IRISH LITERATURE, POST-CLASSICAL

Introduction

The departure of O'Neill and O'Donnell (the defeated native chiefs of Tyrone and Tyrconnell) and their allies for exile on the Continent in September 1607 and the subsequent plantation of Ulster (ULAID) completed a the eclipse of the old GAELIC order: The native lordships were wiped out, Brehon law (see LAW TEXTS) was replaced by English common law, and Gaelic patrician culture began to crumble.

Poets and Poetry

The dominant and defining feature of the literature of the Early Modern Irish period (*c.* 1200–*c.* 1650) is the strict syllabic verse (*dán díreach*) of the professional poets (see BARDIC ORDER). Nevertheless, verse in other forms was also produced in that period, including verse in accentual metres (*abhrán/amhrán*) and in freer syllabic metres (*óglachas*). Such verse was produced in sufficient quantity and was held in high enough esteem—by some patrons at least—as to be seen by the professional composers of strict syllabic verse to constitute a real threat to the dominant position of their product. In the classical period, professional poets used freer syllabic metres in composing satires, love poems, coarse poems, and other works.

The Dominican priest Pádraigín Haicéad (*c.* 1600–54) was undoubtedly the outstanding Irish poet of the 17th century, in terms of the variety and intensity of his poetry and the sophistication of his use of the language and of the metres, both accentual and syllabic. While his public verse is strongly traditional, his personal poems offer a striking revelation, expressed in a truly personal voice, of a complex personality. Although frequently engaged in bitter controversy, he was also capable of extremely warm affection—for Ireland, for music and musicians, and particularly for his friends.

Political and religious poems well are represented in this period as well. Several gloomy, moralizing poems on the *memento mori* theme survive by Muiris Mac Gearailt (*fl.* 1600–26), Tomás Déis, bishop of Meath (An Mhí; 1622–52), and others.

The political *aisling* was to become one of the defining features of 18th-century verse in Irish. Ireland (ÉIRE) as a beautiful but sad woman appears to the poet in rural surroundings; he describes her misfortunes and predicts the arrival of the rightful Stuart king (or another) to save her. This formula, treated with particular linguistic flair by such Munster poets as Seán Clárach Mac Domhnaill (1691–1754), and Eóghan Ruadh Ó Súilleabháin (1748–84), who sought to lift the spirits of their audience, was repeated scores of times until worn threadbare. Meanwhile the Ulster poet Art Mac Cumhaigh (1738–73) expressed the hope that a return of the UÍ NÉILL dynasty would bring salvation.

By the second half of the 18th century, the poets had come to accept what they were: schoolmasters, scribes, casual labourers, ordinary men of the people who composed for the people in their provincial dialects. Occasional poems, including humorous ones, were composed in large numbers, and poems of repentance were common—but so also were mocking, satirical, and scatological poems. The warrant (*barántas*), a genre that consists of an imitation of the legal warrant, became the vehicle for much ribald humour and mockery. Brian Merriman/MAC GIOLLA MEIDHRE (?1745–1805) made the proceedings of the law courts, combined with the setting of the love *aisling*, the basis for his impressive poem, *Cúirt an Mheon-Oíche* (The midnight court), in which he offers a bawdy analysis of matters of sex, fertility, marriage, and celibacy. In *Eachtra Ghiolla an Amarráin*, Donncha Rua Mac Conmara (1715–1810) gives a vibrant account of an emigrant's journey to Newfoundland. The stories and poems of the Fianna continued to be a much-loved part of the folk repertoire (see FIANNAÍOCHT; FINN MAC CUMAILL), and even spawned new literary additions, such as Mícheál Coimín's *Laoi Oisín ar Thír na nÓg* (see OISÍN; TÍR NA NÓG). By the turn of the 18th century, however, Irish verse had begun to lose much of its vigour.

Prose

The first half of the 17th century is remarkable for the volume of religious and historical prose writing produced during this era. Both kinds represent a response to important contemporary challenges, while the authors of some of the significant body of creative literature written during the 17th and 18th centuries also engaged with current issues.

No attempt was made to mediate the tenets of the REFORMATION to the people of Ireland through the medium of IRISH until the reign of Elizabeth I (see TUDUR), and her practical recognition of the fact that Irish was the language of the majority of the Irish population. Eventually, just after Elizabeth's death, William Daniel (Ó Domhnaill, *c.* 1570–1628) in 1603 published the translation of the New Testament that he and his collaborators had made (see BIBLE); in 1608, he followed this work with the publication of his translation of the Book of Common Prayer. William Bedell (1571–1642), an Englishman who became Provost of Trinity College in 1627, learned Irish and set about the mammoth task of having the Old Testament translated into Irish. He completed this project in 1640, but the translation remained unpublished until 1685. The Roman Catholic Counter-Reformation response in Irish came initially from Europe; later works produced in Ireland— those of Seathrún CÉITINN (Geoffrey Keating), for example—were not printed and circulated in manuscript. Beginning with Ó Maolchonaire's *Desiderius* (Louvain, 1616), a substantial series of translations were made. Ó hEodhasa's catechism (Antwerp, 1611; Louvain, 1614; Rome, 1707) closely follows the templates established by Peter Canisius and Robert Bellarmine and itself became a model to be followed by later Irish authors.

At the other end of the spectrum from religious literature are the bawdy satire *Pairlement Chloinne Tomáis* and the large progeny that it spawned. Based on two sessions of a parliament of peasants, the *Pairlement* consists of two parts—the first probably written about 1610–15, the second some fifty years later—in which contempt for the boorishness of the upstart churls of the time is trenchantly expressed. Aogán Ó Rathaille's brief social satire, *Eachtra Thaidhg Dhuibh Uí Chróinín*, is strongly influenced by the *Pairlement*, while two short works closely related to it have an ecclesiastical focus: *Comhairle Mhic Clamha* provides a harsh criticism of the ignorance of the Catholic clergy of the later 17th century, while *Comhairle Comissarius na Cléire* ridicules the holding of ecclesiastical synods, which were very frequently convened in the same period. A further extensive text on the same model and to a significant extent derived from Erasmus's Colloquies is *Párliament na mBan* (The parliament of women), which Domhnall Ó Colmáin composed in 1670: In it, an assembly of upper-class women deliver rather dull speeches on moral and social behaviour appropriate to their class and on behaviour suitable for lower-class people.

Romantic tales, both those based on the Fenian (Fiannaíocht) tradition and imitations of Continental models, continued to be popular in the 17th and 18th centuries, though it is difficult to establish when some of them were composed. Most of the Early Modern Fionn tales are considered older than the 17th century by some scholars. Three Romances that seem to date from the early 17th century show evidence of French and Italian influence: *Eachtra Mhacaoimh an Iolair* by Brian Ó Corcráin (fl. 1608), *Eachtra Mhelóra agus Orlando,* and *Eachtra Ridire na Leomhan* (see ECHTRAI). Much later in the century, a minor explosion of creativity in the southeast Ulster area produced a sizeable collection of Romantic tales, beginning perhaps with *Tóruigheacht Gheanainn Ghruadhsholais* in 1679, which revive the old Ulster Cycle heroes and introduce them into the standard Romantic setting. Toward the end of the century, Fr Maghnus Ó Domhnaill translated three tales from the Spanish of Juan Perez de Montalvan.

In the early years of the 18th century, Seán Ó Neachtain (?1645–1729) composed two interminable pseudo-Ossianic tales in which Fionn (Finn mac Cumaill) and his associates are presented as chivalrous European knights. Another work by Ó Neachtain, *Iacobides et Carina*, is a fictionalization of recent historical events, with the hero of the title being James Fitzjames, duke of Berwick and bastard son of King James II. The same author's *Stair Éamain Uí Chléirigh* brings him almost into the stream of the modern novel: Although this work is an allegory, the main character is rather well drawn and there is a strongly realistic feel to the story's delineation of an alcoholic's decline into degradation and subsequent recovery.

Contemporary English literature may have influenced a late 18th-century rewriting of the Deirdre story (see Derdriu), *Imeacht Dheirdre le Naoise*, which has some remarkably sophisticated touches of characterization and Gothic atmospheric elements. The Gothic influence is strong, too, on a substantial series of sketches written by Amhlaoibh Ó Súilleabháin (1780–1838) in the early 19th century, which he may have intended to form sections of a novel.

The small amount of creative prose produced in Irish in the 18th and 19th centuries might have been sufficient to sustain the tradition and point to new directions, were the voice of Irish prose literature not stifled in the middle of the 19th century. Writing of the song tradition, George Petrie, in the preface to *The Ancient Music of Ireland* (1855), referred to the 'awful, unwonted silence' in which the country was enveloped as a result of the Great FAMINE of 1845–52. The silence that descended on Irish prose remained unbroken almost until the end of the century.

Cathal Ó Háinle

IRISH LITERATURE, 19TH CENTURY (*C.* 1845–*C.* 1922)

Irish Literature Prior to the Gaelic Revival (1893)

The period between the Great FAMINE (1845–52) and the establishment of the Gaelic League (CONRADH NA GAEILGE) in 1893 has often been characterized as the bleakest epoch in the history of Irish literature. Creative prose writing, which had been vigorous in the 17th century, was virtually nonexistent. Poetry, though esteemed and widespread in IRISH-speaking areas, was undistinguished by the thematic and formal experimentation that had characterized the best of 17th- and 18th-century verse. It is no surprise, moreover, that the deterioration of the language and its literature are popularly associated with the Famine. In ten years the percentage of Irish speakers in Ireland declined from approximately 50 percent to approximately 33 percent.

Some important continuities did prevail, without which the linguistic and literary revival that occurred toward the end of the century would have been unimaginable. Gaelic manuscripts were still being compiled at the beginning of this period, and it is clear that the literature in the native language could still attract a listening audience. A new departure was marked, however, by the gradual integration of traditional scribal activities with popular publishing interests. For the first time, Irish was appearing in publications aimed at a large audience, most notably in song collections

Patrick Pearse/Pádraig Anraí Mac Piarais (1879–1916), who wrote in both Irish and English. (Library of Congress)

and in the 'Gaelic Departments' of periodicals such as *The Nation* (1842–), the *Irish-American* (1856–) in New York, the *Tuam News* (1866–), and *The Gael* (1881–) in Brooklyn (see CELTIC LANGUAGES IN NORTH AMERICA). Publishers thus came to play a crucial rôle in maintaining an awareness of a national literature, as well as the potential for its revitalization. John O'Daly (1800–78), for example, with his bookshop and publishing enterprise in BAILE ÁTHA CLIATH (Dublin), brought together disparate groups with an interest in Irish literature: scribes, antiquarians, Young Ireland activists, and other nationalists. His bilingual editions of Edward Walsh's *Reliques of Irish Jacobite Poetry* (1844) and his own *Poets and Poetry of Munster* (1849) and *Irish Language Miscellany* (1876) were highly successful, and served to introduce traditional Irish poetry to a sympathetic non-Irish-speaking audience. As a co-founder and honorary secretary of the Ossianic Society (1853), O'Daly published several volumes of Fionn Cycle material, including both prose texts and verse (see FIANNAÍOCHT; OISÍN). One of the Society's editors, the Louth-born scribe Nicholas O'Kearney (*c*. 1802–65), produced good translations of verse by BURNS and others, as well as some original compositions inspired by historical and contemporary events.

In mid-century Ulster (see ULAID) and north Leinster (see LAIGIN), an efflorescence of poetic composition was largely due to the financial support and enthusiastic encouragement of Robert MacAdam (1808–95), a founding member of the Ulster Gaelic Society (1830) and the editor of the *Journal of the Ulster Archaeological Society* (1853–62). As part of a manuscript-collecting project in the period 1842–58, he employed several Irish-speaking scholar-scribes who were inspired, in turn, to original composition.

Another individual whose educational and publishing interests played an important rôle in the subsequent revival was Canon Ulick Bourke (1829–87), a native of Co. Mayo (Contae Mhaigh Eo). Bourke was a member of the Ossianic Society, and during the 1850s he compiled the *College Irish Grammar* (1856) and supplied 60 'Easy Lessons or Self-Instruction in Irish' for *The Nation* (eventually published in book form in 1860). In the following decade, while president of St Jarlath's College, Tuam, he oversaw the publication of Irish columns in several journals (including the *Tuam News*) and successfully publicized the Irish-language issue on both sides of the Atlantic. Bourke was a founding member of the Society for the Preservation of the Irish Language (Cumann Buan-Choimeádta na Gaeilge, 1876) and the Gaelic Union (1880), and his establishment (along with David Comyn [1854–1907]) of the *Gaelic Journal* (*Irisleabhar na Gaedhilge*) in 1882 was a landmark event in the movement to renew the literary tradition. It is in the *Gaelic Journal* (1882–86) that Bourke published his *Beatha Sheághain Mhic Éil* (The life of John MacHale), the first modern biography in Irish.

Prose of the Gaelic Revival

The revival of creative prose in Modern Irish commences with the serialized publication in the *Gaelic Journal* (1894–97) of Fr Peadar Ó Laoghaire's *Séadna*, the retelling of a folk-tale concerning a man who sells his soul to the devil. With its rural style of humour, lively dialogue, and superb, idiomatic Irish, *Séadna* was an immense success. In addition to convincing the Gaelic League that the sponsorship of creative writing would be a useful venture, Ó Laoghaire's work strengthened the case—in what was a hotly debated issue at the time—for using the spoken Irish of the GAELTACHT as the basis for a new prose standard. *Séadna* was not published in book form until 1904. In the meantime, Fr Patrick Dinneen (Pádraig Ua Duinnín) published *Cormac Ua Conaill* (1901), which has the claim at least of being the first historical novel in Irish.

Irisleabhar na Gaedhilge was adopted as the official organ of the Gaelic League in 1895, and in the following year it decided that a festival modelled on the Welsh EISTEDDFOD would help to stimulate new writing. Accordingly, the first Oireachtas was held in May 1897 (see FEISEANNA). In the following year, a short-story competition was added, which was won by 'Conán Maol' (Pádraig Ó Séaghdha, 1855–1928, a native of Kenmare, Co. Kerry/Contae Chiarraí). The first published collection by 'Conán Maol', *An Buaiceas* (The wick), appeared in 1903, and he is now generally recognized as the first short-story writer of the revival. His stories represent a determined shift away from the model of oral narrative.

Another writer much admired at the time was 'Gruagach an Tobair' (Pádraig Ó Séaghdha, 1864–1955), who published a series of short stories in the *Gaelic Journal* (1903–5) under the title *Annála na Tuatha* (The countryside ANNALS). While the language of these stories was lively and humorous, their dependence on stock comic characters and their want of intellectual substance leave them deficient by any literary criteria. The only author to develop the humorous, rural-based short story in a controlled, sophisticated, and effective way was Pádraig Ó Siochfhradha ('An Seabhac', 1883–1964), a native of Corca Dhuibhne, whose *An Baile Seo' Gainne* (This village of ours [1913]) still makes for delightful reading. Some years later, he reproduced his success in extended form with a comical picaresque novel, *Jimín Mháire Thaidhg* (Jimmy, son of Mary, daughter of Thaidhg, 1921).

One of the challenges facing the revivalists was how to foster an urbane, modern prose that engaged with contemporary social realities. Views on the issue were split between nativists, who regarded the Irish language as a bulwark against the moral degeneracy emanating from ENGLAND and the Continent, and progressives, who hoped to forge a modern literature open to inspiration from without. Patrick Pearse (Pádraig Mac Piarais), the most influential advocate of the progressive position, is properly regarded as the first modernist prose-writer in Irish. He argued that short stories should have a 'definite art form' (rather than an oral-narrative form) and be expressive of an individual point of view. The short stories in his first collection, *Íosagán agus Sgéalta Eile* (Little Jesus and other stories, 1907), largely embodied these desiderata; they are carefully structured, and their characters are delineated with some psychological depth. Pearse's second collection, *An Mhathair agus Sgéalta Eile* (The mother and other stories, 1916), contains his masterpiece, *An Deargadaol* (The devil's coach-horse), a disturbing social critique in the guise of a first-person oral narrative.

It is generally agreed that the finest writer of creative fiction in this period was Pádraic Ó Conaire (1882–1928). Following in the footsteps of Pearse, he urged fellow writers to be honest and fearless in their revelation of life. The best of his early stories, written in London, examine the spiritual desperation of socially alienated individuals. Ó Conaire's willingness to touch on themes such as sexual desire and alcoholism did not endear him to the conservative wing of the literary establishment, however.

Ó Conaire also produced a fine novel, *Deoraíocht* (Exile, 1910). This fictitious autobiography of a maimed Conamara man living in London is a strange and brooding psychological novel, the first of the genre in Irish. Ó Conaire's *Seacht mBuaidh an Eirghe-amach* (Seven victories of the uprising, 1918), a collection of stories dealing with the events of 1916, is of some interest as a literary projection of contemporary attitudes.

Two worthwhile novels dealing with Irish nationalist mentalities before and after 1916 are, respectively, *Caoimhghin Ó Cearnaigh* (Kevin Kearney, 1913) by Liam P. Ó Riain (1867–1942) and *Mo Dhá Róisín* (My two Róisíns, 1920), the first novel by the Donegal writer 'Máire' (Séamas Ó Grianna, 1889–1969), who later came to be recognized as one of the most important and influential stylists of the 20th century.

One of the more interesting progressive writers of the period was Liverpool-born Piaras Béaslaí (1883–1965), whose short stories (from the period 1912–20) remained unpublished until the appearance of *Earc agus Áine agus Scéalta Eile* (Earc and Áine and other stories) in 1946. Béaslaí's remarkable novel *Astronár* (Astronaut), which examines the various responses of individuals to colonial domination in a fictional Eastern European country, was serialized in *The Freeman's Journal* in 1921, but was not published in book form until 1928.

The Gaelic League also published scores of translations, including translations of Old Irish tales, contemporary writings in English, and classics of European and English literature.

Poetry of the Gaelic Revival

The extensive forum opened up by Irish-language journals encouraged the creation of verse addressed to a wide, nonlocal audience. Douglas Hyde (Dubhghlas DE HÍDE, 'An Craoibhín Aoibhinn') was himself one of the most prolific producers of such poetry, and a collection of his verse, written throughout the 1880s and 1890s, *Ubhla den Chraoibh* (Apples of the branch, 1901), holds the claim of being the first book of one poet's verse to be published during the revival.

Within Gaelic League circles, there was great dissatisfaction with poetry composed on English metrical models. Thus, for the first Oireachtas (see FEISEANNA, 1897), it was decided that compositions entered for the poetry competitions should all be in traditional syllabic or assonantal verse. The most successful of the traditional stylists was 'Torna' (Tadhg Ó Donnchadha, 1874–1949), whose *Leoithne Andeas* (Southern breezes) was published in 1905.

Patrick Pearse (Pádraig Mac Piarais) blended the modern and the traditional in *Suantraidhe agus Goltraidhe* (Lullabies and sad music, 1914) and *Collected Works* (1917). Áine Ní Fhoghlú (Aine Ó Néill, 1880–1932) is the only female poet of note; her love poems from the period 1916–19 were published in *Idir na Fleadhanna* (Between the festivities, 1922).

William J. Mahon

IRISH LITERATURE, SINCE 1922

Prose, 1922–39

Most of the original prose produced in the decades following the establishment of the Free State was—in one form or another—a 'regional literature' focusing on the economic struggles of the rural IRISH-speaking community and its forms of social interaction. A classic paradigm for the genre may be found in the realist fiction of Séamus Ó Grianna ('Máire', 1889–1969), the author from Rinn na Feirste (Co. Donegal/Contae Dhún na nGall) who had already enjoyed considerable success with his political Romantic novel *Mo Dhá Róisín* (My two Róisíns) in 1921. In his short-story collection *Cith is Dealán* (Showers and sunshine, 1926), Ó Grianna shifted away from nationalist themes, and depicted instead the foibles and vicissitudes of human nature as manifested in small-village society. His stories are well crafted and marked by an acute and sympathetic sense of irony. *Caisleán Óir* (Golden castle, 1928) is his finest sustained work, a Romantic novel set against a background of rural poverty and EMIGRATION.

Regional fiction was produced by many of Ó Grianna's contemporaries in the 1920s and 1930s. The regional literature of the period also includes the uniquely important Gaeltacht autobiographies. The seminal works in this genre are the three produced by the Great Blasket authors Tomás Ó Criomhthain, Muiris Ó Súilleabháin, and Peig Sayers: *An tOileánach* ('The Islandman', 1929), *Fiche Blian ag Fás* ('Twenty Years A-Growing', 1933), and *Peig* (1936), respectively. Promoted as classics since their first publication, and translated into best-sellers, they played an important part in shaping popular, mid-20th century notions of Irish identity.

From a critical point of view, the most distinctive work in pre-war creative fiction was produced by Seosamh Mac Grianna ('Iolann Fionn', 1901–90) and Liam Ó Flaithearta (Liam O'Flaherty, 1896–1984). Mac Grianna's prose shares the same richness of language as that which characterizes the work of his brother (Séamus Ó Grianna), but his thematic concerns are more profound, and may be seen as a response to the political and cultural malaise of the post–Civil War Free State (see IRISH INDEPENDENCE MOVEMENT). His master-work is *Mo Bhealach Féin* (My own way, 1940), a picaresque autobiographical narrative (largely recounting a foot journey made through Wales/CYMRU), which incessantly registers the author's sense of alienation, his distrust of authority, and his futile search for an unsullied, heroic Irish integrity. Liam Ó Flaithearta's five Irish-language short stories from the period (published in periodicals in 1924 and 1925) are powerful portrayals of animal and human nature, all set against the primitive background of the author's native Aran Islands (OILEÁIN ÁRANN).

Wartime and Post-War Prose

By the end of the 1930s, a younger generation of writers—those who had grown to maturity within the new state—had come to share a critical view of the nation's cultural and political institutions. One axis of this movement emanated from the

GAELTACHT, and is most powerfully represented in the writing of Máirtín Ó Cadhain (1905–70). Ó Cadhain's attack on the Romanticized Gaeltacht is paralleled in the humorous work of Brian Ó Nualláin (pen names Myles na Gopaleen and Flann O'Brien, 1911–66). In *An Béal Bocht* (The poor mouth, 1941)—a merciless parody of the regional literature—the Dublin-based Ó Nualláin ridiculed the popular stereotypes and clichés being promoted by the Gaelic establishment in lieu of an effective rural and urban language policy.

Growing impatience with government lethargy eventually led to a popular revitalization of the language movement (notably, in the university), the establishment of the literary journal *Comhar* (1942), and the appearance of an independent Irish-language publishing house, Sáirséal agus Dill (1945).

Prose from the 1960s

Regional literature was still popular at the onset of the 1960s, but backward-looking and nostalgic narrative modes were being replaced by description and critical assessment of existing conditions. Críostóir Ó Floinn's *Caoin Tú Féin* (Lament yourself, 1955)—a novel set in Corca Dhuibhne—was an early manifestation of this trend.

In terms of thematic and stylistic innovation, the two most influential writers of the 1960s were Máirtín Ó Cadhain and Diarmaid Ó Súilleabháin (1932–85). In his eight novels published between 1959 and 1983, Ó Súilleabháin explores the problem of recovering idealism and cultural wholeness in an increasingly shallow and materialistic Irish society. His challenging prose makes much use of the stream of consciousness.

As an intellectual and a political activist, Ó Cadhain had a strong student following, and his writing had a tremendous influence, which is readily discernible in the prose of the younger writers who emerged in the 1970s. The influence of Ó Cadhain in respect to stylistics has been especially fruitful in the work of the scholar and critic, Alan Titley (1947–), whose work combines political and social astuteness with a keen talent for satire and linguistic playfulness. His first novels, *Méirscrí na Treibhe* (The scars of the race, 1978) and *Stiall Fhial Feola* (A fine strip of meat, 1980), are trenchant political and social critiques.

Post-modern Irish-language fiction emerged in the mid-1980s with the publication of *Cuaifeach Mo Londubh Buí* (My yellow blackbird's squalls, 1983), the first volume of a surreal trilogy by Séamas Mac Annaidh (1961–) in which personal identity is explored through the lenses of Babylonian mythology and international politics. Since then, its themes and techniques have been taken up by many of the best contemporary authors.

Since the 1960s, sexuality has become a major thematic concern in Irish prose and, for that reason, it deserves mention here. Pioneering novels dealing with the topic include *Bríde Bhán* (Fair Bríde, 1967) by Pádraig Ua Maoileoin, *Maeldún* (1972) by Diarmaid Ó Súilleabháin, and *Lig Sinn i gCathú* (Lead us into temptation, 1976) by Breandán Ó hEithir (1930–90); the last was the first novel in Irish to be included on the national bestsellers' list. Beginning with his controversial *Súil le Breith* (Expecting a birth, 1983)—a novel about a priest's sexual relationship with his housekeeper—Pádraig Standún has since explored sex, society, the clergy, and religious culture in a series of eight unpretentious popular novels. Psychological and social issues related to various forms of sexual orientation are starkly dealt with by Micheál Ó Conghaile (1962–), most notably in his short-story collection *An Fear a Phléasc* (1997) and the novels *Sna Fir* (In the men, 1999) and *Seachrán Jeaic Sheáin Johnny* (Jack Seán Johnny's wanderings, 2002).

Poetry

Little extraordinary poetry was produced between the two World Wars. Modern Irish poetry truly came of age in the 1940s with the establishment of *Comhar* (1942) and the publication therein of work by an upcoming generation of modernists. The best of this verse was subsequently republished in Seán Ó Tuama's *Nuabhéarsaíocht, 1939–1949* (New verseology, 1950), a milestone anthology in which the work of three young poets—Máirtín Ó Direáin (1910–88), Seán Ó Riordáin (1916–77), and Máire Mhac an tSaoi (1922–)—was especially prominent.

For Máirtín Ó Direáin, his experience as an Aran islander living in the city formed the artistic basis for a critique of modernity. In his view, the spiritual richness engendered by the struggle for existence (as represented by life on Árann) has been exchanged for a superficial, soulless prosperity. There is a pronounced nostalgia in Ó Direáin's early verse, but it is counterbalanced by a striking use of archetypal landscape imagery (sea, stone, clay, tree) that gives his work a stark immediacy. Ó Direáin wrote in free verse, but his rhythms and use of ornamentation are solidly rooted in traditional verse and the spoken language.

Máire Mhac an tSaoi was the first major female literary figure of the period under discussion, and indeed from the start of the Gaelic revival. In her first published collection, *Margadh na Saoire* (The exchange of freedom, 1956), she explored a variety of personal themes, especially love and relationship between men and women. Her verse is highly flexible in register, but carefully and exquisitely crafted. It displays a deep familiarity with the older literary tradition and a confident sense of working from within it.

The major influence in the spectacular burgeoning of Irish poetry in the 1970s and 1980s was the establishment in 1970 of the University College Cork–based journal *Innti* by Michael Davitt (1950–2005). Indeed, what *Comhar* has been for Seán Ó Tuama's generation, *Innti* was for Davitt and his contemporaries. Collectively, the work published in *Innti* reflects the whole gamut of influences that affected Ireland in the 1960s and 1970s: the questioning of authority and old social paradigms, the sexual revolution, the emergence of a confident sense of Irish identity that envisioned new possibilities for the language, and the rise of international pop music.

William J. Mahon

IRISH MUSIC

The term 'Irish traditional music' is used to designate an eclectic body of music. Much of this music is not Irish in origin, and some of the repertoire is known to have come from Britain and Scotland (ALBA) in the 17th and 18th centuries and from Continental Europe in the 19th century. Nevertheless, there is widespread agreement as to the type of music this designation represents: a living, popular tradition that has been transmitted to the present generation, whether in Ireland (ÉIRE) or in the Irish diaspora (see CELTIC LANGUAGES IN NORTH AMERICA). It is primarily not written, primarily conservative in its aesthetics, and primarily recreational (rather than professional).

The music is conservative in the sense that older tunes and older styles are highly regarded and largely determine the aesthetic parameters within which innovation is felt to be legitimate. Innovations undergo a 'trial period' before the community of practitioners and listeners accept or reject them. The corpus of Irish traditional music comprises several strata that may be set out in a rough chronological order:

1. The oldest stratum is represented by the words and music associated with ritual performances, labour, and children's games. These include laments (or 'keens', Irish *caointe*), lullabies, plough-songs, 'whistles', and gaming rhymes.
2. Next are the *Laoithe* FIANNAÍOCHT (Fenian lays), ballads associated with the legendary hero Fionn mac Cumhaill (older FINN MAC CUMAILL) and his son OISÍN.
3. Much of the present-day dance-music repertoire (including treble-time jigs and marches) appears to have originated in traditional pipe marches dating back to 16th and 17th centuries.
4. Some of the older Gaelic love songs appear to be at least as old as the 17th century, and songs of all kinds—many composed in the 18th and 19th centuries—are still extant in the tradition. These are typically performed as SEAN-NÓS ('old style'), an unaccompanied solo performance characterized in most regions by a considerable degree of vocal ornamentation, subtle variation, and an absence of emotive vocal or physical gestures.
5. Some of the traditional harp music collected by Edward Bunting (1773–1843) and others is associated with musicians who lived in the 16th and 17th centuries.
6. Popular DANCES and melodies were grafted on to the native musical tradition, and developed in characteristically Irish ways. In this period, the 'reel' (particularly in its Scottish form) and the hornpipe took root and flourished in Ireland.

The oldest instruments associated with this music, and still used in performance, are the violin (see FIDDLE), uilleann pipes (see BAGPIPE), and flute. It is likely that some form of tambourine (see BODHRÁN) was used for dance music in an early period.

The earliest published collection of traditional Irish music was John and William Neal's *Collection of the Most Celebrated Irish Tunes* (Dublin, 1724). George Petrie's manuscript collection—containing 2,148 pieces in all—was eventually published as the *Complete Collection of Irish Music, as Noted by George Petrie* (1902–5).

Website
www.itma.ie (Irish Traditional Music Archive)

William J. Mahon

IRISH REPUBLICAN ARMY

The Irish Republican Army (IRA, Óglaigh/Fianna na hÉireann) is an organization whose aim is to establish an independent united republic in Ireland (ÉIRE) by force. It was originally founded under the name Irish Volunteers (Óglaigh na hÉireann) on

25 November 1913 as a militia to defend the introduction of home rule against the opposition from the Ulster Volunteer Force. When the political party Sinn Féin ('We ourselves') won the general elections and set up its own Irish parliament, Dáil Éireann, in 1918, it brought the Volunteers under its authority. Nevertheless, the army refused to accept the Dáil's recognition of the partition of Ireland, leading to a civil war in 1922–23.

Unsuccessful campaigns in the 20th century led to a split within this organization, with the more militant wing becoming the Provisional IRA, while the remainder became known as the Official IRA, which suspended military operations in May 1972. The Provisional IRA has sustained its campaign of violence for almost thirity years, but with changing tactics. The initial belief that an armed uprising could bring about a British withdrawal gave way in the mid-1970s to the concept of the 'long haul', which would gradually sap the British will to stay. Since the early 1980s, the use of violence has been combined with an attempt to establish Sinn Féin as a political force. In 1998, Sinn Féin entered into the compromise political settlement of the 1998 'Good Friday Agreement'. Canadian General John de Chastelain, overseeing the disarmament, confirmed the decommissioning of the IRA's weapons to the Irish and British governments in September 2005.

Joost Augusteijn

IRON AGE

The Iron Age was a cultural as well as a chronological era in which iron was the predominant material for the manufacture of implements and weapons. In historical linguistic terms, iron use among speakers of ancient CELTIC LANGUAGES can be attributed to the COMMON CELTIC horizon; a PROTO-CELTIC word *isarno-* 'iron' can be reconstructed from Gaulish *Isarno-* and INSULAR CELTIC.

Cultural

The earliest datable finds of iron objects point toward Asia Minor as the region where the technologies of iron production and iron working were developed. Iron objects dating back as early as the 5th and 4th millennia BC are known from the areas that constitute modern Iran, Iraq, and Egypt. Through the mediation of Phoenician and Greek colonization, Iron Age cultures developed around the Mediterranean during the 8th and 7th centuries BC. At approximately the same time, the cultures of the Iron Age HALLSTATT period flourished in temperate Europe. In the 7th and 6th centuries BC, Iron Age cultures finally emerged along the Spanish and French coasts. In Britain, iron smelting and forging developed during the 7th century.

Chronological

H. Hildebrand used the finds from the eponymous sites at HALLSTATT (Austria) and LA TÈNE (Switzerland) to describe two groups; the Hallstatt group was further separated into an older phase (Hallstatt A and B, now known as the Urnfield period) and a younger phase (Hallstatt C and D, or just the 'Hallstatt period').

The Hallstatt period occurred in the first half of the 8th century BC, and the transition to the subsequent La Tène period took place during the first half of the 5th century BC. Due to its definition as the last prehistoric period in European prehistory, the end of the La Tène period is usually linked with the expansion of the Roman Empire to the north. Therefore, in France, for example, the La Tène period is regarded as ending as early as 58/52 BC with the conquest of GAUL by Julius Caesar; in southern Germany, its end is connected with the campaigns of Drusus and Tiberius, stepsons of the emperor Augustus, in 15 BC. In southern BRITAIN, the La Tène period came to an end as late as AD 43, with the invasion of the Claudian army. Outside the frontiers of the Roman Empire (for example, in Ireland/ÉRIU and north Britain), the Iron Age is conventionally divided into a pre-Roman Iron Age, lasting approximately to the birth of Christ, and a Roman or peri-Roman Iron Age, usually regarded as ending with the 'Migration Period' of the 4th to 6th centuries AD.

Norbert Baum

ISLE OF MAN

See Ellan Vannin entries.

IUDIC-HAEL

Iudic-hael was a ruler of Armorican DOMNONIA, northern Brittany/BREIZH, *c.* AD 600–*c.* 640. Iudic-hael is also revered as a saint and founder of monasteries. The most informative source about this ruler is the Latin saint's life written by the Breton monk Ingomar, who was active between 1008 and 1034. The text survives in two late manuscripts, and there is also a French epitome of 1505 by the historian Pierre Le Baud.

Iudic-hael is probably of greatest interest to CELTIC STUDIES because of the literary contents of Ingomar's Life (see also BRETON LITERATURE). The Life contains an elaborate conception tale of the hero: Weary after hunting, Iudic-hael's father Iud-hael has a vivid dream of a young woman he knows, named Pritell, who speaks enigmatically to him. When the king awakes, he sends a servant to relate the dream and have it interpreted by the great seer and traveller from overseas named TALIESIN son of DÔN. Taliesin foresees that the son of Iud-hael and Pritell will be a great secular leader and then a great leader of the Breton church; the tale has numerous analogues in other Celtic literatures.

Sovereignty Myth

The interest of Ingomar (or his source) in Taliesin, one of the CYNFEIRDD (early Brythonic poets), is especially significant, given that the Life of Iudic-hael also contains a heroic praise poem in Latin, which shows signs of having been translated from BRYTHONIC and contains themes strikingly similar to those of the early Welsh GODODDIN.

The name Iudic-hael is either the diminutive of his father's name Iud-hael (which means 'Generous lord', and survives in Welsh as *Ithel*) or possibly its old oblique stem *iūdic-*. The first element is probably derived from Latin *iūdex* 'judge', which was used for post-Roman chieftains. *Hael* 'generous' < Celtic *sagilos* is a common honorific.

John T. Koch

JACOBITE POETRY

Jacobite poetry is poetry concerned with the Jacobite cause—namely, to return the main line of Stuarts to the united English and Scottish throne. It has its literary roots in the vernacular praise poetry that celebrates the achievement of the CLAN chief. Following the accession of William and Mary in 1688, the Jacobite viewpoint began to dominate the scene of GAELIC political poetry.

Historical events from the departure of James VII (of Scotland/ALBA) and II (of ENGLAND) in 1688 to the death of Charles Edward Stuart ('Bonnie Prince Charlie') in 1788 are clearly reflected in Gaelic poetry (see also JACOBITE REBELLIONS). Reactions to the accession of William and Mary range from a discussion of their lack of political legitimacy—for instance, Iain Lom MacDomhnaill's *Òran air Rìgh Uilleam agus Banrìgh Màiri* (Song to King William and Queen Mary; MacKenzie) and the political poetry in the Fernaig Manuscript—to a celebration of the battle of Killiecrankie in 1689, such as Iain Lom's *Cath Raon Ruairidh* (The battle of Killiecrankie). The battle was a victory for the Stuart faction, but it did not have wider repercussions in favour of the deposed monarch because of the death in the battle of the leader, John Graham of Claverhouse. The unpopularity in Scotland of the UNION of Parliaments in 1707 is also reflected in Gaelic poetry, such as Iain Lom's *Òran an Aghaidh an Aonaidh* (A song against the Union).

Most extant Jacobite poetry is concerned with the Rising of 1745/6 and its aftermath. The most significant figure is Alasdair Mac Mhaighstir Alasdair. Not only was he the leading poet of the '45, but he also took an active part in the campaign itself, gaining the rank of captain in Charles Edward's army. Mac Mhaighstir Alasdair's range of Jacobite verse is considerable. His *Òran do'n Phrionnsa* (A song to the prince) expresses both expectation of Charles Edward's imminent arrival and the firm belief in victory.

Mac Mhaighstir Alasdair's poetry composed after CULLODEN indicates that Jacobites viewed their defeat in that battle as a temporary setback, not the end of the cause. The expectation of Charles Edward's imminent return and success is also the central premise of *Òran a Rinneadh 'sa Bhliadhna 1746* (A song made in the year 1746); this song anticipates this event in a reference to the ancient belief that the rightful king's rule is attended by wealth and plenty.

The Badenoch poet Iain Ruadh Stiùbhart (John Roy Stewart, 1700–49) was a military man by profession. This perspective is reflected in his songs on the battle of Culloden, composed when he was in hiding following the end of the Rising, such as *Latha Chuil-lodair* (Culloden day).

Mo Rùn Geal Òg (My fair young love), attributed to Christiana Fergusson, shows a different and personal reaction to the Rising. The song is a lament for the poet's husband, who was killed at Culloden, and praises and mourns him in vivid images:

> *Cha tog fidheall no clàrsach,*
> *Pìob no tàileasg no ceòl mi;*
> *Nis o chuir iad thu 'n tasgaidh*
> *Cha dùisg caidreabh dhaoin' òg' mi.*

> No harp or fiddle will lift me,
> No pipe, chess or music;
> Now you've been buried
> Young people's banter can't rouse me.

The song existed in oral tradition in the 20th century.

The prohibition on the wearing of tartan was imposed indiscriminately by the Disclothing Act of 1747 on loyal and Jacobite clans alike, a measure that provoked widespread outrage, which is in turn strongly reflected in poetry.

An Suaithneas Bàn (The white cockade) by Uilleam Ros is an elegy composed on the death of Charles Edward Stuart, and may be regarded as the end-point of Jacobite poetry. Composed nearly 40 years after the Rising, it includes touches of nostalgia that would not have been possible in the poetry contemporary to the '45.

While containing a great deal of conventional praise and dispraise for clans and individuals, Jacobite poetry shows clearly that detailed knowledge of the political arguments of the time was current in the Highlands and was used publicly to win or maintain support for the cause.

Anja Gunderloch

JACOBITE REBELLIONS

The Jacobite rebellions were a series of revolts that wracked the British Isles between 1689 and 1746. Their aim was to restore the fallen House of Stuart to the thrones of its three kingdoms.

The Jacobite movement took its name and inspiration from King James II (of England) and VII (of Scotland/Alba), whose name was 'Jacobus' in Latin, and whose disastrous reign from 1685 to 1688 had ended in the collapse of his regime and in his own humiliating flight into French exile. The Gaelic Irish, together with many of the Highland Scots, saw in Jacobitism a means to safeguard their religious faith and indigenous cultures, and to free themselves, decisively, from the domination of a remote, and Anglicized, central government (see Scottish Parliament). Risings in favour of the exiled James II, and later his son James Edward Stuart (the 'Old Pretender') and grandson Charles Edward Stuart (the 'Young Pretender' and 'Bonnie Prince Charlie' of legend), effectively disfigured the political development of the British Isles for more than half a century.

The early victory of Claverhouse's Highlanders at the battle of Killiecrankie (Coille Chneagaidh), on 27 July 1689, was more than offset by crushing defeats for the Jacobites at Dunkeld (Dùn Chailleann), on 18 August 1689, and at Cromdale, on 1 May 1690. The massacre of the MacDonalds of Glencoe (Gleann

Comhainn) by regular Highland troops loyal to the government on 13 February 1692 effectively signalled the end of the first Scottish rising, as the other CLAN chiefs rushed to make their peace with the authorities. In the meantime, Jacobite resistance in Ireland (ÉIRE) had also collapsed as the result of defeats at the battles of the Boyne (1 July 1690; see BÓAND) and Aughrim (Eachro, 12 July 1691). Scotland was thereafter to be the prime location for all subsequent risings.

In 1715, a major rising in the Highlands backed by French landings offered the prospect of success, but the opportunity was ultimately lost due to poor general-ship. The belated arrival of the Old Pretender on Scots soil did little to lift spirits or to stem the tide of desertions over the winter months, and the clans dispersed back to their homes in February 1716. A fresh rising, backed by Spain, was crushed in 1719. However, in the summer of 1745, the 'Young Pretender' staged an oppor-tunistic landing on the west coast of Scotland. After initial reluctance, the clans ral-lied to his father's banner and government forces scattered before his advance. Edinburgh (DÙN ÈIDEANN) fell to him, and at Prestonpans (21 September 1745) a Hanoverian army was scattered by a daring night attack. Confident of success, the Jacobites headed south into England, but with their supply lines seriously overex-tended they were forced to turn back at Derby (7 December 1745) and begin the long retreat back to Scotland. One last victory was achieved at the battle of Falkirk (An Eaglais Bhreac), but on CULLODEN Moor (16 April 1746) an outnumbered and unfed Jacobite Highland army was decisively defeated in less than 25 minutes by Hanoverian troops. The Prince's subsequent flight entered folklore, but brought the Jacobite risings to a sorry end.

John Callow

JOYCE, JAMES

James Joyce (1882–1941) was born in Rathgar, BAILE ÁTHA CLIATH (Dublin), into a middle-class Catholic family. In 1904, accompanied by Nora Barnacle, his lifelong partner, Joyce fled what he saw as the intellectual, spiritual, and political paralysis of Dublin, and thereafter settled on the European Continent, where he died in 1941.

Joyce largely rejected the Celtic revival as sentimental folklorism aligned with a British imperial image of Irish culture (see PAN-CELTICISM, ROMANTICISM). He portrayed the Dublin that he had left behind in his collection of short stories, *Dubliners* (1912). His stultifying home life, Jesuit education, and sense of social oppression are described in his first novel, *A Portrait of the Artist as a Young Man* (1916). Although the book was initially banned for obscenity, the publication of *Ulysses* (1922) assured Joyce's immense literary reputation. Set in Dublin on 16 June 1904, *Ulysses* dramatizes the relations between the autobiographical Stephen Dedalus, Leopold Bloom, and his wife Molly. It has been praised, among other qual-ities, for its pioneering use of 'stream of consciousness'. *Finnegans Wake* (1939) is composed in a richly allusive portmanteau language—'alphybettyformed verbage' as the book calls it—which was the culmination of Joyce's lifelong narrative exper-imentation. Such self-conscious celebration and subversion of the English language and literary forms characterize his work.

James Joyce. (Library of Congress)

Joyce's achievement was immense: He was soon widely accepted as the leading prose writer in English in the 20th century and a preeminent figure in European modernism. His work revolutionized the novel genre, taking it away from the realistic traditions of the Victorian era and toward the post-modern form of the post-war period, and has been instrumental in the development of post-structural and deconstructive critical thought.

Although Joyce wrote in English, his eclectic and allusive style drew in many Irish-language words, names, and sources.

John Nash

KEATING, GEOFFREY

See Céitinn, Seathrún.

KEEILL

Keeill is a Manx Gaelic term that refers to a small, dry-stone-walled Christian chapel or oratory (see Ellan Vannin for a photograph). There are approximately 180 sites known on the Isle of Man, mostly in rural locations without extant secular structures in the vicinity; a few more may be recalled in the place-name element *kil*. All are now disused and rarely survive to a height of more than half a metre; most are no longer visible above ground. The buildings were superseded by larger, mortared structures once congregational worship and territorial parishes became the norm, probably in the 12th century. Several keeills are associated with an enclosed cemetery (Manx Gaelic *rhullick*, cf. Old Irish *reilic*). At some locations, it is apparent that the extant keeill was built over preexisting graves.

Nick Johnson

KELLS, BOOK OF (*CODEX CENANNENSIS*)

The Book of Kells is the most richly decorated and iconographically complex of the large format, illustrated Latin gospel-books produced in the British Isles between the 7th and 10th centuries. Current scholarly opinion favours the view that it was begun on the Hebridean island of Iona (Eilean Ì) toward the end of the 8th century or early in the 9th century and sent to Kells in Co. Meath, Ireland (Ceanannas, Contae na Mí, Ériu), soon after. The manuscript is incomplete and some leaves are missing, and there is reason to believe that theft of the manuscript from the church at Kells sometime before 1017 may account for the loss of the book's cover and book shrine as well as most of its missing pages. It is now housed at Trinity College, Baile Átha Cliath (Dublin).

The text of the Book of Kells is based on the 4th-century Vulgate Latin Bible, with accompanying canon tables. As many as four scribes, using a bold script known as 'insular majuscule', laboured over the text. At the Gospel openings, Matthew 1:18, the start of the nativity story, is given special prominence. The page displays a greatly enlarged and embellished monogram of the Greek form of Christ's name (chi-rho), and is preceded by two full-page miniatures—the first with an image of Christ Enthroned, the second dominated by a large double-barred cross filled with ornament and set against a minutely detailed ornamented ground. Similarly, a sequence with a full-page Madonna and Child miniature facing an elaborately

Detail of the center of the chi-rho (Christ's monogram in the Greek alphabet) from the Book of Kells, fo. 34r, Trinity College Dublin MS 58 (A.I.6). (Jupiterimages)

ornamented text page appears in the preliminaries, another with a miniature of the Arrest of Christ is found at Matthew 26:31, and a third set with a full-page image of the Temptation of Christ is at Luke 4:1.

The highly embellished incipit pages, full-page miniatures, and canon tables are all elegantly ornamented with figural, animal, foliate, and geometrical details, and even the simpler text pages are filled with an extraordinary and seemingly infinite miscellany of these motifs drawn from the repertoire of Celtic (LA TÈNE), Anglo-Saxon, and Mediterranean styles integrated into the insular or Hiberno-Saxon style of early medieval Britain and Ireland. In terms of delicacy and meticulousness of touch and almost hallucinatory inventiveness, the decoration of the Book of Kells is unmatched in the circumscribed world of insular manuscript design and even the larger sphere of early medieval book art.

Although it represents the summit of insular book production, the Book of Kells stands apart from the insular tradition in two important respects: the multilayered painting technique employed by its artists and the placement of three of the full-page miniatures within the manuscript. In other insular gospel-books, miniatures are placed at the beginning or at the end of the codex and/or at the separate Gospel openings. In the Book of Kells, however, three full-page miniatures do not follow this rule: the Madonna and Child page introduced after the canon tables, and the Arrest and Temptation miniatures, each placed in the body of the manuscript, in Matthew and Luke, respectively.

Martin Werner

KENTIGERN, ST

St Kentigern (†*c.* AD 612) is remembered as the first bishop of Glasgow (Glaschu) and one of the most important of the northern British saints. The saint's name is

Celtic (*Kuno-tegernos*) and means 'hound lord', but he is commonly referred to by his nickname, Mungo.

The earliest traditions relating to the historical Kentigern are contained within two *vitae* commissioned by successive bishops during the 12th century. Aspects of an authentic 7th-century Kentigern tradition survive within the existing *vitae*, but only the barest details concerning his life can be accepted as historically correct. Reduced to its essence, the tradition maintains that Kentigern was the grandson of the British king of Lothian, that he was educated by St Serf at Culross, and that he became a monk. He travelled to Glasgow to bury a holy man named Fergus at the site of an existing cemetery. As a consequence of political disruptions, Kentigern travelled widely through Cumbria as well as Glasgow. At the time of his death, around AD 612, his biographers present him as being founding bishop of Glasgow cathedral, presumably bishop of the northern Britons.

Pre-12th-century church dedications indicate that veneration for Kentigern was strong throughout the Brythonic kingdom of Cumbria; there are eight dedications in the present-day county of Cumbria in England. Among these Kentigern dedications is the early medieval foundation in Annandale at Hoddom, a centre of some importance in both the 8th and 12th centuries.

Stephen Driscoll

KERNOW (CORNWALL)

Kernow (Cornwall) is one of the six regions in which a Celtic language was spoken in modern times (see Alba; Breizh; Cymru; Éire; Ellan Vannin; also Celtic Countries). Situated at the tip of the southwestern peninsula of Britain and covering 1,376 square miles (3,564 km^2), it is physically divided from the rest of the island by the river Tamar, a separationn that has helped to preserve the sense of an independent territory. The 2001 census recorded 501,257 inhabitants in the region.

The Cornish language, which is closely related to Welsh and Breton, is attested in a variety of texts. It went into steep decline after the Reformation (see Bible) and disappeared around 1800, with partially successful attempts at revival being made from the end of the 19th century (see language [revival] movements in the Celtic countries; dictionaries and grammars).

Cornwall and its inhabitants were part of the wider post-Roman kingdom known as Dumnonia. Cornubia was recorded as early as c. AD 700 as the name for the west of Dumnonia. Cornish *Kernow* corresponds exactly to Welsh *Cernyw,* which sometimes refers to a much larger region than the modern county, including what is now Somerset. The English name *Cornwall* combines the Celtic tribal name *Cornovii* and Anglo-Saxon *wealas,* a Germanic term applied to Romanized foreigners and also the source of Modern English *Wales.* Kernev in southwest Brittany is also a form of this name, and post-Roman migration from southwest Britain is a likely explanation for this connection (see Breton migrations).

In AD 936, Æthelstan, king of Wessex, fixed the border between his kingdom and Cornwall at the river Tamar. In 1337, Edward III created the Duchy of Cornwall to provide for his eldest living son and to take control of the Stannaries, an indigenous

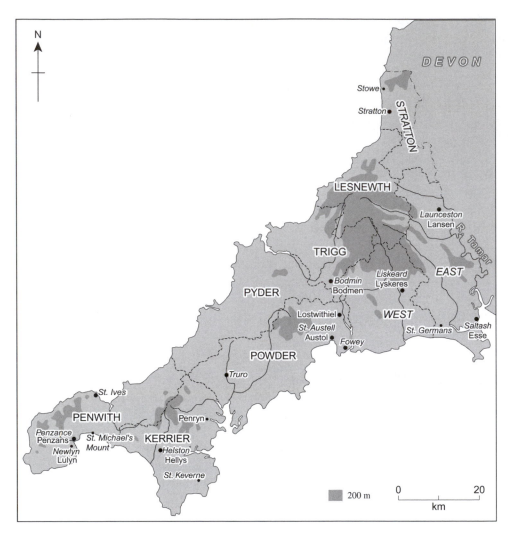

Cornwall/Kernow showing its traditional divisions or 'hundreds'. (Map by Ian Gulley and Antony Smith)

form of government (see Stannary Parliament). Until the 17th century, Cornwall was governed by the household of the Duke of Cornwall, which left it relatively free of administrative interference from the Crown.

Naturally, the long coastline and the sea have played an important part in Cornwall's history and economy, from smuggling in early modern times to today's booming tourist and surfing industry. For centuries, Cornwall has been famous for its pilchards. The relatively rare element tin was abundant in early Cornwall, and its tin and copper stores have been exploited since the Early Bronze Age (c. 2100 BC).

Both copper and tin mining declined after the 1870s, with the last tin mines closing in the 1980s. Thus Cornwall provides a remarkably early example of a post-industrial society. China clay mines have been another source of income for the

Cornish. Although not as numerous as before, the clay mines north of St Austell (Astol) still dominate the local landscape.

Amy Hale and Marion Löffler

KILKENNY, STATUTES OF

In 1366, the Anglo-Irish parliament at Kilkenny (Cill Chainnigh) passed a series of statutes directed at the perceived threat of Gaelicization to the English colony in Ireland (Éire). The Statutes forbade the use of Irish and the expression of Irish culture to the extent that these contrasted with English culture, and amounted to cultural protection legislation for the Anglo-Normans. They also promoted English social institutions—for instance, English common law over Brehon law (see LAW TEXTS)—and denigrated the native Irish institutions such as the BARDIC ORDER. The legislation was haphazardly enforced, and was not entirely successful; it was repealed in the parliament of 1613–15.

Antone Minard

KILTS

The Scottish kilt of today is a men's garment, resembling a knee-length, pleated skirt, typically made from tartan fabric (see TARTANS). The earliest evidence for a garment ancestral to the modern kilt is found in ART and descriptions from around the late 16th century, which indicate that this garment was a large rectangular cloak, fastened about the shoulders and belted around the body.

Seventeenth-century depictions show this style, known variously as the belted plaid, *breacan fèileadh, fèileadh mòr,* or great kilt, and it is a common feature of formal portraits of noblemen with Highland connections. Prohibition of the kilt for ordinary wear as part of the Dress Act of 1746, combined with its popular use as a uniform by some Scottish military units, helped to convert the garment into an icon of national identity. When the Act was repealed in 1782, the kilt had become firmly fixed in the popular imagination not simply as a characteristic Highland garment, but as a national costume for Scotland (ALBA) as a whole.

The expansion of the kilt from a Scottish to a pan-Celtic symbol (see PAN-CELTICISM), sometimes accompanied by distinctive national variants, was a 20th-century development.

Heather Rose Jones

KINGDOM OF MAN AND THE ISLES

Following Viking raiding and later settlement in BRITAIN and Ireland (ÉRIU), the Isle of Man (ELLAN VANNIN), together with the 'Hebrides' (Innse Gall)—thirty-one larger and many hundreds of smaller islands off the west coast of Scotland (ALBA)—became a petty kingdom under the theoretical control of the King of Norway. Place-name, epigraphic, and archaeological evidence suggests considerable mixing of the Norse and native populations (see SCOTTISH PLACE-NAMES). The kings of Man and the Isles themselves appear to be of mixed Norse–Gaelic origin.

During most of the 11th century, power had swayed between kings based in Baile Átha Cliath (Dublin), Man, and Orkney. Somerled (Somhairle Mac Gillbhríde, †1164), ruler of coastal Argyle (Earra-Ghaidheal), defeated the Manx king Godred II twice and forced him to share control of the kingdom, with Somerled taking Mull (Muile) and Islay (Île), and Godred taking Skye (An t-Eilean Sgitheanach) and Lewis (Leòdhas).

Relations between Scotland and Norway came to a head at the battle of Largs in 1263, in which Haakon of Norway was forced to retreat by Alexander III of Scotland. Magnus, the last Norse King of Man, had gone to assist Haakon but did not actually participate in the battle; afterward, he remained virtually a prisoner on Man until his death in 1265. By the Treaty of Perth in 1266, the whole of the Kingdom of the Isles became Scottish. The Chronicles of the Kings of Man and the Isles, written at this time, appear to have as their prime motive a desire to establish the legitimacy of the family.

From 1266 onward, though the Scots claimed Man, it fell increasingly under the authority and finally the control of the English, with power over the island granted by Henry IV to Sir John Stanley in 1406. The core of the remaining parts of the kingdom stayed under the influence of Somerled's sons, albeit not without periods of strife between them. The shadow of the development of central power in Scotland greatly reduced the independence of the Macdonalds, whose Lordship of the Isles, based first at Finlaggan on Islay and later in Skye, represented the direct successor to the Norse island empire.

P. J. Davey

KINGS' CYCLES, MEDIEVAL IRISH

Introduction

The Kings' Cycle, or simply Cycles, is one of the four main classifications of early Irish narrative literature (see TALE LISTS; IRISH LITERATURE). The term embraces several prose sagas, poems, and anecdotes that focus on the exploits of certain early Irish kings and dynasts generally not treated in the ULSTER CYCLE, FIANNAÍOCHT, and the MYTHOLOGICAL CYCLE. The vast majority of these texts are written in Old and Middle IRISH, starting from around the 8th century AD, although stories about particularly famous kings such as CONN CÉTCHATHACH and his grandson CORMAC MAC AIRT continued to be composed in the Early Modern Period (1200–1650). Set against the chronological framework of Irish history and LEGENDARY HISTORY, the stories span a period of almost 1,500 years, from the 3rd or 4th century BC to the 10th or 11th century AD. They are united, however, by their common focus on conflicts and kingships and matters concerning the community groups. Even so, these tales are not historical in the modern sense.

The Kings

According to Irish tradition, the kings who appear in the Kings' Cycle of Tales had, in fact, existed and, therefore, could meaningfully be claimed as ancestors by latter-day tribes and rulers. However, it is doubtful whether this was true of any of the figures belonging to periods earlier than the 5th century AD. The earliest figure in the Cycles is Labraid Loingsech, the mythical ancestor of the Leinstermen.

Although kings from each of the five provinces appear in the Cycles, not all of the ten or so great dynasties of the historical period are represented. In fact, a greater number of the kings in the Cycles have genealogical ties to the Uí Néill lineages of the north and midlands than to any other dynasty. Provincial dynasties are also represented in Kings' Cycle texts. Thus the Cycle includes narratives of Connachta kings such as Dathí mac Fiachrach (†445) and Guaire Aidne (†662), in addition to the legendary prehistoric legendary Connachta (i.e., descendants of the prehistoric Conn Cétchathach), who were also ancestors of the Uí Néill. From Munster (MUMU) legend come figures such as Conall Corc (Corc of Caisel) and Éogan Már; from Leinster (LAIGIN), Brandub mac Echach (†605) and Rónán mac Aedo (†623); and from Ulster (ULAID), Fiachnae mac Baetáin (†626) and Fergus mac Léite, whose death-tale contains the earliest extant reference to the leprechaun (see LUCHORPÁN).

The Individual Cycles

For ease of reference, modern scholars have grouped the kings' tales by the characters who appear in them. The largest grouping involves Cormac mac Airt, progenitor of the Uí Néill. The second largest focuses on Diarmait mac Cerbaill, the Uí Néill king of Tara (TEAMHAIR), who was killed in AD 565. Other kings popular in the literature include Conn Cét-Chathach (Conn of the hundred battles), Mongán mac Fiachna, and Guaire Aidne.

Dan Wiley

KINGSHIP, CELTIC

Introduction

The rôle of kings in ancient and medieval Celtic-speaking lands was in many respects comparable to that in other societies around the world that were also tribal and largely rural, with a hierarchical ranking of classes, a warrior aristocracy, and great emphasis on personal honour. Without a regulated cash economy, surpluses were exchanged as gifts entailing personal obligations between granter and recipient. At the apex of such small-scale societies, the successful king had to begin with a recognized illustrious lineage. He had to excel as a war leader. His share of surplus wealth had to be enhanced, often through leading successful raids against neighbouring tribes, and subsequently to be generously and wisely distributed as gifts to ensure the loyalty of followers.

Archaism and Innovation

At the time of the campaigns of Caesar in GAUL (60–50 BC), many of the tribes had already given up the institution of kingship and were ruled instead by magistrates called *vergobreti*. Such findings of innovation among the free Celtic governing classes do not outweigh the fact that Celtic vocabulary, literature, and legal principles relating to kingship preserve numerous inherited and apparently primitive features, however much these could be disregarded as hollow conventions in practice. Furthermore, even 'hollow' conventions, as long as their significance is appreciated, provide a vocabulary for articulating political claims and were thus skilfully manipulated as propaganda in early Ireland, albeit probably not slavishly adhered to as sacred traditions.

Some Literary Conventions of Kingship

Numerous intriguing features of kingship recur so frequently in early Irish literature and are so well developed that we must assume that they were widely understood, whether or not they were still believed or practised. For instance, the idea that the king must be unblemished (physically perfect) is widespread and is used, for example, to account for the way in which the historical 7th-century king of Ulaid, Congal Caech (Congal the one-eyed, †653), forfeited the kingship of Tara (Teamhair) after being partially blinded by bees, as described in the legal text *Bechbretha* (Bee-judgements). The same idea is found in the Mythological Cycle.

The tribal king figures as a virtual linchpin of the cosmic order, assuring the beneficial harmony between the natural universe and his people, especially the weather and crops. On the opposite side of the coin, in *Cath Maige Mucrama* ('The Battle of Mag Mucrama'), Lugaid Mac Con's reign in Tara ends after a false judgement of his is declared to be such by young Cormac mac Airt: On the spot, the wall of the house collapses at Tara, and no plants grow until Mac Con leaves the kingship. Such examples show how the wasteland theme—which was of central importance to the international Arthurian literature of the Grail—arose from traditional Celtic narrative expressions of the ideology of kingship.

The idea that the king is wedded to the woman personifying the sovereignty of his kingdom—though not confined to Celtic material—has been viewed as the central myth of Celtic tradition and is discussed in the article sovereignty myth.

That Ireland had a single *ard-rí* (high-king) associated with the site of Tara is a pervasive premise in the Kings' Cycles and legendary history. However, in the Ulster Cycle, the kings of the provinces (*cóiceda*, sing. cóiced) seem to be the top tier. Practical control by one king over all or most of Ireland first became a reality only fitfully in the Viking Age (see Ériu).

Parallel concepts are found in Wales, but the idea is absent from the earliest sources; in pre-Roman times, several tribes did coalesce around Cassivellaunos to resist Caesar and, a century later, Caratācos managed to fight on in the west and north with authority as an intertribal war-leader even after the lands of his native Catuvellauni had fallen to his enemies. The closest approximation we have to a pre-Roman peacetime British high-king would be Caratācos's father Cunobelinos, but the fragmentation that provided the opportunity for the Roman invasion of AD 43, a few years after his death, shows pre-Roman high-kingship to have been more of a remarkable accomplishment than a stable institution.

Terms and Their Implications

Two Old Irish words stand out as very old cultural concepts, once general throughout the Celtic world. These words are *rí* 'king' (Gaulish *rīx*, cf. Latin *rēx*) and *tuath* 'people, tribe, tribal land' (Gaulish *toutā*, Welsh and Breton *tud*). Most importantly, the terms define each other reciprocally: A *rí* is one who rules a *tuath*; a *tuath* is what is ruled by a *rí*. As the *tuath* was a dispersed rural population, the *rí* had to gather them together in an *oenach* (assembly; cf. Modern Irish *aonach* 'fair') to direct them in group action. These specially kingly functions regarding his *tuath* included enacting new laws and treaties. The struggles or alliances between tribes, in theory, involved individuals only through their kings, with the average tribesman or tribeswoman having no recognized status at all outside the tribe. This aspect led to the special importance of the border and the transformation of the warrior from refined courtier to bestial manslayer at the frontier (see HEROIC ETHOS). The identity-giving function of the *rí* and his *tuath*—taken together with the idea discussed previously that the ruler maintained not only the social order, but also the natural order—explains the commonplace plot in the tales in which a journey into the wilderness beyond the frontier rapidly descends into a frightful Otherworld adventure. The closed system of the Irish *tuath* has an interesting echo in the tightly closed community of Arthur's court in *Culhwch ac Olwen*; only Arthur himself can break the rules of his own court to admit his cousin, wisely explaining that his own status depended on permitting such noble heroes as Culhwch to approach him for favour.

An early word meaning 'leader' appears on a 5th- or 6th-century inscribed stone as both OGAM Irish and British genitive TOVISACI: *Tywysog* now means 'prince' in WELSH, the regular descriptive title used for Prince Charles, for example. In Ireland, the corresponding *Taoiseach* is now the correct title, in both Irish and English, for the Prime Minister of the Irish Republic (ÉIRE).

John T. Koch

KINSHIP, CELTIC

Celtic kinship is known largely from medieval IRISH and WELSH sources. Both the earliest Irish and Welsh sources exhibit a very complex kinship system. Kinship differed according to which element of social structure was otherwise involved. If it was status, kinship was partly bilateral (taking into account both paternal and maternal ancestry); if it was the holding and transmission of land, kinship was agnatic or patrilineal; if it was alliance, notably in feud, kinship was a bilateral alliance of kindreds who were themselves patrilineal.

For status, the rank of a mother mattered as well as the rank of a father. Kinship and status also interacted within early Irish marriage. An Irish nobleman enjoyed high rank because he had many cattle, which he could advance as fiefs to ordinary commoners. The latter could expect to inherit land, but they needed to become base-clients of a noble to gain enough cattle to sustain normal mixed farming. The inheritance of commoners was largely land, which normally passed down from father to sons. The kinship of inheritance for commoners was thus essentially agnatic. For nobles, the situation was different, as their high rank depended on cattle. The highest form of marital union in Irish law was 'a pairing of joint-contribution', when both bride and bridegroom contributed movable wealth, most importantly cattle, to their farming resources. For a noble, therefore, wealth came both from mother and from father, because movables were as important in his resources as land.

The inheritance of land was normally partible among all the recognized sons, whether or not their parents were married. The sole importance of the illegitimacy was that the father only had the choice to acknowledge or reject a son if that son was born out of wedlock. In Irish law, it is probable that provision was made for a resharing of the land between grandsons and great-grandsons; in Welsh law, this understanding is explicitly stated. Similarly, in the earliest Irish legal texts, it appears that if a line of descent died out, such that their land could not pass down in the normal way from father to sons, it passed to collateral kinsmen within a group known as the *derb-fhine*, 'certain kindred'. This group comprised the descendants of a common great-grandfather. Its counterpart in Welsh, known as the 'joint-heirs', stretched out to the first cousin, *cefnderw*, and second cousin, *cyferderw*. Both these terms for collateral kinsmen contained a word, *derw*, which is cognate with Irish *derb* as in *derbfhine*.

Thus there appears to have been a relative stability in the shallow kindred primarily relevant for inheritance, but much greater change in the deeper kindreds, usually of more political importance.

T. M. Charles-Edwards

L

LA TÈNE, ARCHAEOLOGICAL SITE

The archaeological sites of La Tène and Hallstatt were responsible for shaping archaeological concepts of the European Iron Age well into the 1970s, and the second phase of the Iron Age over much of Continental Europe is still called La Tène, after the type site on the northern shores of Lake Neuchâtel in Switzerland. 'Celtic' was often treated as almost synonymous with 'La Tène' with reference to the period from c. 475 BC to the advance of cultural Romanization. La Tène properly refers to a type of material culture, and Celtic to a set of languages and the associated culture; in most areas, La Tène objects were used by Celtic speakers, but not all, and not all Celtic cultures used La Tène objects in that time period.

The La Tène site itself consists of the remains of two bridges across the river Zihl/Thielle, the remains of houses and palisades, and, perhaps most importantly, numerous WATERY DEPOSITIONS, especially of weapons and other characteristic high-status metal objects. Dendrochronological dating of the wood places the construction of Pont Vouga, the narrower bridge (c. 4 m in width), around 250 BC. A SHIELD found close to the bridge was found to have been made from the wood of a tree felled in 229 BC. In the same area, several skeletons and numerous other finds were discovered.

In total, approximately 2,500 objects have been recovered from the site, in an area that extends for approximately 25 m along the bank downstream from Pont Vouga and about the same length along the course of the bridge into the river. Finds include SWORDS, shields, and other weapons; metal adornments; knives, razors, sickles, scythes, and other tools; bronze CAULDRONS; and iron ingots. Apart from these objects, domestic pottery and other household items have been found, as well as remains of CHARIOTS and carts.

Raimund Karl

LA TÈNE PERIOD

All Iron Age chronological systems have been developed from local typological systems based, to a large degree, on the analysis of grave goods. These systems were never intended to have a pan-European application. Nevertheless, some major common features are shared by the various regional systems.

The late Hallstatt regional groupings of barrow cemeteries with four-wheeled wagons clearly dedicated to the élite are replaced in La Tène A/Ia by groups of similar rich barrow cemeteries with two-wheeled chariots (see VEHICLE BURIALS). These were concentrated in northeastern France, the middle Rhine, and western Bohemia. La Tène Bi/Ib saw a marked reduction of the élite burials, which are

Detail of Iron Age flagons from Basse-Yutz, Moselle, France, *c.* 400 BC. A detail showing one of the 'oriental' handles in canine form, an imported Mediterranean idea executed in local style. (The Trustees of the British Museum/Art Resource, New York)

replaced by flat grave cemeteries. Chronologically, this period is contemporary with a major expansion east and south into northern Italy—the time of the Gaulish invasions. This period saw the development of the Vegetal or Waldalgesheim Style with its obvious influence from Graeco-Etruscan motifs; La Tène Bii/Ic is also related to a continuation of movements east as far as the Balkans and ultimately across to the Anatolian plain. Middle La Tène C/II is seen as a period of consolidation into several distinct regional groups still buried in flat cemeteries with a marked number of graves with weapons suggestive of a warrior class, a view that is supported by classical accounts of the employment of Celtic mercenaries throughout the Mediterranean. This period also saw the introduction of the first indigenous coinage, initially copied from contemporary Hellenistic staters. The final main phase, La Tène D/III, has always been considered as marked by an increase in tribal centralization based on a number of oppida, several of considerable size and larger than many medieval towns. A feature of Late La Tène was a greater degree of uniformity across Europe from eastern Slovakia to northern France, a uniformity that was, in fact, more perceived than real. The Late La Tène phase ends with the gradual spread of the Roman Empire across central and western Europe, which was completed by the middle of the 1st century AD with the conquest of lowland BRITAIN.

Regional refinements have been made in several areas—for example, a distinctive eastern Hallstatt zone has been identified, while in the west the rich graves of Hallstatt C and D have been regarded as marking the first stages of a 'Celtic' culture. Celtic, in this sense, is relatively remote from the linguistic definition; in other words, this usage should *not* be taken to mean that a language that had not previously existed came into being around 750 BC. In contrast, this archaeological sense of 'Celtic' may come close to the early central European groups, which the Greeks first identified as κελτοί *Keltoi*.

Chronological table of the Hallstatt (Ha) and La Tène (LT) periods

	Eastern France	S. Germany / Switzerland	N. Italy	Yugoslavia	Dendro-chronology	Historical Events	Early Celtic Art Styles
BC	Bronze final III	Hallstatt B3 (Late Urnfields)	Villanova III (Benacci II) — Este II			Steppe nomads in Assyria	
700	Hallstatt I — Early Hallstatt	Ha I Ha C1 / Long swords Hill-forts / Ha C2	Vill IVa	Slovenia: Podzemelj 'Thraco-Cimmerian' influence			
600	Ha IIa — Late Hallstatt	Ha II Ha D1 / Daggers Princely graves	Vill IVb (Arnoaldi) — Situlae	Stična I Novo mesto Italian influence Stična II		c.600 Etruscans at Rome / Foundation of Massalia	
500	Ha IIb Les Jogasses	Ha D2 / Ha D3	Certosa — Este III — Etruscans	Horizon with double ridged helmets / Scythian influence	Altrier 464	c.520 Foundation of Spina / 513 Persians in Balkans / 508 End of Etruscan rule in Rome	
400	— Early La Tène —	LT Ia Chieftains' graves / LT A	— Cels	Hallstatt graves with 'Negau' helmets / La Tène influence		Etruria Padana	Early style
300	La Tène I	LT Ib LT B1 Duchcov & Münsingen brooches / LT Ic LT B1		West group: Mokronog 1 — East group: Belgrade 1		387 Sack of Rome / 335 Celtic embassy to Alexander the Great / 279-7 Celts in Balkans Sack of Delphi / 270 Settlement of Asia Minor / 240/30 War of Attalos I against Galatae	Gaulish invasion of Italy/Pannonia / 'Waldalgesheim' or 'Vegetal' / 'Sword' styles — Early 'plastic' — Late 'plastic'
200	LT II — Middle La Tène —	LT II LT C1 / LT C2	— Romans	Mokronog 2-4 — Belgrade 2	La Tène shields 229 / Wederath 208	233/2 Ager gallicus / 225 Battle of Telamon / 222 Defeat of Insubres / 191 Defeat of Boii / 190/81 Pergamene reliefs	Early insular style (Torrs-Witham)
100		Oppida LT III LT D1 / LT D2 Nauheim brooches			Fellbach 123 / Cornaux 120-16 / Manching 105 / Ehrang 70	124/3 Roman conquest of Gallia Narbonensis / 113/101 Invasion of Cimbri & Teutones	
0	LT III — Late La Tène —	LT D3		Mokronog 5-6 — Belgrade 3		Celto-Dacian wars / 58 Defeat of Helvetii / 58/50 Gallic wars / 52 Fall or Alesia End of Oppida / 15 Alpine campaign	Later insular style (mirrors/ harness mounts)
AD						AD43 Claudian invasion of Britain	
100							Ultimate or Late N. British/Irish

Chronological table of the Hallstatt (Ha) and La Tène (LT) periods
Source: after Ruth Megaw & Vincent Megaw, *Celtic Art*

One aspect that certainly seems to mark the beginning of a new culture, at least in material terms, is the ART of the rich or 'chieftainly' graves of La Tène A, which are found mainly in northeastern France and the Middle Rhine and across to Bohemia. These artefacts represent what the classical archaeologist Paul Jacobsthal described in detail in 1944 as 'Early Celtic Art', an art style that he regarded as developing in part from preceding indigenous Hallstatt, but also showing borrowings from, and variations of, classical motifs.

Much of the work on the chronology of the European Iron Age has been concerned with the defining of regional chronologies and the refinement of their dating, which continue to reflect the basic periodization first established by Otto Tischler and Paul Reinecke; brooch typology is still central in this system. For example, one may now subdivide the final La Tène D1 and D2 phases associated with the main period of the south German oppida such as Manching, near Ingolstadt. While their beginnings go back at least to the early 3rd century BC and they cannot have survived the campaigns of Tiberius and Drusus in AD 15, the oppida seem to begin to decline in the middle of the 1st century.

The Iron Age in Britain and Ireland

The chronology of the Iron Age in the British Isles and Ireland (ÉRIU) still presents many difficulties. While movements across the English Channel cannot be entirely discounted, notably with regard to the origins of 'insular' La Tène art, the continuing antipathy toward what has been termed 'the invasion hypothesis' has virtually led to the abandonment of the terms 'Hallstatt' and 'La Tène' as chronological descriptors for the Iron Age of the British Isles and Ireland. This is particularly the case for Ireland, where one of the most troublesome aspects of what has been termed 'the enigma of the Irish Iron Age' is the absence of Continental material, let alone anything that definitely indicates a movement from the Continent.

Limitations and "Celtoscepticism"

There is no doubt that the basic Hallstatt–La Tène chronology has been applied much too widely on the Continent, as in the British Isles. There seems to be little typological—or cultural—support for its use, for example, in the eastern Balkans or around the Black Sea. Some would go further; there has been much debate concerning the equation that is often made between archaeological phases—however defined—and 'cultures', meaning a correlation between material manifestations and regional ethnicities or identities. In particular, a group of English archaeologists has questioned not only the existence of a pan-European Celtic society, but also the view that La Tène (let alone late Hallstatt) periods equal ancient Celtic society. The same scholars deny the very existence of insular Celts at any time in insular prehistory. From this position, it is a small logical step to argue for the abandonment of the very terms 'Hallstatt' and 'La Tène'.

J. V. S. Megaw and M. Ruth Megaw

LAIGIN (LEINSTER)

Laigin (Leinster), Early Modern Irish Laighin, is Ireland's traditional southeastern province.

Definition and Extent

In early historic Ireland (Ériu), Laigin designated a group, with subtribes, as well as a kingdom, also known as Cóiced *Laigen* 'the province of Leinster'. In current usage, the province of Leinster (Cúige Laighean) is understood to mean the counties of Baile Átha Cliath (Dublin), Wicklow (Cill Mhantáin), Wexford (Loch Garman), Kilkenny (Cill Cheannaigh), Carlow (Ceatharlach), Laois, Offaly (Uíbh Fháile), Meath (An Mhí), Westmeath (An Iarmhí), Longford (Longphort), and Louth (Lú). Of these, the first seven lay within the ancient province, while Meath and Westmeath broadly correspond to an area often reckoned to be a central fifth province (*Coíced Midi*) in early Irish literature. Louth had been southeast Ulster (Ulaid, *Coíced Ulad*) and, in fact, figures as Cú Chulainn's home country, with much of the action of the Ulster Cycle taking place there. The geographical boundaries of early historical Leinster were defined by the river Liffey and the bogs of Offaly in the north, and the uplands of Ossory (Osraige) in the west. It was apparently a more coherent tribal territory than other provinces.

Prehistory and Protohistory

Early texts use the group names *Laigin* and *Gáileóin* interchangeably. Archaeological evidence suggests that the Leinster area had significant ties with Roman Britain—for example, the Roman or highly Romanized Stonyford burial, Co. Kilkenny, and material from the fort of Rathgall, Co. Wicklow. On the linguistic side, archaic poems concerned with Leinster's dynasty have a high proportion of rare or otherwise unattested secular Latin loanwords. The tradition of pre-Patrician saints in the southeast is another indication of possible Roman influence. That the name *Laigin* survives attached to some significant places in north Wales (Cymru), such as the *Llŷn* Peninsula, is evidence for the prominence of the *Laigin* in that part of Britain in Roman and/or early post-Roman times.

The church of St Brigit at Kildare (Cill Dara) was of importance to the kings of Leinster; Brigit may have been a Christianized tribal goddess (see Brigantes).

The Early Middle Ages

Once we enter the more solid historical record of the annals from the 6th century, we find Leinster's kingship contested between the rival Uí Dúnlainge and Uí Cheinnselaig lineages. From AD 738 to 1042, Leinster's kingship was monopolized by the Uí Dúnlainge of the Liffey plain, whose power base was located at Naas (Nás na Rí). The earliest annalistic references to the Laigin show them at war with the Uí Néill, who eventually wrested the territory north of the river Liffey from them.

Strife between these two kingdoms continued over the following centuries, much of it caused, ostensibly, by the Cattle Tribute of Leinster (*Bórama Laigen*), a payment demanded annually by the Uí Néill and often contested in battle. The *Bórama's* origins are traced back into the prehistoric period, as a blood-fine (*éraicc*) owed Tuathal Techtmar, a legendary ancestor of the Uí Néill, for the dishonourable deaths of two daughters married to Eochu, king of Leinster.

The Viking Age

The two most notable kings produced by the Laigin were both members of the Uí Cheinnselaig lineage. The first of these, Diarmait mac Mael na mBó, became king of Leinster around 1046 and extended his power by seizing the kingship of Dublin in 1052. Eventually controlling Leinster, Munster, and Osraige, Diarmait was effectively overking of Leth Moga (the southern half of Ireland). His great-great-grandson, Diarmait Mac Murchada, is infamous in Irish history as Diarmait na nGall (Diarmaid of the Foreigners), who created the political alliance that resulted in the Anglo-Norman conquest of most of Ireland.

Anglo-Normans and Gaelic Survival

Leinster was the province most successfully colonized initially by the Norman incursions, which began in 1169. Nonetheless, substantial areas remained in the hands of Gaelic lords descended from the Laigin until the 17th century. The fastnesses of the Wicklow mountains were held by the Ua Broin (O'Byrne), descendants of the Uí Faeláin, while the Ua Mórdha (O'More) retained their independence in Laois, as did the Ua Conchubhair (O'Connor) in Offaly and the Mac Murchada (McMurrough) in northern Wexford. At this time, several of the Irish noble families were more powerful than they had ever been in pre-Norman times, and in this context it is interesting to note that the kingship of Leinster was the longest surviving of all the Irish provincial kingships, with the last Mac Murchada to claim the title dying in 1631.

During the Desmond and Nine Years Wars, the Gaelic lords of Leinster joined the Fitzgeralds and O'Neills against the forces of Elizabeth I. Their greatest military success of this period was achieved in 1580, but the defeat at Kinsale (Cionn tSáile) in 1601 was as disastrous and final for the Gaels of Leinster as elsewhere throughout the country, and its aftermath saw their refuges in the vast forests of Offaly, Wicklow, and Wexford fall to the axes of the colonists.

Simon Ó Faoláin

LAILOKEN

Lailoken is a character who appears in some medieval Scottish texts, a hermit with visionary powers living in extreme hardship in the wild. He closely parallels the Irish Suibne Geilt and the Welsh Myrddin (Merlin), and many writers have regarded the three as sharing a common north British origin. For an overview of the related legends of Lailoken and the other two figures, see Wild Man.

Literary Sources for Lailoken

The Scottish sources for Lailoken occur within material for the Lives of St Kentigern compiled from the 12th-century. Two Lailoken stories are 'Kentigern's encounter with Lailoken' and 'Lailoken in King Meldred's court'. These stories may date back well into the 11th century—even to a time when written or spoken Cumbric sources were available, as the Brythonic name 'Rederech' (Rhydderch) in the text suggests. The wild-man material was probably incorportated from earlier pre-Gaelic vernacular traditions regarding the battle of Arfderydd.

The Identity of Lailoken and Myrddin

In the Cotton Titus manuscript, 'Kentigern's encounter with Lailoken' and 'Lailoken in King Meldred's court' are headed *Vita Merlini Silvestris* (The Life of Merlin Silvester), and Bower heads his version of Kentigern's encounter with Lailoken *De mirabili paenitentia Merlini vatis* (Of the penitential marvels of the seer Merlin). Both manuscripts thus show knowledge of the Merlin of *Vita Merlini* and of Welsh tradition, especially as he was seen by writers of the later 12th century. The scribe of 'Kentigern's encounter with Lailoken' considers the rumour that Lailoken was one and the same as the 'extraordinary prophet of the Britons, Merlyn'. For a 12th-century audience, there was at least a possibility of equating the two figures.

Lailoken's Penitence

'Kentigern's encounter with Lailoken' focuses on worthy partaking of the sacrament. Kentigern's leaving the consecrated host on the altar for Lailoken to receive—neither offering nor refusing it—is motivated by church law regarding participation in communion by the mentally and spiritually afflicted. Following biblical models, Lailoken is to be translated immediately to glory because of his temporal sufferings.

The Name

Lailoken is apparently a Brythonic name corresponding to the Middle Welsh word *llallawc*, and more specifically to its diminutive *llallogan*. In the Myrddin poetry, only the *Cyfoesi* include the epithets *llallawc* or *llallogan*, by which Gwenddydd addresses her brother Myrddin. The terms appear elsewhere only in the Llywarch Hen cycle, in both cases meaning 'brother', 'friend', 'lord', or 'honoured one'. The source is probably *llall* 'other one'.

Brian Frykenberg

LAKE SETTLEMENT

Insular Bronze Age

Excavated examples of lake settlements stretch back more than 10,000 years into the past. In Ireland (Ériu) and Britain, excavations indicate an increase in lake settlement activity in the Late Bronze Age from around 1200 BC. This phenomenon coincides with a more general increase in defended settlements, weaponry production, and a marked climatic downturn. More frequent lake settlement at this time may be linked to the latter factors, reflecting a preference for easily defensible locations in a warlike society where conflict was on the increase and/or where people were being forced to live in agriculturally marginal areas due to climatic deterioration and the resulting population pressure. Some of the Irish sites occupy lakeside positions extending somewhat into the shallows in a similar manner to the Continental pile-dwellings. Other lake settlements of the later prehistoric period in Ireland—such as some of those in Lough Gara, Co. Sligo (Contae Shligigh)—are wholly or largely artificial platforms raised well above the water's surface, constituting islands cut off from the shoreline, a true 'crannog' (Irish *crannóg*)—a term more commonly applied to such structures in early medieval Ireland and Scotland.

Insular Iron Age

For the important Continental Iron Age lake site on Lake Neuchâtel, see La Tène, archaeological site.

In Britain, the Iron Age lake village at Glastonbury was a settlement of round houses, each raised above the water level on its own individual mound of clay, accompanied by outdoor working areas, with the whole grouping being surrounded by a timber palisade. Data from excavations indicate that the settlement was occupied for at least 150 years, beginning around 250 BC, and that the population grew gradually over that time to an estimated 200 or so. Excavations at the slightly earlier Iron Age wetland site at Meare, approximately 5 km from the Glastonbury lake village, suggest that it was a place of periodic gatherings such as markets and/or festivals rather than a settlement. In comparison with the preceding Bronze Age, definite Iron Age lake settlements are rare in Ireland, following the trend for settlement in that period in general.

Late prehistoric lake settlements in Ireland and Britain share several common features. The material recovered from them often indicates that the inhabitants were relatively well off, with decorative artefacts of bronze, amber, and glass not uncommonly turned up by excavations and surveys. Also, evidence of water transport, such as piers (Glastonbury), paddles (Clonfinlough), and boats (Lough Eskragh and Glastonbury), emphasizes the fact that travel would have been primarily on waterways. Lake settlement during this period was mirrored by settlement in other wetland environments, such as the banks and islands of large rivers (e.g., Runnymede Bridge, on the Thames in Surrey, England), estuaries (e.g., Goldcliff on the Severn estuary in Gwent, Wales, and several sites on the Shannon estuary in Ireland), and marshlands (Assendelver Polders, Netherlands).

Medieval and Early Modern Crannogs

In the early medieval period, the use of lake dwellings in the Celtic-speaking lands appears to have been essentially confined to Ireland and Scotland (Alba), where crannogs were a popular form of dwelling (approximately 1,200 have been identified in Ireland and at least several hundred in Scotland). Different definitions have been advanced for crannogs, but—as outlined previously—the main defining features are generally that they are mainly or wholly artificial islands (most often round or oval in plan) built of timber, stone, and peat, raised well above the surrounding water level and endowed with a palisaded perimeter. In some parts of western Ireland, particularly Conamara, Co. Galway (Contae na Gaillimhe), crannogs are surmounted by CASHELS (stone-built early medieval forts), rather than by the more conventional wooden palisade.

Considerable variation exists among investigated crannogs in terms of many attributes, including size, purpose, apparent status of occupants, and length of occupation. Most crannogs appear to have been primarily places of residence, whatever other activities took place upon them, though exceptions are known. Although these settlements were primarily an early medieval site-type, numerous documentary references make it clear that crannogs continued to be inhabited in Ireland, for military purposes at least, until the 15th century. The archaeological evidence supports this point, with later medieval material recovered in significant quantities from several sites (e.g., Lough Faughan, Co. Down; Newtownlow, Co. Westmeath). In Scotland, their use into the 17th century or even the 18th century is related to hunting and feasting by high-status clansmen, as portrayed in contemporary Gaelic verse, and, possibly, as a neutral location at which treaties and disputes could be handled.

Many important questions remain regarding crannogs: Is it valid to regard the early medieval variety as a development of the late prehistoric examples? Moreover, was early medieval crannog construction introduced into Scotland from Ireland, or vice versa? To what extent were these structures' locations decided purely by defensive factors, or was there a special social significance to their situation in lakes that has not yet been fully grasped?

Simon Ó Faoláin

LAND AGITATION, IRELAND

The last quarter of the 19th century witnessed three phases of land agitation in Ireland (ÉIRE) , all broadly similar in methods: the Land League (1879–82), the Plan of Campaign (1886–91), and the United Irish League (1898–1903). The first phase of the agitation is generally termed the 'land war', though some historians extend the term to include the two later phases. The 'land war' was a social revolution rather than a war, which resulted in the demise of Irish landlordism. The economic distress was most acute in western Ireland, which was home to most of the Irish-speaking communities in this period.

Following the massive dislocation and high mortality during the Great FAMINE, Ireland experienced a period of relative prosperity. In the post-Famine decades, insolvent estates changed hands, uneconomic and unsustainable plots of land were consolidated into larger holdings, and there was a switch from tillage to less labour-intensive pastoral farming. From the mid-1850s to the late 1870s, productivity and price increases far outstripped the rise in agricultural rents. In these generally buoyant years, the majority of Irish landlords adopted a relatively benign attitude toward their tenants and, in the main, harmonious relations existed between them.

The years 1877–79 witnessed a succession of wet and cold seasons, poor harvests, falling prices, and reduced demand, all of which threatened the economic gains that the majority of Irish tenant farmers had experienced since the mid-1850s. The agricultural crisis was most severely felt in the west of Ireland, where small farmers were once again threatened with bankruptcy, eviction, and starvation. Tenants looked to their landlords for relief, but there was a general resistance to granting voluntary rent reductions—a reluctance that exposed the vast cultural and political gulf separating landowners and tenants.

The Land League was launched with two declared objectives in 1879: to protect the tenant farmers against their landlords in the short term, and ultimately to turn the farmers into the owners of their holdings. This movement began in Mayo (Contae Mhaigh Eo), one of the country's poorest counties. It was predicated on a form of mass mobilization and motivation, a tenant collectivity that was banded and bonded by a brilliant orchestration of publicity and propaganda, promises and intimidation. 'Moonlighting', or the activities of agrarian secret societies, including physical assaults and threats, arson, and the maiming of farm animals, gave added steel to the widely implemented policy of social ostracism, or boycotting, as it came to be called. The main targets were those involved in evictions and the individuals who took over the farms, dubbed 'landgrabbers'. The more radical nationalists believed that the 'land war' was not merely an assault on the institution of landlordism, but also an attack on the landlord class as part of the English garrison in Ireland.

The 'land war' cut through the layers of traditional deference that the ordinary people of Ireland had displayed to the higher social classes, and brought them to a new level of political consciousness and organization. The recurring phases of agrarian militancy resulted in a series of Land Acts, beginning with that of 1881, which legalized tenant rights and introduced the concept of dual ownership in the land. It culminated in major Land Purchase Acts in 1903 and 1909, which revolutionized land ownership in Ireland. The demise of landlordism did not lead to the transfer of the land of Ireland to the people of Ireland, but it did lead to possession by the occupying tenants.

Laurence M. Geary

LAND AGITATION, SCOTLAND

Scottish land agitation was mainly restricted to the HIGHLANDS, and seems to have been a belated reaction to the CLEARANCES, the potato FAMINE of 1846, and the worsening economic situation of the crofters and cottars as the 19th century progressed. It reached its zenith with the 'Highland land war' or 'Crofters' war' of 1883–88. The action taken by various communities ranged from rent strikes and repossessing grazing rights to the slaughtering of sheep and deer on former common lands and taking up arms against the police. Troops were called to quell the unrest.

The first phase of the 'Highland war' began with the protests of the crofting communities of Glendale (Gleann Dail) and Hùsabost on the Isle of Skye (An t-Eilean

Sgitheanach) in 1882, when rents were withheld and sheriff-officers forcibly evicted tenants. Five of the local leaders, known as the 'Glendale martyrs', were sentenced to two months in prison. In response, the Highland Land League was formed, and its agitation led to a Royal Commission on the Crofters and Cottars of Scotland in 1883. Its members collected evidence in the Highlands in 1883–84, and the published report is an exhaustive monument to the sufferings of the Highland tenantry in the 19th century and a damning indictment of the landlords and those who perpetrated the clearings. The Crofters' Holdings Act, passed in 1886 as a result of its work, gave larger crofts security of tenure.

Marion Löffler

LAND AGITATION, WALES

The land question in 19th-century Wales (Cymru) was not just an economic topic, but also a social, cultural, and political issue. Approximately 60% of the land was at this time parcelled into large estates of more than 1,000 acres, owned by just 571 individuals. This élite, whose members were English-speaking and Anglican, was increasingly distinguished from the rest of the population; the tenantry, by contrast, comprised Welsh-speaking Nonconformists (see Christianity).

Henry Richard (1812–88), an ordained minister and radical journalist, penned a series of 'letters' on conditions in Wales for Cobden's *Morning Star* newspaper in 1866, stating that the tenant's lack of secure tenure rendered him vulnerable to bullying at election time: The price of a 'wrong' vote in Wales, said Richard, was eviction. Richard, who was returned to parliament in 1868, escalated the controversy by claiming in the House of Commons that large numbers of Liberal-voting tenants had been evicted by their Tory landlords following the 1868 election.

The 'tithe war', a period when hard-pressed farmers in north Wales refused to pay their tithes, marked the high point of the conflict over the land question. The idea of a Land Act for Wales along the Irish model was repeatedly canvassed in radical circles. The government instead set up a Royal Commission to examine the Welsh land question. Its report (1896) suggested some additional legislation for Wales. The land question was finally resolved through market forces rather than legislation. By 1914, landholding had lost its social, political, and economic advantages. The great landowners—not only in Wales, but across Britain—sold up, leaving the farmers in charge of their own destiny.

Matthew Cragoe

LANDEVENNEG/LANDÉVENNEC, ABBEY OF

Origins

The only document that gives an account of the foundation of the monastery of Landevenneg (French Landévennec) is the *Vita Sancti Winwaloei*, edited *c.* 880 by its abbot Wrdisten (Uurdisten). It relates that St Uuinuualoe (Modern Breton Gwennole, Modern French Guénolé) founded the monastery with eleven companions.

The medieval monastery of Landévennec (Landevenneg) in Brittany (Breizh). (Wessel Cirkel)

Names in Old Breton that include *Lan(n)*- (cf. Welsh *Llan*-), which literally meant 'enclosure', refer to early churches and monasteries. The monastic education of Uuinuualoe, as well as the foundation of the monastery at the end of the Brest harbour—in a place naturally accessible to new settlers sailing in from western Britain—fits very well into the religious context of this first period of Christian organization, as can be understood from the evidence of these early place-names. Thus *Te-Uuinnoch* is an Old Breton hypocoristic or pet-name for Uuinuualoe; the place-name *Landevenneg* signifies the monastic enclosure of Uuinuualoe.

We have no surviving documentary history for the first three centuries of the monastery founded by Uuinuualoe. The Landevenneg charters that name historical figures of the 4th, 5th, and 6th centuries are all probably later forgeries (see CHARTER TRADITION). However, the monastery's existence in Merovingian times is confirmed by archaeological evidence. The first sound historical reference to it occurs in a decree of 818 by the Frankish emperor Louis the Pious; in it, he imposed the Benedictine Rule on the community.

Soon afterward, documents reveal a period of great and extroverted cultural vigour at Landevenneg, and in Brittany as a whole. The political context favoured Breton expansion in the 9th century under NOMINOË, Erispoë, and Salomon, at the expense of a Frankia badly governed by Charlemagne's successors. At the same period, the Landevenneg scriptorium (a centre for producing and copying manuscripts) produced a lavishly illuminated gospel book, which is found today in New York (Public Library MS 115). It is the earliest manuscript known from Finistère (Penn-ar-Bed) and displays many shared points of comparison with the famous insular gospel books, such as those of KELLS and LINDISFARNE. Two successive Lives of Uuinuualoe were composed—one written by the monk Clement, and one (mentioned previously) by his abbot, Uurdisten; moreover, one life of Saint Paul Aurelian was written by Uurmonoc in 884 for the bishop of Leon. At this time, the abbey was very strongly linked to the local secular power of the Breton dynasty of Cornouaille (Kernev), but it was also already well integrated into the Benedictine Continental mainstream, including the architecture of the monastery buildings.

History

In the following centuries, the prosperity of the monastery remains apparent, but seems to have been rather fragile. The monks themselves were painfully aware of the peril; since the middle of the 9th century Vikings had been raiding all over Brittany, with devastating effects. In the year 913, they plundered the abbey. The monks fled to Montreuil-sur-mer, where they built a second monastery, which was also consecrated to Saint Uuinuualoe (this site was called St Walloy), whose relics they had brought with them. After approximately 40 years, they returned to Brittany, but the relics remained in Montreuil.

The returning monks found a monastery in ruins. In the 11th and 12th centuries, they built a Romanesque ensemble: church, cloister, and dormitories. Those centuries were the golden age of monasticism, in Brittany as well as in France.

Throughout France in the 17th century, the monasteries formed associations to unite against outside pressure, and Landevenneg joined the congregation of St Maur in 1636. Strengthened by this association, monastic life was revived, new buildings were erected, and cultural life experienced a flourishing period. A history of the abbey was published by Dom Noël Mars in 1648, and a Breton–French dictionary between 1728 and 1752 by Dom Louis Le Pelletier.

By the mid-18th century, however, the abbey had entered into an irreparable decline, suffering from the repercussions of the Jansenist controversy (a Catholic theological controversy in the early 18th century) and from the anti-monastic attitudes that accompanied the Enlightenment. The monastic community was effectively reduced to only five or six members. In 1766, the abbey lost its abbatial rights to the Bishop of Cornouaille. In 1792, in the midst of the French Revolution, the last four monks were expelled and the abbey sold off with little notice. Landevenneg fell into oblivion.

Revival

From 1825 onward, the old abbey was reduced to ruins. However, at the beginning of the 20th century, the Christian conscience of the Bretons became increasingly scandalized by these venerable ruins. One important factor in this revival was a monastic community, founded in 1878 near Landevenneg, at Kerbénéat, which recognized in the restoration of Landevenneg a compelling mission on its doorstep. In addition, the Breton cultural movement Bleun-Brug, founded in 1905, started a campaign for the restoration of the site. Finally, in 1950, the monks bought back the property with financial and moral support from all parts of Brittany. They began a programme of rebuilding and reconstruction, whose crowning achievement was the inauguration of a new monastery and, in 1965, the consecration of its church.

Today, still under the patronage of St Gwennole, a community of thirty monks pursues a tradition of more than a thousand years of prayer, work, and brotherly life. In 1981, seven brothers from Landevenneg founded a daughter house in Haiti, the Morne Saint Benoît. In 1985, celebration of the traditional 1,500th anniversary of the original abbey was marked by a programme of religious and cultural events.

Marc Simon, Order of Saint Benedict

LANGUAGE (REVIVAL) MOVEMENTS IN THE CELTIC COUNTRIES

All the modern Celtic languages—BRETON, CORNISH, IRISH, MANX, SCOTTISH GAELIC, and WELSH—have, since early modern times, required efforts to ensure the survival of communities of native speakers. In the case of Cornish and Manx, special efforts have been required to reestablish such communities. As with many smaller languages in Europe, Celtic language movements emerged as part of 19th-century NATIONALISM, and it is due in no small measure to the activities of 'language nationalists' that the Celtic languages have survived at all. The process of language reproduction (transmission from one generation to the next) in minority settings has been an important subfield of the academic discipline of sociolinguistics since World War II, and Celtic language movements have increasingly benefited from the conclusions drawn from sociolinguistic research.

Marion Löffler

LANGUAGE (REVIVAL) MOVEMENTS, BRITTANY

Interest in the Celtic west in the European ROMANTICISM of the 19th century paid special attention to Brittany (BREIZH) and was thus partly instrumental in the creation of the first *emsav* (language revival movement), which lasted until World War I. BARZAZ-BREIZ, a compilation of Breton BALLADS published in 1839 by Kervarker (Hersart de La Villemarqué), was an important milestone for literary modernism in Brittany, coinciding with the starting point of recent BRETON LITERATURE.

The literary revival was accompanied by a strengthening of cultural contacts with the other CELTIC COUNTRIES, symbolized by Celtic congresses and the creation of the Gorsedd des bardes de Bretagne (GOURSEZ) in 1901 (see PAN-CELTICISM).

The first of many petitions in favour of the teaching of Breton was organized in 1870 (see EDUCATION), but was ignored by France's highly centralized government, which banned the use of Breton in both school and church at the very beginning of the 20th century.

Roparz Hemon, a writer of short stories, novels, and dictionaries, as well as a translator, essayist, and poet, dominated the second *emsav*, which lasted until the end of World War II. Beginning in 1925, he directed a new literary magazine,

Gwalarn, in which many famous contemporary works were published. Success in introducing Breton in schools was limited but symbolic: Kerlann opened the first monolingual primary school, while state schools included the history and geography of Brittany in the curriculum and taught Breton for one hour per week. This created a new demand for schoolbooks, grammar books, dictionaries, and lexicons. The Institut Celtique, created in 1941 and directed by Roparz Hemon, federated the various language initiatives. Roparz Hemon could also be heard for an hour each day on Radio-Rennes.

The end of the war in 1945 put a stop to this progress, as the new French government reverted to its pre-war language policy. Furthermore, the post-war purge was used as a means to end all Breton initiatives, whether political, cultural, or linguistic.

After World War II, private initiatives tried to remedy the lack of official Breton teaching. In December 1950, the *loi Deixonne* was passed, which allowed a small amount of teaching of Breton in schools. However, this created a rift among language activists, in part due to conflict over Breton orthography.

By the 1960s, a new kind of activism had emerged that often expressed itself through songs. *Festou-noz* ('Night parties', an avenue for traditional songs and dances, sing. FEST-NOZ), recitals of *kan ha diskan* songs (see BRETON MUSIC; DANCES), recitals, and singers such as Alan Stivell and Glenmor (Ar Skanv) rekindled pride in the language and culture of Brittany.

Lobbying in the 1960s and 1970s led to the Cultural Charter for Brittany (1978). The policy of regionalization in the 1980s allowed elected representatives to subsidize local Breton-language initiatives. Bilingual road signs were erected, and, a few years later, Ofis ar brezhoneg (The Breton language office) was created to help with translations, new terminology, and data collection.

The first network of monolingual Breton schools (Diwan) was opened in 1977. It now covers nursery, primary, and secondary education, with plans for further development. These schools do not have full public status. Progress is steady, but slow, compared to the rapidly declining population of Breton native speakers.

Jacqueline Gibson

LANGUAGE (REVIVAL) MOVEMENTS, CORNWALL

Although the revival of the CORNISH language is often historically attributed to the end of the 19th and early 20th centuries, it may be more productive to assess the most recent revivalist impulse as part of a longer process of resistance against language and culture loss beginning in the 18th century, when a group of Cornish scholars worked to collect and translate Cornish while it was still spoken as a community language.

The modern Cornish revival began in the 1870s, when the Newlyn-based Revd W. S. Lach-Szyrma (1841–1915) and Henry Jenner collected Cornish words still in use by Newlyn (Lulyn) fishermen. Many 20th- and 21st-century revivalists date the start of the revival to the publication of Jenner's *Handbook of the Cornish Language* in 1904. The real pioneer of revived Cornish is actually Robert Morton

Nance, however. He developed Unified Cornish in the 1930s with the express aim of creating a system of Cornish that would be easy to learn and appropriate for speakers and writers, based primarily on medieval texts, which are considered to document a 'golden age' of Cornish.

Over the course of the 20th century, many forms of Cornish have been proposed, based on various phases of the language. External observers should bear in mind that the forms have more commonalities than differences, and as the revived language grows into a community language it will continue its development.

Amy Hale

LANGUAGE (REVIVAL) MOVEMENTS, IRELAND

Language Movements Prior to 1922

During the 18th and early 19th centuries, IRISH was widely spoken, particularly in rural Ireland (ÉIRE). Just before the Great FAMINE (1845–50), the number of Irish speakers was probably at its highest in history in absolute terms, although they represented only 45% of the total population. By the mid-19th century, the Irish population itself had declined, and the share of the population who spoke Irish had declined to less than 30%.

An active concern with the decline in the numbers of Irish speakers developed in the post-Famine years, leading to the establishment of the Society for the Preservation of the Irish Language (Cumann Buan-Choimeádta na Gaeilge) in 1876. *The Gaelic Journal* was founded three years later, and served as an important catalyst in the development of a modern Irish prose style.

The most influential language organization in the 19th century—the Gaelic League (CONRADH NA GAEILGE)—was established in 1893. It went beyond the objectives of earlier organizations. Its founding members included Douglas Hyde (Dubhghlas DE HÍDE), David Comyn, Eoin MacNeill, and Fr. O'Growney (An tAthair Eoghan Ó Gramhnaigh). The Gaelic League was not simply concerned with trying to preserve the Irish language, but rather with bringing about its revival in areas where it had ceased to be spoken, and with creating a new modern literature in Irish (see IRISH LITERATURE). Within 15 years of this organization's foundation, some 950 branches (with an estimated membership of 100,000) had been established. As the movement developed, the basic shape emerged of what later became the language policy of the new Irish Free State, with a strong emphasis on education policy, teaching methods, teacher training, development of a standard language and promotion of a creative literature, employment of competent Irish speakers in the public service, and maintenance of the Irish-speaking heartland.

Language Policy since 1922

The magnitude of this task was revealed by the census of 1926. Only 18% of the population were returned as Irish speakers, nearly half of whom lived in scattered bilingual or monolingual communities along the western and southern coasts (collectively referred to as the GAELTACHT). The remaining Irish speakers, most of whom had learned the language at school, lived in largely English-speaking communities.

Although the population of the Gaeltacht has declined in both absolute and relative terms, there has been a gradual, but continual, revival in the ratios of Irish speakers in other regions. In the 1996 census, 1,430,205 people were returned as Irish speakers. This number represented 43.5% of the population of the Irish Republic, and is encouraging compared with the 18% share in 1926.

National language surveys, however, suggest that census statistics overestimate the numbers fluent or nearly fluent in Irish, and that a more realistic figure would be about 10%. They further indicate that less than 5% of the national population uses Irish as a first or main language, while a further 10% uses Irish regularly, but less intensively.

Public Attitudes

A majority of the Irish public perceive the Irish language as having an important rôle in defining and maintaining national cultural distinctiveness. Thus the general population is willing to accept a considerable commitment of state resources to support the Irish language and its survival.

Although the effort to reestablish Irish as a national language has not been successful, the impact of Irish language policy cannot be described as negligible. Since 1922, there has been some real measure of maintenance and revival, and the pattern of bilingualism has consequently expanded. However, the long-term future of the Irish language is no more secure now than it was then.

Pádraig Ó Riagáin

LANGUAGE (REVIVAL) MOVEMENTS, ISLE OF MAN

The last traditional native speaker of Manx, Ned MADDRELL, died in 1974, but by his death a language revival movement was well under way. Indeed, in September 2002, a Manx Gaelic-medium class was established.

An awareness of the decline of Manx Gaelic was expressed in the press in the 1820s when letters to the editor argued either for its retention or its discontinuation. Nevertheless, it was not until the 1880s that the language revival movement gained significant momentum. Yn Cheshaght Ghailckagh (The Manx Language Society) was founded in 1899. The society aims to preserve and promote the language and its associated culture.

From the 1930s, a small group of language activists (Mark and Tom Braide, Walter Clarke, Charles Craine, Douglas Fargher, Leslie Quirk, and William Radcliffe) sought out the last native speakers to achieve fluency in the language, making recordings in the 1950s. In this way, a sense of continuity has been maintained between past and present speech communities.

Eamonn DE VALERA met Ned Maddrell on a visit to the island in 1947, which prompted him to request the Irish Folklore Commission to make recordings of the last native speakers. This effort was followed in turn by the Manx Museum's Manx Folklife Survey (1940–70), which effectively provided comment on the language as remembered for the period c. 1910.

The official support that had been lacking to the revival came as a result of a motion to Tynwald in 1984, which proposed the following: 'Manx Gaelic should be supported and encouraged by all agencies of Government and Boards of Tynwald'. Coonceil ny Gaelgey, the Manx Gaelic Advisory Council, was established to provide official translations.

The year 1997 saw the significant step of establishing a Manx Gaelic-medium playgroup, Mooinjer Veggey (Little people), out of which came demands for the establishment of Manx-medium primary education. The Manx Heritage Foundation continues to support the language, most notably in the form of Yn Greinneyder (Manx Language Development Officer).

Breesha Maddrell

LANGUAGE (REVIVAL) MOVEMENTS, SCOTLAND

Compared to similar initiatives in Ireland (Éire) and Wales (Cymru), Scottish Gaelic revival movements have always been frail and marginal. Without doubt, this weakness is related to the lack of a nationalist impulse in the Gaelic movements: Gaelic has largely been seen as a Highland phenomenon, and not as an essential or central component of the national identity of Scotland (Alba) as a whole. Although mainstream cultural nationalism in 19th-century Scotland made much use of the trappings of Gaelic culture—tartanry and the like—little interest was expressed in the language of the Gaels. The Ossianic controversy, however, gave particular force to lagnuage revival efforts (see Macpherson; Oisín): The authenticity and value of the Gaelic tradition had been challenged and attacked, prompting efforts at 'the vindication of the Gael'. In particular, Gaelic societies were founded in London (1777), Glasgow (Glaschu, 1780), Edinburgh (Dùn Èideann, 1784), and elsewhere.

A Chair of Celtic was founded in the University of Edinburgh in 1882. The creation of An Comunn Gaidhealach (The Gaelic League) in 1891 was an important milestone, as it was the first organization founded with the objective of defending and promoting Gaelic culture. In the early 20th century, revival efforts involved literary and cultural initiatives by Gaelic intellectuals who endeavoured to modernize the language in various respects. These efforts were followed by the 'Scottish Renaissance' of the 1920s and 1930s, when writers and activists such as Hugh MacDiarmid took a keen interest in Gaelic and relocated it within a new nationalist discourse.

A new burst of energy appeared in the 1960s and then intensified during the 1970s and 1980s. This renewed vigour can be understood as part of the 'ethnic revival' witnessed in peripheral regions of Europe and elsewhere.

Government funding of Gaelic organizations, including An Comunn Gaidhealach and the Gaelic Books Council (Comhairle nan Leabhraichean, founded 1968) began in the mid-1960s; from this point, it can be said that the maintenance of Gaelic became an objective of government policy. It is now customary to speak of a 'Gaelic Renaissance' in Scotland from the early 1980s.

Local government reorganization in 1974 meant that the Western Isles, the strongest Gaelic-speaking area, became a distinct political entity for the first time, with its own local authority, Comhairle nan Eilean (Council of the Isles). The Comhairle quickly introduced a bilingual policy and began a bilingual project in the schools. This initiative marked the first time that Gaelic had really been used in the educational system in Scotland to any meaningful extent. More than 2,000 schoolchildren are now being educated through the medium of Gaelic. Sabhal Mòr Ostaig, the Gaelic college on Skye (Sgiathanach), is now a degree-granting institution within the University of the Highlands and Islands (Oilthigh na Gaidhealtachd's nan Eilean).

Wilson McLeod

LANGUAGE (REVIVAL) MOVEMENTS, WALES

Throughout its history, the language movement in Wales (Cymru) has been closely associated with the idea of Welsh nationhood (see NATIONALISM). From the later 20th century, the movement has also benefited from shifting international attitudes that are increasingly sensitive to, and supportive of, cultural and linguistic diversity.

Antiquarian Beginnings

The roots of the Welsh language movement lie in Romantic nationalism and the efforts of the cultural intelligentsia within the Welsh middle classes to prove that Wales possessed native traditions and national institutions and, therefore, should be considered a distinct nation. The beginnings of this movement can be traced to London (Welsh Llundain), where, in 1751, the Honourable Society of Cymmrodorion was founded to cultivate the language. The early efforts of these societies led to the revival of the Welsh EISTEDDFOD and the honing of the language as a tool of modern expression through the coinage of new words for modern concepts and orthographic reforms.

The Modern Language Movement

Following the introduction of an English state-school system in 1870 and the mass in-migration of English-speaking workers into the coalfields of Wales, the Welsh language became increasingly relegated to the home and family life. After World War II, methods derived from the American civil rights movement were adopted, especially by the Welsh Language Society (CYMDEITHAS YR IAITH GYMRAEG), and new initiatives focused on adult learners of Welsh and the preservation of Welsh-speaking communities.

Cultivating Written and Spoken Welsh

The third Cymmrodorion Society (1873) was no longer dominated by antiquarians. Rather, this national body was an important institutional participant in the National Eisteddfod (EISTEDDFOD GENEDLAETHOL CYMRU), which had itself become a national institution, focused on developing the Welsh language in all fields of life. A Welsh society at Oxford developed a Welsh orthography that became the basis for the principles of the University of Wales' *Orgraff yr Iaith Gymraeg* (Orthography of the Welsh language, 1928); it remains the authoritative standard today.

From the end of the 19th century, a new wave of local Welsh societies organized Welsh lectures, concerts, and St David's Day celebrations (see DEWI SANT). These societies also began to conduct local campaigns for the use of the Welsh language in schools, libraries, law courts, and administration. The sheer sizes of their total membership—the Cardiff Cymmrodorion, for instance, counted more than 1,200 members in 1909—made them a force to be reckoned with.

Legal Status for the Welsh Language

The agenda of the language movement in 20th-century Wales has attached primary importance to gaining legal status for the Welsh language. Clause 17 of the 1536 ACT OF UNION had effectively banned Welsh from public administration and the courts of law at a time when the overwhelming majority of the inhabitants of Wales spoke Welsh only. At the beginning of the 20th century, Welsh speakers still had no right to use their native language in the courts. When the use of Welsh was later permitted, translation costs were charged to the individual. Following a period of local campaigning and a parliamentary report unfavourable to the cause, a united movement comprising the National Union of Welsh Societies, Plaid Cymru (the Party of Wales), and the Welsh League of Youth (Urdd Gobaith Cymru) arose in 1938 to collect signatures on a petition to the British parliament demanding official status for the Welsh language. The petition, with 365,000 signatures, was presented to the House of Commons in 1941, and led to the passing of the Welsh Courts Act 1942, which reconfirmed English as the official language of Wales.

Further campaigns conducted in the 1960s, most notably by the Welsh Language Society established in 1962, led to the passing of the Welsh Language Act 1967. This Act provided that in the courts of Wales 'anything done in Welsh shall have the like effect as if done in English', but added that in cases of doubt the English version of a document should prevail. State agencies were still under no obligation to provide Welsh-language services, however.

The 1967 Act's limited provisions for official equal status for Welsh triggered further campaigns, which were to continue for the following 25 years, until the passage of the Welsh Language Act 1993. This legislation provided that 'in the conduct of public business and the administration of justice in Wales the English and Welsh languages should be treated on the basis of equality', though this principle was considerably weakened by the nebulous qualifying clause 'so far as is both appropriate in the circumstances and reasonably practicable'. The Act also established Bwrdd yr Iaith Gymraeg (The Welsh Language Board). Because of the limited scope of this Act, which places no obligation on the private sector and does not require even state organizations to produce all their material in a bilingual format, a fresh campaign for all-encompassing legislation has been under way since the mid-1990s.

Publishing and the Mass Media

During the 19th century, the Welsh press experienced a 'golden age' unparalleled by any other Celtic language, but it faced steep decline in the first half of the 20th century. Inter-war efforts to generate a revival, beginning with annual book festivals held by the National Union of Welsh Societies and book-selling campaigns by Urdd Gobaith Cymru, eventually led to the establishment of the Welsh Books Council (Cyngor Llyfrau Cymraeg, later renamed Cyngor Llyfrau Cymru) at ABERYSTWYTH in 1964. Compared with similar initiatives for other minority languages, the Welsh Books Council has been extremely successful in sponsoring publications in the Welsh language and English publications relating to Wales, as well as organizing their distribution. Publishing a daily paper, however, has proved difficult.

The growth of Welsh-language mass media has often been described as one of the success stories in the world of lesser-used languages. Nevertheless, when the BBC began transmitting radio programmes in 1923, regular Welsh-language broadcasts were not planned. As late as the the 1970s, only some 15 hours of Welsh broadcasts per week were provided. Energetic campaigning by numerous societies and individuals, led by the Welsh Language Society, resulted in the establishment in 1979 of Radio Cymru, which was broadcasting nearly 112 hours of Welsh-language programmes per week by the end of the 1990s. Major restructuring of schedules in 1998, however, resulted in the introduction of more English-language songs and more frequent use of English words and phrases in these programmes. This move sparked the formation of the pressure group Cylch yr Iaith (The language circle), whose aim is to preserve the integrity of the existing Welsh-language service.

Decades of campaigning for a Welsh-language television channel came to a head in 1980 when Gwynfor EVANS, then president of Plaid Cymru, threatened to go on hunger strike over the matter. The campaigners were successful and Sianel Pedwar Cymru (S4C) began transmitting programmes in November 1982. It was broadcasting approximately 30 hours of Welsh television per week—80% at prime time—by 1998.

Adult Learners of Welsh

During the course of the 20th century, but especially in its second half, interest in learning Welsh by monoglot English speakers in Wales has grown, taking its inspiration from the revival of Hebrew as a spoken language after World War II. Urdd Gobaith Cymru paved the way by introducing the rank of *dysgwr* (learner) in 1932 to enable children who were learning Welsh to join the organization. The movement was boosted when the poet, academic, and prominent Welsh learner, R. M. (Bobi) Jones, published his *Cymraeg i Oedolion* (Welsh for adults) in 1965–66. The National Eisteddfod of Wales holds a *Dysgwr y Flwyddyn* (Learner of the year) competition.

Welsh-Speaking Communities

In the 1970s, Welsh-language organizations began to explore the link between economic infrastructure and language decline, especially in rural areas; there, out-migration of young Welsh speakers because of lack of employment and afford-able housing was paralleled by in-migration of affluent English speakers. In an effort to counteract the underlying causes of these trend, several organizations were estab-lished, including Adfer (Restoration) in 1975, which bought houses to restore and rent to Welsh speakers at affordable prices. In addition, the Welsh Language Society's campaign, *Nid yw Cymru ar werth* (Wales is not for sale), argued against the sale of houses in Welsh-speaking areas as second homes.

Following in the footsteps of Cymdeithas yr Iaith, the organization Cymuned (community) was founded in 2001 to counter the threat posed to the remaining Welsh-speaking communities by the substantial influx of English speakers and the lack of employment for local people. Its slogan, 'Tai, Gwaith, Iaith' (Houses, work, language), highlights the group's approach. Cymuned's aims include stemming the in-migration of English speakers, preventing the sale of housing stock as holiday homes, helping incomers to learn the Welsh language, and galvanizing the resources within the communities.

Websites

www.cwmni-iaith.com; www.cymuned.com; www.nantgwr.com; www.twfcymru.com; www.ybyd.com; www.ylolfa.com.

Marion Löffler

LAW TEXTS, CELTIC, IRISH

Introduction

Early Irish legal texts fall into three main categories: ecclesiastical law written in Latin; 'laws' (*leges*, Irish *rechtgai* or *cánai*) promulgated by mixed ecclesiastical and secular assemblies and written in IRISH; and legal tracts in Irish for the instruction of judges and aspirant judges within the native tradition of law. Despite some over-lap, the main concerns of ecclesiastical law and native Irish law were different. A sin-gle great compilation dominates the surviving textual evidence for each: the ecclesiastical *Collectio Canonum Hibernensis* (The Irish collection of canons) on the one hand, and the SENCHAS MÁR (The great tradition) on the other hand.

Ecclesiastical Law in Latin

The *Collectio Canonum Hibernensis* was compiled between 716 and 725 by two scholars, Ruben from Munster (MUMU) and Cú Chuimne from Iona (EILEAN Ì). Their legal text constantly appealed to textual authority, primarily the Bible, but also a wide variety of ecclesiastical documents and texts, both Roman and post-Roman.

Ecclesiastical Law in Irish

The few surviving ecclesiastical *cánai* are only a remnant of the many promulgated between *c.* 680 and 830. Fortunately, the surviving texts include one of the most important, *Cáin Adomnáin* ('Adomnán's Law'), or, as it is called in the ANNALS, 'The Law of the Innocents', referring to the non-combatants whom it sought to protect.

The mode of enforcement was also distinctive. Ecclesiastical law appears to have remained in force for a limited period, and it could be renewed. The penalties were, in general, higher, but also more equitable, than in the ordinary native law. The penalties attached to infringement of a *cáin* were divided between the church of the saint and local lords; given that all received a share, all had an interest in enforcing a *cáin*. As the ecclesiastical *cánai* show, decrees affecting the whole of Ireland were very rare.

Native Irish Law

The native law, in contrast, claimed to be the law of all the Irish. The old Introduction to the SENCHAS MÁR, the major vernacular Irish law book, begins with a question and answer in the textbook style derived from Latin grammars: 'The *Senchas* of the men of Ireland, what has maintained it? The joint memory of the old men (or: of two old men), transmission from one ear to another, chanting of poets, amplification by the law of the letter, strengthening by the law of nature, for those are the strong rocks by which the judgements of the world are fixed'.

The *Collectio Canonum Hibernensis* was a large-scale statement of the law composed of 'books' devoted to particular legal topics, such as marriage or bishops. To some extent, the arrangement of the whole text follows a logical order, though that is by no means true of the whole. It is even less true of the *Senchas Már*, a law book composed of what modern scholars call 'tracts', comparable in extent to the 'books' of the *Hibernensis*. Some of these tracts are relatively systematic in their internal organization, but it is rarely possible to see what might have connected one tract with its neighbours. Parts of the *Senchas Már* are linked, instead, by having come from a single source; just as the *Hibernensis* was an overview constructed from smaller texts, so also was the *Senchas Már*, and some of these texts came to the compilers in groups. For example, *Bechbretha* (Bee-judgements) was very probably from the same source as its neighbour, *Coibnes Uisci Thairidne* (Kinship of conducted water), a text on legal problems arising from conducting a water supply for a mill across more than one holding of land.

The *Senchas Már* had grand aspirations from the start to be a law book for all the Irish, yet there were also legal texts from Munster (see BRETHA NEMED). The two sources occasionally differ on particular points, though the substance of the law is very similar.

The most likely date for the *Senchas Már* is the first half of the 8th century. Similarly, the *Bretha Nemed* has been dated to the middle years of the 8th century. Some important texts, such as *Críth Gablach*, may not have formed part of any law book, but the material, too, seems to belong to the first half of the 8th century. Some of the tracts within the *Senchas Már* are probably of the 7th century, which suggests that the major compilations of the 8th century were the culmination of an extraordinarily fertile period in legal writing.

Yet, in spite of the parallels between the major texts of Irish law, native and ecclesiastical, their modes of thought are normally very different. Occasionally, vernacular tracts cite textual authority, as when the *Bretha Nemed* quotes the *Hibernensis*, but this is very far from the constant citation of texts that is one of the essential characteristics of the *Hibernensis*. The normal mode of exposition in the *Senchas Már* is a description of what the law is; if the law is what the text says it is, the problem of authority does not arise. The tract purports to set out what judges have judged, are judging, and will judge. Occasionally, one can look behind this easy assumption of the authority of a learned tradition and of judges as its exponents. Individual, even controversial, writing can be found, but that is not the explicit stance of the texts.

T. M. Charles-Edwards

LAW TEXTS, CELTIC, WELSH

Introduction

Medieval Welsh law was separate and distinct from the English common law and Roman canon law. It is uncertain when Welsh law first came into being, but the manuscripts attribute the law to king Hywel ap Cadell, known as HYWEL DDA 'the Good' (†949/50). The law itself is a complicated, compensation-based system; though it contains many archaic elements, it was clearly a sophisticated and highly developed legal system. The Law of Hywel Dda was seen as a unifying factor among the Welsh in the turbulent Middle Ages, but this practice was not without its drawbacks—Welsh law was one of the factors used as a justification for the conquest of Wales (CYMRU) in 1282. Following the conquest, the law was not immediately superseded by English law, but it survived for some time in certain situations; for example, land law was used until the 16th century, and Welsh law survived in the March of Wales until the ACTS OF UNION in 1536–43, with the Marcher lords often adopting the more profitable elements of both Welsh and English law to create a hybrid legal system.

Texts and Surviving Copies

Most of the law texts that survive date from the 12th and 13th centuries. The Welsh law texts have a significance that goes beyond their legal implications, as law manuscripts form a large part of the surviving WELSH-language manuscripts from the Middle Ages, particularly in the 13th century. As prose texts, they are a valuable source of technical and everyday medieval Welsh vocabulary. They demonstrate a variety of styles and techniques, and represent an important body of practical texts written in the vernacular.

Organization and Contents

The prologue is usually the first part of any law book, and it relates the story of Hywel assembling worthies—lay and ecclesiastical—from each CANTREF in Wales to the 'White House', to discuss law. The prologues show that the meeting was not to create law for Wales, but to reform existing law.

Most law texts follow the prologue with the laws of court, which detail the everyday life of the king's court, and list all the officials, their duties, their responsibilities, and their dues. This section was already considered antiquated by the time of writing of the earliest manuscripts, and several scribes omitted the laws of court altogether, explaining that they were no longer in use.

The law of women was preoccupied with the status of women, marriage, divorce, and children; several different recognized unions were listed, and after seven years a couple could divorce and divide all their goods, excluding the land, according to the rules set out. Women were seen in some ways as a commodity, marriage was a contract, and a woman would have an *agweddi*, goods that were paid to her if her husband left her without just cause. Land law gives details of how to conduct cases for land, how the different tenures in Welsh law apply, and how to claim land legally. The suretyship tractate was the law of contract, and in any kind of obligational relationship a person called a surety was used as a guarantee on contracts and debts. An archaic hand-binding ceremony also featured in forming contracts, and the surety would then have to ensure that both sides kept their promises. There is also a short tractate on corn damage, listing the payments due to farmers whose corn was damaged by trespass by another person's animals. Iorwerth redaction manuscripts also have sections on joint ploughing contracts, injury to animals, and church protection, as well as a tractate on children, which covers paternity and offences by children.

The Iorwerth test book (*Llyfr Prawf*), which is stated as the section a lawyer needed to know to practice law, has the value of wild and tame, also found in the other redactions, which is a long list giving the value and purpose of animals, and a list of prices for common household items, essential for paying compensation. The other section of the test book in Iorwerth is the crucial three columns of law; this is criminal law, and the three columns are homicide, theft, and arson. The value of parts of the body and a section on special witnesses whose word is always accepted, the nine tongued-ones, are often found with the three columns in the Blegywryd and Cyfnerth redactions.

In Welsh law, each person had a life value, *galanas*, which was to be paid to the family if the person was killed; it was calculated on a sliding scale according to status. According to the laws, society was hierarchical, with the king at the head of society, the bondmen at the bottom, and the freemen in between. Women were not persons in their own right in law; their value was calculated according to their husbands (or fathers if they were unmarried) and they were not entitled to hold land or speak in court. The other people of low status were the aliens, people from outside Wales. Their position was similar to that of the women. The *sarhaed* (injury value) was half of a person's *galanas*, and was an additional compensation to be paid for a deliberate injury; it was intended to compensate the insult. If a person was killed accidentally, only the *galanas* was paid. In contrast, if a person was killed as a result of a deliberate attack by another, then there was insult involved and the killer would then have to pay both *galanas* and *sarhaed*. *Sarhaed* was also payable for all deliberate injuries; thus, if someone cut off another person's finger, the offender would have to pay the value of the finger and his *sarhaed*.

The death penalty was used only for certain cases of theft in Welsh law; the reasoning may have been that theft was a stealth crime, whereas homicide was (usually) openly committed. A stealth act undermined society and, therefore, was punishable by death. The complicated *galanas* system, in contrast, was developed to prevent blood feud and revenge killings between kindred, so the *galanas* payment would be divided between the murderer's parents, siblings, cousins, second cousins, and so on. When it was paid, it was divided in the same way among the members of the victim's family. In this way, everyone would pay the penalty for the killing, and everyone in the victim's family would be compensated.

Sara Elin Roberts

LEABHAR BHAILE AN MHÓTA

Leabhar Bhaile an Mhóta ('The Book of Ballymote') is an important medieval Irish vellum manuscript. It was written at Ballymote, Co. Sligo (Baile an Mhóta, Contae Shligigh), in the house of the local ruler Tomaltach Mac Donnchaidh. Written toward the end of the 14th century, it is now in the library of the Royal Irish Academy (Acadamh Ríoga na hÉireann).

The Book of Ballymote at present consists of 251 folios, having lost some folios during its turbulent life. It is written in two columns and many capital letters are decorated in a variety of colours. The contents of the Book of Ballymote are very similar to those of the Book of Lecan (*Leabhar Mór Leacáin*), and the scribes of both manuscripts used the same source for at least some of the material. Among the sources cited in the Book of Ballymote are many famous medieval manuscripts such as *Saltair Chaisil* ('The Psalter of Cashel'), Cín Dromma Snechtai ('The Book of Druim Snechta'), and the *Leabhar Gleann Dá Locha* ('The Book of Glendalough'). The texts cover many different areas, ranging from genealogical, historical, and religious matter to prose tales (both classical and other) and legal material, hence illustrating the typically miscellaneous character of medieval Irish manuscripts. Genealogies occupy the largest parts of the manuscript, covering more than 150 folios, followed by a version of the dindshenchas, which takes up some 60 folios. Other important texts included are *Sex Aetates Mundi* (The six stages of the world), Lebar Gabála Érenn ('The Book of Invasions'), *Lebor na Cert* ('The Book of Rights'), *Senchus Fer n-Alban* (Tradition of the men of North Britain), *Senchas Naomh Érenn* (Tradition of the saints of Ireland), *Cóir Anmann* (The appropriateness of names), *Uraicecht Becc* (The small primer), Auraicept na nÉces ('The Scholars' Primer'), *Compert Conchobuir* (The conception of Conchobar), *Echtra Cormaic* (The adventure of Cormac), and the *banshenchas* (The lore of women).

Petra S. Hellmuth

LEABHAR BREAC

Leabhar Breac, earlier *Lebor Brecc* ('The Speckled Book'), is an important medieval Irish vellum manuscript. The entire manuscript seems to have been written between 1408 and 1411 by a single scribe, probably Murchadh Riabhach Ó Cuindlis, a member of a professional scribal family.

Today, 142 folios remain. At some point, probably during the 18th century, the codex was broken up into two volumes. The larger of the two has been in the Royal Irish Academy (Acadamh Ríoga na hÉireann) since 1789. Volume 2, which consists of nine folios plus a single, detached sheet, is now also the property of the Academy. The writing in the manuscript was in double columns, with some coloured illumination. There is considerable variation in the size of the script, with particularly large capital initials at the beginning of paragraphs.

The *Leabhar Breac* contains much religious and devotional material and is an important source of early Irish ecclesiastical and theological writing, including *Fís Adomnáin* ('The Vision of Adomnán') and *Betha Coluimb Chille* (The life of Colum Cille). It also contains a heavily glossed version of *Félire Oengusso* ('The martyrology of Oengus Céile Dé'), a copy of Sanas Chormaic ('Cormac's Glossary'), *Aislinge Meic Con Glinne* (The dream of Mac Con Glinne), and a fragmentary history of Philip and Alexander the Great.

Petra S. Hellmuth

LEABHAR BUIDHE LEACÁIN

Leabhar Buidhe Leacáin ('The Yellow Book of Lecan') is one of the great medieval Irish vellum manuscripts that form the main sources for early Irish literature. It is a composite made up of miscellaneous manuscripts owned by the Welsh antiquarian Edward Lhuyd (*c.* 1660–1709), which he acquired during a tour of Ireland (Éire) between 1699 and 1700. Lhuyd had sixteen codices bound together at random and with columns numbered 1–998. The name *Leabhar Buidhe Leacáin* originally referred only to part of this heterogeneous volume (cols. 370–400 and 573–958), as demonstrated by a marginal entry (col. 380) by Ciothruad mac Taidg Ruaid. The time and place of writing range from the late 14th century to the early 16th century and from Sligo (Sligeach) and Galway (Gaillimh) to Tipperary (Tiobraid Árann) and Cork (Corcaigh).

The entire collection was presented to Trinity College, Baile Átha Cliath (Dublin) in 1786. Prior to this event, the final ten folios (cols. 959–98) had become detached from the rest of the codex and were subsequently sold separately. They now constitute Dublin, National Library of Ireland MS G 4.

Given the nature of its creation, it is not surprising that *Leabhar Buidhe Leacáin* contains a wide selection of literary genres and texts, ranging from religious poetry and other religious material to historical, genealogical, medical, and legal texts. It is also a main source for some of the most famous early Irish literary saga texts, among them a version of the early Irish epic Táin Bó Cuailnge ('The Cattle Raid of Cooley'), Togail Bruidne Da Derga ('The Destruction of Da Derga's Hostel'), Longas mac nUislenn ('The Exile of the Sons of Uisliu'), *Orgain Denna Ríg* ('The Destruction of Dind Ríg'), *Immacallam in Dá Thuarad* ('The Colloquy of the Two Sages'), Fled Bricrenn ('Bricriu's Feast'), Tochmarc Étaíne ('The Wooing of Étaín'), and *Aided Chon Roí* (The violent death of Cú Roí). It also contains early voyage tales, including *Immram Brain maic Febail* (The voyage of Bran mac Febail) and *Echtrae Chonlai* (The adventure of Conlae), as well as one of the two complete extant copies of Sanas Chormaic ('Cormac's Glossary') and a copy of *Amrae Coluimb Chille* (the elegy for Colum Cille attributed to Dallán Forgaill), and also DINDSHENCHAS (lore of high places).

Petra S. Hellmuth

LEBAR GABÁLA ÉRENN

Lebar Gabála Érenn ('The Book of the Takings of Ireland', often called 'The Book of Invasions') is a Middle Irish text, probably first composed in the later 11th century. It details a series of prehistoric invasions of Ireland (Ériu) and the LEGENDARY HISTORY of the Gaels (the ethno-linguistic Irish) from times corresponding to the biblical Genesis down to the Gaels' taking possession of Ireland under the leadership of the sons of Míl Espáine.

The Text and Its Early Transmission

The immediate sources of *Lebar Gabála*'s anonymous author were seven lengthy didactic poems, composed by four poets who worked in the 10th and 11th centuries. *Lebar Gabála* was the single most influential document in the Irish pseudo-historical corpus.

Lebar Gabála enjoyed great and almost immediate success: Within a few generations of its first composition, it existed in at least three recensions, several sub-recensions, and an indefinite number of manuscripts. It was the principal source for Keating/Céitinn's account of Ireland before St Patrick, and continued to exert a powerful influence on such major 20th-century Celtic scholars.

Ireland's Legendary History According to the Lebar Gabála

The versions of *Lebar Gabála* differ in several respects. Some of these differences, notably with regard to the events of the Gaelic migration, are quite pronounced. The précis that follows is based on the version known as the 'first recension', accepted here as the closest approximant to the work's lost exemplar.

Lebar Gabála begins with the biblical story of the Creation, and discusses Noah's descendants with particular attention to his son Japheth's progeny and the peopling of Europe. We are told how Fénius came to Babel and invented the *bélra Féne* (that is, 'the speech of the Irish' or Gaelic). His son Nél went to Egypt and married Scota, the Pharaoh's daughter, who bore Goídel Glas, the eponymous ancestor of the Gaels. Following the flight of the Israelites, Goídel's descendants returned to Scythia. At length, the Gaels were driven out, and wandered for many years, at last sailing the length of the Mediterranean and conquering Spain. Here, Bregon built the city of Brigantia and a tower from whose top his son Íth glimpsed Ireland.

The focus then shifts to Ireland and its several settlements. Before Noah's Flood came Cesair, with three men and a multitude of women. Cesair also descends from Noah; she is his granddaughter through an extra-biblical fourth son, Bith. Two of the men died, and then all of the women; Fintan mac Bóchra alone survived the Flood in a cave, and then lived on until the coming of Christianity to Ireland.

First after the Flood came Partholón, whose time in Ireland was marked by the clearing of plains, the eruption of lakes (see flood legends), and a battle against the sinister and mysterious Fomoiri. His people were annihilated by a plague, leaving only Tuán as a survivor. Next came Nemed, who won several battles against the Fomoiri and enslaved them. After his death, however, they conquered his descendants in turn and subjected them to an onerous tribute. Finally, Nemed's descendants rebelled and attacked the Fomoiri's chief stronghold; both armies were virtually wiped out in the battle and inundation that ensued. Those of Nemed's people who survived dispersed in three groups: The ancestors of the Tuath Dé went to 'the northern islands of the world', the ancestors of the Fir Bolg emigrated to Greece, and a third troop became the first Britons.

After two centuries of slavery in Greece, the Fir Bolg returned to Ireland. They divided the island into 'fifths' (*cóicid*; sing. cóiced 'province'), and established kingship there for the first time. The Fir Bolg were overthrown by the Tuath Dé, who are portrayed as coming to Ireland out of the sky and using their powers to turn day into night. Although *Lebar Gabála* assigns them a human ancestry, a supernatural element is clearly present, and later in the text they are sporadically identified as Fomoiri or demons.

At last, the narrative returns to Spain and the Gaels. We are told how Íth journeyed to Ireland, where he was killed by the jealous Tuath Dé; his nephews, the sons of Míl, led an expedition to avenge him. After conversations with the island's three eponymous goddesses, they confronted the three kings at Tara. Amairgen mac Míled, their chief poet, was called upon to judge between them, and said that his own people should go nine waves' distance back out to sea and then try to land again. With a poem he calmed the magical storm with which the Tuath Dé attempted to prevent this second landing, and the Gaels gained the mastery of Ireland.

Lebar Gabála concludes with a long account of all of the kings who ruled Ireland until the time of Patrick. In some versions, the list was brought down to the time of writing.

John Carey

LEBOR LAIGNECH

Lebor Laignech ('The Book of Leinster') is one of the earliest surviving manuscripts written entirely in the Irish language. It was probably compiled in Co. Tipperary (Contae Thiobraid Árainn), near Lough Derg, between 1151 and 1224. The name 'Book of Leinster' was given to the manuscript by the scholar John O'Donovan (1806–61) because of its strong Leinster provenance. It is now housed in Trinity College, Baile Átha Cliath (Dublin).

The book, which is also (more correctly) known as *Lebor na Nuachongbála*, is the most substantial of the early Irish codices. On some 200 folios, *Lebor na Nuachongbála* contains the cyclopaedic collection of texts typical of medieval Irish codices. The contents range from early Irish tales, poetry, and genealogies to religious material and historical matter, including the earliest version of the metrical

DINDSHENCHAS (Lore of places) and a new redaction of LEBAR GABÁLA ÉRENN ('The Book of Invasions'). Among the saga material are some of the best copies of the ULSTER CYCLE tales, such as TÁIN BÓ CUAILNGE ('The Cattle Raid of Cooley') and MESCA ULAD ('The Intoxication of the Ulstermen').

Petra S. Hellmuth

LEBOR NA HUIDRE

Lebor na hUidre ('The Book of the Dun Cow') is the oldest extant Irish manuscript written entirely in the IRISH (GAELIC) language rather than Latin. The dating of the compilation of the manuscript to 1106, as well as its Clonmacnoise provenance, is based on the identification of a man called Maolmuire as the main scribe. While the exact date and place of writing of the manuscript remain under discussion, it is clear that the language of some texts contained in *Lebor na hUidre* considerably predates 1106.

Little is known of the early history and provenance of the manuscript. The 14th-century tale *Faíllsigud Tána Bóó Cuailnge* (How TÁIN BÓ CUAILNGE was found) claimed that the manuscript was kept in the monastery of Clonmacnoise. It also alleged that it had been made from a miraculous cowhide that could grant eternal life to those who died on it. Another legend connects *Lebor na hUidre* with St Ciarán, claiming that when the saint was about to go to study with St Finnian of Clonard (Cluain Ard), he vainly requested from his parents a cow to take with him. Despite this refusal, one cow, called *Odhar Chiaráin* (Ciarán's dun [cow]), followed the young man and wondrously sustained not only St Ciarán during his studies, but also twelve bishops, their retinues, and their guests. The legend underlines the esteem in which a manuscript containing secular tales was held.

Lebor na hUidre is a collection of texts, ranging from religious, historical material to Romantic tales. It contains the earliest surviving versions of many of the most famous and important early Irish tales: *Táin Bó Cuailnge* ('The Cattle Raid of Cooley') and other tales from the ULSTER CYCLE such as FLED BRICRENN ('Bricriu's Feast'), *Siabarcharpat Con Culainn* ('The Phantom Chariot of CÚ CHULAINN'), SERGLIGE CON CULAINN ('The Wasting Sickness of Cú Chulainn'), and MESCA ULAD ('The Intoxication of the Ulstermen'). The manuscript also contains the early voyage tales (IMMRAMA) *Immram Curaig Maíle Dúin* (The voyage of Mael Dúin's coracle) and IMMRAM BRAIN *maic Febail* (The voyage of Bran mac Febail). Also included is a copy of the very early Gaelic poem, *Amrae Coluimb Chille* (Poem for COLUM CILLE) attributed to Dallán Forgaill.

Petra S. Hellmuth

LEGENDARY ANIMALS

Supernatural beings in Celtic tradition extend beyond the humanoid FAIRIES. In addition to the Welsh afanc, dragons, and the hounds of hell, there are both ancient and modern beliefs describing fairy animals. All of the CELTIC COUNTRIES have traditions of water-horses or water-bulls. Also known as kelpies (cf. Gaelic *cailpeach* 'heifer', 'colt') or pookas (< Irish *púca*) in English, these animals can take human form, and even marry mortals. The Breton story of *Paotr Pen-er-Lo* is typical: A wild horse appears, gentle and mild, but once mounted, the horse gallops into a body of water (a lake, river, a swamp, or the sea), drowning or merely ducking its passengers. Sometimes, as in the Irish tale of *Gille Dheacair*, the horse can extend to take an unusual number of riders. Many of the CELTIC LANGUAGES use the literal 'water-horse', as in Gaelic *each-uisge* 'waterbull', Manx *tarroo-ushtey*, but more specific names also exist, such as Irish *púca*, Manx *glashtyn*, and Welsh (g)*ŵyll*.

Medieval literature from Ireland (ÉRIU), Wales (CYMRU), and Brittany (BREIZH) abounds in magical animals, often men or women who had been transformed. A few of these tales have mythological underpinnings, while others may be inspired by the international FOLK-TALE.

More recently, a belief in feral panther-like animals has been documented in the British Isles, including Wales (CYMRU; e.g., *bwystfil y Bont*) and Cornwall (KERNOW; e.g., the beast of Bodmin Moor). Rational explanations have been proposed, such as a breeding colony of escaped exotic animals, but their existence remains unproven, and in legend they are sometimes given preternatural attributes. It is possible that these legends are related to beliefs about the ferocity of the European wild cat (*felis sylvestris*), widespread in much of Britain until the 19th century but now confined to northern Scotland (ALBA). Another wild animal attributed with magical attributes is the Eurasian common shrew (*sorex araneus*), which was literally 'fairy mouse' (*luch-sith* or *luch-shìth*) in Gaelic. It was believed to cause paralysis of the spine in farm animals.

Antone Minard

LEGENDARY HISTORY, BACKGROUND AND DEFINITIONS

The terms 'legendary history' and 'pseudo-history', used more or less interchangeably, designate writing that purports to be historical but actually deals with a period prior to authentic historical documentation. Such writing reflects the endeavours of a learned class to knit together preexisting legends, speculation, and fresh invention, all to create a coherent framework compatible with established historical models.

In a Christian context, the foreign model to which native traditions had to be accommodated was represented by the Bible, as interpreted and elaborated upon by the Fathers of the Church. Already in the 7th century, we find the claim that the Franks, like the Romans, claim to derive from the Troy of Homer's *Iliad* and Vergil's *Aeneid*. (It is worth remembering that Vergil was himself a native of what had been CISALPINE GAUL, and such claims might therefore be taken as evidence that areas whose cultural background was Celtic had early on proved fertile ground for Trojan origin legends.)

John Carey

LEGENDARY HISTORY, BRITTANY

Although the Breton saints' lives seem to give a coherent picture of the succession of rulers in the 4th to 7th centuries, a great deal of this material is actually medieval historical fiction. Brittany's legendary history begins with Conan Meriadec, said to have landed in Brittany (Breizh) in 396, and later extolled as the founder of the house of Rohan. Following Conan, most of these medieval legendary accounts of Breton origins give the names of the rulers of early Domnonia (Northern Brittany). An 11th-century legendary history with the beginnings of an Arthurian orientation is suggested by the *Livre des faits d'Arthur* and the Life of St Uuohednou (Goueznou). From the 12th century, medieval Breton historians generally adopted Geoffrey of Monmouth's scheme of succession of the rulers of ancient Britain, in which Armorica played a central rôle in numerous key episodes. Geoffrey's authority among Breton historians lasted until the 16th century.

†Gwenaël Le Duc

LEGENDARY HISTORY, GAELIC SCOTLAND

The Scottish Gaelic tradition of legendary history was closely related to the Irish tradition for most of the Middle Ages. The Gaels in Scotland (Alba) were portrayed as an offshoot from Ireland (Ériu) as early as *c.* ad 731, when Bede in his *Historia Ecclesiastica* ('Ecclesiastical History') 1.1 wrote that the Gaels, led by their chieftain Reuda, took Dál Riata by force and treaty from the Picts. According to this tale, the name Dál Riata was taken from their leader Reuda, and meant 'Reuda's portion/share'.

Senchus Fer n-Alban (Tradition of the men of North Britain) portrays the main Dál Riata kindreds as descendants of Erc son of Eochu Munremar. Both the Annals of Tigernach and the Dál Riata king-lists (see Scottish king-lists) state that Fergus Mór mac Eirc took Dál Riata, but these could also be 10th-century or later versions of the legend. Yet another version of the settlement legend is found uniquely in the 9th-century Welsh Latin Historia Brittonum, which states that 'Istoreth son of Istorinus held Dál Riata with his people'; the source of this statement is uncertain.

The destruction of the Picts by Cinaed mac Ailpín (r. 842/3–858) was an important element in the foundation legend of the kingdom of Alba. This idea, first found in the Chronicle of the Kings of Alba, compiled 971×995, had evolved (by the time of the 11th-century verse history of Scottish kings known as the 'Prophecy of Berchán') into a treacherous slaughter of the Pictish nobility in a hall at Scone (perhaps originally Forteviot) by Cinaed mac Ailpín. The tale, which contradicts the contemporary evidence that Cinaed and his successors up to 876×900 viewed themselves as Pictish kings, was clearly designed to explain the disappearance of Pictish language and identity. In later Scottish king-lists, these actions were presented as following the killing of Cinaed's father, Ailpín, in Galloway (Gall Ghàidhil), perhaps indicating that Cinaed avenged his father by destroying the Picts.

From the 10th century, the kings of Alba portrayed themselves (perhaps correctly) as descendants of the Cenél nGabráin kings of Dál Riata, rather than as the successors of Pictish kings. The royal genealogies and the late 11th-century *Duan Albanach* (Scottish poets' book) added the kings of Alba onto Cenél nGabráin genealogies and king-lists. The main difference in *Duan Albanach* is that the name 'Alba' was supposedly derived from its first settler, Albanus, brother of Brutus—a view probably taken from *Historia Brittonum*, many manuscripts of which have an Albanus as brother of

Britto (= Brutus; see Trojan legends). To stress the primary nature of the Scottish settlement, the Gaels were presented as having come to Scotland more directly, rather than via Ireland.

The 'St Andrews' Foundation Legend' was another reaction to English claims, this time by the archbishopric of York to ecclesiastical supremacy in Alba. The foundation legend, written 1093×1107, was St Andrews' reaction—a tale in which 'Ungus', a king of the Picts, won a battle with the help of St Andrew. Then, supposedly, Ungus donated St Andrews (*Cennrígmonaid*) in gratitude, to house the relics of St Andrew, which were brought from Constantinople to St Andrews by St Regulus. In the tale, St Andrews is then made head church of the Picts, and therefore also of the subsequent Gaelic church in Alba.

Nicholas Evans

LEGENDARY HISTORY, GAUL

Within the extant Greek and Roman accounts of the ancient Continental Celts, numerous traditional stories go back to the remote and prehistoric past, and these show points of comparison with the legendary histories of the medieval Celtic countries. Origin legends from Gaul frequently contain eponymous (namesake) founders. For example, the story of the foundation of Gaul preserved by Diodorus Siculus tells of the union of the gigantic and beautiful daughter of an ancient king of Celtica with Hercules, which produced a hero and leader named Galateis, from whom the Gauls (Greek Γαλαταί *Galatae*) were named.

Many of the colourful descriptions of the invasion of Greece in 280–78 BC by the Gauls under Bolgios or Belgios and Brennos of the Prausi have the flavour of hero tales as opposed to history. Thus, according to Timagenes (a Greek writer of the 1st century BC) as preserved by Strabo (6.1.12–13), the treasures deposited in the pools of Tolosa (Toulouse) were said to have been the sacred treasure from Delphi carried back to Gaul by retreating warriors; this watery deposition acted as a talisman protecting the sovereignty of the Tectosages in southwest Gaul until it was looted a second time by the conquering Roman general Caepio in 106 BC.

Ammianus Marcellinus provides an account of doctrines promulgated by the druids concerning the origins of the population of Gaul:

> The Drysidae [druids] say that a part of the people [of Gaul] was in fact indigenous, but that others had poured in from remote islands and the regions across the Rhine, driven from their homes by continual wars and by the inundation of stormy sea. Some assert that after the destruction of Troy a few of those who fled from the Greeks and were scattered everywhere occupied those regions, which were then deserted. But the inhabitants of those countries affirm this beyond all else, and I have also read it inscribed upon their monuments, that Hercules, the son of Amphytrion, hastened to destroy the cruel tyrants Geryon and Tauriscus, of whom one oppressed Spain, the other, Gaul; and having overcome them both that he took to wife some high-born women and begat numerous children, who called by their own names the districts that they ruled. (15.9, trans. Rolfe 1.179)

John T. Koch

LEGENDARY HISTORY, IRELAND

Along with the various versions of the Middle Irish Lebar Gabála Érenn ('The Book of Invasions'), other sources mention the doctrine that all of the Irish descend from a figure named Donn mac Míled, and go after death to an island called Tech Duinn (the house of Donn; see Otherworld). Donn, or Éber Donn, is presented as one of the sons of Míl Espáine (< *miles Hispaniae* 'a soldier from Spain'), a manifestly nontraditional figure; nevertheless, the idea that the ancestor of the race also rules over the realm of the dead cannot be so easily put down to external influence. In fact, it strikingly echoes Julius Caesar's report that the Gauls believed themselves to be the descendants of Dīs Pater, god of the underworld (see Greek and Roman accounts). The Irish sources appear to reflect a tenet of Celtic paganism, for which parallels can be found elsewhere in the Indo-European world.

Lebar Gabála states that the first Gael to set foot in Ireland was named Íth: This curious name, identical with a noun meaning 'fat, lard, grease', can be explained as a close relative of the name Ériu (Ireland), both deriving from the Indo-European root *peih-* 'to be fat, to swell'. This etymological connection would have been apparent only in a prehistoric phase of the language, indicating that Íth himself is a figure of considerable antiquity.

Old Irish Sources

The earliest traces of a blending of native origin legends with monastic learning appear in the dynastic poetry of the Laigin (Leinstermen). Their ancestor Labraid Loingsech is said to have conquered the lands of Éremón mac Míled, one of the sons of Míl Espáine and a figure almost certainly invented by the pseudo-historians.

The grammatical text Auraicept na nÉces ('The Scholars' Primer'), perhaps first written in the 8th century, opens with a story that identifies the origins of the Gaels with that of their language. At the Tower of Babel, where the one original language of humanity had been divided into seventy-two, the eponymous Fénius (< *bélra Féne* 'Fénius' language'—a term applied to Irish legal diction, but also, in a more basic sense, the Irish language) and Goídel 'Gael, Gaelic speaker' create the Irish language by assembling parts of all the other tongues.

Such a synthetic system appears for the first time in a work emanating from Wales, the Historia Brittonum (as redacted 829/30). Besides its testimony regarding British tradition, it furnishes us with two accounts of the legendary history of Ireland. The first of these accounts describes a series of settlements, all apparently originating in Spain. First comes a colony led by Partholomus, which is eventually wiped out by a plague; then another colonization effort is led by Nimeth, who presently takes his people back to Spain; and finally a settlement is led by 'three sons of a Spanish soldier' (*trēs filii militis Hispaniae*), almost all of whom are drowned as they attack a mysterious glass tower. One shipload survives, and from these individuals descend the subsequent inhabitants of Ireland.

The second account, which the author claims to derive from 'the most learned of the Irish', focuses not on the antecedents of Ireland but on those of the Gaels themselves. They are made to descend from a Scythian nobleman resident in Egypt.

Banished following the drowning of Pharaoh's army in the Red Sea, he eventually reaches Spain. His descendants live there for almost a thousand years, then sail to Ireland. The departure from Egypt at the same time as the Israelites, and the forty-two years' wandering on the way to Spain, reflect a deliberate likening of the Gaels to the Hebrews; whereas the Franks and Britons aspired to the same origins as the Romans, the Irish modelled themselves on the Israelites.

Can a mbunadus na nGoidel? (Whence is the origin of the Gaels?) is plausibly attributed to the poet Mael Muru of Fahan (†887). Much of its narrative matches that seen in the *Historia Brittonum* and the *Auraicept*. In other respects, Mael Muru appears to preserve traces of native tradition: The poem speaks of Donn's house as the home of the dead, and of marriage alliances between the Tuath Dé and the sons of Míl, reflecting the idea that the first Gaelic settlers of Ireland intermarried with the Tuath Dé—Tuath Dé, 'People of God', being a term applied to the Israelites as well as to the indigenous immortals.

Middle Irish Sources

The Middle Irish period (roughly AD 900–1200) saw the consolidation and embellishment of the pseudo-historical framework that had evolved in the preceding centuries. The tale *Suidigud Tellaich Temra* (The establishment of the household of TEAMHAIR), perhaps written in the 10th century, includes a summary of Ireland's settlements as proof of the supreme knowledge of a sage consulted concerning the country's landmarks and territories. This is a figure even older than Tuán—Fintan mac Bóchra, who came to Ireland before the Flood with Noah's granddaughter, Cesair. (The name *Fintan* significantly reflects a Celtic etymology *Windo-senos* 'white' + 'old'.)

Fintan reappears as an authority on place-names in the DINDSHENCHAS (lore of places), a massive assemblage of verse and prose devoted to the etymologies of place-names. Of particular importance for this scheme's development were the compositions of didactic poets who were writing in the 10th and 11th centuries and who produced exhaustive verse compendia of historical and pseudo-historical information which dealt both with the Irish past and with Eusebian world history. Many of these accounts were to remain authoritative sources of legendary history as late as the 17th century.

Two more works should be mentioned in any survey of the Middle Irish evidence: *Lebor Bretnach* (The British book) and *Sex Aetates Mundi* (The six stages of the world). The former is a translation into Irish of the *Historia Brittonum*; in his version of the section on Irish legendary history, the translator draws upon his own knowledge to supplement the testimony of the Latin original. The *Sex Aetates* is primarily concerned with biblical chronology and genealogy, but mentions Fénius in passing as the Scythian inventor of the Irish language. *Lebor Bretnach*, *Sex Aetates*, and *Lebar Gabála* show no signs of mutual influence in their earliest versions; subsequent redactors of each, however, drew heavily upon the others.

John Carey

LEGENDARY HISTORY, PICTS

Very little legendary history by the Picts survives; this is not surprising given that the extinction of the PICTISH language and culture probably led to a neglect of Pictish documents. The surviving tales exist because they were retold by outsiders, increasing the likelihood of misunderstandings and alterations, with the result that some of the material may not be Pictish in origin at all. An Irish-influenced source claims that the Picts, having moved to northern Britain, asked the Irish for wives, because they had no women with them. The Irish agreed only if the Picts chose a king from the female line, should the succession come into doubt. In later Gaelic versions of this tale from the 9th century onward, female-line succession is compulsory, but whether this reflected actual Pictish practice is disputed. The *Series Longior* Pictish king-list also included seven sons of Cruithne ('Pict' in Irish), most of whom bore the name of Pictish territories, the so-called Pictish provinces. This sequence was probably based on a story that Pictland was divided by the seven sons of Cruithne, though in the Pictish king-list it is used to stress the essential unity of Pictland from ancient times. Another Pictish tale may be reflected in the Pictish king-list note stating that Drust son of Uerp fought a hundred battles and lived a hundred years. *Series Longior* also includes a condensed foundation legend for Abernethy (Obair Neithich), involving the exile of Nechtan son of Uerp in Ireland, his taking of the Pictish kingdom through St BRIGIT's intercession, and his subsequent gift of Abernethy to God and Brigit; this, possibly, is a later, Gaelic tale, but *Uerp* is arguably a Pictish spelling.

Nicholas Evans

LEGENDARY HISTORY, WALES

The indigenous origin legends of the Welsh have been preserved only in allusions in *Enweu Ynys Brydein* (The names of the island of Britain) and some TRIADS. According to the former, the names by which the island of Britain was first known are *[C]las Merdin*, 'before it was taken and inhabited', *Y Vel Ynys*, 'after it was taken and inhabited', and *Ynys Brydein*, when it was conquered by Prydein son of Aedd Mawr. *Prydein*, Modern Welsh *Prydain*, is the usual Welsh name for BRITAIN. This succession of three names appears to represent two successive occupations of the originally empty island, but nothing is said of the nature of the settlements or the identity of each group of settlers.

Indigenous legendary history had a mythic character, remnants of which remain in the Four Branches of the Mabinogi and the triads, relating to, for example, the families of DÔN, LLŶR, and BELI MAWR, and, in particular, the usurping of the crown of the island of Britain by Beli's son Caswallon (CASSIVELLAUNOS) during the absence of King Bendigeidfran (BRÂN) son of Llŷr in Ireland (ÉRIU). Over time, much of the narrative of indigenous Welsh myth was lost as the European Christian learned traditions became more dominant. In Wales (CYMRU), the native origin legends and their sequential character were displaced by versions of the classical and biblical legends, which carried more authority. The concept of a succession of settlers was lost in favour of a single eponymous hero, called Brutus or Britto (the singular of *Brittones* 'Britons'). The 9th-century Welsh Latin compilation Historia Brittonum (§7) simply refers to 'Brutus, a Roman consul'. Further on, however, the text gives two different explanations: From the 'Annals of the Romans' (§10) comes the story of Britto/Brutus, grandson of Aeneas, who fled after the sack of Troy (see Trojan legends); and, from 'the old books of our elders' (§17), an account of Britto, a descendant of Japheth, Noah's son. Most of the European nations claimed descent from Britto, his brothers, and cousins. In §18, the Trojan and biblical origins are combined. The theme of invaders was not forgotten, though its application changed. Where the native and 'Brutus' legends sought to claim and to justify British hegemony, the development of the traditional history of the Roman and post-Roman periods made reference to the origins of the nations of contemporary Britain: Irish, Picts, Saxons, and Britons. The priority of the Britons within Britain is stressed.

The field of reference of legendary history in *Historia Brittonum* and *Enweu Ynys Brydein*, as well as in the tales and the triads, was the island of Britain, rather than the more compact and recent successor in Wales. *Ynys y Cedyrn*, 'the island of the mighty', is the (mythic) name used in the Four Branches of the Mabinogi. Essential to the concept of the island of Britain is the unity of Britain and the sovereignty of the British (in the sense of speakers of Brythonic), who had formerly ruled 'from sea to sea' and were now represented by their remnant, the Welsh (*Historia Brittonum* §9). Political unity is symbolized in the 'crown of London' and the 'three realms of Britain': Wales, Cornwall (Kernow), and the North (Hen Ogledd). Sovereignty is expressed in the titles 'Lord of Britain' given, rhetorically, to Urien of Rheged (6th century) and Cadwallon of Gwynedd (7th century) and in the war song *Unbeiniaeth Prydein* (Sovereignty of Britain), sung before battle according to the Welsh laws (see law texts); moreover, single kingship is implicit in, for example, the pre-Galfridian genealogy/king-list of Prydein son of Aedd. British unity, hegemony, and sovereignty were themselves myth.

Gildas is the first to express the coming of the English and its aftermath in terms of the 'loss of Britain'. The theme of the loss of sovereignty and unity, with the logical corollary that the English invasions are the turning point in Welsh history, becomes dominant, but also gives rise to the psychological reaction of hope of renewal and restoration expressed through political vaticinations (prophecies). *Historia Brittonum* (§§40–2) gives an account of the red dragon 'of our people' (see Draig Goch), which drives out the white dragon of the English. The 10th-century poem Armes Prydein *Vawr* (The great prophecy of Britain) further develops this theme, which would later inform Geoffrey of Monmouth's *Historia Regum Britanniae* in the 12th century and account for its particular significance for Welsh audiences. Political prophecy would be an integral part of the Welsh literary tradition until its apparent fulfilment in the coming of the partly Welsh Tudur/Tudor dynasty to the 'crown of London', but the central themes never lost their resonance in popular Welsh historiography.

Brynley F. Roberts

LEINSTER

See Laigin.

LEPONTIC

Introduction

'Lepontic' is the traditional designation for a discrete group of approximately 140 INSCRIPTIONS clustered around the town of Lugano in the northern Italian lake district. The large majority are proprietary (signifying ownership) or funerary in nature, though there are two dedicatory inscriptions and sixteen coin legends. The entire corpus is engraved in the Etruscan-derived script of Lugano (see SCRIPTS). This body of Lepontic can be arranged into the following chronological periods: Early (*c.* 600– *c.* 400 BC), Middle (*c.* 400–*c.* 200 BC), and Late (*c.* 200–*c.* 1 BC). The Early and Middle Lepontic texts antedate virtually all other CONTINENTAL CELTIC inscriptions.

There has been considerable controversy concerning the relationship of Lepontic to 'Cisalpine GAULISH' (see also CISALPINE GAUL) in particular, and its position in the Celtic family tree in general, with some arguing that it is essentially an early dialect of an outlying form of Gaulish, and others arguing for its position as a separate Continental Celtic language.

Phonology

As the earliest attested variety of Continental Celtic, Lepontic may well be expected to preserve features that have disappeared elsewhere in Celtic (see CONTINENTAL CELTIC languages for a description of the linguistic features of Continental Celtic in general). Eska argues that the character ν represents /ϕ/ (a sound similar to [f] with both lips together) < Indo-European /p/ in the Early Lepontic form *uvamoKozis* (S–65), the first element of which continues **upamo-*. It is also noteworthy that Indo-European /k^w/ may be preserved in the Lepontic forms *Kualui* (S–29) and *Kuaśoni* (S–20) (though the script conceals whether the character transcribed as *K* represents /k/ or /g/). The diphthong /ei/ is preserved in Lepontic in word-final position in the *n*-stem dative singular forms *aTilonei* (S–12), *Piuonei* (S–26), and *Kionei* (S–1), as well as in the apparent *i*-stem dative singular *sunalei* (S–28).

Morphology

Early Lepontic attests several examples of *o*-stem genitive singulars in *-oiso*, which appear to continue Indo-European **-osjo*. Middle and Late Lepontic (like Cisalpine Gaulish) form thematic genitive singulars in *-i*. In the area of verbal morphology, Lepontic has developed an innovative simple past tense, a *t*-preterite that appears to continue inherited imperfect (habitual past tense) forms in *KariTe* and *KaliTe* (S–119). The Lepontic inscriptions show several suffixes for giving the name of an individual's father: vowel + *-kno-*, *-io-*, and *o*-stem genitive singular *-ī* (all of which are known also in Gaulish). Lepontic alone also uses *-alo-* in this function; its origin remains mysterious.

Joseph Eska

LEWIS, SAUNDERS

Saunders Lewis (1893–1985) was born in Cheshire (swydd Gaer) and was brought up in a conventional nonconformist late Victorian household. His early contact with Wales (CYMRU) was limited to family holidays in Anglesey (MÔN).

During and after World War I, Lewis, influenced by the works of Maurice Barrès and by Emrys ap Iwan (Robert Ambrose Jones, 1848–1906), gradually came to regard himself as a Welsh nationalist. By the early 1920s, when he embarked on an academic career as a lecturer in Welsh literature (a subject he had hardly studied) at Swansea (Abertawe), he began to develop a reputation not only as a writer and critic but also as a political thinker. In 1925, he was a founder member of Plaid Genedlaethol Cymru (the Welsh Nationalist Party; see NATIONALISM), becoming its president a year later. For the next fifteen years, Lewis was the most influential figure within the fledgling party. Developing ideas based on a Welsh-European medieval heritage, his apparent opposition to modern industrial society and his avowed opposition to the English language mystified most Welsh people. Many opponents accused him of having an anti-democratic streak and even of sympathizing with the fascist regimes of the 1930s.

In 1936, aware that his fellow-countrymen were rejecting his message, Lewis, along with Lewis Valentine (1893–1986) and D. J. Williams (1885–1970), committed a symbolic act of arson at Pen-y-berth, on the Llŷn peninsula in northwest Wales, where a medieval Welsh farmhouse with literary connections had been demolished to build an army firing range. For a short time, Lewis and his colleagues enjoyed a great surge of public support, leading to the refusal of a jury at Caernarfon Crown Court to convict.

His one great intervention in later years—his radio lecture, 'Tynged yr Iaith' (The fate of the language), in 1962—saw Lewis deliver a far clearer and more explicit message than in the 1930s. Although intended as an appeal to Plaid Cymru to abandon parliamentary aspirations and become a language movement, it directly led to the formation of the Welsh Language Society (CYMDEITHAS YR IAITH GYMRAEG), one of the catalysts for the regeneration of the language.

Ioan Matthews

LEWIS, SAUNDERS, PLAYWRIGHT

Although still surrounded by controversy, Saunders Lewis (1893–1985) remains the most significant modern Welsh dramatist. From his early days as a student in Liverpool (Welsh Lerpwl) after World War I, he immersed himself in contemporary English and WELSH DRAMA.

Lewis's long career as a dramatist falls into four separate phases that, though they partly reflect changes in the dramatist himself, resulted in the main from the way he responded to the creative opportunities available to him. His apprenticeship falls into two halves: (1) the years from 1919 to 1924 saw the decisive move from English to Welsh, the frustrated attempt to create a new theatre, and the composition of the two first acts of *Blodeuwedd*; and (2) 1936 to 1940, the years immediately before and after his imprisonment for politcally motivated arson, saw the production of the two verse plays for radio, *Buchedd Garmon* ('The Life of St Germanus') and *Amlyn ac Amig*. The period from 1949 to 1954 began with the establishment of Robert Wynne's theatre at Garthewin, Llanfair Talhaearn, Denbighshire (sir Ddinbych), and Morris Jones's theatre company, which spurred Lewis to finish *Blodeuwedd* (1949). At Garthewin, *Eisteddfod Bodran* (1950), *Gan Bwyll* ('With Care', 1952), and *Siwan* (1954) were all staged for the first time. From 1954, however, Lewis responded to new opportunities resulting from increasing collaboration between the Arts Council, BBC Wales, and the National Eisteddfod (Eisteddfod Genedlaethol Cymru). *Gymerwch Chi Sigaret?* ('Will You Have a Cigarette?', 1955) was written for the Arts Council company and performed at Llangefni, Anglesey (Môn). *Brad* ('Treason'), commissioned by the Eisteddfod at Ebbw Vale (Glyn Ebwy), was performed there in 1958. *Esther* (1959) was commissioned by Emyr Humphreys for the BBC, but performed at Llangefni by Cwmni Drama Môn (Anglesey Drama Company). *Excelsior* (1961) and *Problemau Prifysgol* ('University Problems', 1962) were also commissioned by the BBC. *Cymru Fydd* ('The Wales of the Future'), commissioned by the Bala National Eisteddfod in 1967 and toured by Cwmni Theatr Cymru (Theatre Company of Wales) under Wilbert Lloyd Roberts before being televised, ends this phase of the dramatist's career.

Lewis's current reputation as a dramatist suffers partly because the historical importance of his rôle within the ongoing nationalist movement (see NATIONALISM and the previous article) has sharpened resistance to his cultural conservatism. At the same time, the crisis in Welsh-language theatre has persuaded many that his achievement represents a barrier to future progress. The world in which Lewis's plays were created belongs by now to the fairly distant past. If they continue to possess dramatic potential, it will be because they incorporate strategies of response and resistance that continue to be viable for a minority-language culture even in a 21st-century world to which Lewis would have been a stranger.

Ioan Williams

LEWIS, SAUNDERS, POET, NOVELIST, AND LITERARY CRITIC

The range and variety of Saunders Lewis's literary interests are remarkable, and no appraisal of his achievements should ignore his seminal contribution as a literary critic, a novelist, and a poet. Lewis's writing was characterized by a conservative cast of mind that also, paradoxically, was suffused with an extraordinary breadth of learning and a commitment to some of the liberating cultural influences of continental Europe. He first made his mark as a critical writer when he published *A School of Welsh Augustans* (1924), a study of English influences on 18th-century Welsh classical poetry. Three years later he published *Williams Pantycelyn* (1927), a penetrating appraisal of Wales's 'Sweet Singer' within a Romantic context. His oblique approach generated considerable controversy but, undeterred, Lewis pursued his hard-hitting agenda by publishing a series of provocative studies on individual writers, including *Ceiriog* (1929) and *Ieuan Glan Geirionydd* (1931), and celebrated the Welsh Catholic tradition in *Braslun o Hanes Llenyddiaeth Gymraeg* (1932). His essays on literary subjects are available in three volumes: *Ysgrifau Dydd Mercher* (1945), *Meistri'r Canrifoedd* (1973), and *Meistri a'u Crefft* (1981).

In 1930, Lewis published his first novel. *Monica* was a bleak but powerful depiction of the corrosive influence of lust in a petit-bourgeois setting in English-speaking Wales. It caused a considerable stir in Welsh-speaking Nonconformist circles, and more than three decades passed before a second and final novel, *Merch Gwern Hywel* (The daughter of Gwern Hywel, 1964), emerged. This work—described by Lewis as 'a historical Romance'—focused on the relationship between the daughter of an affluent farmer and a less well-to-do Methodist preacher.

During World War II, Lewis blossomed as a poet of considerable merit, though his forthright stance on the industrialization and Anglicization of Wales continued to antagonize his critics. *Y Dilyw, 1939* ('The Deluge', 1939), published in a short collection of poems entitled *Byd a Betws* (The world and the church, 1941), was such an ill-judged indictment of life in depressed industrial valleys that it aroused a storm of protest. His poems *Mair Fadlen* ('Mary Magdalen', 1944) and *Marwnad Syr John Edward Lloyd* (Elegy to Sir John Edward Lloyd, 1948) are held in the highest esteem by literary critics. *Siwan a Cherddi Eraill* (Siwan and other poems) appeared in 1956, and a complete collection was published in *Cerddi Saunders Lewis* (1986).

Lewis was nominated on two occasions for the Nobel Prize for literature. He was a major intellectual force in 20th-century Wales and his literary works continue to attract considerable critical attention and to generate lively debate.

Geraint H. Jenkins

LHUYD, EDWARD

Edward Lhuyd (*c.* 1660–1709) was a Welsh naturalist, antiquary, and pioneering linguist in the field of the CELTIC LANGUAGES. Born Edward Lloyd around 1660, he spent time at Oxford. Although he left without a degree, he became assistant to Dr Robert Plot, Keeper of the Ashmolean Museum, around 1685. Lhuyd himself was made Keeper in 1691. His duties at the museum allowed him to develop his interests in botany, palaeontology, and conchology. His fieldwork rapidly led to his becoming an expert in the flora of Snowdonia (ERYRI). He also greatly expanded the museum's collections of 'formed stones' and shells. He published the first comprehensive classified list of British fossils in 1699.

Lhuyd shared the broad interests of many of his contemporaries and was an enthusiastic, but prudent, antiquary. Invited by Edmund Gibson in 1693 to be responsible for the additions and revisions to the Welsh sections in his new English edition of Camden's *Britannia* (which appeared in 1695), he undertook a tour of Wales (CYMRU) to see for himself and to learn at first hand what he could of the antiquities of the Welsh countryside. He was thus able to supplement his own fieldwork by establishing a network of local observers with whom he corresponded and excerpts from whose letters he could use in his descriptions. This work proved to be a crucial turning point in Lhuyd's career. He acknowledged his commitment to the subject and, inspired by the county and regional surveys upon which he saw colleagues in ENGLAND embarking, and encouraged by some of the gentry, especially in Glamorgan (MORGANNWG), he began to formulate ideas for a comprehensive survey of Wales and the Celtic-speaking countries that would include natural history, antiquities, social customs, literature and languages, and much else.

With a small group of assistants, Lhuyd embarked in 1697 on an extended research tour of Wales, the Scottish HIGHLANDS, Ireland, Cornwall, and, briefly, Brittany (BREIZH). He had planned a series of volumes corporately entitled *Archaeologia Britannica*, but succeeded in writing only the first of these, *Glossography* (1707), before his death in 1709. This volume contains grammars of IRISH, CORNISH, and BRETON; Irish, Breton, and WELSH dictionaries; catalogues of Irish and Welsh manuscripts; descriptions of early Welsh (and 'BRITISH') orthography with directions on how to read ancient manuscripts; and an analytic description of early WELSH POETRY. However, the opening sections of the book—'Comparative etymology' and 'Comparative vocabulary of the original languages of Britain and Ireland'—and a later section—'British etymologicon'—reveal Lhuyd (and one of his pupils) attempting to formulate the patterns of phonetic correspondence between European languages and to establish criteria to distinguish between cognates and chance similarities—an essential endeavour if historians were to be able to track the movements of peoples (see also INDO-EUROPEAN). It is a measure of Lhuyd's greatness that the significance of his linguistic work was not recognized until the new age of linguistics in the 19th century.

Brynley F. Roberts

LINDISFARNE

Lindisfarne, now also called Holy Island, was the site of a major medieval monastery (see MONASTICISM), which served as a centre of Celtic and Anglo-Saxon intellectual and artistic interaction in the 7th and 8th centuries.

According to HISTORIA BRITTONUM (§63), Lindisfarne (there called *insula Medcaut*) had been a base for the pagan Angles of Bernicia in the later 6th century, when it was besieged by a coalition of four Brythonic kings led by URIEN of RHEGED. Urien was then assassinated out of envy by one of his kinsmen and erstwhile allies, Morgan (Old Welsh Morcant). It is likely that this episode near Lindisfarne forms the immediate background to the moving saga *englynion* regarding the head and corpse of Urien. That the place was of interest to the Welsh writer is also shown by the incorrect statement in *Historia Brittonum* (§65) that St Cuthbert (†687) died there.

The name Lindisfarne occurs Latinized in Bede's *Historia Ecclesiastica* as *ecclesiae Lindisfarnensis*, and is of uncertain origin. The first element has been ultimately derived from Celtic *Lindon* (pool); since the island has fresh water on it, Celtic 'pool' makes sense and could be either BRYTHONIC or GOIDELIC. The second element is presumably the same as that which occurs for the nearby Farne islands, but its etymology is also obscure. The completely different Old Welsh name *Medcaut* corresponds to Lindisfarne's Old Irish name *(Inis) Medcóit*. Both of these derive from Latin (insula) medicātus, in the sense of 'island of healing'. If this name is as old as Urien's siege, then Lindisfarne was apparently already known as a holy island, perhaps visited by pilgrims seeking cures, before the monastic foundation.

John T. Koch

LINDOW MOSS

Lindow Moss, near Manchester, ENGLAND, is where an amazingly well-preserved body in the bog, the so-called Lindow Man, and a partly preserved skull, likely of a woman, were discovered in 1984. Lindow Man was approximately 25 years old, had a beard and short hair, and was found naked; he dates from the early 5th century BC, too early to be securely Celtic. He died from

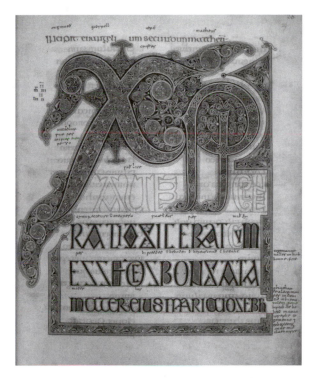

Chi-rho page at the beginning of the Gospel of Matthew from the late 7th- or early 8th-century Lindisfarne Gospels, London, BL, Cotton Nero D.IV, fo. 29. Old English glosses include *godspell* for Latin *euangelium* at the top. (The British Library/StockphotoPro)

a blow to the back of his skull, was strangled, and had his throat cut, all in a rapid succession. Human SACRIFICE and a relation to the threefold or multiple death in early Irish vernacular literature (as in the death tale of King Diarmait mac Cerbaill, for example) have been seen in this evidence. The English place-name *Lindow* is of Celtic origin, Old Welsh *Linn Dub* 'Black pool'; the corresponding Irish phrase *lionn dubh* also means 'melancholy'.

Georg Schilcher

LITERACY AND ORALITY IN EARLY CELTIC SOCIETIES

The Advent of Literacy

Literacy requires writing, but for every region and society in Europe some part of its history predates the advent of writing, stretching back into an unfathomable past. Thus the past everywhere may be visualized as a relatively brief period of recorded history preceded by an immeasurable prehistory. For those regions of Europe where the CELTIC LANGUAGES are, and have been, spoken, it is useful to think of an intermediate stage of 'proto-history' as well. This third term covers a period in real time from the mid-1st millennium BC to the mid-1st millennium AD, during which Celtic-speaking peoples were within the purview of the literate Graeco-Roman world. We have fragmentary indigenous inscriptional remains in various epigraphic SCRIPTS in some of the ancient Celtic languages; however, none has preserved what modern readers would recognize as a full-scale literary text or chronicles of past events.

The medieval CELTIC COUNTRIES contrast with the ancient in that both major literature and documentary history were produced in Latin, and the Celtic vernaculars and the literary traditions have continued without a comparable subsequent break into the modern period.

According to Caesar's *De Bello Gallico* (6.14), the Gaulish DRUIDS considered it improper to entrust their learning to writing, though they made use of the Greek script for other writing.

The Insular Neo-Celtic World

By the 6th or 7th centuries, the Celtic languages, BRYTHONIC and GOIDELIC, were also written—continuously and not just isolated Celtic proper names in Latin texts—with the help of the Latin alphabet. Even before we find Goidelic written with the Latin alphabet, the Irish had used OGAM—an alphabetic script of 20 symbols—to write it. However, this writing system was unsuitable for lengthy texts, which is likely to have been an important factor leading to ogam's eventual replacement by Roman letters.

Putting the various vernaculars into writing was not easy: Sound systems are invariably more complex than the available 24 letters of the Roman and medieval alphabet, so that every system of writing entails a learning process comprising the adaptation of the skeleton of the alphabet to the sound system of a particular language, whose inventory of distinctive sounds or phonemes will always be more numerous. Devising the principles necessary to write the various languages was a major intellectual achievement. Knowing how to write one language does not automatically allow someone to write a second language that he can speak but has never been taught to write. Thus, for example, St PATRICK (working at some time in the 5th century) could write Latin, and two of his little books (*opuscula*) have survived. He could also speak Brythonic and Goidelic, but there is no evidence that he could have written continuous texts in either Celtic language, or that the intellectual revolution which opened the door to full Celtic vernacular literacy had yet occurred.

Material circumstances are also important. The bulk of writing in the Middle Ages was done on animal skin, parchment, or vellum; the latter material, while freely available in cattle-raising societies such as the Celtic countries, was quite expensive. The transformation of the raw material into a surface for writing required great technical expertise and thus an elaborate economic and social context. In addition, writing on animal skin was much more difficult than writing on papyrus. Thus there was a great change in the material context of writing between classical antiquity and the Middle Ages.

Cultural Obstacles

At no time were medieval societies built upon the written word in the manner the Roman world had been. Tradition bearers, working exclusively within oral tradition, and their techniques enjoyed high status. As in the case of the druids of GAUL, the mere availability of alphabetic writing did not upset an established order or preliterate learning.

It requires considerable mental effort for a modern reader to acknowledge that written works were in the Middle Ages still marginal products of a society that functioned predominantly orally and that even the language of these written works was ultimately the product of an oral culture.

The Rôle of the Church

In the early Middle Ages, the only institution that could not do without writing was the Church. In western Europe, Latin was the language most frequently written in a Christian milieu and for the purpose of the religion. In turn, ecclesiastical institutions taught and transmitted the skills of literacy, and it is there that one finds the material and intellectual context for such expertise. In what had been the Western Roman Empire, Vulgar Latin was the regular spoken language for the Christian religion. When the Christian religion was brought into foreign societies, teaching had to be done in the vernacular language of the recipients. Not surprisingly, in many societies the first efforts to write the vernacular took place in the service of the Christian religion. In Old Irish, the likely priority of a highly learned vernacular religious poem such as *Amrae Coluimb Chille*, an elegy for St COLUM CILLE, believed to have been composed on the occasion of his death in AD 597 and attributed to Dallán Forgaill, is an important case in point. Afterward, these technical innovations could be applied outside the immediate concerns of Christianity.

Michael Richter

LLEFELYS/LLEUELIS/LLYWELUS

Llefelys/Lleuelis/Llywelus is one of two protagonists of the Middle WELSH prose tale CYFRANC LLUDD A LLEFELYS (The adventure *or* encounter of Lludd and Llefelys). The name *Llefelys* appears to be a compound, the first element of which is the same as seen in the simplex name of the important pan-Celtic supernatural figure, Welsh LLEU, Old Irish LUG, and CELTIBERIAN and Gaulish LUGUS. The etymology of the second element is less apparent. Lludd's name is explained in the article on NŌDONS. Elements of the Welsh story resonate with features of the story of the Irish Nuadu and Lug, for which the principal source is the Old Irish mythological tale CATH MAIGE TUIRED ('The [Second] Battle of Mag Tuired'), suggesting an inherited Common Celtic source behind *Cyfranc Lludd a Llefelys* and *Cath Maige Tuired*—that is, a myth of Lugus and Nōdons.

Lleuelis, the usual spelling in the LLYFR GWYN RHYDDERCH/LLYFR COCH HERGEST text of the *Cyfranc*, is ambiguous as to how it should be modernized; *Llefelys* is the form used in this encyclopedia, as it is by now the most common form used by Celtic scholars. In the 16th-century text of *Cyfranc Lludd a Llefelys* recorded by Elis Gruffydd, the spelling is *Llywelus*, suggesting that the name was then pronounced like the common Welsh name *Llywelyn*, except for the final consonant.

John T. Koch

LLEU

Lleu Llaw Gyffes (Lleu of the skilful hand) is the protagonist of the Middle WELSH prose tale MATH FAB MATHONWY, also known as the Fourth Branch of the MABINOGI.

Lleu is first introduced into the Mabinogi text as a 'small thing' (to be understood as a foetus, mythologically and possibly biologically) left behind by ARIANRHOD after she has given birth to her son Dylan. This 'small thing' is taken by GWYDION AP DÔN and placed in a chest. Sometime later, Gwydion opens the chest to discover a baby. When Gwydion later approaches Arianrhod, she swears three destinies (Welsh sing. *tynged*; see GEIS) on the boy: Except by her he may not obtain a name, nor weapons, nor may he have a wife of this earth. Gwydion succeeds in outwitting Arianrhod into giving the lad a name, Lleu Llaw Gyffes, and weapons. The third destiny is overcome when Gwydion and Math create a woman out of flowers, BLODEUWEDD.

The name *Lleu/Llew* occurs in four TRIADS, one of which portrays Lleu as a warrior. His name also occurs in *Englynion y Beddau* ('The Stanzas of the Graves', LLYFR DU CAERFYRDDIN 18.106–8), where we are told that his grave is located under the sea.

There are two variants of the name of this character, *Lleu* and *Llew*. The former is probably the original version, proven by rhyme in at least two poems. The Old Welsh form, which would regularly turn into Middle Welsh *Lleu,* is attested in the Old Welsh GENEALOGIES as *Lou Hen map Guidgen*, probably to be understood as 'Lleu the Old, son of Gwydion'. The spelling *Llew* probably arose by analogy with other words in the medieval period. The name *Lleu* is cognate with the name LUG (Modern Lugh) in IRISH tradition and with the name LUGUS, which occurs in CONTINENTAL CELTIC INSCRIPTIONS and has been preserved in various place-names in GAUL and elsewhere in western Europe (e.g., Lyons and Laon); see LUGUDŪNON and LOTHIAN.

Ian Hughes

LLOYD GEORGE, DAVID

David Lloyd George, 1st Earl Lloyd-George of Dwyfor (1863–1945), was born in Manchester (Welsh Manceinion) and brought up at Llanystumdwy, Caernarfonshire (sir Gaernarfon). He was a native WELSH speaker and was British Prime Minister between 1916 and 1922.

Lloyd George became the Liberal Member of Parliament for Caernarfon Boroughs at a by-election in April 1890 and soon acquired a reputation as a spokesman on Welsh matters, such as the Disestablishment of the Church in Wales (see CHRISTIANITY). Having come to national prominence as one of the most outspoken opponents of the Boer War (1899–1902) and as the champion of the campaign against the Balfour Education Act of 1902, Lloyd George first entered the Cabinet in December 1905. In April 1908 Prime Minister Asquith promoted him to be his own successor as Chancellor of the Exchequer, in which position he introduced an array of far-reaching social reforms and launched an attack on the House of Lords by introducing his famous 'People's Budget'. Lloyd George initiated a new land campaign shortly before the outbreak of World War I.

In May 1915 Lloyd George became minister of munitions, then Secretary of State for War in July of the following year, and finally Prime Minister in succession to Asquith in December. In 1918, he was reelected at the head of a Conservative-dominated coalition government, which lasted until 1922. During this period, negotiations took place between the British government and leaders of the Irish Independence Movement (including Eamon de Valera).

As a public speaker noted for his powers of political oratory in Welsh as well as English and for many years a familiar figure at the National Eisteddfod (Eisteddfod Genedlaethol Cymru), Lloyd George had an enduring impact on Welsh national consciousness as well as British political life, in which he earned the nickname 'the Welsh wizard' in recognition of his extraordinary political skills.

J. Graham Jones

LLYFR ANEIRIN

Llyfr Aneirin ('The Book of Aneirin') is a later 13th-century manuscript, the contents of which are broadly synonymous with Y Gododdin, the corpus of early Welsh heroic poetry of which it is the only significant surviving copy. The bulk of *Llyfr Aneirin* (pp. 1–24, 30–38) comprises heroic elegies in the *awdl* metres, called collectively the Gododdin and discussed in that article. On the themes celebrated in the elegies, see heroic ethos.

Even within the verses concerned with Gododdin's heroes and the battle of Catraeth, there is evident unevenness, chronological layers, and verses that make sense as later commentary explaining other verses. For example, in A.45 the poet calls himself 'I and not I, Aneirin', describes himself strangely as a chained worm-covered captive 'who sang the *Gododdin* before the dawn of the following day', and makes reference to the special knowledge of Taliesin. Beyond this mixed core conventionally called *Y Gododdin*, the following verses in the manuscript stand out more overtly as being something different and/or later:

- B1.1=A78 celebrates the victory of the Britons of Dumbarton over Domnall Brecc in December 642.
- B2.2=A.52 is the 'Reciter's Prologue', in which a later poet addresses the court referring to Aneirin's death and the cessation of Brythonic poetry (and, presumably, Brythonic courtly life) in the realm of Gododdin.
- A.44 is a stray verse from the saga *englynion* of Llywarch Hen.
- A.87 is a poem addressed to a child 'Dinogat', charmingly relating his father's hunting adventures and localized in what is now the English Lake District (see further Cumbric).

On pages 25–30, there are four long and difficult poems whose rubrics in the manuscript indicate that they are separate. The title of each one labels it as a special literary form, *gwarchan*: *Gwarchan Tutvwlch, Gwarchan Adebon, Gwarchan Kynvelyn*, and *Gwarchan Maelδerw*. The last is explicitly attributed to Taliesin, rather than Aneirin. The Old Irish verb *for.cain,* which corresponds to *gwarchan,* means 'teaches', etymologically 'sings over'. In the 'Reciter's Prologue', Aneirin's '*gwarchan*' presumably means *Y Gododdin* itself.

John T. Koch

LLYFR COCH HERGEST

Llyfr Coch Hergest ('The Red Book of Hergest'), measuring 34 × 21 cm and now comprising 362 parchment folios, is the largest, thickest, and heaviest of all WELSH manuscripts of the Middle Ages. It contains most of the major pre-1400 prose texts of medieval Welsh literature, together with a large selection of GOGYNFEIRDD poetry, which has led to its being justifiably called a one-volume library. It begins with the historical texts *Ystorya Dared*, BRUT Y BRENHINEDD and BRUT Y TYWYSOGYON, followed by tales from the Charlemagne Cycle, the *Imago Mundi*, and CHWEDLEU SEITH DOETHON RUFEIN (Tales of the seven sages of Rome). Grouped together are the classic literary prose works of medieval Wales: the MABINOGI; the three ARTHURIAN Romances OWAIN *neu Iarlles y Ffynnon*, PEREDUR *fab Efrawg*, and *Ystoria* GERAINT *fab Erbin*; the native Arthurian tale CULHWCH AC OLWEN; and *Breuddwyd* MACSEN WLEDIG, CYFRANC LLUDD A LLEFELYS, and *Ystorya Bown de Hamtwn*. The Arthurian tale BREUDDWYD RHONABWY occurs earlier in the manuscript. Other prose works include *Llyma Prophwydoliaeth Sibli Doeth* (Sibyl's prophecy), TRIADS, two series of proverbs, the medical recipes attributed to MEDDYGON Myddfai, *Brut y Saeson* (Chronicle of the Saxons), and the grammatical treatise attributed to Einion Offeiriad. Absent are the religious and didactic prose texts that were popular in medieval Wales and the texts of Welsh native law (see LAW TEXTS). The Red Book is also one of two main sources for the work of the *Gogynfeirdd*, especially those of the 14th century, with the other key source being the Hendregadredd Manuscript. Although it contains the Llywarch Hen saga *englynion*, the poetry in LLYFR ANEIRIN and most of that in LLYFR TALIESIN is not included.

The manuscript was written sometime after 1382 by three scribes working together, the chief of them being Hywel Fychan ap Hywel Goch of Builth (Buellt), and was probably intended for Hopcyn ap Tomas of Ynysforgan near Swansea (Abertawe), for whom the scribes wrote other manuscripts. By the end of the 15th century, the manuscript had come into the possession of the Vaughans of Tretower, Breconshire (sir Frycheiniog), possibly through forfeiture after Hopcyn's grandson Hopcyn ap Rhys was attainted in 1465. It is now at Oxford.

Graham C. G. Thomas

LLYFR DU CAERFYRDDIN

Llyfr Du Caerfyrddin ('The Black Book of Carmarthen'), the work of a single scribe writing *c.* 1250, is one of the earliest surviving manuscripts written entirely in the WELSH language. Essentially a poetry manuscript, its contents include poems with religious themes such as *Mawl i'r Drindod* (Praise to the Trinity) and *Dadl y Corff a'r Enaid* (Dialogue between the body and the soul), panegyric and elegiac odes such as CYNDDELW Brydydd Mawr's 'Elegy to Madog ap Maredudd' (†1160), and poems relating to legendary heroes of Dark Age Britain, especially MYRDDIN, a warrior of the 'Old North' (see HEN OGLEDD), who went mad during the battle of ARFDERYDD (AD 573) and lived as a WILD MAN in the Caledonian Forest, where he received the gift of PROPHECY. Lines referring to this legend are found in the prophetic poems *Yr Afallennau* (The apple trees) and *Yr Hoianau* (The greetings), although the hero is not named. In *Ymddiddan Myrddin a Thaliesin* (Dialogue between Myrddin and TALIESIN), Myrddin encounters the poet Taliesin, who also possessed the art of prophecy. In addition, this book includes dialogue poems between ARTHUR and the gatekeeper Glewlwyd Gafaelfawr (*Pa Gur yv y Porthaur?*), and between Gwyddno Garanhir and Gwyn ap Nudd, the OTHERWORLD lord. Other legendary verse includes poems recording the legends of Seithenyn and the drowning of Cantre'r Gwaelod (see FLOOD LEGENDS), and Ysgolan and the burning of the books, a series of verses recording the graves of Welsh heroes, and verses to GERAINT fab Erbin.

The book is now in the National Library of Wales at ABERYSTWYTH.

Graham C. G. Thomas

LLYFR GWYN RHYDDERCH

Llyfr Gwyn Rhydderch ('The White Book of Rhydderch') reflects the first known attempt to assemble in a single manuscript the main secular and religious prose of medieval Wales (CYMRU). Originally bound as one volume, it now comprises two separately bound volumes: Peniarth MSS 4 and 5, in the National Library of Wales. Apart from Patrick's Purgatory (*Purdan Padrig*), Peniarth 4 contains secular narrative Welsh prose texts, including *Pedeir Keinc y* MABINOGI; the three ARTHURIAN Romances (TAIR RHAMANT) OWAIN *neu Iarlles y Ffynnon*, Peredur, and Geraint *fab Erbin*; the native Arthurian tale CULHWCH AC OLWEN; and the tales *Breuddwyd* MACSEN WLEDIG and CYFRANC LLUDD A LLEFELYS. The religious and didactic Welsh texts are found in Peniarth 5, and include *Imago Mundi*; the *Efengyl Nicodemus* (The gospel of Nicodemus); Our Lord's Passion; the tales of Judas Iscariot and Pontius Pilate (*Ystorya Bilatus*); the Life of the Blessed Virgin Mary; the lives of Saints Catherine, Margaret, Mary of Egypt, and Martha; and the Miracles of St Edmund. Also present are tales from the Charlemagne Cycle and *Ystorya Bown de Hamtwn*.

Written *c.* 1350 for Rhydderch ab Ieuan Llwyd of Parcrhydderch, Llangeitho, Ceredigion, the book is the work of five contemporary scribes.

Graham C. G. Thomas

LLYFR TALIESIN

Llyfr Taliesin ('The Book of TALIESIN') is a manuscript of the first half of the 14th century. It contains 60 Welsh poems, all of which were probably composed in the 12th century or earlier. Apart from some poems' titles and marginalia, the manuscript is the work of one professional scribe, whose name is unknown. Marged Haycock has detected traces of southern WELSH in the usage of the scribe.

Many of the poems in the collection name Taliesin or otherwise imply attribution to him, refer to characters and episodes of the Taliesin tradition, or appear generally to be the kind of things that medieval poets and scribes might have assumed to be the work of the preeminent BARD and shape-shifting visionary of legend. Among other texts, the manuscript contains *Cad Goddau* [Battle of the trees], ARMES PRYDEIN, *Trawsganu Cynan Garwyn*, PREIDDIAU ANNWFN, *Marwnad* CUNEDDA, and various poems and elegies addressed to or regarding important figures from yr HEN OGLEDD (the Old Welsh North).

John T. Koch

LLŶR

Llŷr is the ancestor of important figures in the Second and Third Branches of the MABINOGI: BRÂN fab Llŷr, BRANWEN ferch Llŷr, and MANAWYDAN fab Llŷr. He has no actions in these tales, but the TRIADS contain a reference to his imprisonment by Euroswydd. The mother of Llŷr's children had other children by Euroswydd, and the conflicts among them fuel the Second Branch. It seems likely that there had been a tale concerning the children's conception.

Llŷr, meaning 'sea', occurs as a common noun in early WELSH POETRY, cognate with Irish *Ler* and a possible parallel with DÔN, etymologically probably 'earth'.

John T. Koch

LLYWELYN AB IORWERTH

Llywelyn ab Iorwerth (known as Llywelyn Fawr, 'Llywelyn the Great', †1240) is remembered for two major achievements: the reintegration of Gwynedd after the divisive conflicts that had afflicted the dynasty in the period following the death of his grandfather, OWAIN GWYNEDD, in 1170, and the broad political supremacy that enabled him to create an alliance of the princes of Wales (Cymru) as the basis for an autonomous Principality of Wales to be held under the king of ENGLAND.

Llywelyn had secured mastery over the entire historic kingdom of Gwynedd by 1199 or very soon afterward. John, king of England, allowed Llywelyn to marry his daughter Joan in 1205, and took no action against him until 1211. In that year, John mounted a major campaign that forced the prince into a formal submission, by which he was required to cede Perfeddwlad (the 'Middle Country' between the rivers Conwy and Dee [Dyfrdwy]) and hand over his bastard son Gruffudd to the king.

Clauses in the Magna Carta of 1215, providing for the abrogation of the submission in 1211 and the release of Gruffudd, mark a partial acknowledgement of Llywelyn's authority in Wales. This document marks the conception of a Welsh principality (*principatus*) in which political power would be concentrated in the hands of a single prince.

After the cessation of hostilities in the realm, the council of the young King Henry III came to an agreement with Llywelyn at Worcester (Welsh Caerwrangon) in 1218. Its terms marked a recognition of the prince's power in Wales. The king was prepared to endorse Llywelyn's decision in 1220 that Dafydd, the son of Llywelyn's marriage with Joan, should succeed him, to the exclusion of Gruffudd.

Llywelyn hoped that Dafydd, helped by the advantage of his kinship with the monarchy, would be able to achieve the political objectives of the dynasty. In due course, Dafydd was forced to accept that his authority would be limited to Gwynedd and that his father's broader supremacy could not be sustained.

Llywelyn's rise to power and his ascendancy are celebrated in poetry, notably in the work of Llywarch ap Llywelyn, known as 'Prydydd y Moch', and his death was mourned in verse.

J. Beverley Smith

LLYWELYN AP GRUFFUDD

Llywelyn ap Gruffudd (†1282), the last independent Welsh prince, also known as Llywelyn the Last (Llywelyn ein Llyw Olaf), was the second of the four sons of Gruffudd ap Llywelyn (†1244) and grandson of Llywelyn ab Iorwerth (Llywelyn the Great).

Llywelyn's military triumphs in GWYNEDD gave him sole control over the region in its entirety, and he moved forthwith to establish, by alliance with the princes, a supremacy over Powys and Deheubarth. By 1258, he was in a position to assume the style 'Prince of Wales', an indication that military alliance was taking the form of a political association, and he pressed King Henry III to grant him the homage of the princes of Wales (Cymru) and to accept his homage for a principality of Wales. The king finally conceded him, by the treaty of Montgomery of 1267, the principality of Wales and the title 'Prince of Wales'. It marked the recognition of the unification under the authority of a single prince, for the first time in the entire history of the nation, of the lands held under Welsh lordship. Llywelyn's rise to power and his ascendancy were celebrated by the poets Dafydd Benfras and Llygad Gŵr.

Llywelyn was killed in combat, in circumstances that are far from clear, near Builth (Llanfair-ym-Muallt) in the March of Wales, on 11 December 1282. His death was commemorated in two magnificent elegies, in contrasting styles, by Bleddyn Fardd and Gruffudd ab yr Ynad Coch.

J. Beverley Smith

LOCHLANN

Lochlann, in Irish narratives, is the name for a region, often with mysterious qualities of an Otherworld, located somewhere north of Ériu (Ireland) across the sea. More concretely, the term can simply refer to Scandinavia. In Irish tales, various deadly invaders come from Lochlann: Fomorians (see FOMOIRI), Norsemen, hideous club-wielding giants called Searban Lochlannach, warriors, raiders, and pirates. In the Old Irish mythological tale CATH MAIGE TUIRED ('The [Second] Battle of Mag Tuired'), Lochlann is the gathering place of the Fomorians and is connected with Scythia, thus implying a vague and anachronistic concept of the geography of northern and eastern Europe. The Welsh *Llychlyn*, which is possibly borrowed from Irish, also refers to Scandinavia and has comparable fantastic overtones.

Paula Powers Coe

LONGAS MAC N-UISLENN

Longas mac nUislenn ('The Exile of the Sons of Uisliu') is a tale of the Ulster Cycle, probably composed in the 9th century or *c.* 900. It is the tragic love story of the beautiful Derdriu and the rivals King Conchobar and the young hero Noísiu mac Uislenn. For modern readers, it stands out as one of the most affecting and creatively satisfying of the early Irish tales. Within the Ulster Cycle, it functions as one of the *remscéla* (fore-tales) of the central epic Táin Bó Cuailnge ('The Cattle Raid of Cooley'). Cf. also Ulster Cycle; Conchobar.

John T. Koch

LORDSHIP OF THE ISLES

Lordship of the Isles is a term, taken from contemporary usage (Latin *dominus insularum*), used to describe the dominion of the Clann Domhnaill as exercised within

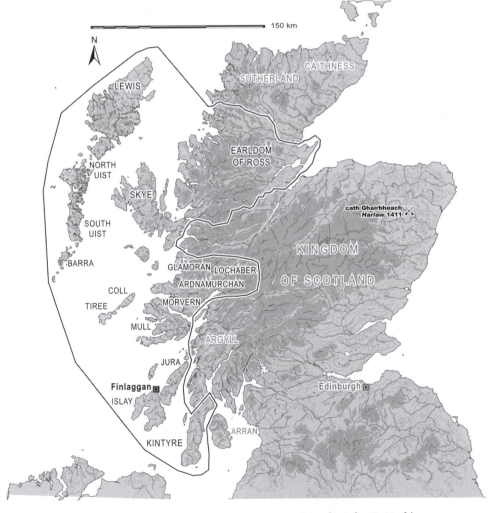

The Lordship of the Isles at its maximum extent in 1424. (Map by John T. Koch)

the framework of the kingdom of the Scots *c.* 1330–1493. This domain was a continuation of the earlier KINGDOM OF MAN AND THE ISLES and inherited the cultural perspective of that kingdom, looking as much to Scandinavian and Irish cultural and political links as to Lowland Scotland, increasingly estranged in its rhetoric from the HIGHLANDS. The grandson of Somerled (Somhairle Mac Gillbhrìde †1164), the first to be accorded the title *dominus insularum*, was Eoin son of Aonghas Óg, from 1354. Something of the scale of his dominion at his death in 1387 is seen in the view of the Irish ANNALS that he was *rí Innse Gall* 'king of the Isles'. Internal dissension and assassination ultimately led to the final forfeiture of the lordship in 1493. Schemes to revive the lordship continued until the death of Domhnall Dubh in 1545. The Clann Domhnaill lordship is generally seen as a beacon of patronage of the Gaelic arts, especially poetry and sculpture, both of which are preserved in abundance. The Book of the DEAN OF LISMORE, in particular, contains many classical SCOTTISH GAELIC poems in praise of patrons from the lordly line or their allies. The Books of Clanranald preserve an impressive Clann Domhnaill-oriented view of Gaelic history.

Thomas Owen Clancy

LOTHIAN

Lothian is a region of southeast Scotland (ALBA). In the present (post-1995) system of regional authorities, West Lothian, Mid Lothian, and East Lothian (SCOTTISH GAELIC Lodainn an Iar, Meadhan Lodainn, Lodainn an Ear) make up a compact urbanized area south of the Firth of Forth and either side of the Scottish capital and southeastern metropolis of Edinburgh (Dùn Èideann). In the Middle Ages, Lothian referred to a larger territory, which extended from the present English border at the river Tweed and Cheviot hills, to Stirling in the northwest, as well as including Edinburgh itself. Lothian was naturally the richest and probably the most densely populated area of pre-industrial Scotland. It is also historically the most deeply Anglicized. Anglian Bernicia (BRYNAICH) under Oswald probably took over Lothian as a result of the siege of Edinburgh, noted in some ANNALS at AD 638. The evidence of Scottish place-names suggests a fairly substantial Anglo-Saxon settlement in the area and contrastingly slight Gaelic and Scandinavian influence. Thus Lothian may be characterized as the cradle of the non-Gaelic Anglian Scots culture of the Scottish Lowlands.

Prior to 638 Lothian had formed part of the northern Brythonic kingdom of GODODDIN. Brythonic place-names are as thick on the ground there as anywhere outside Wales (Cymru), Cornwall (Kernow), or Brittany (Breizh), indicating a high level of survival and a less than overwhelming Anglian settlement. The hagiography of the Celtic St KENTIGERN of Glasgow (Glaschu) looks back to Brythonic Lothian as his home country.

The name *Lothian*, attested as Welsh *Lleuddiniawn*, is of Celtic origin, from **Lugudūniānā* 'the country of the fort of [the god] LUGUS'; see further LLEU; LUGUDŪNON.

John T. Koch

LUCHORPÁN

Luchorpán (pl. *luchorpáin*) is a supernatural figure (see Fairies) whose most obvious characteristic is diminutive size. The most significant early account of these creatures is found in the tale *Echtra Fergusa maic Léiti* (The adventure of Fergus son of Léite). The king of Ulaid falls asleep on the shore and is carried to the sea by three *lúchorpáin*, but awakes when his feet touch the water. He manages to catch three of his little captors and demands three wishes, one of which is to be able to survive underwater. The underwater world is considered as an Otherworld location in early Ireland (Ériu), pointing to the supernatural origin of the *lúchorpáin*. The aquatic associations are further supported by the term *abacc* (corresponding to Welsh *afanc* < Proto-Celtic **abanko-*), which is used as an equivalent to describe the small creatures, and which is supposedly derived from the early Irish word for river (*ab*).

Modern Irish *leipreachán* (and many related forms), Scottish Gaelic *luspardan*, and English 'leprechaun' are all derived from the medieval term, and at least some of the medieval characteristics, such as the being's small size and supernatural origin, as well as a potentially beneficial outcome if one is captured, are retained. However, the 'leprechaun' in modern folklore is most often portrayed as a miniature shoemaker of great wealth and equipped with a magic purse or crock of gold. Modern Irish and Scottish folklore knows of many different methods in which one can benefit from capturing this little craftsman, who is recognized well beyond the Gaelic world.

Luchorpán is a compound, the second element of which is clearly *corpán*, diminutive of *corp* 'body' < Latin *corpus*. The first is probably the name of the mythological figure Lug, originally a Celtic god Lugus, though derivation from Celtic **lagu-* 'small' is also possible.

Petra S. Hellmuth

LUG

Lug (Modern Irish Lugh) is the preeminent figure of the supernatural Tuath Dé of the Irish Mythological Cycle and continuing into modern folklore. He often figures specifically as their king, most notably in the epic Cath Maige Tuired ('The [Second] Battle of Mag Tuired'). Although the Irish Lug belongs to literature of the Christian period, he is often explicitly called a god. In the early Irish literature, Lug has several recurring epithets, most commonly *Lámfota* (Modern Irish *Lámh fada* 'of the long arm'). Other epithets include *Ildánach* or *Samildánach* (having many skills/arts).

Lug is called *mac Ethnenn* or *mac Ethlenn* (from his mother Eithne or *Eithliu), and *mac Céin* (son of Cian son of Dian Cécht, god of healing). Lug is consistently presented as the maternal grandson of the malevolent one-eyed Balor, leader of the Fomoiri, a demonic race who are the mortal enemies of the Tuath Dé. In *Cath Maige Tuired*, Lug assumes the kingship of the Tuath Dé in Tara (Teamhair) during the crisis resulting from the maiming of their king Nuadu (see Nōdons). In the climax of the tale's action, the omnicompetent Lug leads his people to victory against their oppressors and pierces the magical 'destructive eye' of Balor, thereby killing him.

Outside the Mythological Cycle, Lug figures as Cú Chulainn's supernatural father in *Compert Con Culainn* (The conception of Cú Chulainn) and elsewhere in the Ulster Cycle. In *Baile in Scáil* (The phantom's ecstasy), he is the companion of the female personification of the sovereignty of Ireland (Ériu) in the Otherworld and, therefore, has an essential rôle in the confirmation of rightful kingship. Lug is also an important figure in Irish legendary history.

Many modern writers refer to Lug as a 'pan-Celtic' god, since his name is cognate with that of the Lugus worshipped in Celtiberia and Gaul and of the supernatural Lleu of the Welsh Mabinogi. Like its equivalents in Continental Celtic and Brythonic, Irish *Lug* was the base for numerous derived proper names from an early date. The man's name *Lugaid* (< *Lugu-dek-s*) is very common in both medieval Irish literary and historical sources.

Simon Ó Faoláin

LUGNASAD/LUGHNASADH

Lugnasad/Lughnasadh (1 August) marked the beginning of the harvest season. The word (*Lughnasa* in Modern Irish, *Laa Luanys* or *Laa Lunys* in Manx) clearly contains the name of the important Irish mythological figure Lug, and this association may go back to Common Celtic, if the theory is correct that the Roman festival on that date in honour of Augustus in Lugudūnon (modern Lyon, France) began as a Gaulish festival in honour of the Celtic god Lugus.

The *Oenach Tailten* (fair of Tailtiu), held at what is now Telltown, Co. Meath (Contae na Mí), was arguably the most important festival in ancient Ireland (Ériu), held by the claimant to the kingship of Ireland. The annals indicate that it was supposed to be held annually on Lugnasad, barring exceptional circumstances, though after the 9th century it was celebrated irregularly. The English and Scottish festival of Lammas (lit. loaf mass) on the same date is believed to be Celtic in origin, as this date is not celebrated in other Germanic countries.

Antone Minard

LUGUDŪNON

Lugudūnon/Lugudūnum or Lugdūnum, present-day Lyon, was a Gallo-Roman city located at the confluence of the rivers Rhône and Saône. It was founded during the reign of the Emperor Augustus (r. 27 BC–AD 14), reportedly on the site of an older Gaulish town. It was the capital of the Roman province *Gallia Lugdunensis,* which extended northwest from the Rhône toward Armorica (present-day Brittany/Breizh). The name *Lugudūnum* (Gaulish *Lugudūnon*) means 'fortified town of Lugus'. It is closely comparable to the place-name *Dinlleu* (Gwynedd) and *Dinlle* (Shropshire, England), which contain the same two Celtic elements in reverse order. The former is also linked with the figure of Lleu (the Welsh cognate of Lugus) in the tale of Math fab Mathonwy (see also Mabinogi).

At the beginning of August, a festival in honour of the Emperor Augustus was held in Lugudūnum. This custom has been identified with the Irish festival linked with the mythological character Lug—namely, Lugnasad (31 July/1 August; see also calendar).

The name *Lug(u)dūnum* was attested in Roman times at several locations over the territory occupied by Celtic groups: *Lugdunum Convenarum*, now St-Bertrand de Comminges (Garonne); *Lugdunum Consoramorum*, now St-Lizier (Ariège); *Lugdunum Vocontiorum*, now Montlahue (Drôme); *Lugdunum Batavorum* (near Leiden, the Netherlands); *Lugdunum Remorum*, now Laon (Aisne); and *Lucdunus*, now Loudon (Sarthe). The name has also been preserved in many present-day place-names without ancient attestations—for example, *Lion-en-Sullias* (Loiret), *Laons* (Eure-et-Loire), *Laudun* (Gard), *Lauzun* (Lot-et-Garonne), *Monlezun* (Gers), *Montlauzun* (Lot), and *Loudun* (Vienne). The name Λουγιδουνον *Lugidūnon* is given on Ptolemy's map of Germania, and has been located either near the source of the Neisse at the Polish-Czech-German border or in Westphalia in Olden-Lügde, near Pyrmont. Middle Welsh *Lleuddiniawn* occurs for 'Lothian' (in southeast Scotland/Alba).

Peter E. Busse

LUGUS

Lugus is the name of a Celtic god attested in Spain and Gaul. *Lugus* also corresponds exactly to the inherited Proto-Celtic form that became Old Irish *Lug* (Modern *Lugh*), the name of the most centrally important figure of the Tuath Dé in the Mythological Cycle. *Lugus* is also the exact cognate of Welsh Lleu in the Mabinogi. A Latin inscription from Uxama (modern Osma) in Celtiberia is dedicated to a group of divine Lugoues. While there are some uncertainties of interpretation, it is clear that the dedication was made on behalf of a guild of shoemakers, a striking detail considering that Lleu appears as a shoemaker in Math fab Mathonwy and the Welsh triads. Altars from Galicia similarly commemorate lvcovbv and lvcvbo, which appear to be plural forms of the same divine name. Caesar's description of the Gaulish Mercury as *omnium inventor artium* (inventor of all crafts) remains reminiscent of Lug's epithet *samildánach* (possessing many skills), suggesting a common identity as the divine genius of the peripatetic Celtic artisan class. On the place-name evidence, see Lugudūnon and note further Romano-British *Lugu-valium* 'Carlisle', Welsh *Caer-Liwelydd*. Comparable ancient tribal names include *Lugii* in east-central Europe, *Lugi* in northeasternmost Scotland (Alba), and *Lougei* and *Luggoni* in northwest Spain. A great number of Celtic personal names incorporate the element *lugu-*, including Celtiberian *Luguadicus*; Gaulish *Lugudunolus*, *Luguri*, and *Luguselva*; and Ogam Irish luguaedon and lugudeccas. It is also the source of the common Old Irish man's name *Lugaid*, Welsh *Llywarch* < *Lugumarkos*, and *Llywelyn* < *Lugu-belinos*.

John T. Koch

M

MABINOGI/MABINOGION

The Four Branches

Mabinogi refers to *Pedair Cainc y Mabinogi* ('The Four Branches of the Mabinogi'), four tales consisting of more or less related adventures generally known as Pwyll Pendefig Dyfed, Branwen ferch Llŷr, Manawydan fab Llŷr, and Math fab Mathonwy. The earliest complete texts are found in the White Book of Rhydderch (Llyfr Gwyn Rhydderch, *c.* 1350) and the Red Book of Hergest (Llyfr Coch Hergest, *c.* 1400). Portions of the Second and Third Branches appear in Peniarth 6 (*c.* 1250). There is a general consensus that the tales were written down for the first time *c.* 1050–1120, though they circulated orally, in some form or another, prior to this, when tales such as these were the domain of the cyfarwydd (storyteller).

The Eleven Tales

The four tales of the *Mabinogi* form part of a collection of eleven medieval Welsh prose tales known as the *Mabinogion*. This title was popularized by Lady Charlotte Guest in her 19th-century translation of the tales. The term is almost certainly a scribal error for the authentic *mabinogi*, and found in a single manuscript only. However, since the suffix *-(i)on* is a very common plural ending in Welsh, *Mabinogion* has become an extremely convenient label to describe this corpus of native tales and, though a misnomer, it is by now well established.

The tales' content varies greatly. Resonances of Celtic mythology are apparent in the Four Branches of the Mabinogi; Culhwch ac Olwen's dovetailing of two well-known international themes—the Giant's Daughter and the Jealous Stepmother—serves as a framework for a series of independent Arthurian tales in which Arthur, together with warriors such as Cai fab Cynyr and Bedwyr, helps Culhwch win his bride. Peredur, Geraint, and 'The Lady of the Fountain' (or Owain *neu Iarlles y Ffynnon*) also draw on Arthurian material. They betray foreign influences, and correspond in varying ways to the metrical French Romances of Chrétien de Troyes. 'The Encounter of Lludd and Llefelys' (Cyfranc Lludd a Llefelys) first appears, in an abbreviated form, in a 13th-century translation of Geoffrey of Monmouth's Historia Regum Britanniae. In 'The Dream of Macsen Wledig', the Roman emperor Magnus Maximus meets a maiden whom he eventually marries, and this dream-story is followed by a collection of onomastic tales and an account of the founding of Brittany (Breizh). A second dream, 'The Dream of Rhonabwy' (Breuddwyd Rhonabwy), presents a satirical view of the Arthurian past. Despite their differences, the eleven tales of the

Mabinogion draw heavily on oral material and on the storytelling techniques of the medieval *cyfarwydd*. Performance features are an integral part of their fabric, partly because the 'authors' inherited pre-literary modes of narrating, and partly because the written tales were composed for oral delivery, so that their reception and dissemination continued to have an influence on both style and structure.

Sioned Davies

MABON FAB MODRON

Mabon fab Modron is a character with mythological attributes found in medieval Welsh prose literature. He and his mother also have direct pagan Celtic antecedents as MAPONOS (the divine son) and MĀTRONA (the divine mother), often worshipped as a triad of MATRONAE; the cults of both are attested in GAUL and BRITAIN. In CULHWCH AC OLWEN, Mabon fab Modron figures as one of the complex quests (*anoetheu*) set for Culhwch. Mabon was required for the hunt of the monstrous boar TWRCH TRWYTH, and it is told that he was taken away from his mother when he was three nights old. In *Culhwch*, the quest for Mabon sends the Arthurian company on a series of adventurous digressions, including the quests for the oldest animals. The extant TRIADS list the 'Three Exalted Prisoners' as Llŷr Llediaith, Gwair ap Geirioed, and Mabon ap Modron.

Mabon fab Mellt is also named in *Culhwch* among the hunters of the boar Ysgithrwyn and in other WELSH POETRY. This may be a different figure, but it is possible that *Mellt* was the name of Mabon fab Modron's father; *Meldi* occurs as a Gaulish tribal name, and the singular *Meldos* as a divine name (cf. Loucetios 'god of lightning' worshipped at BATH). This Mabon may be a doublet of Mabon fab Modron.

John T. Koch

MAC A' GHOBHAINN, IAIN

Iain Mac a' Ghobhainn (1928–98), also known by the name Iain Crichton Smith, was a writer of short stories, novels, novellas, plays, and poetry in English and SCOTTISH GAELIC. His contribution to modern Gaelic literature is immense, and he is generally acknowledged as one of the greatest of the 20th-century writers of Scotland (ALBA). Although born in Glasgow (Glaschu), Mac a' Ghobhainn was brought up on the Isle of Lewis (Leódhas); his affinity to the island and subsequent personal conflict with island society pervades much of his work.

As the author of five short-story collections in Scottish Gaelic, and of the first collection by a single writer, Mac a' Ghobhainn could easily be attributed with the title of the father of the Gaelic short story. His short stories are possibly the first, and finest, examples of psychological and philosophical stories in Scottish Gaelic. His novella, *An t-Aonaran* (The hermit, 1976), was also highly innovative, and extended the existential themes from his stories to a longer work—again the first of its kind in Scottish Gaelic.

Mac a' Ghobhainn wrote five collections of Gaelic poetry for adults, mostly in free verse. His plays won him awards at national literary festivals, the Mòds, and made a significant contribution to the revitalization of Scottish Gaelic drama. Recurrent themes throughout his work include bilingualism, biculturalism, isolation, mortality, perception, and a quest for self-comprehension.

Michelle Macleod

MAC AN T-SAOIR, DONNCHADH BÀN

Donnchadh Bàn Mac an t-Saoir (Duncan Ban Macintyre, 1724–1812) is not only one of the greatest, but also the best loved, of Scottish Gaelic poets. Born in Campbell (Caimbeul) territory in upper Glen Orchy, Argyll (Gleann Urchaidh, Earra-Ghaidheal), he fought on the Hanoverian side at the battle of Falkirk in 1746. Unable to read or write before leaving the Highlands, he dictated his poems to the Reverend Donald MacNicol (1735–1802) of Lismore; the poetry was eventually published in 1768. Thanks to the magnificent *Moladh Beinn Dóbhrain* (The praise of Ben Doran) and *Òran Coire a' Cheathaich* (The song of the misty corrie), Mac an t-Saoir is principally known for detailed delineations of wild nature, but he was much more than a painter in words: Such poems contain hidden depths, and his range includes satire, bawdry, humour, drinking songs, praise of female beauty, and acute reflections on the times.

Ronald Black

MAC BETHAD/MACBETH

Mac Bethad/Macbeth, king of Scotland (Alba) 1040–57, was a more prosaic character than the tragic tyrant immortalized by Shakespeare. He sprang from a dynasty that seems to have been based around the Moray Firth in the north of Scotland. This head of this dynasty was sometimes accorded the title *rí Alban* (king of Scotland) by Irish chronicles and at other times given the title *mormaer Mureb* (earl of Moray). It is often assumed that the dynasty heads were the rulers of Moray but that they contested the kingship of Alba. Mac Bethad's right to the kingship was ascribed to his maternal descent from Mael Coluim mac Cinaeda (1005–34), a relationship for which there is no early evidence. His wife, Gruoch, belonged to the main line of contemporary Scottish kings. Mac Bethad's reign appears to have been as stable as that of most Scots kings. He faced a rebellion in 1045 led by Crínán, the abbot of Dunkeld (Dùn Chailleann).

In 1054, Mac Bethad was faced with an invasion led by Siward, earl of Northumbria, in which he appears to have been worsted. Siward is said to have set up Malcolm, 'son of the king of the Cumbrians', as king. Although later chroniclers and, following them, Shakespeare, assumed that this was his killer Mael Coluim mac Donnchada (Malcolm III), this event probably refers to the 'liberation' of Strathclyde (Ystrad Clud), in part or in whole, which had been annexed by Mael Coluim II *c.* 1030. Mac Bethad survived as king for several more years. He was mortally wounded in battle at Lumphanan in Aberdeenshire (Lann Fhìonain, Obair Dheathain) in 1057 and died of his wounds. The kingship passed to his stepson and cousin, Lulach.

Alex Woolf

MACGILL-EAIN, SOMHAIRLE

Somhairle MacGill-Eain (Sorley Maclean, 1911–96) is widely regarded as the most influential Scottish Gaelic poet of the 20th century. Born in Oscaig, on the island of Raasay (Òsgaig, Ratharsaigh), his commitment to the language and its oral and literary traditions was undoubtedly nurtured by a family who could, on both sides, boast of singers, pipers, and poets. By the age of sixteen—in the year before he matriculated at the University of Edinburgh (Dùn Èideann)—MacGill-Eain had already begun to compose poetry in both English and Gaelic, largely on the models of the Gaelic song-poetry with which he had been raised. He believed that poetry should be passionately engaged and committed to the improvement of human society.

From a profoundly Marxist perspective, MacGill-Eain related the experience of Gaelic Scotland (ALBA) to currents of politics and literature elsewhere in Europe. In contemporary fascism, for example, he saw the same evils of landlord capitalism and imperialism that resulted in the CLEARANCES of the HIGHLANDS, the depopulation of the *Gaidhealtachd*, and the demise of its language. His first major publication, with Robert Garioch, was *17 Poems for 6d* in 1939. His most important collection, *Dain do Eimhir agus Dain Eile* (Poems to Eimhir and other poems), was published in 1943. This sequence of love poems, exploring the relationship between politics and love, was a landmark in the history of Scottish Gaelic poetry, and convinced a generation of contemporaries that Gaelic could take its place as a modern and relevant literary language.

MacGill-Eain's later publications include contributions to *Four Points of a Saltire* (with George Campbell Hay, William Neill, and Stuart MacGregor) in 1970 and *Nua-bhàrdachd Ghàidhlig* (with Deorsa Mac Iain Deorsa, Ruaraidh MacThòmais [Derick Thomson], Iain Mac a' Ghobhainn, and Domhnall MacAmhlaigh) in 1976. His collected poetry, with English translations, was first published in Manchester under the title *O Choille gu Bearradh/From Wood to Ridge* in 1989. MacGill-Eain died at the age of 85 on 24 November 1996.

William J. Mahon

MAC GIOLLA MEIDHRE, BRIAN

Brian Mac Giolla Meidhre (Brian Merriman, ?1749–1805) held a farm and taught mathematics in the parish of Feakle, Co. Clare (An Fhiacail, Contae an Chláir). He is renowned as the author of *Cúirt an Mheon-Oíche* ('The Midnight Court', [1780]), a boisterous poem of 1,026 lines in assonantal couplets, generally regarded as a masterpiece of Modern Irish literature. In this work—which appears to have a considerable autobiographical element—the dreaming bachelor-poet is arrested by the bailiff of the local fairy court and put on trial before their queen, Aoibheall, for neglecting the sexual and matrimonial expectations of the women of Ireland (ÉIRE). Various 'witnesses', including a young, malcontent wife and her crabbed husband, provide comic dialogue. The *Cúirt* has frequently been described as a parody of the traditional AISLING (dream-vision) poem. While it is true that Mac Giolla Meidhre uses the *aisling* motif as a device for framing the narrative, the poem's internal structure and thematic movement—and even its language—are more closely related to the comic parody of legal warrants found in *barántas* (warrant) poems.

William J. Mahon

MACHA

Macha is the name of a female supernatural figure or goddess in early Irish literature, one of the TUATH DÉ. She appears in CATH MAIGE TUIRED ('The [Second] Battle of Mag Tuired') and the collection of traditions on noteworthy women known as the *banshenchas* as well as the group (usually a triad) of war-goddesses along with the MORRÍGAN.

Macha's most important literary associations are with ULAID (Ulster) and the ULSTER CYCLE of Tales. She is the namesake of the large hilltop Iron Age assembly site EMAIN MACHAE (Twins of Macha) and of the nearby town of Armagh (ARD MHACHA 'High place of Macha'), which has yielded remains suggesting a pagan sanctuary of the 3rd century AD. Macha is the central character of the brief narrative known as *Ces Ulad* or *Noínden Ulad*; the conventional English titles are 'The Debility of the Ulstermen' or 'Pangs of the Ulstermen'. In it, a mysterious woman arrives at the home of a wealthy landowner. She immediately begins keeping the house and then sleeps with him. A long while later she becomes pregnant, and he goes to an *oenach* (tribal assembly or fair), where he foolishly boasts that his wife can run faster than the king's horses. Macha is summoned, runs the race, though giving birth on the spot in agony. She reveals her name, at the same time cursing the Ulstermen that they will henceforth be as weak as a woman in childbirth at the days around SAMAIN. The story of a woman from the Otherworld mistreated by her mortal husband has a Welsh parallel in the tale of Llyn y Fan Fach and *Lanval* in the BRETON LAYS.

Several modern Celtic scholars have seen in Macha's horselike attributes, taken together with the evidence of the pagan Celtic horse-goddess EPONA and the horse-woman RHIANNON of the Welsh MABINOGI, evidence for a centrally important pan-Celtic horse goddess.

John T. Koch

MACPHERSON, JAMES

James Macpherson (1736–96) published a series of poems that he portrayed as his English translations of the 3rd-century epic compositions of the Gaelic poet Ossian (SCOTTISH GAELIC *Oisean*, Irish *Oisín*). The first in the series is the small-scale *Fragments of Ancient Poetry* of 1760, followed by the epics *Fingal* of 1761 and *Temora* of 1763. Most of the subject matter is based ultimately on Scottish

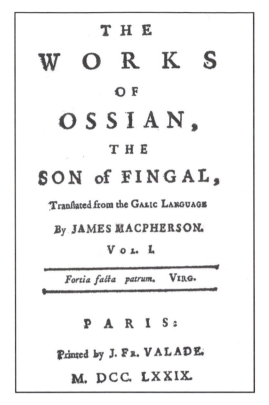

THE
WORKS
OF
OSSIAN,
THE
SON of FINGAL,

Translated from the Galic Language

By JAMES MACPHERSON.

Vol. I.

Fortia facta patrum.   Virg.

PARIS:

Printed by J. Fr. VALADE.

M. DCC. LXXIX.

Title page of *The Works of Ossian, the Son of Fingal*, translated from the Gaelic by James Macpherson (1779 edition). (*The Works of Ossian, the Son of Fingal.* James Macpherson, transl. Paris: J. Fr. Valade, 1779)

Fiannaíocht. Although an instant success with the reading public, Macpherson's poems split the literary establishment into two camps, one arguing in favour of the authenticity of the work and the other against it. A protracted investigation by the Highland Society of Scotland (Alba) concluded that while there were texts attributed to Ossian current in the Highlands, they were very different from the material produced by Macpherson. While some of Macpherson's pieces are more or less loosely based on several genuine Gaelic ballads, much of his work is the product of his own imagination. Although Macpherson acquired several Gaelic manuscripts, among them the Book of the Dean of Lismore, on his collecting tours in the Highlands, he did not find any epics.

Macpherson's poetry first took shape in English, and the Gaelic text of his works, which appeared in 1807, is a translation of these originals into flawed Gaelic. In the wider context of European literature, Macpherson's work is regarded as seminal in the genesis of Romanticism. In Gaelic Scotland, the Ossianic controversy inspired a wave of collecting of Scottish Gaelic poetry from contemporary oral tradition that recorded not only a substantial corpus of Gaelic ballads but also a variety of other verse genres.

Anja Gunderloch

MACSEN WLEDIG

Macsen Wledig is the central character in the Middle Welsh tale *Breuddwyd Macsen* (the dream of emperor Maxen), one of the *Mabinogion* (see Mabinogi). This story and the related accounts discussed in this article are noteworthy as a clear case of the events of Roman Britain forming the basis for medieval Welsh and Breton literature.

Breuddwyd Macsen

In the story, Macsen, king of Rome, has a dream in which he sees a beautiful castle described in detail. He awakes with debilitating lovesickness for a maiden he sees there; after sending messengers to find her, he marries Elen in north Wales (Cymru). Macsen is summoned back by unrest in Rome, accompanied by her brother Cynan and British hosts.

As a Celtic wondertale, *Breuddwyd Macsen* has affinities to several other works in which an irresistible destined bride is seen in the dream of a young ruler: the Old Irish 'Dream of Oengus Mac ind Óc' (see also Brug na Bóinne), the Breton Latin Life of Iudic-hael, and the Scottish Gaelic *Am Bròn Binn*, as well as the French prose Romance *Artus de Bretaigne* (see Arthurian literature). As in the Modern Irish aisling 'dream, vision' genre in general, there can be a political implication to these stories as a type of sovereignty myth conferring legitimacy on the dynasty.

Magnus Maximus

Breuddwyd Macsen is one of several Welsh and Breton literary reflections of the historical Magnus Maximus, a native of Roman Spain, proclaimed emperor by Roman troops in Britain in 383. Maximus and his Romano-British forces crossed to the Continent that year; he defeated and killed the reigning western emperor Gratian, quickly establishing control over Gaul, Spain, and parts of north Africa, as well as Britain, and set up his imperial court in Belgic Gaul at Augusta Treverorum (modern Trier). He was defeated and killed while advancing on Italy in 388.

Legendary History

According to Gildas's *De Excidio Britanniae*, Maximus deprived Britain of its youth. The Welsh Latin Historia Brittonum (redacted in 829/30 and where the name is given as 'Maximianus') tells that his soldiers and their families were settled in Armorica, becoming the founders of Brittany (Breizh).

Genealogies

Maximus became a fashionable ancestor in early medieval Wales and Brittany. In the inscription on Eliseg's Pillar, Maximus is made the ancestor of the Cadelling dynasty of Powys through an otherwise unknown daughter. In the Old Welsh genealogies, *Helen Luidauc* is not Maximus's wife, but rather St Helen, the mother of Constantine the Great (AD 285–337). The historical Christian emperor Constantine, son of Constantius Chlorus and Helen, was proclaimed Caesar by Roman forces in Britain in 306; his story was thus prone to confusion with that of Maximus.

John T. Koch

MADDRELL, NED

Ned Maddrell was the last native speaker of Manx Gaelic. He was born on 20 August 1877 at Corvalley on the Howe, near Cregneash, and died on 26 December 1974, aged 97, at his home in Glen Chass near Port St Mary. Due to the size of his family, he went as a young boy to live in Cregneash with his great-aunt Paaie Humman (Margaret Taubman), who could scarcely speak English. He spent his later life on the land, working for some time as curator of the Manx Folk Museum at Cregneash. In July 1947, Éamonn De Valera, then Taoiseach of Ireland (Éire), visited Cregneash and met him—an occasion that Maddrell cherished for the rest of his life. Maddrell's meeting with De Valera proved the catalyst for a major project to record the last surviving native Manx speakers. These recordings provide essential examples of native spoken Manx to contemporary Manx speakers, who have learned Manx as a second language, and also to Celtic linguists.

It saddened Maddrell that so many of his contemporaries and people older than him were apparently reluctant to admit their knowledge of the Manx language, a sociolinguistic situation common in disadvantaged Celtic-language communities in recent times. By the time he died, however, the decline in the fortunes of Manx had ceased and a new mood of optimism existed among Manx speakers and supporters.

Phil Gawne

MADOG AB OWAIN GWYNEDD

Madog ab Owain Gwynedd ('Prince Madoc') is a figure from Welsh LEGENDARY HISTORY who is credited with the discovery of America in the late 12th century. He landed, according to modern American versions of the story, in Mobile Bay, Alabama. According to the story in its several variants, Madoc was a son of Owain Gwynedd (†1170), who, disillusioned by the internecine warfare of his family following the death of his father, set sail for some unknown land in the far west. The story has parallels with the Irish genre of IMMRAMA, and may reflect beliefs about the location of the otherworld as an island in the west.

Later, Madoc came to be known beyond Wales (Cymru), as attested in early Spanish maps of the New World. The legend took on a new relevance and acquired its familiar geographical bearings in the 16th century with the new awareness of America in Britain during the time of the Tudor (Tudur) dynasty. Dr John Dee, Queen Elizabeth I's astrologer, used Madoc as a way of persuading the Queen to embark on a new 'British Empire' in North America. The legend came into play during the formation of a new national ideology with the American Revolution (1775–83), this time emphasizing the existence of a tribe of Native Americans who might be the descendants of Madoc and his companions. By the 1780s, stories of Welsh Indians had become commonplace in America.

The supposed similarity between Mandan, a Siouan language, and the Welsh language probably arose from the fact that English colonists were inclined to identify the unknown, unfamiliar Native American languages with the unknown language with which they were familiar, Welsh. This linkage may have been aided by the fact that some of the sounds of Welsh—for example, *ch* [χ] and *ll* [ɬ]—are also found in some Native American languages, but not in standard English. Nevertheless, there is no historical linguistic relationship between Welsh and any Native American language.

Robert Southey's poem 'Madoc', published in 1805 and identifying the Welsh Indians with the Aztecs, merely added to the excitement. In Welsh-American circles, articles exploring the 'Welsh Indians' appeared into the 1890s. The legend disappeared from view at the end of World War I, but was resurrected as an academic subject in the latter half of the 20th century.

Prys Morgan

MAELGWN GWYNEDD

Maelgwn Gwynedd (†547) is the best documented 6th-century Welsh king, as he is castigated at length by his contemporary Gildas as the climax of the section of *De Excidio Britanniae*. The genealogies place Maelgwn firmly in Gwynedd: He was Cunedda's great-grandson and the great-great-grandfather of Cadwallon (†634/5). Because of his 547 death notice in *Annales Cambriae* and prominent naming in a synchronizing passage in Historia Brittonum (which makes him contemporary with Ida of Brynaich and the Cynfeirdd), Maelgwn has become a linchpin in the chronology of Dark Age Wales. The idea that Maelgwn belongs to the generation after Arthur is part of the scheme of legendary history in Historia Regum Britanniae and can be understood as based on Geoffrey of Monmouth's use of the *Annales Cambriae* obit. That much of the Welsh legend of Taliesin takes place at Maelgwn's court—where the protagonist challenges the king's uninspired bards—can be seen as a literary development of the idea that Taliesin and Maelgwn were contemporaries (as *Historia Brittonum* says) and that Maelgwn's court poets were wicked sycophants (as Gildas says).

The name *Maelgwn* is a compound of Celtic **maglo-* 'prince' (Old Irish *mál*) and **kuno-* 'hound, wolf'.

John T. Koch

MAG ROTH

Mag Roth, now Moira, Co. Down (Contae an Dún), was the site of a battle fought in 637, in which high-king Domnall mac Aedo of the Northern Uí Néill defeated the coalition of Congal Caech (also known as Congal Claen) of Ulaid and Domnall Brecc of Scottish Dál Riata. Congal was killed in this conflict. The battle of Mag Roth was to have important and historical implications, and pivotal significance is attached to it in several branches of early Irish literature. An important Irish literary figure who, according to tradition, was created as a psychic casualty of Mag Roth was Suibne Geilt, whose battle-induced madness and feral existence in the woods are central to the tales *Buile Shuibne* (Suibne's madness), *Cath Maige Ratha* (The battle of Mag Roth), and *Fled Dúin na nGéd* (The feast of Dún na nGéd); see wild man. As with Suibne, Cenn Faelad's horrific experience at Mag Roth was viewed ironically as beneficial because of the 'stories and poems' he produced in his madness.

John T. Koch

MANANNÁN MAC LIR

Manannán mac Lir is an Irish mythological figure who figures in the native literature as the ruler of a mysterious marine or submarine kingdom, variously called *Emain*

Ablach ('Emain of the apple trees', identified with the Isle of Man [see Ellan Vannin, various entries]), *Mag Mell* ('the plain of games'), or *Tír Tairngiri* ('the land of promise'), all of which are designations for the Otherworld. His name ('Manannán, son of the sea') reinforces the idea that he is a marine deity. In Sanas Chormaic, the glossary of Cormac ua Cuileannáin (†908), Manannán is described as a famous merchant of the Isle of Man, observer of the skies and seasons. His patronym was later reinterpreted as a personal name. Manawydan fab Llŷr in the Welsh Mabinogi is sometimes regarded as a cognate figure; however, the characters Manannán and Manawydan in their respective Irish and Welsh tales have little in common with each other apart from their vaguely similar names and cognate epithets/fathers' names. It is no doubt significant that the name for the Isle of Man, Old Irish *Mano*, genitive *Manann*, and Welsh *Manaw*, appeared to be contained in the two names.

Manannán figures in the early Irish prose tales *Compert Mongáin* (Birth of Mongán), *Immram Brain mac Febail* (The voyage of Bran mac Febail), and Serglige Con Culainn ('The Wasting Sickness of Cú Chulainn'). In these tales his attributes variously include begetting a wondrous child on a mortal woman through shape-shifting into the form of her husband, driving a chariot yoked to dolphins across the sea (which appears to him as a flowery meadow), and bestowing a cloak of forgetfulness that obliterates Cú Chulainn's memory of his lover. In later texts he is counted among the Tuath Dé. Manannán is an important figure in Manx literature and folk-tales, where popular tradition holds that he was the eponymous first king of the island.

Peter E. Busse and John T. Koch

MANAWYDAN FAB LLŶR

Manawydan fab Llŷr (Manawydan son of Llŷr) is the name commonly given to the Third Branch of the Mabinogi. In the Second Branch, Manawydan goes to Ireland (Ériu) with his brother Brân the Blessed (Bendigeidfran), king of Britain, to rescue his sister Branwen ferch Lŷr. Upon his return, he discovers in the Third Branch that his nephew Caswallon has seized the crown of Britain for himself (see Cassivellaunos). Having no wish to fight with Caswallon, Manawydan accepts the land of Dyfed with Rhiannon as a wife. An enchantment falls on Dyfed, and Manawydan rescues his wife and stepson through cleverness. Manawydan is presented in the Third Branch as a wise and patient figure who prefers to use words rather than the sword. The name Manawydan son of Llŷr corresponds closely with Manannán mac Lir, the Irish sea god; however, the characters are very different.

Sioned Davies

MANX LANGUAGE

Like Irish and Scottish Gaelic, Manx (Gaelg in Manx) developed from Old Irish. The language became extinct when the last native speaker, Ned Maddrell, died in 1974. Much material from the last generation of Manx speakers, however, was recorded on ediphone, on tape, and in phonetic transcription. The written remains of Manx include two versions of the Book of Common Prayer, the Bible, numerous ballads and folk-songs, sermons and hymns, and translations of Aesop's fables and of Milton's *Paradise Lost* in rhyming couplets (see MANX LITERATURE).

Manx Orthography

To those familiar with Irish or Scottish Gaelic, Manx orthography is remarkable. Unlike its sister languages, which are written in varieties of the historical Gaelic orthography, Manx uses a spelling system based on English phonetic values. Thus Manx *ching* 'sick', *dreggyr* 'answered', *fockle* 'word', *jannoo* 'to do', and *mish* 'I, me' correspond to Irish *tinn*, *d'fhreagair*, *focal*, *déanamh,* and *mise*, respectively. This orthography first appeared in print in 1707, but likely originated in the mid-16th century. A somewhat different, but related, orthography was used *c.* 1610 by John Phillips, bishop of Man, for his translation of the Book of Common Prayer. Attention has been drawn to the similarities between Manx spelling and the orthography of the Scottish manuscript known as the Book of the DEAN OF LISMORE. It is not unlikely that the distinct spelling system of Manx was introduced into the island during the 16th century from Scotland (ALBA).

Man was Gaelic in speech, yet within the Norse sphere of influence—probably the reason why the language was not written until the Reformation period.

Distinctive Features of Manx

Phonetically, Manx was close to the Irish of east Ulster (see ULAID) and the Gaelic of southwest Scotland. The similarities between Manx and Scottish Gaelic are so great that the two are classified together as Eastern Gaelic. In Eastern Gaelic, the Old Irish present tense has acquired a future sense, and the present is usually expressed by periphrasis. Thus, Irish *tig sé* 'he comes' is etymologically identical with Scottish *thig e* and Manx *hig eh*, which both mean 'he will come'. 'He comes' is *tha e a' tighinn* in Scottish and *t'eh cheet* in Manx, respectively (lit. 'he is coming').

Unlike other Gaelic dialects, Manx did not develop an epenthetic vowel between *r*, *l* and a following consonant. Thus, *jiarg* 'red' and *jiolg* 'thorn' are both monosyllabic. In Manx, the reflex of *-sc-* has become *-st-*, written *sht, st*—for example, *ushtey* 'water' and *fastyr* 'evening' (Old Irish *fescor*). Manx also exhibits the curious phenomenon known as pre-occlusion. When a stressed syllable ends in *m, n,* or *ng*, the consonant has developed an unexploded homorganic stop immediately before it. Thus *trome* 'heavy', *bane* 'white', and *lhong* 'ship' are pronounced [trobm], [be:dn], and [lugŋ], respectively.

Manx also stands apart from Irish and Scottish Gaelic in that its inflection and syntax have been so de-Gaelicized that the language has many of the features of a pidgin. The particle *ag* has become fused with the verbal noun in many verbs that begin in a vowel. Thus *gra* is the Manx verb for 'say' (Irish *ag rá*). Most remarkably, Manx uses the substantive verb *ta* (cognate with Latin *stat* 'stands') where the usage of the other Gaelic languages demands the copula *is* (< Indo-European **esti* 'is'). The partial pidginization of Manx is best ascribed not to English, but rather to the earlier contact with Norse. Some Norsemen had begun to settle in Man as early as *c.* AD 830.

Vocabulary of Manx

The Manx lexicon contains several interesting archaisms. A noteworthy example is the expression *Laa'l chybbyr ushtey* 'Day of the water font' for Epiphany, a reference to the practice of blessing holy water for the following year on 6 January. Another striking term is the common word *eirinagh* 'farmer'. This appears to be an extended use of the Irish *airchinneach* 'lay tenant of a bishop'. Manx surnames are also distinctive. Irish *mac* 'son' is usually reduced to *K*, *C*, or *Qu* in them to give such forms as *Comish < Mac Thomáis* 'son of Thomas', *Kermode < Mac Dhiarmada* 'son of Dermot', and *Quayle < Mac Póil* 'son of Paul'.

Nicholas Williams

MANX LANGUAGE, CULTURAL SOCIETIES IN THE 19TH CENTURY

Before the founding of Yn Cheshaght Ghailckagh in 1899, the 19th-century cultural movement in the Isle of Man had seen two main societies whose objectives related in part to the Manx Gaelic language. The first, the Manks Society for Promoting the Education of the Inhabitants of the Isle of Man, Through the Medium of Their Own Language, was founded in 1821 as a response to organizations in Scotland (ALBA) and Ireland (ÉIRE). The second, the Manx Society for the Publication of National Documents, was founded in 1858. The Society met for the last time in 1892, having published some 33 volumes.

Breesha Maddrell

MANX LANGUAGE, DEATH OF

After Man (ELLAN VANNIN) passed into the English Crown dominions in 1399, English began to establish itself as the language of administration and law, and of the towns, where it existed alongside Manx. Because of Man's isolation and comparatively few English settlers, Manx was initially protected. However, the language became increasingly exposed to English from *c.* 1700 onward, due to a changing set of circumstances brought on essentially by smuggling or 'the Running Trade'; participation in the Trade led to the revesting of Man in the British Crown, which in turn led to impoverishment in Man. This situation resulted in the EMIGRATION of Manxmen (and others) in the latter part of the 18th century. Simultaneous in-migration of English speakers *c.* 1800–20 and further emigration from the Manx heartland during the 19th century began to tilt the balance (*c.* 1840–80) in favour of English. The advent and increase of tourism and a more organized system of EDUCATION imported from ENGLAND during these years hastened this trend, with the result that those born to Manx households *c.* 1860–80 became the last generation to receive Manx from the cradle.

Looking at the decline of Manx in formal linguistic terms, a definite trend toward simplification and reduction can be seen. Language death in Manx affected and attacked right across the spectrum: its phonology (both vowel and consonant phonemes), and its morphophonology (initial and final mutation—i.e., systematic and meaningful modification of sounds used in combining words in sentences), which inevitably led to simplification in its morphology, including grammatical gender. In the phonology, the main results were threefold: (1) wild allophonic variation (i.e., a meaningful sound could be pronounced in widely varying ways), particularly in the vowels, which leads to indistinct perception; (2) loss of the palatalization rule ('broad' versus 'slender' consonants as in Irish and Scottish Gaelic), which leads to indistinctiveness in number marking (corrected by the application of a suffix); and (3) the loss of fortis-lenis and neutral-palatal contrast in the resonants (/L, N, R/).

In addition, the copying and borrowing of idiom and lexemes from English into Manx syntax led to Manx becoming virtually a code for English. Negative social prejudices disadvantaging Manx were significant in the decay and demise of Manx as a community language.

George Broderick

MANX LITERATURE

Early Man and the Gaelic Tradition

Man (Ellan Vannin) seems to have shared a bardic tradition similar to those found in Ireland (Ériu) and Scotland (Alba). Man is mentioned in 'Cormac's Glossary' (Sanas Chormaic); Senchán Torpéist, the celebrated semi-legendary 7th-century Irish bard, is supposed to have described visiting the island and being impressed by its literary school. There is no surviving Manx literature from this period, however.

Early Manx Texts

The earliest datable work in Manx is the so-called *Manannan Ballad* or 'Traditionary Ballad', the composition of which is tentatively dated to *c.* 1500. This poem outlines Manx history from the introduction of Christianity, and was preserved in manuscript form in the 18th century. In the main, surviving or recovered texts in Manx tend to be religious in character and content, and there is a preponderance of translations or adaptations of preexisting texts, usually from English, other Celtic languages, or Latin. A major achievement was the translation into Manx by Bishop John Phillips of the Book of Common Prayer (1610). In 1796, Thomas Christian published an abridged adaptation of Milton's 'Paradise Lost' in heroic couplets. Homilies, catechisms, sermons, and a translation of Bunyan's *Pilgrim's Progress*, all dating from the late 18th and early 19th centuries, survive in manuscript form.

The 'carvals' make up the principal body of original and uniquely Manx texts. These songs on religious themes, ranging from 50 to 300 lines in length, offer the greatest interest. This genre continues the traditions of the professional Gaelic poets of the Middle Ages. Some 150 such songs have been collected, of which A. W. Moore published approximately 75 in 1891 as *Carvalyn Gailckagh*.

Non-religious compositions in Manx included *Baase Illiam Dhone*, a lament for the Manx martyr and patriot William Christian, who was executed in 1662. This eulogy, like the well-loved folk-song *Ny Kirree fo Niaghtey* (The sheep under the snow) dated to 1700, and the 'Fin and Oshin' fragment, from the Gaelic tradition (see FIANNAÍOCHT), were all recovered in the 18th century.

Jennifer Kewley Draskau

MANX LITERATURE, MANX FOLKLORE

Manx folklore is a unique mixture of the folklore of the surrounding countries of the Irish Sea. As a result, many aspects of Manx folklore are variations of broader British and Irish folkloric themes, whereas others are unique to the Isle of Man (ELLAN VANNIN).

The first published account of Manx folklore appeared in 1731 and, in common with other early Manx publications, concentrated on FOLK-TALES. The first accounts, containing calendar customs, rites of passage, and other folkloric themes, were primarily examples of commercial antiquarianism, and appeared in 19th-century guidebooks and tours of the Isle of Man. As a result, little or no folklore was collected in the original Manx Gaelic.

In addition to the importance of FAIRIES, one of the underlying themes running through Manx folklore was 'mischief', similar in nature to the Feast of Misrule. This was expressed in a variety of CALENDAR customs, including young people setting fire to the gorse on the hilltops on May Eve (see BELTAINE) and the twelve nights of singing and dancing during *Y Kegeesh Ommydagh* (the 'foolish fortnight' period over Christmas). It also included legitimized begging by groups of young men, later children, as they went from house to house on *Hop-tu-naa* (see SAMAIN) and throughout Christmas with the White Boys mummer's play, the Mollag band, and Hunt the Wren on St Stephen's Day.

Yvonne Cresswell

MANX LITERATURE, MANX PRAYER BOOK AND BIBLE

The Anglican Book of Common Prayer has twice been translated into Manx. The first version, which represents the first major text extant in Manx in a nearly contemporary manuscript, was completed by John Phillips (a native of north Wales who was bishop of Sodor and Man, 1605–33) in 1610/11. This unique manuscript dates from around 1630. The translation is made from an English version of 1604, issued by James I after the Hampton Court conference, deriving for the most part from the second Prayer Book of Edward VI (1552). Contemporary criticism suggests that the orthography was devised by Phillips himself. Its character is roughly English as regards the consonants, but for the vowels Welsh appears to be the model, including a high frequency for the letters *w* and *y*. (This use of *w* is concealed by the printed edition, which uses *u* to represent both the *u* and *w* of the manuscript.)

The second version is based on the English post-Restoration revision of 1662, in which all the biblical matter (except the Psalter) was replaced by the Authorized Version of 1611. As a consequence, the great bulk of the text had to be translated afresh. The first edition of this second version, in the now established spelling, was printed in London in 1765 and frequently thereafter, with some corrections from the New Testament of 1775.

The liturgical parts of the Prayer Book are complete in the Manx version, except for the Prayers to Be Used at Sea and the Forms of Ordination, but with the rubrics left in English. The 1765 version also omits all the preliminary matter, except the Proper Lessons for Holy Days and Sundays throughout the year, and the Proper Psalms for certain days. In later editions, the Order for reading the Psalter and other Scripture, the Calendar and Lectionary, and the Rules for Feasts and Fasts and for finding Easter were added, entirely in English.

The translation of the Bible begins with Thomas Wilson (bishop 1698–1755). The four Gospels and Acts appeared in 1763, with the Epistles and Revelation being published in 1767. The Old Testament appeared in two volumes printed at Whitehaven: in 1771–2 Genesis to Esther (of which some drafts also survive), and in 1773 Job to Malachi, with Wisdom and Ecclesiasticus from the Apocrypha. A revised edition of the New Testament, uniform with the two volumes of the Old Testament, followed in 1775. The Bible was printed in one volume (without the apocryphal books) in 1819, and a reprint of this version was issued in 1979. The remainder of the Apocrypha, apart from Maccabees, was published from a manuscript of uncertain provenance, also in 1979.

The translation is for the most part made from the text of the English Authorized Version, with occasional use of the marginal alternatives.

Robert Thomson

MANX LITERATURE IN ENGLISH, 20TH-CENTURY SATIRICAL POETRY

The Manx satirical poetry of the 20th century is a form of SATIRE, presented either in oral or written form, generally in the English language, which gives voice to public opinion on the actions of Manx government (see TYNWALD) and locally influential commercial organizations. This genre has a long history, currently unresearched. Even so, in the context of the social and cultural changes experienced by the Isle of Man (ELLAN VANNIN) in the latter part of the 20th century, the poets appear to have been particularly active.

A key feature of this satirical poetry is the humorous but direct criticism of its subjects, who are often seated in the audience when the poems are publicly performed. It has been suggested that to be successful a joke must reflect consensus. Here, the laughter that reveals the audience's agreement leaves the 'subject/victim' in no doubt as to opinion on the issue under scrutiny. In the absence of an official political 'opposition' in the Manx parliament, satirical poetry may be one medium through which the public, via their poet-representative, can express their opinions while retaining good social relations.

In oral form, the poetry is usually performed by the author at various social gatherings, either spoken or set to music, often using traditional Manx tunes (see MANX MUSIC).

Susan Lewis

MANX MUSIC, TRADITIONAL

Although there is a wealth of 19th-century manuscript material and eyewitness accounts, the story of music in the Isle of Man (ELLAN VANNIN) before 1800 is fragmentary and must be pieced together from documentary evidence, comparison with music from neighbouring regions, and a form of musical archaeology.

Several strands emerge. The music of the countryside falls into three broad categories: dance, song, and worship. Dance tunes generally derived from the popular repertoire found elsewhere in the British Isles. Singing has always been a strong tradition in Man. The main song collection is contained in the Clague Notebooks (c. 1890–5), of which many are either directly linked to primitive Methodist hymns or are Manx adaptations of popular British tunes. Several ballads seem to be specifically Manx, including both the major and minor versions of 'Mylecharaine', which was performed on almost every public occasion in the 19th century before becoming the Manx national anthem in 1907. 'Ellan Vannin' is perhaps the best-known Manx song. Composed in 1840, it relates strongly to a group of similar tunes, all of which deal with farewells or loss.

Carvals (carols) were at the heart of Manx song. While a few celebrate Christmas, most deal with other aspects of biblical stories, particularly the prodigal son. The earliest dated survivals are from the 1600s, but some undated tunes proclaim medieval origins. Carvals featured at Oiell Verrees, important events held in church on Christmas Eve after formal services. These have close links with the Welsh *plygain* (traditional morning service at Christmas with unaccompanied carols).

The most popular instrument was the fiddle, but by the end of the 19th century traditional fiddle playing had died out, superseded by popular music of the thriving tourist industry. There are strong indications of links between education, music making, and social mobility as the island became affected by industry and tourism during the course of the 19th century.

Fenella Bazin

MAPONOS

Maponos (the divine son) was a pre-Christian Celtic god, whose cult is attested both in GAUL and in Roman military sites in north Britain. A crescent-shaped silver plaque inscribed DEO MAPONO 'to the god Maponus' was found at the fort of Vindolanda (Chesterholm) on HADRIAN'S WALL. A short distance south of the Wall, three dedications to Apollo Maponus (RIB nos. 1120–2; see INTERPRETATIO ROMANA), associated with objects interpreted as paraphernalia for the HEAD CULT, were found at the fort of Corioritum (Corbridge). At the fort of Bremetenacum (Ribchester, Lancashire), Apollo Maponus is named on an altar or monument, datable to AD 238–44 or possibly later, on which there are figures of two goddesses (RIB no. 583). The place-name *locus Maponi* listed in the Ravenna Cosmography may correspond exactly to *Lochmaben*, meaning 'Lake of Mabon/Maponos', in Dumfriesshire, north of the western terminus of the Wall. In the Gaulish inscription from Chamalières, *Mapon[os]* appears to refer to a god; the fact that this inscription is from near the river Marne (Gaulish *Mātronā* 'the divine mother') is significant. The name and perhaps elements of the myth of Maponos are continued in Welsh Mabon fab Modron.

John T. Koch

MARI LWYD

St Augustine of Hippo (†430) decreed, *Si adhuc agnoscatis aliquos illam sordissimam turpitudinem de hinnicula vel cervula exercere, ita durissime castigate* 'if ever you hear of anyone observing that exceedingly corrupt custom of impersonating a horse or a stag, punish him most severely'. This prohibition interestingly suggests a possible basis in ancient pre-Christian popular practice for a custom common in 19th-century south Wales (CYMRU)—particularly in Glamorgan (MORGANNWG) and Monmouthshire (sir Fynwy)—during the Christmas season. It continues to this day in some Welsh districts, notably about Llangynwyd and Maesteg (in south Wales), and was resurrected for the millennium celebrations in other locations, such as the ABERYSTWYTH area in mid-Wales.

Mari was a horse's skull affixed to a five-foot pole covered with a white sheet (or a multicoloured shawl or cloak), decorated with silk handkerchiefs, ribbons, and rosettes. The jaw was operated by a spring and was snapped shut by a young man crouching under the sheet to operate the Mari. Wearing reins decorated with bells,

The Marie Llwyd at Llangynwyd, **1996 (oil on board), by Huw S. Parsons ('Marie Llwyd' is Parsons's spelling of the Welsh 'Mari Lwyd'). (Private Collection/The Bridgeman Art Library International)**

Mari was led by the Ostler, whose work it was to conduct the party around the neighbourhood in as seemly a manner as possible, calling at each home in turn to distribute good luck and fertility for the coming year. Mari was accompanied by a cast of traditional characters, all played by men—a Sergeant, Corporal, Merryman (who sometimes played the fiddle), Punch, and Judy; their chief qualifications included the ability to rhyme, to provide entertaining company, and to swallow large quantities of beer.

Mari's journey (of many dark evenings) through the neighbourhood was publicized beforehand. Crowds filled the streets to catch a glimpse of the company, but the cast was met by silence at each house door. To gain admittance Mari had to win a rhyming contest by singing extempore verses outside the door, verses that the householders answered and trumped. Sometimes, the battle of wits lasted many hours, until the householders at last surrendered with good grace.

Inside the house, Mari would dance, neigh, nudge, and bite the frightened women and children. Once Mari settled down, Judy would brush the hearth with her broom, banishing evil spirits who worked against the company's efforts to promote fertility. Punch would appear, kissing the women and exciting Judy to jealousy and a frenzied chase with her broom. The revelry would end with beer and cakes for all, with Mari removing her costume for the feast's duration. Before departing, the company would sing a song of thanks for the food and for the money collected, before moving on to the next household. Should one Mari step on another Mari's patch, however, recriminations were merciless: Company members were beaten and bones were often broken.

Many have attempted to explain this peculiar CALENDAR custom, but no theory has proved totally convincing. The hero seeking admittance to a barred feast with a prolonged and spirited bantering exchange is known as a theme in medieval Celtic literatures. Episodes particularly comparable to the Mari Lwyd customs occur in the two early Arthurian texts: CULHWCH AC OLWEN (in which the stunningly attired equestrian Culhwch is denied entry to Arthur's court) and *Pa Gur yv y Porthaur?* (Who is the gatekeeper?) in LLYFR DU CAERFYRDDIN (in which it is Arthur and his company of 'the best men in the world' who are denied entry).

Similar traditions are attested in Cornwall (KERNOW) and Brittany (BREIZH).

Rhiannon Ifans

MASS MEDIA, BRETON

Journals

Breton journals began to appear during the late 19th century, and three of the most important were *Feiz ha Breiz* (Faith and Brittany, 1865–84, 1900–44), the weekly *Kroaz ar Vretoned* (Cross of the Bretons, 1898–1920), and the slightly later *Dihunamb* (Let us awake, 1906–44). With the appearance of *Gwalarn* (Northwest) in 1925, the Breton press developed in a different direction, as this mainly literary journal was written in a standard form of the language and was designed to appeal to a more intellectual readership. Today, the main journals include *Al Liamm*

('The link', literary, founded 1946), *Al Lanv* ('High tide', general), and *Hor Yezh* ('Our language', linguistic, founded in the 1950s), while the most successful current affairs journal is the monthly *Breman* ('Now'). There has never been a daily newspaper in the Breton language.

Radio

Breton was first heard on the air in 1940 on Radio Roazon-Breiz (1940–4) and was transmitted regularly throughout the German occupation. Following the upheaval of the Liberation, Breton-language broadcasting was reestablished in 1946 with Radio-Kimerc'h. Radio Armorique was broadcasting five and a half hours of Breton a week until 1982, but this had decreased to two hours by 1995. In 1982, a new station was added to the Radio-France network, transmitting from Quimper (Kemper), Radio Bretagne-Ouest/Breizh-Izel. Broadcasts never amounted to many hours per week, and the number of broadcast-hours fell in the 1980s and 1990s. However, with the advent of local private radio stations, the number of hours of Breton broadcasts is now increasing, with stations such as Radio Kreiz Breizh (Heart of Brittany Radio) alone providing as many as twenty-one hours of Breton programs per week. In 1998, two new stations were added to the list—Radio Kerne and Arvorig FM—and these devote 80 percent of their air-time to Breton.

Television

The Breton language was first televised in 1964, but the weekly air-time devoted to the language in magazine programmes such as *Breiz o veva* ('Living Brittany', later *Chadenn ar vro* 'Chain of the region') and the daily news bulletins can be counted in minutes rather than hours. TV Breizh was launched in September 2000, as a privately funded cable/satellite television channel—the first bilingual regional generalist channel in Europe.

Gwenno Sven-Myer

MASS MEDIA, CORNISH

The mass media in Cornwall (Kernow) are nearly exclusively controlled by English media institutions, and there is almost no media provision for the Cornish language. Carlton Westcountry Television currently serves the southwest region of Britain, and sought to provide Cornish-language and culturally relevant programming. *Kernopalooza!* was a networked Cornish-language television programme, while the religious series *Illuminations* has also featured some Cornish-language items. Both Carlton and the BBC produce occasional Cornish-focused documentaries concerning culture, economy, and issues of devolution and nationalism. The only Cornish-language news programme on BBC Radio Cornwall—a short programme entitled *An Nowodhow* (The news)—is broadcast on Sundays.

Cornwall is served by one regional daily newspaper, *The Western Morning News*, which, though based in Plymouth, provides a Cornish edition. Weekly newspapers include *The Cornishman*, which serves west Cornwall; *West Briton*, which serves mid-Cornwall; and *Cornish Guardian*, which serves east Cornwall. Although these newspapers address Cornish-language issues, they do not provide any actual coverage in the language. As a result, the following independent magazines and periodicals continue to flourish: *An Baner Kernewek* (The Cornish banner), a literary and historical review; *Cornish Nation*, the magazine of Mebyon Kernow; *An Gannas*, one of the longestrunning Cornish-language magazines; and *Bys Kernowyon* (Cornish world), a specific publication for the Cornish overseas.

There is an emergent small-scale indigenous film industry in Cornwall, partially inspired by European support for minority-language media, and the Celtic Film and Television Festival, which provides a forum for Celtic-language minority programmes. There has been a significant increase in the production of Cornish-language 'shorts', one of which is *Splatt Dhe Wertha* (Plot for sale).

Amy Hale

MASS MEDIA, IRISH

Television

TG4, originally called Teilifís na Gaeilge, first began broadcasting in 1996. It broadcasts primarily in IRISH and include programmes on sport, drama, current affairs, and children's programmes. RTÉ (Radió Telefís Éireann) is the national public service broadcaster of Ireland (Éire). It has two television channels, RTÉ1 and Network 2, which between them broadcast approximately one hour of Irish-language programmes per week, mostly news and current affairs.

Radio

Raidió na Gaeltachta, established in 1972, broadcasts entirely through the medium of Irish, twenty-four hours a day, with a schedule of news and current affairs, magazine programmes, music, sport, discussion, and entertainment. Raidió na Life was founded in 1993, and provides an Irish-language radio service for BAILE ÁTHA CLIATH (Dublin) and its surrounding areas on an educational and community basis.

The radio schedule of BBC Northern Ireland has daily Irish-language programmes in various formats, including those focused on music, discussion, sport, and the arts.

Newspapers

Lá is Ireland's only daily Irish-language newspaper; it was published weekly prior to 2003. *Foinse*, first published in 1996, is a weekly Irish-language newspaper, printed every Saturday in the GAELTACHT and distributed nationwide. It provides a full range of news coverage—local, national, and international.

Magazines

Comhar is a monthly Irish-language magazine that covers current affairs, arts, and literature. It encourages new Irish-language writers and publishes up to three Irish books each year. *Feasta*, whose remit is similar but includes a political dimension, is published monthly.

Irish-Language Publishers

The three main Irish-language publishers are Cló Iar-Chonnachta, which publishes books in Irish and produces traditional Irish music; Cló Mhaigh Eo, which publishes Irish books for children and teenagers; and Cois Life.

Brian Ó Donnchadha

MASS MEDIA, MANX

The *Manx Mercury*, the first newspaper on the Isle of Man (Ellan Vannin) but featuring only occasional Manx, ran from 1792 to 1801. Since the late 1960s, once-a-week news headlines in Manx have been broadcast by Manx Radio, and an hour-long weekly programme featuring Manx has been broadcast since the late 1970s.

R. C. Carswell

MASS MEDIA, SCOTTISH GAELIC

Journals, Magazines, and Newspapers

The level of Scottish Gaelic literacy is low (approximately 60%), and publication in the Gaelic language has always been on a small scale. Various journals appeared during the 19th century, but all proved to be short-lived. The first was *An Rosroine* (1803); among the more successful later publications were *An Teachdaire Gaelach* (The Gaelic messenger, 1829–31), *Cuairtear nan Gleann* (Visitor of the glens, 1840–3), and *An Gaidheal* (The Gael, 1871–7). Today, the only all-Gaelic magazine is the quarterly *Gairm* (Call, 1952–), now largely a literary journal, which publishes principally short stories, poetry, and reviews.

There has never been a daily Gaelic newspaper, and the only Gaelic-language weekly newspaper ran between 1892 and 1904: *Mac Talla*, published in Antigonish, Nova Scotia (see Celtic languages in North America). Monthly newspapers have been produced at various stages—for example, *An Gàidheal Ùr* (The new Gael) since 1997. Weekly or twice-weekly Gaelic columns appear in a number of national and local newspapers.

Radio

Gaelic radio broadcasting began on the BBC in 1923, but was occasional and sporadic until after World War II. Programming became more regular and diverse in the 1950s and 1960s, though still amounting to only about two hours per week. The 1970s saw the beginnings of a genuine Gaelic radio service through Radio Highland and Radio nan Eilean (Radio of the islands), and a programme of consolidated development followed, leading to the introduction of a national service, BBC Radio nan Gaidheal, in 1985. Radio nan Gaidheal now broadcasts some forty-five hours per week, with programming that consists largely of news reports, current affairs, talk shows, and music and arts programmes.

Television

Gaelic television programming began in the 1960s but, as with radio, output was very limited and sporadic before the 1980s. Gaelic television expanded greatly as a result of the Broadcasting Act of 1990, which brought a major funding increase and established the Gaelic Television Committee (Comataidh Telebhisein Gàidhlig, now Gaelic Broadcasting Committee/Comataidh Craolaidh Gàidhlig). Some 350 hours of programming—mostly drama, current affairs, and the arts—are broadcast annually on BBC and ITV channels.

Wilson McLeod

MASS MEDIA, WELSH

Since the early days of radio broadcasting, Wales (Cymru) has been 'fused' in many respects to the west of England. It was not until July 1937 that the BBC's Director General, Sir John Reith, announced during a visit to Cardiff (Caerdydd), that a Welsh Region, separate from England, would be established.

When television came to Wales for the first time in 1952, the country, once again, formed part of the 'Kingdom of Arthur' in the west of the British Isles. In 1958, when Independent Television came to Wales for the first time, the region established embraced 'the West' in addition to Wales. The 1960s saw Wales gain a measure of 'independence' in broadcasting terms. In 1964, BBC Wales was established as an entity in its own right, and in the same year, an Independent Television service for the whole of Wales was created through the merger of the failed Wales (West and North)/Teledu Cymru company and Television Wales and the West (TWW).

The language issue dominated debate on broadcasting during the 1970s, and opinion was polarized between those who complained of being deprived of national (i.e., 'British') network programmes because of Welsh-language broadcasts and those who argued that scant regard was paid to the need for increased Welsh-language broadcasting. The turning point came in 1974 with the publication of the Crawford Committee Report on Broadcasting, which recommended that the fourth channel should, in Wales, give priority to Welsh-language programmes. This ultimately led to the establishment in 1982 of the Welsh Fourth Channel, S4C, under the terms of the 1980 Broadcasting Act. Since that time, the channel has been at the forefront of Welsh-language developments, and over the years its efforts to preserve, promote, and develop the indigenous language and culture of Wales have been praised. Its remit to cater to all shades of opinion and background in terms of the Welsh-language audience has provided a valuable forum for debate and reflection.

The infrastructure for a coherent Welsh-language, print-based media has yet to be established. The National Assembly for Wales (Cynulliad Cenedlaethol Cymru) has no direct control over the Welsh broadcasters and all three major players—the

BBC, HTV, and S4C—are ultimately answerable to the UK parliament in Westminster.

Jamie Medhurst

MATERIAL CULTURE, MEDIEVAL CLOTHING

Medieval clothing in Celtic cultures is known from a variety of sources. Archaeological finds of whole garments are rare; visual depictions (manuscripts, sculpture, metalwork) are plentiful, but are often extremely stylized rather than representational. Vernacular descriptions (e.g., manuscript ART, literary tales, laws) are useful, but can be misleading; likewise, descriptions from outside the culture are often more detailed but may overemphasize minor differences or be slanted for political purposes.

Overall, styles followed general northern European trends, and though there is variation within the CELTIC COUNTRIES, there is no 'Celtic' clothing. Following the Roman era, two distinct styles emerged: a loose, relatively unshaped, sleeved tunic, often worn in multiple layers, full-length for women and either long or short for men, with a mantle (usually an unshaped rectangle) worn over this garment, and usually some type of headdress for adult women. An alternative style (found primarily in Irish sources) involved close-fitting trousers and a short, close-fitting jacket. The loose tunic remained the primary style until roughly the 14th century when the close-fitting, buttoned garments worn elsewhere in Europe begin to be seen.

From the earliest Irish sources, it is possible to identify two styles. The first was worn by both sexes and combines the *léine*, a loose, unshaped, long-sleeved tunic, often described or depicted as being brightly coloured and with ornamental borders, and the *brat*, an unshaped rectangular cloak, often with ornamented edges or fringes. The second style, associated with soldiers or men of lower status, combines a relatively close-fitting jacket called the *ionar* and close-fitting trews of variable length. These one-piece, joined trousers remained distinctive in Ireland through the high medieval period, contrasting with the more pan-European style of separate leg coverings. In the later medieval period, the *léine* evolved into a more shirt-like item, worn under another garment, while the *brat* shifted to a more rounded shape, and was often described and depicted as 'shaggy'. From around the 14th century, a hooded shoulder-cape was introduced, and, in the 15th century, a loose over-gown belted into folds came into vogue.

Works on the history of Scottish clothing tend to focus solely on the HIGHLANDS (whose KILTS and clan TARTANS postdate the medieval period). Plentiful information on Scottish clothing becomes available only in the 16th century. Surviving garments include a hooded shoulder-cape from Orkney (Arcaibh), dating roughly to between the 3rd and the 7th centuries.

No general studies have yet been published on the history of Welsh clothing. Visual sources are scarce, the best being the marginal illustrations in the Peniarth MS 28 law book (13th century), which show men wearing loose, long-sleeved, belted tunics ranging from knee to calf length, and women with similar full-length garments. The law books and the slightly later Romances describe a variety of garments. The basic arrangement was an under-garment usually called a *crys*, typically of linen, covered by a woollen over-garment for which a variety of names are given, but most typically *pais* for men and the generic *gwisg* 'garment' for women. A rectangular *llen* is the older style of cloak, while borrowed names describe more shaped cloaks. In contrast, external descriptions of Welsh dress tend to focus on indications of poverty, such as a lack of woollen garments and a habit of going bare-legged, rather than focusing on distinctions of style. In the later medieval period, there is a shift to more international styles. There appear to be no specific studies of medieval Breton or Cornish clothing.

Heather Rose Jones

MATERIAL CULTURE, MUSICAL INSTRUMENTS

From the early Hallstatt culture to the present age, the Celtic peoples have shared with other European cultures the same basic types of instruments. The earliest archaeological evidence from ancient Celtic Europe reveals a variety of wind instruments, as well as lyres and rattles and other sound makers similar in type to those used by a wide range of peoples across Europe.

Material and iconographic evidence of horns and trumpets such as the vertically held CARNYX are contemporary with comments on their military rôle by classical writers (see GREEK AND ROMAN ACCOUNTS). Horns and trumpets are also generally associated with watchmen and heralds.

From at least the 1st century BC, as in other early societies, the Celtic bards accompanied themselves on the lyre. By AD 1000, the triangular-framed HARP, depicted on PICTISH stone carvings from the 8th to the 10th centuries, replaced the lyre as the main instrument associated with strict-metre poetry. GIRALDUS CAMBRENSIS (*c.* 1188) describes the skill of Irish and Welsh harpers, a statement that also applies to the harpers of Scotland (ALBA), who, according to Giraldus, like those of Ireland additionally used a *timpán* (probably a type of lyre) and those of Wales a *chorus* (crwth).

The high status and privileges accorded to harp, *timpán,* and *crwth* players associated with bardic performance under native rule, as evidenced in the law texts and other literary and documentary sources, had to be constantly justified under English domination (especially from Henry VIII's reign). The Anglicization of the gentry, accelerated by various ACTS OF UNION and the devastating consequences of the anti-Gaelic laws, resulted in the ultimate demise of bardic performance as the traditional patrons either went into exile, some taking musicians with them, or increasingly embraced the current English musical fashions.

Traditional high-art music was governed by a disciplined oral system of education and represents a medieval ART in which highly ornamented, intricate compositional formulae and timbral subtlety were important, complementing the similar qualities of strict-metre poetry. The knowledge of this art was fast being eroded in Wales (CYMRU) when Robert ap Huw compiled his manuscript of harp music (1613) using tablature. The tradition lasted longer in the Gaelic heartland: The last harper to use the old fingernail technique on wire strings was Denis Hempson (1695–1807). Bunting made a transcription of a tuning prelude played by Hempson, then aged about 97, at the 1792 Belfast Harp Festival. Earlier harpers may well have used oral mnemonics similar to the *canntaireachd* used to teach the *piobaireachd* of the Highland bagpipes, whose systematic variation technique resembles the harp music of Robert ap Huw, and may indicate a close affinity with medieval Scottish harp music.

The piper's instrument (Giraldus's Welsh *tibia* and the Irish *cuisle ciuil*) in the early medieval period was probably a single or double reed pipe, possibly a hornpipe, types of which survived in Scotland (stock-and-horn) and Wales (*pibgorn*) as rustic instruments into the 18th century. The Breton duo of BINIOU (BAGPIPE) and bombard (reed pipe) represents an unbroken tradition from the Middle Ages.

In Ireland (ÉIRE) and Scotland by the 16th century, pipes were also well established as military instruments. The hereditary pipers of Highland chieftains, who also provided ceremonial music, enjoyed high status and privileges. By the second half of the 16th century, the new Italian violin (replacing the rebec) became the favourite instrument for DANCING at both the English and Scottish courts, gradually displacing the *crwth* and the older type of fiddle. While the harp's popularity waned in Scotland and Ireland, the violin rapidly gained ground, taking over some of its functions and, despite Nonconformist disapproval of dancing, retained its status along with the bagpipes.

Since *c.* 1800, Irish traditional musicians have expanded their range of instruments to include a variety of fipple and rim-blown flutes, free-reed instruments, and, since the 1950s, bodhrán and bones. Recent years have seen a revival of interest in the older instruments and performance practices of the Celtic countries.

Bethan Miles

MATERIAL CULTURE, NATIONAL COSTUME

The development and adoption of a national costume was part of 19th-century nationalism in most European countries. Often, versions of pre-industrial peasant dress, by then associated with an idealized countryside, were chosen by indigenous élites to serve as the basis for their ideas.

Marion Löffler

MATERIAL CULTURE, NATIONAL COSTUME, BRITTANY

The Bretons are the only Celts who can boast a national costume that continues an unbroken tradition and one that, in its many regional variations, is still worn at Catholic pardons processions and various festivals held over the CALENDAR year. Because of the variety of regional variations, it is difficult to describe the costume; indeed, some observers have even written of Breton national costumes (plural). The core elements for women are petticoats and layers of aprons, with a bodice and corselet, often of black or blue brocade or velvet, adorned with intricate embroidery. A headdress of lace or muslin, the Breton lace *koef*, can be very simple or much

Breton national costume displayed at a 1909 festival. (Branger/Roger Viollet/Getty Images)

more elaborate and built-up, with intricate folds, wings, and long ribbons flowing down the back. R. Y. Creston cites 1,200 variations, grouped within sixty-six main fashion types. The male costume traditionally featured coarse, baggy trousers, taken together at the knee, though nowadays a velvet-trimmed suit seems to be the preferred option. Waistcoats and coats, often of dark velvet with silver buttons, are frequently embroidered, and a broad-rimmed straw hat or black velvet hat with a colourful ribbon is also worn. Silver buckles are a preferred adornment for men.

Gwenno Sven-Myer and Marion Löffler

MATERIAL CULTURE, NATIONAL COSTUME, CORNWALL

As on the Isle of Man, Cornish national costumes were devised in the 20th century. A first costume, based on historic sources, is often worn by dance troupes and during displays at *troyls*. This costume is drawn from the 19th-century tin and copper mining heritage in Cornwall (KERNOW), with men wearing hobnailed boots, gaitered trousers, white shirts, and waistcoats, topped off by early mining helmets, made of lacquered felt with a candle placed in putty or clay on the brim. The female costume is based on the image of the *bal-maiden* (Cornish *bal* 'mine'), who worked at the surface of mines and dressed tin and copper. The women are usually seen wearing boots, long black skirts with white aprons, and white blouses. Traditionally, a white linen bonnet or *gook*, whose variations and styles reflect allegiance to particular parishes or mines, is worn, which may be compared with Brittany's lace *koef*. The historic costume is also seen in maritime towns and villages, though the traditional footwear there tended to be the clog, sometimes called the 'Newlyn clog'. Fishermen also traditionally wore the Cornish Guernsey or 'knit frock'. The stitching of the frock, like the gook, varied according to the area of origin. Fishwives' costumes were further characterized by huge beaver hats, *cawls* (baskets) carried on the back by means of a band passed over the head, and red cloaks.

Tartans in Cornish colours came about in the 20th century. For younger people, the black-and-gold striped shirt of the Cornish rugby team is as much a badge of identity as the tartan or mining costumes, but the latter are still very popular.

Alan M. Kent

MATERIAL CULTURE, NATIONAL COSTUME, IRELAND

Unusually, the national costume of Ireland (Éire) devised by members of the Celtic renaissance at the end of the 19th century was based on early Christian and medieval models. For the men, tunics over which a loose cape (*brat*) was worn and trousers bound up to the knee dominated. Women wore loose, flowing, ankle-length robes modelled on 11th-century European fashion. The clothes were embroidered with 'Kells embroidery'—Celtic zigzag patterns, spirals, and curves—and accessorized with Tara-style brooches. 'Celtic dress' was advertised in Conradh na Gaeilge publications and worn for events such as the Oireachtas (see feiseanna). Although not generally adopted, 'Celtic dress' became the basis for the costume worn for Irish formal dances, recently popularized worldwide by the *Riverdance* company.

Marion Löffler

MATERIAL CULTURE, NATIONAL COSTUME, ISLE OF MAN

The concept of a Manx national costume developed through the early and mid-20th century with the evolution of a series of different types and styles of costume identified as 'a Manx national costume'. Manx historic costume was based on late 18th- to late 19th-century rural working costume—for example, fishermen's *ganseys* (jumpers), homespun *loaghtan* (woollen trousers) for the men, and a *kriss* (belt). The women's outfits often comprised woollen 'bed-jackets', red or striped petticoats, overskirts and aprons, and either long bonnets or small mob caps, reminiscent of those worn in Wales (Cymru) and Brittany (Breizh). In contrast, an ahistorical costume was designed from the beginning to be both practical and attractive, with the emphasis on its specifically Manx design of Celtic interlace and chain decoration and motifs.

Yvonne Cresswell and Marion Löffler

MATERIAL CULTURE, NATIONAL COSTUME, SCOTLAND

Scotland's national costume is mainly associated with kilts and tartans, which are said to denote clan membership. In the kilt's original form, it was simply a large piece of cloth, pleated and fastened around the waist with a leather belt, and with a large BROOCH or pin on the left shoulder to hold both ends together. Known as the *breacan fèileadh* or *fèileadh mòr*, the 'big kilt', this garment was worn by Highlanders only and was regarded by the Lowlanders as a sign of backwardness and barbarism. Like other Highland customs and characteristics, it was banned in 1746 (see CULLODEN).

The *fèileadh beag*, 'small kilt', became the national costume for the whole of the country in the 19th century. The small kilt is usually worn with a *sporran*, a leather purse attached to a leather belt. Both kilts and tartans were popularized by Sir Walter Scott. No corresponding costume for Scottish women was developed, though the wearing of tartan-patterned skirts, shawls, and other accessories in Scottish textile was adopted for celebrations. The mighty influence that the kilt and tartan have exerted can be observed in repeated attempts to incorporate them into the national costumes of Wales (CYMRU), Ireland (ÉIRE), the Isle of Man (ELLAN VANNIN), and Cornwall (KERNOW).

Marion Löffler

MATERIAL CULTURE, NATIONAL COSTUME, WALES

The Welsh national dress was derived from regional Welsh peasant costumes noted by Lady Augusta Hall in an 1834 essay. The more elaborate is the women's dress, consisting of a blouse worn under a corselet or close-fitting mantle, sometimes with petticoats and aprons in various patterns and colours. A (mostly red) shawl covered the often bare arms, and a beaver hat was worn over a close-fitting lace cap. The men's costume consisted of simple trousers or breeches and blazer, made from Welsh wool or corduroy. Nowadays, Augusta Hall's national costume is mainly worn by schoolchildren on Saint David's Day (see DEWI SANT) and by the performers of traditional music. Nevertheless, the red skirt, black shawl, and tall black hat with lace cap remain powerful symbols of Welsh identity.

Marion Löffler

MATH FAB MATHONWY

Math fab Mathonwy is one of the characters in the Middle Welsh tale that is usually referred to by his name, alternatively known as the Fourth Branch of the MABINOGI.

In the Fourth Branch, Math is described as lord of GWYNEDD, the powerful medieval principality of north Wales (CYMRU). Math possesses magical powers and even a magic wand, which at times he wields to mete out justice—for example, turning Gwydion and Gilfaethwy into a succession of different animals in the Mabinogi text. Later on in the story, Math uses his wand to create a wife, BLODEUWEDD, out of flowers, for LLEU Llaw Gyffes.

Math's name is to be found in various GENEALOGIES of the 15th and 16th centuries, where he is often named as the father of several of the characters of the Fourth Branch—Lleu Llaw Gyffes, Dylan Ail Ton, and Blodeuwedd. In these pedigrees, ARIANRHOD daughter of DÔN is named as their mother.

The name *Math* is likely to be connected with two names that appear in early Irish material. In LEBAR GABÁLA ÉRENN ('The Book of Invasions'), Math mac Úmóir is named as druid of the TUATH DÉ. A figure called Mathgen or Matgen is said to be druid of the Tuath Dé in the text CATH MAIGE TUIRED ('The [Second] Battle of Mag Tuired'). Old Irish *Mathgen* derives regularly from the attested Old Celtic name *Matugenos* 'auspiciously born'.

Ian Hughes

MATRONAE

Matronae ('mother goddesses'/divine mothers', sing. Matrona) appear eighty-four times in Gallo-Brittonic dedications of the Roman period. They were worshipped intensively in the Rhineland, in the vicinity of Bonn and Cologne. The name gives rise to those of two figures in Welsh tradition: Modron (discussed later in this article) and Saint Madrun, daughter of Gwerthefyr, both of whom are indeed mythical mothers. The former Welsh name results from the original Celtic form *Mātrona* and the latter from the Latinization *Matrōna*. A British cult of Matrona is also implicit in that of Maponos (the divine son), for which there is abundant evidence. *Mātrona* was the ancient name of the river Marne in northeast Gaul. As with Irish BÓAND, we may understand Mātrona as simultaneously the name of the river and its divine female personification.

Scores of dedications to the *Mātres* ('mothers') can be found in Roman Britain, and the name is often paired with that of a homeland—for example, *Mātres Italae*, *Mātres Gallae*, and *Mātres Germanae*. Some writers have seen the south-Walian name for the fairies, *bendith y mamau* (blessing of the mothers), as survival in folk belief of the Celtic mother goddesses.

In the representations of the Romano-Celtic mother goddesses, these figures are frequently shown in groups of three, commonly with cornucopias and other emblems of harvest and abundance, often with babies and one breast bared, and usually dressed in long gowns. There are more than 1,100 images in total, including images with these features but not inscribed as *Matronae* or *Matres*.

In the early ARTHURIAN tale CULHWCH AC OLWEN, Modron figures as the mother of the primeval prisoner MABON (< Gallo-Brittonic *Maponos*), who was abducted when three nights old. She also has the rôle of a supernatural mother in the TRIADS, where she is the mother of OWAIN and Morfudd by URIEN RHEGED. In a tale dated 1556, a mysterious unnamed woman encounters Urien at the ford of invisible barking dogs (Rhyd y Gyfarthfa), has intercourse with him, later gives birth to Owain and Morfudd, and ultimately reveals herself to be the daughter of the king of ANNWFN, which implies that her patronym, Afallach (see AVALON), is a name of the king of the OTHERWORLD.

John T. Koch

MEATH

See Mide.

MEDB AND AILILL

Medb and Ailill mac Máta (also called Ailill mac Mágach) figure as queen and king of CONNACHT in the tales of the ULSTER CYCLE, often as chief antagonists of the ULAID and their high hero Cú Chulainn, especially in the central epic Táin Bó Cuailnge ('The Cattle Raid of Cooley'). Their principal court is at Crúachu. Their daughter is the beautiful Findabair, whose name is cognate with Welsh Gwenhwyfar.

In general, the most notable attribute of the couple is that Medb is usually dominant and prone to aggressive action, both military and sexual. Consequently, Medb has had particular appeal for modern readers and her personality has lent itself in recent times to feminist interpretations and popular ideas about Celtic women. Her name is Celtic, related to the word for 'mead', Old Irish *mid*, Welsh *medd*, Old Celtic *medu-*. The thematic function of mead in the Welsh Gododdin, but at first the beguiling and luxurious enticement to aristocratic warriors, but ultimately bitter doom on the battlefield, suggests that Medb's complicated and dangerous character is a personification of this paradox of her namesake, mead. *Medb* can be understood as the feminine adjective *medū* 'intoxicating', which could imply that her character originated in the context of the sovereignty myth in the episode in which the goddess or woman representing the sovereignty of the land chooses her spouse, bestowing a libation on the man destined to be king. In fact, Medb does precisely this, rather deceitfully, with each of the three contending heroes of Fled Bricrenn ('Bricriu's Feast'). She then sleeps with the confirmed superhero Cú Chulainn.

Ailill, gen. *Aiello*, later *Ailella*, is a fairly common early Irish man's name. It is possibly the cognate of Welsh *ellyll* 'spirit, phantom, ghost, fairy'; if so, it probably developed into a name as a description of a hero infused with supernatural ardour. The main discussion of Medb and Ailill as literary characters may be found in the article on the Ulster Cycle.

John T. Koch

MEDDYGON MYDDFAI

Meddygon Myddfai, or the Physicians of Myddfai (*fl.* from 1200–30), is the name given to a family of physicians who are reputed to have practised their art at Myddfai in Carmarthenshire (sir Gaerfyrddin) for five centuries. The evidence for their historical existence in the medieval period is sparse. The physicians of Rhys Gryg (†1233), prince of Dinefwr, are listed as Rhiwallon and his three sons, Cadwgan, Gruffudd, and Einion.

Evidence indicates that medicine was practised at Myddfai by the descendants of Rhiwallon until the 18th century. Lewis Morris (1701–65), the antiquarian refers to the last two, David Jones (†1719) and John Jones (†1739), whose gravestone is preserved in the parish church. Handing down a craft or profession through the members of one family is a well-known feature of Celtic society in Ireland (Éire) and Scotland (Alba), where families such as the Beatons practised their medicine for generations.

During more recent centuries, the Physicians of Myddfai became most famous for their association with the legend of Llyn y Fan Fach, the most popular of Welsh folk-tales, which claims the physicians to be descended from a lake fairy (see fairies).

The physicians' names are traditionally associated with medical manuscripts. These compilations consist of a combination of recipes, astrological medical tracts, uroscopies, and instructions for surgery. The contents are not indigenous to Wales (CYMRU) and have their parallels in other languages, deriving ultimately from Latin texts.

Morfydd E. Owen

MEDICAL MANUSCRIPTS, IRELAND AND SCOTLAND

The corpus of medical writing in IRISH comprises more than one hundred manuscripts that are mainly medical in content, written between the beginning of the 15th century and the end of the 17th century. Comprising in total slightly more than 16,000 pages of text, these manuscripts are the most important source extant for the history of medicine and medical education in Ireland (ÉIRE) and Gaelic Scotland (ALBA) during the late medieval and early modern period.

From the 12th century onward, medicine in Ireland was a hereditary profession, organized and practised by distinct physician-kindreds, the names of more than twenty of which are recorded in medical manuscripts, in ANNALS, and in other historical sources. Several of these kindreds maintained medical schools in which academic and practical training was provided for members of their own and other families. The institution about which most detail has survived is a school run by the Ó Conchubhair (O'Connor) family at Aghmacart, Co. Laois (Achadh Mhic Airt, Contae Laoise). In the closing decades of the 16th century, the Aghmacart school was under the patronage of Fínghean Mac Giolla Pádraig (†1613), third Lord Baron of Upper Ossory.

Descended from a branch of the Mac an Leagha family that migrated to Scotland around the end of the 13th century, Scotland's principal medical family, the Beatons, has been studied in depth. For the period 1300 to 1700, there were seventy-six practising physicians among the kindred.

Irish medical manuscripts are essentially textbooks and works of reference written by students and doctors for their own professional use. The treatises they contain are, for the most part, translations or adaptations of Latin texts that expound the Graeco-Arabic learning taught in European medical schools between the 12th and the 17th centuries. Cosmopolitan in origin and wide-ranging in subject matter, the texts deal with various aspects of medieval medicine, such as pathology, anatomy and physiology, diagnosis and prognosis, diet and regimen, surgery, obstetrics, and pharmacology.

The occurrence in the manuscripts of several indigenous compilations—works that draw on Irish versions of Latin texts rather than on the Latin sources themselves—testifies to the complete assimilation by Irish physicians of contemporary European scholastic medicine. The medical texts are invariably written in Early Modern Irish, a standard literary language used by the learned classes of Ireland and Gaelic Scotland throughout the late medieval period.

Aoibheann Ní Chonnchadha

MEDICAL MANUSCRIPTS, WALES

The earliest testimony to medical works written in medieval manuscripts dates from the end of the 14th century. Six manuscripts date from the period before 1500 that consist almost entirely of medical material. These manuscripts, which contain similar material, belong to different parts of Wales (CYMRU) and point to a pan-Welsh tradition of medical writing in the late Middle Ages. Some of the manuscript copies attribute the writings found in them to the Physicians of Myddfai (MEDDYGON MYDDFAI).

The contents of these collections are mixed. There are Latin–Welsh glossaries of the plants that formed part of diet and medicine, passages of medical theory, rules for hygiene, uroscopies, snippets of surgery and references to bloodletting, and three references to surgical procedures for craniotomy, ligation for haemorrhoids, and lithotomy, along with many recipes. These texts are paralleled in Latin and vernacular collections throughout Europe. Among the most popular texts of the collections were the translations of sections of the *Secreta Secretorum*, in the form of a letter written by Aristotle to Alexander the Great. Written down originally in Arabic in the 9th century and translated into Latin in the 12th, this work was influential in the medical school of Salerno.

Much of the Welsh texts consists of long lists of plant and animal recipes aimed at the treatment of disease, sometimes in a head to foot order, together with long lists of the qualities of foodstuffs. Another instance of humoral theory is reflected in the uroscopies, whereby the doctor examined the urine of a patient to discover the nature of a disease. The colour, translucence, and smell of the urine showed the nature of the humours that determined the state of the body and the mind.

Astrology and CALENDARS are often included in the manuscripts. A good example is the series of detailed rules that determined the nature of the importance of the zodiac in a man's life. One belief was that all the signs of the zodiac had particular control over a special part of a man's body in head to foot order, with the first sign of the zodiac—Aries—controlling the head and the last—Pisces—controlling the feet.

Morfydd E. Owen

MEDRAWD

Medrawd is the Welsh Arthurian character who corresponds to the Cornish Modred, usually called Mordred in the Continental and English Romances. The earliest mention of him is an entry in the ANNALS of Wales indicating that he and ARTHUR fell at the battle of CAMLAN. The entry is neutral; negative portrayals of Medrawd do not appear until after GEOFFREY OF MONMOUTH's HISTORIA REGUM BRITANNIAE, c. 1139. In Geoffrey's work, Mordred is described as Arthur's sister's son, and later still as his own son by incest. The tradition of a great hero of the past killing his only son is widespread in Celtic tradition and beyond, as with the Irish CÚ CHULAINN.

John T. Koch and Antone Minard

MEILYR BRYDYDD

Meilyr Brydydd (*fl.* ?1100–*post* 1137) was one of the earliest of the Poets of the Princes (GOGYNFEIRDD), a *pencerdd* (chief poet) and court poet to Gruffudd ap Cynan. He Meilyr Brydydd belonged to a line of hereditary poets whose names are associated with *gwelyau* (tracts of tribal land) in Anglesey (Môn). The political and cultural resurgence of Gwynedd during the reign of Gruffudd ap Cynan and his successors provided the context for a flowering of the bardic order and its craft, with these poets' output making this period one of the most important in the history of Welsh poetry and Welsh prose literature. The extant corpus of the Poets of the Princes is notable for its assured technical mastery: The evident confidence and verve of these poems appear to reflect the conviction of both poets and patrons that a new era had begun.

In their form and substance, Meilyr's poems indicate both tradition and innovation. The *cyhydedd naw ban* metre of his elegy to Gruffudd ap Cynan, as well as aspects of his rhyming system and syntactical usage, point to an earlier poetic diction of which Meilyr may have been among the last proponents. The use in his *marwysgafn* of two metres—*cyhydedd naw ban* and *cyhydedd hir*—are more typical of the metrical developments of the later Poets of the Princes. In their vividness and empathy, the extant poems of Meilyr Brydydd mark him out as an important and distinctive voice.

M. Paul Bryant-Quinn

MELOR, ST

St Melor is a Breton saint whose cult was also known in Cornwall (Kernow) and southwest England. His memory may well reflect a historical individual who lived during the early Middle Ages. According to the medieval hagiography, Melor was the son of a Breton sub-king. He was first mutilated and then decapitated by his uncle Rivod, but miraculously survived. At last, young Melor was assassinated by Rivod's serf, Kerialtan. The place at which Melor died subsequently became the site of a cult, where he was venerated as an innocent, a child of royal lineage doomed to martyrdom. He is one of the very few martyrs in Celtic hagiography. As in many medieval saints' cults and Lives, we are told that Melor's cult site soon afterward became the place of unexplained occurrences, which are suggestive of the special powers of the saint and his relics. The seat of the cult of St Melor is in Lanmeur, in northwest Brittany, Quimper (Kemper), has also claimed to keep the saint's head.

Brittany (Breizh) at this period was highly susceptible to intra-dynastic rivalries, which often culminated in murders within royal families in the struggle over competing hereditary claims to succession. Several such accounts involving real events and people in 6th-century Brittany appear in the contemporary *Historia Francorum* of Gregory of Tours. In addition, for the broader Brythonic world of that era, one may compare the scathing accounts of bloody dynastic intrigues in west Britain in the *De Excidio Britanniae* of Gildas.

The Brythonic and Celtic roots of the legend are reflected in the names of the chief characters. Melor's name is Celtic, deriving from **Maglo-rīχs*, a compound of words meaning 'prince' and 'king'. St Maglorius or Magloire of Dol is treated in Breton tradition as a distinct character, though his name is identical in origin.

The gripping story of Melor's mutilation and decapitation was popular and has many resonances elsewhere in medieval literature. This element of the biography of St Melor is of interest in Celtic studies as it closely parallels the miraculous severed heads of medieval Irish and Welsh stories, and also has similarities with cult practices in the pagan Celtic world (see HEAD CULT). For example, Melor's decapitation and the special powers believed to reside in his animate severed head are comparable to the Welsh account of the undying and talismanically protective head of king BRÂN (or Bendigeidfran) in the MABINOGI.

Perhaps the most striking parallel between the Life of St Melor and Celtic mythological tales is that we find the young saintly prince equipped with a fully mobile prosthetic hand made of silver, received miraculously after his maiming by Rivod. A magic artificial arm of silver is also a feature of the Irish mythological figure Nuadu (see NŌDONS). The same mythological motif is found in early Welsh ARTHURIAN LITERATURE: In the tale CULHWCH AC OLWEN, one of Arthur's vast retinue is named as *Lludd Llawereint* (Lludd 'of the silver hand')—a name and epithet cognate with the Irish *Nuadu Argatlám*.

André Yves Bourgès

MESCA ULAD

Mesca Ulad ('The Intoxication of the Ulstermen') is a major tale of the Irish ULSTER CYCLE. It begins with an account—running closely parallel to that in DE GABÁIL IN T-SÍDA (Concerning the taking of the OTHERWORLD mound)—of the division of Ireland (ÉRIU) and its SÍD mounds between the sons of MÍL ESPÁINE and the TUATH DÉ.

CÚ CHULAINN and CONCHOBAR are portrayed as Ulster's rival kings, preparing rival FEASTS. Following several altercations, an agreement is struck in which the assembled nobles will drink first with Conchobar at EMAIN MACHAE, then with Cú Chulainn at his court in Dún Delgan (Dundalk). The drunken chariot warriors set off, take the wrong road, and arrive implausibly at the other end of Ireland in west Munster (MUMU). A feast is already under way there to celebrate the month-old son of MEDB AND AILILL, who is to be in FOSTERAGE there with Cú Roí.

At the tale's end, the Ulstermen safely return and drink at Cú Chulainn's feast for forty days, and the issue of Conchobar's supreme KINGSHIP is resolved. Surviving premodern copies of *Mesca Ulad* are included in the famous manuscripts LEBOR NA HUIDRE and Lebor Laignech.

John T. Koch

METRICS, MEDIEVAL IRISH

Introduction

Metrics are present both as a part of Irish poetry and in learned tracts by the professional poets. The tracts, focusing mainly on grammatical and also syntactical topics, survive from the Classical Modern Irish period (*c.* 1200–*c.* 1600), and from the preceding Middle Irish period (*c.* 900–*c.* 1200). Several treatises focus on metrics. Irish meter can be accentual (based on the number of accents or stressed syllables per poetic line) or syllabic (based on the total number of syllables per line).

Córus Bard Cona Bairdni

A tract bearing the title *Córus Bard cona Bairdni* (The hierarchy of the BARDS and the poetic composition of that hierarchy) lists and exemplifies the metres of the seven grades—in descending order—of *soerbaird* (noble bards). This is one of the very small number of texts that treat the bards, as distinct from the *filid*, as a class in their own right. The original of the tract illustrated more than forty metrical types. These are all in rhyming syllabic metres, and almost all of the examples cited are four-line stanzas. The metres of the tract are characterized as 'new forms', and the text seems to ascribe the development of most of such rhyming syllabic metres in Irish to people other than the traditional *filid*. The tract as it has come down to us seems to date from the 10th century, though its origins are probably to be traced to the preceding century. Certainly, a great number of its illustrative stanzas seem to belong originally to the 9th century.

Curriculum of the Student-File

Another tract sets forth the curriculum of the student-*file*, originally arranged to cover seven years of study, corresponding to the seven grades of *filid*. The original, later much expanded, was compiled in the early 10th century, though some of the illustrative material seems to be at least two centuries older. The tract as it has survived, however, is a much expanded form of this original. For each year of the course, it catalogues in summary form at the beginning the portions of curriculum to be studied by the student-*file*, with particular reference to his grammatical studies and to the number of tales to be learned by him each year. It should be noted that this tract not only illustrates rhyming syllabic metres, but also contains examples of alliterative accentual metre, *rosc*. *Rosc* measures were, according to the doctrine enunciated in these texts, the prerogative of the *filid*.

Donncha Ó hAodha

MIDE (MEATH)

Mide (Meath) was regarded in mythology as the central province (CÓICED) of Ireland (ÉRIU), bordering all four other provinces. Its focus was the archaeological complex of Uisnech (the Hill of Usnagh, Co. Westmeath/Contae na hIarmhí). In the early Middle Ages, Mide figured as a kingdom dominated by the southern Uí NÉILL dynasty. The name *Mide* is in origin synonymous with Old Irish *mide* 'middle, centre' (< Celtic **mediom*; cf. the Cisalpine Celtic place-name Mediolanon 'Centre of the plain', now Milan, Italy). Uisnech is described as the *umbilicus* of Ireland and, like Tara (TEAMHAIR), was associated with pre-Christian kingship and ceremonies. Mide was at the core of southern Uí Néill kingdoms and was the region from which their dynasties extended eastward to conquer Brega. During the 11th and 12th centuries, the kingdom of 'Mide' also incorporated Brega, and the original kingdom became known as Iarthar Mide (modern Co. Westmeath).

Edel Bhreathnach

MÍL ESPÁINE AND THE MILESIANS

The Milesians, the sons of Míl Espáine (*Miles Hispaniae* 'soldier of Spain'), are credited with conquering Ireland (ÉRIU) and subordinating its previous inhabitants, the TUATH DÉ, according to LEBAR GABÁLA ÉRENN ('The Book of Invasions'), the most important tract on Irish LEGENDARY HISTORY. As in the parallel accounts of DE GABÁIL IN T-SÍDA (Concerning the taking of the OTHERWORLD mound) and the opening section of MESCA ULAD ('The Intoxication of the Ulstermen'), the Tuath Dé were banished below ground, while the land above ground was divided into two halves, north and south, each ruled by one of Míl's sons, Éremón mac Míled and Éber Find. The Latin character of the founder's name *Miles Hispaniae* (as he is called in HISTORIA BRITTONUM §13) shows the legend to be a creation of the Christian literate period. It is also relevant that classical geographers sometimes described Ireland as situated opposite Spain, creating the misleading impression that they were close enough for one place to be seen from the other. Contacts between prehistoric Spain and Ireland are, in fact, found in archaeological evidence—similar types of cauldrons and swords in the Late Bronze Age (*c.* 1200–*c.* 600 BC) and the *castros* of Galicia are typologically similar to Irish ring-forts—but this is now more usually explained as a result of trade or gift exchange rather than mass migration.

Petra S. Hellmuth

MIRACULOUS WEAPONS

Early Irish literature mentions several miraculous weapons, generally of OTHERWORLD origin. The most famous is the Gae Bolga, owned by the hero CÚ CHULAINN of the ULSTER CYCLE. Other examples of miraculous weapons include CALADBOLG, owned by FERGUS MAC RÓICH. The Welsh equivalent of Caladbolg is Caledfwlch, which, via GEOFFREY OF MONMOUTH's Latinized version Caliburnus (in HISTORIA REGUM BRITANNIAE), eventually becomes the Excalibur found in ARTHURIAN LITERATURE. In Welsh tradition, CAULDRONS can be used as weapons, as in the tale of BRANWEN FERCH LŶR.

Petra S. Hellmuth

MÔN

Môn (Anglesey) is a large island off the northwest coast of Wales (CYMRU). Since 1995 it has been known officially as Ynys Môn (the Isle of Anglesey), but from 1284 to 1974 it was sir Fôn (the county or shire of Anglesey). This area has been of long-standing historical importance as a gentle and habitable fertile landscape cut off from easy overland access from the rest of Britain by the rugged massif of Snowdonia (Eryri) and the Menai Straits. Its location places it at the crossroads between Wales, Ireland (ÉIRE), the Isle of Man (ELLAN VANNIN), and southwest Scotland (ALBA). During the protracted Roman conquest of Britain, Anglesey was attacked in AD 60—according to Tacitus, because of the potent anti-Roman ideology of the DRUIDS, the priesthood, who enjoyed particular strength on the island.

In post-Roman times, Anglesey formed the fertile nucleus of the powerful kingdom of GWYNEDD, and the court at ABERFFRAW was one of its most important royal centres from the 7th century to the 13th century. Môn was accordingly often mentioned and praised in the court poetry of the CYNFEIRDD and GOGYNFEIRDD, and continued as a popular subject of literary praise in the works of the CYWYDDWYR and down to modern times. *Môn Mam Cymru* (Anglesey mother of Wales) remains proverbial.

Anglesey's population in the 1801 Census was 33,155; in 2001, it was listed as 66,828. Out of forty districts in the 2001 Census, Cyngar returned the highest proportion (84%) with one or more abilities in communicating in Welsh, a loss of 2 percent since 1991, and Biwmares had the lowest at 40 percent, an increase of 3 percent from 1991; the median of all districts stood between 56 percent and 58 percent.

The name *Môn* is recorded in ancient and medieval Latin as *Mona* (Greek Μονα). The names for Anglesey and the Isle of Man (Welsh *Manaw*, Old Irish *Mano*, gen. *Manann*, Latin *Manavia*) are probably related, and in early texts, both Latin and Welsh, confusion is common.

John T. Koch

MONASTERIES, EARLY IRISH AND SCOTTISH

Monasteries, Society, and Politics

The monks of the earliest Irish monasteries, which date from the 5th or 6th century, sought to know God through a life of solitary contemplation removed from secular society. As time passed, the monastic way of life became absorbed into the Gaelic social system until, by the 8th century, the local monastery was one of the central institutions in the life of the *tuath* (small ethno-political group, loosely 'tribe'), usually with strong links to the secular élite.

The tradition of ascetic monasticism withdrawn from the secular world did not die out, however, but continued, particularly on the western seaboard, where Irish monks found their own form of *desertum* on the islands and rocky headlands of the Atlantic coast and as far afield as Iceland. See also IMMRAMA.

The highly influential monastery of Iona (Eilean Ì) was founded *c.* 563 by COLUM CILLE, who was a member of the Northern Uí NÉILL. Iona's copious literary output favoured this dynasty and, though located geographically alongside or even within Scottish DÁL RIATA, it was a vital a part of Irish intellectual life until the move to Kells (Ceanannas) in the early 9th century. Iona was the burial place of many of the kings of ALBA (Scotland).

Economy of the Monasteries

The economy of the monastery in early medieval Ireland was based primarily on mixed farming (see AGRICULTURE). Grants and gifts were bestowed by the local aristocracy, and the ruling élite also sponsored the production of religious works of ART such as HIGH CROSSES, elaborately decorated shrines, and illuminated manuscripts. Moreover, some monasteries benefited materially from pilgrims attending the shrine of a founding saint. The relics of such saints were often housed in prominent shrines within the monastery graveyard.

Architecture and the Physical Site

The range and scale of buildings and other structural features commonly found on Irish monastic foundations differ to a significant extent between the larger monasteries exemplified by Durrow and the smaller foundations known primarily from the western seaboard. It should be noted, however, that sites of the latter, which are more physically modest in form, are believed to have been widely distributed elsewhere in Ireland but have not survived because they were built mainly of timber.

Irish monasteries were commonly surrounded by an enclosing wall known as a *vallum* or *valla*. Most commonly, these tended to be built of earth or stone and to be circular in plan, with smaller examples often bearing a close resemblance to secular ring-forts. At larger monasteries, the *vallum* was sometimes the outer of two or three concentric rings, with the innermost often defining the area of greatest sanctity, the church and graveyard lying within the walls (e.g., Nendrum [Aon Droim], Co. Down).

The round tower of Glendalough monastery in County Wicklow, Ireland (Gleann Dá Loch, Contae Chill Mhantáin, Éire). (Michael Thompson)

The focus of religious life in the monastery was, of course, the church, as implied by its frequent physically central position. The scale and architecture of the church varied through time, as well as according to the prestige and location of the foundation. It is generally accepted that the earliest Irish churches were small oratories built of wood and wattle or of earthen sods. The peak of pre-Norman church building is clearly represented by structures in the Irish Romanesque style, examples of which are found at the monastery of Clonfert, Co. Galway (Cluain Fhearta, Contae na Gaillimhe). Multiple churches cluster together at many of the larger foundations, such as Clonmacnoise (eight churches).

The monastic graveyard is generally found in proximity to the church. Earth-cut, lintelled, and stone-lined graves occur in these areas, sometimes accompanied by a cross-inscribed grave-slab. Large, decorated cross slabs (such as at Reask) and the succeeding high crosses were also often erected in the graveyard. The cross slabs at the earlier sites were sometimes inscribed with OGAM, as at Maumanorig (Mám an Óraigh), Co. Kerry. In addition to features dating from their original period of use, the graveyards of many early medieval monasteries were reused in the post-medieval period, up until the mid-20th century, as a burial place for infants. Such a burial area for young babies is known by a variety of names, including killeen (cillín) and kalloonagh (ceallúnach). This practice has most often been explained as the covert deposition of infants who died before baptism in what the rural community remembered as ancient consecrated ground, as church rule forbade such burial in contemporary graveyards.

Another structure often positioned near the church was a round tower. The remains of some seventy of these towers are still extant—two of which are in Scotland and one on the Isle of Man (ELLAN VANNIN)—and many more may once have existed. The tallest are more than 30 m in height and even today are impressive architectural achievements, with their tapering form and conical roofs. The function of round towers has long been debated, but multifunction usage seems most likely. Their Irish name—cloigtheach (lit. 'bell-house')—suggests what was probably their main function, as an elevated position from which to ring the hours of the various monastic offices. Moreover, while they may have served as a short-term refuge for the monks in times of danger and as a storeroom for valuables, there can be no doubt they were at least partially conceived as a powerful physical symbol of church authority.

Arts and Crafts

As a self-contained community, each foundation would have required an industrial area serving the practical technological and, in some cases, artistic requirements of the monastic familia. Iron-working evidence has been uncovered at Reask and Killederdadrum and bronze-working evidence at Nendrum. Other crafts undertaken would have been milling, stone-carving, and leatherwork. The last craft was, apart from the more mundane production of shoes, satchels, and the like, related to the preparation of vellum for manuscripts. It is unknown how widespread the practice of producing fine manuscripts was; it may have been restricted to the larger foundations where specialized scriptoria could have existed, though these are not yet attested archaeologically.

Simon Ó Faoláin

MONASTICISM

Monasticism originated in 4th-century Egypt. It took two forms—eremitic (solitaries only gathering for liturgy) and coenobitic (life in a community)—both later found in Ireland (ÉRIU). This eastern, desert pattern was adapted to western Europe by Cassian in southern GAUL in the 5th century, and this 'desert period' remained the monastic ideal. It can be seen in the ideal monasteries in the *Vita Columbae* (Life of Colum Cille) by Adomnán or the Navigatio Sancti Brendani (The voyage of St Brendan), which brings to perfection the notion that the ideal monastic life anticipates heaven, and inspired many later 'reforms'.

Monasticism is first mentioned in Ireland in the 5th-century *Confessio* of Saint Patrick. By 600, in addition to many large monasteries in Ireland, several Irish monasteries were located abroad—for example, Iona/Eilean Ì and Bobbio. This Irish pattern became displaced only with the arrival of the Cistercians in the 12th century (see Cistercian abbeys).

Thomas O'Loughlin

MORGANNWG

Morgannwg is the name of a medieval kingdom and pre-1974 county in south Wales (Cymru). The English equivalent Glamorgan (< Welsh Gwlad Morgan) is generally used for the county only. In the early post-Roman period, the small kingdoms of Ergyng (Archenfield), Gwent, and Glywysing emerged, all continuing Romano-British towns. This pattern no doubt reflects the greater degree of Romanization in the fertile agricultural lands of the southeast as opposed to the rest of Wales. Of these three, Glywysing was the dominant and over-arching kingdom. Ergyng was lost to the English in the 9th century. In the mid-10th century, Morgan ab Owain (†974) became sole king and the region soon afterward came to be called Morgannwg after him.

Although Gower (Gŵyr) became part of the free Welsh kingdom of Deheubarth, most of Gwent and Morgannwg came under the control of the Norman FitzHamon in the late 11th century. With the Acts of Union in 1536–43, the county of Glamorgan was formed, which included Gower on the west, but Gwynllŵg in the Rhymni valley and what had been Gwent further east became Monmouthshire (sir Fynwy). The inventive and influential poet and antiquarian Edward Williams (1747–1826) gave prominence to Morgannwg, not only through his bardic name Iolo Morganwg, but also by expounding the doctrine of a continuous bardic tradition in the region, dating back to pre-Christian druids.

With the Industrial Revolution, Glamorgan became the most industrialized and populous county in Wales. It contained most of the coalfield and iron-working areas, as well as the growing seaports of Cardiff (Caerdydd) and Swansea (Abertawe). Trade unionism and socialist politics have had a particularly strong impact on, and tenacity in, this part of Wales, inspiring internationalist ideals not always readily reconciled with Welsh-language culture. Nevertheless, Glamorgan is famous for such 'iconically Welsh' cultural institutions as the Mari Lwyd, male-voice choirs (*corau meibion*), and rugby, as well as being the birthplace of Welsh international celebrities as Tom Jones, Anthony Hopkins, and Shirley Bassey.

On the millennium of its founder's death, Glamorgan was broken up into three counties—South, West, and Mid Glamorgan—which were reorganized again into smaller electoral districts in 1995, of which only the Vale of Glamorgan/

Bro Morgannwg preserves the old name. Most parts of Glamorgan still had a majority of Welsh speakers at the beginning of the 20th century.

John T. Koch

MORRÍGAN

Morrígan (also Morrígu, pl. *morrígnae*, from Old Irish *mor*, the same root as 'mare' as in 'nightmare' and German *Mahr* [see Fomoiri], and *rígain*, *rígan* 'queen') was an early Irish war-goddess. She appears in Irish literature in two rôles. In the first, she serves as a minister and attendant of fate and battle. Together with the Bodb and Macha, and sometimes Nemain, the Morrígan is part of a tripartite group of war-goddesses. Her second rôle associates her with fertility and wealth, and is illustrated by her identification with the mother of the gods, Anu or Ana. This function is seen, for example, in Cath Maige Tuired ('The [Second] Battle of Mag Tuired'), where the Morrígan mates with the Dagda, one of the leaders of the Tuath Dé. The Morrígan performs these different functions in a variety of shapes, ranging from a hag or maiden to animals such as a deer or crow.

Petra S. Hellmuth

MUMU (MUNSTER)

Mumu (Munster) was the most southerly province of early historic Ireland (Ériu). It is roughly equivalent to the modern province of Munster (Modern Irish An Mhumhain), which comprises six counties: Kerry (Ciarraí), Cork (Corcaigh), Limerick (Luimneach), Tipperary (Tiobraid Árainn), Waterford (Port Láirge), and Clare (An Clár).

Early Munster

In traditions relating to prehistoric times, Munster is often considered to be two provinces, east and west, the latter associated with Cú Roí mac Dáiri. The province has many mythological and traditional associations that represent it as the opposite or mirror image of the rest of Ireland: associations with the dead, women, and goddesses, and with *an Lucht Sídh* (the people of the síd mounds or fairies), among others. Along with southern Leinster [Laigin]), the province remained unpenetrated by the La Tène material culture found elsewhere in Iron-Age Ireland.

Historically, Munster was the province that consistently challenged Uí Néill overlordship of Ireland, first under the Éoganacht and later under the Dál gCais. It was, and remains, the most fertile of the provinces.

Anglo-Normans and Gaelic Survival

Following the Norman incursions of the 12th century, most of Munster came under the control of the invaders, including the good land in the east and centre of the province. Thomond (Tuadhmumhan, north Munster) remained in the hands of the O'Briens (Ua Briain), while the MacCarthys (Mac Cárrthaig) retained control over the mountainous terrain of south Kerry and west Cork, having routed the Norman Fitzgeralds at the battle of Callan in 1261. The rapid Gaelicization of the Fitzgeralds meant that Munster remained essentially Irish culturally and socially throughout the late medieval period.

The Geraldine Wars of the late 16th century eventually resulted in victory for the English. The aftermath of this conflict, along with the final debacle at the battle of Kinsale (Cionn tSáile) in 1601, spelled the end of Gaelic society in Munster and left the province in a state of ruin from which it took a century to recover. Despite this devastation, the art of Irish bardic poetry survived longer in Munster than in other areas (see IRISH LITERATURE).

Modern Munster

During the Great FAMINE of the 1840s, official records indicate that western Munster was, along with Connacht, the most heavily afflicted part of the country. This began a pattern of wholesale EMIGRATION from the west, which was stemmed only in the later 20th century. During the War of Independence (1918–21), Munster was the most militarily active province (see IRISH INDEPENDENCE MOVEMENT).

Of the three modern dialects of Irish, that of Munster is the smallest in terms of numbers of native speakers and is now the vernacular only in the west of Corca Dhuibhne, Co. Kerry, and in some small pockets in counties Cork and (marginally) Waterford.

Simon Ó Faoláin

MYRDDIN

For aspects of the Myrddin legend, see WILD MAN. The following entry deals with background, early dissemination of the legend, the figure of Myrddin, early modern survivals, and the origin of his name.

Background

The main sources are seven Middle Welsh Myrddin poems from 13th-, 14th-, and 15th-century manuscripts, and GEOFFREY OF MONMOUTH's *Vita Merlini*. All of the Myrddin poems except for the earlier *Ymddiddan Myrddin a Thaliesin* probably took shape during the Norman invasion of Wales (CYMRU). The Myrddin poems survive in the Black Book of Carmarthen (LLYFR DU CAERFYRDDIN, *c.* 1250): *Ymddiddan Myrddin a Thaliesin* (Colloquy of Myrddin and Taliesin), *Bedwenni* (Birch-tree stanzas), *Afallennau* (Apple-tree stanzas), and *Hoianau* (Greetings); the Red Book of Hergest (LLYFR COCH HERGEST, *c.* 1400): *Cyfoesi Myrddin a Gwenddydd ei Chwaer* (Colloquy of Myrddin and Gwenddydd his sister) and *Gwasgargerdd Fyrddin yn ei Fedd* (Separation song of Myrddin in his grave); Peniarth 50 (15th century): *Peirian Faban* (Commanding youth) and four stanzas of *Afallennau*; Peniarth MS 12 (the earliest text of *Gwasgargerdd*); a fragment of the White Book of Rhydderch

(Llyfr Gwyn Rhydderch; parts of *Gwasgargerdd*); the Hendregadredd Manuscript; and the *Myvyrian Archaiology of Wales*.

Poems are spoken by Myrddin, and stanzas introduced or concluded by veiled, fragmentary allusions to his story before or after he utters political prophecies. Predictions refer to events of the Norman invasion and of an indistinct time in the future, to important occurrences and persons of earlier Welsh history and tradition, and often to the *Mab Darogan* or 'Son of Destiny'.

Ymddiddan Myrddin a Thaliesin is the oldest of the Myrddin poems in its extant late-11th-century form. Several of the poems refer to a 'king who is not a king' (*brenin na vrenhin*) reigning after Henry II, the last of the historical kings named in the Myrddin poems, and many refer obliquely to legendary material around the battle of Arfderydd. *Gwasgargerdd Fyrddin* depicts Myrddin lying in his grave, declaring his former greatness as a warrior, and uttering political prophecies. In the last stanzas he mentions being spoken to by 'wild-men of the mountain in Aber Caraf'.

Early Dissemination of the Legend

Geoffrey of Monmouth apparently had little knowledge of Myrddin when he wrote his Historia Regum Britanniae *c.* 1139, despite being aware of Myrddin's reputation as a political prophet, as witnessed by the *Prophetia Merlini* in *Historia Regum Britanniae* (originally written as a separate work), which includes material much akin to that of the Myrddin poems. Most of Geoffrey's treatment of 'Merlin' is invented. His Latinized spelling apparently came about to avoid association with Fr. *merde* 'excrement' and was possibly influenced by English 'merlin', the falcon *Falco columbarius*. Offered as history, Geoffrey's fiction received instant acclaim, partly due to its justification of the Norman ruling class (via glorification of the Britons) at the Saxons' expense. *Historia Regum Britanniae* provides nearly all of Merlin's character as found in the works of Wace and of Robert de Boron from the mid-12th century to the early 13th century, in the prose French Romances of the 13th century, and in further Arthurian literature. Some years later, Geoffrey discovered more about Myrddin, and in 1148–51 he completed *Vita Merlini*, a poem devoted entirely to Myrddin. Aside from making political prophecies, many apparently derived from the earlier *Prophetia*, Merlin of *Vita Merlini* corresponds to Myrddin Wyllt of the Myrddin poems, rather than to *Historia Regum Britanniae*'s magician.

The Figure of Myrddin

References to Myrddin are made by the Gogynfeirdd, Dafydd ap Gwilym, other Cywyddwyr, and others, though none of this necessarily confirms Myrddin's historicity. (He is not present in early genealogies.) The 10th-century Armes Prydein alludes to Myrddin's prophetic gift, though there is no certitude that the phrase *Dysgogan Myrddin* ('Myrddin foretells') was original to this early poem. Similarly, the Gododdin reference to Myrddin's prophetic-poetic gift (*gwenwawt*) is present only for the later 'A' text. In the *Descriptio Kambriae* (1.16), Giraldus includes

Merlin as one of the 'muse-inspired seers [who are] ... as though out of their mind[s]' (*awenithion ... quasi mente ductos*).

Early Modern Survivals

Myrddin's forest association with his sister became popular among later storytellers. In an 18th-century Anglesey (MÔN) tale, a lad comes to 'Myrddin ar Bawl' (here a 'Lord of the Animals', who draws a club behind him 'as if it were a tail') seeking judgement for choosing his bride. Myrddin's sister and housekeeper give the youth beer and milk to offer the wild man, who, upon drinking the milk, utters cryptic advice. The 16th-century Chronicle of Elis Gruffydd includes a similar story, with five beverages used to interpret Gwenddydd's five dreams; Gwenddydd ministers to Myrddin out-of-doors, is 'wise and learned', and 'wrote a great book of his utterances'. A modern folk-tale relates the Threefold Death of a youth, Twm Gelwydd Teg (Tom of the Fine Lies), in a way closely paralleling the threefold death predicted by Merlin for a youth in *Vita Merlini* (ll. 387–415). Gruffydd's Chronicle also includes a threefold death story, as well as Myrddin's incarceration by the 'lady of the lake'.

Traditions of Myrddin Wyllt came to France along with much of the Matter of Britain, transferred there via the Breton *conteurs*. For example, Merlin appears as a Lord of the Animals in *L'Estoire de Merlin*; he is a wild man in *Le Livre d'Artus*. Throughout the corpus, he meets Viviane in Broceliande, a mysterious wood similar to the Coed Celyddon (Caledonian Forest) of the Old Welsh North (yr HEN OGLEDD). The late 12th-century *Roman de Fergus* draws upon North British traditions cognisant of the LAILOKEN legend's localization near Newcastleton and Annandale. In *Les Prophécies de Merlin*, of *c*. 1272–79, Merlin makes prognostications from the grave. These presentations of Merlin are indebted no more to *Vita Merlini* than they are to *Historia Regum Britanniae*. Such stories, surrounding both the wild Myrddin and figures analogous to him, have persisted in Breton ballads and local lore practically until the present.

Origin of the Name

To A. O. H. Jarman, the name of this personage is a misinterpretation of *Myrddin* (alternatively *Merddin*) < *Mori-dūnon* 'Sea-fort', seen as the eponymous founder of Carmarthen (Caerfyrddin), after the prefixing of *caer* once the meaning of the old place-name *Myrddin* had become obscure. This eponym of Carmarthen then attracted to himself the North British legend of the prophetic wild man, of whom Lailokan (Welsh *Llallogan*) is the best known.

The forms *llallogan* and *llallawc* occur in early Welsh poetry other than *Cyfoesi*, in each case adjectivally. Their status as proper nouns in *Cyfoesi* is debatable. Further possible origins for the proposed proper noun are the (Gaelic) name Lulath or Lulach, Macbeth's stepson (see MAC BETHAD) found in Scottish chronicles, glossed by such Latin terms for 'fool' as 'ignomine fatuus', 'mimicus', and 'gesticulosus'; and Latin *lallo* (cf. Mod.E 'lulla-by') as a hypocoristic form.

There are alternatives to Jarman's theory of *Myrddin* derived from Carmarthen—for example, *mer* ('foolish', 'witless', cf. *merydd, meredic*) + *dyn* Proto-Celtic <* (*g*)*donios* 'person'. Moreover, early Campbell genealogies and a lost Gaelic tale **Eachtra Smeirbhe Mhóir* mention in an Arthurian context a *Smerevie/Smeirbhe,* or *Merevie/Meirbhe,* 'fool of the forest', a 'wild, undaunted person', born to the south side of An Talla Dearg 'The Red Hall' (Dumbarton). The hypothesis, of course, might allow for other possible Cumbric predecessors for this Gaelic name.

Brian Frykenberg

MYTHOLOGICAL CYCLE

Introduction

Along with the Ulster Cycle, Fiannaíocht, and the Kings' Cycles, the Mythological Cycle is one of the four main classifications of early Irish narrative. It consists of a series of sagas, poems, and anecdotes about the Tuath Dé, a race of magical beings from the remote past of Ireland (Ériu). Although the other cycles contain figures and themes from Irish mythology, the texts that fall under the rubric of the Mythological Cycle deal solely with the exploits of the mythical Tuath Dé and the races of the legendary past whom they encounter: the Fir Bolg, the Fomoiri, and the Sons of Míl Espáine.

In comparison with the other major classifications, the Mythological Cycle contains by far the fewest texts, most of which date from the Middle Irish period (900–1200) or later. Where stories are known to have been lost, scholars can sometimes rely on works such as Lebar Gabála ('The book of the taking [of Ireland]') or the dindsenchas to provide clues about the missing material.

The Mythological Cycle contains many contradictions. For example, Lug mac Céin, the champion of the Tuath Dé at the Second Battle of Mag Tuired (Moytura; see Cath Maige Tuired), is not always depicted as a hero. These discrepancies are part of the vitality of Irish myth, whose variant traditions were never suppressed by an authoritative central text or tradition.

The Medieval Texts

The centrepiece of the Mythological Cycle is the saga *Cath Maige Tuired*, which recounts the triumph of the Tuath Dé over the Fomoiri at a site in Co. Sligo (Contae Shligigh). Equally important are the three early Irish sagas collectively known as Tochmarc Étaíne ('The Wooing of Étaín'). These narratives trace the wanderings of the title character from one incarnation to another until she is at last reunited with her first husband, Midir of Brí Léith. Étaín's transformations have invited comparisons with those of the other mythological figures, such as the Irish Tuán mac Cairill and the Welsh Taliesin. Transformations also play an important rôle in the short Old Irish saga *Aislinge Óenguso* ('The Dream of Óengus'; see aisling). In this story, the title character succumbs to lovesickness after experiencing a vision of a beautiful woman about whom he knows nothing. Along with the Old Irish anecdote entitled DE GABÁIL IN T-SÍDA (Concerning the taking of the OTHERWORLD mound), this is the only other story from the Mythological Cycle that is regarded as one of the *remscéla* or 'fore-tales' to the central tale of the ULSTER CYCLE, TÁIN BÓ CUAILNGE ('The Cattle Raid of Cooley').

The Early Modern Texts

The earliest of the three Early Modern Irish tales included in the Mythological Cycle is the story called *Altromh Tige Dá Medar* (The nurturing of the house of two milk vessels). Dating from perhaps the 13th or 14th century, this narrative traces the fortunes of Eithne ingean Dícon, the foster-daughter of Aenghus Óg mac in Daghdha (see OENGUS MAC IND ÓC; DAGDA), as she undergoes her rite of passage from Otherworld woman to Christian saint. This tale is notable for its prominent religious themes and is open to various literal and metaphorical readings that have yet to be fully explored. The second tale in this category—*Oidheadh Chloinne Tuireann* ('The Violent Death of the Children of Tuireann')—is set before the Second Battle of Mag Tuired. It relates the murder of Lug's father at the hands of the Sons of Tuireann and the terrible price they must pay in expiation of their crime. *Oidheadh Chloinne Tuireann* is of particular interest for its depiction of Tuath Dé society as troubled and unstable, as well as for its portrayal of Lug as spiteful and vindictive; both of these treatments stand in marked contrast to the earlier tradition. The last of the Early Modern tales is *Oidheadh Chloinne Lir* ('The Violent Death of the Children of Lir').

In addition to the major sagas, there are several brief anecdotes about the Tuath Dé that survive from the Old Irish period onward.

Dan Wiley

NATIONALISM, BRITTANY

The beginnings of nationalism in Brittany (BREIZH) consisted mainly of conservative tendencies. Kevredigez Broadus Breiz/Union régionaliste bretonne (URB), founded in 1898, and Unvaniez Arvor/Fédération régionaliste de Bretagne (FRB), founded in 1911, were both regionalist in tone. Though anxious to preserve and promote the region's own unique identity, these organizations believed that Brittany's future lay within the political framework of France.

The most prominent nationalist movement of the first half of the 20th century was the political party commonly known as Breiz Atao (Brittany forever), after the name of its newspaper. Under the leadership of Olier Mordrel (Olivier Mordrelle, 1901–85) and Fañch Debauvais (François Debauvais, 1903–44), the movement's ideals quickly developed into a rejection of regionalism within France amid aspirations for political autonomy. The movement became an official political party in 1927, and called itself Strollad Emrenerien Vreiz/Parti autonomiste breton.

In 1932, a secret society calling itself Gwenn-ha-Du (Black and white, from the colours of the Breton flag) claimed responsibility for destroying the statue in Rennes (Roazhon) that commemorated the union of Brittany with France (see ACTE D'UNION). This particular depiction of Brittany as a subservient maid, kneeling at the feet of a noblewoman representing France, had been a thorn in the side of Breton patriots since its unveiling in 1910. The resulting publicity, and the suppression of all Breton institutions—cultural and political alike—brought much sympathy for the Breton cause.

The German occupation (1940–44) seemed at first to present a golden opportunity, but it became apparent how insignificant Brittany was within Hitler's plans for the new Europe. It now appears that the Bretons who actively collaborated with the Germans were few in number. Nonetheless, many were under suspicion and arrested; though most were released, some lost their civil rights, and others were executed.

After 1945, nationalism in Brittany took on a cultural and economic character. In 1957, a tentative return to politics emerged with the establishment of MOB (Mouvement pour l'organisation de la Bretagne). By 1964, Brittany had a nationalist political party once more in the form of the UDB (Union démocratique bretonne). A more recent separatist movement is Emgann (Battle or struggle), founded in 1983, which is heavily influenced by the Basque, Corsican, and Irish extreme nationalist movements (see IRISH REPUBLICAN ARMY).

Gwenno Sven-Myer

NATIONALISM, CORNWALL

Although organized nationalist political parties did not emerge in Cornwall (KERNOW) until the latter half of the 20th century, the region has always maintained a unique political profile. A certain proto-nationalism by way of assertions of BRYTHONIC identity can be detected in the early wider alignments of the Britons of Cornwall, Wales (CYMRU), Brittany (BREIZH), and north Britain against the ANGLO-SAXON 'CONQUEST' as chronicled by GEOFFREY OF MONMOUTH and other ARTHURIAN LITERATURE. However, modern nationalism in Cornwall—as in many other areas of Europe—has its roots in the developing cultural and ethnic politics of the late 19th century. In Cornwall, this has most often figured within the wider discourses of PAN-CELTICISM.

Mebyon Kernow (Sons of Cornwall) was formed in 1951. Although it served initially as a pressure group, widening support ensured its eventual status as a political party. The earliest aims were to maintain the Celtic character of Cornwall and the right of self-government in domestic affairs. By 1970, Mebyon Kernow had more than 20 branches and some 3000 members. Since then, it has continued to be the most recognized force in Cornish nationalist politics, although it has never had much electoral success.

The frustration over Mebyon Kernow's lack of electoral success led to two splinter movements in the 1970s. The first was the reformation in 1974 of the Cornish STANNARY PARLIAMENT by a modern set of Stannators. This group believed that, to advance the nationalist agenda for Cornwall, the best plan would be to return to the legal and historical documentation that guaranteed Cornwall's constitutional independent status. The revived Stannary is best known today for its direct action campaign against English Heritage in Cornwall. In 1975, a second nationalist party, the Cornish Nationalist Party, was formed.

Although Cornish nationalist political parties have not been overwhelmingly successful in elections, pro-Cornish sentiments certainly influence voting patterns across the board. At all levels of government, Cornwall returns a greater number of independents than anywhere in the southwest. Identity-based politics in Cornwall is certainly becoming more accepted and is having discernible effects on policy. Objective One status within the European Union (assigned areas of economic disadvantage within the EU), gained in 2000, has been based on, and argued for, in terms of regional and cultural distinctiveness.

Amy Hale

NATIONALISM, IRELAND

Origins of Irish Nationalism

The basis of all Irish identity—a subjective sense of difference—was founded on several facets of existence, beginning with an origin myth of the Gaels's descent from the Milesians (see MÍL ESPÁINE). Furthermore, the IRISH LANGUAGE and its literature emphasized the separateness of the Irish peoples. In addition, Ireland possessed a comprehensive native legal system, the Brehon code, as opposed to English common law (see LAW TEXTS). Religion, though ostensibly shared, had its own history and independence (see CHRISTIANITY). The island possessed a tradition of regional rule with provincial kings of well-established lineage, who, depending on their strength, asserted their right to be recognized as 'overking' (cf. KINGSHIP).

The Tudors and Ireland

Despite incursions from Vikings and Anglo-Normans, a tolerable status quo was maintained until the turn of the 15th century under Henry VIII's Tudor conquest (see TUDOR). The long reign of Elizabeth I brought into place a Church Settlement that remained, in essence, in force for four centuries. The Crown policy of active settlement of Scots and English in Ireland laid the basis for future religious and nationalist divisions. The lands necessary for settlement were obtained through Acts of Attainment for disloyalty. The forfeiture of the Earl of Desmond's lands and similar occurrences caused widespread disquiet among Irish lords because of increasing lack of land security. It is significant that Gaelic poetry became overtly political around this time, being directed 'against the foreigner'. The most notable campaign was the Nine Years War (1593–1603), led by Hugh O'Neill (Aodh Ó Néill). His defeat at the battle of Kinsale/Cionn tSáile (1601) is widely seen as the Rubicon of Gaelic demise in Ireland (ÉIRE).

The 17th and 18th Centuries

With the accession of James I (1603) and the 'Flight of the Earls' (1607), the physical, legal, and administrative conquest of Ireland intensified. Common law replaced Brehon law. The Pale, previously the only area of accepted English jurisdiction, was greatly extended. An example of the growing national consciousness can be seen in *Foras Feasa ar Éirinn*. Written by Geoffrey Keating (Seathrún Céitinn), it has been described as the 'first Irish history written toward the conscious bias of nationalism'.

The years 1641–52 marked a decade of rebellion. It led to massive plantation involving the dispossession of the landed Catholic element in all but one of the provinces. The revolt of 1641 was, in the main, a Catholic uprising. The rebels played their part in the English Civil Wars by professing loyalty to Charles I. Cromwell's defeat of the rebels left Ireland by 1652 a conquered colony, with the terms of his settlement classifying 'Irish' and 'Catholic' as synonymous. Gaelic culture in 18th century Ireland was a largely peasant culture: vernacular, oral, and Catholic.

Throughout this century, concern for the idea of a nation, or the stewardship of that nation, rested with a minority élite in an exclusively Protestant parliament. Patrick Darcy, William Molyneux, and Jonathan Swift defended Ireland as a distinct political entity, drawing on the notion of Ireland as an ancient nation. The drive toward parliamentary reform was powered mainly by Presbyterians; they, too, were largely responsible for the formation of the United Irishmen. This movement, which sought the union of Irishmen of all creeds, upheld radical Continental ideology.

It can fairly lay claim to being the first mass movement of Irish nationalism, and at one point its membership was in excess of 280,000.

The 19th Century

The events of the first third of the 19th century revolved around the movement for Catholic emancipation, led by Daniel O'Connell. The longer-term political effect was the identification of the Irish nation with its overwhelmingly Catholic constituents. There was no similar momentum involving people and elected representatives until the Irish Parliamentary Party became involved with the Land League in the 1880s. O'Connell's movement is sometimes projected as the antithesis of what is known as physical force nationalism.

The seismic event in 19th century Ireland, however, was the Great FAMINE. This four-year long trauma left a million people dead and led to the EMIGRATION of another million Irish residents. The single worst social rupture of any country in 19th-century Europe, it shaped the future of Irish politics by fashioning a virulent anti-Englishness.

Toward a Divided Ireland

The years between the first and third Home Rule Acts (1886–1914) have been described as the interlude between a verdict and a sentence, with the facts of Irish political reality forcing the subsequent 1916 Rising. A putatively independent parliament (Dáil Éireann) was set up in 1919. During the subsequent War of Independence, the partition of Ireland according to the Unionist/Nationalist divide was enshrined, somewhat controversially, in the Government of Ireland Act (1920) and the Boundary Commission of 1925.

A lull in extraordinary political events ended in 1968 when the civil rights movement protested at discrimination against Catholics by the Protestant regime in Northern Ireland. The resultant clashes led to the deployment of the British Army to maintain peace between the two communities. A branch of the IRISH REPUBLICAN ARMY (the Provisional IRA) laid claim to the nationalist aspiration of a united Ireland and complete separation from Britain. A civil war spanning three decades ensued, with assassinations and bombing campaigns frequently occurring on both islands. Following the Good Friday Agreement of 1998, and a referendum in the Republic altering its territorial claims to Northern Ireland, a tentative period of peace and self-government exists.

Diarmuid Whelan

NATIONALISM, ISLE OF MAN

Modern Manx nationalism has its basis in the formation of the MecVannin (Sons of Mann) in 1963. The embryonic organization had as its objective the pursuit of independence. In the 1980s, Mec Vannin formally embraced republican objectives.

Manx nationalism draws on the example of Illiam Dhone (William Christian), a 17th-century patriot who gained quasi-independence for a period during the

English Civil Wars and was subsequently executed. MecVannin has agitated on a broad range of social, cultural, and environmental issues, in addition to its political programme. The Party has based its principles on concepts of culture and national identity common throughout the CELTIC COUNTRIES and has advanced this programme by nonviolent means, though individual members were associated with campaigns of direct action that occurred in the 1970s and 1980s. Independence is the ultimate objective.

Bernard Moffat

NATIONALISM, SCOTLAND

1707–1914

Scottish national identity following the Union with ENGLAND in 1707 found new ways to express itself and adapt to the peculiarities of a stateless nation. It was only in the 20th century, however, with the emergence of a mass democracy, that it became possible to say with any conviction that nationalism was anything other than the thoughts of a middle-class élite.

1914–1946

The idea of Scotland as an 'imperial partner' was less valid as the Dominion nations of the British Empire went their own ways. EMIGRATION, which was held up in the 19th century as evidence of the dynamism and entrepreneurism of the Scots, was now seen to be the desperate response of people to poor social and economic opportunities.

Although the Labour Party, which had emerged as the largest party in Scotland after 1922, was committed to home rule, it abandoned the idea when it was realized that the economic dislocation experienced by Scottish society could not be rectified without calling on support from the greater resources of the British state. This volte-face precipitated the creation of the National Party of Scotland (NPS) in 1928, which emerged to champion the cause of Scottish self-government by contesting elections to secure a popular mandate for its objectives. The NPS, however, had supporters who were committed to independence, and others who were satisfied with some form of DEVOLUTION. The party fused with the more devolutionist and right-leaning Scottish Party to create the Scottish National Party (SNP) in 1934.

1946 Onward

In 1967, the SNP won a by-election in Hamilton at a time of mounting unemployment and fears surrounding the devaluation of sterling. The party did well in local elections the following year. The SNP was also helped by an influx of new members and nationalist youth. The mounting economic crisis of the early 1970s, which coincided with the discovery of North Sea oil, helped the nationalists to capitalize on social and economic discontent. In the second general election of 1974, the

SNP won almost a third of the total vote and returned eleven MPs. The growth of nationalism forced the Labour government to concede to the principle of devolution, conceived as a means to halt outright nationalism.

In 1988, the Constitutional Convention was formed; it included the Liberal Democrats, Labour, the trade unions, the churches, and local authorities. The SNP stood on the sidelines, hoping that frustration with Tory rule would crystallize into support for independence. In 1997, the advent of a Labour government, committed to the creation of a Scottish parliament, set up a referendum in September. The result was overwhelmingly in favour of this measure. The Scottish Parliament was formally opened by Queen Elizabeth II on 1 July 1999, and moved into a purpose-built new building in November 2004. In a surprisingly strong showing, the SNP won an outright majority in the election for the Scottish Parliament in 2011. The party members then renewed their pledge to seek a referendum on Scotland's independence from the United Kingdom.

Richard J. Finlay

NATIONALISM, WALES

A sense of nationhood or national consciousness in Wales (CYMRU) dates back at least to the late 6th or early 7th century when the term *Cymry* (deriving from the Brythonic **Combrogī* 'people of the same country') was first used. A distinct sense of Welsh nationalism is manifest in the poem ARMES PRYDEIN (The prophecy of Britain), composed in the earlier 10th century; in the native Welsh laws codified at the time of HYWEL DDA (†950; see LAW TEXTS); and in the remarkable writings of GIRALDUS CAMBRENSIS (Gerald of Wales, 1146–1223). A powerful national awareness also inspired the political activities of Prince LLYWELYN AB IORWERTH (†1240) and his grandson Prince Llywelyn ap Gruffudd (†1282). A more widespread, general sense of Welsh patriotism fuelled the rebellion of OWAIN GLYNDŵR at the beginning of the 15th century, and indeed provided the impetus for the cultural achievements of the 16th-century Welsh humanists.

Following the ACTS OF UNION, a gradual long-term weakening of Welsh national consciousness ensued. The substantial non-Welsh population introduced in the wake of the Industrial Revolution beginning in the 1870s could not be fully assimilated. Some sense of Welsh national consciousness was encouraged by the persistence of the Welsh language, by Antiquarian studies, and by ROMANTICISM. It was followed in the mid-19th century by the rediscovery of the EISTEDDFOD, which fostered a uniquely Welsh musical and literary tradition.

Nationalism became a significant force in Welsh life only during the second half of the 19th century. It was encouraged by developments in Ireland (ÉIRE), which were closely observed in Wales, and by the inspirational writings and activities of Continental European nationalists. Between 1886 and 1896, members of Cymru Fydd (Young Wales) actively sought a measure of Welsh self-government, though firmly staying within the context of Liberal politics. This positioning bore fruit in the establishment of a federal University of Wales in 1893, and a National Library and Museum in 1907.

Political nationalism proved to be a powerful element in 20th-century Wales, but proved not as dominant a force as it was among the Irish and some of the nations of eastern Europe. The establishment of the Welsh Nationalist Party, Plaid Genedlaethol Cymru (later to become PLAID CYMRU), in 1925 heralded a strikingly novel dimension with its emphasis on safeguarding Welsh-speaking communities. Under the inspirational leadership of Saunders LEWIS, it won avid support, though widespread popular support would have to wait for Gwynfor EVANS, the party's president from 1945 until 1981, when it began to win seats in local government elections.

The upsurge of nationalist sentiment in the 1960s gave rise to several new movements, among them Cymdeithas yr Iaith Gymraeg, the Welsh Language Society, formed in 1962. Other bodies, such as the Welsh Arts Council, the Welsh National Opera, and the Welsh Development Agency were also established. A Secretary of State for Wales was appointed in 1964. Education through the medium of Welsh and the University of Wales expanded and prospered. The intensive campaign for a Welsh-language television channel reached a successful outcome in 1982 (see S4C). In a referendum for a Welsh Assembly held on 1 March 1979, however, some 80 percent of those who voted were against the proposal, a negative response that appeared to confirm that Welsh national sentiment was primarily cultural, rather than political, in nature.

A Welsh Language Board (Bwrdd yr Iaith Gymraeg) was set up in 1993 to safeguard the rights of Welsh speakers and the Welsh language. The Labour Party announced new proposals for devolution in May 1995; when Labour won the General Election of 1997, it kept its promise of holding a further referendum in the following September. In a turnout of 50.3 percent of Welsh voters, 559,419 (50.3%) voted in favour, and 552,698 (49.7%) against, devolution of political power to Wales. CYNULLIAD CENEDLAETHOL CYMRU (the National Assembly for Wales) was convened for the first time in May 1999. Between 2007 and 2011, the Welsh Assembly was led by a coalition of Labour and Plaid Cymru.

J. Graham Jones

NATURE POETRY, CELTIC

Celtic nature poetry is a term that refers to early Irish and Welsh poetic compositions concerned with the description and interpretation of the natural world. It is a modern analytical category rather than a native category.

Irish Poetry

The following is a list of the most representative poems (mostly composed in the 9th century) that are commonly considered as examples of Irish nature poetry. The poems are identified by their opening lines:

1. *Daith bech buide a úaim i n-úaim* (The yellow bee is swift from hollow to hollow): 4 lines describing the journey of a bee in a great plain.
2. *Int én gaires asin tsail* (The bird who calls out of the willow): 4 lines describing the voice of a blackbird in a wood.

3. *Ach, a luin, is buide duit* (Ah, blackbird, it is well for you): 4 lines describing the voice of a blackbird and suggesting a similarity between the life of birds and the life of hermits.

4. *Int én bec* (The little bird): 8 lines describing the voice of a blackbird, and using an association between colours and sounds to indicate the complex interaction between the different perceivable layers of the external world.

5. *Énlaith betha bríg cen táir* (Birds of the world, force without shame): also known as 'The Calendar of the Birds', a poem that describes the passage of time in 7 quatrains, beginning with the way in which birds' voices change during the year.

6. *Úar ind adaig i Móin Móir* (The night on the Great Moor is cold): 4 lines describing the cold of a winter night and suggesting a comparison between the sea and the forests.

7. *Fégaid úaib* (Look outward): an 8-line poem, also known as 'The Ocean', which describes the life of the ocean—its vastness, its movements, and the creatures that live in it.

8. *Anbthine mór ar muig Lir* (A great storm on Ler's plain): in 10 stanzas of 5 lines, a description of a storm on the sea, beginning with the various movements caused by the different kinds of winds that cross it; comparisons between the waves and the warriors are frequent, together with a multifaceted perception of the continuously changing colours of the waters.

9. *Táinic gaimred co ngainni* (Winter has come with scarcity): 4 lines describing the coming of winter.

10. *Scél lem dúib* (I have news for you): a 16-line poem, also known as 'Winter', that describes winter's effects on the landscape in 4 quatrains.

11. *Fúit co bráth*! (Cold until doom!): a 16-line poem that describes, in 4 quatrains, the effects of cold weather on lakes, rivers, woods, and the sea.

12. *Fuit, fuit* (Cold, cold): 9 quatrains describing the overflowing of waters following a great storm.

13. *Dubaib ráithib rogeimred* (Black season of deep winter): 10 lines describing a winter landscape.

14. *Hed is annsam do rímaib* (This is the hardest of bad weathers): 4 lines contrasting the beauty of summer with the harshness of winter.

15. *Slíab cúa cúanach corrach dub* (Wolf-haunted, rugged, black Cua Mountain): six lines describing the landscape of Cua Mountain.

16. *Táinic sam slán sóer* (Healthy free summer has come): 7 quatrains on landscape changing with the coming of summer.

17. *Fó sín samrad síthaister* (Peaceful summer is a good season): 6 lines describing a wood in the summer.

18. *Glas úar errach aigide* (Green, cold icy spring): 9 lines describing the appearance of green after the cold season.

19. *Ráithe fó foiss fogamar* (Autumn is a good time for resting): 15 lines describing a landscape in the autumn, its colours and sounds.

20. *Dom-farcai fidbaide fál* (A hedge of a wood thicket looks down on me): 8 lines describing the different perceptions in a wood.

Welsh Poetry

Welsh nature poetry is mainly represented by passages found in the early *englynion*, which together make up what has conventionally taken the names of 'saga poetry' and 'gnomic poetry' (mostly composed in the 9th and 10th centuries). The following can be regarded as the most representative examples:

1. *Eiry mynyδ, gwynn bob tu* (Mountain snow, every surface is white): this poem of 36 three-line *englynion* describes the different effects caused in a landscape by the falling of the snow, interlaced with gnomes (statements of general, timeless truth) about honour, old age, and the life of warriors.

2. *Gorwyn blaen onn* (Delightful is the top of the ash-tree): 33 three-line *englynion* describing the colours and the shapes of different trees, interlaced with gnomes (that is, maxims) about friendship, love, and courage.

3. *Llym awel, llum brin* (Keen the wind, bare the hill): 105 lines of *englynion* describing different parts of a winter landscape, interlaced with gnomes about illness, death, and religion.

4. *Baglawc byδin, bagwy onn* (A spear-carrying host, a cluster of ash): 33 lines describing a mountain landscape on a rainy winter night, interlaced with gnomes and proverbs about human life.

5. *Gnawt gwynt o'r deheu* (Usual the wind from the south): 12 three- and four-line *englynion* listing the normal things in a landscape, and connecting them with events in human life.

6. *Kalan gaeaf* (November 1): 27 lines describing a wintry landscape, interlaced with gnomes about youth and old age.

7. *Bit goch crib keilyawc* (Red is the cock's comb): 54 lines describing different parts of a landscape, with deliberations concerning the life of BARDS and warriors.

8. *Biδ gogor gan iar* (There is cackling from the hen): 42 lines describing the colours and the shapes of lakes and the sea, interlaced with deliberations concerning different aspects of human life.

9. *Mis Ionawr, myglyd dyffryn* (The month of January, the valley is smoky): also known as 'The Verses of the Months', a poem thatdescribes in 12 eight-line stanzas how landscapes change at the coming of different seasons, with added deliberations about human life.

Although *englynion* are often quoted as the only examples of Welsh nature poetry, other texts could be included—for example, a few poems preserved in LLYFR TALIESIN. The 'List of Pleasant Things of Taliesin' (*Addwyn aeron amser cynhaeav*, 'Pleasant are fruits in the season of autumn') is a catalogue of natural elements and human matters. *Cad Goddau* (also known as 'The battle of the trees') is a poem of 250 lines, the central section of which tells the story of a battle fought against an army of Britons by a formation of 34 species of trees. It can be easily read as an example of a landscape epic.

Francesco Benozzo

NAVIGATIO SANCTI BRENDANI

Navigatio Sancti Brendani (The voyage of St Brendan) is a Latin-language prose tale from the end of the 8th century. It is Ireland's most widely read contribution to medieval literature. The tale, which contains a very detailed description of monastic life, concerns the seven-year voyage of the patron of Clonfert, Co. Galway (Cluain Fearta, Contae na Gaillimhe), via many islands to the *Terra Repromissionis*

Sanctorum (Promised land of the saints). The *Navigatio* appears to arise from a sub-genre of voyage episodes in 7th- and 8th-century Hiberno-Latin saints' *vitae* (HAGIOGRAPHY); the tale itself strongly influenced the development of the Irish genre of voyage literature, Old Irish IMMRAMA.

Jonathan M. Wooding

NEMETON

Nemeton is a term for natural space dedicated to pre-Christian Celtic religious activity, implicitly sacralized groves or else the clearings within the groves. In GALATIA, *Drunemeton* 'sacred place of oaks' was the site for annual governing assemblies. Wherever Celts lived, *-nemet-* provided a component of tribal names (*Nemetes*), gods' names (*Nemed, Nemetona, Mars Rigonemetis,* and *Arnemetia*), and place-names (*Aquae Arnemetiae, Medionemeton, Nemetodurum, Nemetobriga, Nemetacum,* and *Vernemeton*). A cartulary from the abbey of Quimperlé (Kemperle), Brittany (BREIZH), dated 1031, mentions woods called *Nemet*, and an 18th-century Belgian document refers to sacred woods called *Nimid* near Lobbes. In Old Irish, *nemed* is an important socio-legal term meaning 'privileged person, dignitary, professional, sacred place, sanctuary, privilege'.

Paula Powers Coe

NEO-DRUIDISM

Contemporary druidry—whether religious, spiritual, or esoteric—is a complex phenomenon that encompasses varied groups and individuals including pagan, Christian, and New Age practitioners. Many modern groups trace their roots to the 18th-century druidic 'revival', particularly the Ancient Order of Druids, which spread widely in America, Canada, Australia, and Europe. The late 19th-century Golden Dawn movement has also been influential in some branches of druidry. Many contemporary practitioners refer to GREEK AND ROMAN ACCOUNTS for information about druidry, accepting from them the importance of learning and the ritual use of mistletoe, oak trees, and sacred groves (see NEMETON), although human sacrifice is more controversial: Some modern druids reject accounts of human sacrifice as a slur by hostile outsiders, while others explain that for a willing victim acting for the good of the community it would have been a great honour.

The contemporary druid's ritual year is shaped by the Celtic or eight-fold CALENDAR, with summer and winter solstices regarded as particularly important—a view reinforced by the 'archaeoastronomy' of writers such as Hawkins, Thom, and Hoyle. The connection between druidry and STONEHENGE, made by Aubrey in the 17th century and reinforced by Stukeley in the 18th century, continues to be articulated and acted upon by contemporary druids.

In some respects, modern druidry appears similar to the cultural bardism of the Welsh GORSEDD BEIRDD YNYS PRYDAIN or the GORSETH of Cornwall (KERNOW). Many groups meet in stone circles in 'the eye of the sun', wear long white 'druidic' robes of the type developed in the 18th and 19th centuries, and recite versions of the Gorsedd Prayer of Edward WILLIAMS (Iolo Morganwg).

Members of the Ancient Order of Druids celebrate the autumnal equinox at Primrose Hill in London, the site where Iolo Morganwg organised the first meeting of Gorsedd Beirdd Ynys Prydain in 1792. (Brian Parkin)

Since some regard druidism as the native spirituality of the British Isles, the incorporation of elements from 'other' indigenous traditions seems logical; thus didgeridoos are commonplace at druid rituals, there are druidic sweat lodges, and 'druid' is commonly equated with 'shaman'. Some druids in North America and Australia use druidry as a means of expressing their Celtic heritage and practising what they consider their ancestral religion.

Views as to whether druidry is a religion, a philosophy, a vocation, or a way of life vary between groups and individuals. Very much in the spirit of Stukeley, who regarded druids as proto-Christians, there are Christian druids. Some regard Celtic CHRISTIANITY as a repository of druidic esoteric wisdom, a hypothetical syncretic blend of pre-Christian religious wisdom and Christianity.

The Order of Bards, Ovates, and Druids (OBOD), formed in 1964, makes the following claim: 'The Order is not a cult or religion—it simply represents a particular way of working with, and understanding the Self and the natural world'. Its aims are to 'help the individual develop his potential—spiritual, intellectual, emotional, physical and artistic' (OBOD publicity leaflet). In 1988, OBOD established a correspondence course in druidry, enabling people to progress, through readings, tapes, and workbooks, through the different grades, from Bard to Ovate to Druid. Other groups and individuals also offer training and formal qualifications in druidry.

Marion Bowman

NIALL NOÍGIALLACH MAC ECHACH

Niall Noígiallach mac Echach ('Niall of the Nine Hostages', †?427/8) is considered the ancestor of the Uí Néill, patrilineal lineages who became the predominant dynasties in early medieval Ireland (Ériu), with their power concentrated particularly in western Ulster (Ulaid) and the Midlands. From the time of Diarmait mac Cerbaill (r. 544–65) down to that of Brian Bóruma (†1014), the Uí Néill overking usually monopolized the prestigious office of *rí Temro* (king of Tara/Teamhair), which evolved toward a notional, and eventually an actual, high-kingship of Ireland. Although we do not have contemporary annals or other written records for Niall, he is so well and consistently attested in genealogies, the tales of the Kings' Cycles, and other early medieval texts that his historicity is not in doubt. In the genealogies, he is a descendant of the legendary king Cormac mac Airt, grandson of Conn Cétchathach; thus his ancestors figure as the opponents of the Ulaid in the legendary struggle that forms the background of the Ulster Cycle.

Niall's epithet *noígiallach* ('of the nine hostages', from *noí* 'nine' and *giall* 'hostage') is sometimes explained as relating to nine tribes who owed him tribute, later known by the collective name Airgialla (lit. 'those who give hostages') of central Ulster.

Petra S. Hellmuth

NINIAN, ST

St Ninian was the most important saint of the monastery, later cathedral, of Whithorn in Galloway, Scotland (Gall Ghàidhil, Alba). As Nynia or Nyniau, he was remembered by historians of the Northumbrian church regime that took over southwestern Scotland in the late 7th or early 8th century. They ascribed to him British origins, a Roman training, missionary work among the 'southern Picts', and a host of miracles, mainly healing ones, at his tomb in the church. Our two main witnesses to these traditions are Bede in his *Historia Ecclesiastica* (731) and an anonymous *Miracula Nynie Episcopi*. In the 12th century, the cult of St Ninian was revived in a climate of reorganization and reform. A revised Life was produced by the Cistercian Aelred of Rievaulx, who used the form Ninianus, the form we know today.

Most of the church dedications to Ninian appear to date from the 12th century or later, when his cult was keenly patronized by Scottish kings. The chronology derived from Aelred, who has Ninian meet monks of St Martin of Tours bringing news of his death (397), has long been thought unlikely among scholars, and is unsupported by the 8th-century material. His Pictish missionary efforts are effectively unsupported by other evidence for attaching early Christian remains north of the Forth to his name. Recently, the fact that there is little or no trace of an early cult in the vicinity of Whithorn has been noticed, and the possibility that there has been some confusion between a local and popular cult of St Uinniau (also known as Finnian of Moville) and an essentially created literary cult of Nyniau has been suggested. None of this debate detracts from the early importance of the ecclesiastical centre at Whithorn, or the importance of Ninian's cult and pilgrimage site in the later Middle Ages.

Thomas Owen Clancy

NŌDONS/NUADU/NUDD

Nōdons in Roman-Britain

Nōdons (also Nōdens and Nūdent-) is the name of a Celtic god whose cult has been attested by several inscriptions from present-day ENGLAND, one from Cockersand Moss in Lancashire and three from Lydney Park in Gloucestershire. One equates Nōdons with Mars (see INTERPRETATIO ROMANA). The archaeological context at Lydney suggests that Nōdons had an acquatic quality, as many bronze plaques of fishermen, ichthyocentaurs (creatures with a human head and torso, the legs and body of a horse, and the tail of a fish or dolphin), and other sea-monsters have also been found at this site. The elaborate Romano-Celtic temple at Lydney is located on a hill-top in what had been a pre-Roman hill-fort (OPPIDUM).

Nuadu

The Irish mythological figure equivalent to Nōdons, in name at least, was Nuadu, gen. Nuadat (attested in a late OGAM inscription). In early Irish literary tradition, Nuadu can be equated with Nechtan, in view of their shared aquatic attributes as well as the combination of the name and the epithet *Nuadu Necht*, found in the early Old Irish genealogical poem.

   In the later 9th- or 10th-century mythological tale CATH MAIGE TUIRED ('The [Second] Battle of Mag Tuired'), Nuadu is a prominent member of the pre-Gaelic inhabitants of Ireland, the TUATH DÉ. In this tale, his regular epithet is *Argatlám* 'silver hand'. The epithet is explained there with an account of how Nuadu has a prosthetic arm of silver made by the Tuath Dé physician, Dian Cécht.

Gwyn ap Nudd and Lludd Llaw Ereint

Later forms of *Nōdons*, the masculine NVDI and NVDINTI (both formally Latin gen-itives), occur in early post-Roman inscriptions from Britain. The Dark Age North British prince *Nuδ Hael mab Senyllt* 'Nudd the Generous, son of Senyllt' figures in the Welsh TRIADS, and both *Nudd* and Irish *Nuadu* occur as personal names in early medieval texts.

   Viewing the name with its epithet, the most exact equivalent to the Irish *Nuadu Argatlám* in Welsh mythology is *Lludd Llaw Ereint* (Lludd of the Silver Hand), who is mentioned twice in CULHWCH AC OLWEN. No story survives to explain the epithet. That the Welsh equivalent of Irish Nuadu should appear sometimes as *Nudd* and sometimes as *Lludd* has probably come about through an irregular change in the ini-tial sound of the name from *n-* > *ll-*. A likely reason for the development of *n-* > *ll-* is the attraction of the alliteration of the epithet that survives as *Llaw Ereint*. An early change is suggested by the place-name *Lydney*, first recorded as Old English *Lideneg* in a source from *c.* 853. The meaning of the place-name is 'Lida's island', where the Anglicized personal name is to be explained as a borrowing from archaic Welsh */Lüδ/* < British *Nōdons*.

In the Welsh tale CYFRANC LLUDD A LLEFELYS, king Lludd of ancient Britain faces three supernatural oppressions or *gormesoedd*. The plot of *Lludd a Llefelys* is broadly comparable to that of *Cath Maige Tuired* in that king Nuadu's people, the Tuath Dé (corresponding to Lludd's ancient British subjects), face supernatural enemies who are routed only by means of the ingenious leadership of the returned exile LUG (corresponding to the Welsh Llefelys). Thus an argument can be made for *Cath Maige Tuired* and *Lludd a Llefelys* preserving cognate versions of an old Celtic myth of the stricken divine king Nōdons and his resourceful rescuer and returned exile Lugus.

Erich Poppe and Peter E. Busse

NOMINOË/NEVENOE

Nominoë/Nevenoe (*c.* 800–51; r. 831–51) is the earliest well-documented ruler of an autonomous and united Brittany (BREIZH). Nominoë first appears in historical sources as count of Vannes (Gwened). He was a vassal of the Frankish ruler Louis the Pious (768–840; r. 814–40), who elevated Nominoë to the status of *missus imperatoris* (emperor's delegate) in 831. Following the death of Louis, the king's three sons quarrelled over the way in which the Frankish Empire was to be divided. Charles the Bald (823–77; r. 843–77) was eventually granted dominion over the Western Empire in 843, but Nominoë rose against him. Charles was defeated at the battle of Ballon in 845, and was forced to recognize the autonomy of Brittany in 846. Nominoë continued to expand the territories which he controlled, moving from Brittany into Maine and Anjou, but he died in 851 at the Vendôme.

Nominoë is described in later medieval sources as king of an independent Brittany; this depiction is evidently intended to make him conform to the trope of the wicked king (cf. ARTHUR in HAGIOGRAPHY).

Antone Minard

NUMANTIA

Numantia was a CELTIBERIAN town north of Soria on the upper Duero river in eastern Castile and Leon, Spain. Its conquest in 133 BC by Scipio Africanus the Younger ended the Celtiberian wars and opened up the central Iberian Peninsula to the Romans. The town was originally a fairly large *castro* 'fort' of around 32 ha, located on a 70-m plateau overlooking the confluence of the Merdancho, Tera, and Duero rivers. It is a major archaeological site, and excavation work has been undertaken here for over two centuries. The Museo Numantino at Soria was established in 1919 to display the finds and control research.

The site has been occupied since the early Bronze Age (the end of the 3rd millennium BC), and the walled Celtiberian town was built on top of an Iron Age *castro*. Its wooden or wattle-and-daub houses were built on a standard 'shotgun' plan, one room wide, with three or four rooms extending in a line back from the street frontage to a yard and storage shed.

The story of Numantia has come down to us in the narrative of Appian of Alexandria (*c.* AD 90–*c.* 162). According to this account, after nearly ten years of war, Scipio was appointed consul and raised an army against Numantia in 134 BC. He blocked all three rivers and created a fortified circle of seven camps, besieging Numantia. These fortifications can still be seen.

The Numantians had only 8,000 fighting men against Scipio's 60,000. In the end, they were starved into submission. Scipio sold most of the Numantians into slavery.

Numantia had never been seriously attacked, but a layer of ash over the Celtiberian remains indicates that it was formally destroyed, at least to ground level. It must have been rapidly rebuilt, for the new town used the old street patterns and house blocks. That the Numantians remained 'Celtic' is supported not only by the ancient sources but also by the presence of Celtiberian names painted on some of their ceramics. In the 1st century AD, Numantia became a *municipium*, a town whose inhabitants had the right to Roman citizenship. It was abandoned, like so many others, in the later 4th century.

Aedeen Cremin

O

O'GRADY, STANDISH JAMES

Standish James O'Grady (1846–1928) was an Irish novelist and historian whose versions of the Irish MYTHOLOGICAL CYCLE earned him the sobriquet 'Father of the Irish Literary Renaissance' (see ANGLO-IRISH LITERATURE). He abandoned a legal career after discovering Sylvester O'Halloran's *An Introduction to the Study of the History and Antiquities of Ireland* (1772). His two-volume *History of Ireland* (1878, 1880) was hugely popular and had a profound influence on W. B. Yeats, T. W. Rolleston (1865–1939), and particularly George Russell (1867–1935).

A journalist for most of his life, O'Grady tried to influence contemporary Irish politics and society. Principally a unionist and conservative, despite his passion for Gaelic culture, he suggested that landlords and tenants work together to revitalize the country in the pamphlet *Toryism and the Tory Democracy* (1886), which also recognized the impending doom of landlordism in Ireland and the growing issue of unemployment (cf. LAND AGITATION). Editor of a small newspaper, *The Kilkenny Moderator* (1898–1902), and founder-editor of the *All-Ireland Review* (1902–6), he became influential in intellectual circles, publishing articles by Æ (pseudonym of George William Russell), Arthur Griffith (Art Ó GRÍOFA), and W. B. Yeats, among others.

Brian Ó Broin

Ó GRIANNA, SÉAMUS

Séamus Ó Grianna ('Máire', 1889–1969) was born in the Donegal GAELTACHT. He edited *Fáinne an Lae* from 1927 until 1929 (see CONRADH NA GAEILGE). In 1930, he joined An Gúm (the Government Publication Office) as a translator. An acknowledged authority on his native dialect, he worked with both Tomás de Bhaldraithe and Niall Ó Dónaill on the preparation of their respective dictionaries. A prolific writer, Ó Grianna published nine novels, thirteen collections of short stories, and three autobiographical accounts.

Pádraigín Riggs

Ó GRÍOFA, ART

Art Ó Gríofa (Arthur Griffith, 1871–1922) is seen as the theoretician behind the Irish struggle for independence. His policy of political abstention—nationalist Irish MPs would refuse to take their seats in the British Parliament to form their own governing body—established a way between the earlier Parliamentarianism and outright armed insurrection. He founded Sinn Féin, whose elected MPs formed the first Dáil Éireann, and led the delegation that signed the Anglo-Irish Treaty of 6 December 1921.

In September 1900, Ó Gríofa's first political organization, Cumann na nGaedheal (Society of the Gaels), advocated the establishment of an Irish republic and established political abstention as a weapon in the struggle for IRISH INDEPENDENCE. Joining forces with his 'National Council', formed in 1903 to protest against King Edward VII's visit to Ireland, and Irish Republican Brotherhood clubs, Sinn Féin was founded in 1905. Conceptualized as an organization embracing the whole spectrum of nationalist opinion, it set about creating a governing body for Ireland by assembling a 'Council of Three Hundred' elected local government delegates.

The failure of the Easter Rising and the indefinite postponement of Home Rule during World War I enabled Sinn Féin to transform itself into a powerful, radical party, which, in December 1918, won an overwhelming victory in the first postwar election in Ireland (ÉIRE). Implementing Griffith's policy of abstention, on 21 January 1919 the Sinn Féin MPs formed Dáil Éireann, in which Griffith became Minister for Home Affairs and Eamon DE VALERA Vice-President. Griffith led the second delegation negotiating the terms of Irish independence with London, signing the first Anglo-Irish Treaty on 6 December 1921. When de Valera resigned on 9 January 1922, following the Dáil's acceptance of the treaty, Griffith became leader of the house, but died that summer after a long illness.

Marion Löffler

OENGUS CÉILE DÉ

Oengus Céile Dé ('The Culdee') lived during the later 8th and early 9th centuries. Apart from the 1645 *Acta Sanctorum Hiberniae* of John Colgan (Seán Mac Colgáin), our only knowledge of him derives from internal evidence in his *Félire* (martyrology, calendar of saints' feasts), and from one Irish poem. Colgan records 11 March as Oengus's feast-day and describes him as a bishop and hagiographer.

The *Félire* is the first extant Irish-language martyrology from Ireland (ÉRIU). It written in verse and was intended as a devotional text, geared toward a wide audience outside the monastery. From the latest entries in the *Félire* we know that it was written between 797 and 808, and that it followed a particular strand of the 'Hieronymian martyrology' found in insular circles; its basis was probably the *Martyrology of Tallaght*. However, in addition to the lists of saints, a high proportion of them Irish, the *Félire* has a prologue and epilogue with two unusual features: (1) a particular theology of saintly intercession on behalf of the whole people, and (2) an implicit critique of the struggles for power among kings in Ireland as being incompatible with the existence of the Irish as a Christian *gens* (nation, people).

Thomas O'Loughlin

OENGUS MAC IND ÓC

Oengus Mac ind Óc is a member of the TUATH DÉ, the supernatural or divine tribe of early IRISH LITERATURE. He is the son of the DAGDA and BÓAND, the female personification of the river Boyne. The stock properties of his character include youth and beauty. His name means 'Oengus the Young Son'. *Oengus* itself is a common name in Goidelic, Modern *Aonghas*, Anglicized *Angus*, but cognates are found also in Old Welsh *Unust* and the variants Onuist and Unuist in the PICTISH king-list, reflecting Proto-Celtic **Oino-gustus* 'Chosen one'. Oengus is closely associated with the great megalithic tomb of Newgrange (BRUG NA BÓINNE), which is often described as his residence (cf. also dubhadh). He is mentioned in texts in the MYTHOLOGICAL CYCLE, LEGENDARY HISTORY, FIANNAÍOCHT, the ULSTER CYCLE, and DINDSHENCHAS.

Two recurrent themes in the various stories of Oengus are, first, a manipulation of time in which one day becomes a much longer period, and, second, fateful entanglement between the affairs of the gods and those of mortals. In Oengus's birth tale, as told in the opening of TOCHMARC ÉTAÍNE ('The Wooing of Étaín'), Oendus was conceived by the Dagda after he had sent Bóand's husband away and cast a spell on him so that the following nine months seemed like one day. Later, the young Oengus is frustrated in the courtship of a mortal woman, who is also sought by others. In the closely related Old Irish tale *Aislinge Oengusa* ('The Dream of Oengus'), Oengus repeatedly sees a beautiful girl in his dreams and falls into a love sickness. His parents intervene and find the girl. As the story of an overpowering dream vision of a destined bride, *Aislinge Oengusa* is thematically comparable to the Welsh *Breuddwyd* MACSEN and the conception episode of the Breton Latin Life of IUDIC-HAEL.

John T. Koch

OFFA'S DYKE
See Clawdd Offa.

OGAM INSCRIPTIONS AND PRIMITIVE IRISH

The oldest surviving Irish texts are a series of about 300 Primitive Irish INSCRIPTIONS carved on stone pillars, apparently during the 5th and 6th centuries. These short and formulaic texts have no literary content, but consist largely of male personal names. There are minor variants on this basic theme, but beyond names the vocabulary is more or less limited to a few terms for kinship and other social rôles. As the only direct evidence for the state of the language in this early period, the inscriptions are of considerable importance to the linguist.

'Primitive Irish' is a term used to describe a state of the language in which the original Old Celtic final syllables of polysyllables were preserved. Irish names and terms begin to be written without their Primitive Irish final syllables in some ogam inscriptions that probably date to the 6th century AD, but more inscriptions are written with the Old Celtic final syllables.

The inscriptions exhibit several remarkable features, but by far the most striking is the SCRIPT in which they are written—not the Roman capitals of contemporary British and Continental inscriptions, but a uniquely Irish script known as *ogam* in Old Irish (Modern Irish *ogham*). The origins of this script are obscure: Although

Standing stone with ogam inscription, Kilmakedar, Dingle Peninsula, County Kerry, Ireland (Cill Mhaoilchéadair, Corca Dhuibhne, Contae Chiarraí, Éire). (Gary Elsner/StockphotoPro)

clearly inspired by the Roman alphabet, ogam exhibits considerable visual and conceptual independence from it. Written from left to right along a continuous line, ogam letters consist of bundles of between one and five short parallel strokes adjoining the central stem (*druim*). Epigraphic ogams are usually inscribed vertically and read from bottom to top. The twenty original letters are arranged in a fixed order in four groups (*aicmi*): Over time additional letters (*forfeda*) were added to this inventory in response to evolving Irish phonology.

Three main phases of ogam usage can be distinguished in the 1,500 years since the invention of the script. Its heyday came during the two centuries before 600 when ogam is found in monumental use in all the Irish-speaking regions of the British Isles. The overwhelming majority of these 'orthodox' inscriptions are found in Munster (Mumu), with particular concentrations in Co. Kerry (Contae Chiarraí) and Co. Cork (Contae Chorcaí). A small number are observed in Scotland (Alba) and the Isle of Man (Ellan Vannin), and rather more numerous groups in Wales, Devon (Welsh Dyfnaint), and Cornwall (Kernow). No ogam-inscribed stones have been discovered on the European mainland. Most of the ogam inscriptions in western Britain are accompanied by Latin versions of the same text. These bilingual dual-script monuments played an important rôle in refining modern knowledge of the correct transliteration of ogam.

Social change in the 7th century brought the tradition of erecting 'individual inscribed memorials' to an end, and with it the main body of evidence for early ogam dries up. A handful of chance survivals, including graffiti, informal inscriptions on domestic objects, and manuscript marginalia, suggest that ogam did continue in limited use beyond the 7th century. Law texts refer to ogam-inscribed stones as evidence of title to land, and descriptions of heroic burial in the sagas mention the carving of the name of the deceased on a pillar above the grave. These matter-of-fact references tally well with the physical evidence. Less secure are the saga descriptions of the non-monumental use of ogam. Táin Bó Cuailnge ('The Cattle Raid of Cooley') cites several instances of ogam carved on a withe and hung on a pillar-stone as a challenge or warning, but there is no corroborating evidence for saga references to the use of ogam for divination or cryptography. There is nothing intrinsically cryptic or occult about ogam, and it must be emphasized that its use in early Ireland was first and foremost as a practical day-to-day script.

The prestige of ogam had diminished by the 7th century, as reflected in its restriction thereafter to private secular and informal, even playful, ecclesiastic contexts. The relative standing of the ogam and Roman alphabets in this 'post-classical' phase echoes in certain respects the relationship between runes and Roman letters in Anglo-Saxon England. There is a definite change in the appearance of ogam at this point: Gone is the three-dimensionality of the orthodox pillars, with letters on adjacent faces of the stone and the arris for a stem; in its place arises a drawn-in stem-line, written across the flat surface as if across a manuscript page. A break with the old spelling system occurred as well. The ogam characters ceased to represent the sounds of Irish directly and became instead a cipher for Old Irish manuscript spelling. As a mere transliteration of Roman letters, ogam could now, in theory, be applied to any language, and in fact there are examples of Latin written in ogam characters.

An important exception to the more marginal status of later ogam is the remarkable effloresence of the script in post-7th-century Scotland, where its prestige was such that it ousted the Roman alphabet as the preferred monumental script. The adaptation of the script to represent the sounds of Pictish is the only instance of the practical use of ogam for a language other than Irish. A scatter of late ogam inscriptions from Shetland (Sealtainn), the Isle of Man, and Ireland (including Viking Dublin [Baile Átha Cliath] and an ogam-runic bilingual monument from Killaloe, Co. Clare [Cill Dalua, Contae an Chláir]), suggest that a revival of interest in the script occurred in Celto-Norse circles in the 10th and 11th centuries. These constitute the latest examples of ogam in practical use. Thereafter, there are texts *about* ogam, but no more texts *in* ogam.

It is a popular misconception that all ogam letters were named for trees. Ogam remained part of the training of a *file* 'poet' until the 17th century (see bardic order), with the letter names surviving thereafter as the names of ordinary Irish letters. The elaborate system of prophetic meanings attached to ogam characters is a recent creation unrelated to genuine ogam tradition or any magical use of ogam letters that may have occurred in the past.

Katherine Forsyth

OGMIOS

Ogmios was a Gaulish god best known from a passage by the Greek writer Lucian of Samosata (*c.* AD 120–after 180). While in Gallia Narbonensis, Lucian had seen an image of the god, showing him with the usual classical attributes of Heracles as psychopomp (conveying souls to the Otherworld). However, this Gaulish Hercules was a bald and sunburnt old man, from whose tongue golden chains pulled his apparently happy followers. It has been suggested that this same scene is represented on an 'Ogmios-type' of coinage. Ogmios is also attested in INSCRIPTIONS; one identifies *Ogmius* as the god of death and the Otherworld. The Irish Ogma *gríanainech* 'Ogma the sun-faced', *trénfher* or 'champion' (lit. 'strongman') of the TUATH DÉ, and inventor of the OGAM SCRIPT has been identified with Ogmios by many modern writers, on the basis of name, attributes of heroic strength, special linguistic skill, and the correspondence of Ogma's epithet and Lucian's description. However, the phonetic correspondence of *Ogmios* to Irish *Ogma(e)* and Welsh *Eufydd* (one of the children of Dôn), Old Welsh *Oumid*, is not exact, though the inconsistencies could be partly explained by a syllable dropped from an earlier **Ogomios* or **Ogumios*.

Helmut Birkhan

OILEÁIN ÁRANN (ARAN ISLANDS)

Oileáin Árann (Aran Islands), Contae na Gaillimhe/Co. Galway, are three islands stretching across the entrance to Galway Bay—Inis Mór (Inishmore, 'Great Island'), Inis Meáin (Inishmaan, 'Middle Island'), and Inis Oirr (Inisheer, 'Eastern Island'). The landscape of the Aran Islands is dominated by large stone forts and stone churches. Some of the forts were originally constructed during the Late Bronze Age (*c.* 1200–*c.* 600 BC)—for example, DÚN AONGHASA—but were reconstructed occasionally into the medieval period.

Early sources suggest that the Aran Islands were subject to the authority of the provincial king of Munster (MUMU) at Cashel (Caisel Muman). The islands were ruled by DÁL GCAIS from the late 8th to the 11th century. Later, the Connacht

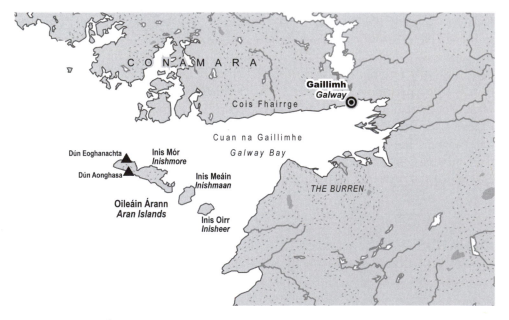

(Map by Simon Ó Faoláin and John T. Koch)

dynasty, Uí Flaithbertaig (O'Flahertys), competed with the Uí Briain for control of these strategic islands.

The people and landscape of the Aran Islands attracted many antiquaries and artists in recent centuries. Some of Ireland's most important antiquaries, including George Petrie and John O'Donovan, recorded and surveyed its monuments. Jack B. Yeats and Charles Lamb painted pictures of the landscape and people. The language and customs inspired authors such as John Millington Synge (see ANGLO-IRISH LITERATURE. Indeed, the themes and language of Synge's writings are deeply rooted in the Aran Islands. Irish continues to be spoken on the islands, and the wealth of this language and its associated traditions has been used by native authors of the 20th century, including Liam O'Flaherty (Ó Flaithearta) and the poet Máirtín Ó Direáin.

Edel Bhreathnach

OISÍN/OSSIAN

Oisín/Ossian is a figure of Irish and Scottish Gaelic legend. Belonging to the cycle known as FIANNAÍOCHT, he is the son of its central hero Finn mac Cumaill. In accounts of his birth, Oisín's mother is portrayed as a supernatural figure who appeared to Finn in the form of a doe (see REINCARNATION); the name Oisín is the diminutive of Irish *os(s)* 'deer'.

In the Middle Irish tale *Acallam na Senórach* ('Dialogue of [or with] the Old Men'), there is an account of how Oisín and his nephew Caílte meet St PATRICK. The figure of Oisín, as well as other members of the Fían (Finn's war-band), was very popular throughout the GAELIC-speaking world; many place-names mentioned in the DINDSHENCHAS relate to *Fiannaíocht*. Oisín was known in the Scottish Highlands as Oisean, a name that was adapted by the Scottish author James MACPHERSON as Ossian for his *Works of Ossian*. The long vitality of this tradition is illustrated by the fact that folk-tales about Oisín were collected from Irish and Scottish Gaelic speakers as recently as the 1960s.

Peter Smith, Peter E. Busse, and John T. Koch

OLD CORNISH VOCABULARY

The 12th-century Cornish-language text known as the *Vocabularium Cornicum*, or the Old Cornish Vocabulary, is found in the larger text known as the Cottonian Vocabulary (part of the Cottonian Library founded by Sir Robert Cotton in the 17th century), which contains some 360 pages and includes other Celtic legendary and historical material.

The Old Cornish Vocabulary is a comparatively short text, forming only seven pages. It is effectively an Old Cornish–Latin thesaurus, possibly assembled by the Anglo-Saxon translator Ælfric of Eynsham *c.* 1100. It is clear that the author or authors had knowledge of both Old Welsh and Old Cornish. The Vocabulary records in considerable detail an early Brythonic Celtic lexical world, framed in a chronological order based loosely on Genesis.

The Vocabulary offers a valuable insight into both the order of this world and the terms and concepts of importance. The vocabulary is of great etymological interest, not least for comparative purposes (see CELTIC LANGUAGES; BRYTHONIC), but also because it reveals the productive word-forming patterns by which Old Cornish generated intelligible new vocabulary. For example, the word for Viking (*ancredwur mor*) is literally 'sea-unbeliever'; the word for a trumpeter (*barth hirgorn*) is literally 'long horn bard'; that for grasshopper (*chelioc reden*) literally 'cock of the bracken'.

Alan M. Kent

ONUIST SON OF UURGUIST

Onuist son of Uurguist (Oengus mac Forguso in GAELIC sources) was a particularly powerful and fairly well-documented king of the PICTS. He was the first of two PICTISH kings with this same name and patronym. Our main source for his activities is the ANNALS of Ulster. Onuist is first mentioned in 727, when he defeated Drest, a rival Pictish prince. In 729, he seized power across Pictland. During his reign, he led several campaigns against DÁL RIATA. Onuist seems to have been overlord not only of the Picts but also of Dál Riata between 736 and 750. In 739, he drowned the Pictish tribal king, Talorgen son of Drustan. Onuist reigned in Pictland until his death in 761.

The name *Onuist* corresponds to Old Welsh *Unust* and the very common Old Irish man's name *Oengus*, all reflecting a Common Celtic **Oino-gustus* 'chosen one'. His father's name *Uurguist* corresponds to Old Breton *Uurgost*, Old Welsh *G(u)urgust,* and the Old Irish *Forggus* 'chosen over others, best' (often confused with *Fergus*).

Peter E. Busse and John T. Koch

OPPIDUM

Oppidum (pl. oppida) is a Latin word. In an Italian context, it means a central or main town. From Caesar's time, *oppidum* came to be used for large proto-urban defended settlements functioning as tribal centres in the Celtic-speaking world. In describing GAULISH architecture, Caesar contrasted *oppidum* with the *aedificium* 'building, structure' and the *vicus* 'village, settlement'. Today, *oppidum* is used in Celtic studies to denote the large, permanently fortified settlements that developed in the final LA TÈNE period (La Tène D) in a substantial part of Celtic Europe. One distinctive characteristic is that oppida were built alongside watercourses and used them as part of their lines of defence.

The rampart is generally made of wooden beams covered with earth with an outside stone facing. East of the Rhine, the rampart has an earthen ramp at the rear rather than an internal vertical wall face. Horizontal beams are present in the core of the earthen rampart. These project forward and join vertical posts at the front, defining a steep outer face, contrasting with the slope at the back. West of the Rhine is the *murus gallicus* 'Gaulish wall' described by Caesar (*De Bello Gallico* 7, 23). The wooden beams are embedded in horizontal beds, and the ends of the beams protrude from the stone facing on the exterior of the ramparts. Iron spikes 20–30 cm long are set into drilled holes where beams cross at right angles, giving rigidity to the wooden framework—a significant innovation in the history of fortification.

Inside the walls of the Gaulish oppida, buildings of all kinds squeeze together, often grouped in enclosures and linked by roads. At some sites the buildings in the oppida resemble those of farmsteads in the countryside. Elsewhere, a distinctively urban architecture emerged. In all cases, there is minimal urban planning. Houses may be made of wood, mud brick, or stone, following the local tradition. Typically British round houses, for example, occur in British oppida. In contrast, in eastern Gaul, the strong influence of Italian urban architecture is apparent. Sanctuaries are present in most of the oppida. The material culture of the oppida is generally very rich, particularly in terms of the products of the numerous craftsmen's workshops that formed a regular core of the settled area. Imports, particularly amphorae (ceramic wine vessels), are a characteristic element of the lifestyle in the oppida, and reflect the rôle of these centres in the ancient world economy. On both the Continent and in Britain, tribal coinage was frequently minted in the oppida.

The oppidum had an economic function comparable to that of a modern provincial town or regional centre. Socio-economic institutions of this sort had previously been unknown to the cultures of the European Iron Age; thus the oppida form a transition between the previous prehistoric hill-forts and the Roman and later medieval towns, whose economic function they anticipate. After Caesar's conquest of Gaul (58–50 BC), the oppidum disappears quickly; the Roman model imposes itself from the 30s BC onward. A general aspect of the Romanization of Celtic society was for the high proto-urban sites to be abandoned in favour of living on nearby plains.

Olivier Buchsenschutz

ORDINALIA

Ordinalia is the conventional title of a Cornish dramatic trilogy written toward the end of the 14th century, composed of three plays: *Ordinale de Origine Mundi* (*Origo Mundi*, the beginning of the world), *Passio Domini Nostri Jhesu Christi* (*Passio Christi*, Christ's Passion), and *Ordinale de Resurrexione Domini* (*Resurrexio Domini*, the Resurrection of the Lord). *Ordinalia* is the plural of Latin *ordinale*, meaning 'prompt' or 'service book'. The language of the plays is Middle Cornish, with different metrical forms used throughout. French, English, and Latin are also incorporated. The place-names of the plays, which combine a biblical landscape with a Cornish one, indicate probable authorship at Glasney College.

Like other Cornish plays, the *Ordinalia* seems to have been staged over three days in open-air amphitheatres, called in Cornish *plen-an-gwary*. Staging and production techniques are indicated by diagrams in the manuscript, which show circles with the characters' names on their peripheries.

The *Ordinalia* is a highly unified work showing the fall and redemption of humanity. Many of its themes are derived from apocryphal sources, the most important of which is the Legend of the Holy Rood. It follows the history of the cross, and begins with three seeds from the tree of life being placed in the mouth of the dead Adam by Seth, who is in search of the oil of mercy. The trilogy is highly comic in places, with earthy humour.

Origo Mundi is an episodic text beginning from the creation of the world. *Passio Christi* opens with the temptation of Christ in the desert leading to a crucifixion both brutal and comic, with the torturers delighting in their task. *Resurrexio Domini* neatly follows on from the Passion, with the release from prison of Nicodemus and Joseph of Arimathea, the Resurrection of Christ and (disguised as a gardener) his encounter with his mother, the harrowing of hell, and the three Marys.

Alan M. Kent

OTHERWORLD

Introduction

The term 'Otherworld' signifies a realm different from that inhabited by normal humanity, variously defined as the dwelling place of the gods, the souls of the dead, or other supernatural beings. No word for 'Otherworld' can be confidently reconstructed for Proto-Celtic, and although legend and folklore furnish many accounts of individual supernatural places, indications of another 'world'—that is, a single unified extended domain distinct from and contrasting with the world we know—are more difficult to find, especially in Gaelic sources. The Roman poet Lucan states that the DRUIDS' doctrine of immortality entailed a belief that the soul after death assumed a body 'in another sphere' or 'region' (*orbe alio*). Other sources may reflect an idea that the dead dwell in islands in the ocean.

Gaelic Tradition

Early Irish sources refer to the 'Otherworld' in various ways. The most common and also the most ambiguous term employed is síd /ʃīð/ (pl. síde). Scholars disagree as to whether the words síd 'Otherworld mound' and síd 'peace' are ultimately identical, or merely homonyms. This term designates an elevation of land inhabited by supernatural beings, or else the subterranean dwelling itself—hence the term *aes síde* ('people of the síd') used generally of the immortal people. Many artificial mounds in the landscape of Ireland (Éire) and other areas of northwest Europe contain prehistoric burials.

Besides referring to an individual cave, síd may designate an extensive region to which access may be obtained in various ways, including travelling underwater. The kingdom conquered by Loegaire is called *Mag Mell* ('Plain of Sports' or 'Delightful Plain'). This name, which recurs in other sources, is not tied to any specific síd. The same is true of other names, whose biblical derivation reflects a partial identification of the native Otherworld with the Christian heaven: *Tír na mBeó* ('Land of the Living') and *Tír Tairngire* ('Land of Promise').

Besides localizations of the Otherworld within hills, under lakes, or beneath the sea, some tales describe supernatural regions beyond the ocean. As noted previously, some classical sources point to a Celtic belief in 'island otherworlds'. Such Irish traditions as the belief that the dead migrate to *Tech Duinn* ('the House of Donn', an island off the Beara peninsula) seem likely to have indigenous roots (see LEGENDARY HISTORY).

Descriptions of the Otherworld focus upon its beauty, harmony, and abundance. Perhaps the last of these characteristics is accorded the most attention. The Otherworld is often described as a place where death and old age do not exist. More generally, time there moves differently from normal time. A short interval there may correspond to a long one here, or vice versa; or it may be summer in the *síd* when it is winter among humankind.

Another trait of the Otherworld is its elusiveness or invisibility. It is only through chance or supernatural favour, or some prophetic gift, that it is usually accessible. An exception is the night of SAMAIN 'Hallowe'en' (see CALENDAR). Many tales of supernatural contact open at dawn on BELTAINE (May Day), suggesting that this was another moment that bridged the worlds.

Besides serving as a venue for marvels and adventures, the Otherworld was seen as a source of authority. CONN CÉTCHATHACH's visit to an Otherworld hall legitimizes his own kingship and that of his successors. The poetic inspiration believed to exist in the waters of the Boyne (BÓAND) flowed from its hidden spring in the *síd* of Nechtan (see also FLOOD LEGENDS).

The Otherworld might be identified with faraway places such as China or the southern hemisphere. In such tales as TOCHMARC EMIRE ('The Wooing of Emer') and *Forfes Fer Fálchae* (The siege of the men of Fálchae), even BRITAIN and the Isle of Man (ELLAN VANNIN) take on Otherworldly attributes. In modern Gaelic folklore, these strands of tradition have been polarized into two distinct 'Otherworlds': (1) the dwellings of the FAIRIES, concretely linked with the actual landscape, and (2) an array of vague faraway regions ('the Great World', 'the Eastern World', 'Land Under Wave') that serve as settings for the fantastic adventures of the wonder tales.

Brythonic Tradition

The evidence for medieval Wales (CYMRU) is much more sparse than for Ireland. We do, however, have a Welsh term that seems to be straightforwardly translatable as 'Otherworld': Middle Welsh *Annwfn*, Modern Welsh ANNWN, variously interpreted by modern scholars to mean 'un-world', 'underworld', 'great world', and 'very deep'.

In the tale of PWYLL, Annwfn is portrayed as a kingdom with an unspecified spatial relationship to the mortal realm. Poems, however, refer to 'Annwfn beneath the earth'; this subterranean localization has probably contributed to an identification of Annwfn with the Christian hell. Other scattered references reflect concepts broadly similar to those attested in Ireland. In the persistent legends that King ARTHUR and various other national heroes have never died, these individuals are portrayed as sleeping in caves in readiness for their people's greatest need. Geoffrey of Monmouth gives an alternative account in his *Vita Merlini* ('Life of Merlin'; see MYRDDIN): Nine sisters take Arthur to an 'island of apples' (see AVALON) to be healed of his wounds after his last battle. Welsh folklore depicts the *tylwyth teg* ('fair folk') or fairies as living beneath hills and lakes, and on magical islands off the coast.

John Carey

OWAIN AB URIEN

Owain ab Urien was probably a historical north British chieftain (see also RHEGED; URIEN) who was active in the later 6th century, though he is not mentioned in any surviving contemporary manuscripts. His name derives from Latin *Eugenius*.

In *Historia Brittonum* §63, unnamed sons of Urbgen (i.e., Urien) are mentioned as bravely fighting the Angles of BRYNAICH. One of the CYNFEIRDD poems in LLYFR TALIESIN is an elegy for him (*Enaid Owain ab Urien*).

Owain ab Urien's grave is mentioned in *Englynion y Beddau* ('The Stanzas of the Graves') in the Black Book of Carmarthen (LLYFR DU CAERFYRDDIN). Scottish HAGIOGRAPHY includes several statements that Euuen son of Ulien (and a variety of similar spellings) was the father of St KENTIGERN, which is at least chronologically possible. He is repeatedly referenced in the TRIADS; for example, Owain and his twin sister Morfudd were one of the 'Three Fair Womb-Burdens'. Against this background, it is not surprising that Owain emerged as a major ARTHURIAN hero, notably as the protagonist of *Owain neu Iarlles y Ffynnon* (Owain or the Lady of the Fountain). For discussions on this tale and its close relationship to the corresponding 12th-century French narrative poem *Yvain*, see TAIR RHAMANT; ROMANCES; CHRÉTIEN DE TROYES. Owain also has a central rôle in the Arthurian dream tale BREUDDWYD RHONABWY.

John T. Koch

OWAIN GLYNDŴR

Owain Glyndŵr (Owain ap Gruffudd Fychan, Owen Glendower, *c.* 1354–*c.* 1416) was the last Welsh-recognized Welsh prince of Wales (CYMRU). He led the last major armed rebellion of the Welsh against the English and, viewed as a national redeemer even in his own time, has become a symbol of modern Welsh nationalism.

In 1400, Glyndŵr was proclaimed Prince of Wales, a position to which he had reasonable claim by virtue of descent from the kings of Powys and the royal line of Deheubarth. In the same year, he began a rebellion that was precipitated by a conflict with his neighbour Reginald Grey, lord of Rhuthun. Social and economic unrest had been growing in Wales since the death of Llywelyn ap Gruffudd in 1282 and the loss of independence. The hardships of English rule were further aggravated by changes in the economic system and by the plague. When Glyndŵr began his war, he was declared an outlaw, but increasing numbers of the Welsh joined him in what was essentially guerrilla warfare. The movement spread to the whole of the country. By 1405, having withstood several expeditions by Henry IV's forces and won important victories, Glyndŵr not only controlled Wales, but had pushed into ENGLAND, formed an alliance (the Tripartite Indenture) with Edmund Mortimer and the Percys of Northumberland, and set up diplomatic and military relations with

France and Scotland (ALBA). Glyndŵr established a parliament, which first met in Machynlleth in 1404 and which—together with his plans for an independent Welsh church and a university system (laid out in the Pennal letters to the King of France in 1406)—seemed to augur both a new golden age and the creation of a modern state. However, in 1406 the balance shifted; by 1409 the war was lost and by 1415 it was over. Events in the early part of the war were depicted by Shakespeare in *Henry IV, Part I*.

In the 19th century, with the rise of Welsh nationalism, Glyndŵr—along with others—was rehabilitated. His fight against English oppression, his war that almost won Welsh independence, and his threefold plan for a Welsh parliament, an independent church, and university turned him into a primary symbol of Welsh NATIONALISM in the 20th century. His name was invoked as a call to action in political speeches and protest songs and by groups such as Meibion Glyndŵr (Sons of Glyndŵr), who burned English-owned summer homes in Wales. In the 21st century and since the creation of the National Assembly for Wales (Cynulliad Cenedlaethol Cymru), he is invoked less as a rebel warrior and more as a model statesman whose threefold plan and links to France presaged Wales as a modern state and a member of the European Union.

Elissa R. Henken

OWAIN GWYNEDD

Owain Gwynedd or Owain ap Gruffudd (†1170) succeeded his father GRUFFUDD AP CYNAN (†1137) as king of the powerful independent kingdom of GWYNEDD in north Wales (CYMRU) and ruled over this dominion for 33 years. His elder brother Cadwallon had been killed in battle in 1132 and Owain, along with his younger brother Cadwaladr, were prominently engaged in warfare during their father's last years.

Despite the opportunity for armed intervention beyond his frontiers that civil war in ENGLAND during the reign of Stephen might appear to have offered, Owain withheld his troops from any incursion into POWYS—a circumspection that indicates his respect for the firm authority exercised there by Madog ap Maredudd. In 1149, however, he wrested the commote of Iâl from Madog, and incurred a combined retaliation on the part of Madog and Earl Ranulph the next year. Renewed conflict caused Henry II to mount a campaign in 1157. Owain was forced to withdraw and agree to terms by which he allowed his brother, by then exiled, to regain his estate within the kingdom of Gwynedd. The death of Madog ap Maredudd in 1160 enabled Owain to secure the districts of Penllyn and Edeirnion in north Wales. By 1165, with Rhys ap Gruffudd finally establishing his power over an extensive part of Deheubarth, Owain judged that it was an opportune time to launch a new offensive in northeast Wales. A major campaign by Henry II, first on the Chester frontier and then through Powys, came to grief, and thereupon Owain assumed leadership of an alliance of Welsh princes of unprecedented strength.

In these last years of his life, Owain, hitherto styled 'king of Gwynedd', assumed the title 'prince of the Welsh' (Latin *princeps Wallensium*)—a title that indicated his desire to transform the military alliance into a new Welsh political entity. Owain took steps toward a church independent of Canterbury and an alliance with France, indications of an incipient Principality of Wales; however, they were cut short by his death and the dynastic conflict that left Gwynedd itself deeply divided for a generation.

J. Beverley Smith

OWAIN LAWGOCH

Owain Lawgoch (Owain ap Thomas ap Rhodri, Yvain de Galles, *c.* 1330–78), a soldier and claimant as prince of Wales (CYMRU), was the great-great-grandson of Llywelyn Fawr (the Great) (LLYWELYN AB IORWERTH), the great-nephew of Llywelyn ap Gruffudd (the last English-recognized Welsh prince of Wales), and the last of the male line and heir to the court of ABERFFRAW. Twice he gathered forces to retake Wales: In 1369, his fleet was turned back by storms; in 1372, he reached Guernsey before being recalled by the French king, for whom he was a mercenary. Owain was assassinated in 1378 by John Lamb at the instigation of the English. According to Welsh legendry, Owain—like Arthur and OWAIN GLYNDŴR—is sleeping in a cave until the time is right for him to return and help the nation.

Elissa R. Henken

OWEN, DANIEL

Daniel Owen (1836–95) was the foremost Welsh novelist of the 19th century. Born and raised in Mold, Flintshire (Yr Wyddgrug, sir y Fflint), his childhood years were marked by poverty. His early literary efforts were in the realm of poetry.

During the following years, Owen began to preach; he enrolled as a ministerial student before returning to work as a tailor in Mold, where he eventually established his own business. His literary career did not begin in earnest until 1876, when a serious illness meant that he had to retire to a great extent from his many and varied social commitments. Owen published a series of sermons in the Calvinistic Methodists' monthly journal, *Y Drysorfa* (The treasury), in 1877 before venturing on his first work of fiction, 'Cymeriadau Ymhlith ein Cynulleidfaoedd' (Characters in our congregations). With its storyline worked around the election of chapel deacons and its depiction of the tensions and hypocrisies of contemporary religious life, its status as a forerunner of Owen's major works is very clear.

Upon receiving a favourable critical response to this work, Owen's career gathered speed. *Hunangofiant Rhys Lewis* (The autobiography of Rhys Lewis, 1885) used the autobiographical convention as a means of deploying Owen's own reminiscences and to convey some of the religious and social tensions of his times. This novel made its author a national hero, and many of its characters—Bob and Mary Lewis, Thomas Bartley and Wil Bryan, for instance—became icons within Welsh cultural life. The next novel, *Profedigaethau Enoc Huws* (The misfortunes of Enoc Huws, 1891), is arguably his crowning achievement. In it, Owen used the local lead-mining scandals as a potent symbol of the hypocrisy and humbug that he believed had permeated every strand of respectable Victorian Wales.

Robert Rhys

P

P-CELTIC AND Q-CELTIC

P-Celtic is a term used for a subgroup of the Celtic languages in which the Proto-Celtic consonant /k^w/ came to be pronounced [p]. Q-Celtic is the contrasting term for the subgroup in which this change did not occur. The word for 'son', for example, is found in Q-Celtic OGAM inscriptions as MAQQI (genitive sing.) and later as Old Irish *mac(c)*, modern *mac*, in the contrasting with *map* in Old Welsh and Old Breton, which were P-Celtic languages.

Although /k^w/ > [p] may seem like an unusual and distinctive change—since the sounds are not easily confused in English—*kw* is, in fact, phonetically similar to *p,* as both are voiceless stops. It is not an uncommon sound change in the languages of the world. As Proto-Celtic had generally lost Indo-European *p* in most positions, it effectively had a gap to be filled in its consonant system.

The individual P-Celtic languages are, of attestation, Lepontic, Gaulish (which shows some Q-Celtic archaic forms or dialect pockets), British (which gave rise to the Brythonic family), Galatian, and Pictish. There are two thoroughly Q-Celtic languages—Celtiberian and Goidelic—and traces of conserving Q-Celtic dialects in the predominantly P-Celtic Gaulish.

In earlier Celtic scholarship, 'Q-Celtic' was sometimes used as though it meant simply the same as Goidelic or Gaelic, so as to imply that all the Celtic languages retaining k^w—even the ancient Continental Celtic languages, Celtiberian and Gaulish—were closely related. However, since the Q-Celtic languages are defined not by innovating, but rather by keeping the original sound system—a non-event—this alone is not evidence to suppose that Goidelic shares any close links with those regions of Gaul where the Q-Celtic forms are found or with ancient Celtic Spain, even though the Q-Celtic language in Spain has misled some modern writers to see a confirmation of the story of the migration of Míl Espáine from Spain to Ireland (Ériu) as told in medieval Irish legendary history.

John T. Koch

PALLADIUS

Palladius is best known from the notice in the Chronicle of Prosper of Aquitaine for the year AD 431: 'Having been ordained by Pope Celestine, Palladius was sent as the first bishop to the Irish who believed in Christ'. It remains unclear whether these words mean that there were a significant number of Irish Christians before 431. Another text by Prosper written in 434 tells how Celestine had made the 'barbarian island'—meaning Ireland (Ériu)—Christian (see Christianity). Dáibhí Ó Cróinín has recently drawn attention to a notice of a young Palladius who, as a promising student of law, came to Rome from Poitou (Pictonia) in western Gaul in the period 417 × 424.

We have no direct evidence on the Roman or the Irish side as to what Palladius actually accomplished. From the 7th century to the present, Irish writers have been at pains to arrange the evidence so that Palladius would not impinge upon the claims for, and the traditions of, Ireland's other 'first bishop'—namely, St Patrick—while carefully avoiding outright refutation of papal authority as represented by Prosper. No universally acceptable solution to the problem of Ireland's two apostles has yet been found. One fundamental difficulty is that the writings of Patrick himself are apparently as ignorant of Palladius as Prosper was of Patrick. As Armagh (Ard Mhacha) gained influence over other Irish churches from the 7th century onward, it is likely that the Patrick story acquired the founding saints of those churches as junior associates; some of these missionaries may in fact have worked with Palladius, but some also with Patrick, and others with neither.

John T. Koch

PAN-CELTICISM

Pan-Celticism encompasses the various movements based on the idea of Celticism, the assumption that the affinity between the Celtic languages indicated common ethnic and historic origins between the Breton, Cornish, Irish, Manx, Scottish, and the Welsh, and might lead to a closer union between the modern peoples.

Introduction

Modern Pan-Celticism is closely bound up with the revival of the term 'Celt' and the rise of Celticism, Celtic Romanticism, and *Celtomanie* ('Celtomania') in the last quarter of the 18th century. Modern Pan-Celticism must be viewed in the context of 19th-century European Romantic nationalism.

Pan-Celticism, like other pan-national movements, flourished mainly before World War I. However, continued 20th-century efforts in this direction were possibly symptomatic of the (post-)modern search for a shared pre-modern identity in a world in which individuals felt increasingly alienated owing to industrialization, urbanization, and other aspects of modernity that undermined traditional community life.

The Rise of Pan-Celticism

During the second decade of the 19th century, antiquarian societies in Scotland (Alba), Wales (Cymru), and France began to exchange correspondence. Notes pointing out similarities between the Irish, the Scottish Highlanders (see Highlands), and the Bretons began to appear in their journals. What might be considered the first Pan-Celtic campaign was conducted by the Welshman Thomas Price (known as Carnhuanawc), who collected money for Le Gonidec's Breton translation of the Bible in the early 1820s (see Christianity). Impressed by the Breton culture and language, he composed a prize-winning essay on the early connections and the contemporary relationship between Brittany (BREIZH) and Wales for the 1823 Powys EISTEDDFOD. In addition, together with Lady Llanofer, Price became one of the organizers of Eisteddfodau'r Fenni, a series of Welsh cultural festivals held in Abergavenny, Monmouthshire (Y Fenni, sir Fynwy), between 1834 and 1854, thus beginning the tradition of linking practical cooperation and support for other 'Celts' with the Romantic paraphernalia and pageantry of the eisteddfod movement and GORSEDD BEIRDD YNYS PRYDAIN.

The Pan-Celtic Association (1900–10)

The Pan-Celtic Association, conceived at the national eisteddfodau of 1898 (Blaenau Ffestiniog) and 1899 (Cardiff) and founded in October 1900 at in BAILE ÁTHA CLIATH (Dublin), constitutes the high point and final development of 19th-century Romantic Pan-Celticism. For the first time, it united Celtic enthusiasts from all the Celtic countries, including members from Yn Cheshaght Ghailckagh (The Manx Society) and Cowethas Kelto-Kernuak (Celtic-Cornish Society), which represented the two smallest Celtic nations. Despite its short life, the Association established a precedent for permanent Pan-Celtic cooperation in education in the Celtic languages and publishing, and the maintenance or revival of indigenous music, dance, and customs. The practice of holding central congresses as focal points for enthusiasts in all the separate countries was adopted by all later organizations.

The organization's most important aspect, however, was its progressive and innovative attitude toward what are now called 'lesser-used languages'. It concerned itself not only with the fate of the Celtic languages, but also with other smaller or oppressed linguistic groups in Europe.

After World War II

The Celtic Congress was resurrected in Dublin in 1947 with the following aims: 'to perpetuate the culture, ideals and languages of the Celtic peoples, and to maintain an intellectual contact and close co-operation between the respective Celtic communities' (Belz, *Hor Yezh* 96.35). On the basis of this brief, it has concentrated since then on cultural matters in the widest sense. Its annual general meeting visits each Celtic country every six years. Conferences and occasional published proceedings since 1947 have tended to focus on particular themes, such as tourism, bilingualism, and the mass media.

The Celtic League (Since 1961)

The Celtic League, founded in 1961 under the presidency of the leader of Plaid Cymru (The Party of Wales) Gwynfor Evans, is a political organization espousing the view that 'the solution of the cultural and economic problems of the Celtic countries requires first self-government' (Thompson, *Recent Developments in the Celtic Countries* 101). The League has a branch in each of the Celtic countries, as well as an international branch and branches in ENGLAND, Nova Scotia (Canada), and the United States. It has increasingly paid attention to developments in the field of minority and women's rights in Europe and worldwide. This perspective has found expression in increasing numbers of resolutions and declarations made to the governments of member states of the European Union and to the Council of Europe.

Other Expressions of Pan-Celticism

The Pan-Celtic idea and current organizations have led to the emergence of a growing number of festivals and institutions, both social and academic. The best known, the annual Inter-Celtic music festivals, founded in 1971 and held at Killarney (Cill Airne) and Lorient (An Oriant), and the annual peripatetic Celtic Film and Television Festival, founded in 1979, have proved helpful for practitioners as well as enormously attractive to visitors.

Marion Löffler

PARNELL, CHARLES STEWART

Charles Stewart Parnell (1846–91), Member of Parliament and 'uncrowned king of Ireland', was the son of an Anglican landowner and an American mother. He was elected Home Rule MP to the United Kingdom Parliament for Meath (Contae na Mí) in 1875, and shortly thereafter became a key figure in the LAND AGITATION, becoming president of the Land League in 1879, which he replaced with the Irish National League in 1882. He was elected leader of the Irish Parliamentary Party in 1880.

Parnell's greatest political achievement was to convert Prime Minister Gladstone and the British Liberal Party to the cause of Irish Home Rule (see NATIONALISM).

Laurence M. Geary

PARTHOLÓN

Partholón (Modern Irish *Parthalán* or *Parthalón*) was, according to the Middle Irish LEBAR GABÁLA ÉRENN ('The Book of Invasions'), the leader of the second settlement of Ireland (ÉRIU) 300 years after Noah's Flood. There are also closely related traditions in texts predating *Lebar Gabála*: the 9th-century Welsh Latin *Historia Brittonum*, where his people figure as Ireland's first settlers, and the Old Irish *Scél Tuáin meic Cairill* ('The Tale of Tuáin son of Cairell'), where Partholón is described as a Greek. The sources agree that his followers died out completely in a plague. According to *Lebar Gabála*, the Partholonians had their main settlement at what is now BAILE ÁTHA CLIATH (Dublin). Later sources describe Partholón as the 'chief of every craft', which suggests identification with LUG Samildánach (the all-skilled), the main deity of the TUATH DÉ. Partholón's name is probably derived from the biblical Bartholomaeus; as an Irish name beginning with *P-*, it cannot be native, but rather may be an early medieval learned invention.

Simon Ó Faoláin

PATAGONIA

Y Wladfa, the Welsh settlement in Chubut, Argentina, is the only place where the WELSH LANGUAGE has greater currency than English.

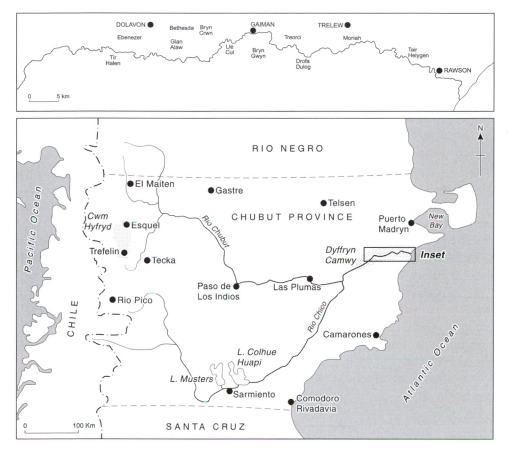

(Map by Ian Gulley and Antony Smith)

The idea of directing organized emigration from Wales (CYMRU) to a specific location to establish a strong community that could withstand the pressures of acculturation was supported by Michael D. Jones (1822–98), later Principal of the Congregational Theological College at Bala, who had experienced rapid linguistic and cultural shift while serving as a pastor in Cincinnati, Ohio, United States (see CELTIC LANGUAGES IN NORTH AMERICA). The subsequent Welsh Colony Movement finally decided on Patagonia as the venue for its 'New Wales', mainly because of an abundance of land and the isolation of the region from the nearest European settlement in the province of Buenos Aires.

In total, 153 Welsh people landed at New Bay on 28 July 1865. The first years were gruelling: Crops failed and by 1867 the population had dwindled to 116 members. The Argentine government offered to resettle these indiviudals elsewhere, but their leaders persuaded them that they would not survive as an independent colony. The idea of a Welsh-speaking colony was still central to the venture, and by the 1890s the colony had become a vibrant success. The Welsh had constructed an effective irrigation system for the Chubut valley and the Irrigation Company was worth an estimated £180,000, a phenomenal sum at the time. Out of desert and chaos the Welsh settlers created fields, gardens, and orchards. They built farms, towns, chapels, roads, and a railway system. They organized an effective local government system in which business was conducted entirely through the medium of Welsh. A Welsh-medium education system was created and was overseen by a school board.

Pressures on the communities to Hispanicize were introduced in 1896 when the Argentine government took over the schools, and a monolingual Spanish policy was rigorously implemented. By the 1930s and 1940s, this policy was bearing fruit in so far as it fostered negative attitudes among the children toward all things Welsh. They were taught that Spanish was the 'national language' and the medium of economic, educational, and social success, whereas Welsh was an impediment to progress.

After 1912, immigration from Wales ceased and contact with Wales along with it until 1965, the centenary year. By the 1970s, most remaining Welsh speakers were older than 40 years of age, and younger people denied any knowledge of the language. Furthermore, Welsh was becoming a restricted language, used only in a finite set of social situations. Since the 1980s, however, attitudes have progressively changed. Cymdeithas Cymru–Ariannin (the Wales–Argentina Society) was instrumental in sending several pastors to minister in Welsh, which in turn led to a call for tutors to teach Welsh. These voluntary tutors have helped rekindle a sense of Welsh identity among the younger generation, and the Welsh language is experiencing a revival.

Robert Owen Jones

PATRICK, ST

St Patrick is currently the most internationally famous of the saints venerated in the CELTIC COUNTRIES. He has been known for many centuries as the patron saint and apostle of Ireland (ÉIRE). There are also significant early dedications and traditions related to St Patrick in the other GAELIC lands (Scotland/ALBA and the Isle of Man/ ELLAN VANNIN) and beyond. St Patrick and the day commemorating his death (17 March) have become icons of Irish identity in the post-FAMINE era of the great diaspora to industrial Britain and the New World.

Patrick is one of the important founders of the Irish church in the 5th century and the starting point of literature in Ireland. Within the medieval Irish literary tradition, beginning in the later 7th century, Patrick is prominent in HAGIOGRAPHY, but also figures in virtually every genre of Irish literature. He is presented as providing divine validation to a great corpus of native law texts. Patrick was also drawn, with ingenious anachronism, into the two great cycles of pre-Christian heroes—into the ULSTER CYCLE by conjuring up the damned soul of CÚ CHULAINN in *Siabarcharpat Con Culainn* ('The Phantom Chariot of Cú Chulainn') and into the FIANNAÍOCHT. His traditional connections with the primatial see of Armagh (ARD MHACHA) confirmed its supremacy (see ÉRIU) up to modern times.

Patrick's Writings and His Life

Two short books in Latin are now generally regarded as Patrick's authentic works. The *Confessio* is autobiographical and tells of his background as a third-generation Christian from a well-to-do family in BRITAIN. Patrick's education was interrupted by Irish slave raiders, who abducted him at age sixteen, along with many others. Six years of slavery in Ireland followed. While tending livestock in isolation and hardship, Patrick found faith. A voice directed him to escape, to travel a great distance for a ship to take him home. He was eventually reunited

The story of Saint Patrick's Purgatory circulated widely in medieval Europe. This image of St Patrick sleeping is from a 13th-century illuminated manuscript in the British Library, Royal 20 D.VII fo. 213v. (The British Library/StockphotoPro)

with his family in Britain. In a key turning point, Patrick had a vivid dream in which a man named Victoricius appeared, bearing innumerable letters. If this is a historical person, it might be Victricius, bishop of Rouen (Rotomagus), who visited Britain in the 390s. On one of the letters, Patrick could read 'the voice of the Irish'; he then saw the place where he had been and heard the Irish people calling to him as with one voice. Thus inspired, he returned to Ireland as a missionary bishop, travelling widely and converting many. The *Confessio* shows a streak of apocalyptism: Patrick believed he was carrying the Word of God to the end of the world in the last days.

Patrick's other work is his 'Letter to the Soldiers of Coroticus' (*Epistola AD milites Corotici*), a response to a crisis in which the chieftain and his war-band had killed several of Patrick's recent Irish converts, abducted the Christian women, and sold them into slavery among the PICTS. Patrick expresses his outrage and excommunicates the raiders, who were thus evidently (nominal) Christians.

The Problem of St Patrick

The ANNALS, hagiography, and other branches of Irish literature from the 7th century onward supply Patrick with dates, contemporaries, numerous foundations, and miraculous deeds. Most of what the later sources claimed was not history, however, but rather served contemporary political motives. Information supplied by the hagiographers was often fanciful, and at worst the willful distortion of any facts that might detract from the reputation of their hero. For example, one great embarrassment was that, according to the papacy, Ireland's first bishop had been Palladius in AD 431. Although Patrick's works do not specifically claim he was the first bishop in Ireland or that there were no Christians there before his mission, propagandists of Patrick and of Armagh's supremacy naturally assumed this from the *Confessio*. The solution to 'who was the first bishop in Ireland?' embodied in Muirchú's late 7th-century *Vita Patricii* is to have Palladius martyred on arrival and Patrick to follow immediately as Palladius's double and virtual first bishop of Ireland. Due to this tradition, we have two sets of dates for Patrick in the annals. In one—compatible with Patrick shadowing Palladius—he dies about 462. In the other, he dies about 493. It is the earlier obit (death date) that looks like a secondary invention, and today most scholars find the later obit more credible. There is also a third solution: Patrick may have preceded Palladius, but the church in Rome was either unaware of his mission or did not regard him as a legitimate bishop. In favour of the early chronology is Patrick's very Romanized view of Britain, along with the negative evidence that Patrick neither mentions nor implies that any of the great 5th-century events had occurred: the end of Roman Britain in 409/10, the ANGLO-SAXON 'CONQUEST', or the theological movement of Pelagius and its condemnation.

A Few Important Texts about Patrick

The earlier and more important sources include Latin texts preserved in the early 9th-century manuscript, the BOOK OF ARMAGH: Tírechán's *Collectanea* (Account of St Patrick's churches) of *c*. 670, Muirchú moccu Macthéni's *Vita Patricii* of *c*. 690, and *Liber Angeli* (The book of the angel). Muirchú's Life is noteworthy in that it introduces elements that became recurrent features of the Patrick story, but had no basis in Patrick's own writings: his four names for Patrick (Patricius, Cothirche/Cothraige/Cothirthiacus, Succat, and Mauonius), his service in slavery to a druid named Miliucc, his sojourn in Gaul, his celebration of Easter near Tara (TEAMHAIR) and confrontation with the king's DRUIDS, and, most importantly, the founding of Armagh. The four subsequent Latin Lives date between the late 8th and late 11th centuries. The vernacular *Bethu Phátraic*, also known as 'The Tripartite Life of Patrick', was produced in Munster (MUMU) in the period 895 × 901. *Bethu Phátraic* also identifies Patrick as being of the Britons Dumbarton (see YSTRAD CLUD), an idea that probably developed from the identification—already found in the Book of Armagh and probably correct—of Coroticus with Ceretic Guletic of Dumbarton.

John T. Koch

PELAGIUS

Pelagius (*c*. AD 350–*c*. 425, active *c*. 400–418) was a theologian who became the central figure in a major controversy of CHRISTIANITY during the first decades of the 5th century. Pelagianism continued openly in Britain and parts of GAUL into the 430s at least, and the writings of Pelagius were copied and correctly attributed to him by Brythonic and Irish scholars in the 7th and 8th centuries. The essence of Pelagian theology was that human beings had complete free will; that they had not inherited the sin of Adam; that death was part of human nature and not God's punishment; and that infants had no original sin and, therefore, infant baptism was pointless. Augustine of Hippo (†430) held beliefs in original sin and the necessity of God's Grace for salvation, which won out as orthodoxy.

Most modern writers regard Pelagius as Romano-British, though he had resided in Rome for many years before coming to prominence during the first decade of the 5th century. GILDAS, probably writing in the 6th century, quotes a Pelagian text, which had presumably survived in Britain.

John T. Koch

PENTREATH, DOLLY

Dolly Pentreath (1692–1777) is often mistakenly referred to as the last speaker of CORNISH. Her reputation grew out of a visit made to Mousehole in 1768 by the English antiquary Daines Barrington, who had travelled to Cornwall (KERNOW) to see whether anyone still spoke the native language. Whether she spoke Cornish as her first language is still open to debate, as is her degree of bilingualism.

Numerous Cornish speakers have been recorded since Pentreath's death, including William Bodinar, a Truro engineer named Thompson, John Nancarrow (who travelled to Philadelphia in 1804), W. J. Rawlings, John Davey, Jane Barnicoat, Ann Wallis, John Tremethack, Mrs Kelynack, Betsey Matthews, and a St Ives policeman called Botheras. Traditional fragments and phrases of the language continued into the 20th century. Recently, many scholars have begun to view the centenary of Pentreath's death in 1877 as the initial impetus for the modern Cornish revival (see LANGUAGE [REVIVAL] MOVEMENTS IN THE CELTIC COUNTRIES).

Alan M. Kent

PEREDUR FAB EFRAWG

Peredur fab Efrawg is the naive or uncouth protagonist and namesake of one of the TAIR RHAMANT (three Romances), 12th- or 13th-century French-influenced Welsh ARTHURIAN tales.

There is no Peredur in the lists of heroes in the earliest Arthurian tale, CULHWCH AC OLWEN. A historical Peredur who died in 580 is known as one of the victorious chieftains at the battle of ARFDERYDD (573). In the GENEALOGIES, this Peredur is the son of Eliffer (OW Eleuthur) and, therefore, a first cousin of URIEN RHEGED. Eliffer is distinct from the Arthurian hero's father Efrawg. *Efrawg* (modern *Efrog*), however, is better known in Welsh as the name of a place—York, Romano-British *Eburācum*—rather than as a man's name; it is therefore possible that the historical Peredur's connection to York was misunderstood as his father's name. As Peredur fab Efrawg does not appear in ARTHURIAN LITERATURE before the Three Romances, it is likely that the name was adopted as the closest approximation within the existing stock of traditional Welsh heroes to *Perceval* and/or *Perlesvaus*, the name of the figure in the French Arthurian Romance that probably inspired the Welsh tale.

John T. Koch

PICTISH KING-LIST

The 'Pictish king-list' is the only non-epigraphic text to survive from Pictland. Extant only in corrupt form in much later manuscripts (the 14th century at the earliest), it lists each king in chronological order, noting his father's name and the length of his reign. Despite its limited form, it provides unique evidence for the nature of Pictish historical writing in the 8th and 9th centuries. Some of the names in this Latin text are precious witnesses to Pictish language and orthography. Internal evidence suggests the list might have been begun as early as the 660s, and it appears to have been maintained as a contemporary record until the reign of Cusantín mac Cinaeda (Constantine son of Kenneth, 862–c. 876). Many of the kings listed are historical figures known from non-Pictish sources, such the ANNALS of Ulster, but others are legendary (e.g., Drust son of Erp 'who reigned a hundred years and fought a hundred battles') or perhaps mere names. The 'prehistoric' section listing the 'thirty Brudes' in the form 'Y; before Y, X' may reflect an oral genealogy.

Katherine Forsyth

PICTISH LANGUAGE AND DOCUMENTS

The Pictish Language

Place-name evidence points overwhelmingly to Pictish being a Brythonic language. Were it not for Bede's statement that Pictish and British were separate languages, the use of elements such as *aber-* 'river mouth', *lanerc* 'grove' (Welsh *llannerch*), *pert* 'bush' (Welsh *perth*), and *tref* 'town' would suggest merely dialectal distinction north and south of the river Forth (Foirthe); there is also first-century evidence for Celtic river names such as *Tava* (Tatha [Tay]) 'silent one', and *Dēva* (Dè [Dee]) and *Dēvona* (Deathan [Don]), both meaning 'goddess'. Cognates in Welsh, Cornish, and Breton are found for the names of historically attested Picts, such as Taran (Welsh *taran* 'thunder'), Onuist (OW *Unust*), Naiton (OW *Neithon*), Drosten (OW *Dristan*), Uurguist (OW *Gurgust*), Uoret (OW *Guoret*), and Alpin (Welsh *Elffin*). Their Roman-period ancestors have unmistakably Celtic names, such as Calgācus ('swordsman'), Vepogenus, and Argentocoxus ('silver leg', a name that recalls the epithet 'Silver-Hand' of the Irish mythological figure Nuadu Argatlám; see NŌDONS).

Apparent Disparities Distinguishing Pictish and Brythonic:

1. There is a dearth of examples showing Pictish turning the voiceless geminate (long or double) stop consonants [*pp, tt, kk*] into simplex spirants [f, θ, χ] as in Welsh, Breton, and Cornish; it seems to have treated them more or less as Irish did. Pictish apparently did not lenite (soften) voiced stops (*b, d, g*) preceded by liquids (*r* and *l*).

2. British $\bar{o}$ (< *eu, ou*) became $\bar{u}$, while in Pictish older *ou* remained $\bar{o}$: e.g., *mons Okhél* (Latin Life of St Serf) corresponding to W *uchel*, MBret. *uhel*, Old Cornish *huhel*, Romano-British *Uxel(l)la*, *Uxellon*, OIr. *úasal* < Celtic **oukselo-*. Proto-Celtic *o* seems to have had different outcomes between British and Pictish in several other contexts, though the seeming divergence may come from distinct Pictish spelling conventions.

3. There is no positive evidence that Brythonic (as opposed to Pictish) ever had *s-*+ nasal. Ptolemy's *Smertae* were situated inland, north of the Moray Firth (*Geography* 2.3). The present-day *Carn Smeart* is more or less precisely in the centre of this territory.

4. One comparatively late innovation is shared by Pictish and Brythonic. The toponymic element *monid* 'mountain', found in several early sources and borrowed as ScG *monadh*, is the cognate of OBret. *monid*, OW *minid*, Cornish *meneth*, Late British *monedo-*, < British **monijo-*.

Pictish Literature?

A Pictish orthography was in use for recording proper names in Latin texts (see Pictish king-list), but if it was ever employed for extended texts in the vernacular these have not survived. Attempts to trawl Scottish literature for faint echoes of genuine Pictish tradition have ranged from the fancifully far-fetched to the plausible but inconclusive. Picts feature in Modern Gaelic folk tradition, but the motifs, of diminutive red-haired people living underground, and the very form of the word used (*Piocaich*) betray the ultimately learned origin of such stories. Figures from Pictland turn up in medieval Welsh and Irish literature (Caw the giant in traditions of the ancestry of St Gildas, Frigriu the craftsman, Llifiau son of Cian in the Gododdin), and among the titles in surviving Irish tale lists, some take place in Pictland, such as *Braflang Scóine* and *Orgain Bene Cé*.

Pictish Symbols

The highly stereotyped curvilinear designs of the Pictish symbols are as unique as they are enigmatic. Their chronological and archaeological distribution throughout northern and eastern Scotland tallies with what is known about the extent of Pictish territory. Despite numerous attempts to crack the code, the meaning of the symbols remains obscure. They reflect a strongly independent Pictish attitude to literacy.

More than thirty individual symbols are known, predominantly geometric designs, with a few naturalistic animals. Among the former there are recognizable mirrors, combs, tongs, and perhaps weapons. The view that the remainder are further, more schematized, representations of everyday objects is widely held, but it is at least as likely that the designs are purely abstract. Symbols almost always occur in combination with one or more other symbols, such combinations apparently governed by a strict syntax. The symbol system is attested in use from as early as the 5th century AD until as late as the 9th century. The bulk of the more than two hundred extant symbol statements are carved on public stone monuments, including undressed pillars and richly carved cross-slabs, but they are also found, for instance, on deluxe metalwork and as cave graffiti. Their usage has many formal parallels with the contemporary use of OGAM. The wide variety of contexts in which symbol statements appear suggests the system was of general application, while its longevity implies its continued usefulness.

Katherine Forsyth

PICTS

Ethnography and Group Names

The Picts were one of three Celtic-speaking peoples inhabiting Scotland (ALBA) in the early medieval period. Descendants of Tacitus's 'Caledonian Britons', they occupied the country north of a line running between the Forth (Foirthe) and the Clyde (Cluaidh), including Orkney (Arcaibh) and probably Shetland (Sealtainn) and the Western Isles (Na h-Eileanan an Iar). The Welsh and Irish names for the Picts were *Prydyn* and Cruithin, respectively, both ultimately from **Pritenī* (cf. **Pritanī*, Romano-Celtic *Britanni*, *Brittones* 'the Britons'). These names support the notion that the Picts were once perceived as part of a British or Brythonic cultural continuum that stretched from the English Channel to the Northern Isles. Whether through the intervention of the Romans in the 1st century or later groups, by the early 8th century the Forth had become an important ethnic boundary with, according to Bede, Britons to the south and Picts to the north.

The Gaelicization of Pictland

From at least the 5th century, the Picts were under political and linguistic pressure from the Gaels of DÁL RIATA. The history of the following centuries reflects the complex ebb and flow of their relative dynastic fortunes. By the mid-9th century, however, the Gaels had succeeded in monopolizing Pictish kingship (see CINAED MAC AILPÍN). The violent political eclipse of the Picts was accompanied by cultural and linguistic decline, already well under way in the 9th century and complete by the 12th century.

Pictish Survival

We now know that the disappearance of the Picts was not as total as it once appeared. The medieval Gaelic kingdom of Alba is seen to be founded on the old political geography of Pictish power. A Pictish institutional legacy is also apparent in the post-9th-century kingdom—for instance, in the development of the office of *mormaer* 'earl' (itself a Pictish term meaning 'great officer') and the comprehensive system of land management reflected in roughly 300 modern place-names commencing with the element *Pit(t)-* or *Pet(t)-* (cf. Welsh *peth* 'thing, some of'). The extent of the impact of the Pictish language on Modern Scottish Gaelic is far from trivial. Vocabulary identified as borrowed from Pictish is almost exclusively toponymic in origin, such as the common nouns *dail* 'field', *monadh* 'mountain', *pòr* 'pasture', and *preas* 'bush'—compare Welsh *dôl*, *mynydd*, *porfa*, and *prys,* respectively. Perhaps more significant is the influence of Pictish on Gaelic syntax. It has long been recognized that the verbal

Relief of a Pict with hooded cloak and Pictish trousers, St. Vigeans, Scotland, 8th or 9th century AD. (C. M. Dixon/StockphotoPro)

system of Scottish Gaelic, and certain aspects of its nominal system, represent the Old Irish inheritance brought almost completely in line with modern spoken Welsh.

Recent historians have begun to recognize the politically necessary but untrue account of genocide for what it is: the entirely successful attempt of the Gaelic ascendancy to present their triumph as inevitable and divinely sanctioned, and the extermination of the Picts as just retribution for past wickedness. The material culture of the Pictish church implies the existence of scriptural, liturgical, and other manuscripts, and this is confirmed by references to the use of such texts by Picts in contemporary Irish and Anglo-Saxon sources. The handful of Roman alphabet inscriptions from Pictland hint at the level of skill in Pictish scriptoria, though none of these manuscripts have survived. That OGAM was the preferred monumental script of the Picts reflects the unique prestige it enjoyed in 8th- and 9th-century Pictland.

A Pictish orthography was in use for recording proper names in Latin texts, but if it was ever employed for extended texts in the vernacular these have not survived. Perhaps the most remarkable aspect of the Pictish sculptural tradition is the wealth of the secular imagery featured on the cross-slabs alongside the more familiar scriptural themes. Some scenes seem to echo episodes or motifs in other Celtic literatures—for example, what appears to be a 'cauldron of rebirth' (see CAULDRONS). Behind the clashing warriors, fearsome giants, dog- and bird-headed men, and the rest, there probably lie long-lost Pictish narratives.

Katherine Forsyth

PIRAN, ST

St Piran is popularly regarded as the patron saint of Cornwall (Kernow), though documented claims to this dignity have also been made on behalf of St Michael and St Petroc. Piran probably acquired his special status in Cornwall given that he is the patron saint of tinners. His standard, which has been adopted as the Cornish flag, is a white vertical cross on a black background.

The traditional biography of Piran is based on that of a 14th-century Life of the Irish St Ciarán of Saighir and the observations of Nicholas Roscarrock. It is not impossible that *Ciarán* and *Piran* ultimately derive from the same name. Piran was reputedly born in Ireland (Ériu), where he performed many miraculous deeds. Jealous of his power, the Irish kings took him to a high cliff, chained him to a millstone, and threw him into the sea. According to his HAGIOGRAPHY, Piran landed on the beach at Perranporth, where he built a small church in the sand dunes and preached, with his first converts being a fox, a badger, and a bear. Piran discovered tin while he was cooking over an open fire and noticed a stream of white metal pouring out of the stone. Piran and St Chewidden were responsible for showing local people how to extract and process tin. Piran lived to be 206 years old, dying in a state of inebriation, with no signs of old age. Roscarrock reports that King Arthur made Piran archbishop of York.

Amy Hale

POWYS

Powys emerged as an independent Welsh kingdom during the post-Roman period; it reappeared as a county in the 1974 reorganization with the amalgamation of three shires created at the time of the 1536 Act of Union: Trefaldwyn (Montgomeryshire), Maesyfed (Radnorshire), and Brycheiniog (Breconshire). The modern county thus extends farther to the south than the historically attested kingdom.

The name *Powys* derives from Latin *pāgēnses* 'people of the rural districts', suggesting formation in the Roman or early post-Roman period and also implying an original relationship with a town, such as Wroxeter (Viroconium Cornoviorum) or Chester (Welsh Caer, Romano-British Deva). With the building of Offa's Dyke (Clawdd Offa) during the later 8th century, Anglo-Saxon Mercia defined the eastern frontier of Powys. The kingdom is mentioned in several 9th-century Welsh texts—*Historia Brittonum*, Eliseg's Pillar, and *Annales Cambriae* (822, 854). In 822, Powys was overrun by the Mercians, but it regained its independence later, as shown by the Eliseg inscription and the ANNAL entry for 854, which reports that King Cyngen died at Rome, having fled the invasion of Powys by the kings of Gwynedd. In 942, Powys was conquered by Hywel Dda. It frequently changed hands during the following centuries—sometimes being part of Gwynedd, sometimes part of Deheubarth, and sometimes independent or fragmented. During the 12th century, Powys again became independent under Madog ap Maredudd, whose court was the centre of a thriving cultural life. Many of the GOGYNFEIRDD of that period were active at the court of Powys. The political centre of Powys at this period was Mathrafal and its religious centre was nearby at Meifod. The politics of 12th-century Powys provide the background of the ARTHURIAN tale BREUDDWYD RHONABWY (Rhonabwy's dream). After Madog's death, the country was ruled by his sons until it was conquered again by the princes of Gwynedd in the 13th century and became part of the Principality of Wales in 1282 following the death of Llywelyn ap Gruffudd.

Modern Powys is geographically the largest electoral county of Wales. It is mostly rural, with little heavy industry, and most heavily Welsh-speaking in the north (the old Montgomeryshire) and the Upper Swansea Valley (Cwm Tawe Uchaf) in the extreme southwest; these areas use two distinct dialects. Major towns include Brecon (Aberhonddu), the home of the annual jazz festival; Builth Wells (Llanfair-ym-Muallt), near the site of the annual Royal Welsh Show; Hay-on-Wye (Y Gelli Gandryll), the site of the annual literary festival; Llandrindod Wells; Llanidloes; Machynlleth; Newtown (Y Drenewydd); Rhayader (Rhaeadr Gwy); and Welshpool (Y Trallwng). The Brecon Beacons National Park (Bannau Brycheiniog) is in the south of the county.

Peter E. Busse and John T. Koch

PRE-CELTIC PEOPLES, PRE-CELTIC SUBSTRATA

Linguistically, 'pre-Celtic' refers to the languages and speakers of those languages which preceded Celtic in the territories where CELTIC LANGUAGES are historically attested. Because the Celtic languages expanded on the threshold of the historical period, they are generally the first language family known in the areas where they appear.

Insular Celtic words that lack any corresponding words in other Indo-European languages—and these make up a fairly high proportion of the attested vocabularies—may reflect ancient borrowings from the aboriginal pre-Celtic languages of Britain and Ireland and/or the pre-Celtic mainland.

Since Celtic speech was established in Britain and Ireland (ÉRIU) by some level of influence from the outside other than extermination of the indigenous population, we must envision a process of bilingualism and language shift. We may think of British and Primitive Irish, as distinct from the parent Common Celtic, coming into being when pre-Celtic aboriginals learned the language of west-central Europe for purposes of trade and/or to enter the society of warlike overlords. Thus the separate Insular Celtic dialects might have come into being more or less immediately with the arrival of Celtic speech in much the same way as the distinctive Hiberno-English or West Indian patois is distinguished by features that originated as substratum interference during the stage of bilingualism.

Some proposed examples of pre-Celtic substratum effects are as follows: (1) phonetic lenition (consonant weakening)—for example, in the development of Proto-Celtic *esio tegos 'his house' to Irish *a theach*, Welsh *ei dŷ*, the consonants have moved toward an articulation more like that of the flanking vowels, in some instances to the point of disappearing; (2) the powerful stress and consequent syllable losses (apocope and syncope)—for example, Proto-Celtic *Cunovalos* developed a strong stress on the first and third syllables, accounting for the dropping of the second and fourth to give Irish *Conall* and Welsh *Cynwal*; and (3) strongly verb–subject–object and noun–adjective word order.

As to which languages might have been spoken in Europe's Atlantic northwest before Celtic, it seems likely that ancestors of Finnish and Basque and the languages of the Caucasus were more extensive before the spread of Indo-European. It is also possible that illiterate ancient Europe contained languages that have disappeared, as have the attested non-Indo-European Iberian, Etruscan, and Minoan. The strongest case so far—though not widely accepted—has been that Celtic was preceded in Britain and Ireland by a language or languages akin to the Afro-Asiatic languages of north Africa and the Middle East.

John T. Koch

PREIDDIAU ANNWFN

Preiddiau Annwfn (Spoils of the OTHERWORLD/Spoils of ANNWN) is an early Welsh ARTHURIAN poem in the *awdl* metre. The unique pre-modern copy survives in the 14th-century manuscript LLYFR TALIESIN (54.16–56.13). The title is written as *Preideu Annwn* in a later hand in the margin and also occurs meaningfully as *preideu Annwfyn* in the first stanza. The poem's contents are recognized to be of significance, as they include early references to several characters, episodes, and themes that find full expression later in medieval Welsh tales and ARTHURIAN LITERATURE. The recurrent central theme is a sea-borne raid on otherworldly strongholds—or perhaps one stronghold called by various names—by Arthur and his unnamed heroes. Characteristic of early Welsh poetry, we are not given narrative per se, but rather allusions to tales and adventures, presumably known in fuller detail and context to the poet and his audience. Thus a mention of 'the tale of Pwyll and Pryderi' in the context of an otherworldly imprisonment (cf. MABON) refers to a tradition closely akin to what survives in the Mabinogi. 'The chieftain of the Otherworld' possesses a wondrous pearl-rimmed cauldron, a treasure comparable to the cauldrons of the quests of CULHWCH AC OLWEN and *Branwen*.

In the last two stanzas, monks are ridiculed for their ignorance regarding natural science and particularly regarding the facts of the separation of day and night and the CALENDAR. The speaker of the poem therefore appears to be the Taliesin persona vaunting his own special knowledge in these areas as superior to that of the adepts of Christian book learning.

John T. Koch

PRINCIPALITY OF WALES

The Principality of Wales had its origins in the political processes by which LLYWELYN AB IORWERTH (†1240) endeavoured to bring the princes of Wales (CYMRU) under his authority in a *principatus* ('principality') that he would hold as a dependency of the Crown of ENGLAND. His proposals were never countenanced by the king, but his objectives were pursued by Llywelyn ap Gruffudd (†1282), who brought the princes into his fealty and assumed the style 'prince of Wales'. In the treaty of

Montgomery (1267), Henry III formally granted Llywelyn and his heirs the principality of Wales with the title 'prince of Wales', the key clause in the agreement being the grant to Llywelyn of the homage and fealty of the Welsh lords of Wales. Princedom and principality lapsed upon his death, but in 1301 Edward I granted his son Edward of Caernarfon the earldom of Chester (Welsh Caer) and the Crown lands in Wales; though unmentioned in the charter, the principality of Wales and the title 'prince of Wales' were also conferred upon the heir to the throne.

The royal lands in Wales continued to form the separate administrations of the principality of North Wales and the principality of West Wales (later South Wales), centred at Caernarfon and Carmarthen (Caerfyrddin), respectively. The princedom was revived in 1343 for Edward the Black Prince, son of Edward III, with the grant of the principality, and the creation was marked by an investiture. Thereafter, the principality of Wales was conferred upon the king's eldest son by investiture. From the ACTS OF UNION of 1536–43, the term 'principality of Wales' described the twelve counties of Wales (Monmouthshire/sir Fynwy excluded), and until 1830 the Courts of Great Sessions established by the Union legislation gave the principality a jurisdiction separate from that of the Westminster courts.

J. Beverley Smith

PRINTING, EARLY HISTORY IN THE CELTIC LANGUAGES

Introduction

With the exception of Breton, printing in the CELTIC LANGUAGES is rare before the second half of the 16th century. Before the 18th century, both oral and manuscript transmission were still of paramount importance to the Celtic languages. Printing in the Celtic languages, however, was immensely important for linguistic survival through the establishment of standard written forms and orthography, the wider dissemination of texts, and the promotion of vernacular literacy.

During the print revolution of late 15th-century Europe, ENGLAND was relatively slow to adopt the new technology, and when it did sought to limit printing to approved centres of production, mainly in southeast England. Together with a continuing lack of economic power, this attempt at royal monopoly was sufficient to ensure that the Celtic countries retained their traditional methods of book production even after the first Celtic-language publications began to appear.

Breton

Some eight million incunabula (books printed before 1500) were printed throughout Europe, but of the CELTIC COUNTRIES only Brittany possesses incunabula. *Le tréspassment de la vierge* was published in 1485, and a Breton edition of the *Catholicon*—a triple dictionary in Latin, French, and Breton—was first printed in 1499. A further five books containing Breton were printed in Brittany in the 16th century, with some twenty titles appearing before 1800.

Welsh

Before 1695, when the Licensing Act that had confined most printing in Britain and Ireland to London finally lapsed, printing in the Celtic languages was not always synonymous with printing in the Celtic countries. The most substantial amount of early Celtic-language printing was in Welsh, though commercial printing in Wales did not begin until the early 18th century. The first book in Welsh, *Yny lhyvyr hwnn* (In this book, 1546), was produced in London, where a group of Welsh humanist scholars including William Salesbury (*c.* 1520–74) produced about 30 Welsh books before 1600, including a Welsh–English dictionary, a Welsh grammar, editions of medieval texts, and a Welsh Bible. Several presses were established in Wales after 1718. By the end of the hand-press era in the early 19th century, some 6,000 titles had been printed in Welsh, substantially more than in all the other Celtic languages.

Cornish and Manx

There was no Cornish in print until the early 18th century; by contrast, the Isle of Man (Ellan Vannin) still had a population of largely monoglot Manx speakers when *Coyrle Sodjeh or Principles and Duties of Christianity* was printed in London, in English and Manx, in 1707. Printing on the island was established in the 18th century in Douglas and Ramsey, but many Manx books were still printed in England.

Irish

An Irish alphabet and catechism appeared in 1571. Printing in Ireland, as in England, was controlled by the English monarchy; in Ireland, the King's Printer's patent was granted to only one printer in Dublin, which limited the range and amount of printing in Ireland until the 18th century.

Scottish Gaelic

Scotland had strong early links with the book trade. Before 1500 there were universities founded at St Andrews, Glasgow (Glaschu), and Aberdeen (Obar Dheathain), and an established trade in bookbinding is attested in the early 15th century. In 1567, *Foirm na n-Urrnuidheadh,* The Book of Common Order, was printed in Edinburgh (Dùn Èideann) in Roman type, the first printed book in Scottish Gaelic. Nothing more was printed in Gaelic until the 17th century.

Geraint Evans

PROPHECY

Prophecy is a formal verbal expression foretelling the future, not necessarily requiring and rituals of divination. Prophecy is a pervasive feature of all the traditional Celtic cultures and their literatures, though hardly unique to the Celtic countries; the main proof that specific features of prophecy were inherited from the Proto-Celtic period is shared vocabulary. For instance, the word 'druid' and its cognates designate a social figure whose functions prominently include prophecy. Similarly, *vātes* 'seers' of ancient

GAUL were prophets, and their name is cognate with Old Irish *fáth* 'prophecy', *fáith* 'prophet', and Welsh *gwawd*, which, in medieval times, meant 'inspired verse, song of praise'. The Early Irish compound verb *do-airchain* 'prophesies' corresponds to Welsh *darogan* < **to-are-wo-kan-* and more loosely to Breton *diougan* < **dī-wo-kan-* meaning the same; the root in all cases is Proto-Celtic **kan-* 'sing, recite poetry'. This points to a formal professional activity closely related to that of musicians and poets.

Gaul

The classical authors offer consistent testimony that the druids were prophets, and several accounts describe female druids uttering prophecies. Lampridius tells of a druidess calling out in Gaulish to Alexander Severus: 'Hurry forward, but do not hope for victory, nor put trust in your soldiers' (*Alexander Severus* 59.5). Vopiscus (*Numerianus* 14) records a story, learned from his grandfather, of how the young Diocletian who was staying in the territory of the Tungri in Gaul settled his account with a druidess who was an innkeeper. She said to him, 'Do not be stingy with your money, Diocletian', to which he replied, as a joke, 'I shall be more generous when I am emperor'. She responded cryptically and auspiciously, 'Don't joke, Diocletian, for you will be emperor when you have slain the boar'. It is likely that the Gaulish word *uidlua* on the Larzac inscription means 'seeress'.

Ireland and the Gaelic World

Early evidence mentions a prohibition against swearing oaths in the pagan manner before a *haruspex* (soothsayer), almost certainly an attempt to express 'druid'. In contrast, the druidism of Muirchú's late 7th-century *Vita Patricii* seems to be a fictionalized inversion of Christianity: the pagan king Loegaire mac Néill is described as having 'sages, druids (*magi*), soothsayers, enchanters, and inventors of every evil art', who make an elaborate and self-consciously benighted prophecy about the coming of Patrick and Christianity and the end of their pagan world order.

In the ULSTER CYCLE, Cathbad makes several prophecies as druid of the Ulaid, notably regarding auspicious times for undertakings, such as the conception of king Conchobar. This practice is comparable to the division of the Gaulish COLIGNY calendar into *mat[us]* 'auspicious' and *anm[atus]* 'inauspicious' time periods.

The disruptions caused by the Viking age seem to have been a stimulus for elaborate apocalyptic prophecies—the main theme of which is a complete upheaval and inversion of the traditional social order—figuring climactically in texts composed at this period, but set in the remote past. The Morrígan's *rosc* at the end of CATH MAIGE TUIRED ('The [Second] Battle of Mag Tuired') is in this category.

As discussed by Aedeen O'Leary, the blending of native and Christian apocryphal traditions in legends of the druid Mug Ruith (lit. 'slave of the wheel') produced a prophecy of imminent doom for Ireland and its people, which was widely believed and which caused serious alarm during the late 11th century. In the tales, Simon Magus of the New Testament (Irish *Símón Druí*) taught *druídecht* (magic, druidry) to the Irishman Mug Ruith, thus linking this practice to the Bible.

In hagiography, true prophecies often figure as miracles validating sainthood. In Adomnán's *Vita Columbae* (Life of Colum Cille), Colum Cille's prophecies are often explicitly political and show how the deceased saint continued to influence the fortunes of the powerful rulers of the period during which these texts were written—the Uí Néill, the kings of Northumbria, and the descendants of Aedán mac Gabráin.

Wales and the Brythonic World

As in the Gaelic world, most of the evidence for prophecy in the Brythonic world can be studied from a modern perspective as literary creations or political propaganda. Only with folk material collected in recent times can we begin to gauge the extent to which prophecies were actually believed or played a part in everyday life. The early ethnographer Giraldus Cambrensis provides details concerning people of his own time, unique to Wales (Cymru), called *awenithion* (Mod. W *awenyddion* 'people possessing awen, poetic inspiration'). He describes them as going into a trance to give oracular utterances in answer to problems put to them, and then needing violent shaking to return them to their senses. Giraldus explains their behaviour as demonic possession.

The two great figures of Welsh prophetic poetry, Taliesin and Myrddin, are discussed in separate articles; see also wild man and Armes Prydein. In 1155, John of Cornwall translated the prophecies of Merlin from Brythonic into Latin verse.

From as early as Historia Brittonum, the central themes of Welsh legendary history have included the former unity of Britain and the eventual triumph of the Britons, whose leader, after driving the English back to the sea, would rule the whole island. In *Historia Brittonum* itself, the boy Ambrosius prophesies that he will be the redeemer. In an important innovation, Geoffrey of Monmouth reconfigures the prophet in this story as a composite Merlin Ambrosius.

The theme of an immortal Arthur as the redeemer of Britain seems to have been widespread as a popular idea and sometimes surfaces in Arthurian literature. A folk-tale of Arthur the sleeping redeemer—often armoured and in a cave or subterranean chamber—have been collected from many places around Britain in both English and Welsh.

In the Welsh poetic tradition, *mab darogan* (lit. 'son of prophecy') is the term for the prophesied redeemer. In *Armes Prydein*, Cynan and Cadwaladr are the expected returning leaders of a great anti-English alliance embracing all the Celtic countries and the Vikings. In later centuries Owain Lawgoch and Owain Glyndŵr were viewed as fulfilling this rôle. In his diplomatic correspondence with potential allies in Scotland and Ireland, Glyndŵr refers to their prophesied successful alliance against England, showing that this political doctrine had remained remarkably stable and could still be taken seriously nearly 500 years after *Armes Prydein*. Glyndŵr disappeared around 1416; the uncertainty regarding when and where he died permitted the belief that he would return to restore Welsh rule to Britain. Lloyd George was sometimes seen fulfilling the prophecy as Britain's Welsh redeemer during the upheavals of World War I. As Glanmor Williams has revealed, Welsh poets showed enthusiasm for Harri Tudur—the future Henry VII (r. 1485–1509) and founder of the Tudor dynasty—as the *mab darogan* and saw in his success a Welshman enthroned in London as king of Britain in fulfilment of the prophecy. In this way, medieval Welsh political prophecy contributed one essential ingredient in forging the modern myth of an imperial Britain as England's successor on the world stage.

John T. Koch

PROTO-CELTIC

Proto-Celtic is the reconstructed intermediate linguistic stage between Proto-Indo-European and the oldest attested individual Celtic languages—in other words, the theoretical common ancestor of the Celtic languages. The Proto-Celtic stage is not directly attested as a written language, but circumstantial evidence supports the widespread view that some early form or forms of Celtic speech were in use among the dominant groups using Hallstatt-type material culture. The location of the original homeland of Proto-Celtic remains unproven, and the mechanism for the spread of Proto-Celtic from its original homeland (by commerce, diffusion, imperialism, and/or migration, or some combination of these) remains a matter of debate. The tiny corpus of Hallstatt-period names that form the oldest indirect attestations of Celtic provide some evidence for Celtic in Etruria, Britain, and Ireland; therefore, Proto-Celtic was already in the mid-1st millennium BC developing the regional variants well known to us from the period of fuller records.

The Phonological Definition of Proto-Celtic

Proto-Celtic is defined by several sound laws partly shared with (but in their specific combination distinguishing) Celtic from other Indo-European languages.

Consonants

1. The three distinct Proto-Indo-European sets of *k*-sounds (see Indo-European) are reduced to just two, as Indo-European palatal *k′* and *g′* and velar *k* and *g* fall together as Proto-Celtic velar *k* and *g*; the same happened in the other branches of the *centum* subgroup of Indo-European languages.
2. Indo-European *gw* (as in the name *Gwen*) became Proto-Celtic *b*.
3. Proto-Indo-European had had a series of voiced aspirated consonants b^h, d^h, g'^h, g^h, and g^{wh} (similar to English *subhuman*, *adhere*, *pigheaded*, *loghouse*, and *egg-white*). The aspiration—that is, the breathy *h*-like component—was lost in Proto-Celtic, so that the first four in the series fell together with IE *b*, *d*, g. g^{wh} became g^w (IE g^w had already become *b*; see above). In most positions, IE *p* was lost in Celtic. It must have become something like a $[\phi]$ first (like [f], but made with both lips, instead of the lower lip and upper teeth). Afterward, in the Indo-European consonant clusters -*pt*- and -*ps*-, this - ϕ - became Celtic -χ-(the sound in Scottish *loch*).
4. Indo-European -*s* + nasal consonant (that is, *m* or *n*) became assimilated to Celtic double nasal—for example, Gaulish *onno*, OIr. *uinn-ius*, W *onn-en* 'ash tree' from IE **os-no-*, Latin *ornus*.
5. Indo-European double dental consonants (*tt* and *dd*) and *st* > [tˢ] or [ˢt], the so-called 'tau gallicum', written variously in Roman script, > *s* in the Insular Celtic languages.

6. *Laryngeals*. The term 'laryngeal' designates a series of breathy sounds that existed in Proto-Indo-European. In Celtic they were mostly lost, but in some contexts resulted in short or long *a*.

Resonants (l, r, m, n)

In Proto-Indo-European, when these sounds were flanked by other consonants, they became syllables, much like in English *battle* and *didn't*, and in American English *batter*. These syllabic resonants are symbolized by writing a ring beneath the usual letter. The Indo-European syllabic nasals *m*, *n* > *an*, *am*. Indo-European *l*, *r* > Celtic *ri*, *li* before k^w, *t*, *k*, k', g^w, *g*, g', *b*, g^{wh}, g^h, g'^h, b^h.

Vowels

Notable vowel changes include Indo-European $\bar{e}$ > Celtic $\bar{i}$ and $\bar{o}$, which became Celtic $\bar{u}$ in final syllables and $\bar{a}$ in non-final syllables.

Stefan Zimmer

PROTO-CELTIC INDUSTRIES (TECHNOLOGIES AND TECHNIQUES)

There are almost 425 words in the technology domain that can be reconstructed for Proto-Celtic, representing more than 10 percent of the reconstructed vocabulary.

Architecture

Proto-Celtic words in the architecture category include words for buildings in general, specific structures such as 'bakery' and 'smithy', parts of a structure such as 'door' and 'floor', and other related terms (bridge, fence, mortar).

Although settlement architecture differed greatly throughout the area in which the Celtic languages were spoken, most of the terminology that can be reconstructed fits well with architectural elements that must have existed in buildings throughout the Celtic world. Even though only rarely attested, smithies, bakeries, and other purpose-specific buildings are known throughout most of the Celtic world. Other architectural features in the landscape, such as fences and bridges, are also well attested in archaeological records, including the famous site of La Tène.

Agriculture

Words in the category of Agriculture include terms for implements (plough, sickle, sieve), actions associated with agriculture (milk, winnow), and farm animals. Artefacts corresponding to most of these terms for implements are well documented in archaeological records, such as parts of ploughs (ard-heads). The practices associated with the agricultural vocabulary are obvious from palaeobotanical and palaeozoological evidence.

Vessels, Pottery, and Other Containers

This category includes words for pot *kelφurno-*, basket, bag *bolgo-*, and cauldrons, sing. *kwarjo-*. Many kinds of vessels, made from metal, ceramics, or organic material, are well attested in archaeological records.

Furniture

The furniture category includes words for bed, seat, and table. Even though such items were usually made from organic materials, such that few have survived until today, a few examples made from metal—such as the bronze couch in the HOCHDORF princely tomb, as well as depictions on Hallstatt situlae (bronze wine buckets)—demonstrate a wide variety of furniture.

Metallurgy and Jewellery

This category includes words for materials (amber *webru-, glass *glanjo-) and types of jewellery (crown, necklace, ring). Metallurgy in copper, bronze, tin, iron, silver, gold, and lead is attested in archaeological records, as is glass production. Crafted from these materials, as well as amber, coral, and stone, were various kinds of jewellery, including the famous Celtic neck ring, the torc, and bracelets, anklets, finger rings, necklaces, crowns, BROOCHES, and beads.

Tools

Words in the tools category include the awl, churn, comb, grinding stone/quern, hook, key and lock, nail, peg, tongs, and whetstone. Many of these tools are also attested in archaeological records, made in bronze or iron, or, like whetstones, from stone.

Textiles

The textiles category includes words for activities associated with textile production (card, spin, weave), general words for garments (clothes *wiska-, dress), words for specific kinds of garments (belt, cloak *bratto-, shirt, shoe, trousers *braka-), words for parts of garments (hood, sleeve), and words for materials (fleece, hemp, leather, linen, wool).

Textiles and leather products are rarely recovered, with the major exception being from the prehistoric salt mines of the DÜRRNBERG BEI HALLEIN and Hallstatt, where fragments of clothing and shoes have been found. Less frequently, remains of cloth have been recovered where metal corrosion has helped to preserve parts of the fabric. However, clothing of all kinds is relatively well known from figurative ART.

Raimund Karl and Caroline aan de Weil

PROTO-CELTIC WEAPONS

Native Celtic Vocabulary

Several weapon words beyond sword and shield can be reconstructed for Proto-Celtic.

Spear is the most important weapon concept, as there are six different Proto-Celtic roots attested in the Celtic languages:

1. Proto-Celtic *gaiso- > Old Irish gae, Scottish Gaelic gath 'dart, sting', and Gaulish γαισον gaison = Gallo-Latin gaesum (neuter) 'heavy iron throwing spear'. This word had several compounds: Proto-Celtic *uɸo-gaiso- (lit. 'under-spear') is attested in MIr. foga 'small spear, javelin', Middle and Modern Welsh gwaew 'lance, spear, javelin', Mod.Bret. goao, and a compound attested in Brythonic with the prefixed element *sukko-(Old Cornish hochwuyu 'hunting-spear, swine spear'). The first element is either what became Welsh hwch 'sow' or swch 'plough-share'.

2. Proto-Celtic *kali- is implied by MIr. cail.

3. Proto-Celtic *kestā- is implied by MIr. cess.

4. Proto-Celtic *kʷarho- is attested in OIr. carr and MW and Mod.W pâr.

5. Proto-Celtic *lagīnā will explain OIr. laigen 'broadheaded spear'. Early Welsh llain 'blade, spear', common in the Gododdin, could not be the exact cognate of the Irish, though it could reflect a borrowing from the Irish of, say, the 4th to 6th centuries AD.

6. Proto-Celtic *s(ɸ?)ligā- can be reconstructed to account for OIr. sleg.

Knife is the next most important weapon concept in inherited Celtic vocabulary. There are three words:

1. Proto-Celtic *skījeno- 'knife' is attested in OIr. scīan, ScG sgian, and MW and Mod.W ysgien 'knife, sword'.

2. Proto-Celtic *gulbo- 'knife, dagger' (< 'beak') is attested in OW gylym, MW geleu, gelyf, Mod.W gylf, Gaulish gulbia 'gouge', and the Romano-British place-name Re-gulbium 'Reculver' (probably lit. 'great beak/point', referring to a headland).

3. Proto-Celtic *ɸaltan- 'razor' is attested in OIr. altan, ScG ealltuinn 'razor', OW elinn, MW and Mod.W ellyn, and OBret. altin, MBret. and Mod.Bret. aotenn.

Further Weapon Vocabulary

Proto-Celtic *sadī- 'hilt' is attested in Mod.W said 'hilt' and ScG saidh, saith, Manx seiy. Finally, there is a word for sling (Proto-Celtic *trok(ʷ)alo-, attested in Ir. trochal).

Early Archaeological Evidence

In archaeological records, spearheads make up the large majority of weapons found in late Bronze Age and Iron Age burials, indicating their importance as the (cheap) weapon of choice during those periods. Within the group of spearheads, types vary from small, leaf-bladed heads in bronze or iron, which could be used on both javelins and ordinary spears, to large, ornately fashioned iron spearheads of up to 50 cm in length, which were probably used either as lances or as decorative heads for battle standards.

Knives are also a frequent find throughout the late Bronze and Iron Ages, though most of them are much more suitable for use as tools than as weapons. Even the rather large iron butchering knives that appear quite regularly in Continental Iron Age burials are almost exclusively found in combination with animal bones. Daggers, known mainly from the Late Bronze Age (c. 1200–c. 750 BC) and the Hallstatt D period (c. 600–c. 475 BC), may have been used as weapons as well.

Slings, attested by the finds of numerous sling-stones, seem to have been used mainly in the British Isles. On the Continent, bows and javelins were preferred as long-range weapons.

The primary defensive weapons were shields, armour, and helmets. Among the various designs of armour, chain-mail suits make their first appearance in Iron Age contexts.

Raimund Karl and Caroline aan de Weil

PWYLL PENDEFIG DYFED

Pwyll Pendefig Dyfed (Pwyll prince of Dyfed) is the name commonly given to the First Branch of the Mabinogi. The opening section tells of Pwyll's encounter with ARAWN, king of ANNWN /ANNWFN. They change places, and Pwyll is given the name Pwyll Head of Annwfn. In the second section, while seated on the mound near his court in DYFED, Pwyll sees a beautiful maiden riding a magical white horse, RHIANNON, and they marry. The third and final section relates how the couple's son disappears on the night of his birth. Rhiannon is falsely accused of murdering him and is punished by being forced to carry visitors to the court on her back. Another lord discovers the child under strange circumstances, and he is adopted and given the name Gwri of the Golden Hair. Eventually he is restored to his father's court and renamed Pryderi (meaning 'worry'), on account of his mother declaring, upon his return, that her 'cares' are now over.

The tale contains resonances of Celtic mythology—it has been suggested, for example, that Rhiannon is functionally cognate with EPONA, the Celtic horse goddess. Also, well-known international tales/motifs abound, such as the calumniated wife, the rash promise, and the giant claw. Against this background of fantasy, the author explores moral issues such as the nature of insult and compensation, and friendship. Pwyll himself matures throughout from an impatient, impetuous young man to a wise and careful ruler, finally deserving his name ('discretion' or 'good sense').

Sioned Davies

R

REFORMATION LITERATURE, BRITTANY

In contrast to Scotland (ALBA) and Wales (CYMRU), the writers of Brittany (BREIZH)—especially Breton-speaking Lower Brittany (Breizh-Izel)—remained predominantly Catholic. Accordingly, the literature covered in this article is connected with the Catholic Counter-Reformation rather than the Protestant Reformation; on the Protestant minority in Brittany and their impact, see CHRISTIANITY IN THE CELTIC COUNTRIES.

Almost all Breton writing before the French Revolution has some connection with religion. Knowledge of Breton was indispensable for confession or preaching in a population of a million Catholics, but this does not mean that the authors who used this language sought to create a cultural language from it. The effects of the later Catholic Counter-Reformation did not truly begin to be felt in the area until the middle of the 17th century, and it is from then on that the works become more numerous.

A first catechism, inspired by the Council of Trent (1545–63), appeared in the 16th century—that of Gilles de Keranpuil (1576), translated from Peter Canisius (1521–97). Other translations of Jesuit works followed, such as those of Tanguy Gueguen, *An mirouer a confession* (The mirror of confession, 1621) and *Doctrin an christenien* (Christians' doctrine, 1622), a Breton version of the catechism of Ledesma.

Writing in Breton was modernized on the initiative of the Jesuit Julian Maunoir, a native of Upper Brittany (Breizh-Uhel) who had learned the language and who, in the 1640s, began a long career as a missionary. He himself published five works—notably the *Sacré Collège de Jésus* (Sacred College of Jesus, 1659), composed of a *dictionnaire* (dictionary), a *grammaire et syntaxe* (grammar and syntax), and a *quenteliou christen* (Christian lessons), a multi-layered catechism. Maunoir is also the author of *Canticou spirituel* (Spiritual canticles). Numerous authors, before and especially after Maunoir, used this genre of canticle, borrowed from the Protestants and well adapted to populations whose majority were illiterate. Collections of canticles are also found dispersed in works of devotion such as those of Charles Le Bris (1660/1665–c. 1737), whose most celebrated work remains the *Heuryou brezonec ha latin* (Breton and Latin hours). This collection of prayers, instructions, and canticles was still used for the mass in the first half of the 20th century.

Claude-Guillaume de Marigo (1693–1759) is best known for his *Buez ar Sænt* (Lives of the saints, 1752), presented as a translation, which furnished, for each day of the year, a pious story followed by moral reflections. The meagre attention given to the Breton saints reflects Marigo's non-Breton sources and probably also his desire to give prominence to the blessed recognized by the Roman Church, as well as his lack of interest in the region. In the 19th and 20th centuries, other authors were to take up the *Buez ar Sænt*, incorporating more of the saints venerated in Brittany.

As civil authorities, the Catholic clergy possessed a *de facto* monopoly on writing in Breton, and thus the discourse of the Catholic Counter-Reformation had a profound spiritual and linguistic impact on Breton-speaking Brittany.

Fañch Roudaut

REFORMATION LITERATURE, IRELAND

Queen Elizabeth I of ENGLAND had already provided a sum of money for printing the New Testament in Irish but, when nothing had happened by the end of 1567, she threatened to withdraw her funds unless action was immediately taken. In 1571, Seán Ó Cearnaigh, treasurer of St Patrick's Cathedral in BAILE ÁTHA CLIATH (Dublin), published the first Gaelic book to be printed in Ireland, *Aibidil Gaoidheilge & Caiticiosma* (The Irish ABC and catechism). Of the 200 copies printed, two survive, and the reference to Elizabeth as 'our pious and all-powerful prince' is a very early acknowledgement in the IRISH LANGUAGE of the English monarch's jurisdiction in Ireland.

Progress on the New Testament was slow. Uilliam Ó Domhnaill (*c.* 1570–1628), one of the first three students to enter Trinity College Dublin on its establishment in 1592, brought the work to completion. In his translation, Ó Domhnaill made use of Erasmus's Greek version, the *Textus Receptus* published in 1516; his willingness to work from the best available Greek text marks his translation of the New Testament as a work of evangelical humanism. Published in 1602, only 500 copies were printed.

Ó Domhnaill's translation of the Book of Common Prayer, *Leabhar na nVrnaightheadh gComhchoidchiond*, appeared in 1608 and is remarkable for its faithful transmission of Cranmer's dignified prose into a natural Gaelic style. Yet, it contains some notable omissions. The ceremonies for the ordination of priests and deacons and for the consecration of bishops are lacking. The omission of the psalter and the lessons from the Old Testament is due to the fact that the Old Testament had not yet appeared in Irish.

In 1627, the Englishman William Bedell (1571–1642), who was competent in Hebrew, was appointed provost of Trinity College Dublin. Soon after his appointment, he started learning Irish under the tutelage of Muircheartach Ó Cionga, a member of an Irish literary family from Co. Offaly (Contae Uíbh Fhailí). While bishop of Kilmore and Ardagh (Ardach), in 1631 he published a little book of 13 pages in both Irish and English: *Aibgitir .i. Theaguisg Cheudtosugheadh an Chriostaidhe* (*The A.B.C. or the Institution of a Christian*).

Much more ambitious was Bedell's plan to translate and publish the Old Testament in Irish with the help of Irish scholars, a project that lasted from 1632 to 1638. The translation, minus the Apocrypha, was eventually published in

London in 1685 under the patronage of the famous scientist, Robert Boyle (1627–91).

Micheál Mac Craith

REFORMATION LITERATURE, SCOTLAND

The formal arrival of the Reformation in Scotland (ALBA) is generally dated to the meeting of the first Reformation Parliament in 1560. It took considerably longer for the Reformation, as a powerful tool for change both spiritual and social, to reach the farthest bounds of the HIGHLANDS AND ISLANDS. The *Book of Common Order* was translated into Gaelic in the 1560s, and published in 1567 by Robert Lekprevik, the Edinburgh printer to the General Assembly of the Reformed Church. The Gaelic version of the *Book of Common Order* was known as *Foirm na n-Urrnuidheadh*, translated by John Carswell into Classical Common Gaelic (with a Scottish flavour), thus distancing the work from vernacular Gaelic and its speakers. Carswell's book was followed in the 1630s by a small succession of translated catechisms produced by the Synod of Argyll (e.g., *Adtimchiol an Chreidimh* of c. 1631).

Non-Biblical Prose and Verse

Protestant interest in the Highlands in the 18th century established a strong tradition of printed Gaelic prose, but a very high proportion of Gaelic prose texts were, in fact, translations from English religious writings: 86 out of a total of 146 by 1800. Of the 86 texts, 68 were produced in the period 1751–1800, suggesting that Gaelic was more favourably regarded in literary circles after the JACOBITE REBELLION of 1745. The Catholic Church also encouraged translation of key texts, albeit in much lesser quantity. A fine and refreshingly idiomatic translation, by the Reverend Robert Menzies (*fl.* 1780), of Thomas á Kempis's *Imitatio Christi* was published in Edinburgh in 1785. Poetry, especially of a hortatory or didactic nature, was also stimulated, and is represented preeminently in the work of Dùgall Bochanan (Dugald Buchanan, 1716–68) of Perthshire (Peairt), whose slim volume of eight poems was published in 1767. Volumes of verse headed the list of original religious works appearing in Gaelic in 1741–99. Bochanan's verse was, however, deeply indebted to composers in English, notably Isaac Watts and Edward Young, and in some instances Bochanan translated directly from Watts, without acknowledgement. Gaelic spiritual verse continued to be a major product of the 19th century, flourishing in the context of frequent religious revivals (see SCOTTISH GAELIC POETRY, 19TH CENTURY).

Imitation and translation of external models, mostly in English, tended to stifle the growth of a properly indigenous Gaelic spiritual literature, particularly in prose. By the 1790s, the balance was being redressed to a certain extent by the gradual publication of printed sermons, composed and delivered by Gaelic-speaking ministers. Curiously, the first surviving printed Gaelic sermons (two homilies, accompanied by three prayers) were published in 1791 in Fayetteville, North Carolina, where many Gaelic-speaking people had settled beginning in the late 1730s (see CELTIC LANGUAGES

IN NORTH AMERICA). It is remarkable that it should have taken so long to produce Gaelic sermons in printed format. Part of the reason for such 'delay' may be that sermons were regarded as essentially 'oral' in their inspiration and delivery, and that printing came about largely in response to changed circumstances, such as emigration, in which it was more difficult to have access to regular Gaelic ministry. It is also noteworthy that the printing of Gaelic sermons began at much the same time as the Scottish Gaelic BIBLE was edging its way slowly toward completion.

Journals and Supplements

Following the completion of the Scottish Gaelic Bible, and the consequent extension of literacy in Gaelic, Gaelic literature as a whole was strengthened by the founding of two Gaelic journals (*An Teachdaire Gaelach* [The Gaelic messenger], 1829–31, and *Cuairtear nan Gleann* [Visitor of the glens], 1840–43) by the Reverend Dr Norman MacLeod. These journals carried original sermons, stories, and traditional tales, and laid the foundation of modern Gaelic literature. Their overall aim was didactic, inculcating moral and spiritual values, but they also imparted knowledge about natural phenomena, foreign countries (with emigrants in mind), and technical achievements. From the second half of the 19th century, the main Protestant churches active in the Highlands have produced Gaelic Pages or Supplements, some of which continue to the present time. The Gaelic Supplement (established 1880) of *Life and Work*, the monthly magazine of the Church of Scotland, has made a particularly important contribution to Gaelic literature in the 20th century.

Overview

Since the Reformation, Gaelic religious literature—both prose and verse—has been produced in some profusion in Scotland, generally by writers and printing presses closely related to the various Protestant churches. Inevitably, much of the material has been doctrinal and didactic, aimed at the propagation of the Christian faith, but, with the gradual expansion of themes and registers, religious composers and publishers have made a vital contribution to the canon of Gaelic literature across the centuries.

Donald E. Meek

REFORMATION LITERATURE, WALES

Scriptural translation forms the basis of Welsh Reformation literature, which demonstrated a Protestant emphasis on lexical fidelity and a humanist emphasis on learning. Its highest achievement was undoubtedly the translation of the Bible into Welsh in 1588. The clarity and dignity of diction and rich idiomatic use of the Welsh language was welcomed, and the Bible provided a firm basis for the development of a standard Welsh language. It also inspired a 'golden age' of Welsh prose writing during the late 16th and 17th centuries, reaching its apogee in the genius of Puritan writers such as Morgan Llwyd (1619–59) and Charles Edwards (1628?– *post* 1690), as well as the Anglican Ellis WYNNE (1671–1734). In the field of poetry,

Edmwnd Prys (1543/4–1623), archdeacon of Merioneth (Meirionnydd), was a learned poet and ardent humanist whose debate with fellow-poet Wiliam Cynwal (†1587/8) crystallizes the tension between Welsh humanists and poets at the time. Prys's outstanding contribution to Welsh Reformation literature was his metrical rendition of the complete Psalter in Welsh, which was published as an appendix to the Welsh Book of Common Prayer in 1621.

Two other Welsh translators of Reformation literature were Huw Lewys (1562–1634), the author of *Perl Mewn Adfyd* (1595), which was a translation of Miles Coverdale's *A Spyrytuall and moost Precious Pearle*; and Morris Kyffin (c. 1555–98), who is primarily known for his translation of Bishop John Jewel's *Apologia Ecclesiae Anglicanae*. *Deffynniad Ffydd Eglwys Loegr* was published in 1595 and its limpid prose style reveals Kyffin's mastery over his medium. In his foreword to the translation, he argued strongly in favour of publishing books in the Welsh language.

Protestantism, and its radical Puritan wing, also produced a large body of Welsh literature, mainly translations, as Welsh prose entered a period of stability and maturity. Notable among original works in Welsh is the short but luminous anti-witchcraft tract by Robert Holland (c. 1556–?1622), written in dialogue form, entitled *Ymddiddan Tudur a Gronw* (c. 1595). This unique example of its genre in Welsh was later printed in Stephen Hughes's *Canwyll y Cymry* in 1681.

Translating the founding texts of Anglicanism into Welsh also produced a large body of illustrious and influential prose writing. Rowland Vaughan was a prolific translator, but he is particularly remembered for *Yr Ymarfer o Dduwioldeb* (1629), a translation of Lewis Bayly's enormously popular handbook of devotion, *Practice of Piety*. John Davies of Mallwyd's *Llyfr y Resolusion* (1632) was a translation of Edmund Bunny's Protestant version of Robert Parsons's *The First Book of the Christian Exercise appertayning to Resolution* and is the sole literary example of Welsh baroque style.

Angharad Price

REINCARNATION AND SHAPESHIFTING

Classical Evidence

Greek and Roman authors speak with unanimous certainty about druids teaching a doctrine of the immortality of the soul. The details of this doctrine, however, are more difficult to recover. Caesar says cryptically that souls 'pass after death from some to others' (*ab aliis post mortem transire AD alios*), a statement that could be taken to refer to birth in a new body. This is surely what Diodorus Siculus has in mind when he attributes to the druids the belief that the soul 'lives again after a certain number of years, the soul having entered another body'. According to the poet Lucan, the druids denied that souls passed into a realm of the dead, claiming rather that 'the spirit governs limbs [i.e., inhabits a body] in another region' (*orbe alio*, which may also be translated as 'otherworld').

Irish Legend

The late Old Irish story of Túan mac Cairill (*Scél Túain meic Cairill*) describes how a man who came to Ireland as part of the first settlement after Noah's Flood lived on through all the subsequent phases of its LEGENDARY HISTORY by passing through the shapes of a stag, a boar, a cormorant, and a salmon; with each metamorphosis, his youth was renewed. In one early anecdote a mysterious youth, whom the author tentatively identifies as the 7th-century Ulster prince Mongán mac Fiachna, tells Colum Cille that he remembers a time when there was a flourishing kingdom on the site of Loch Feabhail (Lough Foyle); subsequently, he has existed as a deer, a salmon, a seal, and a wolf, and then as a man again.

One of the 'fore-tales' of Táin Bó Cuailnge ('The Cattle Raid of Cooley') describes how a quarrel between two swineherds of the Tuath Dé led to their fighting against each other in a lengthy series of transformations. In what seems to be the earliest version of the story, these forms are listed as pairs of ravens, water monsters, stags, warriors, phantoms, and worms. The worms fall into water and are swallowed by cows, who conceive and bear two calves; these grow up to be the bulls on whose account the great war of the Táin is waged.

Welsh Legend

In Wales, the principal figure to be considered in this context is Taliesin, a 6th-century poet to whom many later compositions were attributed. Several of these works portray him as the possessor of knowledge of his former existence in other shapes. Thus the poem *Cad Goddau* (The battle of the trees) opens with the lines 'I was in many shapes before I was set free', and goes on to state that the speaker has been a sword, a shower of rain, starlight, a word, a book, a lantern, and so on. How much of this cryptic diction is simply metaphorical? In the present state of our knowledge, no confident answer can be given.

In the tale of Math fab Mathonwy, Gwydion and his brother Gilfaethwy are condemned to become mating pairs of deer, swine, and wolves; later in the tale, the mortally wounded Lleu turns into an eagle, but is eventually restored to human form. In Culhwch ac Olwen, Arthur and his men interrogate a series of animals, each more ancient than the last, and finally learn the answer from a salmon, which is the oldest creature in the world. We may perhaps compare the story of Túan, where knowledge of the distant past is also mediated by a series of creatures culminating in a salmon.

Celtic Metempsychosis?

It would be strange indeed if the medieval literatures preserved unambiguous testimony to a doctrine of the afterlife that was in fundamental disagreement with Christian teaching. Moreover, in the Pythagorean tradition, the narrative focus is not on the general run of humanity, but rather on those exceptional individuals who are able to remember their prior lives. It is also worth stressing that, while many of the episodes in the tales involve metamorphosis rather than reincarnation per se, the theme of rebirth is seldom wholly absent. One striking piece of evidence seems to bridge the gap between ancient ethnography and medieval legend: The author of the theological treatise *De mirabilibus sacrae scripturae* ('On the miracles of holy scripture', written AD 655) speaks of 'the ridiculous fables of the druids, who say that their ancestors flew through the ages in the form of birds'. Here, shape-shifting and the soul's survival appear to be linked, in a contemporary account of druidic teaching in early Christian Ireland.

Two further points may be mentioned in conclusion. In most of the insular examples, memory of former existences is invoked to provide authority for accounts of the distant past: the doctrine's usefulness in legitimating historical tradition may well have helped it to survive, if only as a narrative motif, following the adoption of Christianity. It should also be stressed that evidence supports several other ideas regarding the soul's fate after death: The Celts, like other peoples, are unlikely to have had a simple or consistent view of this mysterious, absorbing subject.

John Carey

RELIGIOUS BELIEFS, ANCIENT CELTIC

The religious beliefs of the ancient Celts varied across their vast settlement area, with pronounced differences in local practices, and over time. Remnants of the Celtic belief system survive in Celtic hagiography, in secular medieval literature, and in the folk traditions of Britain and Ireland.

Sources

There are many hundreds of short texts in the form of inscriptions, mostly in Greek or Latin with Celtic proper names. There are some important curse inscriptions and a few other texts in the ancient Celtic languages. The interpretation of many of these texts is controversial; for some, no satisfactory reading has been found to date.

Texts by the classical authors have to be placed in context—for example, the famous passage on human sacrifice to the gods TEUTATES, Esus, and TARANIS found in Lucan. It was common for classical authors to contrast the barbarity of Celtic religious beliefs with the sophistication of Roman rule, an agenda very evident in Caesar's *De Bello Gallico* (6.13f., 16–19).

Indigenous depictions go back to the Hallstatt period, especially in the form of the heroic dead or deified ancestors, found on the archaic statues on major burial mounds such as Hirschlanden or Glauberg. There is a tendency to depict severed heads—often with the facial expression of a dead person and probably connected to the ritual display of skulls. It seems that they were intended to transfer the magical power of the skull. Thus head hunting and the head cult, as testified by Posidonius and other authors up to the Middle Ages, surely had religious meaning.

Among the Graeco-Roman–influenced sculptures, the deity at Bouray-sur-Juine (Seine-et-Oise) stands out. This god has stag's hooves and is often seen as Cernunnos. Another depiction of Cernunnos shows a human figure with antlers. In many instances, it is the combination of name and unusual image that points toward a Celtic source.

A Gallo-Roman relief from Reims, France, appears to show the god Cernunnos flanked by two other gods who show iconographic connections to the Roman Apollo and Mercury. (C. M. Dixon/StockphotoPro)

Other archaeological finds connected with settlements, graves, and sacrificial sites have supplied detailed material, but since these finds are 'mute' (i.e., they have no written descriptions), interpretation of their religious meaning must remain speculative. The ritually slain bog man from Lindow Moss raises questions of the relationship between law and religion.

Interpretation

It has usually been assumed that the worship of the god Mercurius among the Celts refers to the Celtic god Lugus (see also INTERPRETATIO ROMANA). The equation of Lugus with Mercurius is not completely certain, however. Another example is the god Belenos, who is often identified with Apollo.

Comparisons within the framework of Indo-European studies are often illuminating. Celtic practices have especially been compared with those in India, using a theoretical approach which assumes that archaic linguistic forms, beliefs, and practices survived on both eastern and western fringes of Indo-European settlement. One example is the sacrifice of a white mare following an implied sacred marriage (*hieros gamos*), including sex with the prince about to be initiated as king, comparable to the horse sacrifice of the Old Indian *Aśvamedha*.

Rituals involving masks are attested by images (such as the horse masks on the Aylesford bucket) and the early Christian decisions of synods in Gaul, in which, for instance, the wearing of stag masks is forbidden.

Deities

While there was apparently no Celtic pantheon (unified system of deities), a range of typically Celtic divine figures is attested. They often occur as couples or trinities, with many Celtic sculptures having three faces perhaps corresponding to an Indo-European three-faced deity or trinity of deities (cf. Old Indian *trimūrti*). The mother goddesses are known as Matronae, whose cult as 'mothers' is linked to that of a divine son, Maponos. They were also seen as goddesses of fertility and helpers in need. The name of a goddess could also correspond to a tribal name, as, for instance, Brigantia (Old Irish Brigit) to the Brigantes and Brigantii. Epona, the horse goddess, most often depicted on the back of a horse, has features in common with the mother goddesses. Because the 'tribal mothers' sought to protect their tribe in peace and in war, they could metamorphize into war goddesses; Brigit appears as the war goddess of Leinster (Laigin), for example.

The father of the tribe and god of the dead was the 'father god'. Teutates (God of the tribe/people) was probably another name for him. The realm of the dead was located very specifically on various, not too far away, islands in the west—for example, Bardsey Island (Enlli) and the Bull near the Bearra Peninsula. Celtic visions of the Otherworld as a land of eternal spring, of plenty, of beautiful women, and of music, as described in the seafarer tales (IMMRAMA), have exerted a lasting influence on the motifs of Western literature.

The god of thunder *Taranis*, *Taranus*, *Tanarus* (cf. the Germanic cognate god *Thor*; both names mean 'thunder') was a male celestial god; his iconography is linked with the bull and the wheel. The sun and his consort and gods of craft, as mythical smiths, cobblers, builders, or doctors, are of special importance. The most important male deity in this group is probably Lugus, and the most important female deity is the goddess corresponding to the Roman Minerva, whose Irish equivalent is Brigit, indicating the close connection between gods of craft and healing; cf. Nōdons.

Responsible for cult and ritual was the priestly caste of the druids. Besides the druids, several names for priests survive, but nothing is known of the relationship between the druids and these other types of priests.

Helmut Birkhan

RENAISSANCE, CELTIC COUNTRIES, OVERVIEW

The European Renaissance may be defined narrowly as the recovery of ancient Greek and Roman texts and artefacts alongside an emphasis on purity and accuracy of written Latin and authenticity in scholarship (humanism). The effects of the new movement generally became influential north of the Alps only at the turn of the 16th century. The delayed northern Renaissance was marked by a special emphasis on humanist scholarship applied to Christian texts, aided by the invention and rapid spread of printing and soon complicated by the Protestant Reformation. Humanists all over Europe in the 16th century showed interest in the potential of the vernacular languages.

Eiléan Ní Chuilleanáin

RENAISSANCE, IRELAND

In Ireland (Éire), the impact of Renaissance ideas was at its height in the 16th and early 17th centuries.

Patronage

In 1522, Aodh Dubh Ó Domhnaill, lord of Donegal, paid 140 cows for a Gaelic manuscript, the Book of Ballymote (Leabhar Bhaile an Mhóta). His son Maghnus Ó Domhnaill, who ruled from 1537 to 1563, was an outstanding example of a Renaissance prince with his skill in love-poetry, Gaelic historical scholarship, and diplomacy, and his patronage of Gaelic bards and foreign-educated scholars.

Urban Centres

Humanist ideas in Europe were especially influential among the political class in urban centres. English-speaking BAILE ÁTHA CLIATH (Dublin) had, in the early 16th century, a tradition of political writing that may show humanist influence; the education received by the pupils—boys from Dublin, Kilkenny (Cill Chainnigh), and Waterford (Port Láirge)—at Peter White's school in Kilkenny in the 1550s and 1560s showed a strong humanist influence.

Richard Stanihurst (1547–1618), a historian, Catholic apologist, and translator of Vergil into English hexameters, wrote a *History of Ireland*, which was incorporated into Holinshed's *Chronicles*. This *History* was based on an earlier history by the English Jesuit Edmund Campion, written when he was Stanihurst's guest during his flight from Oxford to the Continent. Stanihurst ended his career abroad because of his religious convictions.

Elizabethan newcomers such as Lodowyck Bryskett (Ludovico Bruschetto, 1545–c. 1612), who translated the *Tre dialoghi della vita civile* of Giraldi (1504–73) as *A Discourse of Civill Life*, with an introductory dialogue set in Dublin in 1582–85, and, famously, Edmund Spenser, developed the tradition, artfully using the characteristic Renaissance dialogue form, and owing much in the latter case to the greatest theorist of absolute government, Niccolo Machiavelli. Bryskett's introductory dialogue, like those of Italian predecessors such as Castiglione, introduced historical figures such as Sir Robert Dillon, Archbishop Long of Armagh (ARD MHACHA), and Spenser himself. His view of Ireland and, indeed, of the English language too is apologetic: 'This barbarous countrie of Ireland ... where almost no trace of learning is to be seene'. By contrast, Aodh Mac Aingil apologizes in 1618, in his first printed work, for his own Gaelic style and incapacity to rise to the heights of traditional learned prose, while Geoffrey Keating (Seathrún Céitinn) in the introduction to his history of Ireland, *Foras Feasa ar Éirinn*, in the 1630s responds to Spenser and other foreign traducers of Gaelic culture by stressing its antiquity and independence (1.38–40).

Architecture, Visual Art, and Material Culture

Of architecture, visual ART, and material culture generally in this period, little has survived the wars of the 17th century and the demise of the Gaelic and Old English aristocracy. Accounts of the household goods of the Earl of Kildare suggest a magnificent lifestyle, as do the Gaelic poems of Tadhg Dall Ó hUiginn and Eochaidh Ó hEódhasa, which describe the castles of Ó Domhnaill at Ballyshannon (Béal Átha Seanaidh) and Mág Uidhir at Enniskillen (Inis Ceithleann). The Earl of Ormond's 'Great House' at Carrick-on-Suir, Co. Tipperary (Carraig na Siúire, Contae Thiobraid Árainn), still conveys something of the splendour in which Thomas, the ninth earl, friend of Queen Elizabeth and patron of Gaelic poets, lived.

Eiléan Ní Chuilleanáin

RENAISSANCE, SCOTLAND

The *Eneados* (1513, printed in 1553) of Gavin Douglas (*c.* 1475–1522), the first full-length translation of Vergil's *Aeneid* in the British Isles, hailed Scots as a new literary medium. In a similar vein, the miscellaneous anthology of the Book of the Dean of Lismore demonstrates both the catholicity of the taste of bards and their patrons and the series of interconnections between the Gaedhealtachd and the Lowlands of Scotland at the close of the Middle Ages.

European influences were filtered through the new universities of St Andrews/ Cill Rìmhinn (1411), Glasgow/Glaschu (1451), and Aberdeen/Obar Dheathain (1495). John Mair (*c.* 1467–1550) held teaching posts in Paris before returning to become principal of the university of Glasgow. Mair—a philosopher, theologian, and historian, and a colleague of Erasmus in Paris, where they lived in the same house—later returned to St Andrews, becoming the domineering tutor of John Knox. He was the central figure in a circle of clerical scholars, competent in the classical languages and familiar with the great classical texts. The sizeable impact of what may seem a small clique of university men can be measured in different ways. Almost all the libraries of both pre-Reformation bishops and religious houses contained the key works of Erasmus and other Christian humanists, and this period saw both the expansion of grammar schools and the construction of a virtual national curriculum for them, which survived the Reformation.

A second major channel for European cultural influences was the royal court. A patriotic agenda increasingly placed an emphasis on Scots: James V (1513–42) commissioned the translation into Scots of Boece's Latin chronicle, *Scotorum Historiae* (Paris, 1527) in 1535.

A third strand of development—particularly fostered by the arrival of a domestic printing press, first licensed by the Crown in 1507—lay in the emergence of a new, educated lay élite, able to read Latin texts for themselves. Receptive both to humanism and, increasingly, to Protestant ideas, such laymen were influenced by the Latin works of George Buchanan (1506–82), as well as by printed Bibles in English. Although usually supporters of the Reformation, their humanism was infected by a conservative desire to preserve the best of the cultural heritage of the Middle Ages. Cultural continuity, as a result, sat beside religious change.

Michael Lynch

RENAISSANCE, WALES

Sources of Renaissance Culture in Wales

Wales was far removed from the Italian beginnings of the movement in learning and culture known as the Renaissance. It is estimated that, between 1540 and 1642, more than two thousand Welsh students were admitted to the universities of Oxford (Welsh Rhydychen) and Cambridge (Welsh Caer-grawnt), and one or the other university played a vital part in the emergence of Renaissance culture in Wales, where they encountered humanism.

Early Developments in Wales

Many educated Welshmen opted to make their way outside their native country, among them notable figures such as the lawyer William Aubrey (*c.* 1529–95), the Aristotelian scholar Griffith Powell (1561–1620), and the Latin epigrammatist John Owen (?1564–?1628). It was Wales's good fortune that others chose to combine their humanistic learning with a commitment to matters of Welsh scholarly and cultural concern. In 1547, William Salesbury gave expression to his conviction in a call to his fellow-countrymen to insist on having learning, not in Latin or English, but in their own tongue: *mynuch ddysc yn ych iaith* 'demand learning in your language'. The first tentative steps to this end were the publication of *Yny lhyvyr hwnn* (1546) by Sir John Prys (Prise), followed by Salesbury's *A Dictionary of Englyshe and Welshe* and *Oll Synnwyr pen Kembero ygyd* 'All the wisdom of a Welshman's mind brought together' (both 1547). These are short works, but they provide early indications of some of the concerns that were to dominate the work of Welsh Renaissance scholars for a hundred years, culminating in the vast endeavours of Dr John Davies (*c.* 1567–1644) of Mallwyd: matters of language (orthography, grammar, lexicography), the distillation of wisdom (collections of proverbs), and the translation of the Bible and other religious texts.

The Renaissance and the Welsh Language

Scholarly interest in the Welsh language was fuelled both by the humanists' study of the classical languages and by their awareness of the rich vernacular tradition of Wales in earlier centuries. The application of Renaissance rhetorical theory to the work of the Welsh poets is evident in Henri Perri's *Eglvryn Phraethineb* (The exponent of wit, 1595), based on an earlier study by William Salesbury. Linguistic expertise is also demonstrated in works of lexicography, begun by William Salesbury and culminating in Thomas Wiliems's unpublished Latin–Welsh dictionary (Aberystwyth, NLW, Peniarth MS 228) and in John Davies's *Dictionarium Duplex* (1632). In the tradition of Erasmus, Thomas Wiliems and John Davies were also keen compilers of collections of Welsh adages.

Welsh History

Renaissance interests in matters of Welsh history were largely dominated by attempts to counter attacks on the traditions associated with Geoffrey of Monmouth's Historia Regum Britanniae. Over many years, Sir John Prise worked on a reasoned defence of the British history against the attacks made on it in Polydore Vergil's *Anglica Historia*. Prise's *Historiae Brytannicae Defensio*, one of the longest Latin works to emerge from the Renaissance in Wales, was posthumously published in 1573.

Achievement of the Welsh Renaissance

Many aspects of the Continental Renaissance seem to have passed Wales by, though its influence is evident in some of the artistic and architectural styles favoured by the nobility and gentry of the 16th and early 17th centuries. Even in the literary sphere, some common humanistic endeavours were not attempted, and translations of classical literature into Welsh (such as Gruffydd Robert's version of the beginning of Cicero's *De Senectute*) were few.

Ceri Davies

RHEGED

Rheged is mentioned in close connection with Urien in Llyfr Taliesin, regarded as authentic 6th-century court poetry. It must have been a kingdom or, at any rate, a sizeable geographical or political entity. In *Llyfr Taliesin*, Urien is called *glyw Reget* 'lord of Rheged' in the *awdl* on the battle of Gwen Ystrad; *Vryen Reget | Reget δiffreidyat* 'Urien of Rheged, defender of Rheged' appears in the next poem; and the following poem begins *Arδwyre Reget rysseδ rieu* 'Arise, Rheged, great seat of kings'.

Our best evidence as to Rheged's location is in the *Gorhoffedd* of Hywel ab Owain Gwynedd, which places Caerliwelydd (i.e., Carlisle in Cumbria) in Rheged. Assuming that Hywel is well informed, this nonetheless leaves the extent of Rheged open.

The name is Celtic and is related to Welsh *rheg* 'gift', explaining the artful poetic theme of its rulers' renowned generosity.

John T. Koch

RHIANNON

Rhiannon is a character in the Mabinogi. In the First Branch (Pwyll), she appears as a mysterious, unsurpassable horsewoman, who eventually marries Pwyll of Dyfed.

Their wedding initially turns toward disaster, but they marry and together have a son. He, however, is mysteriously abducted, and Rhiannon is falsely accused of killing the child, for which she is compelled to carry people on her back like a horse.

Rhiannon is not prominent in Branwen, the Second Branch, but Brân foretells that the enigmatic 'birds of Rhiannon' will sing above the seven survivors of the calamitous expedition to Ireland (Ériu) as they feast in strange oblivion. In the Third Branch, the widowed Rhiannon is given in marriage by Pryderi to the protagonist Manawydan. Rhiannon goes into a mysterious stronghold (caer) and promptly disappears. She is restored at the end of the tale.

Despite her centrality in the Mabinogi, there is a dearth of references to Rhiannon, by that name at least, elsewhere in medieval Welsh literature.

Rhiannon has a special importance as the figure in the Mabinogi whose antecedents in pre-Christian mythology have been seen as especially clear. Her name indisputably derives from Old Celtic *Rīgantona 'divine queen' (cf. the Irish war-goddess Morrígan). She is compared with the horse goddess Epona for her several equine associations in Pwyll and, like Modron (whose name derives from that of the ancient Matronae 'mother-goddesses'), Rhiannon is a divine mother whose infant son is mysteriously abducted.

John T. Koch

RHODRI MAWR AP MERFYN

Rhodri Mawr ap Merfyn ('Rhodri the Great') was a powerful king of Gwynedd during the 9th century. He became ruler in 844. According to the Irish Annals, Rhodri defeated the Vikings in 856, apparently attracting international attention with his victory. His fame among the Irish is further proved by a Latin poem to Rhodri, as Roricus, written by the Irish monastic scholar Sedulius Scottus. Due to family connections, he gained some level of control over Powys and Ceredigion. Because of this territorial extent, he is often called king of Wales (Cymru)—the only figure besides Hywel Dda and Gruffudd ap Llywelyn to earn this epithet in the pre-Norman period. In 878, Rhodri was killed by 'Saxons', according to Annales Cambriae, probably the forces of the Mercian king Ceowulf II.

Peter E. Busse and John T. Koch

RHUDDLAN, STATUTE OF

The term 'Statute of Rhuddlan' refers to the ordinances given by Edward I of England and his council at Rhuddlan, Flintshire (sir y Fflint), in 1284, following the conquest of Wales (Cymru). The preamble declares that the land of Wales, hitherto subject to the king by feudal right (iure feodali), has now come into the king's own dominion and been united to the Crown of the realm of England as a member of the same body. The ordinances thereby define a constitutional status that would stand until a further change was made by the Acts of Union of 1536–43. As a result of the Statute of Rhuddlan, English criminal law was made obligatory. Welsh civil procedures were allowed to continue, and it was decreed that partible succession (that is, division of inheritance between eligible descendants) would remain the inheritance practice among the inhabitants of the Crown lands, but the procedures of English common law were made available in civil actions.

J. Beverley Smith

RHYDDERCH HAEL

Rhydderch Hael ap Tudwal was king of Dumbarton (Dùn Breatann; see YSTRAD CLUD) in the later 6th century. Adomnán's *Vita Columbae* (Life of Columba) tells how he sought advice from COLUM CILLE (†597), fearing that he would be killed by his enemies. This story shows that the north BRITONS were on good terms with Iona (Eilean Ì) and also that Dumbarton was important enough when Adomnán wrote in the 690s to make this miracle worth including in the Life. According to HISTORIA BRITTONUM, Rhydderch was one of the kings led by URIEN in besieging the Angles on LINDISFARNE. According to the MYRDDIN poetry, as confirmed by GEOFFREY OF MONMOUTH's *Vita Merlini*, Rhydderch was one of the chieftains allied against Gwenddolau at the celebrated battle of ARFDERYDD (573). He also figures as king of Cumbria in the Life of KENTIGERN of Jocelin of Furness and is mentioned several times in the Triads.

Rhydderch was a common CUMBRIC and Welsh name of Celtic orgin < *ro-derkos* 'he who is seen', hence, 'prominent, outstanding'. His father's name *Tudwal*, Old Irish *Tōthal,* reflects Common Celtic *Toutawalos* 'ruler of the tribe' (see TUATH).

John T. Koch

RHYGYFARCH

Rhygyfarch (Ricemarchus, 1056/7–99), a Welsh cleric and scholar, was the eldest son of Sulien, who twice served as bishop of St David's (TYDDEWI). There are three surviving Latin poems by him: one on the psalter (*De Psalterio*), one a lament (*Planctus Ricemarch*) on the hardships the Welsh suffered under the oppression of the Normans, and one on the unhappy harvest (*De Messe Infelici*) destroyed by rain and mice. Rhygyfarch is best known, however, as the author of *Vita Davidis*, the first Life of St David (DEWI SANT; see also HAGIOGRAPHY). Written sometime in the last two decades of the 11th century, the *Vita* became an important tool in the struggle to establish the supremacy of St David's and fend off claims by the Norman-run church and Canterbury.

The Welsh name *Rhygyfarch* is Celtic. *Ricemarchus* is its Old Welsh spelling with a Latinized final syllable. *Cyfarch* is basically a compound verb (Celtic *com-arc-*) meaning 'to entreat' or 'to greet'. *Rhy-* is probably the preverbal particle, Celtic *ro-*, most often adding to the verb a sense of completed action, hence 'the greeted one', perhaps in the sense of 'expected' or 'honoured one'.

Elissa R. Henken

RHYS AP GRUFFUDD

Rhys ap Gruffudd ('The Lord Rhys', *c.* 1132–28 April 1197) was prince of Deheubarth (southwest Wales). The son of Gruffudd ap Rhys (†1137) and Gwenllian (†1136), daughter of Gruffudd ap Cynan of Gwynedd, Rhys succeeded his elder brothers to become sole ruler of Deheubarth in 1155. Although forced to submit to Henry II in 1158 and 1163, Rhys permanently recovered Ceredigion and Cantref Bychan ('The small hundred', between Brycheiniog and the river Tywi) from the Anglo-Norman marcher lords in 1164–65; together with Cantref Mawr ('The great hundred', to the north of the river Tywi) and its castle at Dinefwr, these territories constituted the core of his kingdom. Rhys also joined his uncle, OWAIN GWYNEDD (†1170), at Corwen, Merioneth (Meirionnydd), to resist the king's failed campaign against the Welsh in the summer of 1165. Henry II appointed Rhys 'justice in all south Wales'. Although subject to strains, especially in 1184 and 1186, the détente with Henry II lasted until the king's death in 1189. He held the first known eisteddfod at Cardigan castle (castell Aberteifi) in 1176.

Huw Pryce

RIGOTAMUS/RIOTHAMUS

Rigotamus/Riothamus is called 'king of the Britons' by the 6th-century writer Jordanes in his History of the Goths (*De Rebus Gothicis* §45). In 469, at the request of the western emperor Anthemius, Rigotamus sailed with an army of 12,000 up the Loire (Liger) to the *civitas* of the Biturīges (either modern Bourges or Berry) to join Roman forces. While they were camped there, the aristocratic Gallo-Roman Sidonius Apollinaris, who was bishop of Clermont from *c.* 470, wrote deferentially to king 'Riothamus' on behalf of a local landowner, whose slaves were running away to the Britons. The Rigotamus episode shows that sub-Roman Britons in Gaul were a major and organized factor in the events of the final years of the western Empire, and against this background it is hardly surprising that western ARMORICA has become *Britannia* in sources of the 6th century.

Rīgotamos is composed of the principal Celtic word for 'king' (cf. Old Irish *rí*, genitive *ríg*) with the superlative suffix added—hence 'supreme king' (cf. Gwrtheyrn; kingship). A variation of this same formation is found in the Celtic epithet of the god Mars Rīgisamus. It is possible, therefore, that it was the king's title, rather than his name, a possibility which gave rise to Ashe's theory that Rigotamus was the historical Arthur (see ARTHURIAN SITES).

John T. Koch

RING-FORTS

Ring-forts are a characteristically Irish type of early medieval monument, the upstanding remains of which survive in impressive numbers in Ireland (Éire). More than 45,000 ring-forts have been identified to date. They are commonly referred to by their Irish names: *ráth* or *lios* (Hiberno-English 'liss') in the case of the more common ring-forts of earthen construction, and *caiseal* (Hib.E. 'cashel') or *cathair* (Hib.E. 'caher') in the case of the stone-built variant, which is mostly restricted to the western seaboard (see CASHEL).

Ring-fort at Staigue, County Kerry, Ireland (Caiseal Stéig, Contae Chiarraí, Éire). (C. M. Dixon/StockphotoPro)

The origins of the ring-fort have been the subject of archaeological debate for decades and remain quite poorly understood. As regards the main period of ring-fort use, however, there can be little doubt. Scientific dating of more than 100 samples from 47 ring-forts and associated sites indicates, almost without exception, that their main period of occupation was during the second half of the 1st millennium AD—that is, the early medieval period. Some limited evidence suggests later medieval use and reuse of these structures, but most ring-forts appear to have been abandoned by the 12th century, if not before.

Morphologically, ring-forts are generally circular, or nearly so, in plan, with an internal diameter of between 20 m and 45 m. Most often, their defences consist of a single enclosing rampart accompanied by an external ditch, the upcast from which forms the substance of the bank. Occasionally, two or, very rarely, three banks encompass a site, but the internal area of these multivallate ring-forts usually remains of similar dimensions to that of univallate examples. Evidence from several excavations, such as those at Lisleagh, Co. Cork (Contae Chorcaí), indicates that palisades or fences of timber and wattle were sometimes erected atop the bank, thereby increasing the ring-fort's defensive potential. Entry to a ring-fort interior was via a causeway over the ditch and a corresponding gap in the rampart. Entrances most commonly faced somewhere in the arc from northeast through east to southeast, but could face any direction.

Early Irish law texts on status, particularly *Críth Gablach* (Branded purchase), make it clear that there was a specific relationship between the nature and scale of an individual's ring-fort and its ramparts on the one hand and the individual's social rank and standing on the other hand. There are different schools of thought as to what constituted the primary rationale behind the construction of the bank and ditch that formed the enclosing element of a ring-fort. Some authorities tend to emphasize considerations related to social status, while playing down the defensive rôle of such earthworks. Conversely, others see defence against cattle raiders and wild animals as paramount, with social considerations occupying a secondary place.

Where excavated, the interiors of ring-forts are usually found to have been host to a range of buildings. Both circular and rectangular foundations occur, with some indication that the latter are a later development. Interpretation of the buildings, along with the artefacts and environmental evidence recovered, has led to general agreement on ring-fort function: that they were the dispersed, defended settlements of single families—possibly with slaves and/or retainers—engaged in the type of mixed, but predominantly pastoral, farming widely practised in Irish early medieval society (see AGRICULTURE). Some evidence possibly suggests that ring-forts occasionally served only as cattle enclosures and in other cases may have been used as such when human habitation had, for whatever reason, ceased on the site.

On most excavated ring-forts, the recovered evidence indicates that artefact manufacture was restricted to the basic domestic and agricultural requirements of the inhabitants—for example, iron-working for farming tools such as plough-socks and axes; stone-working to produce querns, whetstones, and spindle-whorls; and the weaving of wool for cloth production. There are, however, several exceptional ring-forts where some of the finds were of a different order: decorative bronze- and silver-working including zoomorphic annular and penannular BROOCHES, production of beads and bangles of glass and lignite, and small intricately wrought decorations in gold. Some of these were the principal residences of early medieval ruling dynasties.

Simon Ó Faoláin

RIOU, JAKEZ

Riou, Jakez (1899–1937) was an important writer of fiction in the Breton language. He was born in Lothey, Finistère, in Brittany (Lotey, Penn-ar-Bed, Breizh), and in 1911 he went to be educated as a missionary in Spain, where he stayed until 1918. His *An ti satanezet* (The haunted house) appeared in book form in 1944. It captures the conviviality of rural Brittany with vivid portraits of a village's more colourful characters. *An ti satanazet* occupies a space in Breton literature between tales of death and the occult, known as *marvailhoù*, and the modern short story.

The short story was Riou's forte, and his collection of short stories—a slim volume entitled *Geotenn ar werc'hez* (literally, 'The virgin's herb')—is unrivalled in modern Breton. It probes a rural community with a modern perspective, and in it Riou illuminates the darker reaches of the Breton and human psyche. The title story describes a young girl's slide into illness and her premature death, which subsequently haunts her father. In *Prometheus ereet* (Prometheus bound), a young artist slips in and out of consciousness in a hospital bed. The staccato repetition of a short sentence suggests the tedium of the ward. The characters are tangible and human, and Rioù transports us into their universe in a few short pages.

Riou's prose works have been translated into several languages, including Esperanto, French, and Welsh. He also wrote several plays, and a volume of his poems, *Barzhonegoù*, was published in 1993.

Diarmuid Johnson

RIVER NAMES

River names are the most conservative features in the linguistic landscape. Old river names are very frequently maintained even after the population of a region has changed language. Names of some major rivers, such as the DANUBE and the Rhine, may predate Celtic, as they have cognates in other INDO-EUROPEAN languages. A number of the most important rivers of Europe bear Celtic names, and many of them also have divine name. For texample, the Seine, which flows through Paris, takes its name from the goddess Sequana, from a root meaning 'follow, pursue'. The Marne comes from *Mātrona*; see MATRONAE. Most of the river-names in BRITAIN, Ireland, and GAUL are Celtic.

Herve Le Bihan

ROADS, PRE-ROMAN

It has long been believed that roads were first seriously introduced in much of Europe by Roman road-building programmes. However, archaeological evidence has revealed that European pre-Roman roads date from at least the Neolithic. Both in the archaeological record and in historical sources, several different kinds of roads are attested in Celtic Europe, and it is possible to distinguish at least three main classes of roads.

Main roads (possibly called Celtic **mantlā*, sing. **mantlom*) are mentioned, for instance, by Caesar (*De Bello Gallico* 1.6.1–3), and appear in the archaeological record as roads 5–10 m wide on average, quite often with surface metalling. Constructed surfaces of gravel, compressed or burnt chalk, compressed clay, sand, clay/gravel mixtures and, where wetland had to be crossed, wooden planking are all attested at various sites. Such main roads probably crossed rivers via bridges, several of which are known in the Swiss archaeological record. Roads of this class seem to be comparable to what would be expected of an Irish *slige* attested in the early medieval literature. A trackway of massive planks and deep-driven stakes crossing a bog at Corlea, Co. Longford (Contae Longfoirt), Ireland, represents a major undertaking closely datable to the mid-2nd century BC.

Ordinary roads (for which a Celtic word was *sentos*) are also attested in historical sources (e.g., *De Bello Gallico* 5.19.2), and are found in the archaeological record as roads 3–5 m wide on average, often as secondary roads in Iron Age fortified settlements. They also frequently display some form of surface metalling. Where such roads crossed rivers, either bridges or fords (attested as British and Gaulish *ritus*) are the most likely possibilities.

The third distinguishable class are minor roads (a Celtic word possibly designating this class was **kammanom*; cf. French *chemin*, Spanish *camino*). These can frequently be detected in wetland contexts as trackways (OIr. *tóchar*) 1.5–3 m wide on average.

Although it was probably not expressedly a legal requirement, where opposing traffic was possible, left-side driving was probably the most common practice in Celtic Europe. Where travellers had to stay overnight, they could probably rely on a common practice of hospitality, attested in various historical texts (e.g., Diodorus Siculus, *Historical Library* 5.28.2–5, 5.34.1; Athenaeus, *Deipnosophistae* 4.150, 152), and also by the numerous *tesserae hospitales* (hospitality tablets) known from the Celtiberian regions of Spain. Along main trade routes and in major population centres (for example, the *oppida* of late La Tène Gaul), where hospitality by individual wayside farmers could not cope with the number of travellers likely to be in need of accommodation, hostels not unlike those described in early medieval Irish literature may well have existed.

Raimund Karl

ROADS, ROMAN (*SARNAU*)

One of the most impressive and enduring aspects of Roman civilization was a road system of legendary reputation. The construction of all-weather roads, and ancillary structures such as bridges, was an integral element of the scheme for the conquest of and the retention of control over the British tribal communities. Using surveying and engineering techniques hitherto entirely unfamiliar in Britain, strategic roads such as Ermine Street and Watling Street provided links between military bases, as well as springboards for further advance, facilitating the needs of military transport and supply—their primary function—and providing Britain with its first integrated communications infrastructure.

In Wales (Cymru), a minimum of 1,025 km of road was in existence. The basic Welsh framework is a great quadrilateral with three north–south axes: between Chester/Caer (deva) and Caerllion (Isca), Caernarfon (Segontium) and Carmarthen/Caerfyrddin (Moridunum), known as Sarn Helen, and a mid-Wales route via Brecon Gaer and Caersws; four east–west axes, between Caernarfon and Chester, Carmarthen and Caerllion, and the valleys of the Severn (Hafren), the Usk (Wysg), and the Tywi; and, finally, several 'diagonal' transmontane routes such as that linking the auxiliary forts at Neath/Castell-Nedd (Nidum) and Brecon Gaer. Some roads seemingly utilized prehistoric routes such as the trackway over the Carneddau, near Bwlch y Deufaen (Caernarfonshire), but the great majority were fresh, the product of Roman military surveyors (*mensores*).

In the post-Roman period many roads, such as Sarn Helen, seem to have become disused and eventually disappeared, while others, such as the Portway in Glamorgan (Morgannwg), survived to become the basis for turnpikes.

Jeffrey L. Davies

ROBERTS, KATE

Kate Roberts (1891–1985) is widely acknowledged as one of the giants of 20th-century Welsh prose literature. The author of numerous novels, novellas, and collections of short stories, the 'queen of our literature' and 'mother of the short story' was also a prolific journalist, a dynamic printer-publisher, and an active supporter of Plaid Cymru (see NATIONALISM) from its inception in 1925.

Roberts first embarked on her writing career while she was a teacher at Ystalyfera school in South Wales. Working with a small female collective similar to the many groups of women who collaborated to produce suffragette plays across ENGLAND at the time, she contributed to several sketches and plays performed by local amateur dramatic societies. Some of these were extremely successful, so much so that they were not only performed, but also published. For example, *Y Canpunt* (The hundred pounds), first performed in 1916, was published in 1923. *Y Fam* (The mother, 1920) won the prestigious de Walden prize in 1919, and *Wel! Wel!* (Well! well!, 1926) attracted the commendation of Saunders LEWIS, who described it in a letter to the author as 'a lively, funny, and true little slice of Welsh life'.

It seems that Roberts's success with the collective in the years during, and immediately following, World War I gave her the confidence to begin submitting her short stories to literary magazines such as *Cymru* and *Y Llenor*. In 1925, her first short-story collection, *O Gors y Bryniau* (From the marsh of the hills), was published to great acclaim, and she rapidly produced another three prose works: two books about children, *Deian a Loli* (Deian and Loli, 1927) and *Laura Jones* (1930), and the short-story collection *Rhigolau Bywyd* (Life's routines, 1929).

Roberts was an ambitious writer who, despite her familiarity with developments in contemporary European literature, was committed to establishing a specifically Welsh form of the short story and the novel, both of which were relatively young genres in Wales. Her political commitment to nationalism resulted in a wholesale rejection of the influence of English modernism: Like many of her compatriots, she deliberately opted for realist narratives peopled by characters drawn from her childhood. One of her most formally conventional pieces of work, the highly politicized family saga *Traed Mewn Cyffion* ('Feet in Chains', 1936), which highlights the plight of minority cultures unwillingly involved in battles between large empires, remains one of her most popular works among Welsh readers. Her focus on women's lives and emotional experiences is particularly marked in the stories in *Rhigolau Bywyd* and in the novel *Y Byw sy'n Cysgu* ('The Living Sleep', 1956), which examines the inexorable unravelling of the fabric of a woman's life following the breakdown of her marriage.

Roberts's journalism, which had always been a feature of her writing career, remained her most significant outlet until the 1950s. She had first contributed to the women's column of the Plaid Cymru newspaper, *Y Ddraig Goch*, in 1926, and continued to produce her own brand of politicized domestic journalism throughout her career, considering such topics as education and careers for women and producing a regular cookery column.

Her retirement from the press enabled Roberts to focus once more on writing novels and short stories, and it was during the 1950s and 1960s that she produced her most arresting and masterfully written works, including *Te yn y Grug* ('Tea in the Heather', 1959), *Y Lôn Wen* (The white road, 1960—her autobiography), and *Hyn o Fyd* (This world, 1964). *Tywyll Heno* (Dark tonight), a remarkable novella about a Nonconformist minister's wife who is hospitalized following a nervous breakdown, was published in 1962. Roberts continued to write and publish until her death in 1985.

Francesca Rhydderch

ROMANCES IN WELSH

'Romances in Welsh' is a shorthand term here for late medieval and early modern translations and adaptations from French. In native Middle Welsh terminology, there was no genre called 'Romance' and the term *rhamant* (see Tair Rhamant for a discussion of the Romances in the Mabinogion) is a purely modern usage.

Y Seint Greal or *Ystoryaeu Seint Greal*, however, is an avowed translation from the French, representing a late 14th-century Welsh version of two early 13th-century Grail Romances, *La Queste del Saint Graal* and *Perlesvaus*. Although the earlier *Peredur* included what approximated to Chrétien's grail procession, the term 'grail' was never used and the vessel carried was not named; therefore, *Y Seint Greal* represents the first specific mention of the grail in Welsh. The redactor knew *Peredur*, and strove to forge links between such earlier stories and his Continental sources. He was also familiar with other French material, notably the prose *Lancelot*, which, together with other Romances of the so-called Vulgate Cycle of French Arthurian Romances now became a quarry for compilers of other material (see Arthurian literature).

Translations or adaptations of foreign originals flourished. These were often based on French or Anglo-Norman sources, but also increasingly on English texts, especially as printed books became more common. The Welsh version of the Travels of Sir John Mandeville was based on a printed exemplar. Besides Welsh versions of books for entertainment or devotion, instructional texts on topics such as hunting, heraldry, and husbandry were produced.

Ceridwen Lloyd-Morgan

ROMANTICISM, BRITTANY

As elsewhere in the Celtic-speaking world, Romanticism in Brittany (Breizh) is the expression of a dramatic reversal in perceptions of a previously despised culture. And, as elsewhere, that reversal comes about through a kind of collusion between writers and artists working outside the area and those on the inside: Brittany 'becomes' Romantic, as it were, from Paris, before adopting and internalizing a Romanticized image of itself. Moreover, as recent critical work has made increasingly clear, Brittany also played a significant rôle in the development of French Romanticism as a whole.

For several decades after the French Revolution of 1789, Brittany was considered an exceptionally primitive backwater of the new French Republic. Descriptions by writers such as Jacques Cambry and J. F. Brousmiche, who toured Finistère (Penn-ar-Bed) in the 1790s and 1830s, are scathing about most aspects of the country, from its food, roads, and climate to the 'superstitious' and insurgent nature of its peasants and the barbaric sound of their language, BRETON. They and other commentators on the province adopted an essentially colonial stance, which sought to civilize a socially and culturally impoverished land.

A potent blend of ideas derived from Jean-Jacques Rousseau and James MACPHERSON neatly reversed the polarities of the primitive, and Brittany's backwardness became desirable. Its geographical isolation and 'ancient' language were now felt to have preserved its inhabitants from the evils of modernity.

A gentler Brittany emerges in the writings of Auguste Brizeux (1803–58), whose collection of poems, *Marie* (1831), aimed at a Parisian audience, evoked a remembered childhood idyll of rural simplicity (see CELTOMANIA). In Brittany, Émile Souvestre (1806–54), whose writings (also for a Parisian audience) dwell on the 'exotic' folk customs and temperaments of his native country, wrote *Les derniers Bretons* (1835–37) and *Le foyer Breton* (1844)—colourful, witty, and nostalgic accounts. Another of the most influential embodiments of Brittany's past was the BARZAZ-BREIZ, a collection of Breton-language BALLADS. Their idealization of the Breton peasantry now appears ideologically rather suspect.

These literary representations of Romantic Brittany have their visual counterparts. Breton costume was an attractive subject (see MATERIAL CULTURE), but most attractive of all was the landscape, with the endless possibilities provided by the interplay of land and sea. Many artists (most particularly a 'realist' group centred on Douarnenez in the 1860s) succumbed to the perennial appeal of the little fishing village. Wilder 'Romantic' scenes of storms and shipwrecks against craggy rocks also had their appeal, as the success of paintings by Théodore Gudin (1802–80) and Eugène Isabey (1803–86) testifies. The vein of myth and legend opened by the *Barzaz-Breiz* became another powerful source of inspiration, allowing the development of a more narrative (and even grotesque) element within the landscape genre. Edouard Yan Dargent's famous painting, *Les lavandières de la nuit* (1861), is directly inspired by Souvestre's account of the ghostly washerwomen at a ford.

The Romantic version of Brittany has proved an enduring one, and continues to contribute linguistic and cultural revival movements.

Mary-Ann Constantine

ROMANTICISM, IRELAND

In the 19th century 'Celtic' was often loosely employed to refer to an ancient (though historically vague) Ireland (ÉRIU), commonly seen to be imaginative, exotic, spiritual, not infrequently melancholy, and almost always strikingly antithetical to the sober Victorian, materialistic present.

The first scientific attempt to argue that the CELTIC LANGUAGES were related is found in the work of Edward LHUYD, whose interest in Irish antiquities garnered him the grateful praise of Irish poets. It was, however, James MACPHERSON's 'discovery' of the Ossianic poems (see OISÍN) that led to a more general awareness of how

Romantically the Celtic past could be viewed, and also to fervent claims that Ireland, rather than Scotland (ALBA), was the rightful home of Ossianic literature. In the translations of Charlotte Brooke (1740–93) and those of her contemporaries—people such as Sylvester O'Halloran (1728–1807), Charles Henry Wilson (1757–1808), Joseph Cooper Walker (1761–1810), Theophilus O'Flanagan (1764–1814), and James Hardiman (1782–1855)—a by and large more honest, albeit not always much more satisfactory, attempt was made to bring to light a culture that had previously been largely despised by educated readers of English. Such interest also led to the founding of several learned associations devoted to antiquarian research, among them the significantly titled Iberno-Celtic Society, the Celtic Society, and the Ossianic Society.

A somewhat analogous process of repossession occurred in the field of music with the work of Edward Bunting (1773–1843), who collected, transcribed, and published many traditional Irish airs (see IRISH MUSIC). Many of these pieces were soon accompanied by the Romantic nationalistic lyrics of Thomas Moore (1779–1852). Another collector of Irish melodies was Sir George Petrie (1789–1866), who was also an avid chronicler of Irish antiquities both pictorially and in his writings, and a successful advocate of the importance of studying the Irish past.

The rediscovery and rehabilitation of Ireland's past was ardently embraced by many nationalists, such as the United Irishmen (founded in 1791), and most notably the Young Ireland movement (founded in 1842), for whom language and culture played a central place in their concept of nationhood (see NATIONALISM).

During the second half of the 19th century, Romantic retellings of early myths and historical events in both prose and verse by such figures as Sir Samuel Ferguson (1810–86) and Standish James O'Grady (1846–1928) found a receptive audience among the nationalistically inclined Irish middle class. Such works inspired W. B. YEATS (1839–1922) to give a new literary expression to aspects of Irish mythology; he, and his like-minded collaborator Lady Augusta Gregory (1852–1932), were pivotal figures in the English-language literary renaissance, sometimes referred to as the Celtic Revival.

In tandem with the attraction of the remote Irish past there also grew a realization that Irish country-dwellers, especially those who remained Irish in speech, still possessed a rich oral legacy. To Yeats, Lady Gregory, and others, this became creative inspiration, as exemplified by Yeats's collection *The Celtic Twilight* (1893, 1902). The harsh, stoic, and apparently timeless way of life still prevailing in the west of Ireland also appealed greatly to a Romantic notion of primitivism.

Interest in the past was reflected visually in the popularity of interlaced Celtic ornament (see ART), and in the great vogue for emblems indicative of early Ireland, such as the HARP, the wolfhound, the HIGH CROSS, and the round tower. The imitation of ancient models was especially noticeable in jewellery, where copies of antique artefacts such as the TARA BROOCH were mass-produced and sold extremely well. This desire for distinctiveness even extended to dress, particularly in the case of formal wear: Women sported dresses and capes, of Irish manufacture and in what were considered Irish colours, modelled upon what native noblewomen of an earlier era were imagined to have worn.

The foundation of the Irish Free State (Saorstát na hÉireann) in 1922 and the subsequent Civil War can be seen to mark a point when Romantic idealism yielded to a harsher modern reality, although the traces of Romanticism certainly live on.

Dewi Wyn Evans

ROMANTICISM, SCOTLAND

The Scottish manifestation of Celtic Romanticism comes from Scotland's partly Celtic, partly non-Celtic cultural background and its relationship with ENGLAND. Scotland (ALBA) shares with other Celtic nations the awkwardess which flows from the exotic, Anglophone genesis of its Celtic Romanticism, which only gradually and gingerly became internalized by SCOTTISH GAELIC culture.

A form of Celtic Romanticism was undoubtedly present in Lowland SCOTS 'Highland Laddie' songs from the early 18th century, which celebrated a figure with an alluring combination of dangerousness and desirability—for instance, the flurry of Romanticized treatments of the Young Pretender's 'adventure' that appeared immediately after the 1745 Rebellion. More subtly, the Romanticization of the Highlander was a by-product of Lowland Scottish identity crisis in the wake of the UNION of the Parliaments.

In the mid-18th century, as the country moved away from the last JACOBITE REBELLIONS, two principal factors combined to stimulate and 'fix' the Scottish version of Celtic Romanticism. First, antiquarian interest in the 'native' past of all parts of BRITAIN was strong. Second, interest in the Celtic traditions of the British Isles was revived, both in the form of local (i.e., Welsh, Scottish, and Irish) investigation and collection, and at the level of a more generalized Celticism.

This was the climate that witnessed (and indeed stimulated) the appearance of James 'Ossian' MACPHERSON's poetry in the early 1760s. His timing was impeccable, and his poems strongly influenced Celticist poets and playwrights in English. As a consequence, Gaelic manuscripts were rescued and revered, Gaelic oral literature was collected, and Gaelic or Highland Societies were formed in the cities. The poetry's 'Romantic' mood percolated widely through into the literary tradition and the cultural consciousness of Gaels in both direct and less obvious ways, often combining with native themes and genres that offered ready-made points of contact.

Celtic Romanticism has also manifested itself in several other ways in Scotland, none of which are wholly independent of 'Ossian'. These include the cult of the martial Highlander, observing 'old' standards of honour and resplendent in Highland dress (see KILTS). Another potent image since at least the later 19th century is that of the naturally devout, deeply religious Gael, heir to the age-old teachings of Celtic CHRISTIANITY (or sometimes of a not dissimilar Celtic paganism). Yet another is the community Gael, with his hospitality, homespun wisdom, and traditional songs and tales: the Gael of the *ceilidh* house. This last is first cousin to the racial stereotype of the melancholy, nostalgic, poetic Gael beloved of television directors. To some extent these Romantic images are reactionary: They represent a 'soft primitivism' that has largely, though not wholly, supplanted the 'hard primitivism' of 19th-century Teutonic thinking, with its hopeless, racially inferior Gael whose removal from the Highlands could be contemplated with equanimity. Examples of Celtic Romanticism are still to be seen in today's media.

William Gillies

ROMANTICISM, WALES

Celtic Romanticism, in its all-embracing, rich, and energizing diversity, witnessed its heyday in Wales (Cymru) over the best part of two generations after 1770. It owed its success to a deliberate attempt to recover the abandoned or lost cultural traditions of Wales and create a more flattering and attractive image for its people. Authors, poets, painters, musicians, and myth-makers jostled with one another as they, in their capacity as self-styled 'ancient Britons' or 'valorous Celts', strove to rescue Wales from the condescension of the English, to rid it of its provincial 'non-historic' image, and to create a distinctive Romantic and national identity. Celtic Romantics in Wales lay great store by nature, primitivism, druidism (see DRUIDS), linguistic and musical traditions, and sheer fantasy, and these preoccupations surfaced in a variety of ways.

In literature, the most intriguing forerunner was Evan Evans (Ieuan Fardd, 1731–88), whose *Some Specimens of the Antient Poetry of the Welsh Bards* (1764) was a critical landmark in the history of Welsh scholarship. In his melancholy *Englynion i Lys Ifor Hael* (Stanzas to the court of Ifor the Generous, 1779), he mourned the passing of the old shrines of patronage that had sustained the poets of yore (see BARDIC ORDER).

Edward Williams (Iolo Morganwg, 1747–1826) not only seized the popular imagination by passing off invented love poetry as the work of Dafydd ap Gwilym but also devised and conducted in 1792 a colourful druidic moot—Gorsedd Beirdd Ynys Prydain (The Gorsedd of the bards of the Island of Britain)—which he advertised and utilized as a means of projecting the cultural, religious, and political principles of the Welsh bardic tradition. From 1819 onward, its ceremonies were incorporated into the EISTEDDFOD.

Thomas Gray's poem *The Bard* (1757) was a seminal influence on Romantic sensibilities, not least in encouraging Welsh radical patriots to excoriate English monarchs such as Edward I, whose army had allegedly massacred the Welsh bards shortly after the death of Llywelyn ap Gruffudd in 1282. This tale caught the imagination of artists such as Paul Sandby (bap. 1731–1809) and Thomas Jones Pencerrig (1742–1803), who depicted one of the last surviving harpist-bards about to leap to his doom into the 'foaming flood' of the river Conwy as the dastardly Norman troops closed in. This image of the Celtic BARD fixed in the public mind the notion that poets, priests, and druids in the Celtic past had long white beards, flowing robes, and melancholy songs to sing. Not surprisingly, therefore, the new Romanticism encouraged musical activity (see WELSH MUSIC).

In many ways, cultural patriots and mythmakers responded positively to the challenge of Romanticism by reviving or inventing institutions, publishing a rich and intriguing corpus of literature, and bringing them into the public domain in attractive and imaginative ways. By the 1830s, however, the proliferation of Nonconformist chapels and the emergence of thriving urban and industrial communities put an end to specifically Welsh Romanticism.

Geraint H. Jenkins

ROME, GAULISH INVASION OF

Only one abridged account from Polybius survives, together with reports in the work of Diodorus Siculus, Livy, Plutarch, and a few fragmentary accounts. Beyond the contradictions, the inventions, and the peculiar narrative colouring that can be found in the ancient sources, there exists a nucleus of credible information that permits us to reconstruct the facts of one of the most traumatic episodes in the thousand-year history of ancient Rome.

Around 390 BC, approximately 30,000 Gauls, predominantly the Senones (see BRENNOS OF THE SENONES), marched against the Etruscan city of Clusium (Chiusi) and besieged it. The terrified inhabitants asked Rome for help. According to Livy, Rome sent the three sons of Marcus Fabius Ambustus (the Fabii) as ambassadors. They intervened in battle on the side of the Etruscans and killed the Celtic chief at Clusium, thereby provoking the Gauls' march on Rome. According to Livy and Plutarch, prince Brennos (Latin *Brennus*) led more than 70,000 Gauls down the valley of the Tiber. There, where the river Allia meets the Tiber, 11 miles (*c.* 18 km) from Rome, they encountered the Roman army.

The Romans numbered at between 24,000 and 40,000, and their defeat against the Gauls at the Allia was traditionally depicted as a stunning reversal and rout. The action should have resulted in a ruinous flight of the Gauls from the Roman forces, who were fighting on familiar ground. That Rome suffered a humiliating defeat is a historical certainty, since this essential fact was known by several Greek authors who were writing a short time after the event in the 4th century BC. However, beyond this kernel, the accounts of the event become elaborate and suspect as to their veracity. Subsequent classical authors enriched their accounts with colourful anecdotes and legendary episodes, which possibly served to paper over some of the ignominious aspects of the event.

The accounts concur regarding the occupation of Rome, the sacking of the city, and the siege of the Capitoline hill (where all the youths fit for military service were barricaded, along with the most courageous senators, their wives, and their children). As to what actually happened, it is unlikely that the intentions of Brennos ever included the permanent occupation of Rome or its systematic destruction, as the accounts would indicate.

Regarding the retreat of the Gauls, Polybius suggests that they returned to their Po valley settlements in CISALPINE GAUL, which were threatened by the Veneti (who lived near Venice). This version involves a march to the north, which would explain the Romans following as far north as Volsinii or to Pisaurum.

Monica Chiabà

ROQUEPERTUSE

Roquepertuse à Vellaux is a prehistoric site located northwest of Massalia (modern Marseille). Its ancient name is not known, but the site was in use from Neolithic times (i.e., roughly 5000–3000 BC) until the 2nd century BC, when it was destroyed by a fire and abandoned, approximately when southern GAUL was annexed by Rome. The site's primary interest for Celtic scholars has been as a source of material evidence for the Celtic HEAD CULT described in the GREEK AND ROMAN ACCOUNTS dependent on the Celtic ethnography of Posidonius, who had travelled in this part of Gaul during the 1st century BC.

The most significant archaeological find was a semicircle structure embedded in the cliff above Roquepertuse. This platform, 50 m wide and 22 m long, was divided in the middle by a staircase. Stone walls to the left and to the right of the stairs formed a terrace. Beside statues of cross-legged sitting male figures, the most remarkable feature of this structure are several pillars with holes in which human stone masks, as well as human skulls, had been placed.

Roquepertuse provides evidence for a cult of the severed head in the territory of the local pre-Roman tribal group known as the Salluvii, who are sometimes tentatively given the ethno-linguistic designation 'Celto-Ligurian'. The nearby site at

Limestone head with two faces from Roquepertuse, France. (A. Dagli Orti/De Agostini/Getty Images)

Entremont has yielded similar relief sculpture of severed human and horse heads, as well as skull niches carved into pillars.

Peter E. Busse

ROSMERTA

Rosmerta, a Celtic goddess, is commemorated in INSCRIPTIONS throughout Europe, notably those from France, Luxembourg, and Germany. She is also frequently depicted with her attribute, the tub or vat, in images found at sites in France, Belgium, Germany, and Britain. Scholars disagree about Rosmerta's function and also about the precise meaning of her name, which is a compound of two elements: *ro-* 'very, great' or a marker of completed verbal action, plus *-smert-*, perhaps meaning 'provisioning', 'foresight', 'brilliance', or 'anointed, smeared'. Rosmerta is frequently paired with Mercurius, one of whose secondary names, *Smertrios*, similarly includes the element *-smert-*; in these instances, her presence preserves the identifying Celtic element of his name, though the indigenous god is subsumed under the Roman name (see INTERPRETATIO ROMANA).

Paula Powers Coe

RUGBY

The game of rugby football is alleged to be lineally descended from its pre-industrial Celtic forerunners: Welsh *cnappan*, Irish *cad*, Cornish HURLING, and Breton *soule*. There were regions in the CELTIC COUNTRIES where the game had acquired a strong working-class flavour by the end of the 19th century. Preeminent among these was south Wales (CYMRU). The game had been formalized and codified with the foundation of the Rugby Union in London in 1871, and its initial practitioners were pupils and old boys of the elite schools and universities. In Wales, scholastic institutions such as Lampeter and Llandovery Colleges were among the first to take up the new game.

The arrival of rugby football in Wales coincided with large-scale industrial development and the growth of towns. Rugby offered a physical release to an industrial workforce, an opportunity for the assertion of collective endeavour, communal loyalties, and, soon, national pride. While the coastal towns of Neath/Castell-Nedd (1871), Llanelli (1872), Swansea/Abertawe (1874), Newport/Casnewydd (1874), and Cardiff/Caerdydd (1875) were among the first to host clubs, the early formation of valley sides such as Treherbert (1874), Pontypridd (1876), and Pen-y-Graig (1878) also attested to a burgeoning club infrastructure that mirrored the location and growth of the Welsh coal industry. The game was controlled by the Welsh Rugby Union (WRU, 1881), which, from its inception, sanctioned cup competitions and local leagues that were anathema to the middle-class administrators in ENGLAND. The strength of the Welsh game, by contrast, was its social inclusiveness, as the WRU turned a blind eye to undercover payments within an ostensibly amateur game.

In Scotland, the founders of the Scottish Rugby Union (SRU) and of the earliest clubs were also products of educational insitutions, as reflected in their names:

Edinburgh Academicals (1857), Glasgow Academicals (1867), Royal High (1867), and Heriot's FP (1890). But Hawick (1873), Gala (1875), Langholm (1872), and Kelso (1876) were of a different cloth, manufactured by the woollen workers and hardy farmers of the Borders (i.e., southern Scotland, near England), whose fondness for cup and league competition distressed the pristine amateurs and social conservatives of the Edinburgh-based Scottish Rugby Union, founded in 1873. It took twenty years before the SRU deigned to award a Borders player an international cap, upon which it dawned on them that here was the Scottish equivalent of the Rhondda forward. In the first decade of the 20th century, whenever Wales failed to win the Triple Crown (in 1901, 1903, and 1907), Scotland did.

Pockets of industry in a predominantly rural setting, in this case tin-mining, were as much features of west Cornwall (KERNOW) as of the Scottish Borders. Here, the population was too thin to sustain professional sport, and, in the absence of other comparable county-wide institutions, the Cornish Rugby Union (1884) came to fulfil an important symbolic rôle as a focus for Cornish sentiment. The success of clubs such as Redruth (1875) and Camborne/Kammbronn (1878) ensured that rugby soon superseded wrestling as the most popular Cornish sport. Cornwall, like Wales, was one of the few places where rugby was not manipulated for social exclusiveness, but became rather an expression of masculinity, patriarchy, and regional identity. Rugby remains one of the ways in which people see themselves as belonging to an imagined Cornish community and, like the Welsh and Scots, subordinate partners in a greater whole, as a means of defining themselves in relation to England.

Meanwhile, the game had a middle-class complexion in Ireland, where it was associated with the Anglo-Irish of BAILE ÁTHA CLIATH (Dublin), though also enjoying a foothold in the Catholic public schools and the universities. In Ulster (see ULAID), it was socially just as exclusive, being the preserve of the Protestant academies and grammar schools; in the north, soccer was the game of the people. In the south, this position was occupied by Gaelic football (see GAMES), though rugby enjoyed a working-class following around Limerick (Luimneach), where some internationals were played before settling on the dual locations of Ravenhill (Belfast/Béal Feirste) and Lansdowne Road (Dublin).

The social and cultural changes of the 1960s and 1970s had a powerful impact on the game in Wales. The enforced loosening of the shackles of an industrial past and the diversifying of a hide-bound political culture resulted in the emergence of a generation of stunningly talented players that made Gareth Edwards, Barry John, and Phil Bennett household names in Wales and well known even outside it. They were celebrated in song, prose, and verse, on canvas and in metal, and the (several) Welsh speakers among them were inducted into the Gorsedd of Bards (GORSEDD BEIRDD YNYS PRYDAIN). The end of this second 'golden era' of six Triple Crowns and three Grand Slams (1969–79) coincided with the defeat of the first referendum for limited self-government in Wales and the beginning of two decades of right-wing Conservative government in the United Kingdom under Prime Ministers Margaret Thatcher and John Major.

In Wales, the 1980s and early 1990s ushered in a period of deindustrialization, severe unemployment, and the unravelling of the entire social and economic fabric that for the best part of a hundred years had sustained the viability and distinctiveness of Welsh rugby. A crippling loss of confidence, reminiscent of the 1920s, was once again reflected in a dizzying decline of Welsh fortunes at the club and international levels. A more confidently devolved Scotland and a politically and economically assured self-governing Ireland came to the fore, enjoying continuous international success against Wales unknown since the 1920s. The birth of the professional era in 1995 allowed England at last to exploit her greater size and resources, and the poor relations that were the Celtic countries were consigned and resigned to forming leagues and alliances among themselves as a massively endowed England moved far ahead of them financially, organizationally, and technically.

What the history of rugby in all the Celtic countries demonstrates, nevertheless, is a clear relationship between sporting prowess and the assertion of national identity, of the persistence of difference.

Gareth Williams

S4C

S4C (Sianel Pedwar Cymru/Channel Four Wales) is a public television service that offers programming through the medium of WELSH around 35 hours per week. The remainder of its programming is taken from Channel 4 as seen elsewhere in the United Kingdom.

In addition to the main analogue channel, S4C is responsible for broadcasting on its digital channels, S4C Digidol and S4C2. The former broadcasts for 80 hours per week in Welsh, simulcasting programmes with the analogue channel and providing additional programmes (such as extended coverage of national events). S4C2, launched in September 1999, provides detailed coverage of the proceedings of the National Assembly for Wales (see CYNULLIAD CENEDLAETHOL CYMRU).

Ten hours per week of programmes is provided from the licence fee by the BBC, but the remainder of the authority's Welsh language output is commissioned from independent producers.

The Welsh channel was established under the terms of the 1980 Broadcasting Act. Its formation needs to be seen as the climax to a lengthy, and often bitter, struggle to establish a separate broadcasting service for Wales that would provide Welsh speakers with Welsh-language MASS MEDIA. The idea of a separate channel for Wales was endorsed by the 1974 Crawford Committee on broadcasting. When it did not happen, acts of civil disobedience included the threat of a hunger strike by the then leader of Plaid Cymru, Gwynfor EVANS, unless the government adhered to its original promise of a separate channel for Wales. S4C broadcast for the first time on 1 November 1982.

Website
www.s4c.co.uk

Jamie Medhurst

SACRIFICE, ANIMAL

Animal sacrifice was practised in a religious context until the advent of CHRISTIANITY, and it continued in a secular context in the Christian era. For example, GIRALDUS CAMBRENSIS gives anecdotal evidence of a horse sacrifice, and literature mentions the *tarbfheis* (Irish 'bull FEAST'; see FEIS).

Animal sacrifice can fulfil many religious and social functions, including the ritual disposal of important or significant animals or the sacrifice of a valuable object in honour of the gods (see WATERY DEPOSITIONS). Neither of these acts normally involves eating the sacrificed animal. In contrast, rituals involving feeding or caring for the gods or ancestors or invoking their presence at significant cultural events probably involved eating the sacrificed animal. The function of animal sacrifice was probably broadly similar to that in the Graeco-Roman world.

Remains of animals discovered in pre-Christian sanctuaries provide evidence for both major categories of sacrifice.

1. *Sacrifices in which the animals were eaten* were the most widespread. Pigs were the most frequently chosen animal (approximately 75% of the remains found), followed by sheep and cattle. Other animals were also sacrificed, including dogs, but they are uncommon. At none of these sites have horses been found among the sacrificial remains.

2. *Sacrificial animals that were not eaten*, primarily cattle and horses, form the second major category. Most of the evidence for this rite comes from Belgic Gaul (see Belgae). These animals were probably never intended to be served as food; work animals were almost never eaten (see foodways). They were invariably adult animals that show traces of having been used as draught animals or mounts. They were put to death by a blow to the skull with a blunt object, and their carcasses often show evidence of having been left to decompose unburied. During this phase, the heads, notably those of the sacrificed cattle, appear to have been intentionally displayed (see head cult).

Patrice Méniel

SACRIFICE, HUMAN

As with Celtic ritual and religious beliefs in general, evidence for human sacrifice is gleaned from classical authors, archaeological finds, and possible reflections in the Insular Celtic literatures. All sources have to be treated with care: Greek and Roman accounts of the ancient Celts are distorted by their authors' attitude toward an enemy and, later, toward their descendants. The archaeological evidence for human sacrifice is rare and its interpretation difficult; the few references in Insular Celtic literature are centuries removed, filtered through Christian attitudes, and probably influenced by international folk-tale motifs. However, there is little doubt that human sacrifice was practised by Continental and Insular Celts alike.

Classical Sources

There are numerous references in Greek and Roman sources to the practice of human sacrifice. The classical authors often refer to this practice in connection with certain gods. Most authors described the custom in connection with the druids and their holy groves (see nemeton). Methods included shooting, impaling, hanging, stabbing, drowning, and burning. Several references identify the practice of using human entrails and remains for divination and communicating with the gods.

According to Diodorus Siculus and other classical sources, prisoners of war were the preferred sacrificial victims. Strabo boasts that it was the Romans who 'put an end to' human sacrifice. In some instances, what is called sacrifice could amount to the religiously sanctioned execution of criminals.

All three of the main classical sources—Diodorus, Caesar, and Strabo—refer to the burning of criminals, prisoners, and the innocent in giant statues of straw and wood or wickerwork constructions, which may be shaped as animals or humans, as a kind of 'thanksgiving' sacrifice (Caesar, *De Bello Gallico* 6.16.4–5; Diodorus Siculus, *Historical Library* 5.32.6; Strabo, *Geography* 4.4.5), a theme that has fascinated modern writers and film makers alike.

Archaeological Evidence

However graphic the classical descriptions, clear archaeological evidence for the sacrificing of humans as part of ritual activity is rare. More often than not, the finds allow for more than one explanation.

The most important sites for our understanding of ritual practices in GAUL are a group of sanctuaries in Picardie, France, which include Gournay-sur-Aronde, Ribemont-sur-Ancre, and Saint-Mauren-Chaussée. So far, all have been found to contain the remains of warriors or prisoners of war (together with substantial amounts of weapons) who had either fallen in battle or had been sacrificed. All skeletal remains were decapitated and seem to have been displayed within the sacred space. At Gournay-sur-Aronde, human adult bones which had been cut off from the body with the help of a knife were discovered. In a different place within the enclosure, six skulls, which had been carefully prepared and showed signs of having been on display, were found (see also HEAD CULT). The most spectacular finds so far have come from the excavated parts of Ribemont-sur-Ancre. Within a space of 60 m^2, more than 10,000 human bones and hundreds of weapons were discovered in a position that seems to indicate they had been kept upright for display, tightly woven into each other. Because no skulls were found in this part of the site, it is assumed that all had been decapitated before display. On two other sites within the sanctuary, fields of bones were discovered, with the longer bones piled crosswise and lengthwise to form a square, the inside of which was filled with pelvic bones arranged around a pit in which yet more bones had been burned.

Among other archaeological finds that seem to testify to human sacrifice is the famous GUNDESTRUP CAULDRON, which (arguably) depicts a man being drowned in what has variously been described as a deep shaft, a well, or a vat.

The so-called bog bodies—well-preserved human remains recovered from peatbogs all over northern and western Europe—constitute the best and most unequivocal archaeological evidence for human sacrifice. The body from LINDOW Moss had suffered the threefold death known from Insular Celtic literature before being submerged in water, naked and with his body painted. An important Irish find has been a late prehistoric adult male dressed only in a leather cloak at Gallagh, Co. Galway (Contae na Gaillimhe). The presence of a band of willow rods around his neck and two pointed wooden stakes at each side of the body may point to sacrificial activity.

Perhaps the earliest evidence for human sacrifice comes from an early Bronze Age ritual timber circle dated 3500–1500 BC excavated at Sarn y Bryn Caled, near

Welshpool (Y Trallwng), in mid-Wales (CYMRU). A central pit contained the cremated bones of young adults, together with four high-quality flint arrowheads, which show signs of having been in the bodies when they were burned. This may indicate that the victims suffered death by shooting, either in war or as part of a ritual.

References in the Insular Celtic Literatures

A classical account of human sacrifice to Teutates has been compared with the deaths by drowning in a vat of mead, beer, or wine ascribed to the Irish kings Diarmait mac Cerbaill and Muirchertach mac Erca. Each king was wounded, trapped in a burning house, and finally perished in a vat of liquor, all at SAMAIN (see KINGSHIP).

In the fantastic story of GWRTHEYRN, the boy AMBROSIUS, and the DRAIG GOCH in HISTORIA BRITTONUM, the king's wizards direct him to sacrifice a fatherless child and sprinkle his blood on a stronghold, to ensure that it can be built successfully.

Events in the saints' lives possibly preserve notions of human sacrifice. For example, St Oran volunteered to be buried under the foundations of Iona (EILEAN Ì) to hallow the soil.

Marion Löffler

SAMAIN

Samain is the Old Irish name (Modern Irish *Samhain*) for a festival celebrated on 31 October to 1 November in the standard western CALENDAR. In contemporary popular understanding, this date marks the beginning of the Celtic year, but, in fact, it is not at all clear when the year began or ended. Samain is known as 'the calends of winter' in the BRYTHONIC tradition (Welsh *Calan Gaeaf*, Breton *Kalan Goañv*).

The date is important in both medieval literature and modern folklore. As a transitional period, the eve of Samain was a liminal time in which boundaries between the mundane world and the OTHERWORLD were more likely to be crossed. Magical events and supernatural beings were more likely to be encountered on Samain; the dead, FAIRIES, and witches were all abroad on Samain.

The abundance of supernatural potential also made Samain a potent time for divination rituals. Many of the charms involved invoking an apparition, either of the dead or of one's future spouse—consider, for example, the practise of sowing hempseed just before midnight while saying a charm, and then turning to see one's future spouse mowing the hemp.

Samain was also a time of games and social gatherings. Bonfires were lit in Scotland (ALBA), and root vegetables such as turnips and rutabagas (swedes) were carved; nowadays, pumpkin carving is more usual. In BAILE ÁTHA CLIATH (Dublin), 'guisers' wore masks and went from house to house, begging for treats and mock-threatening the occupants with mischief if their demands were not satisfied. The night was known as 'Mischief Night' in many places, and pranks, with or without reward, were played in rural areas throughout Ireland and the Americas. All of these beliefs and behaviours have played a rôle in the formation of the contemporary celebration of Hallowe'en.

Samain (Samhain) bonfire, 2004. (Getty Images)

In more practical terms, Samain was the time when rents were collected and animals' values increased as they aged. Irish saga literature pays great attention to the feasts held at Samain. In the medieval literature, Samain is the occasion for both opening tales, as in MESCA ULAD ('The Intoxication of the Ulstermen') and SERGLIGE CON CULAINN ('The Wasting Sickness of Cú Chulainn'), and for significant events within the stories themselves. It is the date of CÚ CHULAINN's vision and, in *Aislinge Oengusa* ('The Dream of Oengus'), the day on which OENGUS MAC IND ÓC's bride-to-be changes from bird to human form. It is also the day on which Oengus claims the KINGSHIP of BRUG NA BÓINNE (Newgrange) in TOCHMARC ÉTAÍNE ('The Wooing of Étaín'). Samain plays an even greater rôle in *Echtrae Nerai* ('The Adventure of Nera'), whose hero journeys in and out of the Otherworld on this day, and in CATH MAIGE TUIRED ('The [Second] Battle of Mag Tuired'), in which the battle is fought on Samain. It is also associated with the deaths of CÚ ROÍ and Conaire Mór (see TOGAIL BRUIDNE DA DERGA).

In the Celtic languages, the name *Samain* is clearly related to that of 'summer'. For example, Modern Irish *samhradh*, Welsh *haf. Samoni*, the GAULISH word, occurs on the COLIGNY calendar as the name of a month.

Antone Minard

SAMSON, ST

The earliest written narrative from Brittany (BREIZH) is a HAGIOGRAPHY, the influential First Latin Life of St Samson of Dol. Basing his dating on textual evidence, Flobert has suggested a date between AD 735 and 772 for the work. The Life was probably composed at Dol, the centre of Samson's cult in Brittany. There are dozens of churches, towns, and parishes associated with Samson in Brittany, Normandy, and the Channel Islands. Samson is also associated with Cornwall (Kernow), including the Isles of Scilly (one of which is named after him). There are no secure dedications to him in Wales (Cymru) though, according to tradition, he was born in Wales and studied there under St Illtud, and a version of his life is found in the Book of Llandaf.

Samson himself appears to be a historical figure. A man named Samson, quite possibly a bishop and potentially St Samson, was present at the Council of Paris in 562. He is often conflated with another Samson, bishop of York, about whom nothing else is known.

Samson is a DRAGON-slaying saint, with several accounts of his banishing a dragon or serpent. There are also several different accounts of his healing or preventing poisonings. In relation to Celtic studies, the most notable events in his Life are the specific parallels to later secular Welsh literature. His parents, unable to conceive a child, make an offering of a silver rod the size of Samson's mother Anna, and she becomes pregnant with Samson. This is comparable to the payment of a rod of gold made to Matholwch in Branwen.

Antone Minard

SANAS CHORMAIC

Sanas Chormaic ('Cormac's Glossary') is an early Irish glossary. It is preserved in Leabhar Breac ('The Speckled Book') and in Leabhar Buidhe Leacáin ('The Yellow Book of Lecan'). The former, a shorter version, may be associated with Cormac ua Cuilennáin (†908), king and bishop of Cashel (Caisel Muman).

The material is listed under headwords ordered by the first letter only but not otherwise alphabetized. The content is extraordinarily varied, ranging from basic dictionary entries where one word is explained with another, through complex etymological analysis of words (a process which that much to Isidore of Seville), to full-blown tales triggered by a headword.

Its purpose remains unclear. While glossaries related to specific texts can be seen as aids to reading, this glossary is textually independent. The term *sanas* (which is the cognate of Welsh *hanes* 'history, narrative') can also refer to the secret council of the king of Cashel in a Munster context, and it is possible that the glossary was regarded as a repository of arcane material within the royal circles of the kings of Cashel.

Paul Russell

SATIRE

Introduction

Laughter and public ridicule were among the most potent of social sanctions in medieval Irish society, which prized the maintenance of individual and familial honour above almost all else. So immediate and real were the effects of public derision believed to be that the sources frequently depict blisters of shame arising upon the face and cheeks of the person being mocked. Moreover, the blistering or reddening (*imdergad, grísad, enechrucce, ruidiud*) of the face or cheek was construed as more than just a physical blemish, since the Old Irish words for 'face' and 'honour' were exactly the same (*enech*). Persons whose 'face' had been marred—in other words, whose reputation had been impugned, or whose behaviour and deeds had been publicly called into question—could all too easily find themselves bereft both of honour and of the privileges and followers to which they would normally be entitled.

Ridicule took many forms in early Ireland (ÉRIU), most of which fell under the general rubric of satire. The most common Old Irish terms for satire, *áer* or *rindad*, covered a wide variety of derisive behaviours. Formal, versified satire was perhaps the most potent type; however, the tales and law texts mention several other types of satirical reproach. Coining an uncomplimentary nickname, or mocking a person's appearance by word or gesture, was construed as satire, as was falsely accusing an individual of a crime, or taunting him, or laughing at him. Perhaps the most intriguing—and certainly the most exotic—species of satire was the mysterious *glám dícenn* (endless revilement), which, in its most extended form at least, seems to have had as much to do with black magic as with other forms of satire.

Many of the tales deal directly or indirectly with the use and abuse of satire: *Imtheacht na Tromdáimhe* (*Tromdám Guaire*, Guaire's band of poets), *Echtra Fergusa maic Léiti* (The adventure of Fergus son of Léite), CATH MAIGE TUIRED ('The [Second] Battle of Mag Tuired'), *Aided Chon Culainn* (The violent death of Cú Chulainn), and, of course, the TÁIN BÓ CÚAILNGE ('The Cattle Raid of Cooley') itself, among many others. The Old Irish legal text BRETHA NEMED (Judgements of privileged persons) provides an extensive discussion of the powers of satire and of the poets who composed it. *Cis lir fodla aíre?* (How many kinds of satire are there?) provides what purports to be a comprehensive list of the many types of satire known in early Ireland. A particularly valuable aspect of this text is its inclusion of examples of actual satirical verse.

It is largely to *Cis lir fodla aíre?* that we owe our current understanding of the workings of formal satire. The text suggests three important distinctions between the types of satire known in early Ireland: public or private; prose or poetry; and varying amounts of information about the person being satirized. In some of the poems cited, for example, the (alleged) offender is referred to only in the vaguest of terms; in others, his or her exact name and residence are given. A glimpse into the psychological subtleties of the genre is provided by poems that hint ominously at the possibility of further disclosure by providing some—but not (yet) enough—information to identify the individual in question. The poems exhibit many different techniques, from excessive and insincere praise, to faint, weak praise, to outright satire. Some are funny, some merely sarcastic. All suggest considerable attention to the language in which the message is conveyed.

The sources strongly suggest that many of the people engaged in the business of satire on a regular basis were a far cry from the literate, monastically educated poets called *filid* (see BARDIC ORDER) whom scholars now tend to associate with the production of metrically sophisticated verse. Indeed, to judge from the plethora of (often sneering) references in the sources to lower-class BARDS or lampooners, satire may well have been a weapon that appealed particularly to outlaws, the disenfranchised, and those whose voices might normally not be heard in the traditional legal process.

Women and Satire

Female satirists figure frequently in the literature. *Bretha im Fhuillema Gell* (The judgements about pledge-interests) allows a 'woman who satirizes' ([*ben*] *rindas*) to seek compensation for a lapsed pledge she has given on behalf of another by satirizing the offender's kindred leader. Similarly, satire offered the otherwise legally invisible bondmaid Dorn a manner in which to exact revenge for the king's mistreatment of her, though she paid a heavy price for her action. It is unclear whether either of the women referred to here would have been specifically trained in the poetic arts, though [*ben*] *rindas* is glossed in the texts with .*i. in banbhard*, 'that is, the female poet'. However, the frequency with which references to female satirists occur and the large number of appellations for women who engage in what must be considered related activities (*birach briathar, ben rindas, banch* *áinte, canait scél, rindele*), suggest that satire, whether spontaneous or ritualized, formal or informal, was an important genre of female speech. In this context, it may be instructive to think about the links between satire and the type of geis (verbal injunction, taboo) by which women or other marginalized figures simultaneously invoke and threaten the honour of those above them in the social scale to get what they want. DERDRIU's demands of Noísiu in LONGAS MAC NUISLENN ('The Exile of the Sons of Uisliu') and Gráinne's demands of Diarmaid in TÓRUIGHEACHT DHIARMADA AGUS GHRÁINNE ('The Pursuit of Diarmaid and Gráinne') may have more in common with satirical verse than is at first apparent.

The Filid and Satire

The *filid* clearly regarded satire as the prerogative of the monastically educated élite; even poets-in-training were not allowed to engage in full formal satire until they had completed their studies. The poetic tract *Uraicecht na Ríar* (The primer of the stipulations) is quite adamant on this point, decrying the attempts of ill-educated *taman* and *drisiuc* poets to engage in public satirizing and implying that any efforts they made in this direction would not be effective. Indeed, the contrast between the socially useful and productive satirizing of learned Christian poets and the greedy and destructive wheedling of the *cáinti* (low-class satirists) is a major theme in many tales. Several texts link *cáinti* with brigandage and the outlaw bands known as *fianna* (see FÍAN), and many go even further to allege the involvement of *cáinti* with paganism and druidry (see DRUIDS). Close parallels were drawn between the satire by the *filid* and the maledictions of Christian saints.

The Public Aspect of Satire

We know from the sources that satire could, and did, serve as a form of legal enforcement. Offenders who were satirized or threatened with satire and did not offer to come before the law forfeited their honour. High-status poets were required to be knowledgeable in the law as well as in the composition of poetry, and poets are often mentioned as playing an active rôle in the enforcing of cross-border claims, levying compensation in places 'where the barbs of satire are answered and the barbs of weapons are not'. Topics include wounding and slaying, women, neighbourhood law, animal law, and FOSTERAGE.

The most common cause envisaged for satire in the sources is the failure by rulers or important churches to maintain decent standards of hospitality. Poets played an important rôle in displaying and forcing rulers to live up to communal standards and expectations: Dues to poets were public dues, and satires (or near-satires) were expressions of communal as well as individual disapproval.

The abuse of hospitality by greedy poets is a common theme in the literature, and one of which the *filid* made deliberate use in disparaging their lesser-educated poetic rivals. Poets might also be appointed by persons in the community to act against others in pursuing a legal claim. They could also be chosen to act on behalf of their tribe, and appointment to tribal office was a sought-after position among the poetic élite. The involvement of the tribe (TUATH) seems to have lessened by the Middle Irish period (*c.* 900–*c.* 1200): the evidence suggests that later poets tended to act on behalf of the king personally rather than the tribes which those kings led.

Satire and Magic

It is difficult to know what to make of the relationship between magic and satire generally. Certainly, it is worth noting that *Uraicecht na Ríar* characterizes the satirical poem by which Caíar's fate was sealed as 'satire through a spell' (*aíre tri bricht*; see BRICTA). In other words, 'normal' satire (as opposed to *glám dícenn,* or satire that explicitly involved the recitation of a magical spell) did not always have to be conceived of as inherently 'magical' or, as Breatnach argues, capable of causing death (*Léachtaí Cholm Cille* 18.14). Its sanction was social rather than supernatural.

Annalistic references to people being 'rhymed to death' date from the 11th century and later, as do the references to 'rat rhyming' for which Ireland later became famous (that is, causing rats to die by reciting metrical verses, alluded to in Shakespeare's *As You Like It* iii.2). Perhaps, as the social context on which early satire had drawn for its sanctions changed over time and poets were thrown more and more back on their own devices in securing patronage and position, magic came more to the fore.

The Celtic and European Context

Curses and anathemas that functioned in a manner similar to satire, at least in Ireland, were commonplace in Europe. However, the only really striking European parallels are to be found in Wales (CYMRU), where satire not only existed as a genre, but also drew on beliefs about honour and poetry that closely resemble those we have examined for Ireland. The relationship between 'honour' and 'face' is reflected in the Old Breton *enepuuert* and the older Welsh word for 'honour-price', *wynebwerth* (literally 'face-worth', later replaced by *sarhaed*). As in Ireland, the Welsh poetical lexicon reflects a belief in poetry as a mantic endeavour, and stories told in Welsh about the acquisition of poetic insight closely parallel Irish tales on the subject. Satire (or at least certain varieties of it) was conceived of as having the potential to harm or even to kill. For example, the poet Rhys Meigen was said to have been slain by a satire of Dafydd ap Gwilym, and Culhwch (see Culhwch ac Olwen) threatened to dishonour Arthur. Military metaphors in which satirical assault is compared to its physical counterpart are not as common in Welsh as they are in Irish, but they certainly exist.

Satire seems to have been far less important in Wales than it was in Ireland, though we know it to have existed in both countries. No satirical verse remains extant from the earliest period, and very little from the period of the Poets of the Princes (*c.* 1100–1282; see Gogynfeirdd). To judge from the surviving poems, Welsh poets would seem to have focused more on praising their patrons than on satirizing on their behalf. There is no evidence from Wales of the use of satire in legal enforcement, though ridicule (especially of the marginalized) was a potent weapon in the maintenance of order.

As in Ireland, suspicions began to be voiced in Wales in the late Middle Ages about satire. However, these reservations seem to have arisen less from a fear of its power as a genre than from its distasteful association with lower-class poets. Denigrating satire was a way in which the élite of the bardic order could limit the participation of those less learned than themselves in the production of poetry at court. In this sense, there are clear similarities with the Irish *filid* and *cáinti*, but each existed within its own individual social and chronological context. Satire in both cultures was deeply embedded in the social and political framework within which the poets who produced it lived and worked. Like other such Common Celtic institutions, its nature and power can be understood only within the context of the medieval society that gave it life.

Robin Chapman Stacey

SAYERS, PEIG

Peig Sayers (1873–1958) was an Irish storyteller whose autobiography is one of the celebrated accounts of life on the Great Blasket Island (An Blascaod Mór). She and her husband had ten children, six of whom survived infancy. One son, Tomás, died in a cliff fall in 1920. The remaining children emigrated to the United States, but one of them, Mícheál/Maidhc, returned. The family left the island in 1942 and settled on the mainland, near Peig's birthplace.

Sayers's storytelling ability and clearly articulated Irish brought her to the attention of scholars such as Robin Flower (1881–1946), who described her as 'one of the finest speakers on the Island'. Persuaded by two visitors, Máire Ní Chinnéide and Léan Ní Chonalláin, to tell her life story, she dictated it to her son Mícheál Ó Guithín, whose own outlook is discernible in the work. *Peig, A Scéal Féin* (Peig, her story)*,* appeared in 1936. Her second book, *Machtnamh Seana-Mhná* (Reflections of an old woman, 1939), consists mainly of folklore and local history.

Scealta ón mBlascaod, Kenneth Jackson's collection of folk-tales from Peig Sayers, was first published in the journal *Béaloideas* in 1938. Seosamh Ó Dálaigh of the Irish Folklore Commission recorded hundreds of items of folklore from her between 1942 and 1951. More than an hour of material was put on disc for Radio Éireann in 1947.

Nollaig Ó Muraíle

SCÉL TUÁIN MEIC CAIRILL

Scél Tuáin meic Cairill (The tale of Tuáin son of Cairell) is a 9th-century Old Irish prose tale about a supernatural figure named *Tuán,* who lived in a succession of animal and human forms through the entire history of Ireland (ÉRIU). St Finnian of Moville induces him to recount his experiences. Tuán tells how he came to Ireland with PARTHOLÓN following the Flood, then lived through all the island's subsequent history, thanks to periodic rejuvenation through assuming the shapes of different creatures.

John Carey

SCÉLA MUCCE MEIC DÁ THÓ

Scéla Mucce Meic Dá Thó ('The Story of Mac Dá Thó's Pig') an early Irish saga of the ULSTER CYCLE. It shares several themes with FLED BRICRENN ('Bricriu's Feast'): the contest for the CHAMPION'S PORTION, the heroic contention at the great FEAST, and beheading (see HEAD CULT). Mac Dá Thó (a name explained in another saga as 'son of two mutes') is the owner of a great hostel (BRUIDEN), unwillingly placed in a dilemma of hospitality when the rival ULAID and Connachta ask, at the same time, for his marvellous dog, Ailbe. He attempts to resolve the problem, and fails disastrously—creating sustained comic tension—by granting the hound to both sides and inviting them all to a great feast. The honour of carving the phenomenal pig seems at last to settle on CONNACHT, until CONALL CERNACH'S sudden appearance reopens the contest; the feast leads to a general mêlée in which Ailbe the dog is killed.

John T. Koch

SCOTLAND

See Alba.

SCOTS/SCOTTI

The meaning of the group name Scots (English)/Scotti (Latin) in modern times is usually geographical and political: the inhabitants of Scotland or people of Scottish origin, without further reference to a specific linguistic or cultural group. *Scots* can also mean the traditional dialect of Anglian English in the Lowlands. Scots is the language of Robert BURNS (1759–96) and many historical and legal documents of the early modern period; it is closely related to English, and, subject to a speaker's linguistic and sociolinguistic factors, may be an accent, dialect, or language. There is also Ulster Scots as the result of Lowland Scottish settlement there in the 16th and 17th centuries (see Ulaid). *Scots Gaelic* is an alternative designation for Scottish Gaelic, Scotland's Celtic language. With reference to the past, the usage is ambiguous; in medieval texts, *Scotia* can mean Ireland as well as Gaelic-speaking Scotland.

Prior to the formation of Alba, *Scotti* 'Scots' must refer to Gaels, Old Irish *Goídil*, early Welsh *Gŵydyl*, speakers of Gaelic or Goidelic, who resided in the earlier Middle Ages in Ireland (Ériu), Dál Riata, and the Isle of Man (Ellan Vannin).

The earliest surviving text to use the term *Scoti* is a list of the Roman provinces and their barbarian enemies, compiled *c.* AD 312, known as *Nomina Provinciarum Omnium*; in this document, these peoples are grouped with the *Picti* (Picts) and the *Caledonii* (Calidones). The word seems to be used synonymously with *Hiberni*. St Patrick calls the Irish both *Scotti* and *Hiberionaci* (cf. Modern Irish *Éireannaí*).

The origin of the name is not certain. The element *Scot-* does occur in some Old Celtic personal names, and there is a record of a tribe known as the *Scotraige* in Ireland. In Lebar Gabála Érenn ('The Book of Invasions'), Scotta is the namesake of the Scotti (Irish); she is the daughter of Pharaoh and mother of Goídel Glas, namesake of the Gaels. They are the ancestors of Éber Scot, who led the Gaels of legendary history from Egypt to Scythia. The linking of the Gaels with Scythia was itself inspired by the similarity between the name *Scotti* and *Scythi*. One of the possible etymologies of *Scotti* is from the same Indo-European form as *Scythi*, both originally meaning 'shooters'.

John T. Koch

SCOTT, SIR WALTER

Sir Walter Scott (15 August 1771–21 September 1832) was born in Edinburgh (Dùn Èideann). His family connections were with the Borders counties, but professional duties also took him as a young man into the Scottish Highlands. His first published works were translations of German narrative poetry, and in 1802–3 he published the *Minstrelsy of the Scottish Border*, a collection of traditional ballads. His own narrative poems, beginning with *The Lay of the Last Minstrel* in 1805, were hugely successful and made Scott famous, rich, and a partner in his publisher, John Ballantyne.

In 1814, Scott began writing novels. Many are set against episodes in Scottish history from the 15th to the late 18th centuries; later titles also explore a variety of European historical contexts. Scott's fiction is usually credited with the invention of the historical novel as a form, and of social realism more generally, though there are Irish antecedents. *Waverley* (1814) and *Rob Roy* (1817) include detailed portrayals of the society from which the Jacobite rebellions (of 1745–46 and 1715, respectively) drew much of their support. Later works such as *The Highland Widow* and *The Two Drovers* (1827) return to the same issues of cultural difference and historical change, as well as showing some basic knowledge of Scottish Gaelic.

Scott's understanding of the difference between the Highlands and the Lowlands is shaped by the Scottish enlightenment, though anticipating Romanticism Scott also represents the values of Gaelic Scotland as admirable, and mourns their loss.

In effect, this perspective turns the 'Celtic' into an aesthetic rather than a linguistic or political category: Scott's works can thus be seen to continue the process, begun by James MACPHERSON and his Ossian poems (see OISÍN), of commodifying Gaelic culture as a series of objects, gestures, and motifs, for sale in the literary marketplaces of Edinburgh and London. Scott's influence extends to the categorization of Scotland as a Celtic nation.

Robert P. Irvine

SCOTTISH GAELIC DRAMA

The first reputed staging of a play in SCOTTISH GAELIC occurred in Edinburgh (DÙN ÈIDEANN) in 1902. Some earlier plays had been published in Gaelic periodicals such as

Sir Walter Scott was a Scottish writer best known for his romantic historical novels. He developed the genre of historical fiction in such novels as *Robin Hood* and *Ivanhoe*. (Library of Congress)

An Gaidheal (The Gael) and *An Teachdaire Gaelach* (The Gaelic messenger).

Although this early drama was originally created by Gaels living in urban areas, drama soon became popular in Gaelic communities in the HIGHLANDS and Islands. Gaelic drama has generally existed in an environment of festivals and competitions. The general rule for amateur competitive drama in Scotland (ALBA) is that plays should be one act in length and should not last longer than half an hour; by far the most common type of play in Gaelic is this one-act half-hour production. A peculiarity of Gaelic drama groups is their reluctance to perform a play that has been seen before, thus providing an impetus for the writing of new plays. To date, there have been only two professional Gaelic theatre companies: *Fir Chlis* (Northern lights, 1977–81) and *Tosg* (1996–).

The drama of the 1960s became less parochial, and the plays were no longer confined to subjects specifically related to the Gaelic way of life. Notable playwrights include Iain MAC A' GHOBHAINN (1928–98), Iain Moireach (1938–), Fionnlagh MacLeòid (1937–), Tormod Calum Domhnallach (1927–98), and Donnaidh Mac-Illeathain (1936–2003).

Michelle Macleod

SCOTTISH GAELIC LANGUAGE

Introduction

Scottish Gaelic belongs to the Goidelic or Gaelic branch of the Celtic languages, along with Irish and Manx. There are Scottish Gaelic speakers in Canada as well as in Scotland (Alba), particularly in Nova Scotia (see Celtic languages in North America). Scotland's Celtic language, Scottish Gaelic, is mainly spoken in parts of the Highlands and the Western Isles, with a small urban community of speakers in Glasgow (Glaschu). At the 2001 Census 58,682 people were able to speak the language, a decrease of 11 percent from the 65,978 speakers counted in 1991 (Registrar General for Scotland, *Registrar General's 2001 Census Report* 17).

Despite the orthographical revision of the 1980s, the spelling of Scottish Gaelic is still to some extent based on 'pronunciation spelling', as can be seen in all but fairly recent publications. Previously, much of the published material was based on the spoken language and reflected the dialect of the author.

Historical Background

The Gaelic language was introduced into western Scotland (Alba) by Irish settlers sometime during the 5th or early 6th century (see Dál Riata). An indication of the settlement pattern of the speakers of Early Irish who had presumably come over from Irish Dál Riata in north Antrim can be gained from the distribution of particular place-names in Scotland, especially those with the elements *baile* 'homestead' and *achadh* 'field' (see Scottish place-names). These distributions show that Gaelic spread at the expense of other Celtic languages once spoken in Scotland—namely, Pictish and Brythonic—and was at some point spoken, at least by the ruling class, in all parts of Scotland.

While contact between Ireland and Scotland was maintained throughout the Middle Ages, as is illustrated by the prolific literature from this period, composed in a shared (and doubtlessly increasingly artificial) literary language (cf. Irish language) used by professional poets on both sides of the Irish Sea, the everyday spoken languages of Scotland and Ireland must have increasingly differed from this learned standard. One early sound change that distinguishes between Irish and Scottish Gaelic is that Irish generally abandons hiatus (two vowels with no intervening consonant sound as separate syllables) before 1200, but Scottish Gaelic retains it: For example, Old Irish *aue* 'grandson' (two syllables) became Middle Irish *úa* (one syllable), but Scottish Gaelic *latha* (still two syllables). The modern Scottish Gaelic language unambiguously appears in written sources from the 17th century onward, consistently displaying various features that mark its independence from Irish.

Scottish Gaelic has borrowed vocabulary from Latin, French (often through Scots English), Norse, and, of course, the English language. Prolonged language contact, particularly with English, has also led to changes in composition and idiom, with calquing (modelling new words and idioms on those of another language, English) now common in the spoken language as well as in all areas of the written language. From the 9th century to early modern times, there was a strong Scandinavian presence in western and northern Scotland, and the phonology of Scottish Gaelic may have been subject to Norse influence, as in the development of the characteristic pre-aspirated consonants (discussed in the next section).

Characteristics

As in Ulster Irish, Scottish Gaelic has retained the initial stress of the older language and has shortened all unstressed vowels. Within a word, stress is generally placed on the first syllable, though loanwords or compounds may have the stress elsewhere. Within each sentence, there is at least one heavily stressed word.

Pre-aspiration is one of the most striking features of Scottish Gaelic and is found in most of its dialects. In most dialects, it means that, when the strong stops *p, t, k* are preceded by a short stressed vowel, an *h*-like or breathing sound is introduced. Hence, *mac* 'son' is pronounced [maχk] vs. Irish [mak] without pre-aspiration (χ is like the final sound in *loch*, as in Loch Ness). The level to which pre-aspiration is realized in the spoken language varies from area to area, and ranges from weaker [ʰp ʰt ʰk] to stronger [χp χt χk].

As in other Celtic languages, initial mutation is a salient feature of Scottish Gaelic. Lenition functions similarly to Irish lenition, but as nasalization is used in fewer grammatical environments, it is not shown in standard spelling.

Basic word order in Scottish Gaelic is verb–subject–object, though a full range of complex structural changes and qualifying clauses are also used. In the absence of a verb indicating ownership or possession, the language uses prepositional sentences—for example, *Tha cat aig Iain* (lit. There-is cat at Ian) for 'Ian has a cat'.

Scottish Gaelic nouns fall into two categories, masculine and feminine, arranged in case paradigms with nominative, genitive, and accusative/dative forms, and some rudimentary vocative forms (used in address). While the masculine and feminine patterns are well developed, there is no distinction between the masculine and feminine plural forms. In spoken Scottish Gaelic, special genitive forms are sometimes simplified or simply replaced by the nominative.

Scottish Gaelic preserves the Old Irish double system of syntactically conditioned verbal endings (absolute versus conjunct) to a certain degree—for example, absolute *beiridh*: conjunct *gu'm beir* 'takes, will take' < Old Irish *beirid*: *-beir*. All dialects make the distinction between past, future, and conditional forms of the verb, though only the verb 'to be' (*bith*) retains both a distinct present and future form. A progressive aspect, to express ongoing action, is shown by using forms of the verb 'to be' in combination with the verbal noun—for example, *tha mi ag iarraidh* 'I am asking'.

As in Irish and the early Brythonic languages, there are two verbs 'to be' in Scottish Gaelic, originally called the substantive verb (forms of *bith*) and the copula (forms of *is*). The copula and substantive verb have different syntax—for example, *is clachair e sin* or *tha e 'na chlachair*, both meaning 'he is a mason'.

Petra S. Hellmuth

SCOTTISH GAELIC LITERATURE (TO C. 1200)

Little literature exists in GAELIC from early medieval Scotland (ALBA). Nearly all of what has survived is preserved in manuscripts of Irish provenance. The major poetry we have derives from the Columban monastic *familia*, and includes a variety of poems in praise of St COLUM CILLE. A strand of anecdotes contained in the 10th-century *Betha Adamnáin* ('Life of Adomnán') has been identified convincingly as deriving from Iona (EILEAN Ì). From the same period come several poems attributed to Mugrón, abbot of Iona. Beyond these works, we are dependent on stray verses contained in metrical treatises and ANNALS. Some verses are in praise of Pictish kings, suggesting that their patronage extended beyond their own linguistic boundaries. One stray satirical verse on Earl David (the future David I, king of the SCOTS, 1124–53) suggests the presence of professional poets within the court circles of the kings of Alba into the 12th century.

The Gaelic translation of the HISTORIA BRITTONUM, the *Lebor Bretnach*, has recently been shown to have been composed in eastern Scotland in the 11th century, and its companion pieces in the dominant manuscript tradition are arguably also Scottish: a king list containing a foundation legend of Abernethy (see SCOTTISH KING-LISTS), and a Middle Gaelic adaptation of Book I of Bede's *Historia Ecclesiastica*. Perhaps dating to the 12th century, but possibly slightly later, is a version of a voyage tale composed on Iona, with newly added verses.

Thomas Owen Clancy

SCOTTISH GAELIC POETRY, CLASSICAL GAELIC

Classical Gaelic poetry in Scotland (ALBA) should be seen as an offshoot of the greater classical Irish poetic tradition (see IRISH LITERATURE). Indeed, most of the Scottish material is classical Irish in form, language, and metre, and the Irish training, orientation, and, occasionally, origin of many of the poets who practised in Scotland is evident. The linkage may begin as early as Muireadhach Albanach Ó Dálaigh, the first certain practitioner of classical verse in Scotland. Among the key learned families practising classical verse under the patronage of Scottish lords we may count the Ó Muirghesain family, originally of Donegal (Dún na nGall); the MacEwen family, who served both the Clann Dubhgaill (MacDougalls) of Lorne and, later, the Campbell lords and earls of Argyll; and the Clann Mhuirich (see CLANN MACMHUIRICH), whose members continued to be capable of composing classical verse into the 18th century. While some Scottish material is preserved in Irish manuscripts—for example, key poems of Muireadhach Albanach, the anonymous Irish poem in praise of Aonghas Mór MacDhomhnaill, Lord of the Isles (*c.* 1250), and the masterly lament for the Scottish Fearchar Ó Maoil Chiarán, composed by his father—the bulk of the Scottish classical material is preserved in the Book of the DEAN OF LISMORE and the Book of CLANRANALD.

Thomas Owen Clancy

SCOTTISH GAELIC POETRY, TO *C.* 1745

Introduction

The earliest recorded poems in vernacular Scottish Gaelic date from the 16th century, though it is clear from the style and quality of the poems that they are part of a well-established tradition. The Book of the Dean of Lismore (mainly compiled between 1512 and 1526) contains a considerable amount of material of Scottish provenance, but much of it is in Classical Common Gaelic—that is, the learned literary language shared by Ireland (Éire) and Scotland (Alba) from *c.* 1200, whose use faded by the later 17th century. However, the popular vernacular tradition draws upon the same broad conventions as the poetry produced by the professional bards who used the classical language (see bardic order; Irish literature). The distinction between poets working in the classical tradition and those composing in the vernacular language is not always absolute: Some Clann MacMhuirich poets who were active toward the end of the classical period produced work in both languages, such as Niall MacMhuirich (*c.* 1630–1716), whose *Marbhrann Mhic Mhic Ailein a Mharbhadh 'sa' Bhliadhna 1715* (Elegy for the son of Clanranald who was killed in the year 1715) is in the vernacular language and metre, but contains imagery shared by both traditions.

Some extant poetry may be described as 'semi-bardic' in recognition that it is vernacular in language, but shares other features with the classical tradition. The metre may be close to a classical metre, the themes and imagery used may be modelled more strongly on bardic imagery than usual, or the poet may use conventions of construction drawn from classical verse, such as the use of an ending to the poem that echoes the beginning by repeating the initial word, phrase, or line (called *dúnadh*, 'encircling, closure'). The practitioners of such verse were sometimes professional poets and sometimes amateurs, usually of some social standing. Semi-bardic features can be identified to a greater or lesser extent in many vernacular poems. One such example of bardic origin is *An Duanag Ullamh* (The polished little poem), dated variously to the first quarter or the middle of the 16th century. The addressee was an earl of Argyll (Earra-Ghaidheal), named as Archibald in the poem, and the poet appears to have been bard to Maclean of Duart.

Where metres are shared between the classical tradition and the vernacular tradition, the vernacular verse handles these much more freely and loosely; this is particularly well illustrated in the Gaelic ballads. The praise tradition inherited from the bardic context is further developed into an extensive and sophisticated code, the so-called panegyric code. Heroic achievement of the leader and warrior dominates in panegyric imagery (see heroic ethos), with some prominence given to the description of prestigious weapons of excellent craftsmanship and the competent handling of such items by their owner. Hunting, horsemanship, and skill in sailing a ship are also present as standard motifs. Often, the chief's household and the musical and literary entertainment offered there are described in great detail, and closely connected is imagery telling of the chief's generosity to the needy and the deserving alike. The noble descent and prestigious connections of the chief within the HIGHLANDS and Islands and farther afield take a prominent place, with some emphasis placed on the chief's ancestors and their achievements. Description of personal beauty is another favourite aspect of the panegyric code. Elegies add imagery pertaining to death, burial, and mourning to the catalogue. Reversal of praise motifs is found in SATIRE. Imagery is also used freely in poetry that does not have an aristocratic subject, emphasizing the importance of the panegyric code in the poetry of the period and well beyond. In this context, originality and innovation are not highly prized attributes of poetry; instead, elaboration of a common motif in fresh and vivid detail is what poets strove for and what audiences expected.

Nearly all poetry belonging to this period was designed to be sung. Many songs remained current in oral tradition and were recorded as late as the 20th century. Printed sources often note tunes for individual songs; this would seem to indicate that many poets were content to compose to existing tunes. In the 18th century it becomes obvious that LOWLAND tunes are increasingly being adopted for Gaelic songs. The céilidh was an important contributory factor in the survival of the songs, as was the waulking tradition, which preserved a substantial number of songs that go back to the 17th century or beyond. While much material by named authors is extant, a considerable body of anonymous material is also known.

Many poets considered themselves as spokespeople for society. They commented on matters of significance for the community or censured inappropriate behaviour, and they expressed shared feelings of grief at the death of a leader.

Clan and Political Poetry

CLAN poetry is a major genre associated with the 17th century and the first half of the 18th century. Important exponents of its different manifestations include Iain Lom MacDhòmhnaill, Sìleas na Ceapaich, Màiri nighean Alasdair Ruaidh, and some of the Maclean poets. The panegyric code is particularly clearly represented in this type of poetry. It is concerned with the rôle of the chief in safeguarding the clan and its lands from external threat, thereby guaranteeing the perpetuation of the traditional values and structures of society. However, strains caused by historical forces (e.g., civil war) and the growing association of the aristocracy and gentry with Lowlands society and values through EDUCATION in English can also be seen in the poetry. The pressure brought on clans such as the MacDonalds, the MacLeods, and the Macleans by Campbell expansionist strategies is also an important facet of clan poetry; anti-Campbell attitudes blend fairly seamlessly with Royalist and later Jacobite sentiments since the Campbells overwhelmingly supported the parliamentary and government sides. Contemporary politics often find expression in such poetry; for example, in Iain Lom's *Òran an Aghaidh an Aonaidh* (A song against the Union), the poet criticizes several individuals who were prominent in the negotiations that led to the UNION of Parliaments in 1707.

A natural development of political verse is the distinctive genre of JACOBITE POETRY in the late 17th and the 18th centuries (see also JACOBITE REBELLIONS).

Eulogy and Elegy

Closely connected with clan poetry are two genres of praise: of the living and of the dead. A mainstay of classical verse, these genres play an important rôle in the vernacular tradition, where verse can be addressed not only to a chief or patron but also to a friend, relative, or lover. Eulogy strives to present the most perfect and positive image possible of its subject, making full use of the tools of the panegyric code. Motifs connected to the Christian faith, piety, and adherence to religious precepts are also a significant part of that code.

Elegy, by comparison, deals with the death of its subject and may possess a cathartic function. While there may be detailed reminiscence of the days when the subject was alive, there is the added dimension of imagery pertaining to death, decay, loss, and the process of grieving. Often, passages describing the closing of the coffin have particular poignancy

In poetry that is predominantly elegiac and eulogistic, there is occasionally a sense that a poem is perfunctory, a mere exercise in the name of duty. In many instances, however, praise imagery is developed in fresh and surprising ways.

Nature

Praise poetry generally contains motifs connected with various aspects of nature, such as the comparison of the subject of the poem with a tree bearing a large crop of fruit. Some poems deal with nature more extensively and not as a mere adjunct of praise. Poetry celebrating nature for its own sake is prominent in the work of Alasdair Mac Mhaighstir Alasdair and Donnchadh Bàn MacIntyre, but their predecessors were active already in the 17th century. *Òran na Comhachaig* (The song of the owl) by Dòmhnall mac Fhionnlaigh nan Dàn (Donald son of Finlay of the Songs, *fl.* 1600) includes in its themes praise of several individuals, the contemplation of old age, and a celebration of nature, which is its most memorable feature. The poet remembers the favourite haunts of his youth in vivid descriptions of both wildlife and landscape; the area covered ranges from Ben Nevis in the west to Badenoch in the east, though the area around Loch Tréig, where Dòmhnall was brought up and spent most of his life, is singled out for description with particular care, focusing repeatedly on Creag Guanach at the southern end of Loch Tréig.

Later in the century, Am Pìobaire Dall composed *Cumha Choire an Easa* (Lament for Coire an Easa), which begins as a lament for Colonel Robert MacKay, who died in 1696. This song is structured as a dialogue between the Piper and the corrie, and half of it is dedicated to the praise of landscape and wildlife.

An Làir Dhonn (The brown mare), by Murchadh Mór mac Mhic Mhurchaidh (Big Murdoch son of the son of Murdoch, *fl.* 1650) follows a somewhat different approach. This song contrasts the poet's present situation, riding a somewhat recalcitrant horse, with his happy memories of the island of Lewis (Leòdhas), where he was the MacKenzie chief's factor. Many laments imagine, in startling images, the body of a drowned loved one in the sea. *Marbhrainn do Mhac Gille Chaluim Ratharsaidh* (Elegy for Iain Garbh MacLeod of Raasay) is said to have been one of a sequence of laments composed by Iain Garbh's sister. The drowning happened in 1671 when Iain Garbh was returning from a visit to Lewis.

The Women's Tradition

Women are well represented both as composers and transmitters of poetry during the period. Many anonymous songs, too, contain historical references or allusions that place their time of composition in the 17th century or earlier. Several of them can be shown to have been composed by women, and such songs were often transmitted through the women's tradition—for instance, as waulking songs or lullabies. Belonging to the early to mid-17th century, *Taladh Dhomhnaill Ghuirm* (Donald Gorm's lullaby) is traditionally ascribed to Donald's nurse or foster-mother. The song is still present in oral tradition, for example, in a version sung by Cathy-Ann MacPhee (*Chì Mi'n Geamhradh* track 11). After several passages in which the subject's seafaring skills, the hospitality of his house, and his possessions are discussed, the poem ends with an invocation intended to ensure prosperity and protection.

Relationships between men and women are also a frequent subject of women's songs. Many are laments for dead lovers, though the dilemma of the unmarried girl who has been left pregnant by a faithless lover is another frequent theme. An example of a successful relationship is dealt with by the anonymous *Bothan Àirigh am Bràigh Raithneach* (The Sheiling in Brae Rannoch). The poet begins with a section of praise for her lover, before listing the gifts that he will bring her.

Again, this song remained current up to the present—for instance, in Cathy-Ann MacPhee's version as learned from William Matheson (MacPhee, *Chì Mi'n Geamhradh* track 9).

Sources

The poetry under discussion was slow to find its way into print, and its collection largely occurred as a result of the Ossianic controversy (see MACPHERSON; OISÍN). Hence, 18th-century collectors began to take down texts from the oral tradition. For instance, the collecting activity of the Reverend James McLagan of Amulree spanned from *c.* 1750 to McLagan's death in 1805. His collection contains Gaelic ballads, versions of songs by most well-known poets of the 17th and 18th centuries, and anonymous material. Relatively little material from such manuscript collections was printed at an early stage, with two important exceptions. One is the Eigg Collection of 1776, which contains material ranging from the poetry of Mac Mhaighstir Alasdair to anonymous songs of the 17th century. The other is the Gillies Collection of 1786, which contains both anonymous and attributed material, and is representative of the breadth of the tradition mostly in the mainland areas. In 1841, John MacKenzie edited the highly influential and much reprinted anthology *Sàr-Obair nam Bàrd Gaëlach or, the Beauties of Gaelic Poetry*; this collection emphasized prestigious material by named bards and includes short biographies. Material by individual poets was edited under the auspices of the Scottish Gaelic Texts Society. Among recent publications, *Gàir nan Clàrsach* (ed. Ó Baoill) gives a choice of 17th-century material, while *An Lasair* (ed. Black) is a substantial anthology of 18th-century texts.

Much of the material continued to flourish in an oral environment. Some examples of survival in the oral tradition are remarkable, such as John MacCodrum's poetry in North Uist. Sorley Maclean (Somhairle MacGill-Eain) remembered versions of many well-known songs from his childhood in Raasay. The Sound Archive of the School of Scottish Studies in Edinburgh (Dùn Èideann) is an extensive repository of the widest range imaginable of material recorded from tradition bearers from all over the Gaelic-speaking regions.

Anja Gunderloch

SCOTTISH GAELIC POETRY, LATER 18TH CENTURY

Scottish Gaelic verse in the late 18th century represents one of the highest achievements of Celtic literature. The six chief poets were (arguably in order of importance) Alexander MacDonald (Alasdair Mac Mhaighstir, *c.* 1698–*c.* 1770), Duncan Macintyre (Donnchadh Bàn Mac an t-Saoir, 1724–1812), Robert MacKay (Rob Donn MacAoidh, 1714–78), William Ross (Uilleam Ros, 1762–?91), Dugald Buchanan (Dùghall Bochanan, 1716–68), and John MacCodrum (Iain Mac Fhearchair, †1779); the underrated Kenneth MacKenzie (1758–*c.* 1837) was perhaps the first homosexual Scottish Gaelic poet.

The work that shaped this period was MacDonald's verse, most of which was published in 1751 in the pointedly named *Ais-eiridh na Sean Chánoin Albannaich* (Resurrection of the ancient Scottish language). It was an illegal book, with most of the contents being either subversive or obscene.

The 18th century ended with the publication of *Orain Ghaidhealacha* (Gaelic songs), which encapsulated how the status of Gaelic poetry had changed since 1700, and foreshadowed what was to come. Until 1715 the leading poets, known by the title of *Aosdàna* (Men of art), enjoyed real political influence in Gaelic society as senior civil servants, intertribal diplomats, and mediators between chief and kindred; *Orain Ghaidhealacha* of 1798 consists of poems by Ailean Dall (Blind Allan MacDougall, *c.* 1750–1828), a pauper who postured brilliantly as family bard while selling charms to the superstitious, and Ewen MacLachlan (Eòghan MacLachlainn, 1773–1822), a shy young academic who became Librarian of King's College, Aberdeen (Obair Dheathain).

Ronald Black

SCOTTISH GAELIC POETRY, 19TH CENTURY

The 19th century in Scottish Gaelic verse is above all the period of the CLEARANCES. Vast numbers of people were displaced, and left facing an uncertain and often dangerous future. The result in terms of poetry is that the period has come, unfairly, to be perceived as a tedious trough between the twin peaks of the mid-18th and mid-20th centuries.

SCOTTISH GAELIC was never a civic or even a national language, but rather tribal, heroic, and spiritual in nature; 19th-century Gaelic verse remains infused with these ideals. JACOBITE heroes having been swept away, pride of place was given to evangelical Presbyterianism, Victorian morality, and the exploits of Gaelic-speaking soldiers in the service of the British Empire.

Gaelic literature did produce an innovator of towering stature, the Reverend Dr Norman MacLeod ('Caraid nan Gaidheal', Friend of the Gaels, 1783–1862), but he was a prose writer, not a poet. It is difficult to understand why an act of ethnic cleansing as ruthless as the clearances should have failed to produce a single poet to denounce them; the nearest to an eye-witness account is Donald Baillie's *Aoir air Pàdraig Sellar* (Satire on Patrick Sellar, 1816), and no other poem by Baillie is known to exist.

Much 19th-century verse appeared in newspapers, a resource not yet fully exploited, and the full corpus has neither been collected nor studied. Innovation did occurr: The first Gaelic poets to write free verse seem to have been William Livingstone (Uilleam MacDhunlèibhe, 1808–70) and Donald Campbell MacPherson (Dòmhnall Mac a' Phearsain, 1838–80), the latter deriving it seamlessly from folklore.

Perhaps the frustrations of the period are best summed up by Dr John MacInnes, who tells us that (as with MacQueen's sermons) the lost verse of the sailor poet Iain Dubh MacLeòid (*fl.* 1880) was much better than the published verse of his merchant brother Niall (1843–1924). In his day, Niall was regarded as one of the greatest Gaelic poets who ever lived.

Ronald Black

SCOTTISH GAELIC POETRY, 20TH CENTURY

A marked feature of 20th century Gaelic literature has been the resilience of the community-based bardic tradition of (primarily) orally composed sung verse, performing the age-old functions of praise and SATIRE, lament, religious devotion, and topical comment. Its tendency toward proxility (in comparison with modern verse's valuing of brevity) and its high verbal dexterity have made it a difficult tradition to sustain, however, given the depletion in the traditional registers and vocabulary. Younger composers in the latter third of the century were much more likely to opt for the imported musical forms of country and western, folk, or soft rock, or to become writers of *nua-bhàrdachd* (modern poetry, non-sung, and usually in free metres).

In sharp contrast to Wales (CYMRU) and Brittany (BREIZH), there has been a disappointing lack of adventurism and development in song writing in contemporary idioms—beyond the few pioneers of the 1960s and 1970s, such as Murchadh MacPhàrlain (1901–82) and the 'Runrig' MacDonald brothers—which raises disturbing questions about younger Gaels' relationship to the language, and their perceptions of language domains in cultural creativity. By contrast, the enthusiastic acceptance of new and imported forms in written poetry has been extraordinary, due in no small part to the example of innovatory giants such as Somhairle

MacGill-Eain and Ruaraidh MacThòmais, as well as the preponderance of such forms in English literature, mediated through the education system.

From 1950, the popular periodical *Gairm* was the principal platform and testing ground for poetry of all kinds. The dominance and successful development of the *nua-bhàrdachd* in the last quarter of the century was in no small part due to the seminal anthology *Nua-bhàrdachd Ghàidhlig* (1976), which presented selections from the work of the most prominent five practitioners (Somhairle MacGill-Eain, George Campbell Hay, Ruaraidh MacThòmais, Iain Mac a' Ghobhainn, and Dòmhnall MacAmhlaigh) with facing translations into English.

Two interesting features of the nontraditional poetry have been the important contribution of women and the rise of the non-native poet, evident in the bilingual anthology *An Aghaidh na Sìorraidheachd/In the Face of Eternity* (1991). Learners of the language have produced some of the most experimental work linguistically and conceptually, while their varied relationship to their working language has inevitably raised questions about cultural and linguistic identity.

Michel Byrne

SCOTTISH GAELIC PROSE, MODERN

The first Gaelic prose text to appear in print was John Carswell's translation of the Book of Common Order (*Foirm na n-Urrnuidheadh*) in 1567. Its publication was followed by a small number of other religious translations. It was only in the 19th century that any significant amount of Scottish Gaelic prose began to be published.

The initial impetus for the growth of published Gaelic prose stemmed from the expansion in EDUCATION in the HIGHLANDS and the need to provide suitable reading material for the increasing number of Gaels with basic literacy skills. The overwhelming majority of this writing appeared in periodicals, which continued to provide an important outlet for prose writing during the 20th century, most notably with Roderick Erskine of Mar's *Guth na Bliadhna* (Voice of the year, 1904–25) and *An Sgeulaiche* (The storyteller, 1909–11), and later with *Gairm* (1952–2003). The writing that appeared in the periodicals during the first half of the 19th century was dominated by the writings of the clergy.

The prose published in periodicals from the later decades of the century saw a shift in emphasis away from the spiritual and toward the secular. Original fiction was still rare, though traditional tales were appearing in print with more frequency, due to the work of folklore collectors such as John Francis Campbell. One writer with a distinctive style who bridged the 19th and 20th centuries was Dòmhnall MacEacharn, whose essays combine humorous tone and philosophical content. It was only from the 1890s onward that any significant number of original stories came to be written for a Scottish Gaelic readership. Many of these writers were Glasgow-based and came under the influence of Roderick Erskine (1869–1960) of Mar, a learner of Gaelic and a fervent nationalist who perceived a need to raise Gaelic literary standards and to use Gaelic in areas other than literature. As the founder of *Guth na Bliadhna* and *An Sgeulaiche*, among other publications, he encouraged writers to follow his example in using Gaelic to discuss politics. He wrote the first detective stories to be written in Gaelic, stories that were heavily influenced by Sherlock Holmes. It was under Mar's influence that the first Gaelic novel, Iain MacCormaic's *Dùn-Àluinn, no an t-Oighre 'na Dhìobarach* (Dùn-Àluinn, or the heir in exile), came to be published in 1912; this adventure story shows the influence of traditional tales and is set against a backdrop of CLEARANCE and emigration.

The short story has tended to be a more popular genre with Gaelic-language writers, and most prominent among these are Iain Mac a' Ghobhainn (e.g., *Bùrn is Aran* [Water and bread]), Cailean T. MacCoinnich (e.g., *Oirthir Tìm* [Coast of time]), Iain Moireach (*An Aghaidh Choimheach* [The mask]), Eildh Watt (e.g., *A' Bhratach Dheàlrach* [The shining banner], *Gun Fhois* [Without knowing]), Tormod Caimbeul (*Hostail* [Hostel]), and Alasdair Caimbeul (*Lìontan Sgaoilte* [Cast nets]). A number of autobigraphies appeared in the later decades of the 20th century, with Aonghas Caimbeul's *A' Suathadh ri Iomadh Rubha* (1973) standing out with its rich account of life in Lewis (Leòdhas). Since 1968, when Comhairle nan Leabhraichean (The Gaelic Books Council) was established with the remit of promoting Gaelic books, and offering publication grants as part of this effort, a steady stream of Gaelic prose has appeared in print.

Sheila Kidd

SCOTTISH KING-LISTS

Scottish king-lists survive in a large number of late medieval manuscripts and contain lists of kings, with reign lengths, from three conflated sources, representing the kingdoms of the PICTS (see PICTISH KING-LIST), DÁL RIATA, and ALBA (i.e., the unified kingdom of Picts and Scots from the mid-9th century onward).

The Dál Riata king-list begins with the legendary Fergus Mór, and continues to *c.* 780. The 11th-century poem *Duan Albanach* (Scottish poets' book) and the later king-lists, added to the Alba list of 1165 × 1214, have different additional kings at the end. They could be additions, designed to fill the gap from *c.* 780 to CINAED MAC AILPÍN (r. 840–58), reckoned as the first king of Alba (i.e., the unified kingdom of the Picts and the Scots under Scottish rule). The Alba king-list was a contemporary record by the late 10th century.

Nicholas Evans

SCOTTISH PARLIAMENT

The Scottish Parliament originated in the 12th century. However, it was not until the 17th century that it began to function in an authoritative manner. The removal of the royal court from Edinburgh (DÙN ÈIDEANN) to London in 1603 had led to an Anglicized, absentee, and—after 1625—increasingly unsatisfactory form of governance over Scotland (ALBA).

The biggest difference between the English and the Scottish Parliaments was that the latter comprised one single chamber, which contained both lords and commons. There was seldom opportunity for debate, since elections were often assured by pressure of KINSHIP, patronage, or even sheer intimidation. Individual members could only signify their assent to, or their rejection of, pre-prepared bills, with no chance of emendation or meaningful comment.

Against a background of civil war, between 1640 and 1651, the Parliament effectively nullified royal authority, pursued an independent legislative programme, and forged an effective framework of militias and regular troops with which to quell both incursions by English Royalist forces and home-grown insurrections in favour of Charles I. This experiment in self-government was brought to an end by military defeat and conquest at the hands of Oliver Cromwell, and the Scottish Parliament was officially abolished, in favour of Westminster, in 1654. A separate Scottish government was restored in 1660, but until 1688 it was subject to tight political control from London.

A Treaty of Union was signed in 1706 by 26 Scottish and 27 English commissioners, and duly committed the northern kingdom to the Hanoverian succession to the crown, the admission of English tax gatherers and excise men, and the abolition of the Scottish Parliament. The last session of the Parliament was adjourned on 25 March 1707, and preparations were immediately made to transfer its powers to Westminster. By the terms of the Act of Union of 1707, the Scottish Parliament was abolished and for nearly 300 years Scotland was ruled directly from Westminster.

This constitutional arrangement came under unprecedented strain in the 1980s. A cross-party Constitutional Convention was formed in the early 1990s. Devolution and constitution reform became major planks in the Labour Party manifesto of 1997, and a referendum held later that year produced a three-to-one majority for the re-establishment of a Scottish Parliament. Accordingly, the new Scottish Parliament was opened in 1999, with 129 members and the power to levy taxes. The new Scottish Paliament building facing Holyrood Park in Edinburgh was officially opened in October 2004.

John Callow

SCOTTISH PLACE-NAMES

Scottish place-names reflect the complex history of Scotland (Alba), with six languages contributing to the bulk of its place-names. Of these six languages, three are Germanic and three are Celtic: Cumbric (also known as British or Brythonic), Pictish, and Scottish Gaelic.

Both Cumbric and Pictish are closely related to Old Welsh and evolved *in situ* from the indigenous British speech. Cumbric, in Southern Scotland, was sufficiently close to Welsh for preforms to be identical to their Welsh equivalents. Typical Cumbric elements are *tref* 'homestead, farm', as in *Tranent*, East Lothian (= *tref* + Cumbric *nant* 'burn, valley') and *Terreagles*, Dumfriesshire (= *tref* + Cumbric *eglwys* 'church'), as well as *pen(n)* 'end, hill' (literally 'head'), as in *Pentland*, Midlothian (*pen* + Cumbric **lann* 'enclosure, church') and *Penpont*, Dumfriesshire (*pen* + Cumbric *pont* 'bridge' < Latin *pont-em*). Many central places in this region are of Cumbric origin, such as *Glasgow* and *Lanark* (cf. Welsh *llannerch* 'glade').

For Pictish, the language of the Pictish kingdom(s) north of the Firth of Forth, typical elements are *abor/aber* 'burn- or river-mouth' (cf. Welsh and Breton *aber*), as in *Arbroath*, Angus (< *Aberbrothoc*), and *Abernethy*, Perthshire and Inverness-shire, as well as **pert* 'wood, grove' (cf. Welsh *perth* 'hedge'), as in *Perth*.

GAELIC, derived from Primitive Irish (see OGAM), was spoken originally in Scottish DÁL RIATA, a division of the kingdom in northeast Ireland (ÉRIU) of the same name. The heartland of Scottish Dál Riata from an early period was also referred to as Argyll (Scottish Gaelic *Earra-Ghàidheal* from earlier *Airir Gáidel* 'Gaels' coastland'). By AD 900, a Gaelic-speaking dynasty and aristocracy was firmly in control in Pictland, and Gaelic dominated not only much of former Pictland and Dál Riata, but also spread south of the firths of Forth and Clyde into Strathclyde and Lothian. The bulk of the settlement names in its heartlands north of the Forth–Clyde line are in Scottish Gaelic. As the kingdom was established, its chief language was used to name new settlements, rename old settlements and topographic features, or Gaelicize older names so as to adapt them to speakers of the language of the new rulers. This last process was probably common, given that the replacing language, Scottish Gaelic, shared much vocabulary with the replaced language, Pictish.

Simon Taylor

SCRIPTS, EPIGRAPHIC

Introduction

The earliest records of the CELTIC LANGUAGES—outside isolated proper names or glosses recorded by classical authors (see GREEK AND ROMAN ACCOUNTS)—are all attested as INSCRIPTIONS. The earliest of these are engraved in the indigenous scripts of the respective areas in which they are attested, or in adaptations of them. Hence, the Iberian script was employed to engrave Celtic inscriptions in the Iberian Peninsula; the Lugano and Sondrio scripts, derived from the Etruscans, in CISALPINE GAUL and adjacent areas; and the Massaliote Hellenic script (Greek alphabet), which emanated from the Greek colony at Massalia (Marseilles), in TRANSALPINE GAUL. In the Iberian Peninsula and Transalpine Gaul, especially, where the Celtic epigraphic tradition continued after Roman colonization, Celtic inscriptions came to be engraved in various Roman scripts. This article focuses on the characteristics and conventions of the indigenous scripts.

The Iberian Script

Background

The large part of the CELTIBERIAN (also known as Hispano-Celtic) linguistic corpus is engraved in an adaptation of the Iberian script, which was employed, in various versions, to engrave inscriptions in a variety of non-INDO-EUROPEAN languages throughout the Iberian Peninsula.

Structure of the Script

The Iberian script is semi-segmental and semi-moraic. The segmental characters represent individual phonemes (i.e., the sounds that are significant and distinct within a given language), while the moraic characters represent the opening of a syllable, specifically one of the Celtiberian stop consonants /t, k, kʷ, b, d, g (, gʷ)/ plus the vowel that forms the nucleus of the syllable. As is made apparent below, the script does not fit the structure of the Celtiberian language well, and this necessitated the development of a variety of orthographic strategies to write it.

Characteristics and Orthographic Conventions

As with many epigraphic scripts, character shapes can vary. Table 1 sets out the character shapes of the Iberian script as engraved in the BOTORRITA I inscription and Table 2 sets out the character shapes, drawn from a variety of inscriptions, of the western school.

The segmental characters of the Celtic adaptation of the Iberian script (i.e., those representing single phonemes) are the vowels *a e i o u*, the sonants *m n l ŕ*, and the sibilants (*s*- like sounds) *ś s*. The characters for the vowels do not distinguish length; hence *a*, for example, may represent /a/ or /á/. The characters representing the high vowels /i u/ are also used to represent the glides /j/ (as in English <u>y</u>es) and /w/, respectively. The digrapheme (double letter) *ei* is employed to write not only the inherited diphthong /ej/ but also /e/ < older unstressed /i/.

In the Iberian language, two *r* sounds are represented; in Celtiberian, only *ŕ* is used, and some scholars do not use the acute diacritic.

Table 1   **Character shapes of the eastern school of Celtiberian epigraphy**

a	▷	m	ᵚ	n	ᴎ
e	ᴇ	l	⌐	ŕ	◊
i	ᴉ	ś	M	s	ᔓ
o	H				
u	↑				
Ca	⅂	Pa	Ⅰ	Ta	X
Ce	ᴦ	Pe	◊	Te	ᗷ
Ci	✓	Pi	⌐	Ti	Ψ
Co	X̵	Po	Ӿ	To	ш
Cu	◈	Pu	▯	Tu	Δ

Table 2   Character shapes of the western school of Celtiberian epigraphy

a	P	ṁ	ⲓ	ń	V
e	E	l	ʌ	ŕ	φ
i	И	ś	M	s	⧣
o	H				
u	↑				

ꟼ

Ca	ʌ	Pa	I	Ta	X
Ce	C	Pe	W	Te	⊗
Ci	✓	Pi	Γ	Ti	Ψ
Co	X̆	Po	⚹	To	⊔
Cu	⊙	Pu	▯	Tu	Δ

There is considerable controversy at present concerning the transcription of what have usually been termed the sibilant characters. Traditionally, **M** has been transcribed as ś and **Ϛ** as s. It had been presumed that both characters represented /s/ and its allophones (i.e., variant pronunciations that were not phonemically significant within the grammatical system), though the variation between the characters in usage was difficult to explain. However, Villar has demonstrated that, while **M** appears to continue Indo-European /s/ unchanged in most instances, **Ϛ** continues it in voiced environments (i.e., where pronounced as /z/), but also original /d/ in certain word-internal environments and in final position. This has led Villar to transcribe **M** as s and **Ϛ** as z (*New Interpretation of Celtiberian Grammar*). Untermann, however, has adopted a different system, whereby **M** = s and **Ϛ** = đ̣. Various scholars have now adopted either Villar's or Untermann's system, though others prefer to continue using the traditional system.

The moraic (or '[semi-]syllabic') characters of the script comprise three series of five consonantal characters at the (p/)b, t/d, and k/g articulatory places. In each instance, the symbol has the value of the following vowel built in. It is normally assumed that these characters represent phonemic plosives (stop consonants) in their initial consonantal sound, as represented above, though it is likely that they could represent fricatives (e.g., Po for /fo/) as well. These characters do not indicate voicing (i.e., the contrast between /t/ and /d/, /k/ and /g/); hence, Ta can represent /ta(:)/ or /da(:)/, or even /t/ or /d/ (with no additional vowel). The latter pair are possible representations because the moraic quality of these characters is an ill fit for

Celtiberian syllable structure, which permits various consonant clusters at the beginnings of syllables. The result is something like using Japanese characters to write English words—comprehensible for someone familiar with English, but difficult for an outsider to master. Thus the script forces the use of 'dead' vowels, which, in transcription, are solely graphemic and without phonetic value.

The Etruscoid Scripts

Background
The entirety of the Cisalpine Celtic epigraphic corpus is engraved in varieties of scripts derived from northern Etruscan usage. Virtually all of it is in the Lugano script. The principal addition that all the Etruscoid scripts share is the addition of the character *o*, which was absent from Etruscan itself. This character, like most additions to the inherited character set, has its origin in forms of the Greek alphabet. Table 3 sets out the character shapes of the Lugano script in their principal variants.

Characteristics and Orthographic Conventions
The vowel characters *a e i o u* do not distinguish length; hence, *e* may represent /e/ or /ē/. The characters *i u* are also employed to represent the glides /j/ (as in English <u>y</u>es) and /w/, respectively.

The characters *K P T* each represent two possible sounds: the phonemic stop consonants /k g/, /p b/, and /t d/, respectively. In other words, they do not distinguish voicing.

Two different characters are attested to convey the *tau Gallicum* phoneme (see CONTINENTAL CELTIC)—namely, *ś* and *z*. The former is far more common. It is noteworthy that one early LEPONTIC inscription from Prestino (S–65) apparently employs both characters to write this sound.

The Greek Script of Massalia

Background
Prior to, and for some period following, Caesar's conquest of TRANSALPINE GAUL, the Massaliote Hellenic script, which was borrowed from the Greek colony at Massalia (Marseilles), was employed to engrave inscriptions in Transalpine Celtic. These are always engraved from left to right. The large majority of Celtic inscriptions engraved in Greek letters are from an area to the immediate northwest of Marseilles.

Characteristics and Orthographic Conventions
As expected, the Transalpine Celtic adaptation of the Greek script was alphabetic (segmental). Vowel length is not distinguished, even by the pairs ε η and ο ω, which in Greek are long and short *e* and *o*, respectively. The vowels /a(:) e(:) o(:)/ are reliably spelled with the single letters α ε/η ο/ω; however, /i/ is occasionally spelled with the two letters ει, in addition to the usual ι, and /u(:)/ is routinely spelled with the two letters ου. The glides /j w/ are represented by ι and ου, respectively.

Most consonants have their expected phonemic values. Geminates (long or double consonants) are normally spelled as such. There are some conventions for the

Table 3   The early and later character shapes of the Lugano script

6TH–5TH CENTURIES BC			3RD–2ND CENTURIES BC	
Λ Λ	a	Λ Ⅎ		
ⱻ	e	Ⅎ Ⅎ		
Ⅎ	v			
‡	z	‡		
⊙	ϑ			
Ι	i	Ι		
⋊	K	⋊	⋊	
⌉ ✓	l	⌐		
ⱉ	m	ⱉ	Μ	
�	n	Ⴜ	Ⴝ	
↑	P	↑		
Ⲙ Μ	ś	Ⲙ	Ⲙ	
◖	r	◖	◁	◖
Ꙅ ⸚ ꙅ ʃ	s	Ꙅ ꙅ		
× +	T	×		
V ∪	u	V		
↓	χ	↓		
◗ ◯	o	◯	◇	⌾

spelling of certain consonant groups: /χt/, for example, was pronounced [κτ], and is found spelled both ways.

The notorious *tau Gallicum* phoneme (see CONTINENTAL CELTIC) is attested spelled with a variety of single- and double-letter spellings: θ θθ σ σσ τ ττ σθ.

Some Comments on the Roman Scripts

Continental Celtic inscriptions engraved in Roman capitals or cursive are attested in the Iberian Peninsula, Transalpine Gaul, and the Balkans. Two inscriptions that may be engraved in Old British (see Bath) may also be mentioned here. The characters of these scripts bear their conventional phonemic values in most cases. Vowel length is not noted; geminate consonants (with a distinctive unlenited, long, or double articulation) may or may not be written as such. A second, taller form of the letter *i*, the *i-longa*, is commonly attested, but it does not appear to be systematically differentiated in its distribution from standard *i*; modern scholars often transcribe it as *í*, but *j* is increasingly becoming standardized. The *tau Gallicum* phoneme is represented by an extensive range of single, double, and triple letters: *t tt tth d dd đ đđ ts ds s ss ss sc sd st.*

Joseph Eska

SEAN-NÓS

Sean-nós (old style) is an improvised solo *a cappella* singing style, usually in the Irish language. It is highly ornamented, and mostly confined to the west coast of Ireland (Éire).

Originating in the popular *amhrán* and *caoineadh* of the 18th century, *sean-nós* songs can be passionate *amhráin mhóra* (big songs), which express great love or sorrow (e.g., *Úna Bhán*, Fair-haired Úna) and mark important events such as drownings (*Anach Cuain*), or lighter, more popular, songs (e.g., *Bean a' Leanna*, The woman of the alehouse).

Sean-nós songs were transmitted orally from generation to generation until very recently and, for this reason, villages and families may have their own preferred songs and styles. When performing publicly, singers are encouraged between verses by the audience and will often hold hands with a neighbour.

The ornamentation of *sean-nós* songs is melismatic or intervallic—that is, with certain main notes in a melody replaced by a group of adjacent auxiliary notes or having the interval between two main notes filled by a stepwise series of notes. Without accompaniment, singers achieve continuity by stretching phrases and by nasalization.

Brian Ó Broin

SENCHAS MÁR

Senchas Már (The great tradition) is the best preserved collection of early Irish law texts. These anonymous texts, which date from the 7th and 8th centuries, were probably organized as a unit around ad 800. Most of the names cited in the texts relate to the northern Irish Midlands and southern Ulster (Ulaid), and it is therefore likely that the material derived from this area.

Originally, the *Senchas Már* consisted of approximately fifty law texts, arranged in three groups. The First Third (*trian toísech*) of the collection starts with an introduction in which there is an account of the rôle St Patrick was believed to have played in the codification of Irish law. *Cáin Lánamna* (The law of couples) has survived in its entirety, and is concerned mainly with marriage and divorce. The last text in the First Third, of which approximately half has survived, is entitled *Córus*

Bésgnai (The arrangement of customary behaviour). It discusses the nature of Irish law, the maintenance of order in society, and the relationship between the Church and the laity. It repeats material from the introduction on the dissolution of contracts, and on St Patrick's involvement with Irish law.

The Middle Third (*trian medónach*) is the best preserved of the three sections. It contains sixteen texts, thirteen of which have been preserved in their entirety; substantial portions of the remaining three texts have also survived. *Bretha Comaithchesa* (The judgements of neighbourhood) deals with trespass by domestic animals, fencing obligations, and similar issues. Specialized treatments of the law of neighbourhood also occur in the Middle Third; for example, *Bechbretha* (Bee-judgements) includes a discussion of trespass by honeybees.

The Last Third (*trian déidenach*) is the least complete section, and there remains a good deal of uncertainty as to its original complement. Only three of the texts belonging to the Last Third are complete: the short text on sick-maintenance (*othras*), and the longer medico-legal texts *Bretha Crólige* (Judgements of sick maintenance) and *Bretha Déin Chécht* (Judgements of Dian Cécht).

Fergus Kelly

SERGLIGE CON CULAINN

Serglige Con Culainn ('The Wasting Sickness of Cú Chulainn') is an Ulster Cycle narrative in mixed prose and verse. It is of interest as a supernatural adventure that offers points of comparison with Fiannaíocht, the Mabinogi, and Arthurian literature, as well as revealing ideas about the Otherworld.

The tale begins at Samain. Cú Chulainn tries to shoot a pair of mysterious birds for his wife, but fails; these are the first shots he has missed since first taking arms. Afterward, he dreams of two strange women who beat him. When he awakes, Cú Chulainn loses the power of speech for a year. The following Samain, a stranger comes to tell him that the otherworld woman, Fand, awaits him. Returning to the place where he had the dream, Cú Chulainn meets a second otherworld woman, Lí Ban (the beauty of women), who offers him Fand's love if he is willing to fight for one day as the champion of Lí Ban's husband at the place called *Mag Mell* (the plain of delights). The Romance and battle are interrupted by a description of the divination ritual called *tarbfheis* (bull-feast; see feis) and the wisdom literature text, *Bríatharthecosc Con Culainn* ('The Word-Teaching of Cú Chulainn'), in which Cú Chulainn instructs his foster-son Lugaid Réoderg, king of Tara (Teamhair). When the story continues, Cú Chulainn's first wife becomes jealous and tries to kill Fand. Cú Chulainn returns to Emer, and Fand's immortal husband, Manannán, returns for her. In the end, Cú Chulainn is made to forget Fand.

John T. Koch

SHIELD

The Proto-Celtic word for shield was **skeito-*, as attested in Old Irish *scíath*, Scottish Gaelic *sgiath*, Old Welsh *scuit*, Middle and Modern Welsh *ysgwyd*, and Modern

A bronze shield recovered from the Thames River at Battersea, London, known as the Battersea Shield, early 1st century BC. (C. M. Dixon/StockphotoPro)

Breton *skoed*. Latin *scūtum* is cognate. The central projection in front of the hand grip, the shield boss, is called *tul*, *taul* in Old Irish, and *tal* in Early Welsh < Proto-Celtic *talu-*.

The shield was probably the most widely used Celtic defensive weapon (see Proto-Celtic weapons). The typical shield of the Continental Iron Age was an oblong oval, less often hexagonal or octagonal, flat wooden shield about 1 to 1.2 m high with a protruding midrib and a metal shield boss across the midrib to strengthen it at the handle. An iron rim was attached for further stability.

British shields seem to have been considerably smaller, only 0.6 to 0.8 m in height, provided that the examples of decorated sheet metal shield covers, as known from the Battersea and Witham shields, are representative. Irish shields seem to have been similarly small, round or rectangular, and constructed from a wooden body with a leather cover, without any metal. The only surviving example has a straight bar of oak functioning as the handle, and a domed wooden boss as the protective cover for the hand. It is fashioned from a single board of alder wood, covered with calf-hide on both sides.

Shields remained in use throughout the medieval period, though later shields mostly followed European designs. The shields described in the Irish epic TÁIN BÓ CUAILNGE ('The Cattle Raid of Cooley') are typical of the general northwestern European shield of the 7th to 10th centuries AD, and show no similarities to the shields of early Ireland (ÉRIU).

Raimund Karl, John T. Koch, and Caroline aan de Weil

SHINTY

Shinty is known in SCOTTISH GAELIC as *iomain* or *camanachd*, literally, 'driving'. A strictly amateur game, it shares a common sporting and literary heritage with the Irish game of HURLING, with both codes featuring extensively in myth, legend, and song. Some similar version of stick-and-ball games is attested widely through-out BRITAIN and Ireland (ÉIRE) and is of great antiquity. A game of this sort is described in *Macgnímrada Con Culainn* ('The Boyhood Deeds of CÚ CHULAINN') in the ULSTER CYCLE.

The origins of shinty are often linked to those of golf and ice hockey, given the nature of the sticks (sing. *caman*, pl. *camain*) used and the method of scoring. In its modern organized form, which dates to the formation of the sport's ruling body, the Camanachd Association, in 1893, the game is played on a rectangular field that is not more than 170 yards (155 m) nor less than 140 yards (128 m) in length, and not more than 80 yards (73 m) nor less than 70 yards (64 m) in breadth, with min-imal markings. To score, the ball must be placed between two upright posts, equi-distant from the corner flags and 4 yards (3.66 m) apart, joined by a horizontal crossbar 3.33 yards (3.05 m) from the ground. The goal has a net attached to the uprights and crossbar, as in association football. The ball is spherical, made of cork and worsted inside, and an outer cover of leather or some other approved material. It is not more than 8 inches (20 cm) and not less than 7.5 inches (19 cm) in circum-ference. Traditionally, shinty was played at New Year as part of local festivities.

Hugh Dan MacLennan

SÍD

Síd, (Early Modern Irish *sídh,* now *sí*) refers to hills or mounds often containing pre-historic burials conceived of as the residence of supernatural beings such as the TUATH DÉ of early Irish tradition and FAIRIES of modern folk belief; cf. Scottish Gaelic *sìth* 'fairy', BEAN SÍ 'woman of the fairy mound, banshee'. *Síd,* or a word with the same form, also means 'peace'. The same double meaning is found in the related BRYTHONIC words (which show a different inherited vowel grade): Welsh *gorsedd* (cf. the magical mound, Gorsedd ARBERTH) and *hedd, heddwch* 'peace'. For the concept of the *síd* in early IRISH LITERATURE, see OTHERWORLD.

John T. Koch

SIÔN CENT

Siôn Cent, a 15th-century Welsh poet, is referred to in the earliest manuscript attes-tations as John Kent or Siôn y Cent. Historical information about him was so heavily confused by later redactors with other similarly named but unconnected religious and secular figures that he became the subject of myth and legend. Siôn's *floruit* remains the subject of debate (variously estimated *c.* 1400–1430/45), as does the authentic canon of his work. Some 170 poems and fragments are attributed to him in the sources, but of these the great majority are apocryphal. The standard edi-tion of his work selects just 17 poems, all of which are in the CYWYDD metre; however, the authenticity of even some of these works is in doubt.

For all the uncertainties, Siôn is one of the most important of the CYWYDDWYR of his time, and probably the single most significant religious poet of the later Middle Ages in Wales. Later tradition associates him with the south and east of Wales and with the family of John Scudamore of Kentchurch, Herefordshire (Welsh swydd Henffordd), said to be the son-in-law of Owain Glyndŵr.

Of the innovative nature of his poetry, however, there can be no doubt. In his *ymryson* (contention) with Rhys Goch Eryri concerning the origin and purpose of the awen (poetic inspiration), Siôn ruthlessly attacks the very basis of the bardic tradition of praise poetry and what he saw as its inherent falsehood. For him, the world's transience and the inconstancy of human nature are mirrored in the terrifying image of death itself. The poet's primary responsibility, therefore, is to analyse human nature and humankind's response to God; to declare uncompromisingly the eschatological choice facing each individual; and to summon all to repentance.

Although the majority of Siôn's poems are undoubtedly didactic, reflecting the religious climate and themes of the time, another important aspect of his work concerns the condition of the Welsh people in the aftermath of the Glyndŵr revolt and the exploitation of the powerless by those who have usurped their property. Siôn draws on the historiography and prophetic literature of the day to remind his people of their past dignity and hope for the future; their unnamed oppressors, in contrast, are castigated by the poet and confronted with the inevitable and eternal consequences of their injustice.

Siôn's trenchant observations, antitheses, satire, and word-play reveal a distinctive and personal perspective that makes him unique among late medieval Welsh religious poets, and that inspired a substantial body of contemporary and later imitators. At its sombre best, the poetry of Siôn Cent is both profound and challenging.

M. Paul Bryant-Quinn

SLAVERY AND THE CELTIC COUNTRIES, ANCIENT AND MEDIEVAL

The institution of slavery was widespread across ancient Europe, producing a thriving slave trade that extended from Ireland (Ériu) to the eastern limits of the Roman Empire. Caesar claimed that actual slaves were burned on their masters' funeral pyres (*De Bello Gallico* 6.19). Slavery among the tribal Celts was probably roughly similar to that among the Greeks and Romans, as well as the medieval Celtic peoples, with the slave population deriving mainly from war, slave raids, and penal and debt servitude. Such slavery became a hereditary condition, but manumission was possible through payment of the slave's worth.

Old Irish *cacht* and Welsh *caeth* both mean 'slave, captive' (Breton *kaezh* 'unfortunate' is cognate), and probably represent a borrowing from Latin *captus* 'captive'.

Irish laws warned that freeing slaves could bring on the failure of the master's crops and milk. In the Domesday Survey of 1086, slaves were not common in eastern England, but were prominent in those parts of Cornwall (Kernow) and Wales (Cymru) that were included in the survey. Slaves are prominent in Brittany (Breizh) at the earliest period of detailed documentation (i.e., the later 9th century), but largely absent from sources of the 12th and later centuries.

Both Irish and Welsh law codified slavery, specifying the responsibilities of slaves (and masters for their slaves) in matters ranging from crimes of violence to sexual relations. From the LAW TEXTS and other early medieval documentary evidence, it appears that the status of slaves in the CELTIC COUNTRIES was generally better than that of the chattel slaves of ancient Rome, though the Celtic slaves lacked the legal rights enjoyed by serfs in the later Middle Ages.

Although most slaves seem to have been tied to plots of land in serfdom, trade in slaves was common enough to result in the word *cumal* (female slave) being used as a unit of value in Ireland. The future St PATRICK is the most famous example of Celtic slave.

Victoria Simmons

SNOWDONIA

See Eryri.

SOUTH CADBURY CASTLE

South Cadbury Castle is a hill-fort situated 18 km southeast of GLASTONBURY in Somerset, ENGLAND. The site encloses 7.28 ha (18 acres) within multivallate defences, consisting of three and four sets of banks and ditches. There are two ancient gateways in the ramparts, with a third, now blocked, still visible. The site was identified as King ARTHUR's Camelot by John Leland in 1542. Antiquarians and early archaeologists reported artefacts that suggested substantial activity had taken place there during the Roman and post-Roman periods. The discoveries culminated in the 1950s with the identification of pottery that shared similarities with imported wares known at TINTAGEL and thought to date from between the 5th and 7th centuries.

Excavation on the hilltop recovered archaeological evidence of almost continuous human occupation from the early Neolithic (*c.* 4500 BC) down to the 11th century AD. The site was evidently stormed by the Roman army in the mid-1st century AD, after which it declined and may have been abandoned. Evidently reoccupied during the late 3rd century, the site was abandoned again for a little less than a hundred years during the 5th century. The site was later refortified *c.* 1010, by which point the rulers of the area were no longer Celtic speakers.

P. W. M. Freeman

SOVEREIGNTY MYTH

One of the most well-known and often studied thematic elements of Celtic myth, the sovereignty goddess is sometimes explicitly a personification of the land or of the right to rule. In the typical sovereignty narrative, the man fated to be king has some kind of real or implied sexual encounter with a mysterious woman who is later revealed to have represented the sovereignty of the place he will rule. Sometimes she is ugly until transformed into a beautiful woman by the meeting with the fated king, as in *Echtra Mac nEchach Muigmedóin* ('The Adventure of the Sons of Eochaid Mugmedón') and in folk-tale motif D732 (the Loathly Lady), known in English ARTHURIAN LITERATURE from Chaucer's *Wife of Bath's Tale*.

Sovereignty has also been identified with equine figures such as EPONA, RHIANNON, and MACHA. Gerald of Wales (GIRALDUS CAMBRENSIS) describes a kingship ritual from

Donegal (Tír Chonaill) in which a king is described as copulating with a mare that was then sacrificed, cut into pieces, and boiled in water, in which the new king then bathed (*History and Topography of Ireland* 3.102). A comparable ceremony from Vedic tradition, the *aśvamedha,* suggests that this ritual derives from the Indo-European heritage, and that horse divinities may indeed have been seen as validating kingship.

Elements of the sovereignty mythos have also been seen in various women of Celtic tradition, from Guenevere (Gwenhwyfar) to the Cailleach Bhéirre. The Greek and Roman accounts of historical Celtic women, such as Camma and Cartimandua, suggest that identification of leading women with goddesses once played an important social function as well as being a narrative theme.

What we might consider characteristic of sovereignty may also overlap with the activities of a consort, a fertility deity, a tutelary goddess, or the ancestress of the tribe. In the case of any given woman in traditional narrative, who may or may not be of divine origin, it may be best to think of sovereignty as one of the more important aspects of a figure who has a transfunctional nature.

Victoria Simmons

SPIRITUALITY, CELTIC

The term 'Celtic spirituality' in contemporary parlance covers a huge variety of beliefs and practices and involves a wide range of people—Christians, neo-pagans (an umbrella term covering a number of religious and spiritual traditions), Druids, and people in the New Age movement. The concept of Celtic spirituality is largely predicated upon the image of the 'spiritual Celt', inherently spiritual and intuitive, in touch with nature and the hidden realms, epitomizing that which is lost but longed for in contemporary society.

While many neo-pagans regard Celtic spirituality as their ancestral, pre-Christian 'native' religion, Celtic neo-paganism is quite varied, and includes assorted forms of Neo-Druidism, some aspects of the western occult tradition and Wicca (contemporary witchcraft), some eco-protest groups, and groups and individuals with a specific area or culture focus.

While Celtic myth, art, and literature are utilized to 'reconstruct' religion, some Celticize contemporary peoples' practices, with 'Celtic Shamanism' being one example of this trend. In what is regarded as the revival or continuance of ancient Celtic tradition, offerings are frequently left at archaeological sites and natural features such as springs and trees. Many see the ancient Celtic deities simply as aspects of the universal sacred female.

Many contemporary Celtic spirituality practitioners observe the so-called 'Celtic' or 'eight-fold' calendar of Samain (Hallowe'en), Imbolc (Candlemas), Beltaine (May Day), Lugnasad, summer and winter solstices, and spring and autumn equinoxes, and they believe the Celtic year started on 1 November.

In contemporary Celtic spirituality, the Celtic church is characterized as gentle, tolerant, 'green', meditative, egalitarian, and holistic—an early 'pure' form of Christianity (whether Orthodox or proto-Protestant) that came directly to the Celtic lands long before Roman Catholic missions.

Contemporary Celtic spirituality owes much to Romanticism, as well as to recent Western religious trends. Its stress is on 'Celticism' as a spiritual quality to be aspired to, rather than on strictly documented historical criteria.

Marion Bowman

SPRING DEITIES

Spring deities were usually female. The goddess Sequana was worshipped at her cult site at the source of the Seine, and shrines and watery depositions of offerings are found at places such as the shrine of Sulis at Bath. In Christian times, these sites often remained popular as holy wells, linked to the legends of saints (usually male); for example, Menacuddle Well in Cornwall (Kernow) was under the protection of St Austell. Sacred springs might also become foci for local folk-tales and legends, such as the Scottish claim that a well-spring had actually changed location from one island to another because a woman had offended it by washing her hands in its water. Improperly cared for, a benign spring could become a catastrophic torrent.

Victoria Simmons

STANNARY PARLIAMENT

The Stannary Parliament is a feature of the government of Cornwall (Kernow) that appears to be independent of, and hence most likely older than, the introduction of English and Norman systems to the region. The term derives from Latin for 'tin' (*stannum*), and charters from 1150 have recognized the ancient customs and privileges of the stannaries of Cornwall, originally defined by four tin-mining areas covering the territory of the region: Foweymore, Blackmore, Tywarnhaile, and Penwith-and-Kerrier.

The Parliament was convened until 1752. It consisted of 24 Stannators and 24 Assistants; thus it was broadly comparable to other bicameral legislatures. The original Parliament had the right to veto any statutes of the Westminster Parliament should they be detrimental to Cornish interests.

On 20 May 1974, the Cornish Stannary Parliament was recalled by the Court of Blackmore, which sought to reactivate the ancient political and legal rights of the Cornish people. Successfully reactivated, the Parliament came into conflict with Westminster in 1990 over the implementation of the Community Charge (Poll Tax), when a considerable number of Cornish people refused to pay the charge because they were exempt under Stannary Law.

Alan M. Kent

STONEHENGE

Stonehenge near Amesbury, Wiltshire, England, is a monument dating from probably pre-Celtic periods (Neolithic to Early Bronze Age). Nonetheless, popular beliefs associating the site with the Celtic period of British history are attested in literary sources as far back as the 12th century.

The prehistoric megalithic monument of Stonehenge in Wiltshire, England. (Corel)

The site of Stonehenge was developed early, with an earthwork enclosure begun around 3000 BC, in the late Neolithic period (New Stone Age). The blue stones that make up the inner circle were brought from the Preseli mountains in Pembrokeshire (sir Benfro), southwest Wales (CYMRU), more than 200 km from the site, around 2300 BC. The larger sarsen stones were brought from the Marlborough Downs in north Wiltshire, and the monument was essentially complete by around 1700 BC, in the Early Bronze Age.

As a stone circle of the later Neolithic to Early Bronze Age, Stonehenge has several parallels throughout Britain and Ireland (ÉRIU), and elsewhere in northwest Europe. It is remarkable but not unique in its large scale and the amount of labour required to build it. Like many megalithic (large-stone) monuments of this period, Stonehenge has astronomical alignments, one focal point in the arrangement of the stones being the summer solstice sunrise. The astronomical content of megalithic religion and science is the subject of widespread popular interest and ongoing archaeological research.

GEOFFREY OF MONMOUTH, writing in the first third of the 12th century AD, recounts an aetiological legend for Stonehenge in his HISTORIA REGUM BRITANNIAE ('The History of the Kings of Britain'). The ruler Aurelius AMBROSIUS wished to create a monument to commemorate the BRITONS who had been killed as a result of the treachery of the Saxon Hengist. Tremorinus, archbishop of Caerleon-on-Usk (Caerllion), suggested to Aurelius that he should hire Merlinus (MYRDDIN) to create a suitable memorial. Merlin proposed to bring the Chorea Gigantum (the giants' ring-dance) from Mount Killaraus in Ireland. It has been suggested that this legend is the inverse of the building of the tower of Vortigern (Gwrtheyrn), told earlier in Geoffrey's narrative and derived from the 9th-century Historia Brittonum. Both episodes illustrate a ruler's legitimacy (or lack thereof) through the edifice Merlin helped to build for him.

Other than Geoffrey's evidence, there is nothing to indicate that Stonehenge was of special significance in British tradition. The architect Inigo Jones (1573–c. 1652) is the first to mention druids in connection with Stonehenge. He rejected the association, indicating that he may have been reacting to popular beliefs already current in his day. The antiquary John Aubrey (1626–97) stated that the druids had definitely built Stonehenge, an idea that has remained current in popular literature.

Antone Minard and John T. Koch

STRATHCLYDE
See Ystrad Clud.

SUIBNE GEILT

Suibne Geilt (Suibne the madman or wild man) is a central figure in a group of Middle Irish texts. His madness is seen as a spiritually ecstatic state, an inspiration to poetry motivated by the outcast life of the *naomhgheilt* (saintly madman). As a prophet and poet, deranged by battle and living in the wild, Suibne is broadly similar to Myrddin/Merlin in Welsh and Arthurian tradition and Lailoken of Stratchclyde (Ystrad Clud). So closely parallel are the three figures, in terms of their attributes, stories, and their north British geographies, that it is widely thought that they go back to a common 6th- or 7th-century Strathclyde tradition of a wild man as mad prophet.

The Early Suibne Tradition in Ireland

This Suibne is mentioned in two texts of Old Irish date. A 9th- to 10th-century legal triad (see triads) in *Bretha Étgid* mentions Suibne's *geltacht* (madness, wildness) at the battle of Mag Roth as giving benefit due to the resulting 'stories and poems'. A contemporary gloss in *Codex Sancti Pauli* attributes to Suibne the marginal, riddling verse description of a treetop perch in terms of a hermit's oratory. These allusions indicate that something very much like the story embodied in the Middle Irish saga *Buile Shuibne* (Suibne's madness) was already well known in the 9th century. Suibne's rôle and stock epithet, meaning approximately 'wild man' or 'mad man', is most likely derived from the Brythonic *gwyllt* (wild), which is the stock epithet of the related figure Myrddin.

Buile Shuibne

The late 12th century saw the culmination of the original Irish-language Suibne traditions. Only scattered references, derived from the earlier sources, exist after this point.

The immediate historical background of *Buile Shuibne* was the battle of Mag Roth, fought in 637 at what is now Moira, Co. Down. It is the horror of this battle that is supposed to have transformed Suibne into a *geilt*. The historical battle saw Domnall Brecc of Scottish DÁL RIATA, in league with Congal Cáech of ULAID, defeated by Domnall mac Aedo maic Ainmirech, high-king of the Northern Uí NÉILL. In *Buile Shuibhne* (as also in *Fled Dúin na nGéd* [The feast of Dún na nGédh] and *Cath Maige Ratha* [The battle of Mag Roth]), Domnall mac Aedo and Congal dispute trivial gifts (birds' eggs) from otherworldly instigators. Ireland's saints curse Congal's ally, Suibne, for his theft of a tunic, the gift of truce. Suibne commits an escalating series of offences at Mag Roth and against St Rónán: the violation of a truce, of persons, of sanctuary, murder, and stripping (*lommrod*) of the raiment bestowed by Congal. In the course of the battle, Suibne is then driven mad by horror, grief, and an overwhelming sense of guilt.

Suibne eventually achieves a spiritual perfection through long suffering—exposure; lack of music, sleep, and food; loss of company. In both *Buile Shuibhne* and the related poetry presented as uttered by St Mo-Ling, Suibne dies and is buried at Mo-Ling's monastery, awaiting resurrection with him.

Modern Versions of Suibne Legend

It is not possible to mention all of the contemporary discussions and treatments of Suibne. From a play by Macnas, a community arts and theatre company, to photographic renderings of the revised text of Heaney's full poetic translation, *Sweeney Astray*, Suibne Geilt has enjoyed a recent revival. Devotees of Flann O'Brien are familiar with Suibne from *At Swim-Two-Birds,* and readers of Seamus Heaney meet the *geilt* often in his poetry.

Brian Frykenberg

SŪLIS

Sūlis was a BRITISH Celtic deity of healing and retribution who was venerated at the thermal waters of Aquae Sulis (now BATH, ENGLAND) during the Romano-British period. She was conflated at times with the Roman goddess Minerva in her healing rôle (see INTERPRETATIO ROMANA). Offerings (see WATERY DEPOSITIONS) of Celtic COINAGE dated to the first century AD attest to the existence of the cult and probably the deity in pre-Roman times. However, not until the development of the associated bath and temple complex in the Flavian era (AD 69–138) did the cult gain overt religious significance, as Roman and native INSCRIPTIONS and *defixiones* (curse tablets) to the goddess testify.

The solar dimension of the cult of Sūlis is similar to that associated with other curative springs in the Romano-Celtic world in stressing the affiliation of water environs and the underworld with that of a sky/solar cult in a healing capacity. Alternatively, or as an additional set of associations, a close phonetic parallel within Celtic is provided by a derivative of this word for 'sun' *sūlis*, with the transferred meaning 'eye', Old Irish *súil*. It is likely that 'eye' is a relevant meaning here in connection with Sūlis's name and myth. In the early HAGIOGRAPHY of St BRIGIT (possibly reflecting myths of the goddess of the same name), there is an episode in which she plucks out her eye and a spring miraculously bursts forth on the ground before her. Furthermore, in Old Welsh the word *licat* (Modern Welsh *llygad*) means both 'eye' and 'spring' and is used for a legendary marvellous spring in HISTORIA BRITTONUM.

Michelle Mann

SUPERSTITIONS AND MAGICAL BELIEFS

Introduction

Superstitions and magical beliefs have often been especially associated with the CELTIC COUNTRIES, but such beliefs are found in all societies. Usually called superstitions when considered (by insiders or outsiders) to have been discredited, so-called magical beliefs are held by societies on the basis of tradition rather than empirical examination. Nevertheless, they have usually developed rationally, springing from traditional standards of evidence, confidence in authorities regarded as credible, and interpretations of cause-and-effect relationships. The accuracy of traditional beliefs is felt to be proved on the grounds of personal experience and is founded on a worldview that has no reason to rule out the existence of magic or supernatural beings. In areas such as the cause and treatment of illnesses, the difference between ordinary traditional belief and magical belief often lies more in an ability to understand a process scientifically than in any distinction drawn by the tradition itself.

Superstitions and magical beliefs attach to all aspects of life. Many beliefs serve useful social functions, from marking the passage of the CALENDAR year to reinforcing identity. Others may be harmful, serving as a basis for isolating or harassing particular members of the community. Finally, there are traditions in folk scepticism as well as folk belief.

Ireland

Ireland (ÉIRE) has an especially well-recorded and well-known tradition of belief in the supernatural powers of the environment and their ability to aid or harm. Crops and livestock were particularly at risk from such agencies as fairies, and were protected with recourse to a vast array of precautions, such as building new houses where they would not block fairy paths and tying red ribbons to the tails of cows. The everyday world was rich with resources for charms and cures. Rowan branches hung over the door warded off bad luck, local standing stones and holy wells were available for cures, and on the feast-days of St BRIGIT and St John, the livestock could be safeguarded by driving them between bonfires. Prescriptions and proscriptions surrounded every major occasion of life, especially those related to death. Lively funeral wakes were among many customs that ensured the dead would rest in peace and not disturb the living. The community also had the benefit of those persons with such gifts as second sight or healing. Many traditional beliefs and practices have died out in Ireland, as elsewhere, but they have been replaced by beliefs common to most of the world.

Scotland

Scotland (ALBA) blends Celtic, Anglo-Saxon, and Norse traditions in its heritage of magical belief, but many beliefs cross regional boundaries. For instance, evil eye beliefs were found all over Scotland, and in ENGLAND as well. Gaelic Scotland shared many beliefs and practices with Ireland.

There was a large catalogue of supernatural creatures, an elaborate tradition of second sight, and an intense belief in ghosts. Witches were repelled in various ways, including nailing rowan above the door and tying red threads about cows and pregnant women. One use of witchcraft in cursing was to make a wax or clay effigy known as the *corp creadha* (clay body), which was then stuck with pins. New Year observances were among the most important of the CALENDAR year, and especially popular throughout Scotland was first-footing, in which people considered lucky would travel from house to house to be the first to cross the threshold. As with the Western Isles, the folklore of Orkney (Arcaibh) and Shetland (Sealtainn) was centred on the sea, and several terrifying sea monsters were elaborated.

Isle of Man

Most authorities who write on Manx superstitions and beliefs concentrate on those involving fairies and witchcraft. The *buitch* or witch could take the form of a hare, and consequently it was bad luck to see a hare cross the road. Some Manx refused to eat the hare because it might be a woman transformed. Witches could cause supernatural afflictions, but some, such as the evil eye, could also be triggered accidentally.

Given the importance of fishing on the Isle of Man (ELLAN VANNIN), it is not surprising to find numerous signs and portents related to the industry. The *lhemeen y skeddan*, 'herring moth', was a sign of a good herring harvest to come. Another insect superstition involved the *creg* or *carraig*, a small black beetle that, if killed, would bring rain.

Wales

In many cultures, the passage from one stage of life to another is often accompanied by signs that foretell the future. In Wales (CYMRU), rain on the morning of a wedding was a sign that the bride, rather than the groom, would be head of the household. The end of life also has its signs, and death does not come without warning. The *aderyn corff* (death bird), sometimes said to be a starling or an owl, but not usually identified, would come to the window of a dying person in Wales and tap on it with its beak. The *cannwyll gorff* (corpse candle) was a pale blue light like the will-o'-the-wisp that proceeded along the route of a funeral. Sometimes the entire phantom funeral or *toili* could be seen. The last sheaf of grain, called the *caseg fedi* (harvest mare) or *y wrach* (the witch), was left uncut, as death would soon follow for anyone who cut it.

Brittany

Many of the beliefs of Brittany (Breizh) relate to the milieu of subsistence farming and fishing. The success or failure of a crop had an enormous impact on the prosperity of the average Breton family and its livestock, and the numerous detailed superstitions relating to planting reflect the importance of a healthy harvest. Less consequential tasks such as doing the laundry also had their superstitions: Washing on Sunday caused the washerwoman to become a *kannerez-noz* (night washer) after death (see Anaon), and washing when someone in the house was ill could be fatal to the sick person. Sailors believed that whistling, often accompanied by prayers to St Clement or St Anthony, brought a wind, but caution should be exercised, because whistling could also turn a breeze into a gale. Boats, too, had to be baptized, or Satan would be able to lead them onto the rocks. Just as many people across Europe believed that animals speak at midnight at Christmas, fishermen in Saint-Brieuc (Sant-Brieg) believed that fish speak at Easter.

Cornwall

The dangers inherent in mining, the primary industry of Cornwall (Kernow), gave rise to many superstitions. Not only were the mines peopled by knockers and other fairies, but it was lucky to see them. Whistling and the sign of the cross were very unwelcome underground. If anyone was plagued by a run of bad luck or otherwise became the victim of black magic, he or she had recourse to a *peller*, the Cornish and Anglo-Cornish name for a sort of white witch. The peller removed bad luck, curses, charms, and other magical complaints. This name does not occur in any other Celtic language or dialect of English, but may derive from Latin *pellis*, 'skin' or 'hide'. Specific maladies would also be cured by turning to the appropriate saint. St Non's well at Altarnun had the virtue of curing the insane, who would be given a blow to the chest and thrown into the water. The magical properties of wells could also apply more generally: A child bathed in the well of St Ludgvan would never be hanged by a rope of hemp, although the water had no effect on ropes of silk.

Antone Minard and Victoria Simmons

SWORDS

Vocabulary

Several distinct native words for sword are attested in the Celtic languages and are thus possibly derived from Proto-Celtic, of which two have widespread attestations.

Proto-Celtic *kolgo, kalgo-* is first attested in the Romano-Celtic personal name *Calgācus* 'swordsman', the leader of the north British forces defeated by the Roman general Agricola in AD 84. The root is found in Old Irish *colg, calg* 'short sword' and a number of other words in the modern langauges for 'awn, beard of corn', 'point, spike', and 'penis'.

Proto-Celtic *kldios lit. 'striking/digging implement' accounts for Latin *gladius* 'short slashing sword' as an early loanword from Celtic. In Brythonic, Modern Welsh *cleddyf*, Middle Cornish *kledha*, and Middle Breton *clezeff* are all 'sword'. Old Irish *claideb* is a borrowing from Welsh.

Artefacts

It is immediately clear as to which of the range of attested weapons these words refer. On etymological grounds, Proto-Celtic *kalgo-* seems to refer to a pointed stabbing weapon, and *kladios* to a striking edge-weapon. *Calg* and *colg* occur more frequently in older Irish texts and, therefore, may refer to an earlier type of sword. The longer slashing La Tène swords of approximately 80 cm in length were unknown in north Britain and Ireland (Ériu) in the Iron Age, which is circumstantial evidence that *Calgācus*'s name refers to a shorter type.

Swords are a frequent find in archaeological contexts claimed to be 'Celtic'. The earliest swords that have been claimed as Celtic are late Bronze Age Carp's-tongue and antennae-hilted swords of the Hallstatt B period, from about 1100/1000 BC. These Late Bronze Age swords have a distinctive leaf-shaped profile and are suitable as edge-weapons; in this way, they differ from the very narrow-pointed rapiers of the Middle Bronze Age (*c.* 1600–*c.* 1300 BC).

Much more commonly accepted is the fact that the Hallstatt C bronze and iron Gündlingen- and Mindelheim-type swords have been used by, among others, the

Detail of a sword scabbard made of iron and bronze, Cisalpine Gaul (northern Italy), late 4th century BC. (C. M. Dixon/StockphotoPro)

earliest historically attested Celts. Swords of these types are widely distributed across western and central Europe.

During the Hallstatt D period (roughly the 6th century BC), daggers replaced the sword as the typical equipment in rich male burials on the Continent, and only during the early La Tène period was the sword reintroduced. The La Tène sword, usually carried in a scabbard on the right hip, developed from a relatively short slashing and stabbing sword with a blade approximately 60 cm in length into a long slashing sword with a blade exceeding 80 cm in length toward the end of the La Tène period.

Exceptions to this pattern are the Irish La Tène swords, which, in comparison with their late Continental and (southern) British counterparts, are more like tooth-picks than swords. Their blade lengths, which range from 37 to 46 cm in the 30 known examples, are considerably shorter than even the early La Tène swords on the Continent.

In the first millennium AD, sword types of Roman, Anglo-Saxon, and then Viking inspiration came into use in Ireland and Celtic areas of Britain. The general trend in early Christian times was toward weapons shorter than the long late La Tène swords had been, with a longer, heavier weapon appearing in the Viking Age (roughly 9th–11th centuries). Literary evidence for the earlier Middle Ages must be used with caution, as many of the texts look back to a distant legendary past (as in the ULSTER CYCLE).

Swords continued to be used until well after the end of the medieval period in the CELTIC COUNTRIES, and tended to follow the general western European pattern in armament. Notable exceptions were the late medieval Scottish broadsword and, of course, the famous claymore (Scottish Gaelic *claidheamh mòr* 'great sword'), a large double-handed late medieval and early modern sword.

Raimund Karl, John T. Koch, and Caroline aan de Weil

TÁIN BÓ CUAILNGE

Táin Bó Cuailnge ('The Cattle Raid of Cooley') is the longest and most famous of the tales of the ULSTER CYCLE of early IRISH LITERATURE. Three principal recensions of this tale have come down to us, though none survives in manuscript form earlier than the 12th century. Internal references and some inconsistencies suggest that it may represent a conflation of several versions that had grown and developed over several centuries.

The second recension alone gives the reason for Queen MEDB's incursion into Ulster (ULAID) to steal the brown bull, the Donn Cuailnge. Her husband, King Ailill, has in his herd a special bull, the Findbennach (white-horned)—for which Medb has no equivalent—and she decides to resolve the predicament by acquiring a great brown bull that belongs to an Ulsterman. Mustering her army at SAMAIN, she marches north, guided by FERGUS MAC RÓICH and the other members of the Ulster exiles.

Samain, a period associated with the dead, is an auspicious time for her to attack Ulster. All adult Ulstermen are at this time struck by a debilitating illness, the result of a curse by MACHA. Mebd's army is harried by Ulster's greatest hero, the youthful CÚ CHULAINN, who ambushes them and kills several of their number. He does not suffer Ulster's affliction, which causes Medb to query Fergus about Cú Chulainn. Fergus then relates *Macgnímrada Con Culainn* ('The Boyhood Deeds of Cú Chulainn') to her.

When they arrive in Ulster, Cú Chulainn stands on the ford over the river Níth defending the province, and engages various Connachtmen in single combat. This event culminates in his encounter with his foster-brother, Fer Diad, who engages in a duel with him that lasts for three days, before falling to Cú Chulainn's powerful weapon, the *Gae Bolga* (see MIRACULOUS WEAPONS; CALADBOLG).

Finally, the Ulstermen arise from their debility and rout the invading army. The two bulls, the Findbennach and the Donn Cuailnge, also lock horns in combat. Having killed the Findbennach, the Donn Cuailnge traverses much of Ireland (ÉRIU) with the remnants of his defeated adversary on its back before reaching Ulster, where the animal falls dead.

A number of *remscéla* (fore-tales) are associated with the *Táin*; this series of independent tales serves to show how certain circumstances connected with the *Táin* came about. The number of the *remscéla* varies between ten and fourteen, but includes tales such as *Táin Bó Fraích* ('The Cattle Raid of Froech'), *Táin Bó Flidais* ('The Cattle Raid of Flidais'), *Echtrae Nerai* ('The Adventure of Nera'), *Aislinge Oengusa* ('The Dream of Oengus'), *Compert Con Culainn* ('The Conception of Cú Chulainn'), *De Chophur in Dá Mucado* (Of the *cophur* of the two swineherds),

Fochann Loingsi Fergusa meic Róig (The cause of Fergus mac Róich's exile), and LONGAS MAC NUISLENN ('The Exile of the Sons of Uisliu').

The connections of some *remscéla* with the existing versions of the *Táin* are at best tangential. *Aislinge Oengusa* relates how OENGUS MAC IND ÓC son of the DAGDA, with the help of Medb and Ailill, manages to find the OTHERWORLD woman Caer Ibormeith, who had appeared to him in a vision (AISLING). In return for this assistance we are told that Oengus helped the royal couple in their expedition in *Táin Bó Cuailnge*. Oengus, however, plays no rôle in the *Táin*. *Táin Bó Fraích* is concerned with the adventures of the Connacht warrior Froech mac Idaith and, while Froech is killed by Cú Chulainn in the *Táin*, the tale is hardly necessary to explain that. It is probable that some of the *remscéla* were stories originally independent of the *Táin* that were later drawn into its orbit.

Conversely, the aeteological tale *Ces Ulad* (The debility of the Ulstermen) is not reckoned among the *remscéla*, even though it tells how Macha cursed the Ulaid for making her race against the king's horses when she was pregnant. While this legend etymologizes the place-name EMAIN MACHAE, it also explains why all adult males of the Ulaid were bedridden at Samain.

Ruairí Ó hUiginn

TAIR RHAMANT

Y Tair Rhamant ('The Three Romances') is a term conventionally used for the three Middle Welsh prose adventure tales known as OWAIN *neu Iarlles y Ffynnon* ('Owain or the Lady of the Fountain'), PEREDUR, and GERAINT. These three are probably the earliest, but not the only, examples of the later medieval to early modern French-derived or -influenced ROMANCES in Welsh. Each of the Three Romances is found in part or wholly in the Red Book of Hergest (LLYFR COCH HERGEST) and the White Book of Rhydderch (LLYFR GWYN RHYDDERCH).

The central literary fact of the Three Romances is that they correspond closely to *Yvain ou le Chevalier au Lion*, *Perceval ou le conte du Graal*, and *Erec et Enide,* respectively, of Chrétien de Troyes. The basis of this close correspondence has long remained controversial. This is the so-called *Mabinogionfrage* (Mabinogion problem): Are the three Welsh Romances native tales with French influence, Chrétien's tales with accretions from Welsh tradition, or descendants of a lost common source? On the one hand, several incidents in the Welsh have no parallel in the French, and some passages in German adaptations of Chrétien's tales are closer to Celtic tradition than to the French Romances; on the other hand, it is clear that the redactor of the extant manuscripts incorporated at least some material from Chrétien's texts. The problem remains unsolved.

John T. Koch

TALE LISTS, MEDIEVAL IRISH

Medieval Irish tale lists consist of titles of tales intended to represent the repertoire of the medieval Irish *filid* (higher grade of poets), whose rôle included that of the professional learned storyteller (see BARDIC ORDER). These long lists of tales have been preserved in important medieval Irish manuscripts. With a few exceptions, the titles in the lists are grouped under native genre-headings, which include *togla* 'destructions', *tána bó* 'cattle raids', *tochmarca* 'wooings', *catha* 'battles', IMMRAMA 'sea-voyages', and *aideda* 'death tales'. This system contrasts with the modern arrangement of placing the tales into tale cycles such as the ULSTER CYCLE and the MYTHOLOGICAL CYCLE.

It is now generally accepted that neither of the two extant lists gives an accurate account of the literature of 10th-century Ireland (ÉRIU); both contain additions and modifications, and certain titles are found in only one of the lists. Nevertheless, they present some indication as to which tales were known and popular during that time. It is noteworthy that the majority of titles relate to tales now associated with the Ulster Cycle of Tales, with only very few titles relating to FINN MAC CUMAILL (see FIANNAÍOCHT).

Petra S. Hellmuth

TALIESIN, HISTORICAL

Throughout the medieval period and into the modern day, Taliesin was regarded as an actual court poet of the heroic age, roughly the 6th century AD. The core of the case for the historical poet is twofold. First, 'Taliessin' is named as one of the five CYNFEIRDD in the 9th-century Welsh Latin HISTORIA BRITTONUM, where these five are synchronized with the independently documented historical rulers Ida of BRYNAICH (r. 547–59) and MAELGWN of GWYNEDD (†547).

The second pillar of the argument is provided by at least nine poems in the *awdl* metre within the diverse 60-odd surviving poems in the 14th-century manuscript known in modern times by the poet's name, LLYFR TALIESIN. This subgroup shows the attitude of contemporary praise poems, both eulogy and elegy, composed for living or recently deceased patrons who can be identified with independently documented chieftains of the early 6th century. Internal attributions to Taliesin occur in two poems of the canonical group, panegyrics addressed to URIEN, ruler of RHEGED. Several close with the same signature quatrain:

> *Ac yny vallwyf (i) hen*
> *y-m dygyn agheu aghen*
> *ny byδif y-m·dirwen*
> *na molwyf Vryen.*

Until I perish in old age, | in death's dire compulsion, | I shall not be joyous, |unless I praise Urien.

There is an implication of common authorship for the poems sharing this verse, and Taliesin is named, together with the signature, in *Canu Taliesin* iv (*Eg gorffowys* 'In [my] rest', *Llyfr Taliesin* 58). ENAID OWAIN AB URIEN (*Canu Taliesin* x), a *marwnad* or 'death-song' for Urien's son, shares information and wording with *Canu Taliesin* vi (*Gweith Argoet Llwyfein* 'The battle before the elm wood') and, therefore, is plausibly assigned to the same poet.

Beyond the corpus of Dark Age court poetry directly or indirectly ascribed to Taliesin, there is the matter of broader context. We know from the contemporary 6th-century record of Gildas's *De Excidio Britanniae* (On the destruction of Britain) that there were, in fact, praise poets at the court of Maelgwn (Gildas's Maglocunus). The 11th-century Breton Latin Life of Iudic-hael places its eloquent soothsayer *Taliösinus bardus filius Donis* in a completely historical late 6th-century context.

An early medieval Brythonic language similar enough to Welsh already existed in the 6th century for poems composed at that time to survive in copies of the Middle Welsh period without impossible linguistic barriers.

John T. Koch

TALIESIN, TRADITION OF

Introduction

The legendary poet Taliesin has attracted attention as a source of mythological and other supernatural elements, including prophecy and passages that describe REINCARNATION and shapeshifting. This Taliesin material has been compared with the fantastic exploits of poets in medieval Irish tales and, more especially, with ancient evidence for Celtic poets (see BARD) and druids in attempts to throw light on pre-Christian Celtic ideology and beliefs.

As a figure of legend, Taliesin occurs importantly in the Breton Latin Life of Iudic-hael. In this text Taliesin is addressed as 'Taliesin the bard, son of Dôn, a prophet who had great foresight through the interpretation of portents; one who with wondrous eloquence, proclaimed in prophetic utterances the lucky and unlucky lives of lucky and unlucky men'. He then interprets the prophetic dream of Iudic-hael's father.

In Wales (Cymru), the first firmly dated evidence for the existence of substantial traditions about a sage and seer, Taliesin, appears in Geoffrey of Monmouth's *Vita Merlini* (mid-12th century), but late Cynfeirdd manuscript poems, notably from the Book of Taliesin, testify to a rich and developed body of material, part of whose content may predate Geoffrey. Taliesin's fame was well known throughout the medieval period.

Medieval Sources

Beyond the main manuscript of Taliesin poems, Llyfr Taliesin, the Black Book of Carmarthen (Llyfr Du Caerfyrddin) contains three relevant items. First, in *Ymddiddan Myrddin a Thaliesin* (Colloquy of Myrddin and Taliesin), the two figures reminisce about the great battles of the past and the prowess of Maelgwn and other heroes. In a second dialogue, Taliesin, on his way to 'the fortress of Lleu and Gwydion', is accosted by Ugnach ap Mydno, who tries to lure him away to his fort flowing with mead and wine. Taliesin, 'challenger in poetic contest', declines. Third, a few lines in *Englynion y Beddau* ('The Stanzas of the Graves') indicate that the stanzas were interpreted as 'his' replies to questions about topographical lore posed in the presence of Elffin. A series of six 12th- or 13th-century prophecies in the Red Book of Hergest, commencing with *Anrheg Urien* (Urien's gift), and containing echoes of the Urien praise poems and other Book of Taliesin poems, are attributed to Taliesin, as are many prophecies, triads, and religious and didactic poems throughout the medieval period. In total, more than 270 items are attached to his name in manuscript attributions. Taliesin was a figure well known to the GOGYNFEIRDD and the CYWYDDWYR, primarily as a prophet and sage; as Elffin's poet, preeminent in bardic contest at Maelgwn Gwynedd's court at Degannwy; and as a praise-poet in Rheged.

The earliest versions of the prose tale *Ystoria* (or *Hanes*) *Taliesin* appear in the 16th century, in Elis Gruffydd's Chronicle of the Six Ages, and Peniarth 111, copied by John Jones of Gellilyfdy. The poems embedded in the prose are all attested in earlier manuscripts, and were clearly very popular with copyists. They (and others not included in the prose tale versions) share many features with the persona poems in the Book of Taliesin, and appear in places to recycle phrases and lines. The prose tale tells how the servant, Gwion Bach, gains inspiration from the cauldron of Ceridwen, undergoes transformations, and as a grain of wheat is eaten by her and reborn. After being set adrift on the sea, he is found and renamed Taliesin by Elffin fab Gwyddno, and taken to Maelgwn's court at Degannwy, where he confounds Heinin and the other court poets with his knowledge and eloquence and frees Elffin from prison.

Marged Haycock

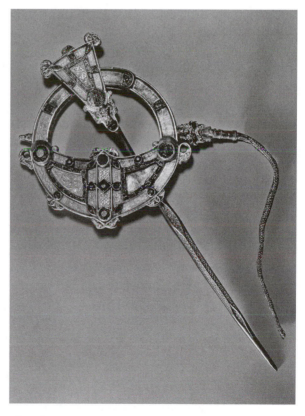

The 8th-century AD Tara Brooch from Bettystown, County Meath (Baile an Bhiataigh, Contae na Mí). (National Museum of Ireland, Dublin, Ireland/The Bridgeman Art Library International)

TARA

See Teamhair.

TARA BROOCH

The Tara brooch is an early 8th-century silver gilt pseudo-penannular brooch—the apparent gap in the design of the ring is decorative and not a true opening—found on the seashore at Bettystown, Co.

Meath (Contae na Mí), in 1850. The diameter of its ring is 8.7 cm, and its pin is 32 cm long. It received its name from a firm of jewellers in the 19th century, possibly for Romantic reasons.

The elaborately and finely wrought zoomorphic interlace and the spiralled triskeles that cover the brooch, together with the cast glass and amber human and bird heads, are all demonstrative of the high degree of artisanship during the early Middle Ages in Ireland (Ériu). In modern times, the brooch counts among the most valued of Irish national treasures. It was acquired by the Royal Irish Academy (Acadamh Ríoga na hÉireann) in 1868 and now forms part of the antiquities collection of the National Museum of Ireland (Ard-Mhúsaem na hÉireann).

Nicola Gordon Bowe

TARANIS

Taranis, Teutates, and Esus comprise Lucan's grim trinity of Gaulish gods who received bloody human sacrifice in a grove near Massalia in France. Dedications to Taranis have been found across Europe, at sites including Godramstein, Heilbronn, and Blockberg in Germany; Orgon and Nîmes in France; Piedmont in Italy; Garunna and Nedan in eastern Europe; and Chester (Welsh Caer) in Britain. The name *Taranis* is based on the word that appears as Welsh *taran* and Old Irish *torann* 'thunderbolt'. Therefore, the widely distributed Celtic representations of thunderbolt-wielding deities may be images of Taranis. Taranis has several points in common with the Roman Iuppiter/Iovis (Jupiter), and Germanic Thunar, both of whom are associated with thunderclaps. Lead hammers recovered from thermal springs, miniature votive hammers, and altars depicting hammers throughout Gaul are variously attributed to Taranis, Sucellus, and Silvanus.

Paula Powers Coe

TARTANS

Tartans may be defined as woven patterns formed by regular repeated symmetrical stripes in both warp and weft. Similar patterns are found worldwide in many eras, but tartan has become popularly associated with Celtic cultures, and specifically with Scotland (Alba). The earliest known Celtic examples are Iron Age finds at Hallstatt. The earliest surviving Scottish example is the 3rd-century 'Falkirk tartan' with the two-colour check pattern.

Paintings of Scottish clothing from the late 16th century onward regularly feature tartan, and formal portraits of the 17th century present it as a cultural icon. It gained the status of political icon when the Dress Act of 1746 banned the use of 'Tartan or partly-coloured plaid or stuff' for certain garments.

The association of particular weaving patterns with specific families or regions before that time is doubtful. The vast majority of standardized, named patterns arose as 'brand names' in the course of expanded industrial cloth production. Virtually no named patterns from the 19th-century pattern books can be matched with surviving pre-1745 fabrics or artwork.

Victorian fondness for a Romanticized Scotland helped to popularize tartan more generally, and today it is common for new patterns to be designed to commemorate groups or events. Pre-modern Irish archaeological finds feature tartan fabric and 19th-century depictions of Welsh clothing feature the tartan and stripe patterns that Lady Llanofer (Augusta Hall) encouraged as a national symbol.

Heather Rose Jones

TARTESSIAN

The name Tartessian is used for a corpus of ninety-seven inscriptions on stone from south Portugal and southwest Spain; this term is also used to denote the language in which those inscriptions are written and its SCRIPT, a writing system derived primarily from the Phoenician alphabet and related to the native script used for the earlier CELTIBERIAN inscriptions. The few Tartessian-inscribed stones with recorded archaeological contexts come from burial grounds of the Early Iron Age (*c.* 750–*c.* 450 BC). There is by now wide agreement among experts that there are at least some Celtic divine and personal names contained in these texts. Some researchers also believe that the language of these 'Southwestern' inscriptions is simply Celtic throughout. In either case, they probably represent the earliest written Celtic now known. The name 'Tartessian' derives from the ancient silver-rich kingdom of Tartessos (Greek Ταρτησσός) ruled by the historical Arganthonios ('Αργανθωνιος, r. *c.* 625–*c.* 545 BC) and probably centred on Huelva on southern Spain's Atlantic coast. A direct connection between Tartessos and the inscriptions is probable but not certain.

John T. Koch

TATTOOING

Tattooing, the permanent marking of the body by inserting pigments under the skin, has been associated with the tribal Celts from the time of the ancient ethnographers down to post-modern neo-tribal enthusiasts. The custom seems to have indicated aristocratic or sacred status in some cases, and low status in others. Strabo and Caesar were among the classical authors who described more elaborate tattooing among the insular Celts, with Caesar specifying that the ink used was a blue dye made from woad (*De Bello Gallico* 5.14).

In the 19th century, tattooing became well known again throughout the western world as a marker of the more marginalized elements of the lower classes, especially sailors and criminals. The punk and neo-tribal movements of the late 20th century brought tattooing back into mainstream fashion, however. Today, there are many 'Celtic' varieties of tattoos—some based on the designs of ancient Celtic metalwork, some on medieval Irish manuscript writing or illuminations, and some imaginatively recreating plausible Celtic tattoos (see ART).

Victoria Simmons

TEAMHAIR (TARA)

Teamhair (Tara) is a prehistoric archaeological complex in Co. Meath (Contae na Mí) that is associated with an extraordinary KINGSHIP often identified as the high-kingship of Ireland (Éru). The Hill of Tara is a topographically insignificant hill lying between the towns of Navan (An Uaimh) and Dunshaughlin (Dún Seachlainn). The principal visible monuments consist of a Neolithic (New Stone Age) passage tomb, a linear earthwork, a hill-fort, a stone standing on the inauguration mound (reputed, though unlikely, to be the ritual stone called *Lia Fáil*), and numerous barrows and enclosures of uncertain date.

The origin of the Old Irish name *Temair* (< Celtic *Temris*) seems to mean 'a sacred place' (cf. Latin *templum* < *tem-lo-m*). It has been regarded as the seat of the high-kings of Ireland. A constant theme in early IRISH LITERATURE is that of the exalted status of the kings of Tara and the all-island nature of their authority; gods and goddesses such as LUG, MEDB, and Eithne frequently appear in tales relating to Tara (see SOVEREIGNTY MYTH).

Tara was a special kingship, the 'kingship of the world', governed by universal principles of kings ruling justly, peacefully, prosperously, and truthfully. This rule is represented by the phrase *fír flathemon* 'the justice of a ruler', typified by the actions of heroic kings.

In political terms, it is unlikely that any king dominated the whole island before the 9th century. Control of Tara was a matter of contention between the LAIGIN (Leinstermen), ULAID (Ulstermen), and the UÍ NÉILL until the 8th century, by which time the first two groups had weakened and the contention was henceforth between the Uí Néill and the ÉOGANACHT dynasties of Munster (MUMU). From the 11th century onward, control of BAILE ÁTHA CLIATH (Dublin) and other cities was more important than control of Tara. Nevertheless, the old capital retained its significance in literature. One of the most popular tales linked to Tara is the dramatic account of St PATRICK lighting the paschal fire in the plain of Brega—traditionally on the Hill of Slane—and of his confrontation with Loegaire mac Néill, king of Tara, and his druids. According to legend, Tara was abandoned when St Ruadán of Lorrha cursed its king Diarmait mac Cerbaill († *c.* 565), the last king of Tara to celebrate the fertility rite, *Feis Temro*.

Edel Bhreathnach

TEUTATES

Teutates (also Toutatis, Tūtuates, Tūtatus, Toutorīx [see TUDUR]) froms a trinity of GAULISH gods along with TARANIS and ESUS in Lucan's *Pharsalia* (1.444–6) to which Gauls near Massalia sacrificed their prisoners of war. The name Teutates occurs alone or as a secondary theonym in combination with Mars, Apollo (see BELENOS), and Mercurius in texts and INSCRIPTIONS, including sites now in Austria, ENGLAND, France, Germany, and Italy. Since his name preserves a root that means 'tribe' or 'people' (compare Old Irish TUATH 'tribe', Welsh and Breton *tud* 'people'), Teutates may be an epithet that allows a better-known Roman god to incorporate a local, tutelary, tribal deity (see INTERPRETATIO ROMANA). The Germanic word either cognate with or, more likely, borrowed from Gaulish *toutā* gives *Deutsch* 'German' and *Dutch*. The early Irish oath formula common in the ULSTER CYCLE—*tongu do dia tongas mo thuath*, roughly 'I swear by the god by whom my tribe swears', and variants—is possibly based on a comparable notion of the god of the *toutā/tuath*.

Paula Powers Coe

TG4

TG4 is the television channel on which the majority of IRISH-language programmes are broadcast. The station has an audience of almost 800,000 viewers each day. The channel's signal covers Ireland and is available worldwide via webcast. TG4 was established as a publisher/broadcaster, and operates under the statutory and corporate aegis of Radió Telefís Éireann (RTÉ), the national broadcaster for Ireland.

As a public-service broadcaster, TG4 provides programmes in Irish and English, including a news service, drama, music, documentaries, sports, children's programming, and live coverage of the national parliament, Dáil Éireann. The station sources most of its programmes from independent production companies, and it also receives a provision of 365 hours of programming (valued at €7.5m) annually from RTÉ. Its regular soap opera *Ros na Rún* is the largest single independent commission in Ireland at €1.6m annually.

Website
www.tg4.ie.

Brian Ó Donnchadha

THAMES, RIVER

The river Thames has been the source of numerous important archaeological finds, from Late Bronze Age SWORDS to very prominent IRON AGE finds, such as the Battersea SHIELD and other WATERY DEPOSITIONS. The river probably formed the southern boundary of the Catuvellauni and the Trinovantes. The relative dearth of pagan Anglo-Saxon material north of the lower Thames suggests that the post-Roman BRITONS still controlled the area well into the 6th century. The easternmost bridgeable crossing at London (ancient *Lōndinion*, Welsh *Llundain*) became the site of the largest town of Roman Britain, and there is literary and archaeological evidence for its continuous occupation throughout the Dark Ages. The name, ancient *Tamēsta*, Welsh *Tafwys*, is probably related to *Taf* in south Wales (CYMRU), *Tamar* between Devon and Cornwall (KERNOW), and similar pre-English river names.

Raimund Karl

TINTAGEL

Tintagel is a village in north Cornwall (KERNOW) that has been linked to ARTHURIAN legend since the 12th century at the latest (see also ARTHURIAN SITES).

Although Tintagel now refers to an entire village, until the 19th century it referred only to the headland area on the coast. It was GEOFFREY OF MONMOUTH in his HISTORIA REGUM BRITANNIAE ('The History of the Kings of Britain', *c.* 1139) who

Aerial view of Tintagel in Cornwall (Kastell Tre war Venydh, Kernow). The 12th-century historian Geoffrey of Monmouth claimed that Tintagel was the birthplace of King Arthur. (David Goddard/Getty Images)

made the earliest surviving literary connection between ARTHUR and Tintagel, though possibly drawing on earlier tradition. According to Geoffrey, Arthur was conceived by magic at Tintagel castle. His father, UTHR BENDRAGON, was transformed by Merlin (MYRDDIN) into Gorlois, the duke of Cornwall, to gain access to the duke's wife, Igraine. The liaison resulted in the conception of Arthur. Many TRISTAN AND ISOLT narratives have King Mark ruling Cornwall from a seat at Tintagel.

The Tintagel slate, a broken inscribed stone with three men's names, belongs to the early post-Roman period (4th–7th centuries). The surviving fragment reads:

> PATERN(.)[
> COLIAVIFICIT [
> ARTOGNOV[
> COL[
> FICIT[
> . . . [inscribed stone] of Paternus [and] of Coliau,
>   Artognou made . . . Col . . . made . . .

The letters are lightly scratched, and the stone may represent a practice piece for a larger inscription. Portions of a more deeply cut A, X, and E remain visible at the top. *Coliau* and *Artognou* are Brythonic Celtic names, with the latter corresponding to Old Breton *Arthnou* < Celtic *Artognāwos* 'knowing the bear'. Due to the literary associations of Tintagel, there has been natural eagerness to associate Artognou with Arthur, but the names are not the same and may not even be etymologically related.

By 1233, Arthur's legendary connection with the site inspired Richard, earl of Cornwall, to build a castle on Tintagel headland, some of which remains today. By the 1330s, the castle had begun to decay and fall into ruin, becoming by the Tudor (Tudur) period a site of antiquarian interest for travellers.

Throughout the 20th century and into the 21st century, Tintagel has remained a focus for tourists.

Amy Hale

TÍR NA N-ÓG, IRISH BACKGROUND

The term *Tír na nÓg* (Land of youth) is one of many used in early Irish literature to denote the Otherworld. Tír na nÓg is a kind of earthly paradise, inhabited by supernatural beings, the *aes síde* (people of the síd). Other terms used include Tír fo Thuinn (Land below the wave), Mag Mell ('Plain of sports' or 'Delightful plain'), Tír na mBeÓ (Land of the living), Tír Tairngire (Land of promise), and Emain Ablach (Emain of apples; see Ellan Vannin [Isle of Man], in early Irish literature; Avalon). All of these names essentially describe the same phenomenon—a land of eternal youth, beauty, abundance, and joy—and a visit to this supernatural realm is a recurrent theme throughout medieval Irish literature. Access to the Otherworld could be gained by many means—for example, through fairy mounds, the *sídh*, or by going across or under water, which was considered one of the boundaries of the Otherworld.

The term Tír na nÓg probably appears for the first time in the Fiannaíocht (Fenian lays), where we find Finn mac Cumaill's son Oisín coming back from a visit to the Otherworld.

Petra S. Hellmuth

TÍR NA N-ÓG, WELSH CONNECTION

Wales (Cymru) has its own 'Land of the Young' in Ynys Afallach or Afallon (the Isle of Avalon). The Irish story of Oisín's love for the otherworldly Niamh and his fatal return home from her Land of the Ever-young became well known in Wales early in the 20th century, thus presenting an example of cultural cross-fertilization between Celtic countries and Celtic languages in modern times. Thomas Gwynn Jones, an a poet and an accomplished scholar of Irish, brought the term to popular notice in his Welsh-language poem *Tir na nÓg,* first published in 1916 and later set to music. His account of Osian and Nia Ben Aur (Golden-haired Niamh) is a melancholy meditation on longing and loss. The popularity of *Nia* as a woman's name in 20th-century and present-day Wales can be traced to his work.

Dewi Wyn Evans

TOCHMARC EMIRE

Tochmarc Emire ('The Wooing of Emer') is a tale of the Ulster Cycle. It tells how Cú Chulainn met and won his wife Emer. It also describes the super-hero's training in arms by Scáthach (whose name means 'shadowy'), a warrior woman of Alba; his brief liaison with Scáthach's daughter Uathach ('frightful'); and his triumph over another warrior woman, Aífe, with whom he fathers a son. In this last episode, *Tochmarc Emire* sets the essential background for the story of Cú Chulainn slaying his own son, AIDED ÉNFIR AÍFE.

The tale holds renewed interest for modern readers and feminist critics on account of its several strong female characters, especially the highly sexualized women warriors. For the study of mythology, it provides a particularly vivid example of Alba (Scotland or BRITAIN) able to function as a virtual OTHERWORLD in the early Irish literary imagination.

John T. Koch

TOCHMARC ÉTAÍNE

Tochmarc Étaíne ('The Wooing of Étaín') is an Irish saga in three diverse parts or else a group of three related sagas. The text's language implies a 9th-century original with 11th-century reworking. Elements of the plot are discussed in the articles on REINCARNATION and the MYTHOLOGICAL CYCLE.

Part I concerns the DAGDA's intrigues to beget OENGUS MAC IND ÓC. Years later, Oengus acts on behalf of his foster-father Midir to woo the beautiful Étaín Echraide (Étaín of the horses). After Oengus performs heroic tasks, Midir obtains Étaín, but Midir's jealous sorceress wife Fuamnach drives her away. Étaín is eventually reborn a thousand years later in ULAID. In Part II, Étaín is the wife of Eochaid Airem, king of Tara (TEAMHAIR). Eochaid's brother Ailill falls into love sickness for Étaín, prefiguring the reappearance of the otherworldly Midir. In Part III, Midir repeatedly plays the board game FIDCHELL with Eochaid and eventually wins Étaín. The lovers fly off as two swans to the síd. When Eochaid sends the men of Ireland (ÉRIU) to dig up Midir's mound at Brí Léith, the king mistakenly chooses and marries his and Étaín's own daughter. The child of that union gives birth to Conaire Mór, the doomed protagonist of TOGAIL BRUIDNE DA DERGA ('The Destruction of Da Derga's Hostel'). The name *Étaín* is intelligible as a diminutive of Old Irish *ét* 'passion, jealousy'.

John T. Koch

TOGAIL BRUIDNE DA DERGA

Togail Bruidne Da Derga ('The Destruction of Da Derga's Hostel') is an early Irish tale. At least the main elements of the story were already known in the 8th or 9th century. Nominally, it is part of the Ulster Cycle, though the setting is in Leinster (LAIGIN), and the main character, Conaire Mór, the prehistoric king of Tara (TEAMHAIR), is an important figure in the legendary framework of the Irish GENEALOGIES. *Togail Bruidne Da Derga* contains an account of an ideal KINGSHIP and the forces of the OTHERWORLD, points of connection with the KINGS' CYCLES and the MYTHOLOGICAL CYCLE.

Within the scheme of Irish LEGENDARY HISTORY, the story of the downfall of Conaire Mór serves to explain why the tribal group known as the Érainn had fallen from a central to a marginal position within Irish dynastic politics before the horizon of reliable Irish history.

The text tells the story of Conaire king of Tara, son King Etarscél's wife. However, Conaire's father is not Etarscél, but a mysterious otherworldly figure who, in the form of a bird, mates with the queen. Following Etarscél's death, Conaire is appointed king of Ireland (ÉRIU) through the custom of *tarbfheis* 'bull-feast', in which a bull is sacrificed (see FEIS); a visionary consumes some of the bull's flesh, then sleeps under the skin of the bull and receives a dream-vision of the man destined to be king. In this case, the PROPHECY is fulfilled through the intervention of Conaire's supernatural bird kin. At the beginning of his reign Conaire is a very successful king, and there is an elaborate and beautiful description of the abundance and harmony of his idealized reign. However, Conaire's foster-brothers begin to plunder the country, as young noble warriors are wont to do (see FÍAN; HEROIC ETHOS). When Conaire fails to punish them, he offends against a king's obligation to follow the justice of the ruler (*fír flathemon*). His doomed reign soon slides toward disaster as a series of improbable circumstances compel him to break several of his personal taboos (*geisi*, sing. GEIS). Conaire is attacked at the hostel of Da Derga, an otherworldly figure whose name etymologically means 'the Red God', by his foster-brothers and the demonic Ingcél Caech (Ingcél the One-eyed), a hideous giant with an eye like a wheel. After fierce resistance, he is overthrown, thus meeting his fate for having broken his *geisi*. In his final moments, as the hostel burns around him, Conaire is overcome by an all-consuming thirst, but all liquid flees from him, even the river Dothra (Dodder, Co. Dublin). In one memorably horrific scene among many, the decapitated head of Conaire thanks his servant for pouring drink into his headless gullet.

Peter E. Busse and John T. Koch

TOGAIL TROÍ

Togail Troí ('The Destruction of Troy') is a Middle Irish adaptation of the late antique forgery attributed to the fictitious Dares Phrygius and purports to be an eye-witness account of the Trojan war (see TROJAN LEGENDS). The most popular and influential of all the classical tales in Ireland (ÉRIU), *Togail Troí* is the centrepiece of the classical corpus. Although it was first translated in the 10th century, the earliest surviving version dates to the 11th century. *Togail Troí* is a free adaptation: The bald narrative of Dares is expanded and effectively retold in native saga style, rendering this reworking similar to the style of the tales of the ULSTER CYCLE. The longest recension includes numerous lengthy additions from the *Thebaid* and the *Achilleid* of Publius Papinius Statius (*c.* AD 45–*c.* 96). It also adds a sequel, *In tres Troí* (The third Troy), concerning the rebuilding of Troy and its ultimate destruction.

Barbara Hillers

TOMBS IN IRON AGE GAUL

The funerary practices of west-central Europe during the Early IRON AGE have their origins in the Late Bronze Age (9th century BC) and are evidenced by the rise in inhumations associated with the building of individual funerary monuments (*tumuli*). This practice became generalized during the 8th and 7th centuries BC. It accompanied a process of concentration of power, which, in the 6th century, led to a reduction in funerary monuments, which became confined to a stratum of burials for the privileged. These were characterized in some important areas by four-wheeled wagons and, soon after, by CHARIOTS—for example, in the Marne, the Middle Rhine, and Bohemia (see VEHICLE BURIALS). The Early LA TÈNE period (5th and 4th centuries BC) saw the development of other forms of burials that have their origins in the peripheral tombs of the *tumuli* of the HALLSTATT period. These cemeteries consist of flat graves containing bodies buried in small, probably family, groups. The differences between the burials essentially denote the distinction between the sexes. There are signs of a major change in the 3rd century BC, when most of the sites were abandoned and new practices developed, particularly associated with cremation.

Laurent Olivier

TONE, THEOBALD WOLFE

Theobald Wolfe Tone (1763–98) is known as the 'father of Irish republicanism'. Although he was a Protestant, and therefore a member of the Ascendancy, he argued in favour of the rights of the Catholic population and sought to unite Catholics and Protestants on the basis of their common political interests. Inspired by the American and French revolutions, he co-founded the Society of United Irishmen in 1791; this non-sectarian organization included both Protestant and Catholic leaders and acted as a political pressure group to demand a reduction in religious discrimination. Under Tone's leadership, aims were extended to include radical demands for an Irish republic and total separation from ENGLAND. Forced into American exile in 1795, Tone travelled to France in 1796 and persuaded leaders there to send a large military expedition to Ireland (ÉIRE) to aid the rebels in their imminent revolution. This unsuccessful campaign was followed by the brutal oppression of the rural population by British troops, which, finally, led to the rebellion of 1798. By then, most of the group's leadership had been arrested, however, and the national idea was lost. Ultimately, more than 30,000 people fell victim to the sectarian fighting that ensued. Tone's arrival with a small French army at Donegal (Dún na nGall) in October 1798 came too late. Captured and convicted of treason, he committed suicide.

Marion Löffler

TORC

Torc is the term used for the typically Celtic neck ring. Derived from a Latin word meaning 'twisted', the term used in the historical texts to refer to this ring is today applied to a wide variety of neck rings and necklaces.

Neck rings were a relatively common form of jewellery in most of Europe from the Bronze Age into the Roman period, when they seem to have gone out of fashion. Early examples are frequently simple bronze rings, though more elaborately

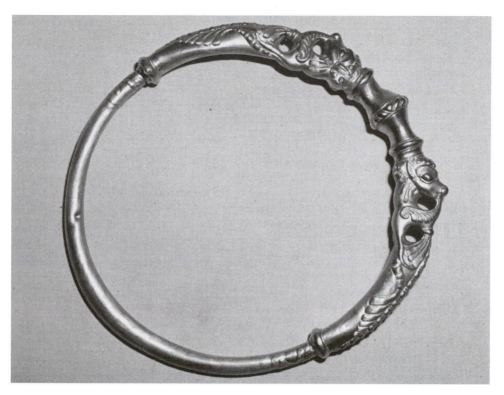

Celtic torc of gold from Erstfeld, Switzerland, 5th or 4th century BC. (C. M. Dixon/ StockphotoPro)

decorated pieces, sometimes crafted in gold, are also known; they show little resemblance to Iron Age neck rings.

Most frequently associated with the term torc, however, are the elaborate bronze and gold rings from the Late HALLSTATT and LA TÈNE periods. Silver and iron examples are rarer.

Torcs also feature frequently in Celtic ART: on statues, figurative art such as the GUNDESTRUP CAULDRON, and COINAGE. Torcs also became part of the classical topos for the depiction and description of Celts, as in the case of the 'dying Gaul' marble statue and Cassius Dio's description of Queen BOUDĪCA.

Raimund Karl

TÓRUIGHEACHT DHIARMADA AGUS GHRÁINNE

Tóruigheacht Dhiarmada agus Ghráinne ('The Pursuit of Diarmaid and Gráinne') is an important tale of the Fenian Cycle (see FIANNAÍOCHT). It shows striking similarities to the internationally popular medieval love story of TRISTAN AND ISOLT (see also DRYSTAN AC ESYLLT). A version of 'Diarmaid and Gráinne' was known in the Middle Irish period, though earliest extant copy survives in a manuscript written by Dáibhidh Ó Duibhgeannáin around the middle of the 17th century.

In the story, the beautiful Gráinne, daughter of King Cormac mac Airt of Tara (Teamhair), is the chosen bride of the ageing hero Finn mac Cumaill. When he comes to Tara to court her, she finds the younger Fenian heroes Oisín and Diarmaid ua Duibhne more appealing. Gráinne gives a sleeping draught to everyone but Oisín and Diarmaid. Both refuse her advances at first, but she then imposes a geis (an honour-threatening verbal injunction) on Diarmaid, requiring that he run off with her against his better judgement. They elope, and a vengeful Finn commences a pursuit that leads them through Ireland (Ériu). After several years, Finn arranges for Diarmaid to participate in the hunt of a supernatural boar, knowing that this will cause his death.

Much of the enduring power of the tale is that the three primary characters are all—despite their flaws and the supernatural plot devices—sympathetic, and motivated by understandable human emotions, which lead directly to irreconcilable conflict and disastrous breaches of social obligations. The story remained popular in Ireland and Gaelic Scotland (Alba) until recent times, and numerous folk versions have been recorded.

Peter Smith, Peter E. Busse, and John T. Koch

TRANSALPINE GAUL

Transalpine Gaul, Latin *Gallia Transalpina* (Gaul beyond the Alps, from the Roman perspective) contrasts with Cisalpine Gaul (*Gallia Cisalpina*). However, without further qualification, Gaul most often referrs to Transalpine Gaul, a region of ancient Europe bounded by the Rhine on the east, the Alps on the southeast, and the Pyrenees on the southwest.

John T. Koch

TREGEAR HOMILIES

John Tregear, writing *c.* 1558, is one of the few priests known to have made translations of Catholic works for his Cornish-speaking congregation. His translation of these Homilies remains the longest piece of prose writing from the Middle Cornish period. The themes of twelve Homilies are the Creation, the supremacy of the Church, and its authority, charity, and transubstantiation. A final thirteenth homily is translated from an unidentified source and is twice as long as the others.

Alan M. Kent

TRIADS, OF IRELAND

The arrangement of ideas in groups of three is common in the literatures of the Celtic-speaking peoples; cf. the Welsh triads (Trioedd Ynys Prydain). The largest Irish collection dates from around the 9th century and in some of the manuscripts is entitled *Trecheng Breth Féne* (A triad of judgements of the Irish). It consists of 214 triads, as well as a few other groupings and occasional single items. Some of these triads may have come from oral tradition, but most seem to have been the work of a single author. As a collection of proverbial truths, the Triads of Ireland

(Ériu) may be thought of as belonging to the more general category of gnomic or wisdom literature (see also Audacht Morainn).

The author's aim is clearly to describe various aspects of life as he saw it around him. Sometimes, his triads consist simply of observation of natural phenomena and general statements about society.

Fergus Kelly

TRIADS, TRIOEDD YNYS PRYDAIN

Trioedd Ynys Prydain (The triads of the Island of Britain) typify the oldest native strata of records detailing the mythology and legendary peoples of insular Brythonic culture. Arranged in threes as aids to memory, the names contained in these triads represent the largest and most diverse mnemonic record of epithets and onomastic lore in the Welsh language, the obscurity and mystery of which attracted the attention of many medieval Welsh poets and storytellers. Both the Cynfeirdd and Gogynfeirdd poets made use of names and narrative elements as triads. They served as an indispensable source of native lore and poetic training. In addition, the triads fell into the orbit of those native materials gravitating to the name of Arthur and subsequent tales associated with that name in Welsh tradition.

Embodied in more than half a dozen medieval and early modern manuscripts, successive enumeration, cataloguing, and copying of the text reveal the process of sifting and reshaping memory with each successive generation. Variants in the texts reflect the literary, sometimes ecclesiastical, and even political interests and attitudes of those involved in their production.

The triads served the native bardic schools as an index to an immense body of narrative materials that young novice poets or storytellers would master as part of an oral apprenticeship (see bardic order). Grouped according to theme rather than age or cycle, the three names in a triad produce a narrative trace of a longer tale or event. Some record narrative details, but many leave only the names of participants and their virtues or faults.

Triads appear as a device within the Mabinogi. Indeed one medieval tale, Cyfranc Lludd a Llefelys (The adventure or encounter of Lludd and Llefelys), is the expansion of a single triad, structured around three supernatural oppressions (*gormesoedd*).

Themes for the triads include tribal thrones and seats; the titles and occupations of men as warriors, chieftains, poets, and various other occupations from seafarers to wanderers; the good and bad qualities of men; the same expansion of titles and qualities of women; the peoples of Arthur's court; saintly peoples and lands; elder animals; the qualities and names of various warriors' horses, oxen, and cows; as well as quests, battles, womb-loads, oppressions, marvels, and other memorable and critical events that affected the history and/or legendary history of the island as a whole.

Chris Grooms

TRISTAN AND ISOLT

The story of Tristan and Isolt is one of the best-known pan-Celtic love stories, and has been retold in various guises throughout the centuries. The following features recur in most retellings. The Cornish knight Tristan and the Irish princess Isolt fall in love by means of a love potion, behind the back of her husband and his uncle, King Mark of Cornwall (Kernow). Eventually they escape through the Cornish landscape. Realizing how destructive their love is, they agree to separate. The love triangle is doomed from the outset, and the narrative ends in tragedy. Other important characters include the Irish champion Morholt, whom Tristan defeats; the dwarf Frocin; and Ogrin the hermit.

The oldest existing texts are by Thomas d'Angleterre (c. 1170) and Béroul (c. 1190), both of which survive only as substantial fragments and are written in the Anglo-Norman dialect of Old French. Meanwhile, Gottfried von Strassburg (c. 1200) composed his German version based on that created by Thomas, and this became the dominant European version, inspiring others such as the modern composer Richard Wagner. In the high Middle Ages, the narrative was incorporated relatively late into the Arthurian corpus.

The 6th-century 'Tristan' stone near Fowey in mid-Cornwall may provide a historical link to the narrative, since it reads DRVSTANVS HIC IACIT CVNOMORI FILIVS (Drustanus [i.e., Tristan?] lies here, son of Cunomorus). Cunomorus has been linked to Mark—the 9th-century Breton Latin Life of St Paul Aurelian mentions a King Marcus, also known as Quonomorius, thus making this historical Tristan the son of Cunomorus, alias Mark. From contemporary Frankish sources, we know that King Cunomor ruled c. 560. A. S. D. Smith's 8,000-line poem in Cornish, *Trystan hag Ysolt* (1951), is one of the most important 20th-century pieces of work in Revived Cornish (see Cornish literature).

On the Celticity of the names *Tristan* and *Isolt*, see Drystan ac Esyllt.

Alan M. Kent

TROJAN LEGENDS IN THE CELTIC COUNTRIES

The Roman historian Ammianus Marcellinus († AD 395) mentions a tradition of the Gauls that they were of Trojan origin; this was perhaps the source of the Trojan origin legend later adopted by the Franks (see legendary history). It is worth noting that Vergil himself was a native of what had been Cisalpine Gaul and may have been Gaulish.

The resemblance of the Irish Ulster Cycle to the Iliad has struck many modern writers, and there are Middle Irish adaptations of Trojan legends: Togail Troí (The destruction of Troy), the Middle Irish *Merugud Uilixis meic Leirtis* ('The Wandering of Ulysses son of Laertes'), and *Imtheachta Aeniasa* (The wanderings of Aeneas).

Britain's legendary history—like that of Gaul, as noted previously, and of Rome—looked back to Trojan origins. The Brythonic tradition of the Trojan refugee Brutus as Britain's namesake and founder appears first in the 9th-century Historia Brittonum; it was greatly elaborated in the 12th century in the Historia Regum Britanniae of Geoffrey of Monmouth. The same story is alluded to in Brittany (Breizh) in the Life of St Uuohednou (Gouieznou) from AD 1019. Brutus's brother Albanus is made the founder of Scotland (Alba) in the late 11th-century *Duan Albanach*. The Trojan framework of the Matter of Britain was still adhered to by the antiquary John Lewis (†1616) and retained its grip on Breton historians to a similarly late date.

John T. Koch

TUATH

Tuath (Old Irish *túath*, genitive *túaithe*) was the term for the basic social unit of early Ireland (ÉRIU), comprising roughly 3,000 people, with approximately 150 such *tuatha* in the country at any given time in the early Middle Ages. It is often translated as 'tribe'. *Tuath* also refers to the territory in which the group lived and where its members' rights and social identities were recognized. The fixed and guarded boundary of the *tuath* was an especially strong concept, with most persons losing their status and legal competence outside its confines. The dual rôle of the warrior—as the man on the frontier—is a commonplace in the hero tales: He is the prestigious protector and recipient of the king's largesse within the *tuath*, but also the bestial marauder outside this area (see further HEROIC ETHOS).

The *tuath* was ruled by a king. Throughout the historical period, we invariably find larger political units built up through subordinate kings submitting to overlords, who did not rule the tribesfolk of their subordinate's *tuatha* directly, but only indirectly in the king-to-king relationship. Over time, the importance of *tuatha* and tribal kings eroded in the face of consolidation of power by such relatively stable dynastic entities as the UÍ NÉILL and ÉOGANACHT.

Tuath is a COMMON CELTIC word traceable to INDO-EUROPEAN. Scottish Gaelic *tuath* 'people, tenantry' corresponds to Welsh *tud* 'people, tribe; country, territory, district' and Breton *tud* 'people'. It is often inferred from this evidence that the social system visible in early Ireland must once have been current throughout the whole Celtic world. If so, that would have been prior to the historical period. In post-Roman Wales, the CANTREF is roughly on the scale of the *tuath* and may represent a subordination of the native *tud* at the time when kingdoms became larger.

John T. Koch

TUATH DÉ

The Name and Its Meaning

Tuath(a) Dé Donann is a designation frequently applied to the immortals of Irish legend in medieval texts, with the later variant *Tuatha Dé Danann* also attested from medieval times.

The first clear evidence for the term occurs in the verse of Eochaid ua Flainn (†1004). Earlier sources speak of the *Fir Dé* (Men of the gods) or *Tuatha Dé* (Tribes of the gods); *Tuatha Dé Donann* would seem to be an expansion of the latter, motivated by a desire to avoid the ambiguity from the use of *Tuath Dé* for both pre-Christian divinities and the 'People of God', the Israelites. Eochaid ua Flainn is also the earliest source for the eponymous 'Donann, mother of the gods', and thus the meaning 'Tribes of the goddess Donann'. There are no other traditions regarding

Donann, and grammatically the name does not behave like a normal Irish proper noun. Proposals for an unattested nominative *Donu* or *Danu* are linguistically unworkable.

Donann may have arisen from a conflation with the mysterious group *trí dé dáno* (three gods of skill), and/or the land goddess ANU (genitive *Anann*), called 'mother of the Irish gods' by CORMAC UA CUILENNÁIN (†908) and often identified with Donann in later sources. A third possibility is influence from the ethnonym *Domnann* (see FIR DOMNANN).

The name *Tuath(a) Dé (Donann)* is equivalent to the expressions *aes síde* (people of the síd; see OTHERWORLD). The only difference in usage is context: *Tuath Dé* tends to be used in tales set in the legendary period before the arrival of the Gaels in Ireland (ÉRIU).

Pagan associations rendered the phrase problematic for Christian authors. One interpretation held that the immortals were fallen angels or, indeed, simply devils. Intriguingly, explicit evidence for the latter view seems again to be attested no earlier than the poetry of Eochaid ua Flainn. The 9th-century SCÉL TUÁIN MEIC CAIRILL (The tale of Túan, son of Cairell) speaks of the settlement of Ireland by the *Tuath Dé ocus Andé* (Tribe of gods and un-gods) 'whose origins the learned do not know; but they think it likely that they belong to the exiles who came from heaven'. This testifies to the keen desire of the Irish literati to find a place for their old gods within the framework of a Christian worldview.

Euhemerism, or the idea that gods are only illustrious figures of the distant past who came to be worshipped by posterity, was first formulated by the rationalists of pagan Greece, but its usefulness for Christians led to its enthusiastic adoption through the medieval period. In Ireland, the idea that the Tuath Dé were a race of mortals—descendants of Noah's son Japheth—who had gained a particular proficiency in magic was a key element in the pseudo-historical scheme from at least the time of Eochaid ua Flainn (see LEBAR GABÁLA ÉRENN).

None of these identifications ever achieved exclusive acceptance. Indeed, texts of the later Middle Irish period still debate whether the Tuath Dé were men or devils, and whether the supernatural encounters of early times should be attributed to diabolical or angelic agency.

An Irish Pantheon?

Cormac ua Cuilennáin not only identifies Anu as mother of the gods, as already noted, but also describes BRIGIT as a goddess worshipped by poets; the traditional etymology of DAGDA's name as meaning 'the good god' also seems to be correct. That such beings as GOIBNIU the smith (cf. the Welsh Gofannon fab DÔN), Dian Cécht the physician, and Flidais the mistress of animals are invoked in incantations is further evidence that they were viewed as having power.

Brigit can scarcely be dissociated from the British tribal goddess Brigantia, nor Nuadu, husband of BÓAND (the river Boyne), from the NŌDONS whose temple in Roman times overlooked the Severn. Ogma, 'strong-man' of the Tuath Dé and inventor of the native alphabet ogam, is clearly cognate with Gaulish OGMIOS, a god of eloquence portrayed with the attributes of the Greek Hercules (see also GREEK AND ROMAN ACCOUNTS). Georges Dumézil has persuasively linked the Irish Nechtan, guardian of the spring of inspiration, with the water deities Apām Nápāt in India and Neptūnus in Italy. The most striking example of all is the supremely accomplished LUG: The cult of the god LUGUS is reflected in dedications and top-onyms throughout most of the rest of the Celtic world.

Despite their origins, neither 'gods' nor 'fairies' are appropriate for understanding the Tuath Dé in medieval Irish literature; 'immortals' is probably the best rendition.

Characteristics

The magical powers most frequently attributed to the Tuath Dé are control over the weather and the ability to transform appearances, including their own. Normally, however, they are described in idealized terms: Their bodies are beautiful and their apparel opulent, and they are immune to age or disease. As with the gods of Norse legend, however, their immortality does not place them beyond the reach of death by violence.

By definition, the 'people of the *síd*' are dwellers in the Otherworld. In concrete terms, the *síde* are hills and mounds; in addition, supernatural regions were believed to exist beneath bodies of water. The immortals were accordingly very much associated with specific places, in a manner recalling the profusion of dedications to local deities among the Continental Celts. In some sources they are explicitly said to control the fertility of the land; thus the brief tract DE GABÁIL IN T-SÍDA (Concerning the taking of the otherworld mound) states that the first Gaels had to establish 'friendship' with the Tuath Dé before they could raise crops or herds.

This intimate link with land and territory goes together with their associations with KINGSHIP. In several tales, a king's right to the sovereignty is signalled or confirmed by an encounter, sometimes sexual, with a supernatural female (see SOVEREIGNTY MYTH).

A final trait to be emphasized in characterizing the Tuath Dé is their close connection with the arts. The 'three gods of skill' and many other immortal artisans are mentioned in the sources, and several of these—Dian Cécht the physician, Goibniu the smith, Creidne the brazier, Luchtaine the carpenter, and Cairpre the poet—are the prototypical representatives of their crafts. Lug, the paragon of the Tuath Dé, is the *samildánach*, the one 'possessing many skills together'. This depiction recalls the persuasive hypothesis that Caesar's description of a Gaulish Mercurius, 'inventor of all the arts', refers to the Continental Lugus.

John Carey

TUDUR (TUDOR) DYNASTY

Tudor was the name of a family from north Wales that gave five monarchs to ENGLAND in the period between 1485 and 1603. The house was descended from Ednyfed Fychan (†1246), seneschal of LLYWELYN AB IORWERTH. The name comes from a lord with the given name Tudur (†1367), whose full patronymic is Tudur ap

Goronwy ap Tudur ap Goronwy ab Ednyfed Fychan. Tudur's youngest son, Maredudd ap Tudur, was the great-grandfather of King Henry VII and openly supported the Owain Glyndŵr rebellion. His son, Owen Tudor, married Katherine of Valois, widow of King Henry V, in 1429. His son Edmund Tudor (†1456) married Margaret Beaufort in 1455. Their only child, Henry Tudor (†1509), known to the Welsh bards as the 'son of PROPHECY' (*mab darogan*), made a bold bid for the throne by sailing with a fleet of soldiers from Brittany (Breizh) to Wales, landing at Aberdaugleddyf (Milford Haven) in 1485. He recruited a sizeable army during a dramatic march through Wales and inflicted a humiliating defeat on Richard III, the last Yorkist king, at the battle of Bosworth on 22 August.

On the name Tudor, see Teutates and tuath.

Geraint H. Jenkins

TUROE STONE

The Turoe stone is the finest of five non-representational carved stones that have been dated to the pre-Christian Iron Age in Ireland (Ériu). The Turoe stone now stands in Bullaun townland, near Loughrea, Co. Galway (Baile Locha Riach, Contae na Gaillimhe), having been moved from its original location in the 1850s. Though it was moved from the vicinity of a small number of undecorated standing stones or boulders and a ring-fort known as the Rath of Feerwore, the original location of the Turoe stone remains unknown.

Turoe Stone, County Galway, Ireland (Contae na Gaillimhe, Éire). (C. M. Dixon/StockphotoPro)

The granite Turoe stone now stands 1.2 m above ground level, with a further 0.48 m below ground. The upper 0.68 m of the stone is decorated with finely executed La Tène ornament, which runs continuously over the top of the stone and is delimited below by a band of relatively crude step pattern. The curvilinear La Tène motifs were carved on three different levels and organized on a quadripartite basis. Motifs employed include roundels, a bird's head, trumpet shapes, comma-shaped leaves, triskeles, and pelta shapes, generally quite similar to metalwork of the 1st century BC/AD from southern ENGLAND and Wales (CYMRU).

Michelle Comber

TWRCH TRWYTH

Twrch Trwyth (originally *Twrch Trwyd*), the supernatural boar, is best known as the focus of the climactic task set for ARTHUR and his heroes in 'Culhwch ac Olwen'. The chase across south Wales (CYMRU) and across the Severn to Cernyw (KERNOW) is used as a framework for accounts of remarkable localities. As well as being remarkable for his size and destructiveness and carrying between his ears the comb, razor, and shears demanded by Ysbaddaden the giant, Twrch Trwyth is said to be the son of the king Tareδ Wledic; according to Arthur, he was 'a king transformed by God into a hog (*hwch*) for his sins' (cf. REINCARNATION; MATH FAB MATHONWY).

Like Arthur's wife GWENHWYFAR, corresponding to Irish *Findabair*, and Arthur's sword *Caledfwlch*, Irish CALADBOLG, Twrch Trwyth is equivalent to *orc tréith*, explained as 'a king's son' in SANAS CHORMAIC ('Cormac's Glossary'). Old Irish *orc* means 'young pig' and *tríath* (gen. *tréith*) can mean either 'king' or 'boar'. In the Middle Irish tract 'The TUATH Dé Miscellany', edited by Carey, we find *Triath rí torcraide* (Triath king of the boars). The Welsh spelling *trwyt* (Modern *trwyd*), which does occur, could be the exact cognate of *triath*, implying Common Celtic **trētos*.

Arthur's hunt of *Porcum Troit* 'the pig Trwyd' and other episodes found in *Culhwch* are mentioned in the *mirabilia* (marvels) of the 9th-century HISTORIA BRITTONUM.

John T. Koch

TYNWALD

The High Court of Tynwald, more commonly known as 'Tynwald', is the parliament of the Isle of Man (ELLAN VANNIN), and comprises the Legislative Council and the House of Keys. The name Tynwald derives from the Scandinavian *thingvollr*, which means assembly field.

Tynwald meets annually on 5 July in the form of an open-air assembly in the centre of the island. Tynwald Hill itself is *Cronk Keeill Eoin* in Manx. For the remainder of the year, Tynwald meets indoors at the Tynwald Chamber, part of the Legislative Buildings in the island's capital, Douglas.

Breesha Maddrell

UFFINGTON, WHITE HORSE OF

The only horse-like hill figure in Wessex, ENGLAND, which has claim to antiquity is the White Horse of Uffington, now in Oxfordshire (before 1974, in Berkshire). The chalk figure was carved in the hill immediately below the prehistoric hill-fort of Uffington Castle. The drawing is about 110 m long. The dating of the horse is difficult, but its origin is usually given as around 50 BC.

Horses with supernatural associations figure in pagan Celtic iconography (for example, EPONA 'divine horse') and in both Irish and Welsh mythological tales. Therefore, there is much comparative Celtic evidence for considering the possible significance of the White Horse of Uffington.

Maria Hinterkörner

UÍ NÉILL

The Uí Néill were an Irish dynasty whose members played a dominant rôle in Irish politics during the early medieval period. The family traced its line back to NIALL NOÍGIALLACH mac Echach (†?427/8), whose descendants came to dominate the midlands and the northwest of Ireland (ÉRIU). The Southern Uí Néill were divided into two collateral branches: Cland Cholmáin in MIDE and Síl nAedo Sláine (descendants of Aed Sláine) in Brega, both claiming descent from the common ancestor, highking Diarmait mac Cerbaill (†565), Niall's great-grandson. Although the rôle of the Uí Néill was sometimes challenged by the ÉOGANACHT of Munster (MUMU) during the 8th and 9th centuries and shaken by the Vikings in the 9th and 10th, it was BRIAN BÓRUMA of the DÁL GCAIS (†1014) who decisively eclipsed Uí Néill power, replacing it with a strengthened high-kingship. The fortunes of the Uí Néill—and their legendary ancestors, including CONN CÉTCHATHACH and CORMAC MAC AIRT—are a central theme of the KINGS' CYCLES.

Petra S. Hellmuth

UINNIAU (FINDBARR, FINNIAN)

Uinniau (Findbarr, Finnian) was a famous monastic scholar and an important authority in the church in the early to mid-6th century. He is known from both Irish and Breton sources. A contemporary Hiberno-Latin list of penances known as *Penitentialis Uinniani* (Finnian's penitential) survives, and Adomnán's *Vita Columbae* (Life of Saint Columba [COLUM CILLE], who died in 597) has several variant forms of the name of Saint Columba's teacher: *Findbarrus*, *Uinniauus*, and *Finnio*. This teacher is probably St Finnian of Clonard (†549), Meath (MIDE). There is a

Aerial view of the White Horse of Uffington in Oxfordshire (historically Berkshire), England. (Fred Ramage/Keystone Features/Getty Images)

second Irish St Finnian (†579), of Moville, Co. Down (Contae an Dún). These personages may have been one historical figure remembered in two local cults. St Ninian or Nyniau of Whithorn may also derive from Finnian/Uinniau, with early insular forms of *u* and *n* being easily confused, as at the end of these names. In total, a fairly impressive composite case emerges for an illustrious monastic figure in the poorly documented generations preceding Columba.

John T. Koch

ULAID

Ulaid, Modern Irish Ulaidh, English Ulster, means different things according to the period and context under consideration. Nowadays, used carefully with reference to modern times, Ulster means one of the four traditional provinces of Ireland (Éire; see cóiced), comprising the nine counties in the northeast: Cavan (an Cabhán), Donegal (Dún na nGall, also called Tír Chonaill), Monaghan (Muineachán), Antrim (Aontroim), Armagh (Ard Mhacha), Derry/Londonderry (Doire), Down (an Dún), Fermanagh (Fear Manach), and Tyrone (Tír Eoghain). Used more loosely with reference to recent politics and current events, Ulster can be a shorthand for Northern Ireland (see Irish independence movement).

In ancient times, Ulster was already reflected in name in Ptolemy's *Geography*, where the Ουολυντιοι *Uoluntii* appear as a tribe in the northeast. This form can correspond exactly to OIr. *Ulaid* if we assume, first, an old variation *Uo-, U-* and, second, that the name had come through an intermediary who falsely restored *-nt-* to *U(o)luti,* a hypercorrection from someone aware that GOIDELIC was already losing *n* before *t*.

In early historical times, the Northern Uí Néill rose to power in west Ulster, but claimed origin from the Connachta and never called themselves Ulaid. Their subordinates, the Airgialla, controlled the region around Emain Machae and Armagh, confining dynasties with Ulaid identity farther east. The kings of Dál Fiatach in present-day Co. Down claimed Ulaid tribal ancestry, whereas the Dál nAraidi in what is now Antrim, though also called Ulaid, were considered CRUITHIN.

The end of the 'GAELIC order' under native aristocracy is often marked by the decisive defeat of Aodh Ó Néill (Hugh O'Neill) and his sometimes ally Aodh Ruadh Ó Domhnaill (Red Hugh O'Donnell) of Tír Chonaill as they attacked the English forces blockading the Spanish fleet at Kinsale (Cionn tSáile) in 1601. Although O'Neill retained his earldom and much of his land in the treaty of 1603, he, O'Donnell, and many followers fled to the Continent in 1607.

The resettlement of Ulster from Britain and the partial displacement of the native population—which has affected the linguistic, religious, and political character of Ulster to such a great extent—began in the 16th century with major migrations from Scotland (ALBA) into Antrim and Down. Following the 'Flight of the Earls' in 1607, James I of ENGLAND acquired Hugh O'Neill's lands and remaining tenants, providing the opportunity for an organized scheme of resettlement or 'plantation' from 1608 onward by Scots, English, and 'deserving' Irish.

Although the Plantation succeeded in establishing the Ulster SCOTS language as an offshoot of the speech of the Scottish Lowlands and undoubtedly contributed to the decline of Irish speech in Ulster, areas of west Donegal have remained Irish speaking to the present, and most parts of the province retained native Irish-speaking communities late enough for a composite view of the Ulster Irish dialect to be possible. Some of its distinctive features show affinities with SCOTTISH GAELIC.

The largest city in Ulster and the capital of Northern Ireland is Belfast (Béal Feirste). Belfast was the seat of the Northern Ireland parliament from its inception in 1921 until it was suspended in favour of direct British rule during the conflict of 1972. Belfast is now the home of the devolved Northern Ireland Assembly under the Belfast Agreement.

John T. Koch

ULSTER CYCLE OF TALES

Introduction

Modern scholarship normally makes a fourfold classification of the Irish saga literature determined primarily by *dramatis personae* and by chronology. These four 'cycles' are the MYTHOLOGICAL CYCLE, the Ulster Cycle, the Fenian Cycle (see FIANNAÍOCHT), and the KINGS' CYCLES. The modern system does not accord with the system of the native literati, whose thematic system for classifying the sagas is usually inherent in the title.

Extent and History of the Cycle

The Ulster Cycle is the dominant corpus of Irish saga literature from the pre-Norman period. Roughly100 items spanning 1,200 years belong to the Cycle, from the long epic Táin Bó Cuailnge ('The Cattle Raid of Cooley') to poems and short passages of DINDSHENCHAS. The list comprises some of the best and most well-known literature of the period, including tales such as Fled Bricrenn ('Bricriu's Feast'), Longas mac nUislenn ('The Exile of the Sons of Uisliu'), Scéla Mucce Meic Dá Thó ('The Story of Mac Dá Thó's Pig'), Tochmarc Emire ('The Wooing of Emer'), Mesca Ulad ('The Intoxication of the Ulstermen'), Ces Ulad (The debility of the Ulstermen), and Táin Bó Flidais ('The Cattle Raid of Flidais').

The earliest literary versions of some of the more celebrated tales appear to have been written down in the 8th or 9th century—that is, the central and later Old Irish linguistic periods. While older tales were continually revised and rewritten, the process of composition did not cease. The 12th century saw the composition of some new material, such as the description of Conchobar's household and warriors found in Scéla Conchobair maic Nessa (Tidings of Conchobar mac Nessa).

Between the 14th and the 16th centuries, many older tales were revised. Aided Énfir Aífe was recast as Oidheadh Chonnlaoich mheic Con Culainn (The violent death of Connlaoch son of Cú Chulainn); Breislech Mór Maige Muirtheimni (The great rout of Mag Muirtheimne), while greatly modernized, appeared under the same name or as Oidheadh Chon Culainn (The death of Cú Chulainn) and Deargruathar Chonaill Chearnaig (Conall Cernach's red [bloody] rout); Longas mac nUislenn was replaced by Oidhe Chloinne Uisnigh (The violent death of the children of Uisniu), though the latter tale differs in many respects from the earlier composition. Many of these later tales appear to have been written in north CONNACHT, a thriving centre of scribal activity in the later Middle Ages.

Of no small importance in the later development of the Ulster Cycle was Keating's history of Ireland, Foras Feasa ar Éirinn, compiled in the 1630s (see CÉITINN). Several of the older death tales were recast and retold therein in Keating's lively and more modern prose style. The final creative phase of the Ulster Cycle followed; in the period 1670–1720, several new texts were composed in southeast Ulster and include Eachtra Chonaill Cheithearnaigh (CONALL CERNACH's adventure). The later tales were written in the verbose style that was favoured in Irish Romances of the 16th century onward and embraced the quest as a central theme.

In the 18th century, material belonging to this cycle was recorded from oral tradition in Scotland. At a later stage, similar material was gathered in Ireland. Many of these oral works can be associated with the 'Connacht Compendium' referred to previously, and were most likely inspired by manuscript versions thereof.

The Tales and Their Heroes

The Ulster Cycle is concerned with the exploits of the legendary ancient ULAID, a people once dominant in the northern part of the country (modern Ulster). Under their king, CONCHOBAR mac Nessa, they were based in the royal fort of EMAIN MACHAE (now Navan Fort, near Ard Macha/Armagh). Native tradition ordained that they were contemporaries of Christ, and the cycle, which is therefore set four centuries before the arrival of St PATRICK, has a strongly pagan atmosphere. Although written in the 8th or 9th century, the tales contain references to pagan gods and druids, to items of material culture, and to customs not known to have been practised in Ireland at the time of their writing. The reader is presented with a picture of an archaic prehistoric society, but it is a picture that displays anachronisms, inconsistencies, and features at variance with the historical and archaeological record.

Some features of the tales may reflect genuine memories of an earlier age and way of life. The tales probably contain some genuinely old material that had been added to and embellished in the course of being written and rewritten over a long period of time. It is not always easy to determine what is genuinely old or what is due to the literary invention of archaizing writers.

The tales are heroic legends concerned with the martial exploits of the legendary Ulaid (see HEROIC ETHOS). The heroes are drawn from the upper echelons of society and are sometimes collectively referred to as the warriors of *Craebruad* (red branch), a name whose origin is not clear. Bravery and valour, nobility of spirit, honour, and generosity are the traits most highly valued in this society. Defeated enemies are usually dealt with in barbarous fashion, suffering decapitation while their heads are kept as trophies by their victorious opponents (see HEAD CULT).

It is acceptable for warriors to boast, provided their boasts are carried out. To be respected as a warrior and remembered as such is the summit of ambition. When the druid CATHBAD was asked how auspicious it would be for a warrior to take arms for the first time on that day, he replied that such a warrior would gain fame and renown, but would have a short life. On hearing this, the young CÚ CHULAINN, the principal warrior of the Ulster Cycle, stated that he did not care whether he lived but for a day provided his deeds would remain on the lips of the men of Ireland. After Cú Chulainn, Conall Cernach is the second warrior of the Cycle.

As might be expected, King Conchobar mac Nessa features prominently in the Ulster Cycle. Like Cú Chulainn, tradition makes him the fruit of multiple conception. A version of *Compert Conchobuir* (The conception of Conchobar) dating perhaps from the 8th century relates how he was conceived through a chance encounter between Nes and the druid Cathbad. Conchobar, who is born on the same day as Christ, gains the kingship of Ulster when the incumbent, FERGUS MAC RÓICH, is tricked into yielding this office to him through the guile of Conchobor's mother Nes. The picture painted of Conchobar as the comely, brave king loved by his people is tarnished in *Longas mac nUislenn*, where he is presented as an envious and treacherous old man. His physical beauty contributes eventually to his death. *Aided Conchobair* (The violent death of Conchobar) relates that the women of Connacht wished to view him on account of his great beauty. Granting them their wish, Conchobar is struck by a shot from a sling cast by Cet mac Mágach, a Connacht warrior who had hidden himself among the Connacht women. The ball that strikes the Ulster king consists of the brain of a slain Leinster warrior, Mes Gegra, which had been mixed with lime and hardened. Conchobar survives for seven years with the ball embedded in his head, until hearing of the death of Christ.

Bricriu Nemthenga (poison-tongue) is an altogether more insidious personage in the tales. In accordance with his sobriquet, he incites strife and dissension among the Ulaid. On refusing an initial invitation to a feast that he had prepared, the Ulaid are informed that Bricriu would stir up enmity between the nobles of Ulster, between father and son, between mother and daughter, and betweem the two breasts of every woman, if they did not come. The strife he incites among Cú Chulainn, Conall Cernach, and Loegaire Buadach, and their respective wives, Emer, Lendabair, and Fedelm Noícride, is the theme of *Fled Bricrenn*. Bricriu's ability to cause enmity and strife is again brought into sharp relief in the later version of *Táin Bó Flidais,* where, under the name Bricne, he incites further conflict among most of the main protagonists in the story.

While the Ulaid encounter many enemies in their adventures, their chief foe is Medb, the warrior queen of Connacht. A formidable character, manipulative and treacherous, she resides in the royal fort of Crúachu (Rathcroghan, Co. Roscommon/Contae Ros Comáin) with her much weaker consort Ailill mac Máta. Medb uses her wiles to get warriors to fight for her, offering them various inducements, not least of which is the openly sexual *cairdes sliasat* 'friendship of thighs'. In fact, she uses this ploy in *Táin Bó Cuailnge* to get Fer Diad to fight against his foster brother Cú Chulainn. Ailill has to suffer his wife's excesses, as he does her relationship with the Ulsterman Fergus mac Róich. After Conchobar had treacherously killed the sons of Uisliu, Fergus and some other of the Ulster nobles go into exile in Connacht, where Fergus enters into a relationship with Medb that is an important part of the Táin Bó Cuailnge.

The Themes of the Tales

Thematically, the dominant group of tales within this cycle are the *Aideda* 'death tales'. The deaths of most of the prominent characters in the cycle are recorded. Other violent native genres include *Catha* 'battle tales' and *Tána bó* 'cattle raids'. Among these can be reckoned *Táin Bó Regemain, Táin Bó Fraích, Táin Bó Flidais,* and the longest of all the Ulster tales, *Táin Bó Cuailnge.* So prominent is this tale that the unqualified term *Táin* is frequently used to refer to it, rather than to any of the other *Tána.*

Supernatural and Mythological Aspects

Many of the characters in the Ulster Cycle are endowed with supernatural features, notably Cú Chulainn, who is comparable to a modern superhero. He has seven pupils in each eye and seven fingers on each hand, and when incited to anger he undergoes a *riastrad,* a series of contortions whereby portions of his three-coloured hair, eyes, and other parts of his body recede and stand out grotesquely.

The characters in this cycle range from the clearly supernatural to the human, with the former sometimes shapeshifting into animal forms. In *Echtrae Nera,* the mortal Connacht warrior Nera finds himself caught fatefully in a time-distorted succession of raids between the court of Crúachu and the *síd*, and in the end he is trapped for all time with his otherworld wife and their child.

Supernatural aspects of some characters are manifested in certain aspects of their behaviour. Medb, for instance, is the queen who takes many lovers and is marked by her promiscuity. She is willing to offer her sexual favours to any man, provided she can gain some advantage thereby. At a deeper level, however, this behavior accords with the native concept of sovereignty, which is usually conceived of as a feminine entity and thus can be personified (see SOVEREIGNTY MYTH). A similar interpretation can be seen in the case of her lover Fergus mac Róich, whose name can be translated as 'manly vigour, son of the great horse'. Physically a giant, his supernatural proportions and gargantuan appetite are described in *Scéla Conchobair maic Nessa*, where we are told that he required seven women to satisfy him if his wife, Flidais, was not with him. Given the meaning of his name and his attributes, Fergus can be seen as a god of virility. As is true for his partner Medb, several other figures in the tradition who bear this name may be alternative realizations of the same deity.

In later tales, supernatural adversaries are frequently encountered in overseas lands or in some imaginary country. Overseas expeditions are not unknown in early texts, but are a marked feature in later compositions. *Oileamhain/Foghlaim Con Culainn* has the Ulster hero travelling to Greece and to Scythia to learn martial arts, as well as encountering and defeating several otherworldly beings. In many cases, the action is played out in an imaginary land such as *Críoch na Sorcha* (The land of brightness) or *Tír an Uaignis* (The land of loneliness).

Place-Names and the Ulster Cycle

As in other branches of Irish literature, *dindshenchas* plays an important part in the Ulster Cycle. A prominent example is the Fer Diad episode in *Táin Bó Cuailnge*, evidently a late addition to the tale that was most likely inspired by and created from the place-name Áth Fir Diad (Fer Diad's ford). *Táin Bó Cuailnge* contains in excess of fifty such legends that purport to explain the origins of certain toponyms encountered in the tale. Down Bricriu (Loughbrickland, Co. Down/Loch Bricrenn, Contae an Dúin) and Fraoch mac Idaith (Carnfree, Co. Roscommon/Carn Fraoich, Contae Ros Comáin) can also be associated with toponyms. In other cases, we find the name of a character assimilated to that of a toponym. Cú Chulainn appears in some later tales as Cú Chuailnge, or Cú Chuillinn, forms that appear to be inspired by the place-names Cuailnge (Cooley, Co. Louth/Contae Lú) and Sliabh gCuilinn (Slievegullion, Co. Armagh/Contae ARD MHACHA).

Ruairí Ó hUiginn

UNION WITH SCOTLAND (1707)

The Treaty of Union between ENGLAND and Scotland (ALBA), which created the United Kingdom of Great Britain, was approved by both English and Scottish parliaments and came into effect on 1 May 1707. Under the terms of the Treaty,

45 Scottish Members of Parliament would sit in the UK Parliament at Westminster, and 16 representative peers would sit in the House of Lords. By population, then, the Scottish people had roughly half the representation the English had.

The Union brought into permanent being uniformity of taxation, duties, and coinage throughout the United Kingdom, with various Scottish exemptions. Scotland was to keep its legal system and its heritable jurisdictions of barony and regality. The two parliaments passed separate acts that preserved the establishment of the Presbyterian Church of Scotland (see CHRISTIANITY) and Scotland's universities.

The key motivation for the Union was the succession to the Crown. By the Act of Settlement of 1701, the English Parliament had excluded all Catholics from succession to the Crown. In doing so, it had excluded the exiled Scottish dynasty, the Stuarts. The SCOTTISH PARLIAMENT had responded by passing several acts asserting Scottish independence—namely, the Act anent Peace and War (1703), which reserved an independent foreign policy for Scotland, and the Act of Security (1704), which reserved to Scotland the right to alter that succession. Pressure was brought to bear for Union as the only solution to the impasse over the succession and Scottish national rights.

The common people of Scotland were heavily to overwhelmingly against Union. Despite the expectation in Scotland that the Union would endure 'without any Alteration thereof . . . for ever', its legal position has always been ambivalent, and a significant number of breaches of the terms of the Union have occurred; see also DEVOLUTION.

Murray G. H. Pittock

URIEN OF RHEGED

Urien of Rheged is probably the best known and best documented of the BRITONS of the 'Old North' (HEN OGLEDD) who fought against the Anglo-Saxons in the 6th century. The son of Cynfarch, Urion is also mentioned in the oldest layer of Welsh poetry. Several *englynion* about Urien concern his death, including the gripping verses on the hero's severed head and headless corpse (cf. HEAD CULT).

There are also eight panegyrics to Urien in the Book of Taliesin (LLYFR TALIESIN), which have been regarded by many Welsh and Celtic scholars as compositions of the historical TALIESIN. These *awdlau* refer to numerous battles, including detailed accounts—vivid in their journalistic immediacy—of battles fought at places called *Gwen Ystrad* (the white or blessed valley) and *Argoed Llwyfain* (before the elm wood).

In the GENEALOGIES, Urien belongs to the Cynferching branch of the descendants of Coel Hen. As to his locality, he is repeatedly associated with several places—most frequently RHEGED, thought to include Carlisle (Caerliwelydd). He is called ruler of CATRAETH twice in the *awdlau*, the most certain geographical identification. Llwyfenydd—perhaps linked to *llwyfain* in the battle-name—has been identified with the river Lyvennet in CUMBRIA. *Erechwydd* means '[land] before the fresh, flowing water'; possible identifications include the English Lake District and the

Yorkshire Dales. Although uncertainties remain, the most plausible localizations for the hereditary lands of Urien are south of Hadrian's Wall.

According to the triads, Urien fathered Owain ab Urien and his twin sister Morfudd on the otherworldly woman Modron daughter of Afallach (cf. Avalon; Matronae). Urien occurs repeatedly in Arthurian literature, but he is usually merely mentioned as a king subordinate to Arthur.

John T. Koch

UTHR BENDRAGON (UTHER PENDRAGON)

Uthr Bendragon (Uther Pendragon) is best known as the father of Arthur since at least the publication of Historia Regum Britanniae ('The History of the Kings of Britain', *c.* 1139). This work includes the story of Arthur's conception at Tintagel in which Uther assumes the guise of the duke of Cornwall (Kernow) to be with his wife, Igraine. Geoffrey of Monmouth's Uther is the brother of Aurelius Ambrosius, who is clearly based on the historical 5th-century leader Ambrosius Aurelianus praised by Gildas.

Uther's earlier origins are more difficult to trace. The name appears in several poems, though not as Arthur's father, and in many cases it may not be a name but rather a simple adjective, *uthr*, which means 'awful' or 'awesome'. *Pendragon* can mean 'dragon's head' as Geoffrey takes it, but since Welsh *draig*, pl. *dragon* could also mean 'chieftain, military leader, hero' (see Draig Goch), *Pendragon* could be 'chief of chieftains' or 'high chieftain'.

Among the *marwnadau* (death songs, elegies) in the 14th-century Book of Taliesin (Llyfr Taliesin), there is a weird elegy issuing from the mouth of the deceased, entitled *Marwnat Vthyr Pen* 'Elegy of the terrible head', with *mar. vthyr dragon* 'El. of the high chieftain Uther' added in another hand at the margin. It contains the string of bloodthirsty boasts:

> It is I who killed a hundred strongholds' mayors.
> It is I who gave out a hundred cloaks.
> It is I who cut off a hundred heads.

John T. Koch

UUINUUALOE, ST

St Uuinuualoe (Modern Gwenole) is an important Breton saint who probably lived in the 6th century. The Life of Uuinuualoe was written *c.* 880 by Uurdisten, the abbot of Landevenneg. When the monks fled before the Vikings in AD 914, they took the body of Uuinuualoe, his relics, and copies of his written Life away from Brittany; the Lives are now in Paris and Quimper, Brittany (Kemper, Breizh), respectively, while the saint's relics are in Saint-Sauve in Montreuil-sur-Mer in Artois, Normandy.

In addition to founding the abbey of Landevenneg, Gwenole is closely associated with stories of King Gradlon or Grallon and the drowned city of Ys (see FLOOD LEGENDS). There is a tradition that St Uuinuualoe used his bell to attract fish from the sea, and his iconography often includes fish.

The name *Uuinuualoe* is composed of two elements: Old Breton *guinn* (Modern *gwenn*) 'white, fair, holy' and the common masculine name element *wal*(*oe*), possibly meaning 'ruler'. The Cornish parish of Gunwalloe takes its name from him. The name is also recorded in a hypocoristic form, with *to-* 'thy' (Irish *tu-/to-*, Welsh *ty-*), and the diminutive *-oc,* in Landévennec in Brittany (BREIZH) and the parishes of Landewednack and Towednack in Cornwall (KERNOW).

Antone Minard

VEHICLE BURIALS

A characteristic feature of rich tombs from the HALLSTATT period in Central Europe and the LA TÈNE period in several areas of Europe is the internment of a wagon or CHARIOT with the deceased as a funeral gift or death-bier.

Hallstatt Tombs and Four-Wheeled Wagons

Four-wheeled wagons frequently appear in aristocratic tombs of the Hallstatt IRON AGE (c. 750–c. 475 BC). The wheels were usually removed from the axles and put alongside one of the walls of the burial chamber. Often, the wagon was also used as a surface on which to put feasting equipment (see FEAST), as at Hochdorf. The presence of a four-wheeled wagon in a burial has been interpreted as one of the most significant markers of the high social status of the person buried in the grave. Two exceptionally rich late La Tène tombs (broadly datable to the 2nd century BC) from what is now France contained four-wheeled wagons.

La Tène Tombs and Two-Wheeled Chariots

Beginning in the later Hallstatt period, but most characteristic of the La Tène period (c. 475 BC to the Roman conquest), is the practice of burying persons with or on a two-wheeled chariot. Most frequently found in Germany, Belgium, the Champagne region of present-day northeast France, and the ARRAS CULTURE of East Yorkshire in ENGLAND, such burials appear sparingly across most of Celtic Europe, with examples from as far as Mezek, Bulgaria and ancient Thrace. These burials often contain very rich grave goods.

Raimund Karl

VERCINGETORĪX

Vercingetorīx, prince of the Arverni, was leader of the Gaulish uprising against Caesar in 52 BC and one of the most famous historical figures of the ancient Celts (see GAUL). He succeeded in uniting the Gaulish tribes—even the Aedui and the Atrebates, who were traditional allies of the Romans. Once he became supreme commander of the Gaulish forces, Vercingetorīx declared himself king. Following a defeat in Avaricum, he withdrew to Gergovia, where he defeated the Roman army. He was finally defeated by Caesar in Alesia, where he was captured. Vercingetorīx lived for six years as a Roman prisoner until he was executed in Tullianum in 46 BC.

Tomb of a Gaulish chief buried with his chariot and his chariot driver, from La Gorge-Meillet, Somme-Tourbe, France, 4th century BC. (Musee des Antiquites Nationales, St. Germain-en-Laye, France/Giraudon/The Bridgeman Art Library International)

The chief source for the career of Vercingetorīx is Book VII of Caesar's *De Bello Gallico*. The name *Vercingetorīx* is Celtic—a three-element compound consisting of the roots *wer-* 'over', *cingeto-* 'hero', and *rīx* 'king', hence 'Great leader of heroes'.

Peter E. Busse

VISION LITERATURE, MEDIEVAL IRISH

Written accounts of existence after death, purportedly related by individuals who visited the afterworld in spirit before having their souls restored to their bodies, are known as vision literature.

Background

Vision narratives have a long history in the Judaeo-Christian literatures. The influence of external sources on insular vision literature is unmistakable, and the genre as a whole is clearly of Continental inspiration. By far the most popular of the apocryphal visions was the Vision of St Paul, originally written in Greek as early as the 3rd century. The text describes how he witnessed the judgement of souls, the beauties of paradise and the 'city of Christ', and the punishments of sinners.

The Visions of Fursa

There are several accounts of the visions of the Irish saint Fursa or Furey († *c.* 650): the earliest are the *Vita prima Fursaei* (?7th century) and a briefer notice in BEDE's *Historia Ecclesiastica* (731). In outline, Fursa's principal vision echoes the sequence of the Vision of St Paul: He is challenged by demons but defended by angels; he is carried aloft and looks down to see the world as a place of flames and darkness; he visits heaven, where he hears the singing of the angels and is given exhortations to carry back to earth; and he sees the damned in the fires of hell. Other elements are innovative: Fursa meets two Irish saints in heaven, whose relics he subsequently takes with him to the Continent. Much attention is given to eschatology (the end of the world).

The Vision of Laisrén

The earliest vernacular Irish vision still extant is preserved only as a fragment. A cleric named Laisrén, following a prolonged fast, experienced his soul's departure from his body. He was denounced by demons, but protected by angels; he flew above dark regions in the north to a valley where the future sufferings of sinners were revealed; he saw hell as a 'sea of fire'. At this point the text breaks off.

Enough remains to show that this text was in the same general tradition as that of the Fursa visions. A new feature is the valley where the punishments of those who can still be saved are disclosed, a place called 'the porch of hell'. This is the first Irish account of an infernal region from which redemption is possible, as distinct from the place of the damned.

Fís Adomnáin

This account of a vision supposedly seen by Adomnán (†704) of Iona (EILEAN Ì) was written in the 10th or 11th century. Once again the basic framework recalls the Vision of St Paul: Adomnán visits a paradisial 'land of saints', sees God enthroned in his heavenly city, is taken to regions of punishment adjacent to the yet more terrible habitation of Satan, and briefly revisits paradise before returning to his body. What most sets *Fís Adomnáin* apart from its predecessors is the extravagant vividness of its descriptions, and the author's evident wish to construct a coherent geography of the afterworld.

Visio Tnugdali

Written in 12th-century Germany by a member of the Irish monastic community at Regensburg, this narrative enjoyed enormous popularity throughout medieval Europe. The young nobleman Tnugdalus (Irish Tnúthgal, often simplified to 'Tundal') sees in hell the ULAID heroes FERGUS MAC RÓICH and CONALL CERNACH (see further ULSTER CYCLE); in paradise he meets various Irish notables, clerical and secular, with whom his monastery had had close ties.

St Patrick's Purgatory

By the end of the 12th century at least, there was a belief that a cave leading to the afterworld was located on a small island in Loch Dearg, Co. Donegal (Contae Dhún na nGall). Whoever survived a night in the cave was held to have expiated his sins in this world, and would not experience further punishments after death.

This 'Purgatory' became famous throughout Europe, and vigils continued to be held in the cave until it was closed by papal order in 1497 and subsequently destroyed. Several accounts of adventures encountered within it circulated during the Middle Ages. In the most popular of these texts, a knight named 'Owein' was said to have visited the Purgatory in the mid-12th century. According to this account, Owein sees regions of torture from which souls will eventually be delivered, slips briefly into the mouth of hell, and crosses a supernatural bridge to the earthly paradise, where those not quite good enough for heaven await the ultimate beatitude.

Miscellaneous

Besides the works listed previously, there is ample further evidence of the importance of vision literature in medieval Ireland. It is difficult to see anything distinctively 'Irish' in vision literature, though the native genre of the AISLING should be noted.

John Carey

VITRIFIED FORTS

Vitrified forts are a type of defended settlement of the Scottish Early IRON AGE. They appear most commonly to be oblong or oval in plan with thick, heavy stone walls, often timber-laced, which occur both singly and in concentric rings. There is little overlap between the distributions of the vitrified forts and the roughly contemporary BROCHS.

The name 'vitrified' is linked to the fact that several of these forts appear to have had their walls fired, with the intense heat of the burning timber frame causing vitrification to an extent in the stone construction. Extremely high temperatures (in excess of 1,000 °C) would have been necessary to achieve this state, achievable by the firing of timber-laced stone walls of the *murus gallicus* or Gaulish wall type.

Scottish vitrified forts are tentatively dated from about the 7th to the 3rd centuries BC, although later reuse can be envisaged for many examples (e.g., the possible Pictish royal sites at Clatchard Craig, Fife [Fìobh], and Craig Phadrig, Inverness [Creag Phàdraig, Inbhir Nis]).

Simon Ó Faoláin

VIX

Vix is the name of a necropolis at the foot of Mont-Lassois in the *département* of Côte-d'Or, France. The tomb of a very rich woman, often known as 'the princess of Vix', consists of a roughly 3 m^3 cubic wooden chamber covered by a cairn.

It contained an imported bronze *krater* (a vessel for mixing wine and water) weighing 280 kg, with a capacity of more than 1,200 litres, the biggest ever found anywhere. The corpse was laid out on the bed of a disassembled four-wheeled wagon (see CHARIOT; VEHICLE BURIALS), and was dressed with a bronze TORC and several other pieces of jewellery.

Close to the skull was a golden torc weighing 480 g, with pear-shaped terminals joined decoratively to the torc's arc with lion's paws and further decorated with a small winged horse. The tomb is dated to *c.* 480 BC, thus placing it very near the end of the HALLSTATT IRON AGE. It has assumed particular importance in discussions of the potential for high status for women in early Celtic societies, trade contacts west-central Europe and the Mediterranean, and Celtic notions of the afterlife as an Otherworld FEAST.

M. Lévery

VORTIGERN
See Gwrtheyrn.

VOYAGE LITERATURE

Introduction

A 'voyage tale', in the context of medieval IRISH LITERATURE, may be defined as a story describing a visit to an OTHERWORLD region or regions, reached after a sea journey. It accordingly contrasts with stories in which a protagonist finds himself in the Otherworld after entering a *síd,* diving beneath a lake, losing his way in a fog, or some other means. In most cases, voyage tales are referred to as IMMRAMA (voyages) in IRISH-language sources, while other stories of Otherworld excursions are called simply ECHTRAI (adventures).

Voyage tales differ from other Otherworld stories in their free use of imported elements. Notably, geographical writing, travel tales, homilies, and the apocrypha all appear to have contributed significantly to the genre.

The First Voyage Tales

The earliest surviving voyage tale may be an *echtrae*, *Echtrae Chonlai* (The adventure of Conlae). Conlae, son of CONN CÉTCHATHACH, king of Tara (TEAMHAIR), is taken to a *síd* in a glass boat. The use of the same vocabulary for the native Otherworld and the Christian paradise and the theme of the sea journey remained key elements in subsequent voyage literature.

IMMRAM BRAIN *maic Febail* (The voyage of Bran son of Febal) appears to draw upon legends concerning the eruption of Lough Foyle (see FLOOD LEGENDS) and exhibits striking resemblances to *Echtrae Chonlai*. A beautiful woman, bearing a silver branch, induces the protagonist to join her beyond the sea; but here the voyage is the central feature of the tale, not merely an appendage. The most memorable scene is perhaps that in which Bran in his ship encounters the immortal Manannán driving his chariot across the sea, and the latter recites a poem describing the delights of the supernatural realm. As in *Echtrae Chonlai*, the inhabitants of the Otherworld are conversant with the mysteries of Christianity.

An early voyage tale of a different type is *Forfes Fer Fálchae* (The siege of the men of Fálchae). It, too, begins with a marvellous token being brought across the sea, but the raiding expedition by Cú Chulainn that ensues has no discernible supernatural elements. Other stories associating voyages with the acquisition of supernatural treasures occur in the lives of the saints. Patrick is said to have visited an island inhabited by an ageless couple, who offered him the staff that became his crosier.

The Otherworld Pilgrimage

The full development of the voyage tale may be attributed to the impact on the Irish imagination of *peregrinatio* (pilgrimage), the monastic practice of voluntary self-exile as a form of devotional austerity. The expansion of Irish monks across the face of Europe was a direct consequence of the zeal for *peregrinatio*; others recklessly sought a 'desert in the ocean' in the trackless North Atlantic, penetrating at least as far as Iceland.

The most celebrated of these pilgrim adventurers was St Brendan: Accounts of his voyages in search of the Land of Promise figure prominently in his Latin and Irish lives, and the Navigatio Sancti Brendani (The voyage of St Brendan) enjoyed great popularity on the Continent throughout the Middle Ages. In the *Navigatio*, the Otherworld voyage becomes the vehicle for a sophisticated monastic allegory, with the circular wanderings of the pilgrims mirroring the round of the religious year. The author presented his tale's fantastic incidents in a vivid, matter-of-fact style, which led readers to look for a historical basis for the legend.

The Later Immrama and Modern Irish Adaptations

Subsequent voyage tales show clear indebtedness to the Brendan legend and to *Immram Brain*, while developing the genre in fresh directions.

Immram Curaig Maíle Dúin (The voyage of Mael Dúin's coracle) is the most flamboyant specimen to have come down to us. Mael Dúin, son of a king and a nun, travels among a series of fantastic islands.

The only full-blown voyage tale to survive from the Early Modern Irish period is 'The Voyage of Tadhg mac Céin', an elaborate and so far little-studied narrative that takes its hero to a transoceanic wonderland ('the fourth paradise of the earth'). There, all the illustrious Irish dead dwell in a series of splendid fortresses. There are abundant references to the earlier literature: Conlae and his immortal mistress appear, with the latter now identified as Veniusa daughter of Adam.

Fantastic voyages figure frequently in the Romantic tales of the period, and in the related wonder tales of the oral tradition; for the most part, these accounts have more in common with adventure stories than with the *immrama* proper. Sometimes, however, direct influence by the latter can be detected. For example, the Romance *Eachtra Cloinne Ríogh na hIoruaidhe* ('Adventures of the Children of the King of Norway') draws material from Mael Dúin's voyage, and echoes of *Echtrae Chonlai* may be present in *Laoidh Oisín air Thír na nÓg* ('Oisín's Lay on the Land of Youth [Tír na nÓg]').

John Carey

WALES
See Cymru.

WALLACE, WILLIAM

William Wallace (*c.* 1274–1305) was the second son of a minor Scottish laird. Little is known of his life before he became a major contender in the struggle for Scottish independence in 1296, but his execution in 1305 made him a martyr to the Scottish cause and a national hero, celebrated in medieval epics and later folklore. Wallace's international recognition and popularity have been greatly enhanced by the 1995 film *Braveheart*, which coincided fortuitously with increasing Scottish nationalist sentiment in the run-up to the referendum on the Scottish Parliament in 1997.

William Wallace was the main force from 1296 onward in rallying support for a military campaign against the English occupation, following ten years of strife over the Scottish Crown after the death of King Alexander III in 1286. Wallace met success at the battle of Stirling Bridge (1297), followed by defeat at Falkirk (1298). He sought assistance from Philip IV of France, returning in 1301, but by 1304 no help had come and the major Scottish leaders had all submitted to the English King Edward's rule. Wallace refused to submit and was captured, tried for treason, and hanged in London. Still alive, he was cut down, drawn, quartered, and beheaded. His head was impaled on a spike on London Bridge. This vivid brutality ensured Wallace's immortality as a martyr and contributed to Robert de Bruce's decision to take up the national struggle, leading to success at the battle of Bannockburn.

Marion Löffler

WARFARE, PROTO-CELTIC VOCABULARY

The warlike culture of the ancient Celtic-speaking peoples was one of the most pervasive themes of the Greek and Roman accounts and is evident in early medieval Celtic literature, as well as reconfirmed by archaeology. Another vantage onto the Celtic attitude toward warfare is afforded by shared, inherited Celtic vocabulary, as can be established by comparing cognate words within the attested Celtic languages.

The most common word in this field is Proto-Celtic **katu-*, found in Galatian proper names and corresponding to Irish *cath* and Old Welsh *cat* 'battle, warband'. There are several inherited compounds: Proto-Celtic **kom-katu-* > Early Irish *cocad* 'war', Middle Welsh *kyngat* 'battle, conflict'; **katu-uiro-* > Early Ir. *cather* 'battle-hero', Old Cornish *cadwur* glossed 'soldier or athlete'.

Proto-Celtic *wik-e/o- is the source of Early Ir. *fichid* 'fights', related to the suffix-*vices* 'fighters' found on GAULISH and BRITISH tribal names (e.g., Ordovices), Early Ir. *fích* 'strife, fight', ScG *fioch* 'wrath', MW *gwic* 'strife, contention, battle'; Proto-Celtic *wik-tā* 'battle' is reflected in Gaulish proper names, Early Ir. *fecht* 'raid, fight, course', ScG *feachd* 'army, host, expedition', OW *gueith* 'battle'.

Proto-Celtic *korios* 'army' occurs in Gaulish tribal names as *-corii*, MW *corδ* 'host, army', and in compounds.

Proto-Celtic *agro-, *agrā* > Early Ir. *ár* 'slaughter', ScG *àr* 'battle, slaughter', Mod.W *aer* 'war, battle; slaughter; host', OCornish *hair* glossed 'slaughter', OBret. *airou* gl. 'massacres'; cf. Proto-Celtic *agro-magos*, Early Ir. *ármag* 'battlefield', MW *aerfa* 'slaughter; battle, army'.

Proto-Celtic *gal-* is probably reflected in the Gaulish name element *-galos* 'power; strong'; in the group names *Galatae, Galli*, Early Ir. *gal* 'bravery', ScG *gal* 'valour, war'; and in the OBret. name element *Gal-, -gal*.

Proto-Celtic *bāg-āko-* > Early Ir. *bágach* 'warlike'; cf. the compound Proto-Celtic *kom-bāgo-* > Early Ir. *combág* 'battle, conflict', MW *kymwy* 'toil, stress, grief', probably related also to MW *kyma* 'battle, conflict'.

Proto-Celtic *nei-t-* is probably reflected in Gaulish *Nētos* (an epithet of Mars, probably 'warrior, hero'), Early Ir. *nía* 'hero, warrior', OGAM Irish NET(T)A-, -NETAS, and possibly CELTIBERIAN *neito*.

MW *tres* 'battle, (military) raid, attack' may be a borrowing from Early Ir. *tress* 'battle' or a common inheritance from *trexsu-*.

Caroline aan de Weil and John T. Koch

WATERY DEPOSITIONS

Watery or aqueous depositions are objects deposited in water—lakes, rivers, bogs, or wells—for ritual purposes. Depositions of this type were a common feature of Celtic ritual practice. Many aqueous deposits date from the Bronze Age, such as the Dowris hoard (*c.* 800–650 BC). Such collections are also found throughout the Iron Age. LA TÈNE, possibly the most famous site of the second Celtic IRON AGE, has been interpreted as an aqueous deposit.

Deposits have been found in wells and rivers (both at the source and along the course). River finds include the numerous items of prestige metalwork discovered in the river THAMES, such as the Battersea SHIELD. Lake deposits have been found at La Tène in Switzerland, Llyn Fawr in Glamorgan, and Llyn Cerrig Bach on Anglesey, and in Loughnashade (Loch na Séad 'lake of the treasures') at the foot of EMAIN MACHAE.

The most famous bog deposits stem from Lindow Moss in Cheshire and Dowris in Co. Offaly/Contae Uíbh Fhailí. Ritual depositions were made at the thermal springs at BATH, ENGLAND.

Metal objects, especially weapons and other equipment of a 'military' nature such as horse harnesses, CHARIOT parts, and trumpets (see CARNYX), as well as sheet metal vessels, make up the main group of finds from such deposits. Another group of objects sometimes discovered in such deposits are ornamented items made of precious metals. In the case of some of the Gaulish wells, the remains of food offerings were recovered, mainly contained in ceramic vessels, along with imported Italian amphorae, which might have originally held wine. Votive goods depicting parts of the human body, similar to those used to this day, are less common.

Human remains are quite commonly recovered from aqueous deposits. The most famous find of this type is 'Lindow Man', but the La Tène lake site and various wells have yielded similar finds. Such finds are often interpreted (probably correctly in most cases) as the remains of victims of human SACRIFICE. Some of the skeletons recovered at La Tène show marks from blows received on the skull, and one of the completely preserved skeletons from La Tène apparently still had a rope around its neck when it was discovered. Human remains recovered from wells, sometimes partly burned and often only isolated human bones, have also been interpreted as remains of human sacrifices.

The practice of depositing offerings to the gods in water, specifically in lakes, is also attested historically. Strabo writes in his *Geography* (4.1.13) that the treasures found in Tolosa (now Toulouse, France)—allegedly the spoils of the sack of Delphi—added up to a total value of 15,000 talents, part of which had been recovered from sacred lakes where the Gauls had deposited them.

Insular Celtic beliefs in an underwater OTHERWORLD may be a reflection of the beliefs that led Iron Age Celts to deposit items in watery contexts. Celtic literature is full of references to the existence of a land beneath the water. Literature and folk tradition recount stories of magical objects or goods that come from under the water, such as the wondrous sword CALADBOLG/Excalibur.

Raimund Karl

WELSH DRAMA

Medieval and 16th Century

The earliest surviving plays in Welsh are two medieval miracle plays: *Y Tri Brenin o Gwlen* (The three kings of Cologne) and *Y Dioddefaint a'r Atgyfodiad* (The Passion and the Resurrection), a Herod and a Passion play. The other surviving medieval text, *Ymddiddan y Corff a'r Enaid* (A dialogue between the body and the soul), is a morality play. Alongside such text-based theatre there existed the theatricals associated with the folk festivals of *Calan Mai* (see BELTAINE), *gwyliau mabsant* (parish wakes), and wassail celebrations. While the Elizabethan and Jacobean periods in ENGLAND witnessed the golden age of theatre, the corresponding periods in Wales (CYMRU) were singularly lacking in dramatic output. The only surviving text that bears witness to a possible interest in plays around 1600 is the Welsh-language verse tragedy *Troelus a Chresyd*, a dramatized adaptation by an anonymous author of Chaucer's *Troilus and Criseyde* (*c.* 1372–86) and Henryson's *Testament of Cresseid* (1532).

17th–18th Century

When an indigenous Welsh theatrical tradition finally emerged in the 18th century, it took the form of the interlude (*anterliwt*), a metrical play performed at fairs and markets. The most accomplished exponent of the interlude was Twm o'r Nant (Thomas Edwards, 1739–1810). He and his troupe of players provided entertainment that combined ribaldry and seriousness, and its popular appeal lay in its robust condemnation of social injustices, incisive SATIRE, sharp wit, colourful language, and masterly use of tried-and-tested comic techniques. While their tenants were enjoying the Welsh-language interludes, staged in the open air on farm carts, the gentry were entertained in style by visiting English companies at their exquisite private theatres, such as Sir Watkin Williams Wynn's theatre at Wynnstay.

19th to Mid-20th Century

Substantial theatres were built in large Welsh towns in the early 19th century, drawing famous actors. The rise of motion pictures effected a dramatic decline on portable and smaller theatres. Performance of interludes ceased altogether, but some of their basic elements survived in the form of the chapel-led *Ymddiddanion* (Colloquies) and *Dadleuon* (Debates). These dramatic dialogues, based on biblical tales and extolling the good and virtuous life, were in essence miniature plays.

The first licensed Welsh-language company was Cwmni Trefriw, which toured to full houses with its stage adaptation of Daniel OWEN's novel, *Rhys Lewis*, with opposition from non-conformist religious groups. By 1910, the Methodist objection to playacting had been sufficiently eroded to allow the widespread performance of plays to raise money for good causes, including the upkeep of chapels. The post–World War I period was to see the golden age of the amateur movement in Wales. It has been estimated that in 1931 there existed in Wales between 400 and 500 dramatic societies, and at least 300 published Welsh plays.

Later 20th Century

In 1965, the important contribution made by the amateur movement to the cultural life of Wales was reflected in the formation of the Drama Association of Wales, a facilitating body serving the needs of amateur companies.

Despite, or possibly because of, the growing influence of television and its visible effects on the size of theatre audiences, the 1950s and 1960s in Wales saw increasing emphasis being placed on the need for greater professionalism. In 1962, the Welsh Arts Council (Cyngor Celfyddydau Cymru) funded a bilingual touring 'Welsh Theatre Company' under the directorship of Warren Jenkins.

In Welsh-language theatre, alternative small-scale companies existed alongside the mainstream Cwmni Theatr Cymru 'The theatre company of Wales'. Theatr Ddieithr staged plays by Wil Sam and Meic Povey, and Theatr O sought to provide new perspectives on classical plays. One company in particular, Theatr yr Ymylon, was established in 1972 by a group of actors specifically to create a new theatrical tradition in Wales. It failed to achieve this goal, but in the first year of its existence the company had performed more plays by promising Welsh dramatists than the ubiquitous Welsh Theatre Company had done in ten years. Perhaps the most innovative company to emerge in the 1970s was the GWYNEDD-based Theatr Bara Caws, which first came to prominence in 1977 with its challenging review satirizing the royal jubilee celebrations. This politically left-wing community theatre company, which continues to flourish, toured its devised shows to pubs, clubs, and village halls throughout north Wales with the specific aim of 'taking theatre to the people'. In south Wales, Whare Teg and Theatr Gorllewin MORGANNWG served their immediate communities, with the latter developing its own distinct, highly theatrical productions, based on local concerns and on broader Welsh-language issues.

However, the talent drain from Wales continues, with young actors such as Daniel Evans, Ioan Gruffudd, Rhys Ifans, and Matthew Rhys having become international names in theatre, film, and television. It is to be hoped that the Welsh-medium Theatr Genedlaethol Cymru, established in 2003 and directed by Cefin Roberts, and the proposed English-medium National Theatre Company will give Welsh audiences the opportunity to see these actors perform at home in large-scale productions. The two new 'national' companies, however, will need to proceed with care and be prepared to learn from the lessons of the past, when prior attempts at such establishments have failed. The strength of Welsh theatre has traditionally been in the popularity of its vigorous amateur and small-scale professional companies. It remains to be seen whether the advent of the National Assembly for Wales (CYNULLIAD CENEDLAETHOL CYMRU) with its own Minister for Culture will, in the 21st century, help to guarantee the success and survival of the designated 'national' theatre companies.

Hazel Walford Davies

WELSH LANGUAGE

The Welsh language (Cymraeg [see CYMRU]) is one of the four CELTIC LANGUAGES that have survived continuously from pre-modern times till today. By most measurements, it appears to be the healthiest of the living Celtic languages. The 2001 census counted 575,604 persons as Welsh speakers, representing 20.5 percent of the population of Wales (CYMRU), an increase from 508,098 in 1991. It must be noted that statistics are not gathered for Welsh speakers outside of Wales, and the census methodology used for Wales does not apply in Celtic countries outside the United Kingdom. There is a small Welsh-speaking area in Shropshire, ENGLAND (swydd Amwythig, Lloegr), as well as a sizeable community in London (Llundain). There are also native Welsh speakers and learners in PATAGONIA and beyond. These far-flung communities are of increasing relevance at present given the ease of travel and communication.

Historical Stages

Old Welsh is the language as attested from *c.* 800–*c.* 1100; *c.* 1100–*c.* 1500 is the Middle Welsh period; *c.* 1500 onward is the Modern Welsh period.

When Did British Become Welsh?

One obvious problem with the preceding scheme is that some surviving texts of early WELSH POETRY are widely believed to date back to the 6th and 7th centuries,

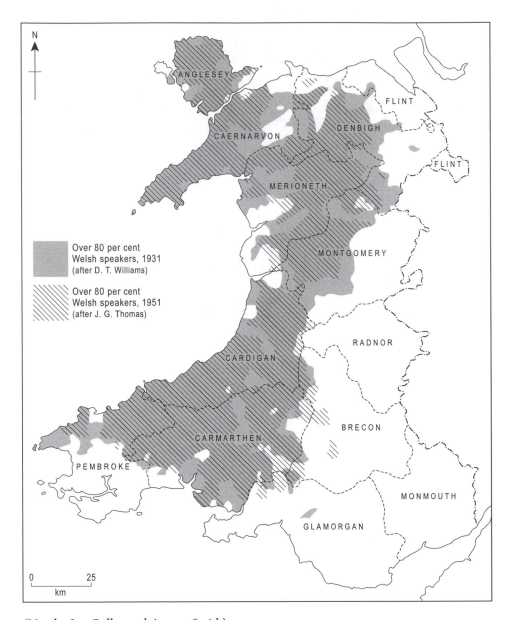

(Map by Ian Gulley and Antony Smith)

the pre-Old Welsh period. Most of the extant poetry attributed to the Cynfeirdd (first poets) is court poetry of north Britain (Hen Ogledd), not in what is now Wales.

When did British (the ancient Celtic language of Britain) become Welsh? This question has two possible interpretations. First, British becoming Welsh is understood as an ancient Celtic language becoming a medieval one, equivalent to Latin becoming French or Spanish—in the Celtic case, essentially a matter of a new syllable structure and sound pattern emerging. Thus a British name written as

Romano-British CVNOMORI (genitive case) comes to be written *Conmor*, with unaccented syllables at the end of polysyllabic elements dropped and consonants that had stood between vowels in ancient Celtic now softened (lenited). From the *Conmor* stage onward, the syllable structure remains stable, and therefore there is no linguistic reason that a poem composed in this early medieval language could not have survived from late British with its metre intact.

Alternatively, 'British becoming Welsh' has been understood as Welsh emerging as distinct from the other 'Neo-Brythonic' languages—that is, Breton, CORNISH, and Cumbric. The original *Hen Ogledd* poetry would have been written in the dialect that became Cumbric, not Welsh. In fact, this is a non-issue. In the first place, a form such as *Conmor* is indistinguishable on linguistic criteria as to whether it is Welsh, Cornish, Breton, or Cumbric, and this is generally true of the archaic forms that occur in the witness lists of the 7th- and 8th-century charters of Llancarfan and the Book of Llandaf, for example. Therefore, to speak of four separate languages—or even distinct dialects, when considering only the written forms—is unwarranted on the basis of the sources we have for the pre-Old Welsh period.

Old Welsh is identifiable on linguistic criteria by *c.* 800. There are three important innovations in this regard: (1) The definite article emerges as /ər/ written *ir*; (2) unaccented /u/ and /i/ fall together as /ə/ (the neutral vowel in English *cut*), written *i* and *e*; and (3) under the word-final accent, /ǫ/ (< Celtic *ā*) becomes the diphthong *au* (as in English *out*), so that *Merchion* (< Latin *Marciānus*) becomes *Merchiaun*, though remaining *Merchion* in Old Breton. This third change does not seem originally to have included the 'Gwenhwyseg' dialect spoken in southeast Wales.

The fact that the ancient Celtic language which became Welsh, Breton, Cornish, and Cumbric underwent the sweeping syllable losses and lenitions in exactly the same way at exactly the same time confirms that they were still one language at the time, not four. Although we may wish to call the new form of Brythonic that appears in the later 6th century 'Welsh' to make the point that it looks and sounds much more like Welsh than the ancient language of the Iron Age and Roman period, there was still one common early medieval Brythonic language spoken along a continuous arc from Dumbarton on the Clyde to southern Brittany (BREIZH). Furthermore, Brythonic Latin texts refer to one language *lingua Britannica* or adverbial *Britannice*. All of this evidence points to the continued unity of the Brythonic literate class down to around the year 1000, even after the languages began to diverge.

Middle Welsh

The MABINOGI to a large extent define Middle Welsh. It is certain that the Four Branches are older than the 14th-century White Book of Rhydderch (LLYFR GWYN RHYDDERCH) and the 15th-century Red Book of Hergest (LLYFR COCH HERGEST) that contain them, but how much older is disputed. This Middle Welsh of the *Mabinogi* is much more readable than Old Welsh for the educated Modern Welsh speaker. The orthography and vocabulary are closer to present-day usage. However, whereas Modern Welsh is verb-initial, Middle Welsh narratives use the now obsolete 'abnormal order', in which the usual sentence consists of a noun phrase or adverbial topic, followed by an unaccented particle followed by the verb, and then the rest of the sentence. This pattern is strikingly similar to the syntax of Cornish and Breton.

Most of the vast corpus of Welsh poetry of this period is credibly attributed and closely datable. Nevertheless, there are reasons not to take the earlier Middle Welsh poetry as representing Middle Welsh in general. In particular, it forms a conservative unbroken tradition with the poetry of the preceding period—in vocabulary, the structure of the verb, and word order in general. Comparison with the prose genres shows that court poetry—not surprisingly—must have differed greatly from everyday speech. Nevertheless, the poets, particularly the *Cywyddwyr*, do give us valuable insights into spoken Welsh. For example, French and English loanwords often make their first appearance in poetry.

Modern Welsh

The Bible of 1588—as a prestigious printed book—was very influential in defining a literary standard for Modern Welsh prose, though a number of features found there are now obsolete in all registers—for example, the abnormal order. The success of the Protestant REFORMATION and Nonconformist revivals in Wales ensured that most of the Welsh-speaking population was heavily influenced by the high-register language of the Bible and the pulpit until the decline of religion in the later 20th century (see CHRISTIANITY).

In poetry, the influence of the *Cywyddwyr* and particularly of DAFYDD AP GWILYM on Welsh has remained much greater than the influence of his younger contemporary Chaucer on Modern English. This is partly a matter of phonology. English has lost many syllables and has changed the pronunciation of all its long vowels since Chaucer's day, and the vocabulary has likewise changed a great deal; thus, while one can simply 'edit' Middle Welsh to render it readable to a modern audience, the same is not true for contemporary Middle English. When poets such as Iolo Morganwg (Edward WILLIAMS) revitalized the bardic tradition, they were able to rely heavily on the Poets of the Nobility as their models.

Dialects

Down into Recent Welsh, one of the features that has continued to distinguish the *Gwenhwyseg* dialect has been the past-tense ending -*ws* (Breton *as*), where other dialects and the standard language have -*odd*. For Middle Welsh, it is likely that preference of *ws*/-*wys* versus -*awδ* in texts indicates a southern versus northern origin.

Modern Welsh, when compared with the other Celtic languages, is remarkable for the strength of its standard literary language and what might be termed the 'verticality' of its varieties—that is, numerous more and less formal, more and less old-fashioned styles belonging to special oral and written social domains, but not limited geographically. Welsh-speaking areas remain geographically contiguous. Until the later 20th century, the strength of the chapels and the appointment of ministers of religion outside their home region were unifying factors. In recent times, the growth of Welsh broadcast media and Welsh-medium education has further diminished dialect variation in the informal speech of the younger generation, in ways not dissimilar to the corresponding processes in contemporary English.

Nonetheless, Welsh dialects persists. The major cleavage is north–south, most immediately obvious in pronunciation. The retracted [ɨ(:)] for orthographic *u* and *y* (the latter when in final syllables of accented words) in the speech of north Wales is immediately obvious (the sound does not occur in English), where southerners have [i(:)] (as in English *see*) for these sounds and also for orthographic *i*. This convergence of vowels can be seen in some 15th-century manuscripts. The dialect of Pembrokeshire (sir Benfro) is noted for its treatment of some diphthongs: thus *oes* 'yes, there is' is [we:s] there, [o:s] elsewhere in the south, and [o:ɨs] in the north.

Common vocabulary differences abound. For example, literary *ef* 'he, him' is *fo, o* in the north and *fe, e* in the south. 'Milk' is *llefrith* in the north, but *llaeth* in standard and southern Welsh.

Social History

The Acts of Union (1536–43) effectively disenfranchized monoglot Welsh speakers within the domains of politics and law. The negative impact was soon offset by the elevation of Welsh as the language of public worship in 1563. Pre-industrial Wales remained overwhelmingly monoglot Welsh. By *c.* 1800, approximately 90 percent of the 687,000 people living in Wales were Welsh speakers—contrasting with 50 percent Irish speakers in Ireland—and some 80 percent of them were monoglot Welsh speakers.

Brad y Llyfrau Gleision (The treachery of the blue books) of 1847 is often viewed as an inflammatory turning point. These three volumes were the work of three English inspectors appointed by Parliament to report on the state of education in Wales. Some negative conclusions were probably true, but the authors also reported that the Welsh people were dirty, lazy, dishonest, prone to drunkenness, and sexually immoral. They blamed the Welsh language and the Nonconformist chapels for this state of affairs. Mid- and later 19th-century Welsh-language publishing over a wide range of edifying subjects, as well as the Welsh temperance movement, took impetus from an urgent desire to prove the commissioners wrong. The 'blue books' remain a rallying issue for Plaid Cymru and Cymdeithas yr Iaith Gymraeg long after critics of the Welsh language and its culture have forgotten the report. In contrast, the Welsh-speaking class in the Victorian period believed that English was the language of progress and getting on in the world. Many of them thus considered Welsh to be fit only for the chapel, the fair, and the hearth.

The more substantial factor working against Welsh by the latter years of the 19th century was tumultuous change brought about by industrialization, particularly in the south. Nonetheless, owing to an overall increase in population, absolute numbers of Welsh speakers continued to rise while declining as a percentage of the total population. Thus, in 1891, there were nearly a million Welsh speakers, but by now they represented only half of the population of Wales. The figures declined both in absolute terms and as a percentage of the total population following World War I, and continued to decline throughout the 20th century, albeit more gradually toward the end of the century, before the upturn of 2001. The latest census figures were based on respondents reporting one or more of four skills in Welsh—reading, writing, speaking, and comprehension of spoken Welsh. The long-term future of the language cannot be foreseen, but some current trends are likely to continue in the next years in view of the career opportunities that now exist in the Welsh Assembly (Cynulliad Cenedlaethol Cymru), in Welsh-medium education, and in Welsh-language mass media: We can expect higher proportions of urban and educated Welsh speakers and of speakers for whom Welsh is a second language.

John T. Koch

WELSH MUSIC, *CANEUON GWERIN*

The collecting of folk-songs in the Welsh language begins effectively with Edward Williams (Iolo Morganwg) at the end of the 18th century. Printed collections appeared in the 1840s. The main body of collecting, however, began with the establishment of Cymdeithas Alawon Gwerin Cymru (The Welsh Folk-Song Society) in 1906.

Calendar-related songs are plentiful, some associated with semi-dramatic Christmas and New Year customs such as the Mari Lwyd and *Hela'r Dryw* (Hunting the wren). Others are related to New Year good-luck visitations by children (*hel calennig*). The religious aspect of the season is sturdily reflected in the carol singing of the *plygain* services (Christmas services made up almost entirely of scriptural carols sung mainly on traditional tunes), representing an unbroken singing tradition of close to three centuries. Love songs of varying kinds are numerous, most of them composed and sung by men. One of their interesting features is the literary convention of using birds as love-messengers, a common theme in medieval Welsh love poetry as well (see Welsh poetry). The largest category of work songs encompass those used in ploughing with a team of oxen, with the call-tag at the end of verses forming their defining characteristic. Remnants of the ballads sung from the 17th to the 19th centuries are well attested. There are also songs that reflect an earlier period in the ongoing practice of *canu penillion*, a form of singing peculiar to Wales (Cymru; see Welsh music, cerdd dant).

Meredydd Evans and Phyllis Kinney

WELSH MUSIC, *CERDD DANT*

Cerdd dant translates as 'the art of the string' and arose initially from renditions by amateur musicians versed in the art of singing *penillion* (stanzas) to harp accompaniment. In modern times, poetry sung to both traditional and modern Welsh airs was supported chiefly through the eisteddfod-sponsored *cerdd dant* competitions. The Powys Eisteddfod of 1824 held such a competition, and an artist's drawing of the occasion shows the competitors, all men, standing in line listening to one soloist's performance. After drawing straws to determine the order of performance, the harper played the chosen air once, and the competitor then sang his verses, using an improvised counter-melody, on that air. The rules of *cerdd dant* insisted that the performer could not begin his recital concurrently with the harp, but at least one bar into the melody, and that he had to finish presenting his stanzas exactly in time with the closing of the last note of the air played on the harp. The next contestant then sang to the same air, presenting a different personal choice of stanzas in the same metre as that chosen by the first contestant, and so on until all the competitors had completed their performances. A second round ensued, with the competitors singing in a different order, to a different air. The winner was the competitor who remained when all others had been eliminated.

Rhiannon Ifans

WELSH MUSIC, CONTEMPORARY

The Welsh National Opera, the National Youth Orchestra of Wales, and the Guild for the Promotion of Welsh Music were all founded during the decade following 1945; the BBC Welsh Orchestra (later to become the National Orchestra of Wales) increased in size, and the Arts Council of Wales (Cyngor Celfyddydau Cymru) recognized the urgent need to patronize contemporary music. Alun Hoddinott (1929–2008) and William Mathias (1934–92) are two of Wales's most individual creative voices to have emerged during this time. Whereas Mathias's incorporation of indigenous themes, such as Welsh history, mythology, folklore, and HAGIOGRAPHY, led to inevitable comparisons between his music and 'nationalist' traits, Hoddinott's style may more accurately be described as 'transnational'.

The legacy of Wales's predominantly vocal musical tradition also continued in the area of mainstream popular music, where the achievements of singers and performers such as Tom Jones and Shirley Bassey during the 1960s outweighed any creative song-writing successes in that era. But the media perspective from outside Wales changed during the 1990s, when a plethora of rock groups converged onto the British pop scene. The Manic Street Preachers' fourth album, *Everything Must Go* (1996), precipitated the collective impact of many

Gruff Rhys of the Super Furry Animals, who perform in both English and Welsh, performing at the Hop Farm Festival 2009. (Simone Joyner/Getty Images)

Welsh rock bands in the UK singles and album charts during this time, including the Stereophonics, Catatonia, Super Furry Animals, and Gorky's Zygotic Mynci. The emphasis on writing original material had been—at least in the case of Catatonia and the Super Furry Animals—inherited through their exposure to WELSH-language pop music, which arguably reached its apex during the late 1970s and early 1980s. Emerging during the 1960s largely as a means of promoting and disseminating nationalist political views and language protest movement messages (see CYMDEITHAS YR IAITH GYMRAEG; NATIONALISM), its early song forms were direct and unadorned. Its most famous exponent was singer-songwriter Dafydd Iwan, who himself had inherited much of the vocal style of the *noson lawen* tradition (lit. 'a merry evening', an evening of informal entertainment comparable to the Irish *céilí* and Scottish *cèilidh*) found in the songs of Hogia Llandegai and Hogia'r Wyddfa from the 1950s onward, but this movement was also influenced by American folk-singer Pete Seeger and by Welsh folk music in general. Dafydd Iwan was also one of the founders of Sain (Sound), which has been the main recording company for recorded songs in the Welsh language since 1969.

Pwyll ap Siôn

WELSH MUSIC, MEDIEVAL

The earliest extant manuscripts of music from Wales (CYMRU) date from the 14th century. They comprise religious music including matins, lauds, and vespers for St David's Day (see DEWI SANT) in Latin with music in neume notation (a system of written music used for plainsong in the later Middle Ages). No other direct evidence has survived beyond terminology; the Welsh LAW TEXTS, for instance, contain references to musical instruments, including the HARP and the CRWTH. The earliest detailed account of musical styles is found in the late 12th-century writings of Gerald of Wales (GIRALDUS CAMBRENSIS), who refers to the music-making of ordinary people on a saint's day as well as sophisticated instrumental music for an aristocratic audience.

During the Tudor (TUDUR) dynasty, the gentry became increasingly Anglicized. In an effort to maintain the craft and status of poets and musicians, an EISTEDDFOD was held at Caerwys, Flintshire (sir y Fflint), in 1523, and another in 1567, with the aim of standardizing the BARDIC ORDER. In 1613, Robert ap Huw of Anglesey (Môn) noted some examples of music of the bardic period in a manuscript that contained various pieces with names such as *gosteg* (series of airs on the harp). The music is in tablature that substitutes the first seven letters of the alphabet for notes on the staff without key or time signatures, few rhythm signs, and no indication of the instrument to be used. It is thought that a Renaissance harp with approximately thirty strings is meant. This music is based on a highly organized treatment of two chords called *cyweirdant* (key-string) and *tyniad* (plucking). The lower hand played the chords and the upper hand varied the melodic line in seventeen different and now obsolete ways, such as the use of the back of the nail (*kefn ewin*) or thumb stops (*takiad y fawd*) or the four-finger plait (*plethiad y pedwarbys*). Recent research has shown that some pieces in the manuscript are attributed to harpers who flourished in the 14th and 15th centuries.

Meredydd Evans and Phyllis Kinney

WELSH POETRY, EARLY AND MEDIEVAL

The earliest poetry attributed to the Cynfeirdd (first or early poets) goes back to the 6th century and, in the case of *Marwnad* Cunedda, possibly the 5th century. See the articles on the bards Aneirin and Taliesin, the manuscripts Llyfr Aneirin and Llyfr Taliesin, and the Gododdin.

A sizeable body of poetry dates from the Old Welsh period (*c.* 800–*c.* 1100), most of them anonymous or with ahistorical attributions. The englyn metre, in its earlier three-line form, was popular at this time. In addition to the *englynion* in the contemporary 9th- or 10th-century Juvencus manuscript, great *englynion* cycles survive from the Old Welsh period about Urien and uttered by the personae Llywarch Hen and Heledd, as well as a series of *englynion* on the death in battle of Geraint and on the battles of Cadwallon, along with the great catalogue of heroes' graves *Englynion y Beddau*. The famous manuscripts Llyfr Du Caerfyrddin and Llyfr Coch Hergest are important sources for saga *englynion* and other poetry of Old Welsh date. Armes Prydein is a datable 10th-century political prophecy in the *awdl* metre from *Llyfr Taliesin*, and this traditional genre continues unbroken to the later Middle Ages. Also from this period are the early Arthurian poems Preiddiau Annwfn (also in *Llyfr Taliesin*) and 'Pa Gur yv y Porthaur?' in *Llyfr Du Caerfyrddin*.

The 12th and 13th centuries form the age of *Beirdd y Tywysogion* (the Poets of the Princes), also known as the Gogynfeirdd (rather early poets). Individual *Gogynfeirdd* include Meilyr Brydydd (*fl.* ?1100–*post* 1137) and Cynddelw Brydydd Mawr (*fl. c.* 1155–*c.* 1195). The most important source for texts of the poetry of the Poets of the Princes is the Hendregadredd Manuscript. Extant examples of the genre of *gorhoffedd* (boastful exultation) include works by Gwalchmai ap Meilyr and Hywel ab Owain Gwynedd.

The downfall of Llywelyn ap Gruffudd and the loss of Welsh independence in 1282/4 understandably marks a major transition in Welsh poetry. The innovative *Beirdd yr Uchelwyr* (Poets of the Nobility), often treated as roughly synonymous with the Cywyddwyr, flourished in the 14th century. Cynghanedd—the intensive use of vowel and consonant harmonies within a line—had been an integral feature of Welsh poetry from its beginning, and parallel patterns of verse ornamentation in Breton and Irish imply a very deep antiquity. Nevertheless, the complete regularization of *cynghanedd* in forms still used in the strict-metre competitions of the National Eisteddfod of Wales (Eisteddfod Genedlaethol Cymru) today is largely a by-product of the period of the Poets of the Nobility. Along with metrical innovations and an expanded vocabulary, new themes become prominent, including love poetry, erotic poetry, and satire, though more traditional elegy and eulogy for noble patrons continued. The most famous poet of the period—and the man widely regarded as the greatest Welsh poet of all time—is Dafydd ap Gwilym (*c.* 1315–*c.* 1350).

The 16th century and down to the Civil Wars (1642–48) is often viewed as a period of decline and transition (see bardic order). The free metres emerge at this time. Although *ymrysonau* (bardic contentions) are also known from earlier and later periods, a famous extended *ymryson* occurred between Wiliam Cynwal (†1587/8) and Edmwnd Prys (1543/4–1623).

John T. Koch

WELSH POETRY, 17TH AND 18TH CENTURIES

Post-medieval Wales (CYMRU) saw the gradual decline of the classical tradition of strict-metre poetry and the appearance of several kinds of verse composed in free metre. These new verse forms, while generally technically less demanding, encompassed a broader range of subject matter and were accessible to a wider audience than the predominantly aristocratic tradition of strict-metre poetry.

The 17th Century

Despite the gradual Anglicization of the Welsh gentry following the ACTS OF UNION under Henry VIII (see TUDUR), the traditional modes of eulogy, elegy, and request poetry in CYWYDD and AWDL metres lingered on well into the 17th century. By the close of the century, however, the era of the professional poet was well and truly at an end (see BARDIC ORDER).

During the 17th centur, love-poetry and poems on moral and religious themes abound, but there is also a fair smattering of humour and SATIRE and a reflection of contemporary events. Like some humble craftsmen and farmers, several acknowledged strict-metre poets made use of the more popular forms, none more successfully than Edmwnd Prys (1543/4–1623), whose *Salmau Cân* of 1621—a polished verse translation of the psalms—is among the century's most enduring literary achievements.

As the century progressed, some of the familiar native metrical forms were rendered redundant by the growing popularity of a more accentual poetry in which the metrical structure was determined by contemporary (and largely English) song tunes. This was to remain the most popular mode of composition throughout the 18th century.

The 17th century is also characterized by an essentially oral tradition of folk poetry. The 'harp-stanzas' (*penillion telyn*), anonymous four-line stanzas sung to the accompaniment of a harp at social gatherings well into the 18th century (see WELSH MUSIC), express the basic human emotions with great conciseness and proverbial wisdom, often with familiar rural imagery.

The 18th Century

The popular literature of 18th-century Wales is well recorded. Few of the hundreds of printed BALLADS correspond to the international narrative type, serving rather a journalistic function by recounting tales of murders, wonders, wars, and disasters; there are love-ballads, biblical stories, morality tales, and satire. The balladeer and playwright Thomas Edwards ('Twm o'r Nant', 1739–1810) was active in northeast Wales where the closely related ballad and interlude (see WELSH DRAMA) traditions were deeply rooted.

The passionate spirituality of the Methodist Revival (see CHRISTIANITY) found its most powerful expression in the writings of William WILLIAMS (1717–91) of Pantycelyn in Carmarthenshire (sir Gaerfyrddin). He composed two ambitious epic poems: *Golwg ar Deyrnas Crist* (A view of the kingdom of Christ, 1756), a history of

Christ's universe since the dawn of Creation, and *Bywyd a Marwolaeth Theomemphus* (The life and death of Theomemphus, 1764), which describes the journey of a man's soul from sin to redemption. It is, however, Pantycelyn's many HYMNS that had the most far-reaching effect. Their central theme is the renunciation of worldly pleasure and the longing for spiritual union with Christ.

During a short but intense period of creativity in the 1750s, Goronwy Owen (1723–69) sought to instil a new seriousness into Welsh poetry through a knowledge of the classics and great English poets. His themes include religion and a longing for his native Anglesey.

Toward the end of the century, poetry of a very different type was composed by Edward WILLIAMS (Iolo Morganwg, 1747–1826), self-styled DRUID and myth-maker. Before concentrating his attentions on the brilliant forgeries that he ascribed to real and imaginary poets of various periods, most notably DAFYDD AP GWILYM, as a young man Williams composed several sensuous *cywyddau* celebrating the joys of love and the natural world. These works, like the later poems that express his radical political beliefs, have more in common with the nascent spirit of ROMANTICISM than with the neo-classicism of Goronwy Owen.

Huw M. Edwards

WELSH POETRY, 19TH CENTURY

Following the scathing official report on Welsh society by the panel of English school inspectors (*Brad y Llyfrau Gleision*, 'Treachery of the Blue Books') in 1847 and the coming of state EDUCATION in 1870, more and more of the Welsh came to see their language not only as inferior to English, but also as a costly hindrance to their advancement in life. The resulting embattled, defensive attitude among poets and the flurry of amateur poets inspired by the rise of the EISTEDDFOD make for a tradition of poetry in the 19th century that has not worn well.

At the heart of 19th-century poetry, a battle raged between the devotees of the strict metres and those of the free metres. Robert Williams (Robert ap Gwilym Ddu, 1766–1850) was a gifted strict-metre poet, but there were few others. In the end, it was decided that the eisteddfod Chair would remain the preserve of the *awdl* metre while a new award, a Crown—equal in status to the Chair—would be established for the free-verse *pryddest*. This arrangement still holds today.

The quest for the Welsh epic forced poets to recognize anew that the strict metres were too short to sustain a lengthy dramatic, narrative poem, with the result that the *pryddest* came more to the fore. The BIBLE and Welsh history were ransacked for epic subject matter. The most powerful attempt at writing in epic mode was that made by William Thomas (Islwyn, 1832–78), who composed two long poems entitled *Y Storm* (The storm) following the death of his fiancée in 1853. It is a remarkable amalgam of grief, soul-searching, purpose-seeking, and God-communing, which, for his contemporaries, set Islwyn apart.

Simple, euphonious lyrics, often laden with *hiraeth* ('longing, yearning'), often musing on the joys and disappointments of love, often vigorously patriotic, often moralistic and pious, often pathetic in the contemplation of death, but infrequently humorous or satirical and never bawdy—such was the poetry that fared well with the Victorian audience. Talhaiarn and Ceiriog were the predominant popular lyricists of the century, both of them making much of their ability to write winning words for traditional Welsh melodies and forming profitable alliances with musicians such as John Owen (Owain Alaw, 1821–83), Brinley Richards (1819–85), and John Thomas (Pencerdd Gwalia, 1826–1913).

Nothing better illustrates the neutering effect that the 'Treachery of the Blue Books' had on 19th-century poetry than the kind of love poem (*rhieingerdd*) and pastoral (*bugeilgerdd*) adopted by the National Eisteddfod for many years as perennial favourites following the remarkable popularity of Ceiriog's *Myfanwy Fychan* in 1858. Literally thousands of girls were named after his 'Myfanwy', who was seen as the prototype of 'innocent Welsh loveliness'.

†Hywel Teifi Edwards

WELSH POETRY, 20TH CENTURY

The earlier years of the 20th century saw new directions as well as continuing Victorian themes. The establishment of institutions such as the University of Wales and the National Library of Wales provided the material basis for the professionalization of Welsh linguistic and literary studies, a development exemplified by the work of John Morris-Jones (1864–1929). During the last decade of the 19th century, the poetry of the Eisteddfod had been dominated by the 'Bardd Newydd' (New poet) school—Nonconformist ministers who wrote tortuously long-winded verse conveying often obtuse theological explorations. Morris-Jones rejected the philosophizing of the 'Bardd Newydd' while also championing rigorous linguistic and metrical standards characterized by the formal standards of medieval Welsh poetry and a purist rejection of the influences of English and dialect on literary Welsh.

Morris-Jones used his classroom at the University of Wales, Bangor (Gwynedd), and his rôle as adjudicator on the very public stage of the National Eisteddfod to promote his educational agenda. His most enduring contribution was Cerdd Dafod (Poetic art, 1925), an authoritative bardic grammar that set out the rules of the medieval strict metres and cynghanedd for a new generation of poets.

T. Gwynn Jones (1871–1949) won the Chair at the 1902 National Eisteddfod with his *awdl Ymadawiad Arthur* (The passing of Arthur), which provided the nation with a strict-metre poem that exemplified the new Morris-Jonesian ideal: formal discipline and linguistic 'purity' combined with a rejection of abstract sermonizing in favour of zesty narrative verse and Romantic foraging in the remnants of the medieval past. T. H. Parry-Williams (1887–1975), having achieved national prominence by winning both the Chair and the Crown twice (in 1912 and 1915), developed his own free-metre *rhigwm* (rhyme), a short and deceptively simple vehicle for meditations ranging from ironic self-mockery to social observation and philosophical enquiry.

While Saunders Lewis and others criticized the National Eisteddfod for pandering to popular tastes, the 1920s and 1930s Crown competitions produced some unique—and at times controversial—poetry, including Caradog Prichard's meditations on insanity and E. Prosser Rhys's poetic exploration of homosexual experience. Bobi JONES (1929–), who began publishing poetry in the 1950s, is another uncompromising poet, following his own late modernist aesthetic irregardless of current trends and tastes.

Waldo WILLIAMS (1904–71) published only one volume of poetry, but his *Dail Pren* ('The Leaves of a Tree', 1956) is one of the century's literary milestones.

One of the fresh new voices to emerge in the early 1960s was Gwyn Thomas (1936–). While he has used various styles over the years, Gwyn Thomas is perhaps best known for the gritty oral idiom that he has brought to bear upon a range of subjects, from the humorous to the darkly meditative. The end of the decade saw the emergence of Gerallt Lloyd OWEN (1944–), who wrote a series of protest poems focusing on the investiture of the Prince of Wales in 1969. One of these, the short cywydd *Fy Ngwlad* (My country), has become one of the most popular of all modern Welsh poems. Its combination of radical NATIONALISM and a masterful use of *cynghanedd* characterizes much of Owen's poetry, including the *awdl Cilmeri* that won the Chair at the 1982 National Eisteddfod.

By 1976, it was clear that a new generation of young poets had mastered the formal complexities of the medieval tradition and were taking it to a renewed level of popularity. The Chair competition of that year was of a very high standard, and the same Eisteddfod also saw the founding of Cymdeithas Cerdd Dafod (The poetry society), with its journal *Barddas* (Poetry) appearing later that same year, edited by the poet Alan Llwyd (1948–).

The poetic counterculture of this period is perhaps best exemplified by the *Beirdd Answyddogol* (Unofficial poets) series of Y Lolfa press. One of these poets, Iwan Llwyd (1957–2010), won the Crown in the 1990 National Eisteddfod with *Gwreichion* (Sparks), a complex series of poems that combines meditations on the state of contemporary Wales with an examination of the nature of artistic creation.

While Dilys Cadwaladr (1902–79) won the Crown in 1953 (the first woman to win either of the main poetry competitions in the National Eisteddfod), women's poetry was largely absent from the literary establishments until recently. This has changed dramatically over the past years, with Mererid Hopwood becoming the first woman to win the Chair at the 2001 National Eisteddfod at Denbigh (Dinbych). See also WELSH WOMEN WRITERS.

Jerry Hunter

WELSH PROSE LITERATURE, EARLY MODERN

Sixteenth-century Welsh manuscript culture preserved several aspects of the earlier tradition, with professional copyists partially modernizing the language and orthography of medieval prose texts. New historiographical works were written, such as the Chronicle of Elis Gruffydd (*c.* 1490–*c.* 1558), a massive history of the world.

The first WELSH book, a short collection of religious texts known simply as *Yny lhyvyr hwnn* (In this book), was published by Sir John Prys (Prise) in 1546, and in 1588 William Morgan (1545–1604) published his Welsh translation of the entire Bible, an event widely viewed as the most important literary development in the post-medieval period. To this day, the 1588 Bible is the most discernible single source for the modern literary language.

Two extremely important prose texts appeared in the early 18th century: Ellis WYNNE (1671–1734) published *Gweledigaetheu y Bardd Cwsc* ('Visions of the Sleeping Bard') in 1703 and Theophilus Evans (1693–1767) first published *Drych y Prif Oesoedd* ('A Mirror of the First Ages') in 1716. While Wynne's text was based on two different English translations of Quevedo's *Los Sueños*, it is an arrestingly original work. Its critique of sin is obviously didactic, yet its lampooning often reaches darkly comic heights. Evans's text was a reworking of the traditional Welsh historiographical tradition combined with a defence of various Anglican practices. It is the style, rather than the content, of both works that was to have an enduring effect on the direction of Welsh prose. Evans wrote his history in a lively narrative register and, as subsequent reprints enthroned the *Drych* as a kind of Welsh national epic, the popularity of the text ensured that future generations of writers drew upon the hardy idiom of his Welsh. Ellis Wynne provided future authors with an example of truly unique literary prose, demonstrating that modern Welsh was a flexible language capable of reaching Rabelaisian comic extremes while also treating political and theological complexities.

Jerry Hunter

WELSH PROSE LITERATURE, MIDDLE WELSH

One of the earliest examples of Welsh prose literature is *Braint Teilo* (Old Welsh *Bryein Teliau* 'The privilege of Teilo'; first part 950×1090, second part 1120×29), which sets out the rights and privileges of the church of St Teilo—that is, Llandeilo Fawr, Carmarthenshire (sir Gaerfyrddin). Welsh LAW TEXTS begin to appear as comprehensive handbooks around the mid-13th century. The law books show many of the features of an oral style of presentation, such as alliteration, triadic groupings (see TRIADS), the use of synonyms, proverbs, and sententious sayings.

The earliest extant narrative is the story of CULHWCH AC OLWEN ('Culhwch and Olwen', probably later 11th century to early 12th century in the text's present form), based on a FOLK-TALE of 'the giant's daughter' type but greatly developed in its literary form. The Mabinogi, composed not long after this tale, is a single work structured in four 'branches'. Although the materials were traditional and mythological in origin, the author appears to have adapted them for his or her own purposes. A native literary narrative style comes to fruition in the 13th century in the Welsh ARTHURIAN 'ROMANCES' (see TAIR RHAMANT) and in idiomatic, confident translations of French *chansons de geste* and Romances. The delightful *Breuddwyd* MACSEN WLEDIG (The dream of Maxen), probably created in the early 13th century, is in the same tradition, as is the later (mid-14th century) CHWEDLEU SEITH DOETHON RUFEIN (Tales of the seven sages of Rome). The author of BREUDDWYD RHONABWY (Rhonabwy's dream; 1150×1250), however, stands outside his own tradition, creating a story and using both the content and stylistics of Welsh narrative to satirize it and to reveal the futility both of the Arthurian ethos and of the rhetorical conventions of oral narrative.

Religious prose of this era, which consists almost entirely of translations, reflects for the most part popular Latin handbooks and instructional treatises, suggesting that these texts were intended for parish priests and laity. The most important are

Elucidarium and the didactic dialogue, *Ystorya Adrian ac Ipotis*; the confessor's handbook *Penityas*; and, most interesting, YMBORTH YR ENAID (Sustenance of the soul). The Welsh writer of the tract, for which no Latin source has been firmly established, uses many of the verbal and stylistic (especially rhetorical) conventions of native narrative prose, and is also able to compose ENGLYNION in the contemporary bardic manner. In HAGIOGRAPHY, the lives of St David (DEWI SANT) and St BEUNO were translated from Latin to Welsh.

Brynley F. Roberts

WELSH PROSE LITERATURE, THE NOVEL

The first Welsh-language novels began appear only at the beginning of the 19th century. Early novels in Welsh tended to be translations from the English (usually lagging about a century behind) or original historical Romances, temperance novels, or simple love stories. Daniel OWEN is the true father of the Welsh novel. In his *Hunangofiant Rhys Lewis* (The autobiography of Rhys Lewis, 1885), the eponymous hero states emphatically that his aim is to tell 'the truth, the whole truth, and nothing but the truth'. Owen's four novels became immediately popular when they were first serialized. Despite weaknesses in the construction of plot, his characterization, his humour, and his soul-searching make Owen an unrivalled novelist in Welsh until this day.

Only a handful of writers chose the novel as their main form of expression over the next half-century. Saunders LEWIS's *Monica* (1930) raised many eyebrows by allowing the lustful anti-heroine to be unashamedly amoral. Elena Puw Morgan (1900–73), who was first a children's writer, published three novels for adults between 1933 and 1943. Kate ROBERTS, a prolific short-story writer, raised the novel to a higher level of excellence with her *Traed Mewn Cyffion* ('Feet in Chains', 1936), a novel set in the harsh environment of a slate-quarrying area in north Wales at the end of the 19th century.

From 1943 to 1947, T. Rowland Hughes (1903–49) published a novel annually and was soon hailed as a 'second Daniel Owen'. Although his fundamental themes are often tragic, he weaves a great deal of humour into his stories, and his characterization is strong. His main aim was to celebrate the courage with which the quarrymen and their families endured hardship. A new note was struck by Islwyn Ffowc Elis, the most professional novelist of the second half of the 20th century. His style is sleek and his plots well wrought. His subject matter does not hark back nostalgically to the past, and his characters are in the main young and full of enthusiasm for the new. Between 1953 and 1971, Elis published nine novels.

The 1960s saw the emergence of a new breed of writers, mostly in their early twenties, who expressed the *Weltanschauung* of the times. Some singular novels made a strong impression, though their authors did not produce a large corpus of fiction. Caradog Prichard published only one novel of distinction, yet his *Un Nos Ola Leuad* ('One Moonlit Night', 1961) has already achieved the status of a classic, and is the only Welsh-language novel to have appeared in the Penguin Twentieth-Century Classics series. Set in the same background as T. Rowland Hughes's

Chwalfa (Dispersal, 1946), it deals with the worlds of madness, perversion, murder, and suicide. Another poet, T. Glynne Davies (1926–88), was the author of *Marged* (1974), possibly the longest novel in the Welsh language, a chronicle of life in the back streets of Llanrwst at the beginning of the 20th century. Dafydd Rowlands (1931–2001) published only one novel, *Mae Theomemphus yn Hen* (Theomemphus is old, 1977), but it is an experimental work with autobiographical undertones, written at the interface between prose and poetry. The playwright John Gwilym Jones (1904–88) published only two novels, but his second, *Tri Diwrnod ac Angladd* (Three days and a funeral, 1979), reverberates with symbolism.

The tables were turned on the traditional historical novel by the young Wiliam Owen Roberts (1960–) with his *Y Pla* ('Pestilence', 1987), which is paradoxical in being written from a Marxist point of view and with the use of postmodernist techniques. It deals with the Black Death of the 14th century. The last quarter of the 20th century saw a renaissance in the Welsh novel, to which Wiliam Owen Roberts made a not insignificant contribution. The most significant recent fiction is that of Robin Llywelyn (1958–), Mihangel Morgan, and Angharad Tomos. Llywelyn's fantasy novels used magical realism. Mihangel Morgan is a gay and blatantly anti-Christian writer who bewilders his readers with his postmodernist techniques. Angharad Tomos is a language activist whose first full-sized novel is openly political, but whose range of themes in subsequent novels makes her a writer of wide sympathies.

John Rowlands

WELSH PROSE LITERATURE, THE SHORT STORY

The Welsh short story emerged as a modern literary form in the early decades of the 20th century. Although short stories of a romantic, moralistic, or historical nature had appeared in two 19th-century women's periodicals, *Y Gymraes* (The Welshwoman) and *Y Frythones* (The [female] Briton), it was only in the journal *Cymru* from 1910 and 1925 that the three authors—Richard Hughes Williams (Dic Tryfan, 1878?–1919), Kate Roberts, and D. J. Williams (1885–1970) developed the modern short story. Richard Hughes Williams was the first to provide the realism of the modern short story. His stories are deeply rooted in his slate-quarrying community in Arfon in northwest Wales, and his stark accounts of the tragic lives of individual quarrymen as they fight against their grim fate have a sense of hopelessness akin to that found in the work of Sherwood Anderson. The early characters of Kate Roberts are almost all sensitive women who strive courageously against impossible circumstances of poverty or illness. Their struggle is of a more psychological nature.

As early as 1927, some critics were concerned about what they called the English influence on the development of the Welsh story. They favoured the more traditional storytelling, and more than any other Welsh short-story writer D. J. Williams was able to extend traditional storytelling to serve a literary purpose. In his first volume *Storïau'r Tir Glas* (Stories of the green land, 1936), he draws upon autobiographical material and celebrates the life of his childhood community.

The Welsh short story reached the height of its popularity in the 1960s and 1970s. Two series of anthologies of short stories appeared during this period: *Storïau'r Dydd* (Stories of the day; 1968–74) and then *Storïau Awr Hamdden* (Leisure time stories; 1974–79). Throughout this period of development, the more traditional model survived in the hands of authors such as J. J. Williams (1869–1954), J. O. Williams (1892–1973), W. J. Griffith (1875–1931), and Islwyn Williams (1903–57). Humour is a vital element in this kind of story writing, and Islwyn Williams's approach to the sufferings of the coalmining community can be compared to that of T. Rowland Hughes (1903–49): Both writers emphasized the courage with which these communities faced tragedy. This more oral style of writing continues to this day in the writings of storywriters such as W. S. Jones (Wil Sam; 1920–2007) and Harri Parri (1935–).

In the 1960s, the Welsh short story was drawn into new directions by authors such as Harri Pritchard Jones (1933–), Pennar Davies (1911–97), and Bobi Jones. Harri Pritchard Jones's short stories deal with life outside Wales and also embrace city life. In the hands of Pennar Davies and Bobi Jones, the Welsh short story broke loose and everyone and everywhere became potential material for this medium.

During the 1980s, the novel surpassed the short story in popularity; in the 1990s, however, the short story gained popularity once more. Young writers such as Martin Davis (1957–) and Meleri Wyn James developed the short story in new directions. Martin Davis's volume *Llosgi'r Bont* (Burning the bridge; 1991) represents one of the earlier attempts at depicting the tensions experienced by immigrants into rural Wales. The two most dazzling contributors to the form in recent years have been Robin Llywelyn and Mihangel Morgan. In their different ways, both have baffled the Welsh reader, one with his creation of fantasy stories and the other with his skilful use of post-modernist techniques.

Megan Tomos

WELSH WOMEN WRITERS (1700–2000)

The bardic order that dominated Welsh literature before the 18th century was reluctant to admit women to its ranks. Of the 4,000 or so WELSH-language poets whose names are on record as having composed verse before the mid-19th century, only 60 were women (see WELSH POETRY).

The Welsh Methodist Revival's emphasis on BIBLE reading (see CHRISTIANITY) and the spread of the CIRCULATING SCHOOLS both increased female literacy in the 19th century. Ann Griffiths, still preeminent among Welsh women poets, was by no means the only woman to have found a literary as well as spiritual voice as a direct result of the Methodist revolution. The first book to appear in Welsh under a woman's name seems to have been Jane Edward's *Ychydig Hymnau a Gyfansoddwyd ar Amrywiol Achosion* (A few hymns composed for various occasions), published in Bala in 1816, but, before that, women had published—under their own names and, no doubt, anonymously—pamphlets of verse associated with the Revival. From the evidence of their poems, as well as the history of the Methodist movement, it would appear that few of these women belonged to the higher social ranks.

At the same time, during the last decade of the 18th century and the first years of the 19th, another group of Welsh women were making a name for themselves in the very different arena of the English-language Romantic novel. Anna Maria Bennett (*c.* 1750–1808), born in Merthyr Tudful in south Wales, but living in London (Welsh Llundain) as the mistress of an English nobleman when she began her writing career, became a best-selling author during her time. Another novelist was Mary Robinson (1756–1800), an in-law of one of the leaders of the Methodist Revival and also, for a period, mistress of the Prince of Wales who became King George IV of the United Kingdom.

To refute the moralistic condemnations of the official 1847 report on Wales (infamous to Welsh patriots as *Brad y Llyfrau Gleision* 'Treachery of the Blue Books'), outraged Nonconformist denominations, including the Methodists, felt that it was not enough that Welsh men should defend them; women's voices were needed to proclaim the innate purity of the Welsh woman. One of the first defenders of the Welsh was Jane Williams (Ysgafell, 1806–85). Under the patronage of her friend Augusta Waddington Hall, Lady Llanofer (1808–96), herself one of the most effective benefactors of mid-19th-century Welsh culture, Jane Williams went on to become a historian of note. Lady Llanofer also gave her support to *Y Gymraes* (The Welshwoman), a periodical that was intended by its editor, Ieuan Gwynedd (Evan Jones, 1820–52), as a vehicle giving Welsh women the opportunity to speak up for themselves.

The majority of the content of *Y Gymraes*'s successor, *Y Frythones* (The [female] Briton), edited by the redoubtable Cranogwen, Sarah Jane Rees (1839–1916), were written by women. The third Welsh-language periodical for women, a second *Cymraes* (1896–34), was the mouthpiece of the women's temperance associations.

Better-known female novelists of the first half of the 20th century include Moelona (Elizabeth Mary Jones, 1878–1953, author of *Teulu Bach Nantoer* [The little family of Nantoer]), Elena Puw Morgan (1900–73, author of *Y Wisg Sidan* [The silk dress]), German-born Kate Bosse-Griffiths (1910–98, author of *Anesmwyth Hoen* [Uneasy joy]), and, of course, Kate Roberts (1891–1985), still preeminent among Welsh-language fiction writers (see Welsh prose literature). In the English language, too, writers such as the best-selling author Allen Raine (Anne Adaliza Beynon Puddicombe, 1836–1900, author of *A Welsh Singer*) and Alis Mallt Williams (1867–1950) contributed to the newfound national confidence that marked the closing decade of the 19th century in Wales, and became the literary predecessors of later 20th-century authors such as Dorothy Edwards (1903–34), Hilda Vaughan (1892–1985), and Margiad Evans (Peggy Eileen Whistler, 1909–58).

Developments in the second half of the century included significant changes in Welsh women's sense of identity and in their capacity to contribute with confidence to their culture. The revolutionary decade of the 1960s brought a new wave of women novelists to the fore within both the linguistic cultures of Wales. In Welsh, Jane Edwards (1938–) and Eigra Lewis Roberts (1939–) explored the dissatisfactions of postwar women, while, in English, Siân James (1932–) and Bernice Rubens (1928–2004), from Cardiff's Jewish community, focused on the limitations of the traditional family from the female point of view. Post-1969, the 'second wave' of the feminist movement had, and continues to have, profound effects on women's writing. One of its outcomes in Wales was the establishment in 1986 of the Welsh feminist press, Honno, which publishes new and out-of-print works by Welsh women writing in both Welsh and English. In the 1970s and 1980s, the peace movement, and green politics generally, as well as the feminist movement, were clearly of paramount concern to a new generation of women poets. Menna Elfyn (1951–) and Nesta Wyn Jones (1946–) are influential Welsh-language poets whose work shows green concerns, perhaps the single most characteristic feature of Welsh women's writing in the second half of the 20th century.

The influence that first incited Meg Elis to write was not the green or feminist movements but rather the Welsh-language movement. Since its founding in 1962, Cymdeithas yr Iaith Gymraeg has inspired many a woman writer, none more so than Angharad Tomos (1958–), who chaired the society in the 1980s. Language issues also loom large in the work of another contributor of note to both of the linguistic cultures of Wales, the bilingual poet Gwyneth Lewis (1959–), who has devoted one entire volume of verse, *Y Llofrudd Iaith* (The language murderer, 1999), to a witty, quasi-detective investigation into the state of the Welsh language's health.

As is evident from this necessarily brief account, the women writers of Wales today are concerned not merely with representing self-consciously feminine points of view, but also in addressing issues that are central to the lives of all Welsh people, as evidenced by Mererid Hopwood, who won the Chair in the 2001 National Eisteddfod at Denbigh (Dinbych).

Jane Aaron

WILD MAN IN CELTIC LEGEND

Introduction

Myrddin Wyllt ('Wild Merlin') of Wales (Cymru), Lailoken of Scotland (Alba), and the Irish Suibne Geilt ('Wild Sweeney') represent developments of a migratory legend that probably originated in Cumbric Strathclyde (Ystrad Clud). Three characteristics of the main character coalesce to distinguish the 'Celtic wild man' from similar figures: (1) the source of his madness as grief or horror due to his transgression, which affected comrades or relations in a catastrophic battle; (2) his encounter and exchange of knowledge with an alter ego or consort, whether friendly or inimical; and (3) his self-predicted demise or threefold death at the consort's behest. The second characteristic corresponds to a legend that first appears in Christian guise as St Jerome's Life of Paul, which describes the first hermit—the 'Legend of the Hairy Anchorite'—in the largely Western subtype, wherein the recluse flees to the wild in penitence. A human who has become wild, the Celtic wild man shares aspects with other exiles. Arising from a 6th- to 7th-century prototype in a region on the border of Brythonic andOld Irish speech, and thriving in derivative areas by the 9th century, his legend is the earliest developed medieval European literary attestation of the 'wild man of the woods'.

Catastrophic Battles and Men Gone Mad

Myrddin and Lailoken go mad in the historical conflict of ARFDERYDD (*c.* AD 573), whereas Suibne suffers this fate after MAG ROTH (AD 637). The Welsh TRIADS, Genealogy of the Men of the North (*Bonedd Gwŷr y Gogledd*), an early entry in *Annales Cambriae* (the Welsh ANNALS), and further sources describe Arfderydd as the North British petty king Gwenddolau's defeat, with this leader being slain by the brothers PEREDUR and Gwrgi. In other versions, Gwendolau's chief opponent is the historical 6th-century king RHYDDERCH HAEL of Dumbarton. Further elaborations of this 'epic of defeat' include Arfderydd's trivial causes (a lark's nest), formulaic length, and truce breaking. The battle site was near the present-day western English–Scottish border at Liddel Strength, in the parish of Arthuret (which preserves the old name), near Carwinley Burn (*Kar-Windelhov* 'Fort of Gwenddolau').

There is no good argument for Myrddin's historicity as a poet or seer. In the Welsh Myrddin tradition, he begins as a petty king or lord serving Gwenddolau, then flees to Coed Celyddon (the Caledonian forest), where he mourns in guilt over loss of comrades or brothers, and for crimes that lost him favour from a woman, often seen as his 'sister'. He has thus conceivably destroyed his sister's son or daughter.

In the same region, Lailoken goes insane in a battle as a heaven-sent punishment for his responsibility in the slaughter of fellow combatants. Like the biblical Nebuchadnezzar (Daniel 3:28–34), he hears a voice from on high; he also sees threatening aerial hosts and, like St Paul (Acts 9:3–4), a blinding light. His penance is insanity and a beast-like life out of doors.

The historical battle of Mag Roth saw Domnall Brecc of Scottish DÁL RIATA's league with Congal Cáech of ULAID defeated by Domnall mac Aedo maic Ainmirech, high-king of the Northern UÍ NÉILL. The primary text linking the legendary Suibne to this conflict, *Buile Shuibne* (Suibne's madness), was probably redacted before AD 1197.

In later texts Suibne, who also has connections to Scotland, is filled with frenzy and fear due to three battle-cries from on high by assembled combatants. He looks up to the sky and anti-heroically flees the battle. In *Buile Shuibne* and other tales, Domnall mac Aedo and Congal quarrel over trivial gifts (birds' eggs) from other-worldly instigators (see OTHERWORLD). Ireland's saints curse Congal's ally, Suibne, for his theft of a tunic, the gift of truce.

The Penitent Hairy Anchorite

The early literary antecedents of the Celtic wild man figure are the desert hermit and the 'beast-man'. Further interacting early and culturally widespread themes include the tension between secular and the sacred (king and hermit), and the attempted seduction and capture, or pursuit and destruction, of the recluse (as in the *Epic of Gilgamesh*). The motive for leaving the world is a single, grievous sin, often seduction by a woman or a demon disguised as a woman, who may also constitute the recluse's temptation in the wilds. The sin became an entry point for *dementia* or demon possession, as with the Biblical Nebuchadnezzar.

Thirteen elements constituting penitent hairy anchorite legend are discernible for the Myrddin, Suibne, and Lailoken legends, and hence for the hypothetical Celtic wild man legend 'prototype'.

1. *The visitant's journey*: a meeting between the wild man and a counterpart, whether saint or sister.
2. *The recluse's ascetic abode and life.*
3. *Animal companions.*
4. *A 'perfect' number of years/age*, whether one, seven, or fifty.
5. *Temptations from the ascetic life.*
6. *Reasons for penance/life in the wilderness.*
7. *The visitant is sent by God and is recognized.*
8. *Perfection.* After years of penance, the wild man achieves a transcendent state.
9. *Dialogue/instruction*, where the wild man holds a conversation with a poetic counterpart or his visitant.
10. *The wild man predicts his own death.*
11. *Miraculous meal/sacrament/last rites.*
12. *Death, burial, salvation.*
13. *Utterances (prophecies) for posterity.*

Poetry and Prophecy, "King and Hermit"

The enviable life of the hermit compared with that of the king is a device occurring throughout the Celtic wild man legend, and one that intimately involves poetry (elegy, nature lyric, and hermit poetry) and PROPHECY (Irish *fáith*, Early Welsh *gwawt*). Aspects of these conceits appear only sparsely in the Lailoken texts. However, Myrddin, Merlin, and Suibne are each variously portrayed as king, poet, and seer.

Poetry and Prophecy

'Kentigern's encounter with Lailoken' and *Buile Shuibne* attribute celebratory verse to both saint and wild man about the hermit's life. Each delights in pure water; simple, vegetarian fare; a secluded abode with only animals for companions; and bird- and deer-song for music. *Buile Shuibne* also mentions nature as a source of discomfort: exposure, lack of music, sleep or food, and loss of company. The Suibne corpus thus resembles the Find Cycle (FIANNAÍOCHT), especially concerning persons on the margins or the outside of society, the dubious or criminal life in the wilds.

The Myrddin/Merlin corpus includes eremitical or celebratory strains in its elegiac, natural, and prophetic verse. Like Suibne, Myrddin complains of the direct pain that nature causes him, addressing animal companions and contrasting present wretchedness with former riches, high rank, and female company. He mourns his fallen lord and comrades; complains of sparse clothing, hunger, cold, snow, and wolves; fears capture; and calls on God to relieve him of his wretched life.

Myrddin's prophecies on behalf of DYFED and Wales resemble Mo-Ling's political prophecy as seen in the Mo-Ling poetry, *The Birth and Life of Moling*, *Vitae Sanctorum Hiberniae*, and in the *Bórama*. Just as Suibne, Myrddin/Merlin, and Lailoken are inspired to predict their own deaths, as well as (like Irish saints) the deaths of monarchs or others, so, too, their predictions carry didactic or even apocalyptic weight.

Emphasis upon political prophecy in Myrddin's legend contributed to his exalted reputation as a seer, at its most pronounced in *Vita Merlini*. Although the poems *Afallennau*, the *Hoianau*, and *Ymddiddan Myrddin a Thaliesin* balance Myrddin's prophetic utterances with saga, in *Ymddiddan Myrddin a Thaliesin* (Merlin's conversation with Taliesin') the wild man is portrayed as an inspired prophet, magnified beyond, or even conflated with, Taliesin. Myrddin's exalted secular status contrasts with Suibne's saintly transformation, in keeping with the powerful influence of the Welsh tradition of political prophecy.

King and Hermit

In *Buile Shuibne* and the Mo-Ling poetry, Suibne resists capture and possible return to kingship. Myrddin is destitute and presented as a prophet, in contrast to his regal opposites. Rhydderch's courtly life is compared not with natural glories, but with Myrddin's misery. In *Vita Merlini*, after his initial entry to the eremitical life, Merlin rejects bribes to return to court, prefers nature's whims to rulership, and spurns wealth and good food to enjoy the beautiful woodlands and a diet of apples.

Deaths of rulers, and especially most threefold deaths of rulers in early IRISH LITERATURE, are predicted as a vindication of otherworldly power over the victim's false rule. The wild man's prediction of his own death is due primarily to his rôle as prophet.

The Wild Man's Consort

Widespread ancient traditions of the fertile wild man as a victim betrayed by a courtesan, through sexual enticement or food and drink, to capture or death at the hands of hunters merged early on with the theme of the penitent hairy anchorite, 'king and hermit', and 'catastrophic battles'. In the penitent hairy anchorite legend, the wild man's consort theme provided a contrast between chastity and unchastity. Women always appear in one or other guise of the consort in the Celtic wild man legend. The Welsh texts uniquely merge a largely benign consort figure with that of the holy visitor (though not without tension). By contrast, Irish and Scottish sources show a harsher asceticism, with the woman appearing as temptress and betrayer.

Suibne's queen, Eorann, who had symbolically stripped the wild man of kingship as he attacked St Rónán, invites him to cohabit with her—an inverse 'king and hermit' setting suggesting that his deprivation is preferable to worldly kingship. However, Suibne barely escapes from a hunting party led by Eorann's lover, the new king and his opponent in this love triangle. Women attempt to lure Suibne from asceticism back to kingship and the world, or back to renewed madness, just as he is about to regain his sanity and rule. Thus, in several episodes, Suibne perches in holy trees by holy wells and is approached by noble consorts.

Myrddin laments that the 'fair, wanton maiden' whose favour he courted under the apple tree no longer prizes or visits him. Gwenddydd is the only woman whom Myrddin names in the Myrddin poems, and in one poem, *Cyfoesi*, he calls her his 'sister'. Elsewhere, Myrddin mourns that he has killed Gwenddydd's son and daughter, or that she neither loves nor greets him. Gwenddydd questions Myrddin 'tenderly', calls him her 'life', and says that she 'pines away' from parting with him.

In this single consort theme, the woman is mostly a would-be visitor, with the wild man expecting or bewailing the absence of a queen, spouse, or former lover who is married to his regal pursuer or usurper and who forsakes the wild man or is forsaken by him. The relationship between wild man, paramour, and regal entourage is ambiguous, and duplication of the consort was perhaps present for earlier stages of the legend. The Welsh consort may have survived—adopted into French Romance through Breton *conteurs*—in the name Vivienne (Niniane), the confidant who uses Merlin's secrets to imprison and supersede him. This name may correspond to the cryptic informant *huimleian* or *chwibleian* of the Myrddin poems, a word consisting of *chwyf-* + *lleian*, 'a wanderer of pallid countenance' or even as 'a wandering nun' or 'wandering veiled woman'.

Pursuit and Capture

The centre of the Celtic wild man's biography is the hunt: Suibne, Myrddin/Merlin, and Lailoken are pursued by kings, retainers, or rustics. These would-be captors are aided by a friendly or inimical woman or relative (often related to the pursuer) who instigates the chase. The relative or king, whether enemy or friend, is consort to the chaste visitant or malevolent temptress—thus a 'love triangle' theme emerges.

The Myrddin poems include these themes most prominently in the *Afallennau* (Apple tree stanzas) and the *Hoianau* (Greetings). Myrddin is chased by King Rhydderch, stewards, men, and hounds crowding about his apple tree. Suibne is pursued by Aonghus Remhar, by Domnall mac Aedo the high-king and victor of Mag Roth, or by a relative or his wife's hostile lover. These pursuers trap him in holy trees to no effect.

Buile Shuibne's pursuit and capture episodes are similar to those described in *Vita Merlini*, and polarize the wild man's preference for, or rejection of, the world. Each text has two pursuit–capture–restoration–escape sequences, attributing three madnesses to the wild man. The chase introduces *Buile Shuibne*'s longest poem, in which the pursuit blends with themes of the hunt and the wild man's impending death. Pursued by hunting packs, Suibne sympathizes with a stag, while (like Merlin of *Vita Merlini*) riding on a stag in the manner of the European wild man of the 'Wild Hunt' and the 'Wild Horde'. His frequent pleas to Christ and allusions to agony, going 'peak to peak' on points of branches and antlers or hilltops, evoke both the Crucifixion and his death variously by spear or antler. Suibne regains sanity briefly again, only to be driven at Rónán's behest into lifelong madness by an apparition.

Later, Merlin appears as 'Lord of the Animals' (cf. Owain *neu Iarlles y Ffynnon* and further Arthurian Romance), wondering at woodland herds, or riding a stag and driving great woodland herds before him as a wedding present for his former wife.

The account of the threefold death in 'Lailoken in King Meldred's court' closely resembles that of Merlin's first wager in *Vita Merlini*, including the leaf, the enigmatic laugh, the accusation of adultery, and the threefold death prediction and sequel, but the order of events is scrambled, with the death predictions coming before any logical reason for their occurrence, and the petty king, Meldred, believing the lunatic rather than his wife. Further indication of familiarity with *Vita Merlini* during some point of the 'Lailoken in King Meldred's court' manuscript tradition is the reference to Merlin the wild man, his death and burial, and an awareness of Merlin as a political prophet.

Lailoken, like Suibne, predicts his own threefold death rather than that of a youth. Only 'Kentigern's encounter with Lailoken' and 'Lailoken in King Meldred's court' include a fatal chase of the wild man, though this theme is implicit in the Myrddin poems and in *Buile Shuibne*.

Temptation, Betrayal, and Death

The wild man's death in a saint's company fell together in two versions of the Celtic wild man legend with stories of the recluse's betrayal by a woman and his threefold death at the hands of rustics. Having predicted to St Kentigern's clerics different deaths for himself on three occasions, Lailoken is beaten and stoned by herdsmen, and falls onto a stake of a fishing weir in the Tweed, where he drowns. As seen, 'Lailoken in King Meldred's court' connects the madman's death with the machinations of a woman and accusation of adultery.

The Lailoken tales resemble accounts of Suibne's demise in the types of death suffered and in the female temptation and betrayal. Certain considerations favour seeing the manner of the threefold death in the Suibne legend as evidence for the legend's British origins. Despite parallels between crimes and punishments that fit the ethos of 'purgation of royal sin' (the primary focus of Irish threefold death accounts), the Suibne–Mo-Ling cycle largely stands apart from other Irish treatments of the motif. The entire threefold death motif seems to be intrusive in his story, occurring first in a text that is cognizant of Suibne's killing by a herdsman. Having no historical grounding as a king of Dál nAraidhe, Suibne is linked in extant sources to both Scottish Dál Riata and British Strathclyde. Although predictions of his death emphasize sacerdotal vindication, these prophecies become to an even greater extent a device accentuating the saint or wild prophet's 'powerful knowledge', a strong characteristic of non-Irish threefold deaths. In its full range of variants and thematic associations, Suibne's death, like those of Lailoken and the *Vita Merlini* youth, fits this context more comfortably than an Irish one.

Lastly, the Celtic wild man's penance as linked to his violent death was elaborated in Welsh legend by the 13th century, as is borne out through references in the GOGYNFEIRDD and CYWYDDWYR in contexts of *amour courtois* and political vaticination, to Myrddin's raving and inspired utterances, transfixed by a stake or deer's antlers. These traditions resemble not only the Middle Welsh/Modern Breton story of the penance of Ysgolan/Skolan—a clerical student who for his crimes (slaying a cow, desecrating a church, drowning a book, and rape) is transfixed on the stake of a fishing weir, whence he utters poetry—but also tales of other religious exiles, such as the *clam* (leper) persecuted in *Cath Almaine* ('The Battle of Allen'), and Myrddin's

Breton alter ego Guenc'hlan, the penitent afflicted with a malaise that partly represents Christ's suffering.

Brian Frykenberg

WILLIAMS, EDWARD

Edward Williams (Iolo Morganwg, 1747–1826), universally known by his bardic nom de plume, is arguably the most gifted, complex, and intriguing figure in the cultural history of Wales (Cymru). In his day this poor stonemason was the major authority in Wales on language, poetry, prose, history, music, architecture, agriculture, archaeology, and the folk traditions of the Welsh people. He was a deeply serious scholar and creative writer (sometimes blurring the boundaries between them) who established the Gorsedd of the Bards (1792), a druidic court that became the first modern national institution in Wales. He also campaigned vigorously on behalf of the establishment of a National Library, a National Academy, and a Welsh College in Wales.

Having toyed with a variety of bardic pseudonyms, Williams eventually settled upon *Iolo Morganwg* (Edward of Glamorgan). Fuelled by copious supplies of laudanum, to which he became addicted from 1773, he endeavoured to combine a variety of business speculations with a literary career, a risky enterprise that led him to fall out with friends and enemies in equal measure. Only his skills as a stone and marble mason saved him and his family from utter destitution.

Gorsedd Beirdd Ynys Prydain (The Assembly of the Bards of Britain) was essentially the product of his fertile mind and imagination. It first met on Primrose Hill, London (Welsh Llundain), in 1792, and from 1819 onward it became an integral part of the National Eisteddfod of Wales (Eisteddfod Genedlaethol Cymru). Ever since, this colourful visual pageant has helped to sustain traditions associated with the language, literature, and history of Wales.

Iolo Morganwg was the presiding genius among the imaginative makers and inventors of the past in late 18th-century Wales. He hoodwinked the Welsh of London (Llundain) by persuading them that his poems were the authentic work of the 14th-century poet Dafydd ap Gwilym, and his fantasies regarding the existence of the Madogwys (the Welsh Native Americans) in America were widely read and believed. His inspired vision about the literary and historical past of Wales were aired in *Poems, Lyric and Pastoral* (2 vols., 1794) and *The Myvyrian Archaiology of Wales* (3 vols., 1801–7). Nevertheless, his most cherished project, *Cyfrinach Beirdd Ynys Prydain* (The Secret of the Bards of the Isle of Britain), remained unpublished until three years after his death in 1826. A fervent advocate of the ideals of the French Revolution, Iolo devised the Gorsedd of the Bards in 1792 as a means of projecting a new vision of history, of a nation reborn in radical liberty. Styling himself the 'Bard of Liberty', he campaigned against war, slavery, high taxes, and political repression, and his oft-quoted motto *Y Gwir yn erbyn y Byd* (Truth against the World) became a leitmotif of the Gorsedd of the Bards and the National Eisteddfod of Wales. Iolo was one of the founder members of the Unitarian

Christian Society of South Wales in 1802, and helped to promote its activities by organizing missionary tours and composing hundreds of HYMNS. He also believed that rousing people from their political slumbers was just as important as filling their minds with glorious images and narratives of their historical past.

Iolo Morganwg's massive corpus of historical lore and literary forgeries survived scrutiny for the best part of a century and it is only recently that scholars have realized that the welding together of language, myth, and history demanded a deep understanding of authenticity debates in the literary world and a keen appreciation of the past. No one can deny the pivotal rôle played by this flawed genius in the cultural inheritance of the Welsh and in the development of Welsh national consciousness in the modern period.

Geraint H. Jenkins

WISDOM LITERATURE, IRISH

Wisdom literature is well represented in the IRISH language, particularly from the early period. The oldest text is AUDACHT MORAINN (The testament of Morann), which dates from around the 7th century and consists largely of advice to the young king Feradach Find Fechtnach. Another text containing instructions to a young king is *Bríatharthecosc Con Culainn* ('The Word-Teaching of CÚ CHULAINN'), which is addressed to Lugaid Réoderg and forms part of the tale SERGLIGE CON CULAINN ('The Wasting Sickness of Cú Chulainn'). It provides general advice on proper behaviour. The short wisdom text *Tecosc Cuscraid* ('The Instruction of Cuscraid'), uttered by CONALL CERNACH to his foster-son, a young king, deals more specifically with royal duties and obligations. *Tecosca Cormaic* ('The Instructions of CORMAC [MAC AIRT]') likewise devotes much attention to the behaviour of kings. This text, which dates from around the 9th century, is set in the form of questions and answers. As in *Audacht Morainn*, there is great emphasis on kingship and the beneficial effects of the king's justice, which causes the earth to be fruitful, the river-mouths to be full of fish, and the trees to be covered with fruit. This text also stresses the necessity for the king to be acquainted with law and other branches of learning. Taken as a whole, these observations from the wisdom literature are of value in indicating what was regarded as acceptable and unacceptable behaviour in early Irish society, though not all are realistic.

The collection known as the TRIADS of Ireland (*Trecheng Breth Féne*) comes from approximately the same period as *Tecosca Cormaic*, but seems to be an example of monastic rather than court literature. Like *Tecosca Cormaic*, it contains a good deal of legal material. Versions of a few triads in this collection have been recorded from modern folk tradition.

Two wisdom texts contain a good deal of overlapping material: *Senbríathra Fíthail* (The ancient words of Fíthal) and *Bríathra Flainn Fhína* (The words of Flann Fína). The former is attributed to the legendary judge Fíthal, and contains precepts and general observations on human behaviour. Unlike Fíthal, Flann Fína was a historical person about whose career a certain amount is known. Flann Fína mac Ossu was the Irish name borne by the Northumbrian king Aldfrith son of Oswydd, who ruled from around 685 to 705. He is reputed to have had an Irish mother and to have been partly educated in Ireland. Although there is no doubt about his learning—he was a friend of Adomnán of Iona (Eilean Ì)—it is uncertain whether he ever actually compiled proverbial material in Irish. *Bríathra Flainn Fhína* contains no linguistic features that would date the text as early as the 7th century.

Fergus Kelly

WYNNE, ELLIS

Ellis Wynne (1671–1734) is recognized as one of the most important writers of Welsh prose literature. In 1701, he published *Rheol Buchedd Sanctaidd* ('The Rule of Holy Living'), a somewhat edited translation of Jeremy Taylor's *The Rule and Exercises of Holy Living*. In 1703, he published his most famous work, *Gweledigaetheu y Bardd Cwsc* ('Visions of the Sleeping Bard'), based loosely on classical and native visions of hell (see vision literature), and more particularly on some sections of the English versions of the Spanish writer Quevedo's *Los Sueños*, one by Sir Roger L'Estrange (1667) and the other by John Stevens (1682). In 1710, Wynne's edition of the Welsh Book of Common Prayer was published; in 1755, some short pieces by him were published in his son Edward's *Prif Addysc y Cristion* ('The Christian's Fundamental Instruction').

Gweledigaetheu consists of three visions: a vision of the world set forth as a City of Destruction and overseen by four daughters of Lucifer—Pride, Pleasure, Profit, and Hypocrisy; a vision of Death's Lower Kingdom; and a vision of Hell. These visions belong to a genre of satirical visions common in England and France in the 17th century.

Gwyn Thomas

YEATS, WILLIAM BUTLER

William Bultler Yeats (1865–1939), poet and playwright, was the foremost contributor to the Irish Literary Revival of the late 19th and early 20th centuries (see ANGLO-IRISH LITERATURE; IRISH LITERATURE). Yeats spent his childhood summers with his maternal grandparents in the west of Ireland (ÉIRE). The FOLK-TALES he heard in Sligo (Sligeach) provided the inspiration for several early poems and some of the material for two collections of prose, *Fairy and Folk Tales of the Irish Peasantry* (1888) and *The Celtic Twilight* (1893; revised and enlarged, 1902). The title of the latter collection came to denote the wistful poetic reveries that Yeats and like-minded contemporaries composed in the 1890s, the apotheosis of which is *The Wind Among the Reeds* (1899). With this volume, Yeats put a symbolist capstone on his experiments in narrative poetry, in *The Wanderings of Oisin* (1889; see also OISÍN), and drama and lyric poetry, in *The Countess Kathleen and Various Legends and Lyrics* (1892).

Yeats's 1894 meeting with Lady Augusta Gregory would culminate eventually in the founding of the Abbey Theatre, with a great deal of Yeats's energies at the turn of the century and thereafter being directed toward the creation of a national drama. His nationalist play *Cathleen Ní Houlihan* was first performed in 1902. His dramatic output includes plays in both verse and prose, the most innovative of which are those modelled after the highly stylized Japanese Noh, such as *At the Hawk's Well*.

Later works find Yeats with a more contemporary perspective on the nation of Ireland and on his own identity as a

William Butler Yeats. (Library of Congress)

member of the Anglo-Irish ascendancy. He continued to publish into the 1930s, with his last work being the posthumously published *On the Boiler* (1939).

Alex Davis

YSTRAD CLUD

Ystrad Clud (Strathclyde) is the river valley (Welsh *ystrad*, Gaelic *srath*) of the Clyde, now in south-central Scotland (ALBA). This term was used as the name of a kingdom recorded from 872, also known as CUMBRIA from the mid-10th century. *Cludwys* (people of the Clyde) occurs in the 10th-century political prophecy ARMES PRYDEIN. Strathclyde has often also been used by modern writers as a shorthand for the kingdom that preceded the destruction of the fortress of Al Clud (Dumbarton Rock) by Vikings in 870. That kingdom centred on the power base of Dumbarton Rock, whose kings were normally referred to in contemporary ANNALS as kings of Al Clud (Gaelic *Ail Cluaithe*), or simply kings of the BRITONS. Although these earlier kings may well have controlled much, if not all, of Clydesdale (modern Lanarkshire), it seems as if that polity ended with the events of 870 and Strathclyde marked the start of a new polity. If we take later medieval territorial jurisdictions as a guide, the kingdom based on Dumbarton Rock may have most easily controlled the Lennox (essentially modern Dumbartonshire) and the southern side of the Firth of Clyde (modern Renfrewshire), as well as Clydesdale itself, but there is little hard evidence to support this supposition.

The kingdom on the Clyde at Dumbarton was the most persistent of the northern British kingdoms in the early Middle Ages. Its king, RHYDDERCH HAEL, appears in the 9th-century text HISTORIA BRITTONUM, in an account set in the late 6th century, as one of the kings allied against the power of Bernicia (BRYNAICH). Rhydderch can also be dated to this period by his appearance in an anecdote in *Vita Columbae* (Life of COLUM CILLE, †597), written *c.* 700 by Adomnán.

A mid-7th century victory at Srath Caruin (now Strathcarron), under Eugein map Beli, appears to have freed parts of the Dumbarton kingdom from the dominance of DÁL RIATA, with whom there was relatively constant strife. There are some question marks over the relationship between Northumbria and northern British kingdoms in the later 7th century; certainly the victory at Nechtanesmere by Eugein's brother, the Pictish king Bruide mac Bili, in 685 appears to have freed the northern Britons from Northumbrian tribute or overlordship.

Dumbarton kings are again prominent in the first half of the 8th century, but in 756 the kings were forced to submit to the allied powers of the Pictish king Unuist son of Uurguist and the Northumbrian Ecgberht. Its kings disappear from record for nearly a century. Both Viking incursions and succession disputes weakened the Pictish kingdom in the 840s, allowing Dumbarton to emerge from its shadow.

The first references to the kingdom of Ystrad Clud occur in the aftermath of the siege and sacking of Dumbarton Rock. The new kingdom had expanded as far south as the river Eamont by the mid-10th century. New people- and kingdom-names came about to describe a polity no longer limited to Ystrad Clud itself: Welsh *Cymry*, Latin *Cumbrenses* and *Cumbria*, Old English *Cumbras* and *Cumbraland*.

The kingdom certainly lasted until 1018, when its king Owain ap Dyfnwal died fighting alongside the king of Alba, Mael Coluim mac Cinaeda. Nevertheless, the description of Siward, earl of Northumbria, waging war on MAC BETHAD mac Findlaich and trying to place on the throne of Alba one 'Malcolm, son of the king of the Cumbrians' in 1054/5 reminds us that the kingship may have lasted somewhat longer—though Malcolm may have been Owain's son. It has long been thought that this Malcolm was the future Mael Coluim (III) mac Donnchada, and that Donnchad was therefore 'king of the Cumbrians' before he became king of Alba, but this equation is now thought to be highly unsound.

David I could address the inhabitants of land around Carlisle as Cumbrenses, and speak of Ranulf le Meschin of Carlisle as holding power in 'his land of Cumberland'. David moreover describes himself in his Inquest into the properties of the cathedral of Glasgow (Glaschu) as *Cumbrensis regionis princeps*, and this Inquest initiated a reclamation by the Glasgow diocese of its Cumbrian and 'Welsh' identity in the face of pressure from York, which claimed Glasgow to be its subordinate. The diocese's identification of itself with the former kingdom of Cumbria preserved the memory of that kingdom long after its political existence was at an end. By this point, Ystrad Clud itself, Clydesdale, had been settled by land grants to many of David's trusted retainers, men largely from Flanders, Brittany, Normandy, and ENGLAND. Thus the articulation of a Cumbrian identity for the region happened simultaneously with its permanent linguistic and cultural transformation.

Thomas Owen Clancy

YSTRAD-FFLUR

Ystrad-fflur (Strata Florida) was a Cistercian abbey in Ceredigion (see CISTERCIAN ABBEYS IN WALES; CYMRU), founded in 1164 by Robert Fitz Stephen, lord of Pennardd, but after that date given new impetus and patronage by the Lord Rhys (RHYS AP GRUFFUDD) of the independent Welsh kingdom of Deheubarth. Eight representatives of the princely Deheubarth dynasty are buried there. The convent became what has been called a 'significant custodian' of the native Welsh cultural tradition. It was here in the late 13th century that the now lost Latin work that formed the basis of BRUT Y TYWYSOGYON ('The Chronicle of the Princes') was composed. The poet DAFYDD AP GWILYM is reputed to have been buried within the precincts in the late 14th century.

Work on Strata Florida, under the patronage of the Lord Rhys, was under way by 1184, and certainly the chancel, crossing, and transepts of the church were substantially complete by 1201, when the community occupied it. Work continued on the new church and cloister buildings until at least 1250. The site was damaged during an occupation by the forces of Edward I during the revolt of 1294–95, but the monastery became a strong point for the forces of Henry IV in 1407 during the rebellion of OWAIN GLYNDŴR. The abbey was suppressed in 1539, during the reign of Henry VIII.

John Morgan-Guy

Bibliography

The resources used to compile this encyclopedia run to nearly 10,000 primary sources and scholarly works in more than a dozen languages. ABC-Clio has published a full Celtic studies bibliography as part of *Celtic Culture: A Historical Encyclopedia* (2006). Further Celtic studies bibliographies are available online, such as the bibliography maintained by the Celtic Studies Association of North America at www.humnet.ucla.edu/humnet/Celtic/csanabib.html. For the aims of the present encyclopedia, it will be more useful to compile the most essential and accessible resources in English, offering thematic lists of 10–15 items of further reading for each of the following areas.

Celtic Studies (General)

Books

Aldhouse-Green, Miranda, and Peter Webster, eds. *Artefacts and Archaeology: Aspects of the Celtic and Roman World*. Cardiff: University of Wales Press, 2002.

Green, Miranda J., ed. *The Celtic World*. London: Routledge, 1995.

James, Simon. *The World of the Celts*. New York: Thames and Hudson, 2005.

Koch, John T., and John Carey, eds. *The Celtic Heroic Age: Literary Sources for Ancient Celtic Europe and Early Ireland and Wales*. 4th ed. Celtic Studies 1. Aberystwyth: Celtic Studies, 2003.

Koch, John T., et al. *An Atlas for Celtic Studies: Archaeology and Names in Ancient Europe and Early Medieval Britain and Brittany*. Celtic Studies 12. Oxford: Oxbow Books, 2007.

Koch, John T., et al. *Celtic Culture: A Historical Encyclopedia*. Santa Barbara, CA: ABC-Clio, 2006.

Kruta, Venceslas. *The Celts*. London: Hachette Illustrated, 2004.

Maier, Bernhard. *Dictionary of Celtic Religion and Culture*. Trans. Cyril Edwards. Woodbridge: Boydell, 1997.

Parsons, David N., and Patrick Sims-Williams, eds. *Ptolemy: Towards a Linguistic Atlas of the Earliest Celtic Place-Names of Europe: Papers from a Workshop, Aberystwyth, 11–12 April 1999*. Aberystwyth: Cambrian Medieval Celtic Studies, 2000.

Powell, T. G. E. *The Celts*. Reprint ed. Ancient Peoples and Places. London: Thames and Hudson, 1980. First published, 1958.

Rees, Alwyn, and Rees, Brynley. *Celtic Heritage: Ancient Tradition in Ireland and Wales*. New York: Thames and Hudson, 1989.

Website

Mary Jones's Celtic Encyclopedia: http://www.maryjones.us/jce/jce_index.html.

Celtic Archaeology and Ancient History

Books

Cunliffe, Barry. *The Ancient Celts*. London: Penguin, 1999. First published, Oxford: Oxford University Press, 1997.

Cunliffe, Barry. *The Celtic World*. London: Bodley Head, 1979.

Cunliffe, Barry. *Europe between the Oceans: 9000 BC–AD 1000*. New Haven, CT: Yale University Press, 2008.

Cunliffe, Barry. *Facing the Ocean: The Atlantic and Its Peoples 8000 BC–AD 1500*. Oxford: Oxford University Press, 2001.

Cunliffe, Barry. *Iron Age Communities in Britain: An Account of England, Scotland and Wales from the Seventh Century BC until the Roman Conquest*. 4th ed. London: Routledge, 2005. First published, 1974.

Flanagan, Laurence. *Ancient Ireland: Life before the Celts*. Dublin: Gill and Macmillan, 1998.

Jacobsthal, Paul. *Early Celtic Art*. 2 vols. Oxford: Clarendon, 1970. First published, 1944.

James, David, and Stuart Booth, eds. *New Visions in Celtic Art: The Modern Tradition*. London: Blandford, 1999.

Megaw, Ruth, and J. V. S. Megaw. *Celtic Art: From Its Beginnings to the Book of Kells*. Rev. and expanded ed. London: Thames and Hudson, 2001.

Megaw, Ruth, and J. V. S. Megaw. *Early Celtic Art in Britain and Ireland*. 2nd ed. Shire Archaeology 38. Princes Risborough: Shire, 2005. First published, 1986.

Moscati, Sabatino, et al., eds. *The Celts*. London: Thames and Hudson, 1991. Reprinted, New York: Rizzoli, 1999.

Powell, T. G. E. *The Celts*. Reprint ed. Ancient Peoples and Places. London: Thames and Hudson, 1980. First published, 1958.

Rankin, David. *Celts and the Classical World*. 2nd ed. London: Routledge, 1996.

Website

Visual-Arts-Cork.com: http://www.visual-arts-cork.com/cultural-history-of-ireland/celtic-culture.htm.

Celtic Linguistics

Books

Anderson, James M. *Ancient Languages of the Hispanic Peninsula*. Lanham, NY: University Press of America, 1988.

Ball, Martin J., and James Fife, eds. *The Celtic Languages*. Routledge Language Family Descriptions. London: Routledge, 1993.

Borsley, Robert D., and Ian Roberts, eds. *The Syntax of the Celtic Languages: A Comparative Perspective*. Cambridge: Cambridge University Press, 1996.

Durkacz, Victor. *The Decline of the Celtic Languages*. Edinburgh: John Donald Publishers, 1996.

Evans, D. Ellis. *Gaulish Personal Names: A Study of Some Continental Celtic Formations*. Oxford: Clarendon Press, 1967.

Jackson, Kenneth H. *Language and History in Early Britain: A Chronological Survey of the Brittonic Languages 1st to 12th c. AD*. 2nd rev. ed. Dublin: Four Courts Press, 1994. First published 1953.

MacAulay, Donald, ed. *The Celtic Languages*. Cambridge: Cambridge University Press, 1992.

Meid, Wolfgang. *Gaulish Inscriptions: Their Interpretation in the Light of Archaeological Evidence and Their Value as a Source of Linguistic and Sociological Information*. Budapest: Archaeological Institute of the Hungarian Academy of Sciences, 1992.

Ó Néill, Diarmuid, ed. *Rebuilding the Celtic Languages: Reversing Language Shift in the Celtic Countries*. Talybont: Y Lolfa, 2005.

Russell, Paul. *An Introduction to the Celtic Languages*. Longman Linguistics Library. London: Longman, 1995.

Website

TITUS project, Frankfurt University: http://titus.uni-frankfurt.de/indexe.htm.

Celtic Literature (Medieval)

Books

Carson, Ciaran. *The Táin: Translated from the Old Irish* Táin Bó Cuailinge. Penguin Classics. New York: Penguin, 2009.

Cross, Tom Peete, and Clark Harris Slover, eds. *Ancient Irish Tales*. London: Harrap, 1936. Reprinted, New York: Barnes and Noble, 1996.

Davies, Sioned. *The Mabinogion*. Oxford World's Classics. Oxford: Oxford University Press, 2007.

Ford, Patrick K., trans. *The Mabinogi and Other Medieval Welsh Tales*. Berkeley: University of California Press, 1977.

Gantz, Jeffrey. *Early Irish Myths and Sagas*. Penguin Classics. New York: Penguin, 1996.

Jarman, A. O. H., and Gwilym Rees Hughes, eds. *A Guide to Welsh Literature 1*. Rev. ed. Cardiff: University of Wales Press, 1992. First published, Swansea: Christopher Davies, 1976.

Jarman, A. O. H., and Gwilym Rees Hughes, eds. *A Guide to Welsh Literature 2: c. 1282–1550*. Rev. ed. Cardiff: University of Wales Press, 1997. First published, Swansea: Christopher Davies, 1979.

Kinsella, Thomas, trans. *The Táin*. Dublin: Dolmen, 1969. New ed., Oxford: Oxford University Press, 2002.

Ní Bhrolcháin, Muireann. *An Introduction to Early Irish Literature*. Dublin: Four Courts Press, 2009.

Sjoestedt, Marie-Louise. *Celtic Gods and Heroes*. Mineola, NY: Dover Publications, 2000 (originally *Gods and Heroes of the Celts*, 1949).

Williams, J. E. Caerwyn, and Patrick K. Ford. *The Irish Literary Tradition*. Cardiff: University of Wales Press, 1992.

Websites

Mary Jones's Celtic Texts: http://www.maryjones.us/ctexts/index.html.

Corpus of Electronic Texts (CELT Project): http://www.ucc.ie/celt/.

Celtic Mythology

Brunaux, Jean-Louis. *The Celtic Gauls: Gods, Rites and Sanctuaries*. Trans. Daphne Nash. London: Seaby, 1988.

D'Arbois de Jubainville, H. *The Irish Mythological Cycle and Celtic Mythology*. Trans. R. I. Best. New York: Lemma, 1970. First published, Dublin: Hodges, Figgis, 1903.

Green, Miranda J. *Celtic Goddesses: Warriors, Virgins and Mothers*. London: British Museum Press, 1995.

Green, Miranda J. *Dictionary of Celtic Myth and Legend*. London: Thames and Hudson, 1992.

Green, Miranda J. *Exploring the World of the Druids*. London: Thames and Hudson, 1997.

Green, Miranda J. *The Gods of the Celts*. Stroud: Sutton, 1997. First published, 1986.

Mac Cana, Proinsias. *Celtic Mythology*. Library of the World's Myths and Legends. London: Chancellor, 1996.

MacKillop, James. *Celtic Mythology*. Oxford: Oxford University Press, 1998.

MacKillop, James. *A Dictionary of Celtic Mythology*. Oxford: Oxford University Press, 2000.

Ó hÓgáin, Dáithí. *The Sacred Isle: Pre-Christian Religions in Ireland*. Woodbridge: Boydell Press, 1999.

Ross, Anne. *Everyday Life of the Pagan Celts*. London: Batsford, 1970.

Website

Internet Sacred Text Archive: http://www.sacred-texts.com/neu/celt/index.htm.

Celtic Women

Books

Aaron, Jane, ed. *A View across the Valley: Short Stories by Women from Wales, c. 1850–1950*. Honno Classics. Dinas Powys: Honno, 1999.

Aaron, Jane, et al., eds. *Our Sisters' Land: The Changing Identities of Women in Wales*. Cardiff: University of Wales Press, 1994.

Hingley, Richard, and Christina Unwin. *Boudica: Iron Age Warrior Queen*. London: Hambledon Continuum, 2006.

Jenkins, Dafydd, and Morfydd E. Owen, eds. *The Welsh Law of Women: Studies Presented to Professor Daniel A. Binchy on his Eightieth Birthday*. Cardiff: University of Wales Press, 1980.

John, Angela V. *Our Mothers' Land: Chapters in Welsh Women's History 1830–1939*. Cardiff: University of Wales Press, 1991.

Kerrigan, Catherine, ed. *An Anthology of Scottish Women Poets*. Edinburgh: Edinburgh University Press, 1991.

Meek, Christine, and Katharine Simms, eds. *The Fragility of Her Sex? Medieval Irish Women in Their European Context*. Dublin: Four Courts Press, 1996.

O'Dowd, Mary, and Sabine Wichert, eds. *Chattel, Servant or Citizen: Women's Status in Church, State and Society*. Historical Studies 19. Belfast: Institute of Irish Studies, Queen's University of Belfast, 1995.

Webster, Graham. *Boudica: The British Revolt against Rome AD 60*. Rev. ed. Roman Conquest of Britain. London: Batsford, 1993.

Christianity in the Celtic Countries

Books

Bowen, E. G. *Saints, Seaways and Settlements in the Celtic Lands*. Cardiff: University of Wales Press, 1977.

Carey, John. *King of Mysteries: Early Irish Religious Writing*. Dublin: Four Courts Press, 1998.

Carey, John. *A Single Ray of the Sun: Religious Speculation in Early Ireland*. Aberystwyth: Celtic Studies Publications, 2011.

Carey, John, et al., eds. *Studies in Irish Hagiography: Saints and Scholars*. Dublin: Four Courts Press, 2001.

Cartwright, Jane, ed. *Celtic Hagiography and Saints' Cults*. Cardiff: University of Wales Press, 2003.

Chadwick, Nora K. *The Age of the Saints in the Early Celtic Church*. Riddell Memorial Lectures, 32nd Series. London: Oxford University Press, 1961. Facsimile reprint, Felinfach: Llanerch, 1998.

Clancy, Thomas Owen, and Gilbert Márkus. *Iona: The Earliest Poetry of a Celtic Monastery*. Edinburgh: Edinburgh University Press, 1995.

Davies, Oliver. *Celtic Christianity in Early Medieval Wales: The Origins of the Welsh Spiritual Tradition*. Cardiff: University of Wales Press, 1996.

Meek, Donald E. *The Quest for Celtic Christianity*. Edinburgh: Handsel, 2000.

Ó Catháin, Séamas. *The Festival of Brigit: Celtic Goddess and Holy Woman*. Dublin: DBA, 1995.

O'Loughlin, Thomas. *Celtic Theology: Humanity, World, and God in Early Irish Writings*. London: Continuum, 2000.

Pearson, Joanne, ed. *Belief beyond Boundaries: Wicca, Celtic Spirituality and the New Age*. Aldershot: Ashgate, 2002.

Sharpe, Richard. *Medieval Irish Saints' Lives: An Introduction to Vitae Sanctorum Hiberniae*. Oxford: Clarendon Press, 1991.

Website

Celtic and Old English Saints: http://celticsaints.org/.

King Arthur

Books

Alcock, Leslie. *Arthur's Britain: History and Archaeology* AD *367–634*. London: Penguin, 1990.

Ashe, Geoffrey. *The Discovery of King Arthur*. London: Debrett's Peerage, 1985.

Barron, W. R. J., ed. *The Arthur of the English: The Arthurian Legend in Medieval English Life and Literature*. Rev. ed. Arthurian Literature in the Middle Ages 2. Cardiff: University of Wales Press, 2001.

Bromwich, Rachel et al., eds. *The Arthur of the Welsh: The Arthurian Legend in Medieval Welsh Literature*. Cardiff: University of Wales Press, 1991.

Geoffrey of Monmouth, and Michael Faletra. *The History of the Kings of Britain*. Peterborough: Broadview Press, 2007.

Gowans, Linda. *Cei and the Arthurian Legend*. Arthurian Studies 18. Cambridge: Brewer, 1988.

Grimbert, Joan Tasker, ed. *Tristan and Isolde: A Casebook*. Arthurian Characters and Themes 2. New York: Routledge, 2002.

Hale, Amy, et al., eds. *Inside Merlin's Cave: A Cornish Arthurian Reader 1000–2000*. London: Francis Boutle, 2000.

Jackson, W. H., and S. A. Ranawake, eds. *The Arthur of the Germans: The Arthurian Legend in Medieval German and Dutch Literature*. Arthurian Literature in the Middle Ages 3. Cardiff: University of Wales Press, 2000.

Lacy, Norris J., ed. *Medieval Arthurian Literature: A Guide to Recent Research*. Garland Reference Library of the Humanities 1955. New York: Garland, 1996.

Lacy, Norris J., et al. *The New Arthurian Encyclopedia.* London, New York: Garland, 1996. First published, 1986.

Morris, John. *The Age of Arthur: A History of the British Isles from 350 to 650.* New ed. London: Weidenfeld and Nicolson, 1993. First published, 1973.

Padel, O. J. *Arthur in Medieval Welsh Literature.* Writers of Wales. Cardiff: University of Wales Press, 2000.

Thomas, Charles. *English Heritage Book of Tintagel: Arthur and Archaeology.* Cambridge: Batsford, 1993.

Wilhelm, James. *The Romance of Arthur: An Anthology of Medieval Texts in Translation.* Garland Reference Library of the Humanities 1267. New York: Garland, 1994.

Website

Internet Sacred Texts Archive: http://www.sacred-texts.com/neu/eng/index.htm#arthurian.

Brittany

Books

Badone, Ellen. *The Appointed Hour: Death, Worldview, and Social Change in Brittany.* Berkeley: University of California Press, 1989.

Chadwick, Nora K. *Early Brittany.* Cardiff: University of Wales Press, 1969.

Davies, Wendy. *Small Worlds: The Village Community in Early Medieval Brittany.* London: Duckworth, 1988.

Davies, Wendy, et al. *Inscriptions of Early Medieval Brittany/Les inscriptions de la Bretagne du haut Moyen Âge.* Celtic Studies 5. Oakville, CT: Celtic Studies, 2000.

Denez, Per. *Brezhoneg, Buan hag Aes: A Beginner's Course in Breton.* Cork: Cork University Press, 1977.

Denez, Per. *Brittany: A Language in Search of a Future.* European Languages 7. Brussels: European Bureau for Lesser Used Languages, 1998.

Giot, Pierre-Roland, et al. *The British Settlement of Brittany: The First Bretons in Armorica.* Stroud: Tempus, 2003.

Jones, Michael. *The Creation of Brittany: A Late Medieval State.* London: Hambledon, 1988.

McDonald, Maryon. *'We Are Not French!': Language, Culture and Identity in Brittany.* London: Routledge, 1989.

Reece, Jack E. *The Bretons against France: Ethnic Minority Nationalism in Twentieth-Century Brittany.* Chapel Hill: University of North Carolina Press, 1977.

Spence, Keith. *Brittany and the Bretons.* London: Victor Gollancz, 1978.

Spence, Lewis. *Legends and Romances of Brittany.* London: Constable, 1997. First published, New York: Frederick A. Stokes, 1917.

Cornwall

Books

Bottrell, William. *Traditions and Hearthside Stories of West Cornwall: A Facsimile Selection.* Facsimile reprint. Felinfach: Llanerch, 1989. First published, Penzance: W. Bottrell, 1870.

Brown, Wella. *A Grammar of Modern Cornish.* Saltash: Cornish Language Board, 1984. 2nd rev. ed., 1993.

Brown, Wella. *Skeul an Yeth: A Complete Course in the Cornish Language, Books 1–3.* Cornwall: Cornish Language Board, 1996–98.

Courtney, M. A. *Cornish Feasts and Folk-Lore*. Penzance: Oakmagic, 1998. Revised and reprinted from the Folk-Lore Society Journals, 1886–87.

Doble, Gilbert H. *The Saints of Cornwall*. 4 vols. Felinfach: Llanerch, 1998. First published, Truro: Cathedral Chapter, 1965.

Elliott-Binns, Leonard Elliott. *Medieval Cornwall*. London: Methuen, 1955.

Hunt, Robert, ed. *Popular Romances of the West of England: or, The Drolls, Traditions, and Superstitions of Old Cornwall*. 3rd ed. London: Chatto and Windus, 1881. Facsimile ed., *The Drolls, Traditions, and Superstitions of Old Cornwall: Popular Romances of the West of England*. 2 vols. Felinfach: Llanerch, 1993.

Padel, O. J. *A Popular Dictionary of Cornish Place-Names*. Penzance: Alison Hodge, 1988. (See also Padel, O. J., *Cornish Place-Name Elements*. English Place-Name Society 56/57. Nottingham: English Place-Name Society, 1985.)

Payton, Philip. *The Cornish Overseas*. Fowey: Alexander Associates, 1999.

Saunders, Tim, ed. *Nothing Broken: An Anthology of Contemporary Poetry in Cornish 1980–2000*. London: Francis Boutle, 2002.

Saunders, Tim, ed. *The Wheel: An Anthology of Modern Poetry in Cornish 1850–1980*. London: Francis Boutle, 1999.

Ireland

Books

Bartlett, Thomas. *Ireland: A History*. New York: Cambridge, 2010.

Duffy, Seán, ed. *Atlas of Irish History*. Dublin: Gill and Macmillan, 2000.

Freeman, Philip. *St Patrick of Ireland: A Biography*. New York: Simon and Schuster, 2004.

Foster, R. F., ed. *The Oxford History of Ireland*. Oxford: Oxford University Press, 1989.

Lalor, Brian, ed. *The Encyclopaedia of Ireland*. Dublin: Gill and Macmillan, 2003.

Meehan, Bernard. *The Book of Kells: An Illustrated Introduction to the Manuscript in Trinity College Dublin*. London: Thames and Hudson, 1994.

Ó Riain, Pádraig, et al. *Historical Dictionary of Gaelic Placenames/Foclóir Stairiúil Áitainmneacha na Gaeilge*. London: Irish Text Society, 2003.

Ó Súilleabháin, Seán. *Folktales of Ireland*. London: Routledge and Kegan Paul, 1966.

Ó Súilleabháin, Seán. *Irish Folk Custom and Belief*. 2nd ed. Irish Life and Culture 15. Cork: Mercier Press, 1977. First published, Dublin: Three Candles, 1967.

Ó Súilleabháin, Seán. *Irish Wake Amusements*. Cork: Mercier, 1967.

Ó Súilleabháin, Seán. *Legends from Ireland*. London: Batsford, 1977.

Ó Súilleabháin, Seán. *Storytelling in Irish Tradition*. Cork: Mercier, 1973.

Ryan, Michael, ed. *The Illustrated Archaeology of Ireland*. Dublin: Country House, 1991.

Isle of Man

Books

Belchem, John, ed. *A New History of the Isle of Man 5: The Modern Period 1830–1999*. Liverpool: Liverpool University Press, 2000.

Broderick, George. *Place-Names of the Isle of Man*. 7 vols. Tübingen: Niemeyer, 1994–2004.

Douglas, Mona. *This Is Ellan Vannin: A Miscellany of Manx Life and Lore*. Douglas: Times, 1965.

Douglas, Mona. *This Is Ellan Vannin Again: Folklore*. Times Longbooks. Douglas: Times, 1966.

Killip, Margaret. *The Folklore of the Isle of Man*. London: Batsford, 1975.

Moore, A. W. *The Folklore of the Isle of Man: Being an Account of Its Myths, Legends, Superstitions, Customs, and Proverbs*. Facsimile reprint. Felinfach: Llanerch, 1994. First published, London: Nutt, 1891.

Penrice, Harry, ed. *Fables, Fantasies and Folklore of the Isle of Man*. Douglas: Manx Experience, 1996.

Radcliffe, F. J. *Manx Farming and Country Life*. Douglas: Manx Heritage Foundation, 1991.

Solly, Mark. *Government and Law in the Isle of Man*. Castletown: Parallel Books, 1994.

Thomson, Robert L., and A. J. Pilgrim. *Outline of Manx Language and Literature*. [Isle of Man]: Yn Cheshaght Ghailckagh, 1988.

Wilkins, Frances. *The Isle of Man in Smuggling History*. Kidderminster: Wyre Forest Press, 1992.

Wilkins, Frances. *Manx Slave Traders: A Social History of the Isle of Man's Involvement in the Atlantic Slave Trade*. Kidderminster: Wyre Forest Press, 1999.

Scotland

Books

Anderson, Alan O., and Marjorie O. Anderson, eds. *Adomnán's Life of Columba*. Rev. ed. Oxford Medieval Texts. Oxford: Clarendon, 1991.

Anderson, Marjorie O. *Kings and Kingship in Early Scotland*. Rev. ed. Edinburgh: Scottish Academic, 1980.

Armit, Ian. *Celtic Scotland*. London: Batsford Historic Scotland, 1997.

Campbell, John Gregorson. *The Gaelic Otherworld: Superstitions of the Highlands and Islands of Scotland and Witchcraft and Second Sight in the Highlands and Islands*. Ed. Ronald Black. Edinburgh: Birlinn, 2005.

Mackie, J. D. *A History of Scotland*. New York: Penguin, 1984.

Nicolaisen, W. F. H. *The Picts and Their Place Names*. Rosemarkie: Groam House Museum Trust, 1996.

Nicolaisen, W. F. H. *Scottish Place-Names: Their Study and Significance*. London: Batsford, 1976. Reprinted, Edinburgh: Donald, 2001.

Ritchie, Anna. *Picts: An Introduction to the Life of the Picts and the Carved Stones in the Care of the Secretary of State for Scotland*. Edinburgh: HMSO, 1989. Reprinted, Edinburgh: HMSO, 1999.

Ritchie, Graham, and Anna Ritchie. *Scotland: Archaeology and Early History*. Edinburgh: Edinburgh University Press, 1991.

Ross, Anne. *Folklore of the Scottish Highlands*. Stroud: Tempus, 2000. First published, London: Batsford, 1976.

Shaw, M. F. *Folksongs and Folklore from South Uist*. London: Routledge and Kegan Paul, 1955. 2nd ed., Edinburgh: Birlinn, 1999.

Thomson, Derick S. *An Introduction to Gaelic Poetry*. 2nd ed. Edinburgh: Edinburgh University Press, 1989. First published, London: Victor Gollancz, 1974.

Wales

Books

Aitchison, John, and Harold Carter. *A Geography of the Welsh Language 1961–1991*. Cardiff: University of Wales Press, 1994.

Aitchison, John, and Harold Carter. *Language, Economy and Society: The Changing Fortunes of the Welsh Language in the Twentieth Century*. Updated ed. Cardiff: University of Wales Press, 2000.

Davies, John. *A History of Wales*. New ed. London: Penguin, 1994.

Davies, John, et al., eds. *The Welsh Academy Encyclopaedia of Wales*. Cardiff: University of Wales Press, 2008.

Davies, Wendy. *Wales in the Early Middle Ages*. Studies in the Early History of Britain. Leicester: Leicester University Press, 1982.

Jenkins, Geraint H., and Mari A. Williams, eds. *"Let's Do Our Best for the Ancient Tongue": The Welsh Language in the Twentieth Century*. A Social History of the Welsh Language. Cardiff: University of Wales Press, 2000.

Palmer, Roy. *The Folklore of (Old) Monmouthshire*. Almeley: Logaston, 1998.

Palmer, Roy. *The Folklore of Radnorshire*. Almeley: Logaston, 2001.

Rhŷs, John. *Celtic Folklore: Welsh and Manx*. 2 vols. London: Wildwood, 1980. First published, Oxford: Clarendon, 1901.

Sikes, Wirt. *British Goblins: Welsh Folklore, Fairy Mythology, Legends and Traditions*. London: Low, Marston, Searle and Rivington, 1880.

Turvey, Roger. *The Welsh Princes: The Native Rulers of Wales, 1063–1283*. London: Longman, 2002.

Williams, J. E. Caerwyn. *The Poets of the Welsh Princes*. Rev. ed. Cardiff: University of Wales Press, 1994. First published, 1978.

The Editors and Contributors

General Editor

John T. Koch is Research Professor and Senior Research Fellow at the University of Wales Centre for Advanced Welsh and Celtic Studies, and was the leader of the Centre's research project on the Celtic Languages and Cultural Identity. That project was succeeded in 2008 by the Ancient Britain and the Atlantic Zone Project. John Koch previously taught Celtic Studies at Harvard University and Boston College. He received the degrees of A.M. (1983) and Ph.D. (1985) in Celtic Languages and Literatures from Harvard University and also studied at Jesus College, Oxford, and the University of Wales, Aberystwyth. He has published extensively on early Welsh and Irish language and literature, Continental Celtic, and the coming of Celtic speech to Ireland and Britain. His books include *The Gododdin of Aneirin* (University of Wales Press, 1997), *Tartessian* (Celtic Studies Publications, 2009), *Tartessian 2* (Centre for Advanced Welsh and Celtic Studies, 2011), and, with John Carey, *The Celtic Heroic Age* (Celtic Studies Publications, 1994, fourth edition 2003). He is currently working on a book on the historical Taliesin and a historical grammar of the early Brythonic languages. As well as this *Encyclopedia,* a collaborative *Proto-Celtic Vocabulary* and *An Atlas for Celtic Studies* (Oxbow, 2007) have appeared as fruits of the Celtic Languages and Cultural Identity Project.

Editor

Antone Minard is a lecturer in the Department of Classical, Near Eastern, and Religious Studies at the University of British Columbia and in the Humanities Department at Simon Fraser University. He received the degrees of M.A. (1996) and Ph.D. (2002) from the University of California, Los Angeles, in Folklore and Mythology with a specialty in Celtic Studies. He has published on folk belief and narrative in medieval Celtic literature.

Contributors

Jane Aaron
Pwyll ap Siôn
Joost Augusteijn
Andrew D. M. Barrell
Norbert Baum
Fenella Bazin
Francesco Benozzo
Gareth A. Bevan
Edel Bhreathnach
Jörg Biel
Helmut Birkhan

Ronald Black
Jacqueline Borsje
André Yves Bourgès
Nicola Gordon Bowe
Marion Bowman
Dorothy Bray
George Broderick
Terence Brown
M. Paul Bryant-Quinn
Olivier Buchsenschutz
Peter E. Busse

Michel Byrne
T. W. Cain
John Callow
José Calvete
John Carey
Jean-Yves Carluer
A. D. Carr
R. C. Carswell
T. M. Charles-Edwards
Hugh Cheape
Monica Chiabà
Thomas Owen Clancy
Paula Powers Coe
Michelle Comber
Mary-Ann Constantine
Matthew Cragoe
Aedeen Cremin
Yvonne Cresswell
Elizabeth Cumming
Barry Cunliffe
Bernadette Cunningham
Mary E. Daly
R. Iestyn Daniel
P. J. Davey
Ceri Davies
Eirug Davies
Hazel Walford Davies
Jeffrey L. Davies
Sioned Davies
Wendy Davies
Alex Davis
Robert A. Dodgshon
Jennifer Kewley Draskau
Stephen Driscoll
Huw M. Edwards
†Hywel Teifi Edwards
Nancy Edwards
Gwenno Angharad Elias
Joseph Eska
Dewi Wyn Evans
Geraint Evans
J. Wyn Evans
Meredydd Evans
Nicholas Evans
Alexander Falileyev
William Ferguson
Richard J. Finlay
Katherine Forsyth

James E. Fraser
Philip Freeman
P. W. M. Freeman
Brian Frykenberg
Helen Fulton
Neal Garnham
Phil Gawne
Laurence M. Geary
Egon Gersbach
Jacqueline Gibson
William Gillies
Margo Griffin-Wilson
Chris Grooms
Jean-Marie Guilcher
Anja Gunderloch
Mitja Guštin
Amy Hale
Andrew Hawke
Marged Haycock
Petra S. Hellmuth
Elissa R. Henken
Barbara Hillers
Maria Hinterkörner
John Hooker
Nerys Howells
Ian Hughes
Fraser Hunter
Jerry Hunter
Rhiannon Ifans
Robert P. Irvine
Dafydd Islwyn
Karen Jankulak
Geraint H. Jenkins
Elizabeth Jerem
Andrew Johnson
Diarmuid Johnson
Nick Johnson
Dafydd Johnston
Bill Jones
Ffion M. Jones
Glyn T. Jones
Graham Jones
Heather Rose Jones
J. Graham Jones
R. M. Jones
Robert Owen Jones
Tegwyn Jones
Vernon Jones

Paul Joyner
Raimund Karl
Flemming Kaul
Fergus Kelly
Alan M. Kent
Lukian Kergoat
Sheila Kidd
Phyllis Kinney
Victor Kneale
John T. Koch
Herve Le Bihan
†Gwenaël Le Duc
Thierry Lejars
Jutta Leskovar
Philippe Le Stum
M. Lévery
Ceri W. Lewis
Susan Lewis
Ceridwen Lloyd-Morgan
Alan Llwyd
Marion Löffler
Peter Lord
Michael Lynch
Patricia Lysaght
Mícheál Mac Craith
Seosamh Mac Donnacha
Gearóid Mac Eoin
Hugh Dan MacLennan
Michelle Macleod
Séamus Mac Mathúna
Alan Macquarrie
Charles W. MacQuarrie
Ailbhe MacShamhráin
Breesha Maddrell
William J. Mahon
J. P. Mallory
Michelle Mann
Stéphane Marion
Ioan Matthews
Catherine McKenna
Wilson McLeod
Damian McManus
Jamie Medhurst
Donald E. Meek
J. V. S. Megaw
M. Ruth Megaw
Patrice Méniel
Bernard Merdrignac

Bethan Miles
Antone Minard
Bernard Moffat
Prys Morgan
John Morgan-Guy
R. S. Moroney
Kay Muhr
Joseph Falaky Nagy
John Nash
Bronagh Ní Chonaill
Aoibheann Ní Chonnchadha
Eiléan Ní Chuilleanáin
Máirín Ní Dhonnchadha
Kenneth E. Nilsen
Brian Ó Broin
Donnchadh Ó Corráin
Cathair Ó Dochartaigh
Brian Ó Donnchadha
Simon Ó Faoláin
Cathal Ó Háinle
Donncha Ó hAodha
Éamonn Ó hArgáin
Ruairí Ó hUiginn
Lillis Ó Laoire
Laurent Olivier
Thomas O'Loughlin
Nollaig Ó Muraíle
Dónall Ó Riagáin
Pádraig Ó Riagáin
Pádraig Ó Riain
Nicholas Orme
Pádraig Ó Siadhail
Ann Parry Owen
Morfydd E. Owen
Chris Page
Dylan Phillips
Murray G. H. Pittock
Alheydis Plassmann
Erich Poppe
Angharad Price
Huw Pryce
F. J. Radcliffe
Francesca Rhydderch
Robert Rhys
Michael Richter
Pádraigín Riggs
Erwan Rihet
Brynley F. Roberts

Sara Elin Roberts
Boyd Robertson
Fañch Roudaut
John Rowlands
Paul Russell
Georg Schilcher
Susan Self
Michael Siddons
Victoria Simmons
Marc Simon, Order of Saint Benedict
Tom Sjöblom
J. Beverley Smith
Peter Smith
Robin Chapman Stacey
Thomas Stöllner
Gwenno Sven-Myer
Simon Taylor
Graham C. G. Thomas
Gwyn Thomas
M. Wynn Thomas
Robert Thomson
Megan Tomos
Robyn Tomos
Lauran Toorians

Geraint Tudur
Seán Ua Súilleabháin
Ríonach uí Ógáin
Otto Helmut Urban
Lucian Vaida
Daniele Vitali
Caroline aan de Weil
Martin Werner
Diarmuid Whelan
Dan Wiley
Colin H. Williams
Gareth Williams
Heather Williams
Ioan Williams
J. E. Caerwyn Williams
Nicholas Williams
Patricia Williams
Stephen D. Winick
Andrew Wiseman
Dagmar Wodtko
Jonathan M. Wooding
Alex Woolf
Kurt Zeller
Stefan Zimmer

Index

Note: Phrases in Celtic languages that begin with the definite article *al, an, ar, na, ny, y, yn,* or *yr* ("the") have been alphabetized under that word rather than under the second word of the phrase.